PART 6: THE ECONOMICS OF LABOUR MARKETS

The special features of labour markets, in which most people earn most of their income.

PART 7: TOPICS FOR FURTHER STUDY

Additional topics in microeconomics include household decision making, asymmetric information, political economy, and behavioural economics.

EIGHTH
CANADIAN
EDITION

PRINCIPLES OF MICRO ECONOMICS

N. Gregory Mankiw
HARVARD UNIVERSITY

Ronald D. Kneebone
UNIVERSITY OF CALGARY

Kenneth J. McKenzie
UNIVERSITY OF CALGARY

NELSON

NELSON

**Principles of Microeconomics,
Eighth Canadian Edition**

by N. Gregory Mankiw, Ronald D.
Kneebone, and Kenneth J. McKenzie

VP, Product Solutions, K–20:
Claudine O'Donnell

Director, Quantitative Publishing:
Paul Fam

Publisher:
Katherine Baker-Ross

Marketing Manager:
Marcia Siekowski

Technical Reviewer:
Racquel Lindsay

Content Manager:
Sandy Matos

Photo and Permissions Researcher:
Julie Pratt

Senior Production Project Manager:
Natalia Denesiuk Harris

Production Service:
MPS Limited

Copy Editor:
Kelli Howey

Proofreader:
MPS Limited

Indexer:
Jerry Ralya

Design Director:
Ken Phipps

Post-secondary Design PM:
Pamela Johnston

Cover Design:
John Montgomery

Cover Image:
AstroStar/Shutterstock

Compositor:
MPS Limited

Library and Archives Canada Cataloguing in Publication

Title: Principles of microeconomics /
  N. Gregory Mankiw (Harvard University), Ronald D.
  Kneebone (University of Calgary), Kenneth J. McKenzie
  (University of Calgary).

Other titles: Principles of micro economics

Names: Mankiw, N. Gregory, author. |
  Kneebone, Ronald D. (Ronald David), author. |
  McKenzie, Kenneth J. (Kenneth James), author.

Description: Eighth Canadian edition. | Includes index. |
  Previously published: Toronto, Ontario: Nelson
  Education, 2016.

Identifiers: Canadiana (print) 20190150858 | Canadiana
  (ebook) 20190150890 | ISBN 9780176872823 (softcover) |
  ISBN 9780176888060 (PDF)

Subjects: LCSH: Microeconomics—Textbooks. | LCGFT:
  Textbooks.

Classification: LCC HB172 .M36 2019 | DDC 338.5—dc23

ISBN-13: 978-0-17-687282-3
ISBN-10: 0-17-687282-5

To Catherine, Nicholas, and Peter, my other
contributions to the next generation

To our parents and Cindy, Kathleen, and Janetta—
thanks for your support and patience

© Kevin LeBlanc

N. Gregory Mankiw is Professor of Economics at Harvard University. As a student, he studied economics at Princeton University and MIT. As a teacher, he has taught macroeconomics, microeconomics, statistics, and principles of economics. He even spent one summer long ago as a sailing instructor on Long Beach Island.

Professor Mankiw is a prolific writer and a regular participant in academic and policy debates. His work has been published in scholarly journals such as the *American Economic Review, Journal of Political Economy,* and *Quarterly Journal of Economics,* and in more popular forums such as *The New York Times, The Financial Times, The Wall Street Journal,* and *Fortune.* He is also author of the best-selling intermediate-level textbook *Macroeconomics* (Worth Publishing). In addition to his teaching, research, and writing, Professor Mankiw has been a research associate of the National Bureau of Economic Research, an adviser to the Federal Reserve Bank of Boston and the Congressional Budget Office, and a member of the Educational Testing Service (ETS) test development committee for the advanced placement exam in economics. From 2003 to 2005, he served as Chairman of the President's Council of Economic Advisers.

Ronald D. Kneebone is Professor in the Department of Economics and The School of Public Policy at the University of Calgary. He received his Ph.D. from McMaster University. Professor Kneebone has taught courses in public finance and in macroeconomics from principles through to the Ph.D. level, and he is a two-time winner of the Faculty of Social Sciences Distinguished Teacher Award at the University of Calgary. His research interests are primarily in the areas of public-sector finances and fiscal federalism, but he has recently worked on the problems of homelessness and poverty reduction. He shared with Ken McKenzie the Douglas Purvis Memorial Prize for the best published work in Canadian public policy in 1999. He is currently the Scientific Director of the Social Policy and Health research division in The School of Public Policy, where he leads a group of researchers investigating issues related to poverty, cognitive and physical disabilities, the organization and financing of health care, and homelessness.

Kenneth J. McKenzie is Professor in the Department of Economics and The School of Public Policy at the University of Calgary. He received his Ph.D. from Queen's University. Specializing in public economics with an emphasis on taxation and political economy, Professor McKenzie has published extensively in these areas. He is the winner of the 1996 Harry Johnson Prize (with University of Calgary colleague Herb Emery) for the best article in the *Canadian Journal of Economics,* a two-time winner of the Douglas Purvis Memorial Prize for a published work relating to Canadian public policy (1999 with Ron Kneebone and 2011 with Natalia Sershun), and a Faculty of Social Sciences Distinguished Researcher Award winner at the University of Calgary. He is a former editor of *Canadian Public Policy* and currently co-editor of the *Finances of the Nation* feature of the *Canadian Tax Journal.* Professor McKenzie has taught microeconomics and public economics from the principles to the graduate level, and has received several departmental teaching awards.

BRIEF CONTENTS

CONTENTS

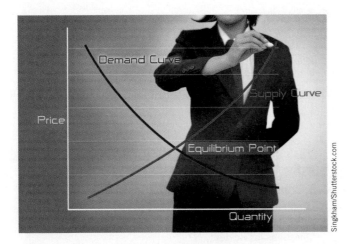

PART 1 INTRODUCTION

PhilipR/Shutterstock.com

PART 2 SUPPLY AND DEMAND I: HOW MARKETS WORK

Brian Summers/First Light

PART **3** SUPPLY AND DEMAND II: MARKETS AND WELFARE

CHAPTER **6**

Supply, Demand, and Government Policies   121

CHAPTER **7**

Consumers, Producers, and the Efficiency of Markets   145

Jeff Kowalsky/Bloomberg/Getty Images

PART 5 FIRM BEHAVIOUR AND THE ORGANIZATION OF INDUSTRY

Norm Betts/Bloomberg/Getty Images

Ditty_about_summer/Shutterstock.com

PART 7 TOPICS FOR FURTHER STUDY

CHAPTER 22

Frontiers of Microeconomics 487

As soon as we got our hands on the first U.S. edition of *Principles of Micro-economics*, it was clear to us that "this one is different." If other first-year economics textbooks are encyclopedias, Gregory Mankiw's was, and still is, a handbook.

Between us, we have many years of experience teaching first-year economics. Like many instructors, we found it harder and harder to teach with each new edition of the thick, standard textbooks. It was simply impossible to cover all of the material. Of course, we could have skipped sections, features, or whole chapters, but then, apart from the sheer hassle of telling students which bits to read and not to read, and worries about the consistencies and completeness of the remaining material, we ran the risk of leaving students with the philosophy that what matters is only what's on the exam.

We do not believe that the writers of these other books set out with the intention of cramming so much material into them. It is a difficult task to put together the perfect textbook—one that all instructors would approve of and that all students would enjoy using. Therefore, to please all potential users, most of the books end up covering a wide range of topics. And so the books grow and grow.

Professor Mankiw made a fresh start in the first U.S. edition. He included all the important topics and presented them in order of importance. And in the eighth U.S. edition, he has resisted the temptation to add more and more material. We have, in adapting the text for Canadian students, taken a minimalist approach: "If it isn't broken, don't fix it!" While the book is easily recognizable as Mankiw's, we have made changes that increase its relevance to Canadian students. Some of these changes reflect important differences between the Canadian and U.S. economies. For example, the Canadian economy is much smaller and more open than the U.S. economy, and this fact is explicitly recognized in this edition. Other changes reflect important institutional differences between the two countries, including the structure of the tax system and the nature of competition policy. Finally, the Canadian edition focuses on issues and includes examples that are more familiar and relevant to a Canadian audience.

We would not have agreed to participate in the Canadian edition if we were not extremely impressed with the U.S. edition. Professor Mankiw has done an outstanding job of identifying the key concepts and principles that every first-year student should learn.

It was truly a pleasure to work with such a well-thought-out and well-written book. We have enjoyed teaching from the earlier Canadian editions and we look forward to using the eighth Canadian edition. We hope you do, too.

How the Book Is Organized

To write a brief and student-friendly book, Mankiw considered new ways to organize familiar material. What follows is a whirlwind tour of this text. The tour, we hope, will give you a sense of how the pieces fit together.

Introductory Material

Chapter 1, "Ten Principles of Economics," introduces students to the economist's view of the world. It previews some of the big ideas that recur throughout economics, such as opportunity costs, marginal decision making, the role of incentives, the gains from trade, and the efficiency of market allocations. Throughout the text an effort is made to relate the discussion back to the ten principles of economics introduced in Chapter 1. The interconnections of the material with the ten principles are clearly identified throughout the text.

Chapter 2, "Thinking Like an Economist," examines how economists approach their field of study, discussing the role of assumptions in developing a theory and introducing the concepts of an economic model. It also discusses the role of economists in making policy. The appendix to this chapter offers a brief refresher course on how graphs are used and how they can be abused.

Chapter 3, "Interdependence and the Gains from Trade," presents the theory of comparative advantage. This theory explains why individuals trade with their neighbours, as well as why nations trade with other nations. Much of economics is about how market forces coordinate many individual production and consumption decisions. As a starting point for this analysis, students see in this chapter why specialization, interdependence, and trade can benefit everyone.

The Fundamental Tools of Supply and Demand

The next three chapters introduce the basic tools of supply and demand. Chapter 4, "The Market Forces of Supply and Demand," develops the supply curve, the demand curve, and the notion of market equilibrium. Chapter 5, "Elasticity and Its Application," introduces the concept of elasticity and uses it to analyze events in three different markets. Chapter 6, "Supply, Demand, and Government Policies," uses these tools to examine price controls, such as rent-control and minimum-wage laws, and tax incidence.

Chapter 7, "Consumers, Producers, and the Efficiency of Markets," extends the analysis of supply and demand using the concepts of consumer surplus and producer surplus. It begins by developing the link between consumers' willingness to pay and the demand curve, and the link between producers' costs of production and the supply curve. It then shows that the market equilibrium maximizes the sum of the producer and consumer surplus. Thus, students learn early about the efficiency of market allocations.

The next two chapters apply the concepts of producer and consumer surplus to questions of policy. Chapter 8, "Application: The Costs of Taxation," shows why taxation results in deadweight losses and what determines the size of those losses. Chapter 9, "Application: International Trade," considers who wins and who loses from international trade and presents the debate over protectionist trade policies.

More Microeconomics

Having examined why market allocations are often desirable, the book then considers how the government can sometimes improve on them. Chapter 10, "Externalities," explains how external effects such as pollution can render market outcomes inefficient and discusses the possible public and private solutions to those inefficiencies. Chapter 11, "Public Goods and Common Resources," considers the problems that arise when goods, such as national defence, have no market price. Chapter 12, "The Design of the Tax System," describes how the government raises the revenue necessary to pay for public goods. It presents some institutional background about the Canadian tax system and then discusses how the goals of efficiency and equity come into play when designing a tax system.

The next five chapters examine firm behaviour and industrial organization. Chapter 13, "The Costs of Production," discusses what to include in a firm's costs and introduces cost curves. Chapter 14, "Firms in Competitive Markets," analyzes the behaviour of price-taking firms and derives the market supply curve. Chapter 15, "Monopoly," discusses the behaviour of a firm that is the sole seller in its market, the inefficiency of monopoly pricing, the possible policy responses, and the attempts by monopolies to price-discriminate. Chapter 16, "Monopolistic Competition," looks at behaviour in a market in which many sellers offer similar but differentiated products. It also discusses the debate over the effects of advertising. Chapter 17, "Oligopoly," covers markets in which there are only a few sellers, using the prisoners' dilemma as the model for examining strategic interaction.

The next three chapters present issues related to labour markets. Chapter 18, "The Markets for the Factors of Production," emphasizes the link between factor prices and marginal productivity. Chapter 19, "Earnings and Discrimination," discusses the determinants of equilibrium wages, including compensating differentials, human capital, and discrimination. Chapter 20, "Income Inequality and Poverty," examines the degree of inequality in Canadian society, alternative views about the government's role in changing the distribution of income, and various policies aimed at helping society's poorest members.

The final two chapters present optional material. Chapter 21, "The Theory of Consumer Choice," analyzes individual decision making using budget constraints and indifference curves. Chapter 22, "Frontiers of Microeconomics," introduces the topics of asymmetric information, political economy, and behavioural economics. Some instructors may skip all or some of this material. Instructors who do cover these topics may choose to assign these chapters earlier than they are presented in this text, and they have been written to give that flexibility.

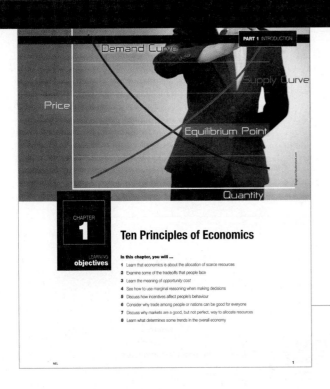

The purpose of this textbook is to help students learn the fundamental lessons of economics and to show how such lessons can be applied to the world in which they live. Toward that end, various learning tools recur throughout the book.

Chapter Openers Well-designed chapter openers act as previews that summarize the major concepts to be learned in each chapter.

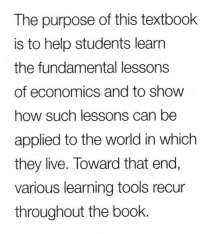

Case Studies Economic theory is useful and interesting only if it can be applied to understanding actual events and policies. Updated or replaced with more current Canadian examples, the numerous case studies apply the theory that has just been developed.

New "Ask the Experts" Boxes Feature Opinions from the World's Most Prominent Economists. This timely learning feature highlights the IGM Economics Experts Panel, a longitudinal survey of several dozens of the world's most prominent economists. Every few weeks these experts review a proposition and respond whether they agree with it, disagree with it, or are uncertain. The insights from this feature demonstrate to your students situations when economists are united, when they are divided, and when they simply don't know what to think.

Figures and Tables Colourful and eye-catching visuals are used to make important economic points and to clarify Canadian and other key economic concepts. They have also proved to be valuable and memorable teaching aids.

FIGURE 2A.5

Calculating the Slope of a Line

To calculate the slope of the demand curve, we can look at the changes in the x- and y-coordinates as we move from the point (21 novels, $6) to the point (13 novels, $8). The slope of the line is the ratio of the change in the y-coordinate (-2) to the change in the x-coordinate ($+8$), which equals $-1/4$.

© 2018 Cengage Learning

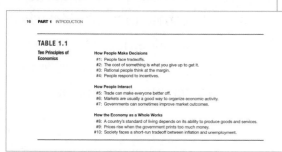

16 PART 1 INTRODUCTION

TABLE 1.1

Ten Principles of Economics

How People Make Decisions
#1: People face tradeoffs.
#2: The cost of something is what you give up to get it.
#3: Rational people think at the margin.
#4: People respond to incentives.

How People Interact
#5: Trade can make everyone better off.
#6: Markets are usually a good way to organize economic activity.
#7: Governments can sometimes improve market outcomes.

How the Economy as a Whole Works
#8: A country's standard of living depends on its ability to produce goods and services.
#9: Prices rise when the government prints too much money.
#10: Society faces a short-run tradeoff between inflation and unemployment.

"In the News" Features One benefit that students gain from studying economics is a new perspective and greater understanding about news from Canada and around the world. To highlight this benefit, excerpts from many Canadian news articles, including opinion columns written by prominent economists, show how basic economic theory can be applied.

CHAPTER 1 TEN PRINCIPLES OF ECONOMICS 7

IN THE news Even Criminals Respond to Incentives

Principle #4, people respond to incentives, is at the core of the study of economics. As the following article explains, this principle applies to all sorts of activities, even of the criminal kind.

Risk, Reward and the Economics of the Criminal Mind

By Todd Hirsch

Last week's *Economist* magazine carried a headline reading, "The Curious Case of the Fall in Crime." It seems that all around the industrialized world—including Canada—all kinds of criminal activity are on the decline. Contrary to the belief that evil thugs lurk around every corner, we are actually safer than we have been in decades. In today's underground economy, identity theft makes better economic sense than stealing a flat-screen television.

The magazine's editorial offers only guesses as to why crime rates are falling. Aging demographics may play a role, along with better theft-prevention technologies. Stiffer punishment and "get tough on crime" policies might make for good political posturing, but they seem to have little impact: Crime rates are falling in countries where sentencing has become tougher as well as where it has been loosened.

The Economist failed to mention the most obvious reason for the change: economic incentives. Thieves are simply doing what most of us do every day: They are responding to market signals.

This is particularly true of property crimes such as residential break-and-enter, car theft and armed robbery. The possible payoff for stealing from a home is dwindling. What is there worth taking? Electronics are increasingly less valuable—a computer or a television in the 1980s would have been worth thousands of dollars on the street; now they would fetch a few

hundred bucks. Why buy a stolen iPod dock out of the back of some guy's truck when you can get a new one for less than $100?

Car theft is down dramatically, too. According to Statistics Canada, car theft in Ontario plunged to 141 per 100,000 people last year, down from 443 in 1998. Better technology, car alarm systems and anti-theft devices have deterred most would-be thieves. And lower-priced cars without car alarms probably are not worth stealing anyway. The bad guys aren't less bad, they're just good economists.

Muggings and purse snatchings are increasingly less common as well. But let's not overthink the reasons why fewer thieves are snatching purses. It has nothing to do with the culprit's age or job situation. Whether there was a father present in the thief's childhood or whether he or she played violent video games are irrelevant. The reason is that there's just not much of value inside purses or wallets anymore. Cash has been largely replaced by debit and credit cards, and as long as the PIN is secure, the thief gets away with nothing more than plastic cards and chewing gum. Cellphones are more costly, but stolen ones are difficult to wipe and resell.

Criminals, like all of us, respond to market signals. If the potential payoff for any activity is too low, we weigh the risks and decide it isn't worth it. For noncriminals, the question isn't "Should I steal this car?" but something along the lines of "Should I put in new bathroom tile before I list my house?" People are quite good at reading and responding to market signals.

Still, we shouldn't think that poor economic incentives are making crime go away. Crime

is simply morphing. Traditional crime statistics tend to focus on activities such as robbery, property theft and murder. Fewer long-term trend statistics are available for crimes that are doubtless increasing, such as identity theft and cybercrime. Not only are they potentially more lucrative, they are global in scope and much more difficult to track.

Thieves are also getting smarter, using technology for evil deeds. Internet scams abound, and bank-card skimming and credit-card fraud is a serious problem. Banks have had to fight back with their own technology and it has been costly.

Economic incentives play a huge role motivating us in almost everything we do. Certain actions are no doubt spurred by altruism and generosity, such as helping our neighbour shovel snow or donating to charity (although we still want the tax receipt). Weighing the financial incentives against the potential risks is the basis of our economy. Criminals may not know they're doing it, but they're just responding to market signals—and doing a good job of it.

Source: "Risk, Reward and the Economics of the Criminal Mind," by Todd Hirsch, August 1, 2013, *The Globe and Mail*. Reproduced by permission of the author.

56 PART 1 INTRODUCTION

FYI The Legacy of Adam Smith and David Ricardo

Economists have long understood the principle of comparative advantage. Here is how the great economist Adam Smith put the argument:

It is a maxim of every prudent master of a family, never to attempt to make at home what it will cost him more to make than to buy. The tailor does not attempt to make his own shoes, but buys them of the shoemaker. The shoemaker does not attempt to make his own clothes but employs a tailor. The farmer attempts to make neither the one nor the other, but employs those different artificers. All of them find it for their interest to employ their whole industry in a way in which they have some advantage over their neighbors, and to purchase with a part of its produce, or what is the same thing, with the price of part of it, whatever else they have occasion for.

This quotation is from Smith's 1776 book *An Inquiry into the Nature and Causes of the Wealth of Nations*, which was a landmark in the analysis of trade and economic interdependence.

Smith's book inspired David Ricardo, a millionaire stockbroker, to become an economist. In his 1817 book *Principles of Political Economy*

and Taxation, Ricardo developed the principle of comparative advantage as we know it today. His defence of free trade was not a mere academic exercise. Ricardo put his economic beliefs to work as a member of the British Parliament, where he opposed the Corn Laws, which restricted the import of grain.

The conclusions of Adam Smith and David Ricardo on the gains from trade have held up well over time. Although economists often disagree on questions of policy, they are united in their support of free trade. Moreover, the central argument for free trade has not changed much in the past two centuries. Even though the field of economics has broadened its scope and refined its theories since the time of Smith and Ricardo, economists' opposition to trade restrictions is still based largely on the principle of comparative advantage.

© Bettmann/Corbis

"FYI" Features These features provide additional material "for your information." Some of them offer a glimpse into the history of economic thought. Others clarify technical issues. Still others discuss supplementary topics that instructors might choose either to discuss or to skip in their lectures.

nefit of a cleaner environment and the improved health that comes with it, they
ve the cost of reducing the incomes of the regulated firms' owners, workers,
d customers.

Another tradeoff society faces is between efficiency and equity. **Efficiency**
eans that society is getting the maximum benefits from its scarce resources.
juity means that the benefits of those resources are distributed fairly among
ciety's members. In other words, efficiency refers to the size of the economic
, and equity refers to how the pie is divided into individual slices.

When government policies are designed, these two goals often conflict. Con-
ler, for instance, policies aimed at achieving a more equal distribution of
onomic well-being. Some of these policies, such as the welfare system or
nployment Insurance, try to help those members of society who are most in
ed. Others, such as the individual income tax, ask the financially successful to
ntribute more than others to support the government. Though they achieve
eater equality, these policies may reduce efficiency. When the government
distributes income from the rich to the poor, it reduces the reward for working

efficiency
the property of society
getting the most it can from
its scarce resources

equity
the property of distributing
economic prosperity fairly
among the members of
society

QUICK Quiz Describe an important tradeoff you recently faced. • Give an example of some action that has both a monetary and nonmonetary opportunity cost. • Describe an incentive your parents and/or guardians offered to you in an effort to influence your behaviour.

Quick Quizzes After each major section, students are offered a quick quiz
to check their comprehension of what
they have just learned. If students
cannot readily answer these quizzes,
they should stop and reread the material
before continuing.

Key Concept Definitions When key concepts are
introduced in the chapter, they are presented in **bold**
typeface. In addition, their definitions are placed in the
margin and in the Glossary at the back of the book. This
treatment helps students learn and review the material.

Chapter Summaries Each chapter ends with a brief
summary that reminds students of the most important
lessons that they have just learned. Later in their study,
it offers an efficient way to review for exams.

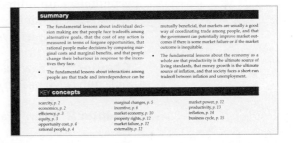

summary

- The fundamental lessons about individual decision making are that people face tradeoffs among
  alternative goals, that the cost of any action is
  measured in terms of forgone opportunities, that
  rational people make decisions by comparing marginal costs and marginal benefits, and that people
  change their behaviour in response to the incentives they face.
- The fundamental lessons about interactions among
  people are that trade and interdependence can be

  mutually beneficial, that markets are usually a good
  way of coordinating trade among people, and that
  the government can potentially improve market outcomes if there is some market failure or if the market
  outcome is inequitable.
- The fundamental lessons about the economy as a
  whole are that productivity is the ultimate source of
  living standards, that money growth is the ultimate
  source of inflation, and that society faces a short-run
  tradeoff between inflation and unemployment.

KEY concepts

scarcity, p. 2	marginal changes, p. 5	market power, p. 12
economics, p. 2	incentive, p. 6	productivity, p. 13
efficiency, p. 3	market economy, p. 10	inflation, p. 14
equity, p. 3	property rights, p. 12	business cycle, p. 15
opportunity cost, p. 4	market failure, p. 12	
rational people, p. 4	externality, p. 12	

CHAPTER 8 APPLICATION: THE COSTS OF TAXATION **189**

KEY concepts

deadweight loss, p. 176	marginal cost of public	marginal benefit of public
elasticity of the tax base, p. 179	funds, p. 182	funds, p. 187

QUESTIONS FOR review

1. What happens to consumer and producer surplus
   when the sale of a good is taxed? How does the
   change in consumer and producer surplus compare to
   the tax revenue? Explain.

2. Draw a supply-and-demand diagram with a tax on
   the sale of the good. Show the deadweight loss. Show
   the tax revenue.

3. How do the elasticities of supply and demand affect
   the deadweight loss of a tax? Why do they have this
   effect?

4. Why do experts disagree about whether labour taxes
   have small or large deadweight losses?

5. What happens to the deadweight loss and tax revenue
   when a tax is increased?

QUICK CHECK multiple choice

1. In which of the following circumstances does a tax
   on a good have a deadweight loss?
   a. the reduction in consumer and producer surplus is
      greater than the tax revenue
   b. the tax revenue is greater than the reduction in con-
      sumer and producer surplus
   c. the reduction in consumer surplus is greater than
      the reduction in producer surplus
   d. the reduction in producer surplus is greater than
      the reduction in consumer surplus

2. Jane pays Chuck $50 to mow her lawn every week.
   When the government levies a mowing tax of $10
   on Chuck, he raises his price to $60. Jane continues
   to hire him at the higher price. What is the change in
   producer surplus, change in consumer surplus, and
   deadweight loss?
   a. $0, $0, $10
   b. $0, −$10, $0
   c. +$10, −$10, $10
   d. +$10, −$10, $0

3. Eggs have a supply curve that is linear and upward
   sloping and a demand curve that is linear and downward sloping. If a tax of 2 cents per egg is increased to
   3 cents, what happens to the deadweight loss of the tax?
   a. it increases by less than 50 percent and may even
      decline
   b. it increases by exactly 50 percent

c. it increases by more than 50 percent
d. The answer depends on whether supply or
   demand is more elastic.

4. Peanut butter has an upward-sloping supply curve
   and a downward-sloping demand curve. If a tax of
   10 cents per kilogram is increased to 15 cents, what
   happens to the government's tax revenue?
   a. it increases by less than 50 percent and may even decline
   b. it increases by exactly 50 percent
   c. it increases by more than 50 percent
   d. The answer depends on whether supply or
      demand is more elastic.

5. The Laffer curve illustrates that, in some circumstances, the government can reduce a tax on a good
   and increase which of the following?
   a. deadweight loss
   b. government's tax revenue
   c. equilibrium quantity
   d. price paid by consumers

6. If a policymaker wants to raise revenue by taxing
   goods while minimizing the deadweight losses, he
   should look for goods with ___ elasticities of demand
   and ___ elasticities of supply.
   a. small, small
   b. small, large
   c. large, small
   d. large, large

PROBLEMS AND applications

1. The market for pizza is characterized by a downward-
   sloping demand curve and an upward-sloping supply
   curve.

   NEL

a. Draw the competitive market equilibrium. Label
   the price, quantity, consumer surplus, and producer
   surplus. Is there any deadweight loss? Explain.

List of Key Concepts A list of key concepts at the end
of each chapter offers students a way to test their understanding of the new terms that have been introduced. Page
references are included so that students can review terms
they do not understand in the original context.

Questions for Review At the end of each chapter are
questions for review that cover the chapter's primary lessons. Students can use these questions to check their comprehension and to prepare for exams.

Quick Check Multiple Choice These end-of-chapter
questions provide a quick check of the student's understanding of the material in a multiple-choice format.

Problems and Applications Each chapter also contains
a variety of problems and applications that ask students to
apply the material they have learned. Some instructors may
use these questions for homework assignments. Others may
use them as a starting point for classroom discussion.

New in This Eighth Canadian Edition

The eighth Canadian edition of *Principles of Microeconomics* has been carefully revised to ensure its contents are current and its examples reflect the interests and concerns of the student market. In a previous edition, responding to reviewers who requested additional but unobtrusive mathematics support, we supplemented four chapters with new appendices: "The Mathematics of Market Equilibrium" (Chapter 4), "The Mathematics of Market Equilibrium with Taxes" (Chapter 6), "The Mathematics of Consumer and Producer Surplus" (Chapter 7), and "The Mathematics of Deadweight Loss" (Chapter 8). This is continued in the eighth Canadian edition, relying more on a numerical approach, carrying the same demand and supply curves throughout the appendices. We have also included technical questions in all end-of-appendix assignments and assured their difficulty level. Examples, key figures, and graphs have been updated throughout the text. Most photos have been replaced and many new photos are added throughout the new edition. The all-new "Ask the Experts" boxes feature opinions from the world's most prominent economists. The insights from this feature demonstrate to your students situations when economists are united, when they are divided, and when they simply don't know what to think.

Here is a chapter-by-chapter list of significant changes:

Chapter 1 A new case study on crosswalk countdown signals to illustrate principle number 4: people respond to incentives.

Chapter 2 A new Graphing Functions section in the appendix.

Chapter 4 A new In the News feature on Tesla and the Canadian town of Cobalt, Ontario. A new case study on marijuana legalization and black markets.

Chapter 6 An updated discussion on the minimum wage, including a new In the News feature.

Chapter 7 An expanded discussion of the nature of equilibrium in competitive markets, focusing on the coordinating role of markets. A new case study on Uber and consumer surplus and a related In the News feature on the way Taylor Swift sells online concert tickets.

Chapter 8 Major changes emphasizing the relationship between DWL and the behavioural shrinkage in the tax base. New discussion of the marginal cost of public funds, including a case study based on Canadian taxes. More emphasis on the tradeoffs governments make in determining how "big" government should be.

Chapter 9 Inclusion of a general discussion of globalization with a new In the News feature. An enhanced discussion of the "winners" and "losers" from trade, and a brief discussion of the politics of free trade.

Chapter 10 A new case study on climate policy in Canada. A new In the News feature on some externalities associated with marijuana.

Chapter 11 A new section expanding on the difference between public and private goods. A new case study on the elimination of the tolls on Vancouver's Port Mann Bridge.

Chapter 12 Tables and figures updated throughout this chapter. Expanded discussion on the incidence of corporate taxes in Canada.

Chapter 13 A new In the News feature discussing the implications of artificial intelligence (AI) on the future of work.

Chapter 17 A new In the News feature on the "athlete's dilemma," applying game theory to doping in sports.

Chapter 18 Updated case study on productivity and wages in Canada.

Chapter 19 Updated case study on the education wage gap. Updated case study on the gender wage gap.

Chapter 20 Expanded discussion of measuring poverty in Canada.

Instructor Resources

The **Nelson Education Teaching Advantage (NETA)** program delivers research-based instructor resources that promote student engagement and higher-order thinking to enable the success of Canadian students and educators. Visit Nelson Education's **Inspired Instruction** website at nelson.com/inspired/ to find out more about NETA.

The following instructor resources have been created for Mankiw, *Principles of Microeconomics*, Eighth Canadian Edition. Access these ultimate tools for customizing lectures and presentations at nelson.com/instructor.

NETA Test Bank

This resource was written by Angela Trimarchi, Wilfrid Laurier University. It includes over 2800 multiple choice questions written according to NETA guidelines for effective construction and development of higher-order questions. The technical check was performed by Ross Meacher. Also included are approximately 340 true/false and 170 short-answer questions, as well as 120 problems.

The NETA Test Bank is available in a new, cloud-based platform. **Nelson Testing Powered by Cognero®** is a secure online testing system that allows instructors to author, edit, and manage test bank content from anywhere Internet access is available. No special installations or downloads are needed, and the desktop-inspired interface, with its drop-down menus and familiar, intuitive tools, allows instructors to create and manage tests with ease. Multiple test versions can be created in an instant, and content can be imported or exported into other systems. Tests can be delivered from a learning management system, the classroom, or wherever an instructor chooses. Nelson Testing Powered by Cognero for Mankiw, *Principles of Microeconomics*, Eighth Canadian Edition, can be accessed through nelson.com/instructor.

NETA PowerPoint

Microsoft® PowerPoint® lecture slides for every chapter have been created by Marc Prud'Homme, University of Ottawa. There is an average of 35–45 slides per chapter, many featuring key figures, tables, and photographs from Mankiw, *Principles of Microeconomics*, Eighth Canadian Edition. These slides also include instructor notes of suggested classroom activities and links to videos and news articles for classroom discussion. NETA principles of clear design and engaging content have been incorporated throughout, making it simple for instructors to customize the deck for their courses.

Image Library

This resource consists of digital copies of figures, short tables, and photographs used in the book. Instructors may use these jpegs to customize the NETA Power-Point or create their own PowerPoint presentations.

Polling Questions

Another valuable resource for instructors are polling questions created specifically for *Principles of Microeconomics*, Eighth Canadian Edition, by Lavinia Moldovan, Mount Royal Unviersity. Using your favourite polling solution, access a bank of questions created in PowerPoint for use with the eighth Canadian edition.

NETA Instructor's Manual

The Instructor's Manual to accompany Mankiw, *Principles of Microeconomics*, Eighth Canadian Edition, has been prepared by Phil Ghayad and Michel Mayer at Dawson College. This manual contains sample lesson plans, learning objectives, suggested classroom activities, and a resource integration guide to give instructors the support they need to engage their students within the classroom.

Instructor's Solutions Manual

This manual, prepared by the text authors, Ronald D. Kneebone and Kenneth J. McKenzie at the University of Calgary, has been independently checked for accuracy by Racquel Lindsay, University of Toronto. It contains complete solutions to the text's Quick Quizzes, Questions for Review, Quick Check Multiple Choice questions, and Problems.

Aplia + MindTap

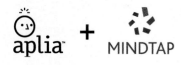

MindTap is the digital platform that propels students from memorization to mastery, helping to challenge them, build their confidence, and empower them to be unstoppable. **Aplia**™ is an application in the MindTap platform that has proven to significantly improve outcomes and elevate thinking by increasing student effort and engagement. Aplia makes it easy to assign frequent online homework assignments and assessments, ensuring students master important concepts. Developed by teachers, Aplia assignments connect concepts to the real world and focus on the unique course challenges faced by students. The MindTap content for *Principles of Microeconomics*, Eighth Canadian Edition, was updated and revised by Anupam Das, Mount Royal University. The Aplia problems for *Principles of Microeconomics*, Eighth Canadian Edition, were updated and revised by Marian Miles, University of Calgary.

The challenging and interactive activities within Aplia guide students through assignments, moving them from basic knowledge and understanding to application and practice. Look for the Aplia logo in the MindTap app dock to explore all that Aplia has to offer. With Aplia, instructors can do the following:

- easily set their course with pre-built, flexible homework assignments;
- author questions (single choice, multiple choice, true/false, essay and numeric entry);
- create custom assignments and populate them with self-authored—and Aplia-authored—questions; and
- inspire students to learn from their mistakes and reward them for effort with the Grade It Now feature that enables three attempts at different versions of a question.

Student Ancillaries

Study Guide

Revised by Peter Fortuna, Algonquin College, and Troy Joseph, Carleton University, this Study Guide was prepared to enhance student success. Each chapter includes learning objectives, a description of the chapter's context and purpose, a chapter review, key terms and definitions, advanced critical thinking questions, and helpful hints for understanding difficult concepts. Students can develop their understanding by doing practical problems and short-answer questions and then assess theory mastery of the key concepts with the self-test, which includes true/false and multiple choice questions prepared and edited under the NETA program for effective question construction. Solutions to all problems are included in the study guide (ISBN: 978-0-17-688809-1).

Aplia + MindTap

Stay organized and efficient with MindTap—a single destination with all your course materials and study tools you need to succeed. Leverage the latest learning technology to stay on track with your learning. For this generation of digital natives, guidance is key to student confidence and engagement. MindTap makes learning a more constant part of your life, motivating you to take a more active role in learning and course preparedness.

- Personalized content in an easy-to-use interface helps you achieve better grades.
- The new MindTap Mobile App allows for learning anytime, anywhere with flashcards, quizzes and notifications.
- The MindTap Reader lets you highlight and take notes online, right within the pages, and easily reference them later.
- ReadSpeaker will read the text to you.

Aplia guides you through assignments, moving from basic knowledge and understanding to application and practice. These challenging and interactive activities are designed to reinforce important concepts. With Aplia, you can do the following:

- learn from mistakes and reinforce your learning with Grade It Now, which provides three attempts at a question;
- get immediate step-by-step feedback; and
- gain understanding through real-world application of concepts.

ACKNOWLEDGMENTS

The success of each Canadian edition of *Principles of Macroeconomics* and *Principles of Microeconomics* has been due, in part, to the reviewers who helped us shape this text, edition after edition. We have benefited enormously from their advice and suggestions.

Rauf Azhar, University of Guelph–Humber

Michael Barber, Queen's University

Catherine Boulatoff, Dalhousie University

Cornelius Christian, Brock University

Samuel Gamtessa, University of Regina

Pierre-Pascal Gendron, Humber College Institute of Technology & Advanced Learning

David Gray, University of Ottawa

Troy Joseph, Carleton University

Ambrose Leung, Mount Royal University

Joy Liu, Vancouver Island University

Logan McLeod, Wilfrid Laurier University

Eric Moon, University of Toronto

Saeed Moshiri, St. Thomas Moore College, University of Saskatchewan

Don Reddick, Kwantlen Polytechnic University

Aqeela Tabassum, Humber College

Mike Tucker, Fanshawe College

Canadianizing this book has been a team effort from the very start. We would like to acknowledge the editorial, production, and marketing teams at Nelson for their professionalism, advice, and encouragement throughout the process. Deserving special attention are Publisher Katherine Baker-Ross and Content Manager Sandy Matos for guiding us through the eighth Canadian edition.

We would also like to thank our colleagues at the University of Calgary who provided invaluable informal input and useful examples and applications. We, of course, bear full responsibility for any misinterpretations and errors.

The student and instructor ancillaries are a key component of this book and we gratefully acknowledge the work of the authors:

Anupam Das, Mount Royal University

Peter Fortura, Algonquin College

Phil Ghayad, Dawson College

Troy Joseph, Carleton University

Michel Mayer, Dawson College

Marian Miles, University of Calgary

Lavinia Moldovan, Mount Royal Unviersity

Marc Prud'Homme, University of Ottawa

Angela Trimarchi, Wilfrid Laurier University

Russell Turner, Fleming College

Lucia Vojtassak, University of Calgary

Finally, we are grateful to our families for their indulgence and encouragement throughout the research and writing process. Their patience and understanding are greatly appreciated.

Ronald D. Kneebone

Kenneth J. McKenzie

August 2019

Singkham/Shutterstock.com

CHAPTER

1

LEARNING
objectives

Ten Principles of Economics

In this chapter, you will ...

1 Learn that economics is about the allocation of scarce resources

2 Examine some of the tradeoffs that people face

3 Learn the meaning of *opportunity cost*

4 See how to use marginal reasoning when making decisions

5 Discuss how incentives affect people's behaviour

6 Consider why trade among people or nations can be good for everyone

7 Discuss why markets are a good, but not perfect, way to allocate resources

8 Learn what determines some trends in the overall economy

The word *economy* comes from the Greek word for "one who manages a household." At first, this origin might seem peculiar. But, in fact, households and economies have much in common.

A household faces many decisions. It must decide which members of the household do which tasks and what each member gets in return: Who cooks dinner? Who does the laundry? Who gets the extra dessert at dinner? Who gets to choose what to binge watch? Who gets to drive the car? In short, the household must allocate its scarce resources (time, dessert, car mileage) among its various members, taking into account each member's abilities, efforts, and desires.

Like a household, a society faces many decisions. A society must decide what jobs will be done and who will do them. It needs some people to grow food, other people to make clothing, and still others to design computer software. Once society has allocated people (as well as land, buildings, and machines) to various jobs, it must also allocate the output of goods and services that they produce. It must decide who will eat caviar and who will eat potatoes. It must decide who will drive a Tesla and who will take the bus.

scarcity
the limited nature of society's resources

The management of society's resources is important because resources are scarce. **Scarcity** means that society has limited resources and therefore cannot produce all the goods and services people wish to have. Just as each member of a household cannot get everything he or she wants, each individual in a society cannot attain the highest standard of living to which he or she might aspire.

economics
the study of how society manages its scarce resources

Economics is the study of how society manages its scarce resources. In most societies, resources are allocated not by an all-powerful dictator but through the combined actions of millions of households and firms. Economists, therefore, study how people make decisions: how much they work, what they buy, how much they save, and how they invest their savings. Economists also study how people interact with one another. For instance, they examine how the multitude of buyers and sellers of a good together determine the price at which the good is sold and the quantity that is sold. Finally, economists analyze forces and trends that affect the economy as a whole, including the growth in average income, the fraction of the population that cannot find work, and the rate at which prices are rising.

The study of economics has many facets but it is unified by several central ideas. In this chapter, we look at ten principles of economics. Don't worry if you don't understand them all at first or if you aren't completely convinced. We explore these ideas more fully in later chapters. The ten principles are introduced here just to give you an overview of what economics is all about. Consider this chapter a "preview of coming attractions."

1-1 How People Make Decisions

There is no mystery to what an economy is. Whether we are talking about the economy of Vancouver, of Canada, or of the whole world, an economy is just a group of people interacting with one another as they go about their lives. Because the behaviour of an economy reflects the behaviour of the individuals who make up the economy, we start our study of economics with four principles of individual decision making.

1-1a Principle #1: People Face Tradeoffs

You may have heard the old saying, "There ain't no such thing as a free lunch." Grammar aside, there is much truth to this adage. To get one thing that we like, we usually have to give up another thing that we like. Making decisions requires trading off one goal against another.

Consider a student who must decide how to allocate her most valuable resource—her time. She can spend all of her time studying economics, spend all of it studying psychology, or divide it between the two fields. For every hour she studies one subject, she gives up an hour she could have used studying the other. And for every hour she spends studying, she gives up an hour that she could have spent napping, bike riding, streaming videos, or working at her part-time job for some extra spending money.

Consider parents deciding how to spend their family income. They can buy food, clothing, or a family vacation. Or they can save some of the family income for retirement or the children's college or university education. When they choose to spend an extra dollar on one of these goods, they have one less dollar to spend on some other good.

When people are grouped into societies, they face different kinds of tradeoffs. One classic tradeoff is between "guns and butter." The more society spends on national defence and security (guns) to protect its shores from foreign aggressors, the less it can spend on consumer goods (butter) to raise the standard of living at home. Also important in modern society is the tradeoff between a clean environment and a high level of income. Laws that require firms to reduce pollution raise the cost of producing goods and services. Because of the higher costs, these firms end up earning smaller profits, paying lower wages, charging higher prices, or some combination of these three. Thus, while pollution regulations give us the benefit of a cleaner environment and the improved health that comes with it, they have the cost of reducing the incomes of the regulated firms' owners, workers, and customers.

Another tradeoff society faces is between efficiency and equity. **Efficiency** means that society is getting the maximum benefits from its scarce resources. **Equity** means that the benefits of those resources are distributed fairly among society's members. In other words, efficiency refers to the size of the economic pie, and equity refers to how the pie is divided into individual slices.

efficiency
the property of society getting the most it can from its scarce resources

equity
the property of distributing economic prosperity fairly among the members of society

When government policies are designed, these two goals often conflict. Consider, for instance, policies aimed at achieving a more equal distribution of economic well-being. Some of these policies, such as the welfare system or Employment Insurance, try to help those members of society who are most in need. Others, such as the individual income tax, ask the financially successful to contribute more than others to support the government. Though they achieve greater equality, these policies may reduce efficiency. When the government redistributes income from the rich to the poor, it reduces the reward for working hard; as a result, people work less and produce fewer goods and services. In other words, when the government tries to cut the economic pie into more equal slices, the pie gets smaller.

Recognizing that people face tradeoffs does not by itself tell us what decisions they will or should make. A student should not abandon the study of psychology just because doing so would increase the time available for the study of economics. Society should not stop protecting the environment just because environmental regulations reduce our material standard of living. The poor should not be ignored just because helping them distorts work incentives. Nonetheless, people are likely to make good decisions only if they understand the options, and the associated costs and benefits, that they have available. Our study of economics, therefore, starts by acknowledging life's tradeoffs.

1-1b Principle #2: The Cost of Something Is What You Give Up to Get It

Because people face tradeoffs, making decisions requires comparing the costs and benefits of alternative courses of action. In many cases, however, the cost of an action is not as obvious as it might first appear.

Consider the decision whether to go to college or university. The main benefits are intellectual enrichment and a lifetime of better job opportunities. But what are the costs? To answer this question, you might be tempted to add up the money you spend on tuition, books, and room and board. Yet this total does not truly represent what you give up to spend a year in college or university.

There are two problems with the calculation. First, it includes some things that are not really costs of going to college or university. Even if you quit school, you would need a place to sleep and food to eat. Room and board are costs of going to college or university only to the extent that they are more expensive there than elsewhere. Second, this calculation ignores the largest cost of going to college or university—your time. When you spend a year listening to lectures, reading textbooks, and writing papers, you cannot spend that time working at a job. For most students, the wages given up to attend school are the largest single cost of their education.

opportunity cost
whatever must be given up to obtain some item

The **opportunity cost** of an item is what you give up to get that item. When making any decision, decision makers should be aware of the opportunity costs that accompany each possible action. In fact, they usually are. College or university-age athletes who can earn millions if they drop out of school and play professional sports are well aware that their opportunity cost of a postsecondary education is very high. It is not surprising that they often decide that the benefit of this education is not worth the cost. Remember, an opportunity cost is an opportunity lost.

You can use forgone wages to measure the opportunity cost of any activity. For example, say you decide to take the day off from work to binge watch the latest season of *Game of Thrones*. The average hourly wage rate for full-time employees in Canada is about $28. The average worker works about 30 hours per week, or about 6 hours per working day (assuming weekends off). Thus, the opportunity cost of taking the day off to binge watch *Game of Thrones* is $168 in forgone wages!

Indeed, you can use any good as the reference good to determine opportunity cost. Depending where you live, the price of a medium double-double at Tim Hortons is about $1.75. So with the $168 in forgone wages you could have bought 96 double-doubles. So, the opportunity cost of binge watching *Game of Thrones* is the 96 double-doubles you could have bought instead.

1-1c Principle #3: Rational People Think at the Margin

Economists normally assume that people are rational. In the final chapter of this book (Chapter 22) we examine some insights from behavioural economics, which considers the implications of systematic departures from rationality. However, for the most part the assumption that people are rational serves us very well. **Rational people** systematically and purposefully do the best they can to achieve their objectives, given the opportunities they have. As you study economics, you will encounter firms that decide how many workers to hire and how much of their product to manufacture and sell to maximize profits. You will also encounter individuals who decide how much time to spend working and what goods and services to buy with the resulting income to achieve the highest possible level of satisfaction.

rational people
those who systematically and purposefully do the best they can to achieve their objectives

Rational people know that decisions in life are rarely black and white, but usually involve shades of grey. At dinnertime, the decision you face is not "Should I fast or eat like a glutton?" More likely, you will be asking yourself "Should I take that extra spoonful of mashed potatoes?" When exams roll around, your decision is not between blowing them off or studying 24 hours a day, but whether to spend an extra hour reviewing your notes instead of watching TV. Economists use the term **marginal changes** to describe small incremental adjustments to an existing plan of action. Keep in mind that "margin" means "edge," so marginal changes are adjustments around the edges of what you are doing. Rational people often make decisions by comparing *marginal benefits* and *marginal costs.*

marginal changes
small incremental adjustments to a plan of action

For example, suppose you are considering calling a friend on your cell phone. You decide that talking with her for 10 minutes would give you a benefit that you value at about $7. Your cell phone service costs you $40 per month plus $0.50 per minute for whatever calls you make. You usually talk for 100 minutes a month, so your total monthly bill is $90 ($0.50 per minute times 100 minutes, plus the $40 fixed fee). Under these circumstances, should you make the call? You might be tempted to reason as follows: "Because I pay $90 for 100 minutes of calling each month, the average minute on the phone costs me $0.90. So a 10-minute call costs $9. Because that $9 cost is greater than the $7 benefit, I am going to skip the call." That conclusion is wrong, however. Although the *average* cost of a 10-minute call is $9, the *marginal* cost—the amount your bill increases if you make the extra call—is only $5. You will make the right decision only by comparing the marginal benefit and the marginal cost. Because the marginal benefit of $7 is greater than the marginal cost of $5 ($0.50 per minute $\times$ 10 minutes = $5), you should make the call. This is a principle that people innately understand: Cell phone users with unlimited minutes (that is, minutes that are free at the margin) are often prone to make long and frivolous calls.

Thinking at the margin works for business decisions as well. Consider an airline deciding how much to charge passengers who fly standby. Suppose that flying a 200-seat plane across Canada costs the airline $100 000. In this case, the average cost of each seat is $100 000/200, which is $500. One might be tempted to conclude that the airline should never sell a ticket for less than $500. Actually, a rational airline can often find ways to raise its profits by thinking at the margin. Imagine that a plane is about to take off with 10 empty seats, and a standby passenger is waiting at the gate willing to pay $300 for a seat. Should the airline sell the ticket? Of course it should. If the plane has empty seats, the cost of adding one more passenger is tiny. Although the *average* cost of flying a passenger is $500, the *marginal* cost is merely the cost of the bag of peanuts and can of soda that the extra passenger will consume. As long as the standby passenger pays more than the marginal cost, selling him a ticket is profitable.

Marginal decision making can help explain some otherwise puzzling economic phenomena. Here is a classic question: Why is water so cheap, while diamonds are so expensive? Humans need water to survive, while diamonds are unnecessary; but, for some reason, people are willing to pay much more for a diamond than for a cup of water. The reason is that a person's willingness to pay for a good is based on the marginal benefit that an extra unit of the good will yield. The marginal benefit, in turn, depends on how many units a person already has. Water is essential but the marginal benefit of an extra cup is small because water is plentiful. By contrast, no one needs diamonds to survive, but because diamonds are so rare people consider the marginal benefit of an extra diamond to be large.

A rational decision maker takes an action if and only if the marginal benefit of the action exceeds the marginal cost. This principle can explain why people use their cell phones as much as they do, why airlines are willing to sell a ticket below average cost, and why people are willing to pay more for diamonds than for water. It can take some time to get used to the logic of marginal thinking, but the study of economics will give you ample opportunity to practise.

1-1d Principle #4: People Respond to Incentives

incentive
something that induces a person to act

An **incentive** is something (such as the prospect of a punishment or a reward) that induces a person to act. Because rational people make decisions by comparing costs and benefits, they respond to incentives. You will see that incentives play a central role in the study of economics. One economist went so far as to suggest that the entire field could be summarized simply: "People respond to incentives. The rest is commentary."

Incentives are crucial to analyzing how markets work. For example, when the price of an apple rises, people decide to eat fewer apples. At the same time, apple orchards decide to hire more workers and harvest more apples. In other words, a higher price in a market provides an incentive for buyers to consume less and an incentive for sellers to produce more. As we will see, the influence of prices on the behaviour of consumers and producers is crucial for how a market economy allocates scarce resources.

Public policymakers should never forget about incentives. Many policies change the costs or benefits that people face and, as a result, alter their behaviour. A tax on gasoline, for instance, encourages people to drive smaller, more fuel-efficient cars. That is one reason why people drive smaller cars in Europe, where gasoline taxes are high, than in Canada, where gasoline taxes are lower. A higher gasoline tax also encourages people to carpool, take public transportation, and live closer to where they work. If the tax were larger, more people would drive hybrid cars, and if it were large enough, they would switch to electric cars.

When policymakers fail to consider how their policies affect incentives, they often end up with unintended consequences. For example, consider public policy regarding auto safety. Today all cars have seat belts, but that was not true 50 years ago. In the 1960s, Ralph Nader's book *Unsafe at Any Speed* generated much public concern over auto safety. Parliament responded with laws requiring seat belts as standard equipment on new cars.

How does a seat belt law affect auto safety? The direct effect is obvious: When a person wears a seat belt, the probability of surviving an auto accident rises. But that's not the end of the story, because the law also affects behaviour by altering incentives. The relevant behaviour here is the speed and care with which drivers operate their cars. Driving slowly and carefully is costly because it uses the driver's time and energy. When deciding how safely to drive, rational people compare the marginal benefit from safer driving to the marginal cost. As a result, they drive more slowly and carefully when the benefit of increased safety is high. For example, when road conditions are icy, people drive more attentively and at lower speeds than they do when road conditions are clear.

Consider how a seat belt law alters a driver's cost–benefit calculation. Seat belts make accidents less costly because they reduce the likelihood of injury or death. In other words, seat belts reduce the benefits to slow and careful driving. People respond to seat belts as they would to an improvement in road conditions—by

IN THE **news**

Even Criminals Respond to Incentives

Principle #4, people respond to incentives, is at the core of the study of economics. As the following article explains, this principle applies to all sorts of activities, even of the criminal kind.

Risk, Reward and the Economics of the Criminal Mind

By Todd Hirsch

Last week's *Economist* magazine carried a headline reading, "The Curious Case of the Fall in Crime." It seems that all around the industrialized world—including Canada—all kinds of criminal activity are on the decline. Contrary to the belief that evil thugs lurk around every corner, we are actually safer than we have been in decades. In today's underground economy, identity theft makes better economic sense than stealing a flat-screen television.

The magazine's editorial offers only guesses as to why crime rates are falling. Aging demographics may play a role, along with better theft-prevention technologies. Stiffer punishment and "get tough on crime" policies might make for good political posturing, but they seem to have little impact: Crime rates are falling in countries where sentencing has become tougher as well as where it has been loosened.

The Economist failed to mention the most obvious reason for the change: economic incentives. Thieves are simply doing what most of us do every day: They are responding to market signals.

This is particularly true of property crimes such as residential break-and-enter, car theft and armed robbery. The possible payoff for stealing from a home is dwindling. What is there worth taking? Electronics are increasingly less valuable—a computer or a television in the 1980s would have been worth thousands of dollars on the street; now they would fetch a few

hundred bucks. Why buy a stolen iPod dock out of the back of some guy's truck when you can get a new one for less than $100?

Car theft is down dramatically, too. According to Statistics Canada, car theft in Ontario plunged to 141 per 100,000 people last year, down from 443 in 1998. Better technology, car alarm systems and anti-theft devices have deterred most would-be thieves. And lower-priced cars without car alarms probably are not worth stealing anyway. The bad guys aren't less bad, they're just good economists.

Muggings and purse snatchings are increasingly less common as well. But let's not overthink the reasons why fewer thieves are snatching purses. It has nothing to do with the culprit's age or job situation. Whether there was a father present in the thief's childhood or whether he or she played violent video games are irrelevant. The reason is that there's just not much of value inside purses or wallets anymore. Cash has been largely replaced by debit and credit cards, and as long as the PIN is secure, the thief gets away with nothing more than plastic cards and chewing gum. Cellphones are more costly, but stolen ones are difficult to wipe and resell.

Criminals, like all of us, respond to market signals. If the potential payoff for any activity is too low, we weigh the risks and decide it isn't worth it. For noncriminals, the question isn't "Should I steal this car?" but something along the lines of "Should I put in new bathroom tile before I list my house?" People are quite good at reading and responding to market signals.

Still, we shouldn't think that poor economic incentives are making crime go away. Crime

is simply morphing. Traditional crime statistics tend to focus on activities such as robbery, property theft and murder. Fewer long-term trend statistics are available for crimes that are doubtless increasing, such as identity theft and cybercrime. Not only are they potentially more lucrative, they are global in scope and much more difficult to track.

Thieves are also getting smarter, using technology for evil deeds. Internet scams abound, and bank-card skimming and credit-card fraud is a serious problem. Banks have had to fight back with their own technology and it has been costly.

Economic incentives play a huge role motivating us in almost everything we do. Certain actions are no doubt spurred by altruism and generosity, such as helping our neighbour shovel snow or donating to charity (although we still want the tax receipt). Weighing the financial incentives against the potential risks is the basis of our economy. Criminals may not know they're doing it, but they're just responding to market signals—and doing a good job of it.

Source: "Risk, Reward and the Economics of the Criminal Mind," by Todd Hirsch, August 1, 2013, *The Globe and Mail.* Reproduced by permission of the author.

driving faster and less carefully. The result of a seat belt law, therefore, is a larger number of accidents. The decline in safe driving has a clear, adverse impact on pedestrians, who are more likely to find themselves in an accident but (unlike the drivers) don't have the benefit of added protection.

At first, this discussion of incentives and seat belts might seem like idle speculation. Yet in a classic 1975 study, economist Sam Peltzman argued that auto-safety laws have had many of these effects. According to Peltzman's evidence, these laws produce both fewer deaths per accident and more accidents. He concluded that the net result is little change in the number of driver deaths and an increase in the number of pedestrian deaths.

Peltzman's analysis of auto safety is an offbeat and controversial example of the general principle that people respond to incentives. When analyzing any policy, we must consider not only the direct effects but also the indirect effects that work through incentives. If the policy changes incentives, it will cause people to alter their behaviour.

case study   **Ready, Set, Go . . .**

Another auto safety example of how the behavioural responses of individuals can lead to unintended consequences involves crosswalk countdown signals. Standard crosswalk signals are being replaced in many cities with countdown signals, which indicate how much time is left for pedestrians to cross the street. The rationale for these signals is to increase safety by giving pedestrians more information about how much time they have to cross the street before the walk light changes.

An important question, then is this: Have these countdown signals actually made intersections safer? Two Canadian economists, Arvind Magesan and Sacha Kapoor, address this question using data on accidents from Toronto. The title of their paper is "Paging Inspector Sands: The Costs of Public Information." Who, you may ask, is Inspector Sands? We will get to that, but first let's look at their study.

When Toronto city officials looked at the data on traffic accidents at intersections where the countdown signals were installed, they noted that accidents were lower at those intersections after the signals were installed. Thus, they concluded, the new signals seem to have worked as intended—accidents declined at intersections where the new signals were installed.

However, this conclusion does not necessarily follow. The reason is that there may have been a general decline in accidents over the time period that had nothing to do with the installation of countdown signals. Maybe accidents were trending downward in any event, independently of the countdown signals.

It turns out that the way that the signals were installed in Toronto generated what economists call a natural experiment. In particular, they were installed randomly at different intersections at different times. This generated a natural control group (intersections without countdown signals) and a treatment group (intersections with signals).

Magesan and Kapoor exploited this natural experiment using what is called the difference-in-differences approach. This involves first calculating the difference (the change) in accidents over a particular time period for both the control and treatment groups. They found that accidents decreased *both* in intersections where the new signals were installed and in intersections where they were not installed. This suggests that there does indeed seem to have been something that caused a general reduction in accidents in all intersections. They then calculated the difference in this difference between the control and the treatment groups. Interestingly, they found that accidents decreased more in intersections where the countdown signals were not installed (the control group) than in intersections where the signals were installed (the treatment group). This suggests that, controlling for the general secular decline in accidents, installing countdown signals actually led to more accidents, not fewer!

How could this be? People respond to incentives. The countdown signals provide more information to both pedestrians and drivers. As a result of this increased information, both pedestrians and drivers tend to act more aggressively at intersections with countdown signals. We have all witnessed pedestrians dashing across the street with just five seconds left on the countdown signal and drivers quickly turning right or left in front of them as they see that same five seconds remaining.

This is a good example of how changes in behaviour in response to a government policy can give rise to unintended consequences. It also suggests that providing more information may not necessarily help people make better decisions. We will briefly revisit this case study in Chapter 2 when we discuss cause and effect and the interpretation of economic data.

Which brings us to the title of the paper. "Paging Inspector Sands" is the code phrase used by public transportation authorities in the United Kingdom to alert staff and police to a potential emergency without alerting the public, possibly causing a panic. So if you happen to be on the London Underground and hear "Would Inspector Sands please report to Platform 3" on the PA system, you may want to consider running for your life. ■

"For $5 a week you can watch baseball without being nagged to cut the grass!"

 QUICK Quiz *Describe an important tradeoff you recently faced. • Give an example of some action that has both a monetary and nonmonetary opportunity cost. • Describe an incentive your parents and/or guardians offered to you in an effort to influence your behaviour.*

1-2 How People Interact

The first four principles discussed how individuals make decisions. As we go about our lives, many of our decisions affect not only ourselves but other people as well. The next three principles concern how people interact with one another.

1-2a Principle #5: Trade Can Make Everyone Better Off

You may have heard on the news that the Americans are our competitors in the world economy. In some ways this is true, for Canadian and U.S. firms do produce many of the same goods. Companies in Canada and the United States compete for the same customers in the markets for clothing, toys, solar panels, automobile tires, and many other items.

Yet it is easy to be misled when thinking about competition among countries. Trade between Canada and the United States is not like a sports contest, where one side wins and the other side loses. In fact, the opposite is true: Trade between two countries can make each country better off.

To see why, consider how trade affects your family. When a member of your family looks for a job, he or she competes against members of other families who are looking for jobs. Families also compete against one another when they go shopping because each family wants to buy the best goods at the lowest prices. In a sense, each family in an economy competes with all other families.

Despite this competition, your family would not be better off isolating itself from all other families. If it did, your family would need to grow its own food, make its own clothes, and build its own home. Clearly, your family gains much from its ability to trade with others. Trade allows each person to specialize in the activities he or she does best, whether it is farming, sewing, or home building. By trading with others, people can buy a greater variety of goods and services at lower cost.

Like families, countries also benefit from the ability to trade with one another. Trade allows countries to specialize in what they do best and to enjoy a greater variety of goods and services. The Americans, as well as the French and the Egyptians and the Mexicans, are as much our partners in the world economy as they are our competitors.

1-2b Principle #6: Markets Are Usually a Good Way to Organize Economic Activity

The collapse of communism in the Soviet Union and Eastern Europe in the 1980s was one of the last century's most important changes. Communist countries operated on the premise that government officials were in the best position to allocate the economy's scarce resources. These central planners decided what goods and services were produced, how much was produced, and who produced and consumed these goods and services. The theory behind central planning was that only the government could organize economic activity in a way that promoted economic well-being for the country as a whole.

market economy
an economy that allocates resources through the decentralized decisions of many firms and households as they interact in markets for goods and services

Most countries that once had centrally planned economies have abandoned this system and are trying to develop market economies. In a **market economy**, the decisions of a central planner are replaced by the decisions of millions of firms and households. Firms decide whom to hire and what to make. Households decide which firms to work for and what to buy with their incomes. These firms and households interact in the marketplace, where prices and self-interest guide their decisions.

At first glance, the success of market economies is puzzling. In a market economy, no one is looking out for the economic well-being of society as a whole. Free markets contain many buyers and sellers of numerous goods and services, and all of them are interested primarily in their own well-being. Yet, despite decentralized decision making and self-interested decision makers, market economies have proven remarkably successful in organizing economic activity to promote overall economic well-being.

In his 1776 book *An Inquiry into the Nature and Causes of the Wealth of Nations*, economist Adam Smith made the most famous observation in all of economics: Households and firms interacting in markets act as if they are guided by an "invisible hand" that leads them to desirable market outcomes. One of our goals in this book is to understand how this invisible hand works its magic.

As you study economics, you will learn that prices are the instrument with which the invisible hand directs economic activity. In any market, buyers look at the price when determining how much to demand, and sellers look at the price when deciding how much to supply. As a result of the decisions that buyers and sellers make, market prices reflect both the value of a good to society and the cost to society of making the good. Smith's great insight was that prices adjust to guide these individual buyers and sellers to reach outcomes that, in many cases, maximize the aggregate well-being of society as a whole.

Smith's insight has an important corollary: When the government prevents prices from adjusting naturally to supply and demand, it impedes the invisible hand's ability to coordinate the millions of households and firms that make up the economy. This corollary explains why taxes adversely affect the allocation of resources: They distort prices and thus the decisions of households and firms. It also explains the harm that can be caused by policies that directly control prices, such as rent control. And it explains the failure of communism. In communist countries, prices were not determined in the marketplace but were dictated by central planners. These planners lacked the necessary information about consumers' tastes and producers' costs, which in a market economy is reflected in prices. Central planners failed because they tried to run the economy with one hand tied behind their backs—the invisible hand of the marketplace.

Adam Smith Would Have Loved Uber

case study You probably have never lived in a centrally planned economy, but if you have ever tried to hail a cab in a major city you likely have experienced a highly regulated market. In many cities, the local government imposes strict controls in the market for taxis. The rules usually go well beyond regulation of insurance and safety. For example, the government may limit entry into the market by approving only a certain number of taxi medallions or permits. It may determine the prices that taxis are allowed to charge. The government uses its police powers—that is, the threat of fines or jail time—to keep unauthorized drivers off the streets and to prevent all drivers from charging unauthorized prices.

Recently, however, this highly controlled market has been invaded by a disruptive force: Uber. Launched in 2009, this company provides an app for smartphones that connects passengers and drivers. Because Uber cars do not roam the streets looking for taxi-hailing pedestrians, they technically are not taxis and so are not subject to the same regulations. But they offer much the same service. Indeed, rides from Uber cars often are more convenient. On a cold and rainy day, who wants to stand on the side of the road waiting for an empty cab to drive by? It is more pleasant to remain inside, use your smartphone to arrange for a ride, and stay warm and dry until the car arrives.

Uber cars often charge less than taxis, but not always. Uber allows drivers to raise their prices significantly when there is a surge in demand, such as during a sudden rainstorm or late on New Year's Eve, when numerous tipsy partiers are looking for a safe way to get home. By contrast, regulated taxis are typically prevented from surge pricing.

Not everyone is fond of Uber. Drivers of traditional taxis complain that this new competition eats into their source of income. This is hardly a surprise: Suppliers of goods and services usually dislike new competitors. But vigorous competition among producers makes a market work well for consumers.

That is why economists love Uber. A 2014 survey of several dozen prominent economists asked whether car services such as Uber increased consumer well-being. Yes, said every single economist. The economists were also asked whether surge pricing increased consumer well-being. Yes, said 85 percent of them. Surge pricing makes consumers pay more at times, but because Uber drivers respond to incentives it also increases the quantity of car services supplied when they are most needed. Surge pricing also helps allocate the services to those consumers who value them most highly and reduces the costs of searching and waiting for a car.

If Adam Smith were alive today, he would surely have the Uber app on his phone. We will revisit Uber later on, in Chapter 7. ■

1-2c Principle #7: Governments Can Sometimes Improve Market Outcomes

If the invisible hand of the market is so great, why do we need government? One purpose of studying economics is to refine your view about the proper role and scope of government policy.

One reason we need government is that the invisible hand can work its magic only if the government enforces the rules and maintains the institutions that are key to a market economy. Most important, market economies need institutions to enforce **property rights** so individuals can own and control scarce resources. A farmer won't grow food if she expects her crop to be stolen, a restaurant won't serve meals unless it is assured that customers will pay before they leave, and an entertainment company won't make their movie available for streaming if too many potential customers avoid paying by making illegal copies. We all rely on government-provided police and courts to enforce our rights over the things we produce—and the invisible hand counts on our ability to enforce our rights.

Another reason we need government is that, although the invisible hand is powerful, it is not omnipotent. There are two broad reasons for a government to intervene in the economy and change the allocation of resources that people would choose on their own: to promote efficiency and to promote equity. That is, most policies aim either to enlarge the economic pie or to change how the pie is divided.

Consider first the goal of efficiency. Although the invisible hand usually leads markets to allocate resources to maximize the size of the economic pie, this is not always the case. Economists use the term **market failure** to refer to a situation in which the market on its own fails to produce an efficient allocation of resources. As we will see, one possible cause of market failure is an **externality**, which is the impact of one person's actions on the well-being of a bystander. The classic example of an externality is pollution. When the production of a good pollutes the air and creates health problem for those who live near the factories, the market left to its own devices may fail to take this cost into account. Another possible cause of market failure is **market power**, which refers to the ability of a single person or firm (or a small group) to unduly influence market prices. For example, if everyone in town needs water but there is only one well, the owner of the well is not subject to the rigorous competition with which the invisible hand normally keeps self-interest in check; she may take advantage of this opportunity by restricting the output of water so she can charge a higher price. In the presence of externalities or market power, well-designed public policy can enhance economic efficiency.

Now consider the goal of equity. Even when the invisible hand yields efficient outcomes, it can nonetheless leave sizable disparities in economic well-being. A market economy rewards people according to their ability to produce things that other people are willing to pay for. The world's best basketball player earns more than the world's best chess player simply because people are willing to

---

property rights
the ability of an individual to own and exercise control over scarce resources

market failure
a situation in which a market left on its own fails to allocate resources efficiently

externality
the impact of one person's actions on the well-being of a bystander

market power
the ability of a single economic actor (or small group of actors) to have a substantial influence on market prices

pay more to watch basketball than chess. The invisible hand does not ensure that everyone has sufficient food, decent clothing, and adequate health care. This inequality may, depending on one's political philosophy, call for government intervention. In practice, many public policies, such as the income tax and welfare systems, aim to achieve a more equitable distribution of economic well-being.

To say that the government *can* improve on market outcomes at times does not mean that it always *will*. Public policy is made not by angels but by a political process that is far from perfect. Sometimes policies are designed simply to reward the politically powerful. Sometimes they are made by well-intentioned leaders who are not fully informed. As you study economics you will become a better judge of when a government policy is justifiable because it promotes efficiency or equity, and when it is not.

QUICK Quiz *Why is a country better off not isolating itself from all other countries? • Why do we have markets and, according to economists, what roles should government play in them?*

1-3 How the Economy as a Whole Works

We started by discussing how individuals make decisions and then looked at how people interact with one another. All these decisions and interactions together make up "the economy." The last three principles concern the workings of the economy as a whole.

1-3a Principle #8: A Country's Standard of Living Depends on Its Ability to Produce Goods and Services

The differences in living standards around the world are staggering. In 2014, the average Canadian had an income of about $49 000. In the same year, the average American earned about $55 000, the average Mexican about $17 000, the average Chinese about $13 000, and the average Nigerian earned only $6000. Not surprisingly, this large variation in average income is reflected in various measures of the quality of life. Citizens of high-income countries have more TV sets, more cars, better nutrition, better health care, and longer life expectancy than citizens of low-income countries.

Changes in living standards over time are also large. In Canada, individuals' incomes have historically grown about 2 percent per year (after adjusting for changes in the cost of living). At this rate, average income doubles every 35 years. Over the past century, average Canadian income has risen about eightfold.

What explains these large differences in living standards among countries and over time? The answer is surprisingly simple. Almost all variation in living standards is attributable to differences in countries' **productivity**—that is, the amount of goods and services produced from each unit of labour input. In nations where workers can produce a large quantity of goods and services per hour, most people enjoy a high standard of living; in nations where workers are less productive, most people endure a more meagre existence. Similarly, the growth rate of a nation's productivity determines the growth rate of its average income.

productivity
the quantity of goods and services produced from each hour of a worker's time

The fundamental relationship between productivity and living standards is simple, but its implications are far-reaching. If productivity is the primary determinant of living standards, other explanations must be of secondary importance. For example, it might be tempting to credit labour unions or minimum-wage laws for the rise in living standards of Canadian workers over the past century. Yet the real hero of Canadian workers is their rising productivity. As another example, some commentators have claimed that increased competition from Japan and other countries explained the slow growth in Canadian incomes during the 1970s and 1980s. Yet the real villain was not competition from abroad but flagging productivity growth in Canada.

The relationship between productivity and living standards also has profound implications for public policy. When thinking about how any policy will affect living standards, the key question is how it will affect our ability to produce goods and services. To boost living standards, policymakers need to raise productivity by ensuring that workers are well educated, have the tools needed to produce goods and services, and have access to the best available technology.

1-3b Principle #9: Prices Rise When the Government Prints Too Much Money

inflation

an increase in the overall level of prices in the economy

In January 1921, a daily newspaper in Germany cost 0.30 marks. Less than two years later, in November 1922, the same newspaper cost 70 000 000 marks. All other prices in the economy rose by similar amounts. This episode is one of history's most spectacular examples of **inflation**, an increase in the overall level of prices in the economy.

Although Canada has never experienced inflation even close to that in Germany in the 1920s, inflation has at times been an economic problem. During the 1970s, for instance, average inflation was 8 percent per year and the overall level of prices more than doubled. By contrast, inflation in the 1990s was about 2 percent per year; at this rate it would take 35 years for prices to double. Because high inflation imposes various costs on society, keeping inflation at a low level is a goal of economic policymakers around the world.

What causes inflation? In almost all cases of large or persistent inflation, the culprit is growth in the quantity of money. When a government creates large quantities of the nation's money, the value of the money falls. In Germany in the early 1920s, when prices were on average tripling every month, the quantity of money was also tripling every month. Although less dramatic, the economic history of Canada points to a similar conclusion: The high inflation of the 1970s was associated with rapid growth in the quantity of money, and the low inflation of the 1990s was associated with slow growth in the quantity of money.

1-3c Principle #10: Society Faces a Short-Run Tradeoff between Inflation and Unemployment

Although a higher level of prices is, in the long run, the primary effect of increasing the quantity of money, the short-run story is more complex and more controversial. Most economists describe the short-run effects of monetary injections as follows:

- Increasing the amount of money in the economy stimulates the overall level of spending and thus the demand for goods and services.

- Higher demand may over time cause firms to raise their prices, but in the meantime it also encourages them to increase the quantity of goods and services they produce and to hire more workers to produce those goods and services.
- More hiring means lower unemployment.

This line of reasoning leads to one final economy-wide tradeoff: a short-run tradeoff between inflation and unemployment.

Although some economists still question these ideas, most accept that society faces a short-run tradeoff between inflation and unemployment. This simply means that, over a period of a year or two, many economic policies push inflation and unemployment in opposite directions. Policymakers face this tradeoff regardless of whether inflation and unemployment both start out at high levels (as they did in the early 1980s), at low levels (as they did in the late 1990s), or somewhere in between. This short-run tradeoff plays a key role in the analysis of the **business cycle**—the irregular and largely unpredictable fluctuations in economic activity, as measured by the production of goods and services or the number of people employed.

business cycle

fluctuations in economic activity, such as employment and production

Policymakers can exploit the short-run tradeoff between inflation and unemployment using various policy instruments. By changing the amount that the government spends, the amount it taxes, and the amount of money it prints, policymakers can influence the combination of inflation and unemployment that the economy experiences. Because these instruments of monetary and fiscal policy are potentially so powerful, how policymakers should use these instruments to control the economy, if at all, is a subject of continuing debate.

This debate heated up in 2008. In 2008 and 2009, the Canadian economy, as well as many other economies around the world, experienced a deep economic downturn. Problems in the financial system spilled over to the rest of the economy, causing incomes to fall and unemployment to soar. Policymakers responded in various ways to increase the overall demand for goods and services. The Canadian government introduced a major stimulus package of increased government spending. At the same time, the Bank of Canada increased the supply of money. The goal of these policies was to reduce unemployment. Some feared, however, that these policies might over time lead to an excessive level of inflation. This has not happened yet, but some argue that pent up inflationary pressures may emerge in time.

 List and briefly explain the three principles that describe how the economy as a whole works.

1-4 Conclusion

You now have a taste of what economics is all about. In the coming chapters we develop many specific insights about people, markets, and economies. Mastering these insights will take some effort, but it is not an overwhelming task. The field of economics is based on a few basic ideas that can be applied in many different situations.

Throughout this book we will refer back to the *Ten Principles of Economics* highlighted in this chapter and summarized in Table 1.1. Keep these building blocks in mind: Even the most sophisticated economic analysis is founded on the ten principles introduced here.

TABLE 1.1

Ten Principles of Economics

How People Make Decisions

#1: People face tradeoffs.

#2: The cost of something is what you give up to get it.

#3: Rational people think at the margin.

#4: People respond to incentives.

How People Interact

#5: Trade can make everyone better off.

#6: Markets are usually a good way to organize economic activity.

#7: Governments can sometimes improve market outcomes.

How the Economy as a Whole Works

#8: A country's standard of living depends on its ability to produce goods and services.

#9: Prices rise when the government prints too much money.

#10: Society faces a short-run tradeoff between inflation and unemployment.

summary

- The fundamental lessons about individual decision making are that people face tradeoffs among alternative goals, that the cost of any action is measured in terms of forgone opportunities, that rational people make decisions by comparing marginal costs and marginal benefits, and that people change their behaviour in response to the incentives they face.

- The fundamental lessons about interactions among people are that trade and interdependence can be mutually beneficial, that markets are usually a good way of coordinating trade among people, and that the government can potentially improve market outcomes if there is some market failure or if the market outcome is inequitable.

- The fundamental lessons about the economy as a whole are that productivity is the ultimate source of living standards, that money growth is the ultimate source of inflation, and that society faces a short-run tradeoff between inflation and unemployment.

KEY concepts

scarcity, *p. 2*
economics, *p. 2*
efficiency, *p. 3*
equity, *p. 3*
opportunity cost, *p. 4*
rational people, *p. 4*

marginal changes, *p. 5*
incentive, *p. 6*
market economy, *p. 10*
property rights, *p. 12*
market failure, *p. 12*
externality, *p. 12*

market power, *p. 12*
productivity, *p. 13*
inflation, *p. 14*
business cycle, *p. 15*

QUESTIONS FOR review

1. What is a tradeoff? Give three examples of tradeoffs that you face in your life.

2. What is the opportunity cost of seeing a movie?

3. Water is necessary for life. Is the marginal benefit of a glass of water large or small?

4. Why should policymakers think about incentives?

5. Why isn't trade among countries like a game, with some winners and some losers?

6. What does the "invisible hand" of the marketplace do?

7. Explain the two main causes of market failure and give an example of each.

8. Why is productivity important?

9. What is inflation, and what causes it?

10. How are inflation and unemployment related in the short run?

QUICK CHECK **multiple choice**

1. Economics is best defined as the study of which of the following?
   a. how society manages its scarce resources
   b. how to run a business most profitably
   c. how to predict inflation, unemployment, and stock prices
   d. how the government can stop the harm from unchecked self-interest

2. What is your opportunity cost of going to a movie?
   a. the price of the ticket
   b. the price of the ticket plus the cost of any soda and popcorn you buy at the theatre
   c. the total cash expenditure needed to go to the movie plus the value of your time
   d. zero, as long as you enjoy the movie and consider it a worthwhile use of time and money

3. Which of the following describes a marginal change?
   a. one that is NOT important for public policy
   b. one that incrementally alters an existing plan
   c. one that makes an outcome inefficient
   d. one that does NOT influence incentives

4. What is Adam Smith's "invisible hand"?
   a. the subtle and often hidden methods that businesses use to profit at consumers' expense
   b. the ability of free markets to reach desirable outcomes despite the self-interest of market participants
   c. the ability of government regulation to benefit consumers even if the consumers are unaware of the regulations
   d. the way in which producers or consumers in unregulated markets impose costs on innocent bystanders

5. When policymakers make policies that change the costs and benefits that people face, what is the result for society?
   a. people's behaviours are altered
   b. people ignore incentives
   c. inflation occurs
   d. government revenue is reduced

6. If a nation has high and persistent inflation, what is the most likely explanation?
   a. the central bank is creating excessive amounts of money
   b. unions are bargaining for excessively high wages
   c. the government is imposing excessive levels of taxation
   d. firms are using their monopoly power to enforce excessive price hikes

PROBLEMS AND **applications**

1. Describe some of the tradeoffs faced by each of the following.
   a. a family deciding whether to buy a new car
   b. a member of Parliament deciding how much to spend on national parks
   c. a company president deciding whether to open a new factory
   d. a professor deciding how much to prepare for class

2. You are trying to decide whether to take a vacation. Most of the costs of the vacation (airfare, hotel, forgone wages) are measured in dollars, but the benefits of the vacation are psychological. How can you compare the benefits to the costs?

3. You were planning to spend Saturday working at your part-time job, but a friend asks you to go skiing. What is the true cost of going skiing? Now suppose that you had been planning to spend the day studying at the library. What is the cost of going skiing in this case? Explain.

4. You win $100 in a hockey pool. You have a choice between spending the money now or putting it away for a year in a bank account that pays 5 percent interest. What is the opportunity cost of spending the $100 now?

5. The company that you manage has invested $5 million in developing a new product, but the development is not quite finished. At a recent meeting, your salespeople report that the introduction of competing products has reduced the expected sales of your new product to $3 million. If it would cost $1 million to finish development and make the product, should you go ahead and do so? What is the most that you should pay to complete development?

6. The welfare system provides income for people who are very poor, with low incomes and few assets. If a recipient of welfare payments decides to work and earn some money, the amount he or she receives in welfare payments is reduced.
   a. How does this affect the incentive to work?
   b. How does this feature of the welfare represent the tradeoff between equality and efficiency?

7. Your roommate is a better cook than you are, but you can clean more quickly than your roommate can. If your roommate did all of the cooking and you did all of the cleaning, would your chores take you more or less time than if you divided each task evenly? Give a similar example of how specialization and trade can make two countries both better off.

8. Nations with corrupt police and court systems typically have lower standards of living than nations with less corruption. Why might that be the case?

9. Explain whether each of the following government activities is motivated by a concern about equity or a concern about efficiency. In the case of efficiency, discuss the type of market failure involved.
   a. regulating cable TV prices
   b. providing some poor people with free prescription drugs
   c. prohibiting smoking in public places
   d. preventing mergers between major banks
   e. imposing higher personal income tax rates on people with higher incomes
   f. instituting laws against driving while intoxicated

10. Discuss each of the following statements from the standpoints of equity and efficiency.
    a. "Everyone in society should be guaranteed the best health care possible."
    b. "When workers are laid off, they should be able to collect unemployment benefits until they find a new job."

11. In what ways is your standard of living different from that of your parents or grandparents when they were your age? Why have these changes occurred?

12. Suppose Canadians decide to save more of their incomes. If banks lend this extra saving to businesses, which use the funds to build new factories, how might this lead to faster growth in productivity? Who do you suppose benefits from the higher productivity? Is society getting a free lunch?

Thinking Like an Economist

In this chapter, you will ...

1 See how economists apply the methods of science

2 Consider how assumptions and models can shed light on the world

3 Learn two simple models—the circular flow and the production possibilities frontier

4 Distinguish between microeconomics and macroeconomics

5 Learn the difference between positive and normative statements

6 Examine the role of economists in making policy

7 Consider why economists sometimes disagree with one another

Every field of study has its own language and its own way of thinking. Mathematicians talk about axioms, integrals, and vector spaces. Psychologists talk about ego, id, and cognitive dissonance. Lawyers talk about venue, torts, and promissory estoppel.

Economics is no different. Supply, demand, elasticity, comparative advantage, consumer surplus, deadweight loss—these terms are part of the economist's language. In the coming chapters, you will encounter many new terms and some familiar words that economists use in specialized ways. At first, this new language may seem needlessly arcane. But, as you will see, its value lies in its ability to provide you with a new and useful way of thinking about the world in which you live.

The purpose of this book is to help you learn the economist's way of thinking. Just as you cannot become a mathematician, psychologist, or lawyer overnight, learning to think like an economist will take some time. Yet with a combination of theory, case studies, and examples of economics in the news, this book will give you ample opportunity to develop and practise this skill.

Before delving into the substance and details of economics, it is helpful to have an overview of how economists approach the world. This chapter, therefore, discusses the field's methodology. What does it mean to think like an economist?

2-1 The Economist as Scientist

Economists try to address their subject with a scientist's objectivity. They approach the study of the economy in much the same way as a physicist approaches the study of matter and a biologist approaches the study of life: They devise theories, collect data, and then analyze these data in an attempt to verify or refute their theories.

To beginners, it can seem odd to claim that economics is a science. After all, economists do not work with test tubes or telescopes. The essence of science, however, is the *scientific method*—the dispassionate development and testing of theories about how the world works. This method of inquiry is as applicable to studying a nation's economy as it is to studying Earth's gravity or a species' evolution. As Albert Einstein once put it, "The whole of science is nothing more than a refinement of everyday thinking."

Although Einstein's comment is as true for social sciences such as economics as it is for natural sciences such as physics, most people are not accustomed to looking at society through a scientific lens. Let's discuss some of the ways economists apply the logic of science to examine how an economy works.

2-1a The Scientific Method: Observation, Theory, and More Observation

Isaac Newton, the famous seventeenth-century scientist and mathematician, allegedly became intrigued one day when he saw an apple fall from a tree. This observation motivated Newton to develop a theory of gravity that applies not only to an apple falling to Earth but also to any two objects in the universe. Subsequent testing of Newton's theory has shown that it works well in many circumstances (although, as Einstein would later emphasize, not in all circumstances). Because Newton's theory has been so successful at explaining observation, it is still taught today in undergraduate physics courses around the world.

This interplay between theory and observation also occurs in economics. An economist might live in a country experiencing rapidly increasing prices and be moved by this observation to develop a theory of inflation. The theory might assert that high inflation arises when the government prints too much money. To test this theory, the economist could collect and analyze data on prices and money from many different countries. If growth in the quantity of money were not at all related to the rate at which prices are rising, the economist would start to doubt the validity of his theory of inflation. If money growth and inflation were strongly correlated in international data, as in fact they are, the economist would become more confident in his theory.

Although economists use theory and observation like other scientists, they do face an obstacle that makes their task especially challenging: In economics, conducting experiments is often impractical. Physicists studying gravity can drop many objects in their laboratories to generate data to test their theories. By contrast, economists studying inflation are not allowed to manipulate a nation's monetary policy simply to generate useful data. Economists, like astronomers and evolutionary biologists, usually have to make do with whatever data the world happens to give them.

To find a substitute for laboratory experiments, economists pay close attention to the natural experiments offered by history. When a war in the Middle East interrupts the supply of crude oil, for instance, oil prices skyrocket around the world. For consumers of oil and oil products, such an event depresses living standards. For economic policymakers, it poses a difficult choice about how best to respond. But for economic scientists, the event provides an opportunity to study the effects of a key natural resource on the world's economies. Throughout this book, therefore, we consider many historical episodes. These episodes are valuable to study because they give us insight into the economy of the past and, more important, because they allow us to illustrate and evaluate economic theories of the present.

2-1b The Role of Assumptions

If you ask a physicist how long it would take for a marble to fall from the top of a ten-storey building, she will answer the question by assuming that the marble falls in a vacuum. Of course, this assumption is false. In fact, the building is surrounded by air, which exerts friction on the falling marble and slows it down. Yet the physicist will point out that friction on the marble is so small that its effect is negligible. Assuming the marble falls in a vacuum simplifies the problem without substantially affecting the answer.

Economists make assumptions for the same reason: Assumptions can simplify the complex world and make it easier to understand. To study the effects of international trade, for example, we might assume that the world consists of only two countries and that each country produces only two goods. In reality, there are numerous countries, each of which produces thousands of different types of goods. But by considering a world with only two countries and two goods, we can focus our thinking on the essence of the problem. Once we understand international trade in this simplified imaginary world, we are in a better position to understand international trade in the more complex world in which we live.

The art in scientific thinking—whether in physics, biology, or economics—is deciding which assumptions to make. Suppose, for instance, that instead of dropping a marble from the top of the building, we were dropping a beach ball of the same weight. Our physicist would realize that the assumption of no friction is less accurate in this case: Friction exerts a greater force on a beach ball because it is much larger than a marble. The assumption that gravity works in a vacuum is reasonable for studying a falling marble but not for studying a falling beach ball.

Similarly, economists use different assumptions to answer different questions. Suppose that we want to study what happens to the economy when the government changes the number of dollars in circulation. An important piece of this analysis, it turns out, is how prices respond. Many prices in the economy change infrequently; the newsstand prices of magazines, for instance, are changed only every few years. Knowing this fact may lead us to make different assumptions when studying the effects of the policy change over different time horizons. For studying the short-run effects of the policy, we may assume that prices do not change much. We may even make the extreme and artificial assumption that all prices are completely fixed. For studying the long-run effects of the policy, however, we may assume that all prices are completely flexible. Just as a physicist uses different assumptions when studying falling marbles and falling beach balls, economists use different assumptions when studying the short- and long-run effects of a change in the quantity of money.

2-1c Economic Models

High-school biology teachers teach basic anatomy with plastic replicas of the human body. These models have all the major organs—the heart, the liver, the kidneys, and so on—which allow teachers to show their students very simply how the important parts of the body fit together. Because these plastic models are stylized and omit many details, no one could mistake them for real people. Despite this lack of realism—indeed, because of this lack of realism—studying these models is useful for learning how the human body works.

Economists also use models to learn about the world, but unlike plastic manikins, they are most often composed of diagrams and equations. Like a biology teacher's plastic model, economic models omit many details to allow us to see what is truly important. Just as the biology teacher's model does not include all of the body's muscles and capillaries, an economist's model does not include every feature of the economy.

As we use models to examine various economic issues throughout this book, you will see that all the models are built with assumptions. Just as a physicist begins the analysis of a falling marble by assuming away the existence of friction, economists assume away many of the details of the economy that are irrelevant to the question at hand. All models—in physics, biology, or economics—simplify reality in order to improve our understanding of it.

2-1d Our First Model: The Circular-Flow Diagram

The economy consists of millions of people engaged in many activities—buying, selling, working, hiring, manufacturing, and so on. To understand how the economy works, we must find some way to simplify our thinking about all these activities. In other words, we need a model that explains, in general terms, how the economy is organized and how participants in the economy interact with one another.

circular-flow diagram
a visual model of the economy that shows how dollars flow through markets

Figure 2.1 presents a visual model of the economy, called a **circular-flow diagram**. In this model, the economy is simplified to include only two types of decision makers—households and firms. Firms produce goods and services using inputs such as labour, land, and capital (buildings and machines). These inputs are called the *factors of production*. Households own the factors of production and consume all the goods and services that the firms produce.

Households and firms interact in two types of markets. In the *markets for goods and services*, households are buyers and firms are sellers. In particular, households buy the output of goods and services that firms produce. In the *markets for the*

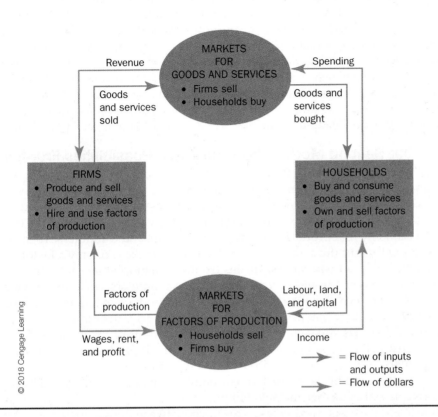

© 2018 Cengage Learning

FIGURE 2.1

The Circular Flow

This diagram is a schematic representation of the organization of the economy. Decisions are made by households and firms. Households and firms interact in the markets for goods and services (where households are buyers and firms are sellers) and in the markets for the factors of production (where firms are buyers and households are sellers). The outer set of arrows shows the flow of dollars, and the inner set of arrows shows the corresponding flow of inputs and outputs.

factors of production, households are sellers and firms are buyers. In these markets, households provide the inputs that the firms use to produce goods and services. The circular-flow diagram offers a simple way of organizing the economic transactions that occur between households and firms in the economy.

The two loops of the circular-flow diagram are distinct but related. The inner loop represents the flows of inputs and outputs. The households sell the use of their labour, land, and capital to the firms in the markets for the factors of production. The firms then use these factors to produce goods and services, which in turn are sold to households in the markets for goods and services. The outer loop of the diagram represents the corresponding flow of dollars. The households spend money to buy goods and services from the firms. The firms use some of the revenue from these sales to pay for the factors of production, such as the wages of their workers. What's left is the profit of the firm owners, who themselves are members of households.

Let's take a tour of the circular flow by following a dollar coin as it makes its way from person to person through the economy. Imagine that the dollar begins at a household—say, in your wallet. If you want to buy a cup of coffee, you take the dollar to one of the economy's markets for goods and services, such as your local Tim Hortons coffee shop. There you spend it on your favourite drink. When the dollar moves into the Tim Hortons cash register, it becomes revenue for the firm. The dollar doesn't stay at Tim Hortons for long, however, because the firm uses it to buy inputs in the markets for the factors of production. Tim Hortons might use the dollar to pay rent to its landlord for the space it occupies or to pay the wages of its workers.

In either case, the dollar enters the income of some household and, once again, is back in someone's wallet. At that point, the story of the economy's circular flow starts once again.

The circular-flow diagram in Figure 2.1 is a very simple model of the economy. It dispenses with details that, for some purposes, are significant. A more complex and realistic circular-flow model would include, for instance, the roles of government and international trade. (Some of that dollar you gave to Tim Hortons might be used to pay taxes and/or to buy coffee beans from a farmer in Brazil.) Yet these details are not crucial for a basic understanding of how the economy is organized. Because of its simplicity, this circular-flow diagram is useful to keep in mind when thinking about how the pieces of the economy fit together.

2-1e Our Second Model: The Production Possibilities Frontier

Most economic models, unlike the circular-flow diagram, are built using the tools of mathematics. Here we consider one of the simplest such models, called the *production possibilities frontier*, and see how this model illustrates some basic economic ideas.

Although real economies produce thousands of goods and services, let's consider an economy that produces only two goods—cars and computers. Together the car industry and the computer industry use all of the economy's factors of production. The **production possibilities frontier** is a graph that shows the various combinations of output—in this case, cars and computers—that the economy can possibly produce given the available factors of production and the available production technology that firms use to turn these factors into output.

Figure 2.2 shows this economy's production possibilities frontier. If the economy uses all of its resources in the car industry, it produces 1000 cars and no computers. If it uses all of its resources in the computer industry, it produces 3000 computers and no cars. The two endpoints of the production possibilities frontier represent these extreme possibilities.

More likely, the economy divides its resources between the two industries, producing some cars and some computers. For example, it can produce 600 cars and

production possibilities frontier

a graph that shows the combinations of output that the economy can possibly produce given the available factors of production and the available production technology

---

FIGURE 2.2

The Production Possibilities Frontier

The production possibilities frontier shows the combinations of output—in this case, cars and computers—that the economy can possibly produce. The economy can produce any combination on or inside the frontier. Points outside the frontier are not feasible given the economy's resources.

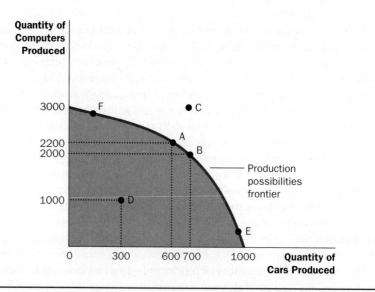

© 2018 Cengage Learning

2200 computers, shown in the figure by point A. Or by moving some of the factors of production to the car industry from the computer industry, the economy can produce 700 cars and 2000 computers, represented by point B.

Because resources are scarce, not every conceivable outcome is feasible. For example, no matter how resources are allocated between the two industries, the economy cannot produce the number of cars and computers represented by point C. Given the technology available for manufacturing cars and computers, the economy does not have enough of the factors of production to support that level of output. With the resources it has, the economy can produce at any point on or inside the production possibilities frontier, but it cannot produce at points outside the frontier.

An outcome is said to be *efficient* if the economy is getting all it can from the scarce resources it has available. Points on (rather than inside) the production possibilities frontier represent efficient levels of production. When the economy is producing at such a point, say point A, there is no way to produce more of one good without producing less of the other. Point D represents an *inefficient* outcome. For some reason, perhaps widespread unemployment, the economy is producing less than it could from the resources it has available: It is producing only 300 cars and 1000 computers. If the source of the inefficiency is eliminated, the economy can increase its production of both goods. For example, if the economy moves from point D to point A, its production of cars increases from 300 to 600, and its production of computers increases from 1000 to 2200.

One of the ten principles of economics discussed in Chapter 1 is that people face tradeoffs. The production possibilities frontier shows one tradeoff that society faces. Once we have reached an efficient point on the frontier, the only way of producing more of one good is to produce less of the other. When the economy moves from point A to point B, for instance, society produces 100 more cars but at the expense of producing 200 fewer computers.

This tradeoff helps us understand another of the ten principles of economics: The cost of something is what you give up to get it. This is called the *opportunity cost*. The production possibilities frontier shows the opportunity cost of one good as measured in terms of the other good. When society moves from point A to point B, it gives up 200 computers to get 100 additional cars. That is, at point A, the opportunity cost of 100 cars is 200 computers. Put another way, the opportunity cost of each car is two computers. Notice that the opportunity cost of a car equals the slope of the production possibilities frontier. (If you don't recall what slope is, you can refresh your memory with the graphing appendix to this chapter.)

The opportunity cost of a car in terms of the number of computers is not a constant in this economy but depends on how many cars and computers the economy is producing. This is reflected in the shape of the production possibilities frontier. Because the production possibilities frontier in Figure 2.2 is bowed outward, the opportunity cost of a car is highest when the economy is producing many cars and fewer computers, such as at point E, where the frontier is steep. When the economy is producing few cars and many computers, such as at point F, the frontier is flatter, and the opportunity cost of a car is lower.

Economists believe that production possibilities frontiers often have this bowed shape. When the economy is using most of its resources to make computers, such as at point F, the resources best suited to car production, such as skilled autoworkers, are being used in the computer industry. Because these workers probably aren't very good at making computers, increasing car production by one unit will cause only a slight reduction in the number of computers produced. At point F, the opportunity cost of a car in terms of computers is small, and the frontier is relatively flat. By contrast, when the economy is using most of its resources to make cars, such as at point E, the resources best suited to making cars are already at use in the car industry. Producing an additional car means moving some of the best computer technicians out of the computer industry and making them autoworkers. As a result, producing an additional car will mean a substantial loss of computer output. The opportunity cost of a car is high, and the frontier is steep.

The production possibilities frontier shows the tradeoff between the outputs of different goods at a given time, but the tradeoff can change over time. For example, suppose a technological advance in the computer industry raises the number of computers that a worker can produce per week. This advance expands society's set of opportunities. For any given number of cars, the economy can now make more computers. If the economy does not produce any computers, it can still produce 1000 cars, so one endpoint of the frontier stays the same. But if the economy devotes some of its resources to the computer industry, it will produce more computers from those resources. As a result, the production possibilities frontier shifts outward, as shown in Figure 2.3.

This figure illustrates what happens when an economy grows. Society can move production from a point on the old frontier to a point on the new frontier. Which point it chooses depends on its preferences for the two goods. In this example, society moves from point A to point G, enjoying more computers (2300 instead of 2200) and more cars (650 instead of 600).

The production possibilities frontier simplifies a complex economy to highlight some basic but powerful ideas: scarcity, efficiency, tradeoffs, opportunity cost, and economic growth. As you study economics, these ideas will recur in various

FIGURE 2.3

A Shift in the Production Possibilities Frontier

A technological advance in the computer industry enables the economy to produce more computers for any given number of cars. As a result, the production possibilities frontier shifts outward. If the economy moves from point A to point G, then the production of both cars and computers increases.

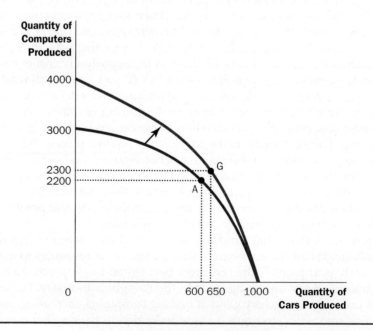

© 2018 Cengage Learning

forms. The production possibilities frontier offers one simple way of thinking about them.

2-1f Microeconomics and Macroeconomics

Many subjects are studied on various levels. Consider biology, for example. Molecular biologists study the chemical compounds that make up living things. Cellular biologists study cells, which are made up of many chemical compounds and, at the same time, are themselves the building blocks of living organisms. Evolutionary biologists study the many varieties of animals and plants and how species change gradually over the centuries.

Economics is also studied on various levels. We can study the decisions of individual households and firms. Or we can study the interaction of households and firms in markets for specific goods and services. Or we can study the operation of the economy as a whole, which is the sum of the activities of all these decision makers in all these markets.

The field of economics is traditionally divided into two broad subfields. **Microeconomics** is the study of how households and firms make decisions and how they interact in specific markets. **Macroeconomics** is the study of economy-wide phenomena. A microeconomist might study the effects of rent control on housing in Toronto, the impact of foreign competition on the Canadian auto industry, or the effects of compulsory school attendance on workers' earnings. A macroeconomist might study the effects of borrowing by the federal government, the changes over time in the economy's rate of unemployment, or alternative policies to raise growth in national living standards.

Microeconomics and macroeconomics are closely intertwined. Because changes in the overall economy arise from the decisions of millions of individuals, it is impossible to understand macroeconomic developments without considering the associated microeconomic decisions. For example, a macroeconomist might study the effect of a cut in the federal income tax on the overall production of goods and services. But to analyze this issue, he or she must consider how the tax cut affects the decisions of households about how much to spend on goods and services.

Despite the inherent link between microeconomics and macroeconomics, the two fields are distinct. Because they address different questions, each field has its own set of models, which are often taught in separate courses.

microeconomics
the study of how households and firms make decisions and how they interact in markets

macroeconomics
the study of economy-wide phenomena, including inflation, unemployment, and economic growth

QUICK Quiz *In what sense is economics like a science? • Draw a production possibilities frontier for a society that produces food and clothing. Show an efficient point, an inefficient point, and an infeasible point. Show the effects of a drought. • Define microeconomics and macroeconomics.*

2-2 The Economist as Policy Adviser

Often economists are asked to explain the causes of economic events. Why, for example, is unemployment higher for teenagers than for older workers? Sometimes economists are asked to recommend policies to improve economic outcomes. What, for instance, should the government do to improve the economic well-being of teenagers? When economists are trying to explain the world, they are scientists. When they are trying to help improve it, they are policy advisers.

2-2a Positive versus Normative Analysis

To help clarify the two roles that economists play, we begin by examining the use of language. Because scientists and policy advisers have different goals, they use language in different ways.

For example, suppose that two people are discussing minimum-wage laws. Here are two statements you might hear:

POLLY: Minimum-wage laws cause unemployment.
NORM: The government should raise the minimum wage.

Ignoring for now whether you agree with these statements, notice that Polly and Norm differ in what they are trying to do. Polly is speaking like a scientist: She is making a claim about how the world works. Norm is speaking like a policy adviser: He is making a claim about how he would like to change the world.

In general, statements about the world are of two types. One type, such as Polly's, is positive. **Positive statements** are descriptive. They make a claim about how the world *is*. A second type of statement, such as Norm's, is normative. **Normative statements** are prescriptive. They make a claim about how the world *ought to be.*

A key difference between positive and normative statements is how we judge their validity. We can, in principle, confirm or refute positive statements by examining evidence. An economist might evaluate Polly's statement by analyzing data on changes in minimum wages and changes in unemployment over time. By contrast, evaluating normative statements involves values as well as facts. Norm's statement cannot be judged using data alone. Deciding what is good or bad policy is not merely a matter of science. It also involves our views on ethics, religion, and political philosophy.

Positive and normative statements are fundamentally different, but they are often intertwined in a person's set of beliefs. In particular, positive views about how the world works affect normative views about what policies are desirable. Polly's claim that the minimum wage causes unemployment, if true, might lead her to reject Norm's conclusion that the government should raise the minimum wage. Yet normative conclusions cannot come from positive analysis alone; they involve value judgments as well.

As you study economics, keep in mind the distinction between positive and normative statements because it will help you stay focused on the task at hand. Much of economics is positive. It just tries to explain how the economy works. Yet those who use economics often have normative goals: They want to learn how to improve the economy. When you hear economists making normative statements, you know they are speaking not as scientists but as policy advisers.

2-2b Economists in Ottawa

U.S. President Harry Truman once said that he wanted to find a one-armed economist. When he asked his economists for advice, they always answered, "On the one hand, … On the other hand, …."

positive statements
claims that attempt to describe the world as it is

normative statements
claims that attempt to prescribe how the world should be

Truman was right in realizing that economists' advice is not always straight-forward. This tendency is rooted in one of the ten principles of economics: People face tradeoffs. Economists are aware that tradeoffs are involved in most policy decisions. A policy might increase efficiency at the cost of equity. It might help future generations but hurt current generations. An economist who says that all policy decisions are easy or clear-cut is an economist not to be trusted. The Government of Canada, like other governments, relies on the advice of economists. Economists at Finance Canada help design tax policy. Economists at the Competition Bureau help design and enforce Canada's competition laws. Economists at Global Affairs Canada help negotiate trade agreements with other countries; the agency also employs economists, both on staff and as consultants, to give advice on overseas development projects. Economists at Employment and Social Development Canada analyze data on workers and on those looking for work to help formulate labour-market policies. Economists at Environment and Climate Change Canada help design environmental regulations. Statistics Canada employs economists to collect the data analyzed by other economists and then give policy advice. The Bank of Canada, the quasi-independent institution that sets Canada's monetary policy, employs more than 200 economists to analyze financial markets and macroeconomic developments.

Economists outside the government also give policy advice. The C.D. Howe Institute, the Fraser Institute, the Institute for Research on Public Policy, the Canadian Centre for Policy Alternatives, and other independent organizations publish reports by economists that analyze current issues such as poverty, unemployment, and the deficit. These reports try to influence public opinion and give advice on government policies.

The influence of economists on policy goes beyond their role as advisers: Their research and writings often affect policy indirectly. Economist John Maynard Keynes offered this observation:

> The ideas of economists and political philosophers, both when they are right and when they are wrong, are more powerful than is commonly understood. Indeed, the world is ruled by little else. Practical men, who believe themselves to be quite exempt from intellectual influences, are usually the slaves of some defunct economist. Madmen in authority, who hear voices in the air, are distilling their frenzy from some academic scribbler of a few years back.

These words were written in 1935, but they remain true today. Indeed, the "academic scribbler" now influencing public policy is often Keynes himself.

2-2c Why Economists' Advice Is Not Always Followed
Any economist who advises government knows that his or her recommendations are not always heeded. Frustrating as this can be, it is easy to understand. The process by which economic policy is actually made differs in many ways from the idealized policy process assumed in economics textbooks.

Throughout this text, whenever we discuss economic policy, we often focus on one question: What is the best policy for the government to pursue? We act as if policy were set by a benevolent monarch. Once the monarch figures out the right policy, he or she has no trouble putting the ideas into action.

In the real world, figuring out the right policy is only part of the job for the government, sometimes the easiest part. For example, consider a political party that forms the government receiving advice from its economic advisers about what policy is best from their perspective. This is just the beginning of the process. Communication advisers will then assess how best to explain the proposed policy to the public, and they will try to anticipate any misunderstandings that might make the challenge more difficult. Press advisers will anticipate how the news media will report on the proposal and what opinions will likely be expressed on the nation's editorial pages. Political advisers will weigh in to discuss which groups will organize to support or oppose the proposed policy, how this proposal will affect party standing among different groups in the electorate, and whether it will affect support for other policy initiatives. After hearing and weighing all of this advice, a decision will be made on how to proceed.

Making economic policy in a representative democracy is a messy affair—and there are often good reasons why politicians do not advance the policies that economists advocate. Economists offer crucial input into the policy process, but their advice is only one ingredient of a complex recipe.

 Give an example of a positive statement and an example of a normative statement. • Name three parts of government that regularly rely on advice from economists.

2-3 Why Economists Disagree

"If all economists were laid end to end, they would not reach to a conclusion." This quip by George Bernard Shaw is revealing. Economists as a group are often criticized for giving conflicting advice to policymakers.

Why do economists so often appear to give conflicting advice to policymakers? There are two basic reasons:

- Economists may disagree about the validity of alternative positive theories about how the world works.
- Economists may have different values and, therefore, different normative views about what a policy should try to accomplish.

Let's discuss each of these reasons.

2-3a Differences in Scientific Judgments

Several centuries ago, astronomers debated whether Earth or the Sun was at the centre of the solar system. More recently, meteorologists have debated whether Earth is experiencing global warming and, if so, why. Science is a search for understanding about the world around us. It is not surprising that as the search continues, scientists can disagree about the direction in which truth lies.

Economists often disagree for the same reason. Economics is a young science, and there is still much to be learned. Economists sometimes disagree because they have different hunches about the validity of alternative theories or about the size of important parameters that measure how economic variables are related.

For example, economists disagree about whether the government should tax a household's income or its consumption (spending). Advocates of a switch from the current income tax to a consumption tax believe that the change would encourage households to save more because income that is saved would not be taxed. Higher saving, in turn, would free resources for capital accumulation, leading to more rapid growth in productivity and living standards. Advocates of the current income tax system believe that household saving would not respond much to a change in the tax laws. These two groups of economists hold different normative views about the tax system because they have different positive views about the responsiveness of saving to tax incentives.

2-3b Differences in Values

Suppose that Peter and Paula both take the same amount of water from the town well. To pay for maintaining the well, the town taxes its residents. Peter has income of $150 000 and is taxed $15 000, or 10 percent of his income. Paula has income of $30 000 and is taxed $6000, or 20 percent of her income.

Is this policy fair? If not, who pays too much and who pays too little? Does it matter whether Paula's low income is due to a medical disability or to her decision to pursue an acting career? Does it matter whether Peter's high income is due to a large inheritance or to his willingness to work long hours at a dreary job?

These are difficult questions on which people are likely to disagree. If the town hired two experts to study how the town should tax its residents to pay for the well, we would not be surprised if they offered conflicting advice.

This simple example shows why economists sometimes disagree about public policy. As we know from our discussion of normative and positive analysis, policies cannot be judged on scientific grounds alone. Sometimes, economists give conflicting advice because they have different values. Perfecting the science of economics will not tell us whether it is Peter or Paula who pays too much.

2-3c Perception versus Reality

Because of differences in scientific judgments and differences in values, some disagreement among economists is inevitable. Yet one should not overstate the amount of disagreement. Economists agree with one another to a much greater extent than is sometimes understood.

Table 2.1 contains 17 propositions about economic policy. In surveys of professional economists, these propositions were endorsed by an overwhelming majority of respondents. Most of these propositions would fail to command a similar consensus among the general public.

The first proposition in the table is about rent control, a policy that sets a legal maximum on the amount landlords can charge for their apartments. Almost all economists believe that rent control adversely affects the availability and quality of housing and is a costly way of helping the neediest members of society. Nonetheless, some provincial governments choose to ignore the advice of economists and place ceilings on the rents that landlords may charge their tenants.

The second proposition in the table concerns tariffs and import quotas, two policies that restrict trade among nations. For reasons we discuss more fully later in this text, almost all economists oppose such barriers to free trade. Nonetheless, over the years, Parliament has often chosen to restrict the import of certain goods.

Why do policies such as rent control and trade barriers persist if the experts are united in their opposition? It may be that the realities of the political process stand as immovable obstacles. But it also may be that economists have not yet convinced the general public that these policies are undesirable. One purpose of this book is to help you understand the economist's view of these and other subjects and, perhaps, to persuade you that it is the right one.

TABLE 2.1

**Propositions about Which
Most Economists Agree**

Proposition (and percentage of economists who agree)

1. A ceiling on rents reduces the quantity and quality of housing available. (93%)
2. Tariffs and import quotas usually reduce general economic welfare. (93%)
3. Flexible and floating exchange rates offer an effective international monetary arrangement. (90%)
4. Fiscal policy (e.g., tax cut and/or government expenditure increase) has a significant stimulative impact on a less than fully employed economy. (90%)
5. The government should not restrict employers from outsourcing work to foreign countries. (90%)
6. Economic growth in developed countries like Canada leads to greater levels of well-being. (88%)
7. Agricultural subsidies should be eliminated. (85%)
8. An appropriately designed fiscal policy can increase the long-run rate of capital formation. (85%)
9. Local and state governments should eliminate subsidies to professional sports franchises. (85%)
10. If the federal budget is to be balanced, it should be done over the business cycle rather than yearly. (85%)
11. Cash payments increase the welfare of recipients to a greater degree than do transfers-in-kind of equal cash value. (84%)
12. A large federal budget deficit has an adverse effect on the economy. (83%)
13. The redistribution of income is a legitimate role for the government. (83%)
14. Inflation is caused primarily by too much growth in the money supply. (83%)
15. A minimum wage increases unemployment among young and unskilled workers. (79%)
16. The government should restructure the welfare system along the lines of a "negative income tax." (79%)
17. Effluent taxes and marketable pollution permits represent a better approach to pollution control than imposition of pollution ceilings. (78%)

Source: Richard M. Alston, J. R. Kearl, and Michael B. Vaughn, "Is There Consensus among Economists in the 1990s?" *American Economic Review* (May 1992): 203–209; Dan Fuller and Doris Geide-Stevenson, "Consensus among Economists Revisited," *Journal of Economics Education* (Fall 2003): 369–387; Robert Whaples, "Do Economists Agree on Anything? Yes!" *Economists' Voice* (November 2006): 1–6; Robert Whaples, "The Policy Views of American Economic Association Members: The Results of a New Survey," *Econ Journal Watch* (September 2009): 337–348.

Ask the Experts

Ticket Resale

"Laws that limit the resale of tickets for entertainment and sports events make potential audience members for those events worse off on average."

What do economists say?

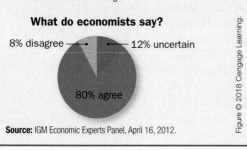

8% disagree — 12% uncertain

80% agree

Figure © 2018 Cengage Learning.

Source: IGM Economic Experts Panel, April 16, 2012.

As you read the book, you will occasionally see feature boxes called "Ask the Experts." These are based on the IGM Economic Experts Panel, an ongoing survey of several dozen of the world's most prominent economists. Every few weeks, these experts are offered a proposition and then asked whether they agree with it, disagree with it, or are uncertain. The results in these boxes will give you a sense of when economists are united, when they are divided, and when they just don't know what to think.

You can see an example here regarding the resale of tickets to entertainment and sporting events. Lawmakers sometimes try to prohibit reselling tickets, or "scalping" as it is sometimes called. The survey results show that many economists side with the scalpers rather than the lawmakers.

QUICK **Quiz**   *Why might economic advisers to the Prime Minister disagree about a question of policy?*

2-4 Let's Get Going

The first two chapters of this book have introduced you to the ideas and methods of economics. We are now ready to get to work. In the next chapter we start learning in more detail about the principles of economic behaviour and economic policy.

As you proceed through this book, you will be asked to draw on many of your intellectual skills. You might find it helpful to keep in mind some advice from the great economist John Maynard Keynes in *Essays in Biography* (1933):

> The study of economics does not seem to require any specialized gifts of an unusually high order. Is it not … a very easy subject compared with the higher branches of philosophy or pure science? An easy subject, at which very few excel! The paradox finds its explanation, perhaps, in that the master-economist must possess a rare *combination* of gifts. He must be mathematician, historian, statesman, or philosopher—in some degree. He must understand symbols and speak in words. He must contemplate the particular in terms of the general, and touch abstract and concrete in the same flight of thought. He must study the present in the light of the past for the purposes of the future. No part of man's nature or his institutions must lie entirely outside his regard. He must be purposeful and disinterested in a simultaneous mood; as aloof and incorruptible as an artist, yet sometimes as near the earth as a politician.

> This is a tall order. But with practice, you will become more and more accustomed to thinking like an economist.

summary

- Economists try to address their subject with a scientist's objectivity. Like all scientists, they make appropriate assumptions and build simplified models in order to understand the world around them. Two simple economic models are the circular-flow diagram and the production possibilities frontier.

- The field of economics is divided into two subfields: microeconomics and macroeconomics. Microeconomists study decision making by households and firms and the interaction among households and firms in the marketplace. Macroeconomists study the forces and trends that affect the economy as a whole.

- A positive statement is an assertion about how the world *is*. A normative statement is an assertion about how the world *ought to be*. When economists make normative statements, they are acting more as policy advisers than scientists.

- Economists who advise policymakers sometimes offer conflicting advice either because of differences in scientific judgments or because of differences in values. At other times, economists are united in the advice they offer, but policymakers may choose to ignore the advice because of the many forces and constraints imposed by the political process.

KEY **concepts**

circular-flow diagram, *p. 22*

production possibilities frontier, *p. 24*

microeconomics, *p. 27*

macroeconomics, *p. 27*

positive statements, *p. 28*

normative statements, *p. 28*

QUESTIONS FOR **review**

1. In what ways is economics like a science?

2. Why do economists make assumptions?

3. Should an economic model describe reality exactly?

4. Name a way that your family interacts in the factor market and a way that it interacts in the product market.

5. Name one economic interaction that isn't covered by the simplified circular-flow diagram.

6. Draw and explain a production possibilities frontier for an economy that produces milk and cookies.

What happens to this frontier if disease kills half of the economy's cows?

7. Use a production possibilities frontier to describe the idea of "efficiency."

8. What are the two subfields into which economics is divided? Explain what each subfield studies.

9. What is the difference between a positive and a normative statement? Give an example of each.

10. Why do economists sometimes offer conflicting advice to policymakers?

QUICK CHECK **multiple choice**

1. What is an economic model?
   a. a mechanical machine that replicates the functioning of the economy
   b. a fully detailed, realistic description of the economy
   c. a simplified representation of some aspect of the economy
   d. a computer program that predicts the future of the economy

2. What does the circular-flow diagram illustrate in terms of markets for the factors of production?
   a. Households are sellers and firms are buyers.
   b. Households are buyers and firms are sellers.
   c. Households and firms are both buyers.
   d. Households and firms are both sellers.

3. Is a point inside the production possibilities frontier efficient and feasible?
   a. efficient but not feasible
   b. feasible but not efficient
   c. both efficient and feasible
   d. neither efficient nor feasible

4. An economy produces hot dogs and hamburgers. If a discovery of the remarkable health benefits of hot dogs were to change consumers' preferences, what would happen?
   a. expand the production possibilities frontier
   b. contract the production possibilities frontier

   c. move the economy along the production possibilities frontier
   d. move the economy inside the production possibilities frontier

5. Which of the following topics does NOT fall within the study of microeconomics?
   a. the impact of cigarette taxes on the smoking behaviour of teenagers
   b. the role of Microsoft's market power in the pricing of software
   c. the effectiveness of antipoverty programs in reducing homelessness
   d. the influence of the government budget deficit on economic growth

6. Which of the following is a positive, rather than a normative, statement?
   a. Law X will reduce national income.
   b. Law X is a good piece of legislation.
   c. Parliament ought to pass Law X.
   d. Law X will change the distribution of income unfairly.

PROBLEMS AND **applications**

1. Draw a circular-flow diagram. Identify the parts of the model that correspond to the flow of goods and services and the flow of dollars for each of the following activities.
   a. Selena pays a storekeeper $2 for a litre of milk.
   b. Stuart earns $15 per hour working at a fast-food restaurant.
   c. Shanna spends $30 to get a haircut.
   d. Salma earns $10 000 from her 10 percent ownership of Acme Industrial.

2. Imagine a society that produces military goods and consumer goods, which we'll call "guns" and "butter."
   a. Draw a production possibilities frontier for guns and butter. Explain why it most likely has a bowed-out shape.
   b. Show a point that is impossible for the economy to achieve. Show a point that is feasible but inefficient.
   c. Imagine that the society has two political parties, called the Hawks (who want a strong military) and the Doves (who want a smaller military). Show a point on your production possibilities frontier that the Hawks might choose and a point the Doves might choose.
   d. Imagine that an aggressive neighbouring country reduces the size of its military. As a result, both the Hawks and the Doves reduce their desired production of guns by the same amount. Which party would get the bigger "peace dividend," measured by the increase in butter production? Explain.

3. The first principle of economics discussed in Chapter 1 is that people face tradeoffs. Use a production possibilities frontier to illustrate society's tradeoff between a clean environment and the quantity of industrial output. What do you suppose determines the shape and position of the frontier? Show what happens to the frontier if engineers develop an automobile engine with almost no emissions.

4. Classify the following topics as relating to micro economics or macroeconomics.
   a. a family's decision about how much income to save
   b. the effect of government regulations on auto emissions
   c. the impact of higher national saving on economic growth

   d. a firm's decision about how many workers to hire
   e. the relationship between the inflation rate and changes in the quantity of money

5. Classify each of the following statements as positive or normative. Explain.
   a. Society faces a short-run tradeoff between inflation and unemployment.
   b. A reduction in the rate of growth of money will reduce the rate of inflation.
   c. The Bank of Canada should reduce the rate of growth of money.
   d. Society ought to require welfare recipients to look for jobs.
   e. Lower tax rates encourage more work and more saving.

6. If you were Prime Minister, would you be more interested in your economic advisers' positive views or their normative views? Why?

7. An economy consists of three workers: Larry, Moe, and Curly. Each works for ten hours per day and can produce two services: mowing lawns and washing cars. In an hour, Larry can either mow one lawn or wash one car, Moe can either mow one lawn or wash two cars, and Curly can either mow two lawns or wash one car.
   a. Calculate how much of each service is produced under the following circumstances, which we label A, B, C, and D:
      • All three spend all their time mowing lawns. (A)
      • All three spend all their time washing cars. (B)
      • All three spend half their time on each activity. (C)
      • Larry spends half his time on each activity, while Moe only washes cars and Curly only mows lawns. (D)
   b. Graph the production possibilities frontier for this economy. Using your answers to part (a), identify points A, B, C, and D on your graph.
   c. Explain why the production possibilities frontier has the shape it does.
   d. Are any of the allocations calculated in part (a) inefficient? Explain.

Graphing: A Brief Review

Many of the concepts that economists study can be expressed with numbers—the price of bananas, the quantity of bananas sold, the cost of growing bananas, and so on. Often these economic variables are related to one another: When the price of bananas rises, people buy fewer bananas. One way of expressing the relationships among variables is with graphs.

Graphs serve two purposes. First, when developing economic theories, graphs offer a way to visually express ideas that might be less clear if described with equations or words. Second, when analyzing economic data, graphs provide a powerful way of finding and interpreting patterns. Whether we are working with theory or with data, graphs provide a lens through which a recognizable forest emerges from a multitude of trees.

Numerical information can be expressed graphically in many ways, just as there are many ways to express a thought in words. A good writer chooses words that will make an argument clear, a description pleasing, or a scene dramatic. An effective economist chooses the type of graph that best suits the purpose.

In this appendix, we discuss how economists use graphs to study the mathematical relationships among variables. We also discuss some of the pitfalls that can arise in the use of graphical methods.

Graphs of a Single Variable

Three common types of graphs are shown in Figure 2A.1. The *pie chart* in panel (a) shows how total income in Canada is divided among the sources of income, including wages and salaries, corporation profits, and so on. A slice of

FIGURE 2A.1

Types of Graphs

The pie chart in panel (a) shows how national income is derived from various sources. The bar graph in panel (b) compares the average income in three countries. The time-series graph in panel (c) shows the unemployment rate in Canada from January 2000 to December 2012.

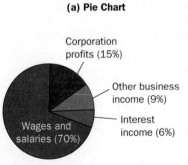

(a) Pie Chart

Corporation profits (15%)
Other business income (9%)
Interest income (6%)
Wages and salaries (70%)

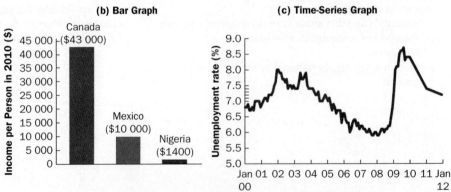

(b) Bar Graph

Income per Person in 2010 ($)

Canada ($43 000)
Mexico ($10 000)
Nigeria ($1400)

(c) Time-Series Graph

Unemployment rate (%)

Jan 01 02 03 04 05 06 07 08 09 10 11 Jan
00   12

the pie represents each source's share of the total. The *bar graph* in panel (b) compares income for three countries. The height of each bar represents the average income in each country. The *time-series graph* in panel (c) traces the Canadian unemployment rate over time. The height of the line shows the unemployment rate in each month. You have probably seen similar graphs in newspapers and magazines.

Graphs of Two Variables: The Coordinate System

The three graphs in Figure 2A.1 are useful in showing how a variable changes over time or across individuals, but they are limited in how much they can tell us. These graphs display information only on a single variable. Economists are often concerned with the relationships between variables. Thus, they need to display two variables on a single graph. The *coordinate system* makes this possible.

Suppose you want to examine the relationship between study time and grade point average. For each student in your class, you could record a pair of numbers: hours per week spent studying and grade point average. These numbers could then be placed in parentheses as an *ordered pair* and appear as a single point on the graph. Albert E., for instance, is represented by the ordered pair (25 hours/ week, 3.5 GPA), while his "what-me-worry?" classmate Alfred E. is represented by the ordered pair (5 hours/week, 2.0 GPA).

We can graph these ordered pairs on a two-dimensional grid. The first number in each ordered pair, called the *x-coordinate*, tells us the horizontal location of the point. The second number, called the *y-coordinate*, tells us the vertical location of the point. The point with both an *x*-coordinate and a *y*-coordinate of zero is known as the *origin*. The two coordinates in the ordered pair tell us where the point is located in relation to the origin: *x* units to the right of the origin and *y* units above it.

Figure 2A.2 graphs grade point average against study time for Albert E., Alfred E., and their classmates. This type of graph is called a *scatterplot* because

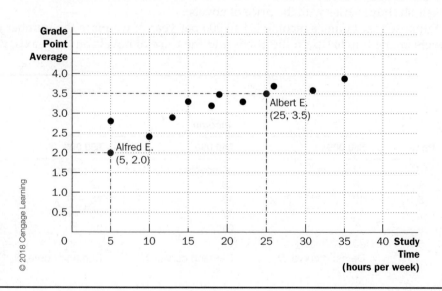

© 2018 Cengage Learning

FIGURE 2A.2

Using the Coordinate System

Grade point average is measured on the vertical axis and study time on the horizontal axis. Albert E., Alfred E., and their classmates are represented by various points. We can see from the graph that students who study more tend to get higher grades.

it plots scattered points. Looking at this graph, we immediately notice that points farther to the right (indicating more study time) also tend to be higher (indicating a better grade point average). Because study time and grade point average typically move in the same direction, we say that these two variables have a *positive correlation.* By contrast, if we were to graph party time and grades, we would likely find that higher party time is associated with lower grades; because these variables typically move in opposite directions, we would call this a *negative correlation.* In either case, the coordinate system makes the correlation between the two variables easy to see.

Curves in the Coordinate System

Students who study more do tend to get higher grades, but other factors also influence a student's grade. Previous preparation is an important factor, for instance, as are talent, attention from teachers, and even eating a good breakfast. A scatterplot like Figure 2A.2 does not attempt to isolate the effect that studying has on grades from the effects of other variables. Often, however, economists prefer looking at how one variable affects another, holding everything else constant.

To see how this is done, let's consider one of the most important graphs in economics—the *demand curve.* The demand curve traces the effect of a good's price on the quantity of the good consumers want to buy. Before showing a demand curve, however, consider Table 2A.1, which shows how the number of novels that Emma buys depends on her income and on the price of novels. When novels are cheap, Emma buys them in large quantities. As they become more expensive, she instead borrows books from the library or chooses to go to the movies instead of reading. Similarly, at any given price, Emma buys more novels when she has a higher income. That is, when her income increases, she spends part of the additional income on novels and part on other goods.

We now have three variables—the price of novels, income, and the number of novels purchased—which are more than we can represent in two dimensions. To put the information from Table 2A.1 in graphical form, we need to hold one of the three variables constant and trace the relationship between the other two. Because the demand curve represents the relationship between price and quantity demanded, we hold Emma's income constant and show how the number of novels she buys varies with the price of novels.

Suppose that Emma's income is $40 000 per year. If we place the number of novels Emma purchases on the x-axis and the price of novels on the y-axis, we

TABLE 2A.1

Novels Purchased by Emma

This table shows the number of novels Emma buys at various incomes and prices. For any given level of income, the data on price and quantity demanded can be graphed to produce Emma's demand curve for novels, as shown in Figures 2A.3 and 2A.4.

| | Income | | |
Price	$30 000	$40 000	$50 000
$10	2 novels	5 novels	8 novels
9	6	9	12
8	10	13	16
7	14	17	20
6	18	21	24
5	22	25	28
	Demand curve, D_3	Demand curve, D_1	Demand curve, D_2

© 2018 Cengage Learning

can graphically represent the middle column of Table 2A.1. When the points that represent these entries from the table—(5 novels, $10), (9 novels, $9), and so on— are connected, they form a line. This line, pictured in Figure 2A.3, is known as Emma's demand curve for novels; it tells us how many novels Emma purchases at any given price. The demand curve is downward sloping, indicating that a higher price reduces the quantity of novels demanded. Because the quantity of novels demanded and the price move in opposite directions, we say that the two variables are *negatively related.* (Conversely, when two variables move in the same direction, the curve relating them is upward sloping, and we say the variables are *positively related.*)

Now suppose that Emma's income rises to $50 000 per year. At any given price, Emma will purchase more novels than she did at her previous level of income. Just as earlier we drew Emma's demand curve for novels using the entries from the middle column of Table 2A.1, we now draw a new demand curve using the entries from the right column of the table. This new demand curve (curve D_2) is pictured alongside the old one (curve D_1) in Figure 2A.4; the new curve is a similar line drawn farther to the right. We therefore say that Emma's demand curve for novels *shifts* to the right when her income increases. Likewise, if Emma's income were to fall to $30 000 per year, she would buy fewer novels at any given price and her demand curve would shift to the left (to curve D_3).

In economics, it is important to distinguish between *movements along a curve* and *shifts of a curve.* As we can see from Figure 2A.3, if Emma earns $40 000 per year and novels cost $8 apiece, she will purchase 13 novels per year. If the price of novels falls to $7, Emma will increase her purchases of novels to 17 per year. The demand curve, however, stays fixed in the same place. Emma still buys the same

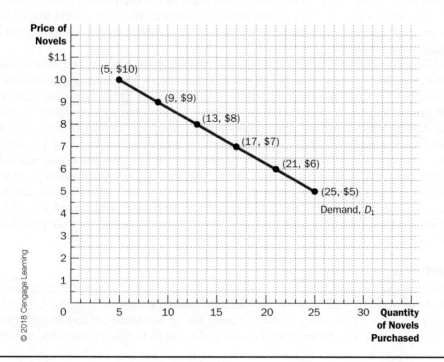

FIGURE 2A.3

Demand Curve

The line D_1 shows how Emma's purchases of novels depend on the price of novels when her income is held constant. Because the price and the quantity demanded are negatively related, the demand curve slopes downward.

© 2018 Cengage Learning

FIGURE 2A.4

Shifting Demand Curves

The location of Emma's demand curve for novels depends on how much income she earns.
The more she earns, the more novels she will purchase at any given price, and the farther to the right her demand curve will lie. Curve D_1 represents Emma's original demand curve when her income is $40 000 per year. If her income rises to $50 000 per year, her demand curve shifts to D_2. If her income falls to $30 000 per year, her demand curve shifts to D_3.

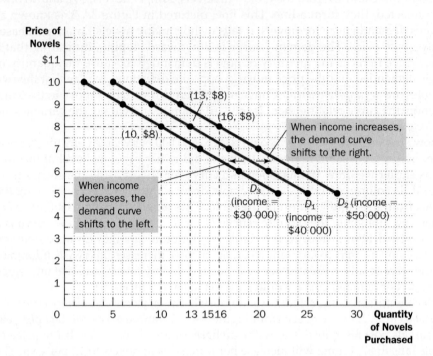

number of novels *at each price,* but as the price falls she moves along her demand curve from left to right. By contrast, if the price of novels remains fixed at $8 but her income rises to $50 000, Emma increases her purchases of novels from 13 to 16 per year. Because Emma buys more novels *at each price,* her demand curve shifts out, as shown in Figure 2A.4.

There is a simple way to tell when it is necessary to shift a curve: When a relevant variable that is not named on either axis changes, the curve shifts. Income is on neither the *x*-axis nor the *y*-axis of the graph, so when Emma's income changes, her demand curve must shift. The same is true for any change that affects Emma's purchasing habits, with the sole exception of a change in the price of novels. If, for instance, the public library closes and Emma must buy all the books she wants to read, she will demand more novels at each price, and her demand curve will shift to the right. Or, if the price of movies falls and Emma spends more time at the movies and less time reading, she will demand fewer novels at each price, and her demand curve will shift to the left. By contrast, when a variable on an axis of the graph changes, the curve does not shift. We read the change as a movement along the curve.

Slope

One question we might want to ask about Emma is how much her purchasing habits respond to price. Look at the demand curve pictured in Figure 2A.5. If this curve is very steep, Emma purchases nearly the same number of novels regardless of whether they are cheap or expensive. If this curve is much flatter, the number

FIGURE 2A.5

Calculating the Slope of a Line

To calculate the slope of the demand curve, we can look at the changes in the *x*- and *y*-coordinates as we move from the point (21 novels, $6) to the point (13 novels, $8). The slope of the line is the ratio of the change in the *y*-coordinate (−2) to the change in the *x*-coordinate (+8), which equals −1/4.

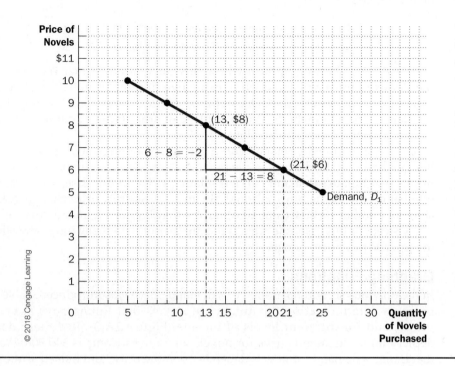

of novels Emma purchases is more sensitive to changes in the price. To answer questions about how much one variable responds to changes in another variable, we can use the concept of *slope*.

The slope of a line is the ratio of the vertical distance covered to the horizontal distance covered as we move along the line. This definition is usually written out in mathematical symbols as follows:

$$\text{Slope} = \frac{\Delta y}{\Delta x}$$

where the Greek letter Δ (delta) stands for the change in a variable. In other words, the slope of a line is equal to the "rise" (change in y) divided by the "run" (change in x). The slope will be a small positive number for a fairly flat upward-sloping line, a large positive number for a steep upward-sloping line, and a negative number for a downward-sloping line. A horizontal line has a slope of zero because in this case the y-variable never changes; a vertical line is said to have an infinite slope because the y-variable can take any value without the x-variable changing at all.

What is the slope of Emma's demand curve for novels? First of all, because the curve slopes down, we know the slope will be negative. To calculate a numerical value for the slope, we must choose two points on the line. With Emma's income at $40 000, she will purchase 21 novels at a price of $6 or 13 novels at a price of $8. When we apply the slope formula, we are concerned with the change between these two points; in other words, we are concerned with the difference between them, which lets us know that we will have to subtract one set of values from the other, as follows:

$$\text{Slope} = \frac{\Delta y}{\Delta x} = \frac{\text{First } y\text{-coordinate} - \text{Second } y\text{-coordinate}}{\text{First } x\text{-coordinate} - \text{Second } x\text{-coordinate}} = \frac{6 - 8}{21 - 13} = -\frac{2}{8} = -\frac{1}{4}$$

Figure 2A.5 shows graphically how this calculation works. Try computing the slope of Emma's demand curve using two different points. You should get exactly the same result, $-1/4$. One of the properties of a straight line is that it has the same slope everywhere. This is not true of other types of curves, which are steeper in some places than in others.

The slope of Emma's demand curve tells us something about how responsive her purchases are to changes in the price. A small slope (a number close to zero) means that Emma's demand curve is relatively flat; in this case, she adjusts the number of novels she buys substantially in response to a price change. A larger slope (a number farther from zero) means that Emma's demand curve is relatively steep; in this case, she adjusts the number of novels she buys only slightly in response to a price change.

Graphing Functions

In the previous section the notion of a demand curve was introduced. Table 2A.1 presents data indicating the number of novels that Emma buys at various prices, and for different levels of income. Figure 2A.3 plots these data to depict Emma's demand curve for novels when her income is $40 000. We saw that Emma's demand for novels depends upon the price, and indeed as the price of novels increases Emma purchases fewer novels, which is to say that Emma's quantity demanded for novels depends negatively on the price. Another way of saying this is that Emma's demand for novels is a *function* of their price—in this case a negative function, where "function of" means "depends upon."

We can express the idea that Emma's demand for novels is a function of (depends upon) the price mathematically, in general terms, by writing $Q^D = f(P)$, where P is the price of a novel and Q^D is Emma's quantity demanded at that price. The term $f(P)$ means simply that Emma's quantity demanded (Q^D) is a function of (depends upon) the price (P). The specific way in which her quantity demanded depends on the price of novels depends upon the *functional form* of $f(P)$. As is evident in Figure 2A.3, and as described above, the relationship between quantity demanded and price in Emma's case is a linear one—her demand curve for novels is a straight line. This is evident visually in the graph, and more precisely because the slope of the demand curve is constant (has the same slope everywhere).

The general functional form for a linear demand curve is:

$$Q^D = f(P) = a - bP$$

where a and b are called the parameters of the function, and represent positive numbers. The negative sign in front of bP therefore indicates that a negative relationship exists between the price of novels and Emma's quantity demanded—as the price goes up, her quantity demanded goes down. The precise values of a and b determine the exact placement and slope of the demand curve. Once we know the values of a and b, we can plug any price into this linear function and determine Emma's demand for novels. For Emma's demand curve depicted in Figure 2A.3—which, remember, assumes that her income is

$40 000—the values for a and b are 45 and 4, respectively, and the precise functional form of her demand curve is:

$$Q^D = 45 - 4P$$

Plug any value for P into this linear demand curve and you will get the quantity of novels demanded by Emma when her income is $40 000. For example, at $P = 10$, $Q^D = 45 - 4(10) = 45 - 40 = 5$; at $P = 9$, $Q^D = 45 - 4(9) = 45 - 36 = 9$; and so on, which coincides exactly with Table 2A.1 and Figure 2A.3.

There are two points on Emma's demand curve that are particularly useful. These are the points where the demand curve intersects the x- and the y-axes (the quantity and price axis, respectively). The point where her demand curve intersects the x-axis, called the x-intercept, coincides with her demand for novels when the price of novels is zero. To determine this, simply plug $P = 0$ into the function depicting Emma's demand curve, giving $Q^D = 45 - 4(0) = 45 - 0 = 45$. The point where her demand curve intersects the y-axis, the y-intercept, coincides with the price at which her quantity demanded is zero. To determine this, plug $Q^D = 0$ into her demand curve and solve for P:

$$0 = 45 - 4P$$
$$4P = 45$$
$$P = 45/4$$
$$P = 11.25$$

So when the price of novels is $11.25 Emma will buy zero novels.

The graph of Emma's demand curve for novels with the x- and y-intercepts identified is shown in Figure 2A.6.

As discussed earlier, we can determine the slope of Emma's demand curve by calculating the "rise" over the "run." To do this, we look at the changes in the x- and y-coordinates as we move from one point on the demand curve to another. Because her demand curve is a straight line the slope is constant, and we can use any two points on the curve to determine its slope. Previously we used the points (21 novels, $6) and (13 novels, $8). Using these two points on her demand curve gave us a change in the y-coordinate, the rise, of $(6 - 8 = -2)$, and a change

FIGURE 2A.6

Emma's Demand Curve with Income of $40 000

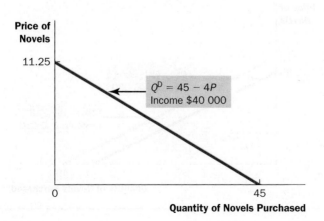

This is Emma's demand curve for novels when her income is $40 000. In this case her demand curve is given by the linear equation $Q^D = 45 - 4P$, which gives an x-intercept of 45, a y-intercept of 11.25, and a slope of $-1/4$.

in the x-coordinate, the run, of $(21 - 13 = 8)$. Taking the ratio of the rise over the run gave us a slope of $-2/8 = -1/4$. Since we can use any two points on a linear demand curve to determine its slope, we can also use the x- and y-intercepts. The y-intercept is associated with the coordinate (0 novels, $11.25), and the x-intercept with the coordinate (45 novels, $0), which gives us a rise equal to $0 - 11.25 = -11.25$, which is the negative of the y-intercept, and a run equal to $45 - 0 = 45$, which is the x-intercept. Taking the ratio of the rise over the run, which is just the negative of the ratio of the y-intercept over the x-intercept, gives us $-11.25/45 = -.25 = -1/4$, just as above. So calculating the x- and y-intercepts of a linear demand curve gives us an easy way to determine its slope.

By writing Emma's quantity of novels demanded as a function of the price of novels alone, we are holding everything else that might affect her demand for novels constant. For example, the demand curve given by $Q^D = 45 - 4P$ assumes that her income is $40 000. If her income increases to $50 000, we saw in Table 2A.1 and Figure 2A.4 that her demand curve shifts to the right and she demands more novels at every price. It turns out that her demand curve when her income is $50 000 is:

$$Q^D = 48 - 4P$$

Using the same approach as above we see that when her income is $50 000 the x-intercept of the associated demand curve is 48 and the y-intercept is 12. The slope of this demand curve is then $-12/48 = -1/4$, which is exactly the same as the demand curve associated with income of $40 000. So we see that in this case a change in income shifts Emma's demand curve for novels in a parallel manner to the right—that is, both the x- and y-intercepts increase by the same proportion but the slope does not change. The demand curve associated with income of $50 000 is shown in Figure 2A.7, along with her demand curve when her income is $40 000.

Cause and Effect

Economists often use graphs to advance an argument about how the economy works. In other words, they use graphs to argue about how one set of events

---

FIGURE 2A.7

Emma's Demand Curve with Different Incomes

This figure shows Emma's demand curves and the associated x- and y-intercepts when her income is $40 000 and $50 000. An increase in her income shifts her demand curve up in a parallel manner, increasing both intercepts but maintaining the slope.

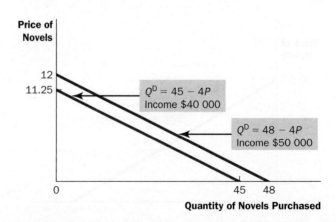

causes another set of events. With a graph like the demand curve, no doubt exists about cause and effect. Because we are varying price and holding all other variables constant, we know that changes in the price of novels cause changes in the quantity Emma demands. Remember, however, that our demand curve came from a hypothetical example. When graphing data from the real world, it is often more difficult to establish how one variable affects another.

The first problem is that it is difficult to hold everything else constant when studying the relationship between two variables. If we are not able to hold variables constant, we might decide that one variable on our graph is causing changes in the other variable, when those changes are actually being caused by a third *omitted variable* not pictured on the graph. Even if we have identified the correct two variables to look at, we might run into a second problem—*reverse causality.* In other words, we might decide that A causes B when in fact B causes A. The omitted-variable and reverse-causality traps require us to proceed with caution when using graphs to draw conclusions about causes and effects.

Omitted Variables

To see how omitting a variable can lead to a deceptive graph, let's consider an example. Imagine that the government, spurred by public concern about the large number of deaths from cancer, commissions an exhaustive study from Big Brother Statistical Services Inc. Big Brother examines many of the items found in people's homes to see which of them are associated with the risk of cancer. Big Brother reports a strong relationship between two variables: the number of cigarette lighters that a household owns and the probability that someone in the household will develop cancer. Figure 2A.8 shows this relationship.

What should we make of this result? Big Brother advises a quick policy response. It recommends that the government discourage the ownership of cigarette lighters by taxing their sale. It also recommends that the government require warning labels: "Big Brother has determined that this lighter is dangerous to your health."

FIGURE 2A.8

Graph with an Omitted Variable

The upward-sloping curve shows that members of households with more cigarette lighters are more likely to develop cancer. Yet we should not conclude that ownership of lighters causes cancer, because the graph does not take into account the number of cigarettes smoked.

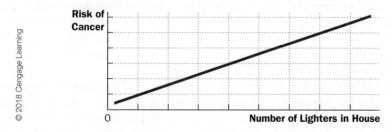

In judging the validity of Big Brother's analysis, one question is key: Has Big Brother held constant every relevant variable except the one under consideration? If the answer is no, the results are suspect. An easy explanation for Figure 2A.8 is that people who own more cigarette lighters are more likely to smoke cigarettes and that cigarettes, not lighters, cause cancer. If Figure 2A.8 does not hold constant the amount of smoking, it does not tell us the true effect of owning a cigarette lighter.

This story illustrates an important principle: When you see a graph used to support an argument about cause and effect, it is important to ask whether the movements of an omitted variable could explain the results you see.

In fact, in Chapter 1 we saw an example of how omitted variables can change our interpretation of data, resulting in an incorrect inference. In the case study on the impact of crosswalk countdown signals, we saw that Toronto city officials improperly concluded that because accidents declined at intersections where crosswalk signals were installed, the signals reduced pedestrian accidents. We saw, however, that accidents declined in all intersections—those with and without countdown signals. This suggests that there was an omitted variable accounting for a secular decline in accidents. As was discussed, the researchers employed a difference-in-differences approach, which involved comparing the decline in accidents in a control group (intersections without countdown signals) to a treatment group (intersections with countdown signals). This enabled them to account for a possible omitted variable that affected both groups and draw a very different inference regarding the impact of countdown signals.

Reverse Causality

Economists can also make mistakes about causality by misreading its direction. To see how this is possible, suppose the Association of Canadian Anarchists commissions a study of crime in Canada and arrives at Figure 2A.9, which plots the number of violent crimes per thousand people in major cities against the number of police officers per thousand people. The anarchists note the curve's upward slope and argue that because police increase rather than decrease the amount of urban violence, law enforcement should be abolished.

If we could run a controlled experiment, we would avoid the danger of reverse causality. To run an experiment, we would randomly assign different numbers of police to different cities and then examine the correlation between police and crime. Figure 2A.9, however, is not based on such an experiment. We simply observe that more dangerous cities have more police officers. The explanation for this may

The upward-sloping curve shows that cities with a higher concentration of police are more dangerous. Yet the graph does not tell us whether police cause crime or crime-plagued cities hire more police.

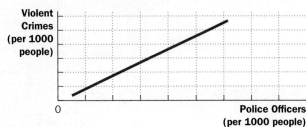

be that more dangerous cities hire more police. In other words, rather than police causing crime, crime may cause an increase in police. Nothing in the graph itself allows us to establish the direction of causality.

It might seem that an easy way to determine the direction of causality is to examine which variable moves first. If we see crime increase and then the police force expand, we reach one conclusion. If we see the police force expand and then crime increase, we reach the other. Yet there is also a flaw with this approach: Often people change their behaviour not in response to a change in their present conditions but in response to a change in their *expectations* of future conditions. A city that expects a major crime wave in the future, for instance, might hire more police now. This problem is even easier to see in the case of babies and minivans. Couples often buy a minivan in anticipation of the birth of a child. The minivan comes before the baby, but we wouldn't want to conclude that the sale of minivans causes the population to grow!

There is no complete set of rules that says when it is appropriate to draw causal conclusions from graphs. Yet just keeping in mind that cigarette lighters don't cause cancer (omitted variable) and minivans don't cause larger families (reverse causality) will keep you from falling for many faulty economic arguments.

PROBLEMS AND **applications**

A1. Consider the linear demand curve:

$$Q^D = 56 - 4P$$

    a. Determine the x- and y-intercepts of this demand curve.

    b. Determine the slope of this demand curve.

A2. Using the general functional form for a linear demand curve, $Q^D = a - bP$, and the data in Table 2A.1,

    a. Determine the values for a and b for Emma when her income is $30 000.

    b. Determine the x- and y-intercepts of this demand curve.

    c. Determine the slope of this demand curve.

    d. Draw it on a diagram along with the demand curves when her income is $40 000 and $50 000, identifying the x- and y-intercepts in each case.

Interdependence and the Gains from Trade

In this chapter, you will ...

1 Consider how everyone can benefit when people trade with one another

2 Learn the meaning of *absolute advantage* and *comparative advantage*

3 See how comparative advantage explains the gains from trade

4 Apply the theory of comparative advantage to everyday life and national policy

Consider your typical day. You wake up in the morning, and you pour yourself juice from oranges grown in Florida and coffee from beans grown in Brazil. Over breakfast, you watch a news program broadcast from Toronto on your television set made in China. You get dressed in clothes made of cotton grown in Georgia and sewn in factories in Thailand. You drive to class in a car made of parts manufactured in more than a dozen countries around the world. Then you open up your economics textbook written by authors living in Massachusetts and Alberta, published by a company located in Ontario, and printed on paper made from trees grown in New Brunswick.

Every day, you rely on many people, most of whom you have never met, to provide you with the goods and services that you enjoy. Such interdependence is possible because people trade with one another. Those people providing you with goods and services are not acting out of generosity. Nor is some government agency directing them to satisfy your desires. Instead, people provide you and other consumers with the goods and services they produce because they get something in return.

In subsequent chapters, we examine how our economy coordinates the activities of millions of people with varying tastes and abilities. As a starting point for this analysis, in this chapter we consider the reasons for economic interdependence. One of the ten principles of economics highlighted in Chapter 1 is that trade can make everyone better off. We now examine this principle more closely. What exactly do people gain when they trade with one another? Why do people choose to become interdependent?

The answers to these questions are key to understanding the modern global economy. Most countries today import from abroad many of the goods and services they consume, and they export to foreign customers many of the goods and services they produce. The analysis in this chapter explains interdependence not only among individuals but also among nations. As we will see, the gains from trade are much the same whether you are buying a haircut from your local barber or a T-shirt made by a worker on the other side of the globe.

3-1 A Parable for the Modern Economy

To understand why people choose to depend on others for goods and services and how this choice improves their lives, let's look at a simple economy. Imagine that there are two goods in the world: meat and potatoes. And there are two people in the world—a cattle rancher named Rose and a potato farmer named Frank—each of whom would like to eat both meat and potatoes.

The gains from trade are most obvious if Rose can produce only meat and Frank can produce only potatoes. In one scenario, Frank and Rose could choose to have nothing to do with each other. But after several months of eating beef roasted, boiled, broiled, and grilled, Rose might decide that self-sufficiency is not all it's cracked up to be. Frank, who has been eating potatoes mashed, fried, baked, and scalloped, would likely agree. It is easy to see that trade would allow them to enjoy greater variety: Each could then have a steak with a baked potato or a burger with fries.

Although this scene illustrates most simply how everyone can benefit from trade, the gains would be similar if Frank and Rose were each capable of producing the other good, but only at great cost. Suppose, for example, that Rose is able to grow potatoes but her land is not very well suited for it. Similarly, suppose that Frank is able to raise cattle and produce meat but he is not very good at it. In this case, Frank and Rose can each benefit by specializing in what he or she does best and then trading with the other person.

The gains from trade are less obvious, however, when one person is better at producing *every* good. For example, suppose that Rose is better at raising cattle *and* better at growing potatoes than Frank. In this case, should Rose choose to remain self-sufficient? Or is there still reason for her to trade with Frank? To answer this question, we need to look more closely at the factors that affect such a decision.

3-1a Production Possibilities

Suppose that Frank and Rose each work 8 hours a day and can devote this time to growing potatoes, raising cattle, or a combination of the two. The table in Figure 3.1 shows the amount of time each person requires to produce 1 kg of each good. Frank can produce a kilogram of potatoes in 15 minutes and a kilogram of meat in 60 minutes. Rose, who is more productive in both activities, can produce a kilogram of potatoes in 10 minutes and a kilogram of meat in 20 minutes. The last two columns in the table show the amounts of meat or potatoes Frank and Rose can produce if they devote 8 hours to producing only that good.

Panel (b) of Figure 3.1 illustrates the amounts of meat and potatoes that Frank can produce. If Frank devotes all 8 hours of his time to potatoes, he produces 32 kg of potatoes (measured on the horizontal axis) and no meat. If he devotes all his time to meat, he produces 8 kg of meat (measured on the vertical axis) and no potatoes. If Frank divides his time equally between the two activities, spending 4 hours on each, he produces 16 kg of potatoes and 4 kg of meat. The figure shows these three possible outcomes and all others in between.

This graph is Frank's production possibilities frontier. As we discussed in Chapter 2, a production possibilities frontier shows the various mixes of output that an economy can produce. It illustrates one of the ten principles of economics in Chapter 1: People face tradeoffs. Here Frank faces a tradeoff between producing meat and producing potatoes.

You may recall that the production possibilities frontier in Chapter 2 was drawn bowed out. In that case, the rate at which society could trade one good for the other depended on the amounts being produced. Here, however, Frank's technology for producing meat and potatoes (as summarized in Figure 3.1) allows him to switch between one good and the other at a constant rate. Whenever Frank spends 1 hour less producing meat and 1 hour more producing potatoes, he reduces his output of meat by 1 kg and raises his output of potatoes by 4 kg—and this is true regardless of how much he is already producing. As a result, the production possibilities frontier is a straight line.

Panel (c) of Figure 3.1 shows the production possibilities frontier for Rose. If Rose devotes all 8 hours of her time to potatoes, she produces 48 kg of potatoes and no meat. If she devotes all her time to meat, she produces 24 kg of meat and no potatoes. If she divides her time equally, spending 4 hours on each activity, she produces 24 kg of potatoes and 12 kg of meat. Once again, the production possibilities frontier shows all the possible outcomes.

If Frank and Rose choose to be self-sufficient rather than trade with each other, then each consumes exactly what he or she produces. In this case, the production possibilities frontier is also the consumption possibilities frontier. That is, without trade, Figure 3.1 shows the possible combinations of meat and potatoes that the farmer and rancher can each consume.

FIGURE 3.1

The Production Possibilities Frontier

Panel (a) shows the production opportunities available to Frank the farmer and Rose the rancher. Panel (b) shows the combinations of meat and potatoes that Frank can produce. Panel (c) shows the combinations of meat and potatoes that Rose can produce. Both production possibilities frontiers are derived assuming that Frank and Rose each work 8 hours a day. If there is no trade, each person's production possibilities frontier is also his or her consumption possibilities frontier.

(a) The Production Opportunities

	Minutes Needed to Produce 1 kg of:		Amount of Meat or Potatoes Produced in 8 Hours	
	Meat	Potatoes	Meat	Potatoes
Frank	60 min/kg	15 min/kg	8 kg	32 kg
Rose	20 min/kg	10 min/kg	24 kg	48 kg

(b) Frank's Production Possibilities Frontier

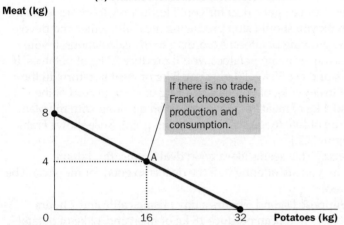

If there is no trade, Frank chooses this production and consumption.

(c) Rose's Production Possibilities Frontier

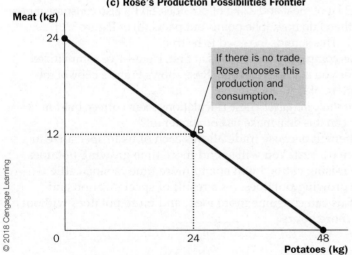

If there is no trade, Rose chooses this production and consumption.

© 2018 Cengage Learning

These production possibilities frontiers are useful in showing the tradeoffs that Frank and Rose face, but they do not tell us what Frank and Rose will actually choose to do. To determine their choices, we need to know the tastes of Frank and Rose. Let's suppose they choose the combinations identified by points A and B in Figure 3.1. Based on his production opportunities and food preferences, Frank decides to produce and consume 16 kg of potatoes and 4 kg of meat, while Rose decides to produce and consume 24 kg of potatoes and 12 kg of meat.

3-1b Specialization and Trade

After several years of eating combination B, Rose gets an idea and goes to talk to Frank:

Rose: Frank, my friend, have I got a deal for you! I know how to improve life for both of us. I think you should stop producing meat altogether and devote all your time to growing potatoes. According to my calculations, if you work 8 hours a day growing potatoes, you'll produce 32 kg of potatoes. If you give me 15 of those 32 kg, I'll give you 5 kg of meat in return. In the end, you'll get to eat 17 kg of potatoes and 5 kg of meat, instead of the 16 kg of potatoes and 4 kg of meat you now get. If you go along with my plan, you'll have more of *both* foods. [To illustrate her point, Rose shows Frank panel (a) of Figure 3.2.]

Frank: *(sounding skeptical)* That seems like a good deal for me. But I don't understand why you are offering it. If the deal is so good for me, it can't be good for you too.

Rose: Oh, but it is! Suppose I spend 6 hours a day raising cattle and 2 hours growing potatoes. Then I can produce 18 kg of meat and 12 kg of potatoes. After I give you 5 kg of my meat in exchange for 15 kg of your potatoes, I'll end up with 13 kg of meat and 27 kg of potatoes. So I'll also consume more of both foods than I do now. [She points out panel (b) of Figure 3.2.]

Frank: I don't know…. This sounds too good to be true.

Rose: It's really not as complicated as it seems at first. Here—I've summarized my proposal for you in a simple table. [Rose shows Frank a copy of the table at the bottom of Figure 3.2.]

Frank: *(after pausing to study the table)* These calculations seem correct, but I'm puzzled. How can this deal make us both better off?

Rose: We can both benefit because trade allows each of us to specialize in doing what we do best. You will spend more time growing potatoes and less time raising cattle. I will spend more time raising cattle and less time growing potatoes. As a result of specialization and trade, each of us can consume more meat and more potatoes without working any more hours.

Draw an example of a production possibilities frontier for Robinson Crusoe, a shipwrecked sailor who spends his time gathering coconuts and catching fish. Does this frontier limit Crusoe's consumption of coconuts and fish if he lives by himself? Does he face the same limits if he can trade with natives on the island?

FIGURE 3.2

How Trade Expands the Set of Consumption Opportunities

The proposed trade between Frank the farmer and Rose the rancher offers each of them a combination of meat and potatoes that would be impossible in the absence of trade. In panel (a), Frank gets to consume at point A* rather than point A. In panel (b), Rose gets to consume at point B* rather than point B. Trade allows each to consume more meat and more potatoes.

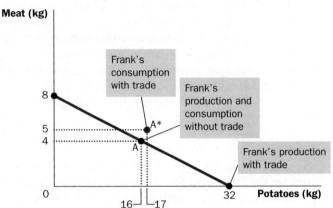

(a) Frank's Production and Consumption

Frank's consumption with trade

Frank's production and consumption without trade

Frank's production with trade

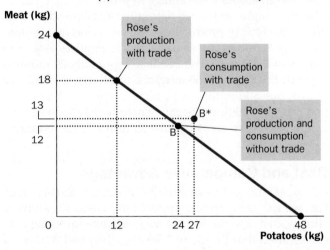

(b) Rose's Production and Consumption

Rose's production with trade

Rose's consumption with trade

Rose's production and consumption without trade

(c) The Gains from Trade: A Summary

	Frank		Rose	
	Meat	**Potatoes**	**Meat**	**Potatoes**
Without Trade:				
Production and Consumption	4 kg	16 kg	12 kg	24 kg
With Trade:				
Production	0 kg	32 kg	18 kg	12 kg
Trade	Gets 5 kg	Gives 15 kg	Gives 5 kg	Gets 15 kg
Consumption	5 kg	17 kg	13 kg	27 kg
Gains from Trade:				
Increase in Consumption	+11 kg	+11 kg	+11 kg	+13 kg

3-2 Comparative Advantage: The Driving Force of Specialization

Rose's explanation of the gains from trade, although correct, poses a puzzle: If Rose is better at both raising cattle and growing potatoes, how can Frank ever specialize in doing what he does best? Frank doesn't seem to do anything best. To solve this puzzle, we need to look at the principle of *comparative advantage*.

As a first step in developing this principle, consider the following question: In our example, who can produce potatoes at lower cost—Frank or Rose? There are two possible answers, and in these two answers lie the solution to our puzzle and the key to understanding the gains from trade.

3-2a Absolute Advantage

absolute advantage
the comparison among producers of a good according to their productivity

One way to answer the question about the cost of producing potatoes is to compare the inputs required by the two producers. Economists use the term **absolute advantage** when comparing the productivity of one person, firm, or nation to that of another. The producer that requires a smaller quantity of inputs to produce a good is said to have an absolute advantage in producing that good.

In our example, time is the only input, so we can determine absolute advantage by looking at how much time each type of production takes. Rose has an absolute advantage in producing both meat and potatoes because she requires less time than Frank to produce a unit of either good. Rose needs to input only 20 minutes to produce a kilogram of meat; Frank needs 60 minutes. Similarly, the rancher needs only 10 minutes to produce a kilogram of potatoes, whereas the farmer needs 15 minutes. Based on this information, we can conclude that Rose has the lower cost of producing potatoes, if we measure cost in terms of the quantity of inputs.

3-2b Opportunity Cost and Comparative Advantage

opportunity cost
whatever must be given up to obtain some item

There is another way to look at the cost of producing potatoes. Rather than comparing inputs required, we can compare the opportunity costs. Recall from Chapter 1 that the **opportunity cost** of some item is what we give up to get that item. In our example, we assumed that Frank and Rose each spend 8 hours a day working. Time spent producing potatoes, therefore, takes away from time available for producing meat. When reallocating time between the two goods, Rose and Frank give up units of one good to produce units of the other, thereby moving along the production possibilities frontier. The opportunity cost measures the tradeoff between the two goods that each producer faces.

Let's first consider Rose's opportunity cost. According to the table in panel (a) of Figure 3.1, producing 1 kg of potatoes takes her 10 minutes of work. When Rose spends those 10 minutes producing potatoes, she spends 10 minutes less producing meat. Because Rose needs 20 minutes to produce 1 kg of meat, 10 minutes of work would yield 0.5 kg of meat. Hence, Rose's opportunity cost of producing 1 kg of potatoes is 0.5 kg of meat.

Now consider Frank's opportunity cost. Producing 1 kg of potatoes takes him 15 minutes. Because he needs 60 minutes to produce 1 kg of meat, 15 minutes of work would yield 0.25 kg of meat. Hence, Frank's opportunity cost of 1 kg of potatoes is 0.25 kg of meat.

Table 3.1 shows the opportunity costs of meat and potatoes for the two producers. Notice that the opportunity cost of meat is the inverse of the

TABLE 3.1

The Opportunity Cost of Meat and Potatoes

	Opportunity Cost of:	
	1 kg of Meat	**1 kg of Potatoes**
Frank the farmer	4 kg potatoes	0.25 kg meat
Rose the rancher	2 kg potatoes	0.50 kg meat

opportunity cost of potatoes. Because 1 kg of potatoes costs Rose 0.5 kg of meat, 1 kg of meat costs Rose 2 kg of potatoes. Similarly, because 1 kg of potatoes costs Frank 0.25 kg of meat, 1 kg of meat costs Frank 4 kg of potatoes.

Economists use the term **comparative advantage** when describing the opportunity cost faced by two producers. The producer who gives up less of other goods to produce Good X has the smaller opportunity cost of producing Good X and is said to have a comparative advantage in producing it. In our example, Frank has a lower opportunity cost of producing potatoes than Rose: A kilogram of potatoes costs Frank only 0.25 kg of meat, while it costs Rose 0.50 kg of meat. Conversely, Rose has a lower opportunity cost of producing meat than Frank: A kilogram of meat costs Rose 2 kg of potatoes, while it costs Frank 4 kg of potatoes. Thus, Frank has a comparative advantage in growing potatoes, and Rose has a comparative advantage in producing meat.

Although it is possible for one person to have an absolute advantage in both goods (as Rose does in our example), it is impossible for one person to have a comparative advantage in both goods. Because the opportunity cost of one good is the inverse of the opportunity cost of the other, if a person's opportunity cost of one good is relatively high, the opportunity cost of the other good must be relatively low. Comparative advantage reflects the relative opportunity cost. Unless two people have exactly the same opportunity cost, one person will have a comparative advantage in one good, and the other person will have a comparative advantage in the other good.

comparative advantage

the comparison among producers of a good according to their opportunity cost

3-2c Comparative Advantage and Trade

The gains from specialization and trade are based not on absolute advantage but rather on comparative advantage. When each person specializes in producing the good for which he or she has a comparative advantage, total production in the economy rises. This increase in the size of the economic pie can be used to make everyone better off.

In our example, Frank spends more time growing potatoes, and Rose spends more time producing meat. As a result, the total production of potatoes rises from 40 to 44 kg, and the total production of meat rises from 16 to 18 kg. Frank and Rose share the benefits of this increased production.

We can also look at the gains from trade in terms of the price that each party pays the other. Because Frank and Rose have different opportunity costs, they can both get a bargain. That is, each of them benefits from trade by obtaining a good at a price that is lower than his or her opportunity cost of that good.

Consider the proposed deal from Frank's viewpoint. Frank receives 5 kg of meat in exchange for 15 kg of potatoes. In other words, Frank buys each kilogram of meat for a price of 3 kg of potatoes. This price of meat is lower than his opportunity cost for 1 kg of meat, which is 4 kg of potatoes. Thus, Frank benefits from the deal because he gets to buy meat at a good price.

FYI

The Legacy of Adam Smith and David Ricardo

Economists have long understood the principle of comparative advantage. Here is how the great economist Adam Smith put the argument:

It is a maxim of every prudent master of a family, never to attempt to make at home what it will cost him more to make than to buy. The tailor does not attempt to make his own shoes, but buys them of the shoemaker. The shoemaker does not attempt to make his own clothes but employs a tailor. The farmer attempts to make neither the one nor the other, but employs those different artificers. All of them find it for their interest to employ their whole industry in a way in which they have some advantage over their neighbors, and to purchase with a part of its produce, or what is the same thing, with the price of part of it, whatever else they have occasion for.

This quotation is from Smith's 1776 book *An Inquiry into the Nature and Causes of the Wealth of Nations*, which was a landmark in the analysis of trade and economic interdependence.

Smith's book inspired David Ricardo, a millionaire stockbroker, to become an economist. In his 1817 book *Principles of Political Economy*

and Taxation, Ricardo developed the principle of comparative advantage as we know it today. His defence of free trade was not a mere academic exercise. Ricardo put his economic beliefs to work as a member of the British Parliament, where he opposed the Corn Laws, which restricted the import of grain.

The conclusions of Adam Smith and David Ricardo on the gains from trade have held up well over time. Although economists often disagree on questions of policy, they are united in their support of free trade. Moreover, the central argument for free trade has not changed much in the past two centuries. Even though the field of economics has broadened its scope and refined its theories since the time of Smith and Ricardo, economists' opposition to trade restrictions is still based largely on the principle of comparative advantage.

© Bettmann/Corbis

Now consider the deal from Rose's viewpoint. Rose buys 15 kg of potatoes for a price of 5 kg of meat. That is, the price of potatoes is one-third of a kilogram of meat. This price of potatoes is lower than her opportunity cost of 1 kg of potatoes, which is 0.5 kg of meat. Rose benefits because she can buy potatoes at a good price.

The story of Rose the rancher and Frank the farmer has a simple moral, which should now be clear: Trade can benefit everyone in society because it allows people to specialize in activities in which they have a comparative advantage.

3-2d The Price of Trade

The principle of comparative advantage establishes that there are gains from specialization and trade, but it raises a couple of related questions: What determines the price at which trade takes place? How are the gains from trade shared between the trading parties? The precise answer to these questions is beyond the scope of this chapter, but we can state one general rule: *For both parties to gain from trade, the price at which they trade must lie between the two opportunity costs.*

In our example, Rose and Frank agreed to trade at a rate of 3 kg of potatoes for each 1 kg of meat. This price is between Rose's opportunity cost (2 kg of potatoes per 1 kg of meat) and Frank's opportunity cost (4 kg of potatoes per 1 kg of meat). The price need not be exactly in the middle for both parties to gain, but it must be somewhere between 2 and 4.

To see why the price has to be in this range, consider what would happen if it were not. If the price of 1 kg of meat was below 2 kg of potatoes, both Frank and Rose would want to buy meat because the price would be below their opportunity costs. Similarly, if the price of meat were above 4 kg of potatoes, both would want to sell meat, because the price would be above their opportunity costs. But there are only two members of this economy. They cannot both be buyers of meat, nor can they both be sellers. Someone has to take the other side of the deal.

A mutually advantageous trade can be struck at a price between 2 and 4. In this price range, Rose wants to sell meat to buy potatoes, and Frank wants to sell potatoes to buy meat. Each party can buy a good at a price that is lower than his or her opportunity cost. In the end, both of them specialize in the good for which he or she has a comparative advantage and is, as a result, better off.

QUICK Quiz   *Robinson Crusoe can gather 10 coconuts or catch 1 fish per hour. His friend Friday can gather 30 coconuts or catch 2 fish per hour. What is Crusoe's opportunity cost of catching one fish? What is Friday's? Who has an absolute advantage in catching fish? Who has a comparative advantage in catching fish?*

3-3 Applications of Comparative Advantage

The principle of comparative advantage explains interdependence and the gains from trade. Because interdependence is so prevalent in the modern world, the principle of comparative advantage has many applications. Here are two examples, one fanciful and one of great practical importance.

3-3a Should Connor McDavid Shovel His Own Sidewalk?

Connor McDavid spends a lot of time on the ice. One of the most talented hockey players in the world, he can shoot a puck with a speed and accuracy that most recreational hockey players can only dream of doing. Most likely, he is talented at other physical activities as well. For example, let's imagine that McDavid can shovel his sidewalk faster than anyone else. But just because he *can* shovel his walk quickly, does this mean he *should*?

To answer this question, we can use the concepts of opportunity cost and comparative advantage. Let's say that McDavid can shovel his walk in one hour. In that same hour, he could film a television commercial and earn $30 000. By contrast, Forrest Gump, the boy next door, can shovel McDavid's walk in two hours. In that same two hours, he could work at McDonald's and earn $30.

In this example, McDavid has an absolute advantage in shovelling sidewalks because he can do the work with a lower input of time. Yet because McDavid's opportunity cost of shovelling the sidewalk is $30 000 and Gump's opportunity cost is only $30, Gump has a comparative advantage in shovelling sidewalks.

The gains from trade in this example are tremendous. Rather than shovelling his own sidewalk, McDavid should make the commercial and hire Gump to shovel the walk. As long as McDavid pays Gump more than $30 and less than $30 000, both of them are better off.

Connor McDavid

The Future of Free Trade in Canada

Canada is a trading nation, and has benefited greatly from trade over its history. A new trade and economic era for Canada is now at hand. While Canada did negotiate a new trade agreement with the U.S. and Mexico in 2018, a rise in protectionism has been underway for a decade. This article asks whether Canada is ready to act decisively to shape and strengthen its position in this new era.

Canada's Next Trade and Economic Era

By Glen Hodgson

Over the past hundred years, Canada's economy has evolved through two quite different economic eras, guided by trade policy.

A new trade and economic era for Canada is now at hand. A protectionist Trump administration is accelerating the emergence of this era, but the trends have been under way for a decade. This next trade and economic era is globally oriented, has more of a role for services and investment and is about emerging technologies and services in areas such as a low-carbon future. Is Canada ready to act decisively to shape and strengthen its position in this new era?

Let's briefly consider how Canada's trade and economic development has evolved. Early colonial economic development was based on immigration and expansion westward, and on the export of commodities to European consumers.

This approach was set aside during the 20th century, when trade policy became more central to defining Canada's economic evolution and performance. The first trade and economic era of the 20th century was shaped by high tariffs on imported manufactured goods introduced at the end of the First World War. The policy goal was to grow Canadian manufacturing behind protectionist trade barriers and replace imported goods.

Some Canadian companies, like farm-machinery manufacturers, succeeded under this approach, but foreign manufacturing firms eventually dominated the Canadian market.

By the 1960s, the majority of manufacturing in Canada was U.S.-owned, with factories and businesses designed to specifically serve the Canadian market. Critics at the time, and resulting government policy, focused largely on the symptoms—foreign ownership of branch-plant manufacturing—and not the root policy cause, which was trade protectionism.

The next trade and economic era saw Canada's progressive economic integration into the U.S. and North American economy. Global tariff reductions under the General Agreement on Tariffs and Trade (GATT) began to set the conditions, but the first major milestone was the Canada-U.S. Auto Pact of 1965, which gave automobiles made in Canada duty-free access to the U.S. market.

The defining policy stroke for this era was the Canada-U.S. free-trade agreement in 1989,

3-3b Should Canada Trade with Other Countries?

Just as individuals can benefit from specialization and trade with one another, as Frank and Rose did, so can populations of people in different countries. Many of the goods and services that Canadians enjoy are produced abroad, and many of the goods and services produced in Canada are sold abroad. Goods and services produced abroad and sold domestically are called **imports**. Goods and services produced domestically and sold abroad are called **exports**.

An interesting question concerns the sources of comparative advantage. For individuals, some of their comparative advantage is "natural"—Connor McDavid clearly has an innate talent for hockey that most of us do not. This is also true at the country level. Canada has a clear comparative advantage in the provision of natural resources. We are a leading provider of oil, forest products, and agriculture goods to the world market because of our natural geographic, geological, and topological advantages. For example, Canada is a large exporter of pulp and paper products to the United States. This is due both to our large forest areas and to our access to cheap hydroelectricity, which provides the power required to process pulp.

imports
goods and services produced abroad and sold domestically

exports
goods and services produced domestically and sold abroad

followed by the North American Free Trade Agreement (NAFTA). There is widespread consensus that North American free trade was a success for Canada, with growing economic integration and strong growth in exports and imports, jobs and GDP.

But there were also consequences—namely, very heavy Canadian trade dependence on the U.S. market. Canadian exports to the U.S. peaked at 87 per cent of exports in early 2000s and still represent 70 per cent of what we sell internationally.

Arguably, this second economic era of deep U.S. integration has run its course. Most Canadians recognize that freer trade and investment are central to our national wealth creation. Canadian international trade and investment has been steadily diversifying over the past decade, with significant trade growth with Asia generally, and China in particular. Trade with the U.S. has been essentially flat over the same period. Canada has also finally committed itself to pursuing free trade with large regions, notably the Comprehensive Economic and Trade Agreement (CETA) with the European Union.

We see three elements to a fully developed new trade and economic era, each of them requiring accompanying shifts in policy.

Element one: Position Canada as an open, integrating hub for global trade and investment. Canada could build upon the success of CETA and actively seek to conclude other major free-trade deals, notably with Japan, and with China under the right conditions. It could position itself as a preferred investment destination and trade enabler for global firms, offering tariff-free market access to both the U.S. and EU. Asian businesses in particular could be attracted to invest more in Canada, in order to gain duty-free access to these markets.

Element two: Seek a global leadership position in services trade and investment. Many Canadian firms are already taking advantage of the new trade and technology paradigm based on services, data, people and investment. For example, a significant expansion in Canada's international financial services business has quietly taken place, in banking, life insurance and wealth management.

Other attractive services trade sectors include computing, professional services, education, and entertainment and culture. A trade policy explicitly aimed at promoting high-value services, and technology-driven digital trade, could produce even better results. Canada has the highly educated, multicultural and multilingual workforce necessary to play such a role.

Element three: Develop and sell low-carbon expertise in technology and services to the world. Canada has much to offer in shaping the low-carbon economy, but we are late to the party; Europe and now China are ahead in adapting to lower greenhouse-gas emissions. We have not yet provided adequate support to low-carbon tech and service providers in terms of home-market demand, availability of financing and global marketing support. Canadian low-carbon businesses will need to consider going global from the outset, especially if only parts of the U.S. market (like California) have the right enabling conditions in place.

These three elements are not mutually exclusive. They could be acted upon together, in whole or in part. But regardless, the second trade and economic era of deep U.S. integration has reached a point of maturity. Beyond domestic policy reforms being considered to reinforce economic growth, embracing a new trade era will likely be required to re-energize the Canadian economy.

Source: Glen Hodgson, "Canada's Next Trade and Economic Era," *The Globe and Mail*, January 12, 2017: https://www.theglobeandmail.com/report-on-business/economy/economic-insight/canadas-next-trade-and-economic-era/article33593947/. Reproduced by permission of the author.

However, hard work, training, education, and experience can create, or enhance, comparative advantage. Raw talent is only part of the reason that some individuals rise to the top of their professions. This is also true at the country level. The Canadian workforce is highly educated, healthy, and productive relative to many countries. This gives Canada a comparative advantage in the production of high-value-added goods that require a skilled labour force.

To see how countries can benefit from trade, suppose there are two countries, Canada and Japan, and two goods, food and cars. Imagine that the two countries produce cars equally well: A Canadian worker and a Japanese worker can each produce 1 car per month. By contrast, because Canada has more and better land, it is better at producing food: A Canadian worker can produce 2 tonnes of food per month, whereas a Japanese worker can produce only 1 tonne of food per month.

The principle of comparative advantage states that each good should be produced by the country that has the smaller opportunity cost of producing that good. Because the opportunity cost of a car is 2 tonnes of food in Canada but only 1 tonne of food in Japan, Japan has a comparative advantage in producing cars. Japan should produce more cars than it wants for its own use and export some of them to Canada. Similarly, because the opportunity cost of a tonne of food is 1 car in Japan but only 1/2 car in Canada, Canada has a comparative advantage in producing food. Canada should produce more food than it wants to consume and export some of it to Japan. Through specialization and trade, both countries can have more food and more cars.

In reality, of course, the issues involved in trade among nations are more complex than this example suggests. The most important among these issues is that each country has many citizens with different interests. This means that international trade can make some individuals worse off, even if it makes the country as a whole better off; there can be winners and losers from trade. When Canada exports food and imports cars, the impact on Canadian farmers is not the same as the impact on Canadian autoworkers. Yet, contrary to the opinions sometimes voiced by politicians and political commentators, international trade need not be like a war, in which some countries win and others lose. The concept of comparative advantage suggests that trade can allow all countries to achieve greater prosperity. However it is important to recognize that there may be winners and losers within a country, generating the inevitable tradeoffs. Indeed, as is seen in the Ask the Experts box, economists are in general agreement that these tradeoffs exist. These issues will be explored in more detail in the discussion of international trade in Chapter 9.

QUICK **Quiz**   *Suppose that a skilled brain surgeon also happens to be the world's fastest typist. Should he do his own typing or hire a secretary? Explain.*

3-4 Conclusion

You should now understand more fully the benefits of living in an interdependent economy. When Canadians buy tube socks from China, when residents of Manitoba drink apple juice from British Columbia, and when a homeowner hires the kid next door to shovel the sidewalk, the same economic forces are at work. The principle of comparative advantage shows that trade can make everyone better off.

Having seen why interdependence is desirable, you might naturally ask how it is possible. How do free societies coordinate the diverse activities of all the people involved in their economies? What ensures that goods and services will get from those who should be producing them to those who should be consuming them? In a world with only two people, such as Rose the rancher and Frank the farmer, the answer is simple: These two people can bargain and allocate resources between themselves. In the real world with billions of people, the answer is less obvious. We take up this issue in the next chapter, where we see that free societies allocate resources through the market forces of supply and demand.

Ask the Experts

Trade with China

"Trade with China makes most Canadians better off because, among other advantages, they can buy goods that are made or assembled more cheaply in China."

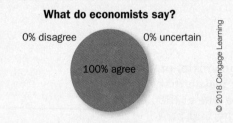

"Those who work in the production of competing goods, such as clothing and furniture, are made worse off by trade with China."

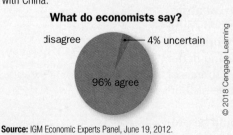

Source: IGM Economic Experts Panel, June 19, 2012.

summary

- Each person consumes goods and services produced by many other people, both in Canada and around the world. Interdependence and trade are desirable because they allow everyone to enjoy a greater quantity and variety of goods and services.

- There are two ways to compare the ability of two people in producing a good. The person who can produce the good with the smaller quantity of inputs is said to have an *absolute advantage* in producing the good. The person who has the smaller opportunity cost of producing the

good is said to have a *comparative advantage*. The gains from trade are based on comparative advantage, not absolute advantage.

- Trade makes everyone better off because it allows people to specialize in those activities in which they have a comparative advantage.

- The principle of comparative advantage applies to countries as well as to people. Economists use the principle of comparative advantage to advocate free trade among countries.

KEY concepts

absolute advantage, *p. 54*
opportunity cost, *p. 54*

comparative advantage, *p. 55*
imports, *p. 58*

exports, *p. 58*

QUESTIONS FOR review

1. Under what conditions is the production possibilities frontier linear rather than bowed out?

2. Explain how absolute advantage and comparative advantage differ.

3. Give an example in which one person has an absolute advantage in doing something but another person has a comparative advantage.

4. Is absolute advantage or comparative advantage more important for trade? Explain your reasoning using the example in your answer to question 3.

5. If two parties trade based on comparative advantage and both gain, in what range must the price of the trade lie?

6. Why do economists tend to oppose policies that restrict trade among nations?

QUICK CHECK multiple choice

1. In an hour, Ken can wash 2 cars or mow 1 lawn, and Ron can wash 3 cars or mow 1 lawn. Who has the absolute advantage in car washing, and who has the absolute advantage in lawn mowing?
   a. Ken in washing, Ron in mowing
   b. Ron in washing, Ken in mowing
   c. Ken in washing, neither in mowing
   d. Ron in washing, neither in mowing

2. Once again, in an hour, Ken can wash 2 cars or mow 1 lawn, and Ron can wash 3 cars or mow 1 lawn. Who has the comparative advantage in car washing, and who has the comparative advantage in lawn mowing?
   a. Ken in washing, Ron in mowing
   b. Ron in washing, Ken in mowing
   c. Ken in washing, neither in mowing
   d. Ron in washing, neither in mowing

3. What results when two individuals produce efficiently and then make a mutually beneficial trade based on comparative advantage?
   a. they both obtain consumption outside their production possibilities frontier
   b. they both obtain consumption inside their production possibilities frontier
   c. one individual consumes inside her production possibilities frontier, while the other consumes outside hers
   d. each individual consumes a point on her own production possibilities frontier

4. Which goods will a nation typically import?
   a. those goods in which the nation has an absolute advantage
   b. those goods in which the nation has a comparative advantage

c. those goods in which other nations have an absolute advantage

d. those goods in which other nations have a comparative advantage

5. Suppose that in Canada, producing an aircraft takes 10 000 hours of labour and producing a shirt takes 2 hours of labour. In China, producing an aircraft takes 40 000 hours of labour and producing a shirt takes 4 hours of labour. What will these nations trade?
   a. China will export aircraft, and Canada will export shirts.
   b. China will export shirts, and Canada will export aircraft.

c. Both nations will export shirts.

d. There are no gains from trade in this situation.

6. Mark can cook dinner in 30 minutes and wash the laundry in 20 minutes. His roommate takes half as long to do each task. How should the roommates allocate the work?
   a. Mark should do more of the cooking based on his comparative advantage.
   b. Mark should do more of the washing based on his comparative advantage.
   c. Mark should do more of the washing based on his absolute advantage.
   d. There are no gains from trade in this situation.

PROBLEMS AND **applications**

1. Maria can read 20 pages of economics in an hour. She can also read 50 pages of sociology in an hour. She spends 5 hours per day studying.
   a. Draw Maria's production possibilities frontier for reading economics and sociology.
   b. What is Maria's opportunity cost of reading 100 pages of sociology?

2. Canadian and Japanese workers can each produce 4 cars per year. A Canadian worker can produce 10 tonnes of grain per year, whereas a Japanese worker can produce 5 tonnes of grain per year. To keep things simple, assume that each country has 100 million workers.
   a. For this situation, construct a table analogous to panel (a) in Figure 3.1.
   b. Graph the production possibilities frontier of the Canadian and Japanese economies.
   c. For Canada, what is the opportunity cost of a car? Of grain? For Japan, what is the opportunity cost of a car? Of grain? Put this information in a table analogous to Table 3.1.
   d. Which country has an absolute advantage in producing cars? In producing grain?
   e. Which country has a comparative advantage in producing cars? In producing grain?
   f. Without trade, half of each country's workers produce cars and half produce grain. What quantities of cars and grain does each country produce?
   g. Starting from a position without trade, give an example in which trade makes each country better off.

3. Pat and Kris are roommates. They spend most of their time studying (of course), but they leave some time for their favourite activities: making pizza and brewing root beer. Pat takes 4 hours to brew 5 L of root beer and 2 hours to make a pizza. Kris takes 6 hours to brew 5 L of root beer and 4 hours to make a pizza.
   a. What is each roommate's opportunity cost of making a pizza? Who has the absolute advantage in

making pizza? Who has the comparative advantage in making pizza?
   b. If Pat and Kris trade products with each other, who will trade away pizza in exchange for root beer?
   c. The price of pizza can be expressed in terms of litres of root beer. What is the highest price at which pizza can be traded that would make both roommates better off? What is the lowest price? Explain.

4. Suppose that there are 10 million workers in Canada, and that each of these workers can produce either 2 cars or 30 tonnes of wheat in a year.
   a. What is the opportunity cost of producing a car in Canada? What is the opportunity cost of producing a tonne of wheat in Canada? Explain the relationship between the opportunity costs of the two goods.
   b. Draw Canada's production possibilities frontier. If Canada chooses to consume 10 million cars, how much wheat can it consume without trade? Label this point on the production possibilities frontier.
   c. Now suppose that the United States offers to buy 10 million cars from Canada in exchange for 20 tonnes of wheat per car. If Canada continues to consume 10 million cars, how much wheat does this deal allow Canada to consume? Label this point on your diagram. Should Canada accept the deal?

5. England and Scotland both produce scones and sweaters. Suppose that an English worker can produce 50 scones per hour or 1 sweater per hour. Suppose that a Scottish worker can produce 40 scones per hour or 2 sweaters per hour.
   a. Which country has the absolute advantage in the production of each good? Which country has the comparative advantage?
   b. If England and Scotland decide to trade, which commodity will Scotland trade to England? Explain.
   c. If a Scottish worker could produce only 1 sweater per hour, would Scotland still gain from trade? Would England still gain from trade? Explain.

6. The following table describes the production possibilities of two cities:

	Red Sweaters per Worker per Hour	Blue Sweaters per Worker per Hour
Montreal	3	3
Toronto	2	1

   a. Without trade, what is the price of blue sweaters (in terms of red sweaters) in Montreal? What is the price in Toronto?
   b. Which city has an absolute advantage in the production of each colour of sweater? Which city has a comparative advantage in the production of each colour of sweater?
   c. If the cities trade with each other, which colour of sweater will each export?
   d. What is the range of prices at which trade can occur?

7. Are the following statements true or false? Explain in each case.
   a. "Two countries can achieve gains from trade even if one of the countries has an absolute advantage in the production of all goods."
   b. "Certain very talented people have a comparative advantage in everything they do."
   c. "If a certain trade is good for one person, it can't be good for the other one."
   d. "If a certain trade is good for one person, it is always good for the other one."
   e. "If trade is good for a country, it must be good for everyone in the country."

8. Canada exports oil and pulp and paper to the rest of the world, and it imports computers and clothing from the rest of the world. Do you think this pattern of trade is consistent with the principle of comparative advantage? Why or why not?

9. Conrad and Barbara produce food and clothing. In an hour, Conrad can produce 1 unit of food or 1 unit of clothing, while Barbara can produce 2 units of food or 3 units of clothing. They each work 10 hours a day.
   a. Who has an absolute advantage in producing food? Who has an absolute advantage in producing clothing? Explain.
   b. Who has a comparative advantage in producing food? Who has a comparative advantage in producing clothing? Explain.
   c. Draw the production possibilities frontier for the household (that is, Conrad and Barbara together) assuming that each spends the same number of hours each day as the other producing food and clothing.
   d. Barbara suggests that, instead, she specialize in making clothing. That is, she will do all of the

clothing production, unless her time is fully devoted to clothing, and then Conrad will chip in. What does the household production possibilities frontier look like now?
   e. Conrad suggests that Barbara specialize in producing food. That is, Barbara will do all the food production, unless her time is fully devoted to food, and then Conrad will chip in. What does the household production possibilities frontier look like under Conrad's proposal?
   f. Comparing your answers to parts (c), (d), and (e), which allocation of time makes the most sense? Relate your answer to the theory of comparative advantage.

10. Suppose that in a year a Canadian worker can produce 100 shirts or 20 computers, while a Chinese worker can produce 100 shirts or 10 computers.
   a. Graph the production possibilities curve for the two countries. Suppose that without trade the workers in each country spend half their time producing each good. Identify this point in your graph.
   b. If these countries were open to trade, which country would export shirts? Give a specific numerical example and show it on your graph. Which country would benefit from trade? Explain.
   c. Explain at what price of computers (in terms of shirts) the two countries might trade.
   d. Suppose that China catches up with Canadian productivity so that a Chinese worker can produce 100 shirts or 20 computers. What pattern of trade would you predict now? How does this advance in Chinese productivity affect the economic well-being of the citizens of the two countries?

11. An average worker in Brazil can produce 30 mL of soy milk in 20 minutes and 30 mL of coffee in 60 minutes, while an average worker in Peru can produce 30 mL of soy milk in 50 minutes and 30 mL of coffee in 75 minutes.
   a. Who has the absolute advantage in coffee? Explain.
   b. Who has the comparative advantage in coffee? Explain.
   c. If the two countries specialize and trade with each other, who will import coffee? Explain.
   d. Assume that the two countries trade and that the country importing coffee trades 60 mL of soy milk for 30 mL of coffee. Explain why both countries will benefit from this trade.

12. A German worker takes 400 hours to produce a car and 2 hours to produce a case of wine. A French worker takes 600 hours to produce a car and X hours to produce a case of wine.
   a. For what values of X will gains from trade be possible? Explain.
   b. For what values of X will Germany export cars and import wine? Explain.

CHAPTER

4

LEARNING
objectives

The Market Forces of Supply and Demand

In this chapter, you will ...

1 Learn the nature of a competitive market

2 Examine what determines the demand for a good in a competitive market

3 Examine what determines the supply of a good in a competitive market

4 See how supply and demand together set the price of a good and the quantity sold

5 Consider the key role of prices in allocating scarce resources in market economies

When a cold snap hits Florida, the price of orange juice rises in supermarkets throughout Canada. When the weather turns warm in Quebec every summer, the price of hotel rooms in Cuba plummets. When a war breaks out in the Middle East, the price of gasoline in Canada rises and the price of a used SUV falls. What do these events have in common? They all show the workings of supply and demand.

Supply and *demand* are the two words economists use most often—and for good reason. Supply and demand are the forces that make market economies work. They determine the quantity of each good produced and the price at which it is sold. If you want to know how any event or policy will affect the economy, you must think first about how it will affect supply and demand.

This chapter introduces the theory of supply and demand. It considers how buyers and sellers behave and how they interact with one another. It shows how supply and demand determine prices in a market economy and how prices, in turn, allocate the economy's scarce resources.

4-1 Markets and Competition

The terms *supply* and *demand* refer to the behaviour of people as they interact with one another in competitive markets. Before discussing how buyers and sellers behave, let's first consider more fully what we mean by a "market" and "competition."

4-1a What Is a Market?

A **market** is a group of buyers and sellers of a particular good or service. The buyers as a group determine the demand for the product, and the sellers as a group determine the supply of the product.

market
a group of buyers and sellers of a particular good or service

Markets take many forms. Some markets are highly organized, such as the markets for many agricultural commodities. In these markets, buyers and sellers meet at a specific time and place, where an auctioneer helps set prices and arrange sales.

More often, markets are less organized. For example, consider the market for ice cream in a particular town. Buyers of ice cream do not meet together at any one time. The sellers of ice cream are in different locations and offer somewhat different products. There is no auctioneer calling out the price of ice cream. Each seller posts a price for an ice-cream cone, and each buyer decides how much ice cream to buy at each store. Nonetheless, these consumers and producers of ice cream are closely connected. The ice-cream buyers are choosing from the various ice-cream sellers to satisfy their cravings, and the ice-cream sellers are all trying to appeal to the same ice-cream buyers to make their businesses successful. Even though it is not as organized, the group of ice-cream buyers and ice-cream sellers forms a market.

4-1b What Is Competition?

The market for ice cream, like most markets in the economy, is highly competitive. Each buyer knows that there are several sellers from which to choose, and each seller is aware that his product is similar to that offered by other sellers. As a result, the price and quantity of ice cream sold are not determined by any single buyer or seller. Rather, price and quantity are determined by all buyers and sellers as they interact in the marketplace.

competitive market
a market in which there are many buyers and many sellers so that each has a negligible impact on the market price

Economists use the term **competitive market** to describe a market in which there are so many buyers and so many sellers that each has a negligible impact on the market price. Each seller of ice cream has limited control over the price because other sellers are offering similar products. A seller has little reason to charge less than the going price, and if he charges more, buyers will make their purchases elsewhere. Similarly, no single buyer of ice cream can influence the price of ice cream because each buyer purchases only a small amount.

In this chapter, we assume that markets are *perfectly competitive.* To reach this highest form of competition, a market must have two characteristics: (1) the goods offered for sale are all exactly the same, and (2) the buyers and sellers are so numerous that no single buyer or seller has any influence over the market price. Because buyers and sellers in perfectly competitive markets must accept the price the market determines, they are said to be *price takers.* At the market price, buyers can buy all they want, and sellers can sell all they want.

There are some markets in which the assumption of perfect competition applies perfectly. In the wheat market, for example, there are thousands of farmers who sell wheat and millions of consumers who use wheat and wheat products. Because no single buyer or seller can influence the price of wheat, each takes the price as given.

Not all goods and services, however, are sold in perfectly competitive markets. Some markets have only one seller, and this seller sets the price. Such a seller is called a *monopoly.* Your local cable television company, for instance, may be a monopoly. Residents of your town probably have only one cable company from which to buy cable service. Other markets fall between the extremes of perfect competition and monopoly.

Despite the diversity of market types we find in the world, assuming perfect competition is a useful simplification and, therefore, a natural place to start. Perfectly competitive markets are the easiest to analyze because everyone participating in the market takes the price as given by market conditions. Moreover, because some degree of competition is present in most markets, many of the lessons that we learn by studying supply and demand under perfect competition apply in more complicated markets as well.

 QUICK Quiz *What is a market? • What are the characteristics of a competitive market?*

4-2 Demand

We begin our study of markets by examining the behaviour of buyers. To focus our thinking, let's keep in mind a particular good—ice cream.

4-2a The Demand Curve: The Relationship between Price and Quantity Demanded

quantity demanded
the amount of a good that buyers are willing and able to purchase

The **quantity demanded** of any good is the amount of the good that buyers are willing and able to purchase. As we will see, many things determine the quantity demanded of any good, but in our analysis of how markets work, one determinant plays a central role: the price of the good. If the price of ice cream rose to $20 per scoop, you would buy less ice cream. You might buy frozen yogurt instead. If the price of ice cream fell to $0.20 per scoop, you would buy more. This relationship between price and quantity demanded is true for most goods in the

FIGURE 4.1

Catherine's Demand Schedule and Demand Curve

The demand schedule shows the quantity demanded at each price. The demand curve, which graphs the demand schedule, shows how the quantity demanded of the good changes as its price varies. Because a lower price increases the quantity demanded, the demand curve slopes downward.

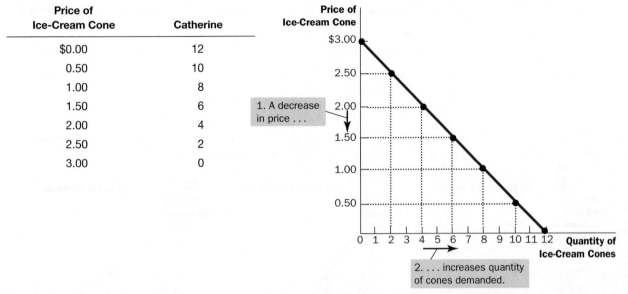

Price of Ice-Cream Cone	Catherine
$0.00	12
0.50	10
1.00	8
1.50	6
2.00	4
2.50	2
3.00	0

1. A decrease in price . . .

2. . . . increases quantity of cones demanded.

© 2018 Cengage Learning

economy and, in fact, is so pervasive that economists call it the **law of demand**: Other things equal, when the price of a good rises, the quantity demanded of the good falls, and when the price falls, the quantity demanded rises.

The table in Figure 4.1 shows how many ice-cream cones Catherine buys each month at different prices of ice cream. If ice cream is free, Catherine eats 12 cones. At $0.50 per cone, Catherine buys 10 cones each month. As the price rises further, she buys fewer and fewer cones. When the price reaches $3.00, Catherine doesn't buy any cones at all. This table is a **demand schedule**, a table that shows the relationship between the price of a good and the quantity demanded, holding constant everything else that influences how much of the good consumers want to buy.

The graph in Figure 4.1 uses the numbers from the table to illustrate the law of demand. By convention, the price of ice cream is on the vertical axis, and the quantity of ice cream demanded is on the horizontal axis. The line relating price and quantity demanded is called the **demand curve**. The demand curve slopes downward because, other things being equal, a lower price means a greater quantity demanded.

4-2b Market Demand versus Individual Demand

The demand curve in Figure 4.1 shows an individual's demand for a product. To analyze how markets work, we need to determine the *market demand*, which is the sum of all the individual demands for a particular good or service.

The table in Figure 4.2 shows the demand schedules for ice cream of the two individuals in this market—Catherine and Nicholas. At any price, Catherine's

law of demand
the claim that, other things equal, the quantity demanded of a good falls when the price of the good rises

demand schedule
a table that shows the relationship between the price of a good and the quantity demanded

demand curve
a graph of the relationship between the price of a good and the quantity demanded

FIGURE 4.2

Market Demand as the Sum of Individual Demands

The quantity demanded in a market is the sum of the quantities demanded by all the buyers at each price. Thus, the market demand curve is found by adding horizontally the individual demand curves. At a price of $2, Catherine demands 4 ice-cream cones, and Nicholas demands 3 ice-cream cones. The quantity demanded in the market at this price is 7 cones.

Price of Ice-Cream Cone	Catherine		Nicholas		Market
$0.00	12	+	7	=	19
0.50	10		6		16
1.00	8		5		13
1.50	6		4		10
2.00	4		3		7
2.50	2		2		4
3.00	0		1		1

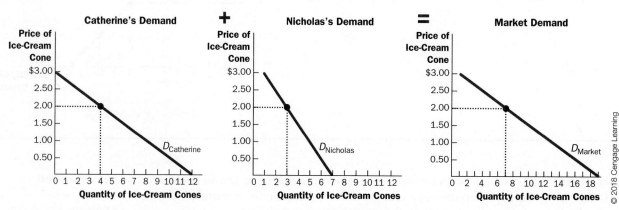

© 2018 Cengage Learning

demand schedule tells us how much ice cream she buys, and Nicholas's demand schedule tells us how much ice cream he buys. The market demand at each price is the sum of the two individual demands.

The graph in Figure 4.2 shows the demand curves that correspond to these demand schedules. Notice that we sum the individual demand curves *horizontally* to obtain the market demand curve. That is, to find the total quantity demanded at any price, we add the individual quantities, which are found on the horizontal axis of the individual demand curves. Because we are interested in analyzing how markets work, we will work most often with the market demand curve. The market demand curve shows how the total quantity demanded of a good varies as the price of the good varies, while all the other factors that affect how much consumers want to buy are held constant.

4-2c Shifts in the Demand Curve

Because the market demand curve holds other things constant, it need not be stable over time. If something happens to alter the quantity demanded at any given price, the demand curve shifts. For example, suppose the Canadian Medical Association discovered that people who regularly eat ice cream live longer, healthier lives. The discovery would raise the demand for ice cream. At any given

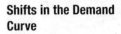

Any change that raises the quantity that buyers wish to purchase at a given price shifts the demand curve to the right. Any change that lowers the quantity that buyers wish to purchase at a given price shifts the demand curve to the left.

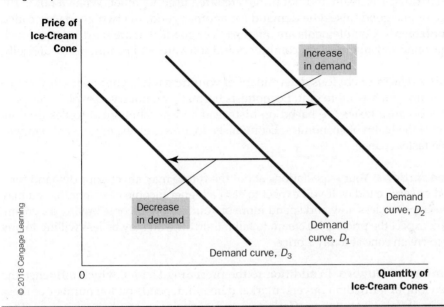

price, buyers would now want to purchase a larger quantity of ice cream, and the demand curve for ice cream would shift.

Figure 4.3 illustrates shifts in demand. Any change that increases the quantity demanded at every price, such as our imaginary discovery by the Canadian Medical Association, shifts the demand curve to the right and is called *an increase in demand*. Any change that reduces the quantity demanded at every price shifts the demand curve to the left and is called *a decrease in demand*.

Many variables can shift the demand curve. The ones that follow are the most important.

Income What would happen to your demand for ice cream if you lost your job one summer? Most likely, it would fall. A lower income means that you have less to spend in total, so you would have to spend less on some—and probably most—goods. If the demand for a good falls when income falls, the good is called a **normal good**.

Normal goods are the norm, but not all goods are normal goods. If the demand for a good rises when income falls, the good is called an **inferior good**. An example of an inferior good might be bus rides. As your income falls, you are less likely to buy a car or take a cab and more likely to ride a bus.

Prices of Related Goods Suppose that the price of frozen yogurt falls. The law of demand says that you will buy more frozen yogurt. At the same time, you will probably buy less ice cream. Because ice cream and frozen yogurt are both cold, sweet, creamy desserts, they satisfy similar desires. When a fall in the price of one good reduces the demand for another good, the two goods are called **substitutes**.

normal good
a good for which, other things equal, an increase in income leads to an increase in demand

inferior good
a good for which, other things equal, an increase in income leads to a decrease in demand

substitutes
two goods for which an increase in the price of one leads to an increase in the demand for the other

Would this be your lunch if you had a higher income?

complements

two goods for which an increase in the price of one leads to a decrease in the demand for the other

Substitutes are often pairs of goods that are used in place of each other, such as hot dogs and hamburgers, sweaters and sweatshirts, and movie tickets and streaming services.

Now suppose that the price of hot fudge falls. According to the law of demand, you will buy more hot fudge. Yet, in this case, you will buy more ice cream as well because ice cream and hot fudge are often used together. When a fall in the price of one good raises the demand for another good, the two goods are called **complements**. Complements are often pairs of goods that are used together, such as gasoline and automobiles, computers and software, and peanut butter and jelly.

Tastes   The most obvious determinant of your demand is your tastes. If you like ice cream, you buy more of it. Economists normally do not try to explain people's tastes because tastes are based on historical and psychological forces that are beyond the realm of economics. Economists do, however, examine what happens when tastes change.

Expectations   Your expectations about the future may affect your demand for a good or service today. If you expect to earn a higher income next month, you may choose to save less now and spend more of your current income buying ice cream. If you expect the price of ice cream to fall tomorrow, you may be less willing to buy an ice-cream cone at today's price.

Number of Buyers   In addition to the preceding factors, which influence the behaviour of individual buyers, market demand depends on the number of these buyers. If Peter were to join Catherine and Nicholas as another consumer of ice cream, the quantity demanded in the market would be higher at every price and market demand would increase.

Summary   The demand curve shows what happens to the quantity demanded of a good when its price varies, holding constant all the other variables that influence buyers. When one of these other variables changes, the demand curve shifts. Table 4.1 lists the variables that influence how much consumers choose to buy of a good.

TABLE 4.1

Variables That Influence Buyers

Source: © 2018 Cengage Learning

This table lists the variables that affect how much consumers choose to buy of any good. Notice the special role that the price of the good plays: A change in the good's price represents a movement along the demand curve, whereas a change in one of the other variables shifts the demand curve.

Variable	A Change in This Variable ...
Price of the good itself	Represents a movement along the demand curve
Income	Shifts the demand curve
Prices of related goods	Shifts the demand curve
Tastes	Shifts the demand curve
Expectations	Shifts the demand curve
Number of buyers	Shifts the demand curve

If you have trouble remembering whether you need to shift or move along the demand curve, it helps to recall a lesson from the appendix to Chapter 2. A curve shifts when there is a change in a relevant variable that is not measured on either axis. Because the price is on the vertical axis, a change in price represents a movement along the demand curve. By contrast, income, the prices of related goods, tastes, expectations, and the number of buyers are not measured on either axis, so a change in one of these variables shifts the demand curve.

case study **Two Ways to Reduce the Quantity of Smoking Demanded**

Because smoking can lead to various illnesses, public policymakers often want to reduce the amount that people smoke. There are two ways that policy can attempt to achieve this goal.

One way to reduce smoking is to shift the demand curve for cigarettes and other tobacco products. Public service announcements, mandatory health warnings on cigarette packages, and the prohibition of cigarette advertising on television are all policies aimed at reducing the quantity of cigarettes demanded at any given price. If successful, these policies shift the demand curve for cigarettes to the left, as in panel (a) of Figure 4.4.

Alternatively, policymakers can try to raise the price of cigarettes. If the government taxes the manufacture of cigarettes, for example, cigarette companies pass much of this tax on to consumers in the form of higher prices. A higher price

What is the best way to stop this?

If warnings on cigarette packages convince smokers to smoke less, the demand curve for cigarettes shifts to the left. In panel (a), the demand curve shifts from D_1 to D_2. At a price of $10.00 per pack, the quantity demanded falls from 20 to 10 cigarettes per day, as reflected by the shift from point A to point B. By contrast, if a tax raises the price of cigarettes, the demand curve does not shift. Instead, we observe a movement to a different point on the demand curve. In panel (b), when the price rises from $10.00 to $20.00, the quantity demanded falls from 20 to 12 cigarettes per day, as reflected by the movement from point A to point C.

FIGURE 4.4

Shifts in the Demand Curve versus Movements along the Demand Curve

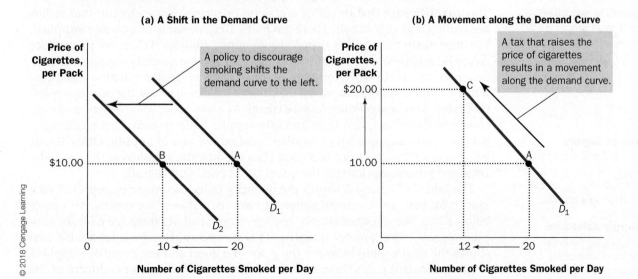

(a) A Shift in the Demand Curve

A policy to discourage smoking shifts the demand curve to the left.

(b) A Movement along the Demand Curve

A tax that raises the price of cigarettes results in a movement along the demand curve.

encourages smokers to reduce the number of cigarettes they smoke. In this case, the reduced amount of smoking does not represent a shift in the demand curve. Instead, it represents a movement along the same demand curve to a point with a higher price and lower quantity, as in panel (b) of Figure 4.4.

How much does the amount of smoking respond to changes in the price of cigarettes? Economists have attempted to answer this question by studying what happens when the tax on cigarettes changes. They have found that a 10-percent increase in the price causes a 4-percent reduction in the quantity demanded. Teenagers are especially sensitive to the price of cigarettes: A 10-percent increase in the price causes a 12-percent drop in teenage smoking.

A related question is how the price of cigarettes affects the demand for other drugs, such as marijuana, which has recently been legalized in Canada. Opponents of cigarette taxes often argue that tobacco and marijuana are substitutes, so that high cigarette prices encourage marijuana use. By contrast, many experts on substance abuse view tobacco as a "gateway drug" leading the young to experiment with other harmful substances. Most studies of the data are consistent with this view: They find that lower cigarette prices are associated with greater use of marijuana. In other words, tobacco and marijuana appear to be complements rather than substitutes. We discuss other issues related to the legalization of marijuana later in the chapter. ■

 Make up an example of a monthly demand schedule for pizza, and graph the implied demand curve. • Give an example of something that would shift this demand curve. • Would a change in the price of pizza shift this demand curve?

4-3 Supply

We now turn to the other side of the market and examine the behaviour of sellers. Once again, to focus our thinking, let's consider the market for ice cream.

4-3a The Supply Curve: The Relationship between Price and Quantity Supplied

quantity supplied
the amount of a good that sellers are willing and able to sell

law of supply
the claim that, other things equal, the quantity supplied of a good rises when the price of the good rises

supply schedule
a table that shows the relationship between the price of a good and the quantity supplied

The **quantity supplied** to sell of any good or service is the amount that sellers are willing and able to sell. There are many determinants of quantity supplied, but once again price plays a special role in our analysis. When the price of ice cream is high, selling ice cream is profitable, and so the quantity supplied is large. Sellers of ice cream work long hours, buy many ice-cream machines, and hire many workers. By contrast, when the price of ice cream is low, the business is less profitable, so sellers produce less ice cream. At a low price, some sellers may even choose to shut down, and their quantity supplied falls to zero. This relationship between price and quantity supplied is called the **law of supply**: Other things being equal, when the price of a good rises the quantity supplied of the good also rises, and when the price falls the quantity supplied falls as well.

The table in Figure 4.5 shows the quantity of ice-cream cones supplied each month by Ben, an ice-cream seller, at various prices of ice cream. At a price below $1.00, Ben does not supply any ice cream at all. As the price rises, he supplies a greater and greater quantity. This is the **supply schedule**, a table that shows the relationship between the price of a good and the quantity supplied, holding constant everything else that influences how much producers of the good want to sell.

FIGURE 4.5

Ben's Supply Schedule and Supply Curve

The supply schedule shows the quantity supplied at each price. This supply curve, which graphs the supply schedule, shows how the quantity supplied of the good changes as its price varies. Because a higher price increases the quantity supplied, the supply curve slopes upward.

Price of Ice-Cream Cone	Quantity of Cones Supplied
$0.00	0
0.50	0
1.00	1
1.50	2
2.00	3
2.50	4
3.00	5

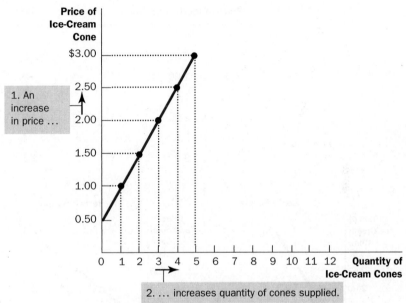

The graph in Figure 4.5 uses the numbers from the table to illustrate the law of supply. The curve relating price and quantity supplied is called the **supply curve**. The supply curve slopes upward because, other things equal, a higher price means a greater quantity supplied.

4-3b Market Supply versus Individual Supply

Just as market demand is the sum of the demands of all buyers, market supply is the sum of the supplies of all sellers. The table in Figure 4.6 shows the supply schedules for two ice-cream producers—Ben and Jerry. At any price, Ben's supply schedule tells us the quantity of ice cream Ben supplies, and Jerry's supply schedule tells us the quantity of ice cream Jerry supplies. The market supply is the sum of the two individual supplies.

The graph in Figure 4.6 shows the supply curves that correspond to the supply schedules. As with demand curves, we sum the individual supply curves *horizontally* to obtain the market supply curve. That is, to find the total quantity supplied at any price, we add the individual quantities, which are found on the horizontal axis of the individual supply curves. The market supply curve shows how the total quantity supplied varies as the price of the good varies, holding constant all other factors that influence producers' decisions about how much to sell.

4-3c Shifts in the Supply Curve

Because the market supply curve is drawn holding other things constant, when one of these factors changes, the supply curve shifts. For example, suppose the

supply curve

a graph of the relationship between the price of a good and the quantity supplied

FIGURE 4.6

Market Supply as the Sum of Individual Supplies

The quantity supplied in a market is the sum of the quantities supplied by all the sellers at each price. Thus, the market supply curve is found by adding horizontally the individual supply curves. At a price of $2, Ben supplies 3 ice-cream cones, and Jerry supplies 4 ice-cream cones. The quantity supplied in the market at this price is 7 cones.

Price of Ice-Cream Cone	Ben		Jerry		Market
$0.00	0	+	0	=	0
0.50	0		0		0
1.00	1		0		1
1.50	2		2		4
2.00	3		4		7
2.50	4		6		10
3.00	5		8		13

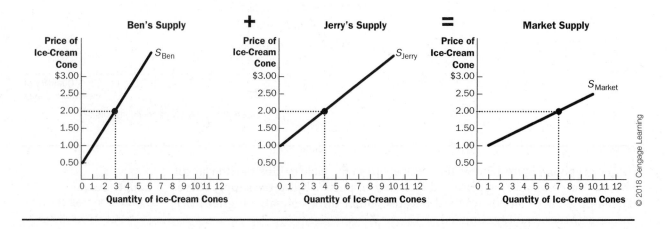

price of sugar falls. Sugar is an input into the production of ice cream, so the fall in the price of sugar makes selling ice cream more profitable. This raises the supply of ice cream: At any given price, sellers are now willing to produce a larger quantity. As a result, the supply curve for ice cream shifts to the right.

Figure 4.7 illustrates shifts in supply. Any change that raises quantity supplied at every price, such as a fall in the price of sugar, shifts the supply curve to the right and is called *an increase in supply.* Any change that reduces the quantity supplied at every price shifts the supply curve to the left and is called *a decrease in supply.*

There are many variables that can shift the supply curve. Let's consider the most important.

Input Prices   To produce their output of ice cream, sellers use various inputs: cream, sugar, flavouring, ice-cream machines, the buildings in which the ice cream is made, and the labour of workers who mix the ingredients and operate the machines. When the price of one or more of these inputs rises, producing ice cream

FIGURE 4.7

Shifts in the Supply Curve

Any change that raises the quantity that sellers wish to produce at a given price shifts the supply curve to the right. Any change that lowers the quantity that sellers wish to produce at a given price shifts the supply curve to the left.

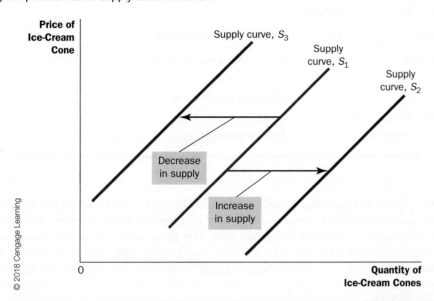

is less profitable, and firms supply less ice cream. If input prices rise substantially, a firm might shut down and supply no ice cream at all. Thus, the supply of a good is negatively related to the price of the inputs used to make the good.

Technology The technology for turning inputs into ice cream is another determinant of supply. The invention of the mechanized ice-cream machine, for example, reduced the amount of labour necessary to make ice cream. By reducing firms' costs, the advance in technology raised the supply of ice cream.

Expectations The amount of ice cream a firm supplies today may depend on its expectations about the future. For example, if a firm expects the price of ice cream to rise in the future, it will put some of its current production into storage and supply less to the market today.

Number of Sellers In addition to the preceding factors, which influence the behaviour of individual sellers, market supply depends on the number of sellers. If Ben or Jerry were to retire from the ice-cream business, the supply in the market would fall.

Summary The supply curve shows what happens to the quantity supplied of a good when its price varies, holding constant all the other variables that influence sellers. When one of these other variables changes, the supply curve shifts. Table 4.2 lists the variables that influence how much producers choose to sell of a good.

TABLE 4.2

Variables That Influence Sellers

Source: © 2018 Cengage Learning

This table lists the variables that affect how much producers choose to sell of any good. Notice the special role that the price of the good plays: A change in the good's price represents a movement along the supply curve, whereas a change in one of the other variables shifts the supply curve.

Variable	A Change in This Variable …
Price of the good itself	Represents a movement along the supply curve
Input prices	Shifts the supply curve
Technology	Shifts the supply curve
Expectations	Shifts the supply curve
Number of sellers	Shifts the supply curve

Once again, to remember whether you need to shift or move along the supply curve, keep in mind that a curve shifts only when there is a change in a relevant variable that is not named on either axis. The price is on the vertical axis, so a change in price represents a movement along the supply curve. By contrast, because input prices, technology, expectations, and the number of sellers are not measured on either axis, a change in one of these variables shifts the supply curve.

4-4 Supply and Demand Together

Having analyzed supply and demand separately, we now combine them to see how they determine the price and quantity of a good sold in the market.

4-4a Equilibrium

Figure 4.8 shows the market supply curve and market demand curve together. Notice that there is one point at which the supply and demand curves intersect. This point is called the market's **equilibrium**. The price at this intersection is called the **equilibrium price**, and the quantity is called the **equilibrium quantity**. Here the equilibrium price is $2.00 per cone, and the equilibrium quantity is 7 ice-cream cones.

The dictionary defines the word *equilibrium* as a situation in which various forces are in balance. This definition applies to a market's equilibrium as well. *At the equilibrium price, the quantity of the good that buyers are willing and able to buy exactly balances the quantity that sellers are willing to sell.* The equilibrium price is sometimes called the *market-clearing price* because, at this price, everyone in the market has been satisfied: Buyers have bought all they want to buy, and sellers have sold all they want to sell.

The actions of buyers and sellers naturally move markets toward the equilibrium of supply and demand. To see why, consider what happens when the market price is not equal to the equilibrium price.

Suppose first that the market price is above the equilibrium price, as in panel (a) of Figure 4.9. At a price of $2.50 per cone, the quantity of the good

equilibrium
a situation in which the price has reached the level where quantity supplied equals quantity demanded

equilibrium price
the price that balances quantity supplied and quantity demanded

equilibrium quantity
the quantity supplied and the quantity demanded at the equilibrium price.

FIGURE 4.8

**The Equilibrium of
Supply and Demand**

The equilibrium is found where the supply and demand curves intersect. At the equilibrium price, the quantity supplied equals the quantity demanded. Here the equilibrium price is $2: At this price, 7 ice-cream cones are supplied, and 7 ice-cream cones are demanded.

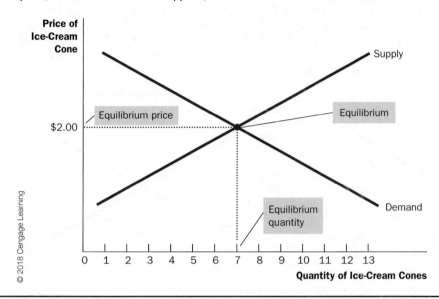

© 2018 Cengage Learning

supplied (10 cones) exceeds the quantity demanded (4 cones). There is a **surplus** of the good: Suppliers are unable to sell all they want at the going price. A surplus is sometimes called a situation of *excess supply*. When there is a surplus in the ice-cream market, sellers of ice cream find their freezers increasingly full of ice cream they would like to sell but cannot. They respond to the surplus by cutting their prices. Falling prices, in turn, increase the quantity demanded and decrease the quantity supplied. These changes represent movement along the supply and demand curves (not shifts in the curves). Prices continue to fall until the market reaches the equilibrium.

Suppose now that the market price is below the equilibrium price, as in panel (b) of Figure 4.9. In this case, the price is $1.50 per cone, and the quantity of the good demanded exceeds the quantity supplied. There is a **shortage** of the good: Demanders are unable to buy all they want at the going price. A shortage is sometimes called a situation of *excess demand.* When a shortage occurs in the ice-cream market, buyers have to wait in long lines for a chance to buy one of the few cones available. With too many buyers chasing too few goods, sellers can respond to the shortage by raising their prices without losing sales. These price increases cause the quantity demanded to fall and the quantity supplied to rise. Once again, these changes represent movements *along* the supply and demand curves, and they move the market toward the equilibrium.

Thus, regardless of whether the price starts off too high or too low, the activities of the many buyers and sellers automatically push the market price toward the equilibrium price. Once the market reaches its equilibrium, all buyers and sellers are satisfied, and there is no upward or downward pressure on the price. How quickly equilibrium is reached varies from market to market depending

surplus

a situation in which quantity supplied is greater than quantity demanded

shortage

a situation in which quantity demanded is greater than quantity supplied

FIGURE 4.9

Markets Not in Equilibrium

In panel (a), there is a surplus. Because the market price of $2.50 is above the equilibrium price, the quantity supplied (10 cones) exceeds the quantity demanded (4 cones). Suppliers try to increase sales by cutting the price of a cone, and this moves the price toward its equilibrium level. In panel (b), there is a shortage. Because the market price of $1.50 is below the equilibrium price, the quantity demanded (10 cones) exceeds the quantity supplied (4 cones). With too many buyers chasing too few goods, suppliers can take advantage of the shortage by raising the price. Hence, in both cases, the price adjustment moves the market toward the equilibrium of supply and demand.

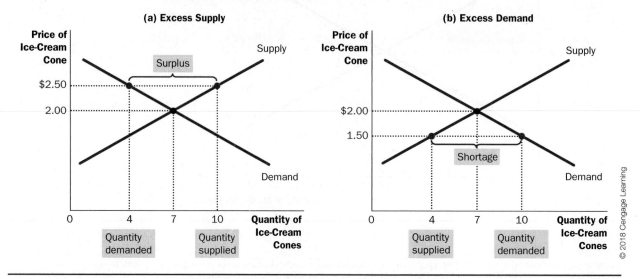

© 2018 Cengage Learning

on how quickly prices adjust. In most free markets, surpluses and shortages are only temporary because prices eventually move toward their equilibrium levels. Indeed, this phenomenon is so pervasive that it is called the **law of supply and demand**: The price of any good adjusts to bring the quantity supplied and quantity demanded for that good into balance.

law of supply and demand

the claim that the price of any good adjusts to bring the quantity supplied and the quantity demanded for that good into balance

4-4b Three Steps to Analyzing Changes in Equilibrium

So far we have seen how supply and demand together determine a market's equilibrium, which in turn determines the price and quantity of the good that buyers purchase and sellers produce. The equilibrium price and quantity depend on the position of the supply and demand curves. When some event shifts one of these curves, the equilibrium in the market changes, resulting in a new price and a new quantity exchanged between buyers and sellers.

When analyzing how some event affects the equilibrium in a market, we proceed in three steps. First, we decide whether the event shifts the supply curve, the demand curve, or, in some cases, both. Second, we decide whether the curve shifts to the right or to the left. Third, we use the supply-and-demand diagram to compare the initial equilibrium with the new one, which shows how the shift affects the equilibrium price and quantity. Table 4.3 summarizes these three steps. To see how this recipe is used, let's consider various events that might affect the market for ice cream.

1. Decide whether the event shifts the supply or demand curve (or perhaps both).
2. Decide in which direction the curve shifts.
3. Use the supply-and-demand diagram to see how the shift changes the equilibrium price and quantity.

TABLE 4.3

A Three-Step Program for Analyzing Changes in Equilibrium

Source: © 2018 Cengage Learning

Example: A Change in Market Equilibrium Due to a Shift in Demand Suppose that one summer the weather is very hot. How does this event affect the market for ice cream? To answer this question, let's follow our three steps.

1. The hot weather affects the demand curve by changing people's taste for ice cream. That is, the weather changes the amount of ice cream that people want to buy at any given price. The supply curve is unchanged because the weather does not directly affect the firms that sell ice cream.
2. Because hot weather makes people want to eat more ice cream, the demand curve shifts to the right. Figure 4.10 shows this increase in demand as the

FIGURE 4.10

How an Increase in Demand Affects the Equilibrium

An event that raises quantity demanded at any given price shifts the demand curve to the right. The equilibrium price and the equilibrium quantity both rise. Here, an abnormally hot summer causes buyers to demand more ice cream. The demand curve shifts from D_1 to D_2, which causes the equilibrium price to rise from \$2.00 to \$2.50 and the equilibrium quantity to rise from 7 to 10 cones.

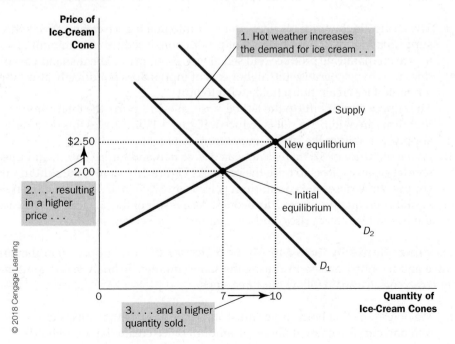

shift in the demand curve from D_1 to D_2. This shift indicates that the quantity of ice cream demanded is higher at every price.

3.   At the old price of $2, there is now an excess demand for ice cream, and this shortage induces firms to raise the price. As Figure 4.10 shows, the increase in demand raises the equilibrium price from $2.00 to $2.50 and the equilibrium quantity from 7 to 10 cones. In other words, the hot weather increases the price of ice cream and the quantity of ice cream sold.

Shifts in Curves versus Movements along Curves   Notice that when hot weather increases the demand for ice cream and drives up the price, the quantity of ice cream that firms supply rises, even though the supply curve remains the same. In this case, economists say there has been an increase in "quantity supplied" but no change in "supply."

"Supply" refers to the position of the supply curve, whereas the "quantity supplied" refers to the amount suppliers wish to sell. In this example, supply does not change because the weather does not alter firms' desire to sell at any given price. Instead, the hot weather alters consumers' desire to buy at any given price and thereby shifts the demand curve to the right. The increase in demand causes the equilibrium price to rise. When the price rises, the quantity supplied rises. This increase in quantity supplied is represented by the movement along the supply curve.

To summarize, a shift in the supply curve is called a "change in supply," and a shift in the demand curve is called a "change in demand." A movement along a fixed supply curve is called a "change in the quantity supplied," and a movement along a fixed demand curve is called a "change in the quantity demanded."

Example: A Change in Market Equilibrium Due to a Shift in Supply
Suppose that, during another summer, a hurricane destroys part of the sugarcane crop and drives up the price of sugar. How does this event affect the market for ice cream? Once again, to answer this question, we follow our three steps.

1.   The change in the price of sugar, an input into making ice cream, affects the supply curve. By raising the costs of production, it reduces the amount of ice cream that firms produce and sell at any given price. The demand curve does not change because the higher cost of inputs does not directly affect the amount of ice cream households wish to buy.

2.   The supply curve shifts to the left because, at every price, the total amount that firms are willing to sell is reduced. Figure 4.11 illustrates this decrease in supply as a shift in the supply curve from S_1 to S_2.

3.   At the old price of $2, there is now an excess demand for ice cream, and this shortage causes firms to raise the price. As Figure 4.11 shows, the shift in the supply curve raises the equilibrium price from $2.00 to $2.50 and lowers the equilibrium quantity from 7 to 4 cones. As a result of the sugar price increase, the price of ice cream rises, and the quantity of ice cream sold falls.

Example: Shifts in Both Supply and Demand   Now suppose that the heat wave and the hurricane occur during the same summer. To analyze this combination of events, we again follow our three steps.

1.   We determine that both curves must shift. The hot weather affects the demand curve because it alters the amount of ice cream that households

An event that reduces quantity supplied at any given price shifts the supply curve to the left. The equilibrium price rises, and the equilibrium quantity falls. Here, an increase in the price of sugar (an input) causes sellers to supply less ice cream. The supply curve shifts from S_1 to S_2, which causes the equilibrium price of ice cream to rise from $2.00 to $2.50 and the equilibrium quantity to fall from 7 to 4 cones.

FIGURE 4.11

How a Decrease in Supply Affects the Equilibrium

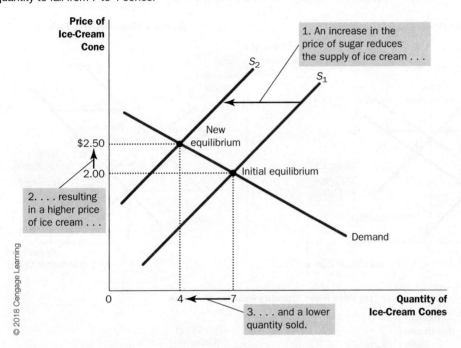

© 2018 Cengage Learning

want to buy at any given price. At the same time, when the hurricane drives up sugar prices, it alters the supply curve for ice cream because it changes the amount of ice cream that firms want to sell at any given price.

2. The curves shift in the same directions as they did in our previous analysis: The demand curve shifts to the right, and the supply curve shifts to the left. Figure 4.12 illustrates these shifts.

3. As Figure 4.12 shows, there are three possible outcomes that might result, depending on the relative size of the demand and supply shifts. In all cases, the equilibrium price rises. In panel (a), where demand increases substantially while supply falls just a little, the equilibrium quantity also rises. By contrast, in panel (b), where supply falls substantially while demand rises just a little, the equilibrium quantity falls. In panel (c), supply and demand both change by the same magnitude such that the equilibrium quantity stays the same but the price rises. Thus, these events certainly raise the price of ice cream, but their impact on the amount of ice cream sold is ambiguous (that is, it could go either way).

Summary We have just seen three examples of how to use supply and demand curves to analyze a change in equilibrium. Whenever an event shifts the supply

FIGURE 4.12

A Shift in Both Supply and Demand

Here we observe a simultaneous increase in demand and decrease in supply. Three outcomes are possible. In panel (a), the equilibrium price rises from P_1 to P_2, and the equilibrium quantity rises from Q_1 to Q_2. In panel (b), the equilibrium price again rises from P_1 to P_2, but the equilibrium quantity falls from Q_1 to Q_2. Finally, in panel (c), the equilibrium price rises from P_1 to P_2, but the equilibrium quantity remains unchanged at Q_1.

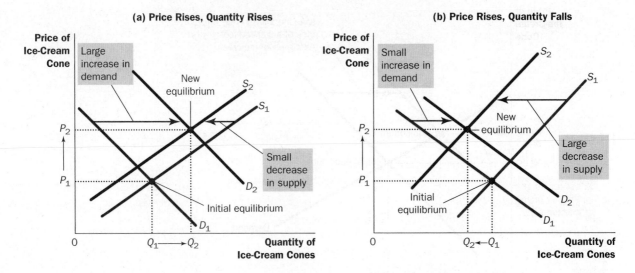

(a) Price Rises, Quantity Rises

(b) Price Rises, Quantity Falls

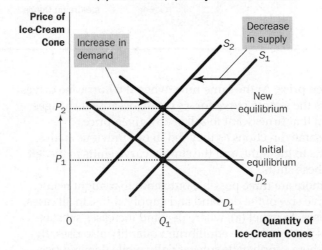

(c) Price Rises, Quantity Remains the Same

curve, the demand curve, or perhaps both curves, you can use these tools to predict how the event will alter the price and quantity sold in equilibrium. Table 4.4 shows the predicted outcome for any combination of shifts in the two curves. To make sure you understand how to use the tools of supply and demand, pick a few entries in this table and make sure you can explain to yourself why the table contains the prediction it does.

TABLE 4.4

	No Change in Supply	An Increase in Supply	A Decrease in Supply
No Change in Demand	P same Q same	P down Q up	P up Q down
An Increase in Demand	P up Q up	P ambiguous Q up	P up Q ambiguous
A Decrease in Demand	P down Q down	P down Q ambiguous	P ambiguous Q down

What Happens to Price and Quantity When Supply or Demand Shifts?

As a quick quiz, make sure you can explain each of the entries in this table using a supply-and-demand diagram.

Source: © 2018 Cengage Learning

case study **Marijuana Legalization**

Canada legalized the selling of marijuana in October of 2018. The legalization of marijuana falls under the Criminal Code, and is therefore a matter for the federal government. However, the regulations governing the buying and selling of marijuana are a provincial responsibility. The provinces have taken different approaches to regulation. For example, in many provinces marijuana can be sold only in provincially run or controlled retail stores, often associated with liquor board stores. However, in other provinces, notably British Columbia and Alberta, retail sales are allowed at both public and private stores.

It is difficult to obtain prices on illegal goods. Prior to the legalization of marijuana Statistics Canada launched an experimental crowdsourcing website, cleverly called StatsCannabis, to collect data on the price and consumption of marijuana. Figure 4.13 shows Statistics Canada's estimate of the average price of non-legal marijuana going all the way back to 1961. As is evident in the

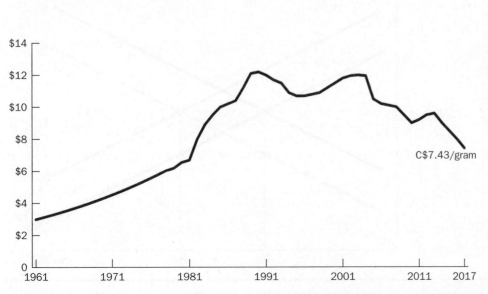

FIGURE 4.13

Marijuana Prices in Canada 1961–2017, CDN$ per gram

Source: Based on Statistics Canada, "The Price of Cannabis in Canada," https://www150.statcan.gc.ca/n1/pub/13-607-x/2016001/1286-eng.htm

C$7.43/gram

figure, the price has generally fallen since the mid-2000s, prior to legalization, from a high (pardon the pun) of about $12 per gram to an average of $7.43 per gram in 2017. Statistics Canada estimates that Canadians spent approximately $5.7 billion on marijuana in 2017, which means total sales were approximately 790 million grams.

We can use our simple demand and supply diagrams to explore some issues associated with the legalization of marijuana. Figure 4.14 shows a stylized market for marijuana prior to legalization. It shows an equilibrium price of P_{N0} per gram and quantity of Q_{N0}, given by the intersection of the demand (D_{N0}) and supply (S_{N0}) curves. Figure 4.14 also illustrates one possible representation of the effects of legalization. The supply curve shifts from S_{N0} to S_{L0}, as the supply of marijuana increases under legalization. This occurs because of the entry of legal firms into the market, the reduction in costs associated with legal production and distribution, and so on. The demand curve shifts from D_{N0} to D_{L0} as demand also increases, reflecting factors like the increased convenience and safety of the legal product and the elimination of the risk of prosecution for possession. The equilibrium illustrated in the diagram indicates in this scenario the legal price, P_{L0}, remains at the non-legal price of P_{N0}. Note, however, that even though the price doesn't change, the equilibrium quantity increases to Q_{L0}, reflecting the fact that the demand for marijuana has increased under legalization. In this

FIGURE 4.14

Marijuana Market, High Legal Supply

The initial equilibrium for non-legal marijuana is determined by the intersection of the demand and supply curves, D_{N0} and S_{N0}, giving rise to an equilibrium price P_{N0} and quantity Q_{L0}. Legalization shifts both curves, the demand curve to D_{L0} and the supply curve to S_{L0}. In this scenario, the equilibrium price remains the same, at $P_{N0} = P_{L0}$, but the quantity increases to Q_{L0}.

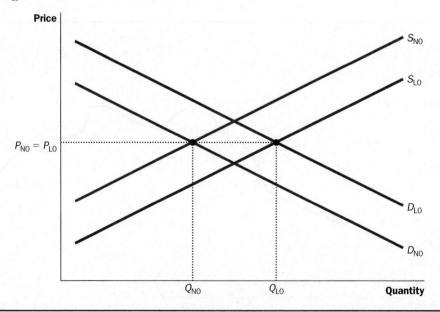

FIGURE 4.15

Marijuana Market, Low Legal Supply

In this scenario the supply curve shifts, but not by as much. Thus, the equilibrium price rises and P_{L1} is above the initial price in the non-legal market, P_{N0}.

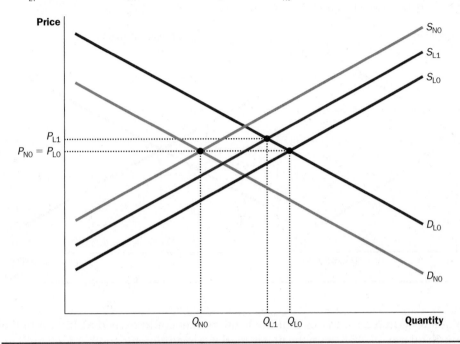

scenario, the supply curve for legal marijuana shifts out enough to maintain the non-legal price, effectively eliminating the illegal market. This is just one possibility, however.

As indicated above, the provinces have taken different approaches to the sale and regulation of marijuana. In some provinces the supply is restricted to provincially controlled stores, while in other provinces sales are allowed in private stores. Moreover, other government regulations relating to online sales, taxes, and so on vary across provinces. There is a risk that because of these regulations, the supply curve under legalization does not shift as much as shown in Figure 4.14. This is illustrated in Figure 4.15, where the supply curve now shifts to S_{L1}. The equilibrium price in this case is P_{L1}, which is higher than the non-legal price of P_{L0}.

If regulation results in a legal price of marijuana that is too high, this could lead to a *split market*, illustrated in Figure 4.16. Here, there are two markets for marijuana, the legal market in panel (a), with a price P_{L2}, and the non-legal market in panel (b), with a lower price of P_{N2}. In this case, overregulation drives some marijuana purchases underground into the illegal black market.

The "day one" prices of marijuana following legalization on October 17, 2018 ranged from about $7.00 to $17.25 per gram depending on the province and the quality. Significant shortages of marijuana were reported in many retail outlets. This was due in part to supply chain issues and a higher than anticipated demand.

FIGURE 4.16

Split Marijuana Market   If the legal price is too high the market will split, with some consumers staying in the legal market in panel (a), paying a price of P_{L2}, and other consumers moving to the non-legal black market, paying a lower price of P_{N2}.

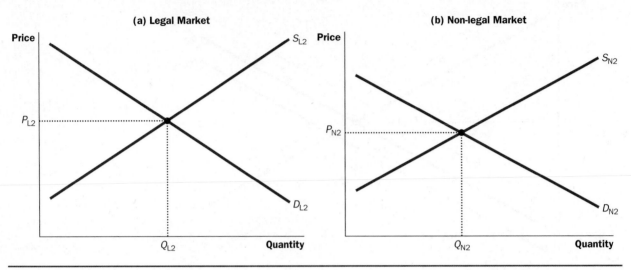

Statistics Canada estimates that the legal market could exceed $1 billion in the fourth quarter of 2018, with the illegal market accounting for another $300 million. It is anticipated that the market will adjust as time goes by, but concern remains that a black market may continue for some time.

One of the key considerations in legalizing marijuana is the desire to eliminate the black market. At the same time, governments want to regulate the market to ensure safe, controlled, and limited access. This analysis suggests that if regulation is too onerous it can drive up the price of legal marijuana, enticing some people into the illegal black market, resulting in a split market. A similar consideration surfaced in connection with the taxation of cigarettes in the 1990s, when the federal government actually cut taxes imposed on cigarettes to curtail a substantial increase in smuggling and black market activity. Concerns over high tax rates on cigarettes and the contraband market continue today.

Provincial governments are still working out how to balance these tradeoffs in connection with the regulation and taxation of marijuana. Regulations will no doubt change over time as the market evolves. This analysis emphasizes, however, that no one, most especially governments, can escape the fundamental laws of demand and supply. ■

QUICK Quiz   *On the appropriate diagram, show what happens to the market for pizza if the price of tomatoes rises. • On a separate diagram, show what happens to the market for pizza if the price of hamburgers falls.*

Supply, Demand, and Technology

This article discusses how technology and changes in demand for electric vehicles are revitalizing a Canadian mining town.

The Canadian Ghost Town That Tesla Is Bringing Back to Life

By Danielle Bochove

Ironically, Cobalt, Ontario—population 1,100—was built on silver.

Remnants of a boom that transformed the town more than a century ago are everywhere. A mine headframe still protrudes from the roof of the bookstore, which was previously a grocery. The butcher used to toss unwanted bones down an abandoned 350-foot shaft in the middle of the shop floor and keep meat cool in its lowered mine cage.

While the last silver mines closed almost 30 years ago, a global push for the village's namesake metal is promising to breathe new life into the sleepy town 500 kilometers (300 miles) north of Toronto. The whitish element (which "blooms" pink when exposed to air) was initially ignored by the area's prospectors and later mined mainly as a by-product of silver. Now, global demand for cobalt, a component in batteries used to power electric cars for automakers from Tesla Inc. to Volkswagen AG, is changing the game.

Call it a cobalt rush in Cobalt.

. . . Cobalt, both the town and the metal, are attracting renewed attention as a buffer to rising political risks in the Democratic Republic of Congo, which accounted for more than half the world's 123,000-ton production in 2016, according to Natural Resources Canada. China and Canada were a distant second and third, each contributing roughly 6 percent of supply, followed by Russia and Australia. But as concerns grow about country risk in the DRC, even as demand swells, those smaller players stand to benefit.

. . . [I]t was silver that first drew prospectors to Cobalt 115 years ago. Contractors looking for lumber to expand the Canadian railroad discovered visible silver in the loose rock. Within two years, 600 prospecting licenses had been issued and by 1907, that had swelled to almost 10,000, according to records housed in the Cobalt Mining Museum. The newly born town was simultaneously cosmopolitan and raucous: while mine owners enjoyed an opera house and a gentlemen's club, their employees let off steam at "blind pigs," illegal watering holes named for the unfortunate animals on which bootlegged alcohol was tested.

Fortunes were made with little mining expertise because rich silver deposits lay so close to surface. In 1911 alone, more than 31.5 million ounces of silver were pulled out of the "camp," roughly one-eighth of the world's production, according to a book on the area written by historian Doug Baldwin. Speaking to Toronto's Empire Club in 1909, the book recounts, Reverend Cannon Tucker told of a widely traveled American who, asked where Toronto was, replied: "Oh yes, that is the place where you change trains for Cobalt."

Today, the remains of those heady days are still visible in the crumbled foundations, capped mine shafts and piles of waste rock scattered in back yards throughout the town. More than 420 million ounces of silver came out of the Cobalt camp during its first 60 years and the town is built on a "honeycomb" of old mining tunnels and trenches, according to its mayor, Tina Sartoretto.

. . . Sartoretto's hope is that future mining will include plans for sustainable economic development tied to the metal. "If you were producing cobalt here, it would be nice if you could produce batteries here," she said.

. . . Prospectors regularly come into the bookstore, hoping to discover old mine maps and surveys. Owner Chitaroni is always on hand to tick off the advantages of Cobalt compared with more remote mining jurisdictions, including access to power, hydro and expertise.

"We call it Tim Hortons's exploration," he said, referring to the convenience of the ubiquitous Canadian doughnut-and-coffee chain, which has a store near Cobalt. "If you've got a breakdown, in half an hour, I've got parts. Try doing that in the Congo."

Source: Danielle Bochove, "The Canadian Ghost Town That Tesla Is Bringing Back to Life," Bloomberg, October 31, 2017. https://www.bloomberg.com/news/features/2017-10-31/the-canadian-ghost-town-that-tesla-is-bringing-back-to-life. Used with permission of *Bloomberg* L.P. Copyright © 2017. All rights reserved.

4-5 Conclusion: How Prices Allocate Resources

This chapter has analyzed supply and demand in a single market. Our discussion has centred around the market for ice cream, but the lessons learned here apply to most other markets as well. Whenever you go to a store to buy something, you are contributing to the demand for that item. Whenever you look for a job, you are contributing to the supply of labour services. Because supply and demand are such pervasive economic phenomena, the model of supply and demand is a powerful tool for analysis. We use this model repeatedly in the following chapters.

One of the ten principles of economics discussed in Chapter 1 is that markets are usually a good way to organize economic activity. Although it is still too early to judge whether market outcomes are good or bad, in this chapter we have begun to see how markets work. In any economic system, scarce resources have to be allocated among competing uses. Market economies harness the forces of supply and demand to serve that end. Supply and demand together determine the prices of the economy's many different goods and services; prices in turn are the signals that guide the allocation of resources.

For example, consider the allocation of beachfront land. Because the amount of this land is limited, not everyone can enjoy the luxury of living by the beach. Who gets this resource? The answer is whoever is willing and able to pay the price. The price of beachfront land adjusts until the quantity of land demanded exactly balances the quantity supplied. Thus, in market economies, prices are the mechanism for rationing scarce resources.

Similarly, prices determine who produces each good and how much is produced. For instance, consider farming. Because we need food to survive, it is crucial that some people work on farms. What determines who is a farmer and who is not? In a free society, there is no government planning agency making this decision and ensuring an adequate supply of food. Instead, the allocation of workers to farms is based on the job decisions of millions of workers. This decentralized system works well because these decisions depend on prices. The prices of food and the wages of farm workers (the price of their labour) adjust to ensure that enough people choose to be farmers.

If a person had never seen a market economy in action, the whole idea might seem preposterous. Economies are enormous groups of people engaged in a multitude of independent activities. What prevents decentralized decision making from degenerating into chaos? What coordinates the actions of the millions of people with their varying abilities and desires? What ensures that what needs to be done does, in fact, get done? The answer, in a word, is *prices*. If an invisible hand guides market economies, as Adam Smith famously suggested, then the price system is the baton that the invisible hand uses to conduct the economic orchestra.

summary

- Economists use the model of supply and demand to analyze competitive markets. In a competitive market, there are many buyers and sellers, each of whom has little or no influence on the market price.

- The demand curve shows how the quantity of a good demanded depends on the price. According to the law of demand, as the price of a good falls, the quantity demanded rises. Therefore, the demand curve slopes downward.

- In addition to price, other determinants of how much consumers want to buy include income, the prices of substitutes and complements, tastes, expectations, and the number of buyers. If one of these factors changes, the demand curve shifts.

- The supply curve shows how the quantity of a good supplied depends on the price. According to the law of supply, as the price of a good rises, the quantity supplied rises. Therefore, the supply curve slopes upward.

- In addition to price, other determinants of how much producers want to sell include input prices, technology, expectations, and the number of sellers. If one of these factors changes, the supply curve shifts.

- The intersection of the supply and demand curves determines the market equilibrium. At the equilibrium price, the quantity demanded equals the quantity supplied.

- The behaviour of buyers and sellers naturally drives markets toward their equilibrium. When the market price is above the equilibrium price, there is a surplus of the good, which causes the market price to fall. When the market price is below the equilibrium price, there is a shortage, which causes the market price to rise.

- To analyze how any event influences a market, we use the supply-and-demand diagram to examine how the event affects the equilibrium price and quantity. To do this we follow three steps. First, we decide whether the event shifts the supply curve or the demand curve (or both). Second, we decide which direction the curve shifts. Third, we compare the new equilibrium with the initial equilibrium.

- In market economies, prices are the signals that guide economic decisions and thereby allocate scarce resources. For every good in the economy, the price ensures that supply and demand are in balance. The equilibrium price then determines how much of the good buyers choose to purchase and how much sellers choose to produce.

KEY **concepts**

market, *p. 65*
competitive market, *p. 66*
quantity demanded, *p. 66*
law of demand, *p. 67*
demand schedule, *p. 67*
demand curve, *p. 67*
normal good, *p. 69*

inferior good, *p. 69*
substitutes, *p. 69*
complements, *p. 70*
quantity supplied, *p. 72*
law of supply, *p. 72*
supply schedule, *p. 72*
supply curve, *p. 73*

equilibrium, *p. 76*
equilibrium price, *p. 76*
equilibrium quantity, *p. 76*
surplus, *p. 77*
shortage, *p. 77*
law of supply and demand, *p. 78*

QUESTIONS FOR **review**

1. What is a competitive market? Briefly describe the types of markets other than perfectly competitive markets.

2. What are the demand schedule and the demand curve, and how are they related? Why does the demand curve slope downward?

3. Does a change in consumers' tastes lead to a movement along the demand curve or a shift in the demand curve? Does a change in price lead to a movement along the demand curve or a shift in the demand curve?

4. Popeye's income declines and, as a result, he buys more spinach. Is spinach an inferior or a normal good? What happens to Popeye's demand curve for spinach?

5. What are the supply schedule and the supply curve, and how are they related? Why does the supply curve slope upward?

6. Does a change in producers' technology lead to a movement along the supply curve or a shift in the supply curve? Does a change in price lead to a movement along the supply curve or a shift in the supply curve?

7. Define the equilibrium of a market. Describe the forces that move a market toward its equilibrium.

8. Beer and pizza are complements because they are often enjoyed together. When the price of beer rises, what happens to the supply, demand, quantity supplied, quantity demanded, and the price in the market for pizza?

9. Describe the role of prices in market economies.

QUICK CHECK **multiple choice**

1. A change in which of the following will NOT shift the demand curve for hamburgers?
   a. the price of hot dogs
   b. the price of hamburgers
   c. the price of hamburger buns
   d. the income of hamburger consumers

2. An increase in ___ will cause a movement along a given demand curve, which is called a change in ___.
   a. supply, demand
   b. supply, quantity demanded
   c. demand, supply
   d. demand, quantity supplied

3. Movie tickets and film streaming services are substitutes. If the price of film streaming increases, what happens in the market for movie tickets?
   a. The supply curve shifts to the left.
   b. The supply curve shifts to the right.
   c. The demand curve shifts to the left.
   d. The demand curve shifts to the right.

4. The discovery of a large new reserve of crude oil will shift the ___ curve for gasoline, leading to a ___ equilibrium price.
   a. supply, higher
   b. supply, lower
   c. demand, higher
   d. demand, lower

5. If the economy goes into a recession and incomes fall, what happens in the markets for inferior goods?
   a. prices and quantities both rise
   b. prices and quantities both fall
   c. prices rise, quantities fall
   d. prices fall, quantities rise

6. Which of the following might lead to an increase in the equilibrium price of jelly and a decrease in the equilibrium quantity of jelly sold?
   a. an increase in the price of peanut butter, a complement to jelly
   b. an increase in the price of Marshmallow Fluff, a substitute for jelly
   c. an increase in the price of grapes, an input into jelly
   d. an increase in consumers' incomes, as long as jelly is a normal good

PROBLEMS AND **applications**

1. Explain each of the following statements using supply-and-demand diagrams.
   a. When a cold snap hits Florida, the price of orange juice rises in supermarkets throughout Canada.
   b. When the weather turns warm in Quebec every summer, the prices of hotel rooms in Caribbean resorts plummet.
   c. When a war breaks out in the Middle East, the price of gasoline rises, while the price of a used SUV falls.

2. "An increase in the demand for notebooks raises the quantity of notebooks demanded, but not the quantity supplied." Is this statement true or false? Explain.

3. Consider the market for minivans. For each of the events listed below, identify which of the determinants of demand or supply are affected. Also indicate whether demand or supply is increased or decreased. Then show the effect on the price and quantity of minivans.
   a. People decide to have more children.
   b. A strike by steelworkers raises steel prices.
   c. Engineers develop new automated machinery for the production of minivans.
   d. The price of SUVs rises.
   e. A stock market crash lowers people's wealth.

4. Over the past 40 years, technological advances have reduced the cost of computer chips. How do you think this has affected the market for computers? For computer software? For typewriters?

5. Using supply-and-demand diagrams, show the effect of the following events on the market for sweatshirts.
   a. A hurricane in South Carolina damages the cotton crop.
   b. The price of leather jackets falls.
   c. All universities require morning calisthenics in appropriate attire.
   d. New knitting machines are invented.

6. Suppose that in the year 2010, the number of births was temporarily high. How will this baby boom affect the price of baby-sitting services in 2015 and 2025? (*Hint:* Five-year-olds need baby-sitters, whereas fifteen-year-olds can *be* baby-sitters.)

7. Ketchup is a complement (as well as a condiment) for hot dogs. If the price of hot dogs rises, what happens to the market for ketchup? For tomatoes? For tomato juice? For orange juice?

8. The market for pizza has the following demand and supply schedules:

Price	Quantity Demanded	Quantity Supplied
$4	135	26
5	104	53
6	81	81
7	68	98
8	53	110
9	39	121

Graph the demand and supply curves. What is the equilibrium price and quantity in this market? If the actual price in this market was *above* the equilibrium price, what would drive the market toward the equilibrium? If the actual price in this market was *below* the equilibrium price, what would drive the market toward the equilibrium?

9. Because bagels and cream cheese are often eaten together, they are complements.
   a. We observe that both the equilibrium price of cream cheese and the equilibrium quantity of bagels have risen. What could be responsible for this pattern—a fall in the price of flour or a fall in the price of milk? Illustrate and explain your answer.
   b. Suppose instead that the equilibrium price of cream cheese has risen but the equilibrium quantity of bagels has fallen. What could be responsible for this pattern—a rise in the price of flour or a rise in the price of milk? Illustrate and explain your answer.

10. Suppose that the price of hockey tickets at your school is determined by market forces. Currently, the demand and supply schedules are as follows:

Price	Quantity Demanded	Quantity Supplied
$4	10 000	8000
8	8 000	8000
12	6 000	8000
16	4 000	8000
20	2 000	8000

   a. Draw the demand and supply curves. What is unusual about this supply curve? Why might this be true?
   b. What are the equilibrium price and quantity of tickets?
   c. Your school plans to increase total enrollment next year by 5000 students. The additional students will have the following demand schedule:

Price	Quantity Demanded
$4	4000
8	3000
12	2000
16	1000
20	0

Now add the old demand schedule and the demand schedule for the new students to calculate the new demand schedule for the entire school. What will be the new equilibrium price and quantity?

11. Consider the markets for film streaming services, TV screens, and tickets to movie theatres.
   a. For each pair, identify whether they are complements or substitutes:
      • Film streaming and TV screens
      • Film streaming and movie tickets
      • TV screens and movie tickets
   b. Suppose a technological advance reduces the cost of manufacturing TV screens. Draw a diagram to show what happens to the market for TV screens.
   c. Draw two more diagrams to show how the change in the market for TV screens affects the markets for film streaming and movie tickets.

12. A survey shows an increase in drug use by young people. In the ensuing debate, two hypotheses are proposed:
   • Reduced police efforts have increased the availability of drugs on the street.
   • Cutbacks in educational efforts have decreased awareness of the dangers of drug addiction.
   a. Use supply-and-demand diagrams to show how each of these hypotheses could lead to an increase in the quantity of drugs consumed.
   b. How could information on what has happened to the price of drugs help us to distinguish between these explanations?

13. Consider the following events: Scientists reveal that consumption of oranges decreases the risk of diabetes and, at the same time, farmers use a new fertilizer that makes orange trees more productive. Illustrate and explain what effect these changes have on the equilibrium price and quantity of oranges.

The Mathematics of Market Equilibrium

The appendix to Chapter 2 presented a discussion of how economists use graphs to help explain mathematical relationships among variables. We have already seen that these are very valuable tools to help us understand economic relationships. In this appendix, we illustrate how simple mathematical methods can help us solve algebraically for a market's equilibrium price and quantity using supply and demand curves.

In Figure 4.8, we saw how the equilibrium price and quantity for a good are determined by the intersection of the supply and demand curves. Although they don't have to be, for simplicity, we often draw these curves as linear (so our "curves" are actually straight lines!).

Consider the following example of a linear demand curve:

$$Q^D = 56 - 4P$$

where Q^D is the quantity demanded and P is the price of the good.

As we saw in the appendix to Chapter 2, for a linear demand curve we can determine its intercept with the price axis (the y-intercept), where quantity demanded is zero, by setting $Q^D = 0$ and solving the demand equation for P. For our demand curve the y-intercept is therefore determined by $0 = 56 - 4P$; solving for P gives $4P = 56$, $P = 56/4 = 14$. Similarly, the intercept with the quantity axis (the x-intercept), where price is equal to zero, is determined by setting $P = 0$ and solving for Q^D, which simply gives $Q^D = 56$. Figure 4A.1 plots the demand curve given by the equation $Q^D = 56 - 4P$, identifying the x- and y-intercepts determined above.

FIGURE 4A.1

Linear Demand Curve

The demand curve $Q^D = 56 - 4P$ is plotted here, with the y-intercept (14) and x-intercept (56) identified. The slope of the demand curve is determined by taking the ratio of the negative of the y-intercept to the x-intercept, $\Delta y/\Delta x = -14/56 = -1/4$.

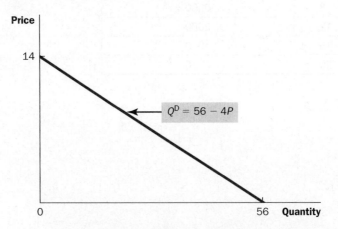

We also saw in the appendix to Chapter 2 that the slope of a linear demand curve is equal to the "rise over the run" as we move from one point on the demand curve to another. The "rise" is the change in price measured along the y-axis (Δy, where you'll recall that Δ is the Greek letter delta, which stands for "change in") as we move from one point on the demand curve to another; the "run" is the change in quantity demanded measured along the x-axis (Δx). So the slope of the demand curve is measured as $\Delta y / \Delta x$, as we move from one point on the demand curve to another.

Since the slope of a line is constant all along the line (that is what makes it a line!), we can use any two points on the demand curve to determine its slope. As discussed in the appendix to Chapter 2, two particularly useful points on the demand curve are the x- and y-intercepts determined above. We can use these points to determine the "rise over the run" from moving from the point on the demand curve that intersects the x-axis to the point on the demand curve that intersects the y-axis. In this case, the "rise" is just the y-intercept and the "run" is the negative of the x-intercept. So for this demand curve $\Delta y = 14$ and $\Delta x = -56$, and the slope is the negative of the ratio of the y-intercept and x-intercept, $\Delta y / \Delta x = -14/56 = -1/4$.

An example of a linear supply curve is:

$$Q^S = -4 + 2P$$

where Q^S is quantity supplied and P is again the price of the good.

As with the demand curve, we can determine the intercept of the linear supply curve with the price axis (the y-intercept), where quantity supplied is zero, by setting $Q^S = 0$ and solving the supply equation for P. The y-intercept is therefore determined by $0 = -4 + 2P$ and solving for P: $2P = 4$, $P = 4/2$, $P = 2$. Similarly, the intercept with the quantity axis (the x-intercept), where the price is zero, is determined by setting $P = 0$ and solving for Q^S, which gives $Q^S = -4$.

Note that because supply curves are upward sloping, in general they can intersect the x- or y-axis at either a positive or negative number. In our example the intersection with the x-axis is negative and with the y-axis is positive, which is often the case. Figure 4A.2 plots our supply curve given the intercepts calculated above. Because the intersection with the x-axis is negative, which corresponds to a negative supply and is clearly not possible, we show the "projection" of the curve into the negative quadrant with a dashed line.

As with the demand curve we can use any two points on the supply curve to determine its slope. Again, it is convenient to use the x- and y-intercepts of the supply curve determined above. In this case the "rise" is the y-intercept, giving $\Delta y = 2$, and the "run" is the negative of the x-intercept, so $\Delta x = 4$. The slope of the supply curve is the negative of the negative of the ratio of the y-intercept and the x-intercept, $\Delta y / \Delta x = 2/4 = 1/2$.

We have seen that the market equilibrium price and quantity are determined by the intersection of the demand and supply curves. In other words, the equilibrium price is such that the quantity demanded exactly equals the quantity supplied. To determine the equilibrium price, we start by using our linear demand and supply curves and set quantity demanded equal to quantity supplied ($Q^D = Q^S$):

$$56 - 4P = -4 + 2P$$

FIGURE 4A.2

Linear Supply Curve

The supply curve $Q^S = -4 + 2P$ is plotted here, with the y-intercept (2) and the x-intercept (−4) identified. The slope of the supply curve is determined by taking the negative of the ratio of the y-intercept and the x-intercept, $\Delta y/\Delta x = 2/4 = 1/2$.

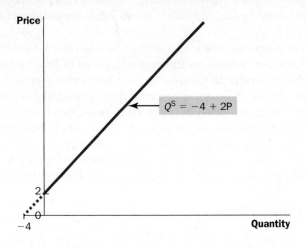

We now solve this equation for P. To do this, we use algebra to gather terms with P on the left-hand side and the other terms on the right-hand side and then solve for P as follows:

$$-2P - 4P = -4 - 56$$
$$-6P = -60$$
$$6P = 60$$
$$P = 60/6$$
$$P = 10$$

Therefore, for our example, the equilibrium price that clears the market and results in the quantity demanded equal to the quantity supplied is $P = 10$.

To determine the equilibrium quantity demanded in the market, substitute the equilibrium price into the equation for quantity demanded to get:

$$Q^D = 56 - 4P = 56 - 4(10) = 56 - 40 = 16$$

And to determine the equilibrium quantity supplied, use the supply curve to get:

$$Q^S = -4 + 2P = -4 + 2(10) = -4 + 20 = 16$$

As we would expect, at the equilibrium price the quantity demanded equals quantity supplied.

Figure 4A.3 plots the demand and supply curves for this example and shows the equilibrium price and quantity.

This diagram illustrates a linear demand curve given by $Q^D = 56 - 4P$ and a linear supply curve given by $Q^S = -4 + 2P$. The equilibrium price is determined by setting $Q^D = Q^S$ and solving for $P = 10$. The equilibrium quantity is determined by substituting the equilibrium price into either the demand or supply curve and solving for $Q = 16$.

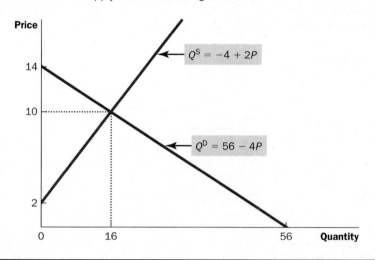

PROBLEMS AND applications

A1. Say that the demand schedule for a good is given by $Q^D = 20 - 2P$ and the supply schedule is given by $Q^S = -10 + 4P$.
   a. Graph the demand and supply curves, showing the x- and y-intercepts for each.
   b. Determine the equilibrium price and quantity.

A2. The demand and supply functions for hockey sticks are given by

$$Q^D = 286 - 20P$$
$$Q^S = 88 + 40P$$

   a. Graph the supply and the demand curves, clearly showing the intercepts and indicating the slopes of the two curves.
   b. Determine the equilibrium price and quantity of hockey sticks.
   c. Suppose that both the men's and the women's teams win Olympic gold medals, causing an increase in the demand for hockey sticks across the country to $Q^D = 328 - 20P$. What impact does this have on the price of hockey sticks and the quantity sold?

A3. Suppose that the demand curve for concert tickets is linear. When the price of a ticket is $5.00, the number of tickets purchased is 1000; when the price of a ticket is $15.00, the number of tickets purchased is 200. Find the slope of the demand curve.

A4. At a price of $320 per tonne, the supply of wheat in Canada is 25 million tonnes and the demand is 26 million tonnes. When the price increases to $340 per tonne, the supply increases to 27 million tonnes and the demand decreases to 22 million tonnes. Assume that both the demand and supply curves are linear.
   a. What is the equation for the demand curve for wheat?
   b. What is the equation for the supply curve for wheat?
   c. Using these equations, what is the equilibrium price and quantity of wheat?

A5. Market research has revealed the following information about the market for chocolate bars: The demand schedule can be represented by the equation $Q^D = 1600 - 300P$, where Q^D is the quantity demanded and P is the price. The supply schedule can be represented by the equation $Q^S = 1400 + 700P$, where Q^S is the quantity supplied.

a. Calculate the equilibrium price and quantity in the market for chocolate bars.

b. Say that in response to a major industry ad campaign, the demand schedule for chocolate bars shifted to the right, as represented by the equation $Q^D = 1800 - 300P$. What happens to the equilibrium price and quantity of chocolate bars in this case?

c. Returning to the original demand schedule, say that the price of cocoa beans, a major ingredient in the production of chocolate bars, increased because of a drought in sub-Saharan Africa, a major producer of cocoa, changing the supply schedule to $Q^S = 1100 + 700P$. What happens to the equilibrium price and quantity in this case?

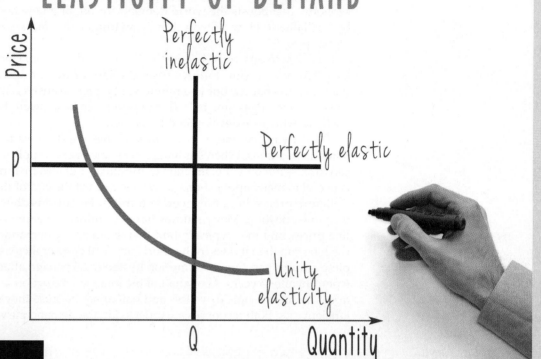

ELASTICITY OF DEMAND

Elasticity and Its Application

In this chapter, you will ...

1 Learn the meaning of the elasticity of demand
2 Examine what determines the elasticity of demand
3 Learn the meaning of the elasticity of supply
4 Examine what determines the elasticity of supply
5 Apply the concept of elasticity in three very different markets

Imagine that some event drives up the price of gasoline in Canada. It could be a war in the Middle East that disrupts the world supply of oil, a booming Chinese economy that boosts the world demand for oil, or a new tax on gasoline passed by Parliament. How do you think Canadian consumers would respond to the higher price?

It is easy to answer this question in a broad fashion: Consumers would buy less. This conclusion follows from the law of demand, which we learned in the previous chapter. But you might want a precise answer: By how much did the consumption of gasoline fall? This question can be answered using the concept of *elasticity*, which we develop in this chapter.

Elasticity is a measure of how much buyers and sellers respond to changes in market conditions. When studying how some event or policy affects a market, we can discuss not only the direction of the effects but also their magnitude. Elasticity is useful in many applications, as we see toward the end of the chapter.

Before proceeding, however, you might be curious about the answer to the gasoline question. Many studies have examined consumers' response to gasoline prices, and they typically find that the quantity demanded responds more in the long run than it does in the short run. A 10 percent increase in the price of gasoline reduces gasoline consumption by about 2.5 percent after one year and about 6 percent after 5 years. About half of the long-run reduction in quantity demanded arises because people drive less and half arises because they switch to more fuel-efficient cars. Both responses are reflected in the demand curve and its elasticity.

5-1   The Elasticity of Demand

When we introduced demand in Chapter 4, we noted that consumers usually buy more of a good when its price is lower, when their incomes are higher, when the prices of its substitutes are higher, or when the prices of its complements are lower. Our discussion of demand was qualitative, not quantitative. That is, we discussed the direction in which quantity demanded moves, but not the size of the change. To measure how much consumers respond to changes in these variables, economists use the concept of **elasticity**.

elasticity

a measure of the responsiveness of quantity demanded or quantity supplied to one of its determinants

price elasticity of demand

a measure of how much the quantity demanded of a good responds to a change in the price of that good, computed as the percentage change in quantity demanded divided by the percentage change in price

5-1a   The Price Elasticity of Demand and Its Determinants

The law of demand states that a fall in the price of a good raises the quantity demanded. The **price elasticity of demand** measures how much the quantity demanded responds to a change in price. Demand for a good is said to be *elastic* if the quantity demanded responds substantially to changes in the price. Demand is said to be *inelastic* if the quantity demanded responds only slightly to changes in the price.

The price elasticity of demand for any good measures how willing consumers are to buy less of the good as its price rises. Because the demand curve reflects the many economic, social, and psychological forces that shape consumer preferences, there is no simple, universal rule for what determines the demand curve's elasticity. Based on experience, however, we can state some rules of thumb about what influences the price elasticity of demand.

Availability of Close Substitutes   Goods with close substitutes tend to have more elastic demand because it is easier for consumers to switch from that good to others. For example, butter and margarine are easily substitutable. A small increase in the price of butter, assuming the price of margarine is held fixed, causes the quantity of butter sold to fall by a large amount. By contrast, because eggs are a food without a close substitute, the demand for eggs is less elastic than the demand for butter. A small increase in the price of eggs does not cause a sizeable drop in the quantity of eggs sold.

Necessities versus Luxuries Necessities tend to have inelastic demands, whereas luxuries have elastic demands. When the price of a visit to the dentist rises, people will not dramatically alter the number of times they go to the dentist, although they might go somewhat less often. By contrast, when the price of sail-boats rises, the quantity of sailboats demanded falls substantially. The reason is that most people view dentist visits as a necessity and sailboats as a luxury. Whether a good is a necessity or a luxury depends not on the intrinsic properties of the good but on the preferences of the buyer. For an avid sailor with little concern about his teeth, sailboats might be a necessity with inelastic demand and dentist visits a luxury with elastic demand.

Definition of the Market The elasticity of demand in any market depends on how we draw the boundaries of the market. Narrowly defined markets tend to have more elastic demand than broadly defined markets because it is easier to find close substitutes for narrowly defined goods. For example, food, a broad category, has a fairly inelastic demand because there are no good substitutes for food. Ice cream, a narrower category, has a more elastic demand because it is easy to substitute other desserts for ice cream. Vanilla ice cream, a very narrow category, has a very elastic demand because other flavours of ice cream are almost perfect substitutes for vanilla.

Time Horizon Goods tend to have more elastic demand over longer time horizons. When the price of gasoline rises, the quantity of gasoline demanded falls only slightly in the first few months. Over time, however, people buy more fuel-efficient cars, switch to public transportation, or move closer to where they work. Within several years, the quantity of gasoline demanded falls substantially.

5-1b Computing the Price Elasticity of Demand

Now that we have discussed the price elasticity of demand in general terms, let's be more precise about how it is measured. Economists compute the price elasticity of demand as the percentage change in the quantity demanded divided by the percentage change in the price. That is,

$$\text{Price elasticity of demand} = \frac{\text{Percentage change in quantity demanded}}{\text{Percentage change in price}}$$

For example, suppose that a 10 percent increase in the price of an ice-cream cone causes the amount of ice cream you buy to fall by 20 percent. We calculate your elasticity of demand as

$$\text{Price elasticity of demand} = \frac{20 \text{ percent}}{10 \text{ percent}} = 2$$

In this example, the elasticity is 2, reflecting that the change in the quantity demanded is proportionately twice as large as the change in the price.

Because the quantity demanded of a good is negatively related to its price, the percentage change in quantity will always have the opposite sign as the percentage change in price. In this example, the percentage change in price is a *positive* 10 percent (reflecting an increase), and the percentage change in quantity demanded is a *negative* 20 percent (reflecting a decrease). For this reason, price elasticities of demand are sometimes reported as negative numbers. In this book we follow the common practice of dropping the minus sign and reporting all price elasticities of demand as positive numbers. (Mathematicians call this the *absolute value*.) With this convention, a larger price elasticity implies a greater responsiveness of quantity demanded to changes in price.

5-1c The Midpoint Method: A Better Way to Calculate Percentage Changes and Elasticities

If you try calculating the price elasticity of demand between two points on a demand curve, you will quickly notice an annoying problem: The elasticity from point A to point B seems different from the elasticity from point B to point A. For example, consider these numbers:

Point A:	Price = $4	Quantity = 120
Point B:	Price = $6	Quantity = 80

Going from point A to point B, the price rises by 50 percent and the quantity falls by 33 percent, indicating that the price elasticity of demand is 33/50, or 0.66. By contrast, going from point B to point A, the price falls by 33 percent and the quantity rises by 50 percent, indicating that the price elasticity of demand is 50/33, or 1.5. This difference arises because the percentage changes are calculated from a different base.

One way to avoid this problem is to use the *midpoint method* for calculating elasticities. The standard procedure for computing a percentage change is to divide the change by the initial level. By contrast, the midpoint method computes a percentage change by dividing the change by the midpoint (or average) of the initial and final levels. For instance, $5 is the midpoint of $4 and $6. Therefore, according to the midpoint method a change from $4 to $6 is considered a 40 percent rise, because $(6 - 4)/5 \times 100 = 40$. Similarly, a change from $6 to $4 is considered a 40 percent fall.

Because the midpoint method gives the same answer regardless of the direction of change, it is often used when calculating the price elasticity of demand between two points. In our example, the midpoint between point A and point B is

Midpoint:	Price = $5	Quantity = 100

According to the midpoint method, when going from point A to point B, the price rises by 40 percent and the quantity falls by 40 percent. Similarly, when going from point B to point A, the price falls by 40 percent and the quantity rises by 40 percent. In both directions, the price elasticity of demand equals 1.

The following formula expresses the midpoint method for calculating the price elasticity of demand between two points, denoted (Q_1, P_1) and (Q_2, P_2):

$$\text{Price elasticity of demand} = \frac{(Q_2 - Q_1)/[(Q_2 + Q_1)/2]}{(P_2 - P_1)/[(P_2 + P_1)/2]}$$

The numerator is the percentage change in quantity computed using the midpoint method, and the denominator is the percentage change in price computed using the midpoint method. If you ever need to calculate elasticities, you should use this formula.

In this book, however, we rarely perform such calculations. For most of our purposes, what elasticity represents—the responsiveness of quantity demanded to a change in price—is more important than how it is calculated.

5-1d The Variety of Demand Curves

Economists classify demand curves according to their elasticity. Demand is considered *elastic* when the elasticity is greater than 1, which means the quantity moves proportionately more than the price. Demand is considered *inelastic* when the elasticity is less than 1, which means the quantity moves proportionately less than the price. If the elasticity is exactly 1, the percentage change in quantity equals the percentage change in price, and demand is said to have *unit elasticity.*

Because the price elasticity of demand measures how much quantity demanded responds to changes in the price, it is closely related to the slope of the demand curve. The following rule of thumb is a useful guide: The flatter the demand curve that passes through a given point, the greater the price elasticity of demand. The steeper the demand curve that passes through a given point, the smaller the price elasticity of demand.

Figure 5.1 shows five cases. In the extreme case of a zero elasticity, shown in panel (a), demand is *perfectly inelastic,* and the demand curve is vertical. In this case, regardless of the price, the quantity demanded stays the same. As the elasticity rises, the demand curve gets flatter and flatter, as shown in panels (b), (c), and (d). At the opposite extreme shown in panel (e), demand is *perfectly elastic.* This occurs as the price elasticity of demand approaches infinity and the demand curve becomes horizontal, reflecting the fact that very small changes in the price lead to huge changes in the quantity demanded.

Finally, if you have trouble keeping straight the terms *elastic* and *inelastic,* here's a memory trick for you: *I*nelastic curves, such as in panel (a) of Figure 5.1, look like the letter *I.* This is not a deep insight, but it might help on your next exam.

5-1e Total Revenue and the Price Elasticity of Demand

When studying changes in supply or demand in a market, one variable we often want to study is **total revenue**, the amount paid by buyers and received by sellers of the good. In any market, total revenue is $P \times Q$, the price of the good times the quantity of the good sold. We can show total revenue graphically, as in Figure 5.2. The height of the box under the demand curve is P, and the width is Q. The area of this box, $P \times Q$, equals the total revenue in this market. In Figure 5.2, where $P = \$4$ and $Q = 100$, total revenue is $\$4 \times 100$, or $\$400$.

How does total revenue change as one moves along the demand curve? The answer depends on the price elasticity of demand. If demand is inelastic, as in panel (a) of Figure 5.3, then an increase in the price causes an increase in total revenue. Here an increase in price from $4 to $5 causes the quantity demanded to fall only from 100 to 90, and so total revenue rises from $400 to $450. An increase in price raises $P \times Q$ because the fall in Q is proportionately smaller than the rise in P. In other words, the extra revenue from selling units at a higher price (represented by area A in Figure 5.3) more than offsets the decline in revenue from selling fewer units (represented by area B).

total revenue (in a market)

the amount paid by buyers and received by sellers of a good, computed as the price of the good times the quantity sold

FIGURE 5.1

The Price Elasticity of Demand   The price elasticity of demand determines whether the demand curve is steep or flat. Note that all percentage changes are calculated using the midpoint method.

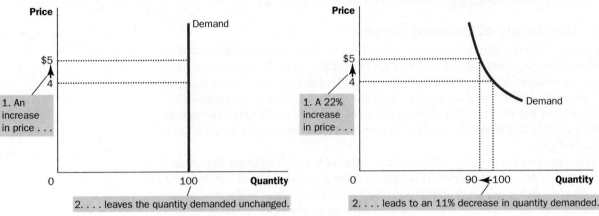

(a) Perfectly Inelastic Demand: Elasticity Equals 0

1. An increase in price . . .

2. . . . leaves the quantity demanded unchanged.

(b) Inelastic Demand: Elasticity Is Less Than 1

1. A 22% increase in price . . .

2. . . . leads to an 11% decrease in quantity demanded.

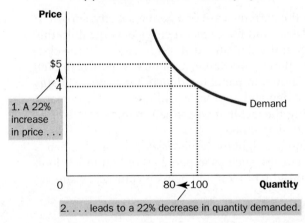

(c) Unit Elastic Demand: Elasticity Equals 1

1. A 22% increase in price . . .

2. . . . leads to a 22% decrease in quantity demanded.

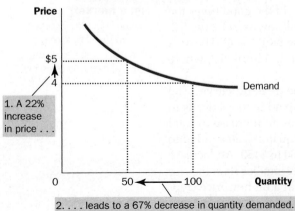

(d) Elastic Demand: Elasticity Is Greater Than 1

1. A 22% increase in price . . .

2. . . . leads to a 67% decrease in quantity demanded.

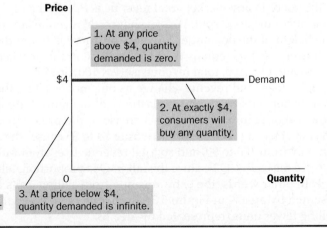

(e) Perfectly Elastic Demand: Elasticity Equals Infinity

1. At any price above $4, quantity demanded is zero.

2. At exactly $4, consumers will buy any quantity.

3. At a price below $4, quantity demanded is infinite.

© 2018 Cengage Learning

FIGURE 5.2

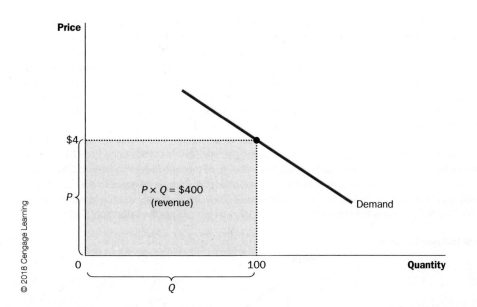

Total Revenue

The total amount paid by buyers, and received as revenue by sellers, equals the area of the box under the demand curve, $P \times Q$. Here, at a price of $4, the quantity demanded is 100, and total revenue is $400.

© 2018 Cengage Learning

FYI # A Few Elasticities from the Real World

We have talked about what elasticity means, what determines it, and how it is calculated. Beyond these general ideas, you might ask for a specific number. How much, precisely, does the price of a particular good influence the quantity demanded?

To answer such a question, economists collect data from market outcomes and apply statistical techniques to estimate the price elasticity of demand. The following are some price elasticities of demand, obtained from various studies, for a range of goods:

Eggs	0.1
Health care	0.2
Rice	0.5
Housing	0.7
Beef	1.6
Restaurant meals	2.3
Mountain Dew	4.4

These kinds of numbers are fun to think about, and they can be useful when comparing markets. We see some of the determinants of elasticities reflected in these estimates. For example, goods with few close substitutes, like eggs and rice, have quite low elasticities. On the other hand, other soft drinks are a very close substitute for Mountain Dew, which is reflected in its very high elasticity. Similarly, restaurant meals and beef have both close substitutes and might be considered luxuries rather than necessities. Health care has a very low elasticity because of the absence of a close substitute and the fact that in many cases it is a necessity.

We should take these estimates with a grain of salt, however. One reason is that the statistical techniques used to obtain them require some assumptions about the world, and these assumptions might not be true in practice. (The details of these techniques are beyond the scope of this book, but you will encounter them if you take a course in econometrics.) Another reason is that the price elasticity of demand does not need to be the same at all points on a demand curve, as we will see shortly in the case of a linear demand curve. For both reasons, you should not be surprised if different studies report different price elasticities of demand for the same good.

FIGURE 5.3

How Total Revenue Changes When Price Changes

The impact of a price change on total revenue (the product of price and quantity) depends on the elasticity of demand. In panel (a), the demand curve is inelastic. In this case, an increase in the price leads to a decrease in quantity demanded that is proportionately smaller, so total revenue increases. Here an increase in the price from $4 to $5 causes the quantity demanded to fall from 100 to 90. Total revenue rises from $400 to $450. Area A is the extra revenue from selling units at a higher price; it is equal to ($5 − $4) × 90 = $90. Area B is the decline in revenue from selling fewer units; it is equal to $4 × (100−90) = $40. Area A is larger than area B by $50, which is the increase in revenue from an increase in the price from $4 to $5. In panel (b), the demand curve is elastic. In this case, an increase in the price leads to a decrease in quantity demanded that is proportionately larger, so total revenue decreases. Here an increase in the price from $4 to $5 causes the quantity demanded to fall from 100 to 70. Total revenue falls from $400 to $350. In this case the extra revenue from selling units at a higher price (area A) is equal to $70, and the decline in revenue from selling fewer units (area B) is $120. In this case, area A is smaller than area B by $50, which is the decrease in revenue from an increase in the price from $4 to $5.

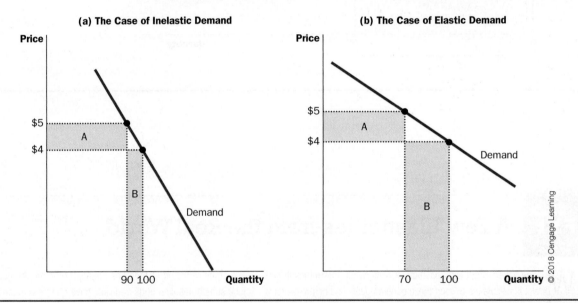

(a) The Case of Inelastic Demand   **(b) The Case of Elastic Demand**

© 2018 Cengage Learning

We obtain the opposite result if demand is elastic: An increase in the price causes a decrease in total revenue. In panel (b) of Figure 5.3, for instance, when the price rises from $4 to $5, the quantity demanded falls from 100 to 70, and so total revenue falls from $400 to $350. Because demand is elastic, the reduction in the quantity demanded is so great that it more than offsets the increase in the price. That is, an increase in price reduces $P \times Q$ because the fall in Q is proportionately greater than the rise in P. In this case, the extra revenue from selling units at a higher price (area A) is smaller than the decline in revenue from selling fewer units (area B).

The examples in Figure 5.3 illustrate some general rules:

- When demand is inelastic (a price elasticity less than 1), price and total revenue move in the same direction: If the price increases, total revenue also increases.
- When demand is elastic (a price elasticity greater than 1), price and total revenue move in opposite directions: If the price increases, total revenue decreases.
- If demand is unit elastic (a price elasticity exactly equal to 1), total revenue remains constant when the price changes.

5-1f Elasticity and Total Revenue along a Linear Demand Curve

Let's examine how elasticity varies along a linear demand curve, as shown in Figure 5.4. We know that a straight line has a constant slope. Slope is defined as "rise over run," which here is the ratio of the change in price ("rise") to the change in quantity ("run"). This particular demand curve's slope is constant because each $1 increase in price causes the same 2-unit decrease in the quantity demanded.

Even though the slope of a linear demand curve is constant, the elasticity is not. This is true because the slope is the ratio of *changes* in the two variables, whereas the elasticity is the ratio of *percentage changes* in the two variables. You can see this by looking at the table in Figure 5.4, which shows the demand schedule for the linear demand curve in the graph. The table uses the midpoint method to calculate the price elasticity of demand. The table illustrates the following: *At points with a low price and high quantity, the demand curve is inelastic. At points with a high price and low quantity, the demand curve is elastic.*

The explanation for this fact comes from the arithmetic of percentage changes. When the price is low and consumers are buying a lot, a $1 price increase and 2-unit reduction in quantity demanded constitute a large percentage increase in the price and a small percentage decrease in quantity demanded, resulting in a small elasticity. When the price is high and consumers are not buying much, the

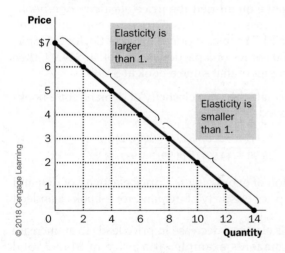

FIGURE 5.4

Elasticity of a Linear Demand Curve

The slope of a linear demand curve is constant, but its elasticity is not. The demand schedule in the table was used to calculate the price elasticity of demand by the midpoint method. At points with a low price and high quantity, the demand curve is inelastic. At points with a high price and low quantity, the demand curve is elastic.

Price	Quantity	Total Revenue (price × quantity)	Percentage Change in Price	Percentage Change in Quantity	Elasticity	Description
$7	0	$0	15	200	13.3	Elastic
6	2	12	18	67	3.7	Elastic
5	4	20	22	40	1.8	Elastic
4	6	24	29	29	1.0	Unit elastic
3	8	24	40	22	0.6	Inelastic
2	10	20	67	18	0.3	Inelastic
1	12	12	200	15	0.1	Inelastic
0	14	0				

same $1 price increase and 2-unit reduction in quantity demanded constitute a small percentage increase in the price and a large percentage decrease in quantity demanded, resulting in a large elasticity.

Giakita/Shutterstock.com

case study **Price Elasticity, Amazon, and the Pricing of E-Books**

In 2014, a well-publicized dispute broke out between Amazon and Hachette over the pricing of e-books. Amazon, of course, is the world's largest distributor of e-books, with about 65 percent of the North American market. Hachette is a large publishing company with more than 2500 authors, including best sellers such as J.K. Rowling, David Baldacci, Stephen King, Malcolm Gladwell, Michael Pollan, James Patterson, and Donna Tartt, among others.

While the dispute concerned many things, one of the headline points of contention was the control of e-book pricing. In a nutshell, Amazon wanted to price most e-books at its ubiquitous $9.99, while Hachette wanted to set its own prices depending on the author, the release date, the book's success, and so on. As part of the dispute, Amazon stopped the sale of some Hachette e-books and delayed the release of others.

In a public letter defending its position, Amazon made the following statement based on work from its in-house economists:

> . . . e-books are highly price elastic. This means that when the price goes down, customers buy much more. We've quantified the price elasticity of e-books from repeated measurements across many titles. For every copy an e-book would sell at $14.99, it would sell 1.74 copies if priced at $9.99. So, for example, if customers would buy 100,000 copies of a particular e-book at $14.99, then customers would buy 174,000 copies of that same e-book at $9.99.

We can use this information to calculate the price elasticity of demand for e-books using the midpoint formula presented above,

$$\text{Price elasticity of demand} = \frac{(174 - 100)/[(174 + 100)/2]}{(9.99 - 14.99)/[(14.99 + 9.99)/2]} = 1.35$$

where we have used the convention of expressing the price elasticity of demand as a positive number. At 1.35, the price elasticity of demand for e-books is indeed elastic, as it exceeds 1.

As we have shown, if demand is elastic, a decrease in price leads to an increase in revenue. Continuing with Amazon's example, at a price of $14.99 total revenue would be $14.99 × 100 000 = $1 499 000, while at a price of $9.99 total revenue would be $9.99 × 174 000 = $1 738 260. The essence of Amazon's defence for charging $9.99 for e-books is that because the demand for e-books is elastic, the lower price is good for all parties involved: the customer pays 33 percent less, the author gets a royalty cheque that is 16 percent higher, and the book is being read by an audience that is 74 percent larger. As Amazon put it, "The pie is simply bigger." Everybody wins!

Yet Hachette continued to oppose Amazon's pricing strategy. And, indeed, a group of best-selling authors including Gladwell, King, and Tartt wrote a public letter to Amazon's board protesting the policy. However, authors were not unanimous in their opposition to Amazon. A group of lesser known authors, largely self-published "indie authors," penned another letter in support of Amazon's lower pricing strategy. If everybody wins, why the opposition?

Again, the issue is complicated, but one possibility is the following. The 1.35 price elasticity of demand calculated by Amazon can be thought of as an average over all e-books. One might think that the elasticity of demand for some types of books is higher than for other types of books. In particular, one might expect that the elasticity of demand for best-selling authors may be somewhat lower than 1.35, and indeed it may be less than 1 and therefore inelastic. For these books and their authors, if the price elasticity is less than 1, total revenue from sales would decline in response to the lower price; best-selling authors could be worse off under Amazon's lower pricing policy. On the other hand, the price elasticity for lesser known indie authors may be even higher than 1.35; they would be better off, as shown above. This may explain, in part, the different reactions to Amazon's pricing policy.

Amazon and Hachette resolved their dispute at the end of 2014 with Hachette maintaining control of e-book prices, including the use of "dynamic pricing" that adjusts prices according to market conditions. ■

The table also presents total revenue at each point on the demand curve. These numbers illustrate the relationship between total revenue and elasticity. When the price is $1, for instance, demand is inelastic, and a price increase to $2 raises total revenue. When the price is $5, demand is elastic, and a price increase to $6 reduces total revenue. Between $3 and $4, demand is exactly unit elastic, and total revenue is the same at these two prices.

The linear demand curve illustrates that the price elasticity of demand need not be the same at all points on a demand curve. A constant elasticity is possible (in which case the demand curve will not be linear), but it is not always the case.

5-1g Other Demand Elasticities

In addition to the price elasticity of demand, economists also use other elasticities to describe the behaviour of buyers in a market.

The Income Elasticity of Demand The **income elasticity of demand** measures how the quantity demanded changes as consumer income changes. It is calculated as the percentage change in quantity demanded divided by the percentage change in income. That is,

$$\text{Income elasticity of demand} = \frac{\text{Percentage change in quantity demanded}}{\text{Percentage change in income}}$$

As we discussed in Chapter 4, most goods are *normal goods*: Higher income raises quantity demanded. Because quantity demanded and income move in the same direction, normal goods have positive income elasticities. A few goods, such as bus rides, are *inferior goods*: Higher income lowers the quantity demanded. Because quantity demanded and income move in opposite directions, inferior goods have negative income elasticities.

Even among normal goods, income elasticities vary substantially in size. Necessities, such as food and clothing, tend to have small income elasticities because consumers choose to buy some of these goods even when their incomes are low. Luxuries, such as caviar and diamonds, tend to have large income elasticities because consumers feel that they can do without these goods altogether if their income is too low.

The Cross-Price Elasticity of Demand The **cross-price elasticity of demand** measures how the quantity demanded of one good responds to a change in

income elasticity of demand
a measure of how much the quantity demanded of a good responds to a change in consumers' income, computed as the percentage change in quantity demanded divided by the percentage change in income

cross-price elasticity of demand
a measure of how much the quantity demanded of one good responds to a change in the price of another good, computed as the percentage change in quantity demanded of the first good divided by the percentage change in the price of the second good

the price of another good. It is calculated as the percentage change in quantity demanded of good 1 divided by the percentage change in the price of good 2. That is,

$$\text{Cross-price elasticity of demand} = \frac{\text{Percentage change in quantity demanded of good 1}}{\text{Percentage change in price of good 2}}$$

Whether the cross-price elasticity is a positive or negative number depends on whether the two goods are substitutes or complements. As we discussed in Chapter 4, substitutes are goods that are typically used in place of one another, such as hamburgers and hot dogs. An increase in hot dog prices induces people to grill hamburgers instead. Because the price of hot dogs and the quantity of hamburgers demanded move in the same direction, the cross-price elasticity is positive. Conversely, complements are goods that are typically used together, such as computers and software. In this case, the cross-price elasticity is negative, indicating that an increase in the price of computers reduces the quantity of software demanded.

 QUICK Quiz *Define the price elasticity of demand. • Explain the relationship between total revenue and the price elasticity of demand.*

5-2 The Elasticity of Supply

When we introduced supply in Chapter 4, we noted that producers of a good offer to sell more of it when the price of the good rises. To turn from qualitative to quantitative statements about quantity supplied, we once again use the concept of elasticity.

5-2a The Price Elasticity of Supply and Its Determinants

price elasticity of supply

a measure of how much the quantity supplied of a good responds to a change in the price of that good, computed as the percentage change in quantity supplied divided by the percentage change in price

The law of supply states that higher prices raise the quantity supplied. The **price elasticity of supply** measures how much the quantity supplied responds to changes in the price. Supply of a good is said to be *elastic* if the quantity supplied responds substantially to changes in the price. Supply is said to be *inelastic* if the quantity supplied responds only slightly to changes in the price.

The price elasticity of supply depends on the flexibility of sellers to change the amount of the good they produce. For example, beachfront land has an inelastic supply because it is almost impossible to produce more of it. Manufactured goods, such as books, cars, and televisions, have elastic supplies because firms that produce them can run their factories longer in response to a higher price.

In most markets, a key determinant of the price elasticity of supply is the time period being considered. Supply is usually more elastic in the long run than in the short run. Over short periods of time, firms cannot easily change the size of their factories to make more or less of a good. Thus, in the short run, the quantity supplied is not very responsive to the price. By contrast, over longer periods, firms can build new factories or close old ones. In addition, new firms can enter a market, and old firms can exit. Thus, in the long run, the quantity supplied can respond substantially to price changes.

5-2b Computing the Price Elasticity of Supply

Now that we have a general understanding about the price elasticity of supply, let's be more precise. Economists compute the price elasticity of supply as the percentage change in the quantity supplied divided by the percentage change in the price. That is,

$$\text{Price elasticity of supply} = \frac{\text{Percentage change in quantity supplied}}{\text{Percentage change in price}}$$

For example, suppose that an increase in the price of milk from $2.85 to $3.15 per four-litre container raises the amount that dairy farmers produce from 9000 to 11 000 L per month. Using the midpoint method, we calculate the percentage change in price as

$$\text{Percentage change in price} = (3.15 - 2.85)/3.00 \times 100 = 10 \text{ percent}$$

Similarly, we calculate the percentage change in quantity supplied as

$$\text{Percentage change in quantity supplied} = (11\,000 - 9000)/10\,000 \times 100 = 20 \text{ percent}$$

In this case, the price elasticity of supply is

$$\text{Price elasticity of supply} = \frac{20 \text{ percent}}{10 \text{ percent}} = 2.0$$

In this example, the elasticity of 2 reflects the fact that the quantity supplied moves proportionately twice as much as the price.

5-2c The Variety of Supply Curves

Because the price elasticity of supply measures the responsiveness of quantity supplied to the price, it is reflected in the appearance of the supply curve. Figure 5.5 shows five cases. In the extreme case of a zero elasticity, as shown in panel (a), supply is *perfectly inelastic* and the supply curve is vertical. In this case, the quantity supplied is the same regardless of the price. As the elasticity rises, the supply curve gets flatter, which shows that the quantity supplied responds more to changes in the price. At the opposite extreme shown in panel (e), supply is *perfectly elastic*. This occurs as the price elasticity of supply approaches infinity and the supply curve becomes horizontal, meaning that very small changes in the price lead to very large changes in the quantity supplied.

In some markets, the elasticity of supply is not constant but varies over the supply curve. Figure 5.6 shows a typical case for an industry in which firms have factories with a limited capacity for production. For low levels of quantity supplied, the elasticity of supply is high, indicating that firms respond substantially to changes in the price. In this region, firms have capacity for production that is not being used, such as plants and equipment sitting idle for all or part of the day. Small increases in price make it profitable for firms to begin using this idle capacity. As the quantity supplied rises, firms begin to reach capacity. Once capacity is fully used, increasing production further requires the construction of new plants. To induce firms to incur this extra expense, the price must rise substantially, so supply becomes less elastic.

Figure 5.6 presents a numerical example of this phenomenon. When the price rises from $3 to $4 (a 29-percent increase, according to the midpoint method), the quantity supplied rises from 100 to 200 (a 67-percent increase). Because quantity supplied moves proportionately more than the price, the supply curve has

FIGURE 5.5

The Price Elasticity of Supply   The price elasticity of supply determines whether the supply curve is steep or flat. Note that all percentage changes are calculated using the midpoint method.

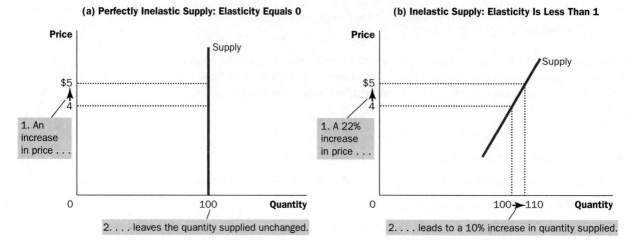

(a) Perfectly Inelastic Supply: Elasticity Equals 0

1. An increase in price . . .
2. . . . leaves the quantity supplied unchanged.

(b) Inelastic Supply: Elasticity Is Less Than 1

1. A 22% increase in price . . .
2. . . . leads to a 10% increase in quantity supplied.

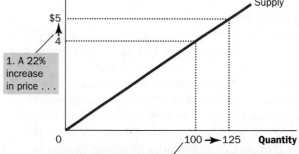

(c) Unit Elastic Supply: Elasticity Equals 1

1. A 22% increase in price . . .
2. . . . leads to a 22% increase in quantity supplied.

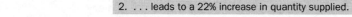

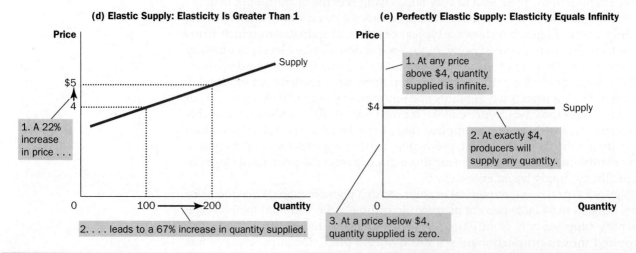

(d) Elastic Supply: Elasticity Is Greater Than 1

1. A 22% increase in price . . .
2. . . . leads to a 67% increase in quantity supplied.

(e) Perfectly Elastic Supply: Elasticity Equals Infinity

1. At any price above $4, quantity supplied is infinite.
2. At exactly $4, producers will supply any quantity.
3. At a price below $4, quantity supplied is zero.

© 2018 Cengage Learning

FIGURE 5.6

How the Price Elasticity of Supply Can Vary

Because firms often have a maximum capacity for production, the elasticity of supply may be very high at low levels of quantity supplied and very low at high levels of quantity supplied. Here, an increase in price from $3 to $4 increases the quantity supplied from 100 to 200. Because the increase in quantity supplied of 67 percent (computed using the midpoint method) is larger than the increase in price of 29 percent, the supply curve is elastic in this range. By contrast, when the price rises from $12 to $15, the quantity supplied rises only from 500 to 525. Because the increase in quantity supplied of 5 percent is smaller than the increase in price of 22 percent, the supply curve is inelastic in this range.

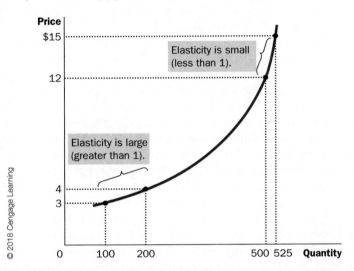

elasticity greater than 1. By contrast, when the price rises from $12 to $15 (a 22-percent increase), the quantity supplied rises from 500 to 525 (a 5-percent increase). In this case, quantity supplied moves proportionately less than the price, so the elasticity is less than 1.

QUICK Quiz *Define the price elasticity of supply. • Explain why the price elasticity of supply might be different in the long run than in the short run.*

5-3 Three Applications of Supply, Demand, and Elasticity

Can good news for farming be bad news for farmers? Why did Organization of the Petroleum Exporting Countries (OPEC), the international oil cartel, fail to keep the price of oil high? Does drug interdiction increase or decrease drug-related crime? At first, these questions might seem to have little in common. Yet all three questions are about markets, and all markets are subject to the forces of supply and demand. Here we apply the versatile tools of supply, demand, and elasticity to answer these seemingly complex questions.

5-3a Can Good News for Farming Be Bad News for Farmers?

Imagine yourself as a Saskatchewan wheat farmer. Because you earn all of your income from selling wheat, you devote much effort to making your land as productive as possible. You monitor weather and soil conditions, check your fields for pests and disease, and study the latest advances in farm technology. You know that the more wheat you grow, the more you will have to sell after the harvest, and the higher your income and your standard of living will be.

One day, the University of Saskatchewan announces a major discovery. Researchers in its College of Agriculture and Bioresources have devised a new hybrid of wheat that raises by 20 percent the amount that farmers can produce from each hectare of land. How should you react to the news? Does this discovery make you better or worse off than you were before?

Recall from Chapter 4 that we answer such questions in three steps. First, we examine whether the supply or demand curve shifts (or perhaps both shift). Second, we consider the direction in which the curve shifts. Third, we use the supply-and-demand diagram to see how the market equilibrium changes.

In this case, the discovery of the new hybrid affects the supply curve. Because the hybrid increases the amount of wheat that can be produced on each hectare of land, farmers are now willing to supply more wheat at any given price. In other words, the supply curve shifts to the right. The demand curve remains the same because consumers' desire to buy wheat products at any given price is not affected by the introduction of a new hybrid. Figure 5.7 shows an example of such a change. When the supply curve shifts from S_1 to S_2, the quantity of wheat sold increases from 100 to 110, and the price of wheat falls from $3 to $2.

Does this discovery make farmers better off? As a first cut at answering this question, consider what happens to the total revenue received by farmers. Farmers' total revenue is $P \times Q$, the price of the wheat times the quantity sold. The discovery affects farmers in two conflicting ways: The hybrid allows farmers to produce more wheat (Q rises), but now each tonne of wheat sells for less (P falls).

FIGURE 5.7

An Increase in Supply in the Market for Wheat

When an advance in farm technology increases the supply of wheat from S_1 to S_2, the price of wheat falls. Because the demand for wheat is inelastic, the increase in the quantity sold from 100 to 110 is proportionately smaller than the decrease in the price from $3 to $2. As a result, farmers' total revenue falls from $300 ($3 × 100) to $220 ($2 × 110).

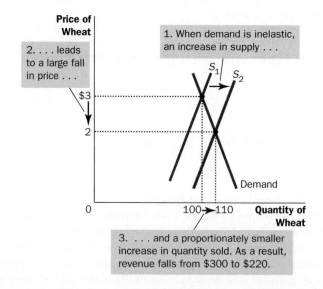

1. When demand is inelastic, an increase in supply . . .

2. . . . leads to a large fall in price . . .

3. . . . and a proportionately smaller increase in quantity sold. As a result, revenue falls from $300 to $220.

© 2018 Cengage Learning

The price elasticity of demand determines whether total revenue rises or falls. In practice, the demand for basic foodstuffs such as wheat is usually inelastic because these items are relatively inexpensive and have few good substitutes. When the demand curve is inelastic, as it is in Figure 5.7, a decrease in price causes total revenue to fall. You can see this in the figure: The price of wheat falls substantially, whereas the quantity of wheat sold rises only slightly. Total revenue falls from $300 to $220. Thus, the discovery of the new hybrid lowers the total revenue that farmers receive for the sale of their crops.

If farmers are made worse off by the discovery of this new hybrid, one might wonder why they adopt it. The answer goes to the heart of how competitive markets work. Because each farmer is a small part of the market for wheat, he or she takes the price of wheat as given. For any given price of wheat, it is better to use the new hybrid to produce and sell more wheat. Yet when all farmers do this, the supply of wheat rises, the price falls, and farmers are worse off.

This example may at first seem hypothetical, but it helps explain a major change in the Canadian economy over the past century. Two hundred years ago, most Canadians lived on farms. Knowledge about farm methods was sufficiently primitive that most people had to be farmers to produce enough food to feed the nation's population. Yet, over time, advances in farm technology increased the amount of food that each farmer could produce. This increase in food supply, together with inelastic food demand, caused farm revenues to fall, which in turn encouraged people to leave farming.

A few numbers show the magnitude of this historic change. As recently as 1950, about 25 percent of the Canadian labour force worked on farms. Today, less than 3 percent of the labour force of employed Canadians work on farms. This change coincides with tremendous advances in farm productivity: Despite the huge percentage drop in the number of farmers, Canadian farms now produce more than twice the output of crops and livestock that they did in 1950.

This analysis of the market for farm products also helps to explain a seeming paradox of public policy: Certain farm programs try to help farmers by restricting the amount that they produce. For example, in Canada the supply of milk and eggs that farmers are allowed to produce is restricted by way of quota programs. The purpose of these programs is to reduce the supply of milk and eggs and thereby raise prices. With inelastic demand for their products, farmers as a group receive greater total revenue if they supply a smaller amount of milk and eggs to the market. No single farmer would choose to restrict supply on her own, since each takes the market price as given. But if all farmers do so together, each of them can be better off.

When analyzing the effects of farm technology or farm policy, it is important to keep in mind that what is good for farmers is not necessarily good for society as a whole. Improvement in farm technology can be bad for farmers because it makes a large quantity of farmers increasingly unnecessary, but it is surely good for consumers who pay less for food. Similarly, a policy aimed at reducing the supply of farm products may raise the incomes of farmers, but it does so at the expense of consumers.

5-3b Why Did OPEC Fail to Keep the Price of Oil High?

Many of the most disruptive events for the world's economies over the past several decades have originated in the world market for oil. In the 1970s, members of the OPEC decided to raise the world price of oil to increase their incomes. These countries accomplished this goal by jointly agreeing to reduce the amount of oil they supplied. As a result, the price of oil (adjusted for overall inflation) rose more than 50 percent from 1973 to 1974. Then, a few years later, OPEC did the same thing again: From 1979 to 1981, the price of oil approximately doubled.

Yet OPEC found it difficult to maintain a high price. From 1982 to 1985, the price of oil steadily declined about 10 percent per year. Dissatisfaction and disarray soon prevailed among the OPEC members. In 1986, cooperation among OPEC members completely broke down, and the price of oil plunged 45 percent. In 1990, the price of oil (adjusted for overall inflation) was back to where it began in 1970, and it stayed at that low level throughout most of the 1990s.

In the first decade of the twenty-first century, the price of oil fluctuated substantially once again, but the main driving force was changes in world demand rather than OPEC supply restrictions. Early in the decade, oil demand and prices spiked up, in part because of a large and rapidly growing Chinese economy. Prices plunged in 2008–09 as the world economy fell into a deep recession and then started rising once again as the world economy started to recover. In 2014, prices fell drastically, by over 40 percent, as the recovery weakened and large new supplies of oil came on the market because of advances in oil extraction technology, primarily associated with fracking.

The OPEC episode of the 1970s and 1980s shows how supply and demand can behave differently in the short run and in the long run. In the short run, both the supply and demand for oil are relatively inelastic. Supply is inelastic because the quantity of known oil reserves and the capacity for oil extraction cannot be changed quickly. Demand is inelastic because buying habits do not respond immediately to changes in price. Thus, as panel (a) of Figure 5.8 shows, the short-run supply-and-demand curves are steep. When the supply of oil shifts from S_1 to S_2, the price increase from P_1 to P_2 is large.

The situation is very different in the long run. Over long periods of time, producers of oil outside of OPEC respond to high prices by increasing oil exploration and by building new extraction capacity. Consumers respond with greater conservation, such as by replacing old inefficient cars with newer efficient ones. Thus, as panel (b) of Figure 5.8 shows, the long-run supply-and-demand curves are more elastic. In the long run, a shift in the supply curve from S_1 to S_2 causes a much smaller increase in the price.

This analysis shows why OPEC succeeded in maintaining a high price for oil only in the short run. When OPEC countries agreed to reduce their production of oil, they shifted the supply curve to the left. Even though each OPEC member sold less oil, the price rose by so much in the short run that OPEC incomes rose. By contrast, in the long run when supply and demand are more elastic, a similar

FIGURE 5.8

When the supply of oil falls, the response depends on the time horizon. In the short run, supply and demand are relatively inelastic, as in panel (a). Thus, when the supply curve shifts from S_1 to S_2, the price rises substantially. By contrast, in the long run, supply and demand are relatively elastic, as in panel (b). In this case, a similar size shift in the supply curve (S_1 to S_2) causes a smaller increase in the price.

A Reduction in Supply in the World Market for Oil

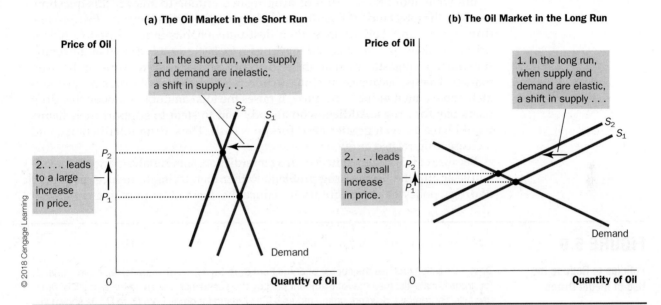

(a) The Oil Market in the Short Run

Price of Oil

1. In the short run, when supply and demand are inelastic, a shift in supply . . .

S_2 S_1

P_2

2. . . . leads to a large increase in price.

P_1

Demand

0   Quantity of Oil

(b) The Oil Market in the Long Run

Price of Oil

1. In the long run, when supply and demand are elastic, a shift in supply . . .

S_2 S_1

2. . . . leads to a small increase in price.

P_2

P_1

Demand

0   Quantity of Oil

© 2018 Cengage Learning

reduction in supply, measured by the horizontal shift in the supply curve, caused a smaller increase in the price. Thus, OPEC's coordinated reduction in supply proved less profitable in the long run. The cartel learned that raising prices is easier in the short run than in the long run.

5-3c Does Drug Interdiction Increase or Decrease Drug-Related Crime?

A persistent problem facing our society is the use of illegal drugs, such as heroin, cocaine, ecstasy, and methamphetamine. Drug use has several adverse effects. One is that drug dependence can ruin the lives of drug users and their families. Another is that drug addicts often turn to robbery and other violent crimes to obtain the money needed to support their habit. To discourage the use of illegal drugs, Canadian governments devote millions of dollars each year to reducing the flow of drugs into the country. Let's use the tools of supply and demand to examine this policy of drug interdiction.

Suppose the government increases the number of officers devoted to the war on drugs. What happens in the market for illegal drugs? As usual, we answer this question in three steps. First, we consider whether the supply or demand curve shifts (or perhaps both shift). Second, we consider the direction of the shift. Third, we see how the shift affects the equilibrium price and quantity.

Although the purpose of drug interdiction is to reduce drug use, its direct impact is on the sellers of drugs rather than on the buyers. When the government stops some drugs from entering the country and arrests more smugglers, it raises the cost of selling drugs and, therefore, reduces the quantity of drugs supplied at any given price. The demand for drugs—the amount buyers want at any given price—is not changed. As panel (a) of Figure 5.9 shows, interdiction shifts the supply curve to the left from S_1 to S_2 and leaves the demand curve the same. The equilibrium price of drugs rises from P_1 to P_2 and the equilibrium quantity falls from Q_1 to Q_2. The fall in the equilibrium quantity shows that drug interdiction does reduce drug use.

But what about the amount of drug-related crime? To answer this question, consider the total amount that drug users pay for the drugs they buy. Because few drug addicts are likely to break their destructive habits in response to a higher price, it is likely that the demand for drugs is inelastic, as it is drawn in the figure. If demand is inelastic, then an increase in price raises total revenue in the drug market. That is, because drug interdiction raises the price of drugs proportionately more than it reduces drug use, it raises the total amount of money that drug users pay for drugs. Addicts who already had to steal to support their habits would have an even greater need for quick cash. Thus, drug interdiction could increase drug-related crime.

Because of this adverse effect of drug interdiction, some analysts argue for alternative approaches to the drug problem. Rather than trying to reduce the supply of drugs, policymakers might try to reduce the demand by pursuing a policy of

FIGURE 5.9

Policies to Reduce the Use of Illegal Drugs

Drug interdiction reduces the supply of drugs from S_1 to S_2, as shown in panel (a). If the demand for drugs is inelastic, then the total amount paid by drug users rises, even as the amount of drug use falls. By contrast, drug education reduces the demand for drugs from D_1 to D_2, as shown in panel (b). Because both price and quantity fall, the amount paid by drug users falls.

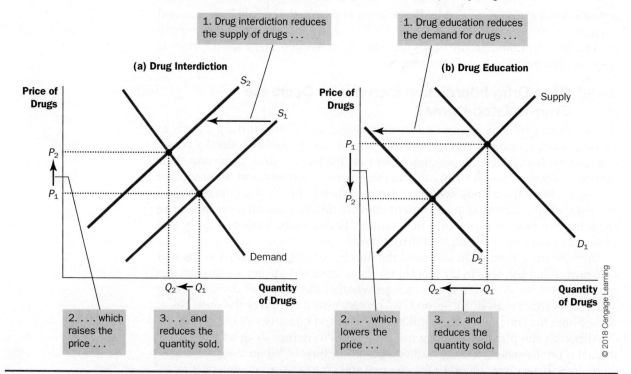

1. Drug interdiction reduces the supply of drugs . . .

(a) Drug Interdiction

Price of Drugs

S_2

S_1

P_2

P_1

Demand

$Q_2 \leftarrow Q_1$ **Quantity of Drugs**

2. . . . which raises the price . . .

3. . . . and reduces the quantity sold.

1. Drug education reduces the demand for drugs . . .

(b) Drug Education

Price of Drugs

Supply

P_1

P_2

D_1

D_2

$Q_2 \leftarrow Q_1$ **Quantity of Drugs**

2. . . . which lowers the price . . .

3. . . . and reduces the quantity sold.

© 2018 Cengage Learning

drug education. Successful drug education has the effects shown in panel (b) of Figure 5.9. The demand curve shifts to the left from D_1 to D_2. As a result, the equilibrium quantity falls from Q_1 to Q_2 and the equilibrium price falls from P_1 to P_2. Total revenue, $P \times Q$, also falls. Thus, in contrast to drug interdiction, drug education can reduce both drug use and drug-related crime.

Advocates of drug interdiction might argue that the long-run effects of this policy are different from the short-run effects because the elasticity of demand depends on the time horizon. The demand for drugs is probably inelastic over short periods because higher prices do not substantially affect drug use by established addicts. But demand may be more elastic over longer periods because higher prices would discourage experimentation with drugs among the young and, over time, lead to fewer drug addicts. In this case, drug interdiction would increase drug-related crime in the short run while decreasing it in the long run.

QUICK Quiz *How might a drought that destroys half of all farm crops be good for farmers? If such a drought is good for farmers, why don't farmers destroy their own crops in the absence of a drought?*

5-4 Conclusion

According to an old quip, even a parrot can become an economist simply by learning to say "supply and demand." These last two chapters should have convinced you that there is much truth in this statement. The tools of supply and demand allow you to analyze many of the most important events and policies that shape the economy. You are now well on your way to becoming an economist.

summary

- The price elasticity of demand measures how much the quantity demanded responds to changes in the price. Demand tends to be more elastic if close substitutes are available, if the good is a luxury rather than a necessity, if the market is narrowly defined, or if buyers have substantial time to react to a price change.

- The price elasticity of demand is calculated as the percentage change in quantity demanded divided by the percentage change in price. If quantity demanded moves proportionately less than the price, then the elasticity is less than 1 and demand is said to be inelastic. If quantity demanded moves proportionately more than the price, then the elasticity is greater than 1 and demand is said to be elastic.

- Total revenue, the total amount paid for a good, equals the price of the good times the quantity sold. For inelastic demand curves, total revenue moves in the same direction as the price. For elastic demand curves, total revenue moves in the opposite direction as the price.

- The income elasticity of demand measures how much the quantity demanded responds to changes in consumers' income. The cross-price elasticity of demand measures how much the quantity demanded of one good responds to changes in the price of another good.

- The price elasticity of supply measures how much the quantity supplied responds to changes in the price. This elasticity often depends on the time horizon under consideration. In most markets, supply is more elastic in the long run than in the short run.

- The price elasticity of supply is calculated as the percentage change in quantity supplied divided by the percentage change in price. If quantity supplied moves proportionately less than the price, then the elasticity is less than 1 and supply is said to be inelastic. If quantity supplied moves proportionately more than the price, then the elasticity is greater than 1 and supply is said to be elastic.

- The tools of supply and demand can be applied in many different kinds of markets. This chapter uses them to analyze the market for wheat, the market for oil, and the market for illegal drugs.

KEY **concepts**

elasticity, *p. 98*
price elasticity of demand, *p. 98*

total revenue (in a market), *p. 101*
income elasticity of demand, *p. 107*

cross-price elasticity of demand, *p. 107*
price elasticity of supply, *p. 108*

QUESTIONS FOR **review**

1. Define the price elasticity of demand and the income elasticity of demand.

2. List and explain the four determinants of the price elasticity of demand discussed in the chapter.

3. If the elasticity is greater than 1, is demand elastic or inelastic? If the elasticity equals zero, is demand perfectly elastic or perfectly inelastic?

4. On a supply-and-demand diagram, show equilibrium price, equilibrium quantity, and the total revenue received by producers.

5. If demand is elastic, how will an increase in price change total revenue? Explain.

6. What do we call a good whose income elasticity is less than zero?

7. How is the price elasticity of supply calculated? Explain what this measures.

8. If a fixed quantity of a good is available, and no more can be made, what is the price elasticity of supply?

9. A storm destroys half of the apple crop. Is this event more likely to hurt apple farmers if the demand for apples is very elastic or very inelastic? Explain.

QUICK CHECK **multiple choice**

1. Which of the following will a life-saving medicine without any close substitutes tend to have?
   a. a small elasticity of demand
   b. a large elasticity of demand
   c. a small elasticity of supply
   d. a large elasticity of supply

2. The price of a good rises from $8 to $12, and the quantity demanded falls from 110 to 90 units. Calculated with the midpoint method, what is the elasticity?
   a. 1/5
   b. 1/2
   c. 2
   d. 5

3. Which of the following describes a linear, downward-sloping demand curve?
   a. inelastic
   b. unit elastic
   c. elastic
   d. inelastic at some points and elastic at others

4. The ability of firms to enter and exit a market over time means that which of the following occurs in the long run?
   a. the demand curve is more elastic
   b. the demand curve is less elastic
   c. the supply curve is more elastic
   d. the supply curve is less elastic

5. An increase in the supply of a good will decrease the total revenue producers receive in which of the following circumstances?
   a. the demand curve is inelastic
   b. the demand curve is elastic
   c. the supply curve is inelastic
   d. the supply curve is elastic

6. The price of coffee rose sharply last month, while the quantity sold remained the same. Each of five people suggests an explanation:

   TOM: Demand increased, but supply was perfectly inelastic.

   DICK: Demand increased, but it was perfectly inelastic.

   HARRY: Demand increased, but supply decreased at the same time.

   LARRY: Supply decreased, but demand was unit elastic.

   MARY: Supply decreased, but demand was perfectly inelastic.

   Who could possibly be right?

   a. Tom, Dick, and Harry
   b. Tom, Dick, and Mary
   c. Tom, Harry, and Mary
   d. Dick, Harry, and Larry

PROBLEMS AND **applications**

1. For which of the following pairs of goods would you expect to have more elastic demand, and why?
   a. required textbooks or mystery novels
   b. Beethoven recordings or classical music recordings in general
   c. heating oil during the next six months or heating oil during the next five years
   d. root beer or water

2. Suppose that business travellers and vacationers have the following demand for airline tickets from Toronto to Montreal:

Price	Quantity Demanded (business travellers)	Quantity Demanded (vacationers)
$150	2100 tickets	1000 tickets
200	2000	800
250	1900	600
300	1800	400

   a. As the price of tickets rises from $200 to $250, what is the price elasticity of demand for (i) business travellers and (ii) vacationers? (Use the midpoint method in your calculations.)
   b. Why might vacationers have a different elasticity than business travellers?

3. Suppose that your demand schedule for DVDs is as follows:

Price	Quantity Demanded (income = $10 000)	Quantity Demanded (income = $12 000)
$8	40	50
10	32	45
12	24	30
14	16	20
16	8	12

   a. Use the midpoint method to calculate your price elasticity of demand as the price of DVDs increases from $8 to $10 if (i) your income is $10 000, and (ii) your income is $12 000.
   b. Calculate your income elasticity of demand as your income increases from $10 000 to $12 000 if (i) the price is $12, and (ii) the price is $16.

4. Emily has decided always to spend one-third of her income on clothing.
   a. What is her income elasticity of clothing demand?
   b. What is her price elasticity of clothing demand?
   c. If Emily's tastes change and she decides to spend only one-fourth of her income on clothing, how does her demand curve change? What are her income elasticity and price elasticity now?

5. *The Globe and Mail* (December 16, 1997) reported that milk consumption declined following price increases: "Since the early 1980s, the price of milk in Canada has increased 22 per cent. As prices rose, the demand for milk fell off. Total [consumption] of milk on a per capita basis dropped … to 2.62 hectolitres in 1995 from 2.92 hectolitres in 1986."
   a. Use these data to estimate the price elasticity of demand for milk.
   b. According to your estimate, what happens to milk producers' revenue when the price of milk rises?
   c. Why might your estimate of the elasticity be unreliable? (*Hint:* Notice that *The Globe and Mail* is careless about the distinction between demand and quantity demanded.)

6. Two drivers—Walt and Jesse—each drive up to a gas station. Before looking at the price, each places an order. Walt says, "I'd like 40 litres of gas." Jessie says, "I'd like $40 worth of gas." What is each driver's price elasticity of demand?

7. You are the curator of a museum. The museum is running short of funds, so you decide to increase revenue. Should you increase or decrease the price of admission? Explain.

8. Consider public policy aimed at smoking.
   a. Studies indicate that the price elasticity of demand for cigarettes is about 0.4. If a pack of cigarettes currently costs $10 and the government wants to reduce smoking by 20 percent, by how much should it increase the price?
   b. If the government permanently increases the price of cigarettes, will the policy have a greater effect on smoking one year from now or five years from now?
   c. Studies also find that teenagers have a higher price elasticity than do adults. Why might this be true?

9. Suppose that the price elasticity of demand for heating oil is 0.2 in the short run and 0.7 in the long run.
   a. If the price of heating oil rises from $0.45 to $0.55 per litre, what happens to the quantity of heating oil demanded in the short run? In the long run? (Use the midpoint method in your calculations.)
   b. Why might this elasticity depend on the time horizon?

10. Pharmaceutical drugs have an inelastic demand, and computers have an elastic demand. Suppose that technological advance doubles the supply of both products (that is, the quantity supplied at each price is twice what it was).
    a. What happens to the equilibrium price and quantity in each market?
    b. Which product experiences a greater change in price?
    c. Which product experiences a greater change in quantity?
    d. What happens to total consumer spending on each product?

11. Some years ago, flooding along the Red River in Manitoba destroyed thousands of hectares of wheat.
    a. Farmers whose crops were destroyed by the floods were much worse off, but farmers whose crops were not destroyed benefited from the floods. Why?
    b. What information would you need about the market for wheat to assess whether farmers as a group were hurt or helped by the floods?

12. Explain why the following might be true: A drought around the world raises the total revenue that farmers receive from the sale of grain, but a drought only in Alberta reduces the total revenue that Alberta farmers receive.

13. A price change causes the quantity demanded of a good to decrease by 30 percent, while the total revenue of that good increases by 15 percent. Is the demand curve elastic or inelastic? Explain.

14. Cups of coffee and donuts are complements. Both have inelastic demand. A hurricane destroys half the coffee bean crop. Use appropriately labelled diagrams to answer the following questions:
    a. What happens to the price of coffee beans?
    b. What happens to the price of a cup of coffee? What happens to total expenditure on cups of coffee?
    c. What happens to the price of donuts? What happens to total expenditure on donuts?

15. You have the following information about good X and good Y:
    • Income elasticity of demand for good X: -3
    • Cross-price elasticity of demand for good X with respect to the price of good Y: 2
    Would an increase in income and a decrease in the price of good Y unambiguously decrease the demand for good X? Why or why not?

16. Consider two demand curves. The first is linear, with the demand curve given by $Q^D = 100 - 20P$. The second is nonlinear, with the demand curve given by $Q^D = 60/P$. For each of these demand curves, compute the quantity demanded at prices of $1, $2, $3, $4, $5, and $6. Graph each of the demand curves. Use the midpoint method to calculate the price elasticity of demand between $1 and $2, and between $4 and $5 for each demand curve. Compare the price elasticities in these cases. In particular, how does the elasticity of the nonlinear demand curve for the two price movements differ from the elasticity of the linear demand curve for the same price movements?

© Lavinia Moldovan

CHAPTER 6

LEARNING objectives

Supply, Demand, and Government Policies

In this chapter, you will ...

1 Examine the effects of government policies that place a ceiling on prices

2 Examine the effects of government policies that put a floor under prices

3 Consider how a tax on a good affects the price of the good and the quantity sold

4 Learn that taxes levied on buyers and taxes levied on sellers are equivalent

5 See how the burden of a tax is split between buyers and sellers

Economists have two roles. As scientists, they develop and test theories to explain the world around them. As policy advisers, they use their theories to help change the world for the better. The focus of the preceding two chapters has been scientific. We have seen how supply and demand determine the price of a good and the quantity of the good sold. We have also seen how various events shift supply and demand and thereby change the equilibrium price and quantity. And we have developed the concept of elasticity to gauge the size of these changes.

This chapter offers our first look at policy. Here we analyze various types of government policy using only the tools of supply and demand. As you will see, the analysis yields some surprising insights. Policies often have effects that their architects did not intend or anticipate.

We begin by considering policies that directly control prices. For example, rent-control laws dictate a maximum rent that landlords may charge tenants. Minimum-wage laws dictate the lowest wage that firms may pay workers. Price controls are usually enacted when policymakers believe that the market price of a good or service is unfair to buyers or sellers. Yet, as we will see, these policies can generate inequities of their own.

After discussing price controls, we consider the impact of taxes. Policymakers use taxes to raise revenue for public purposes and to influence market outcomes. Although the prevalence of taxes in our economy is obvious, their effects are not. For example, when the government levies a tax on the amount that firms pay their workers, do the firms or the workers bear the burden of the tax? The answer is not at all clear—until we apply the powerful tools of supply and demand.

6-1　Controls on Prices

To see how price controls affect market outcomes, let's look once again at the market for ice cream. As we saw in Chapter 4, if ice cream is sold in a competitive market free of government regulation, the price of ice cream adjusts to balance supply and demand: At the equilibrium price, the quantity of ice cream that buyers want to buy exactly equals the quantity that sellers want to sell. To be concrete, let's suppose that the equilibrium price is $3 per cone.

Some people may not be happy with the outcome of this free-market process. The Canadian Association of Ice-Cream Eaters complains that the $3 price is too high for everyone to enjoy a cone a day (their recommended daily allowance). Meanwhile, the Canadian Organization of Ice-Cream Makers complains that the $3 price—the result of "cutthroat competition"—is too low and is depressing the incomes of its members. Each of these groups lobbies the government to pass laws that alter the market outcome by directly controlling the price of an ice-cream cone.

price ceiling
a legal maximum on the price at which a good can be sold

price floor
a legal minimum on the price at which a good can be sold

Because buyers of any good always want a lower price while sellers want a higher price, the interests of the two groups conflict. If the Ice-Cream Eaters are successful in their lobbying, the government imposes a legal maximum on the price at which ice cream can be sold. Because the price is not allowed to rise above this level, the legislated maximum is called a **price ceiling**. By contrast, if the Ice-Cream Makers are successful, the government imposes a legal minimum on the price. Because the price cannot fall below this level, the legislated minimum is called a **price floor**. Let us consider the effects of these policies in turn.

6-1a How Price Ceilings Affect Market Outcomes

When the government, moved by the complaints and campaign contributions of the Ice-Cream Eaters, imposes a price ceiling on the market for ice cream, two outcomes are possible. In panel (a) of Figure 6.1, the government imposes a price ceiling of $4 per cone. In this case, because the price that balances supply and demand ($3) is below the ceiling, the price ceiling is *not binding*. Market forces naturally move the economy to the equilibrium, and the price ceiling has no effect on the price or the quantity sold.

Panel (b) of Figure 6.1 shows the other, more interesting, possibility. In this case, the government imposes a price ceiling of $2 per cone. Because the equilibrium price of $3 is above the price ceiling, the ceiling is a *binding constraint* on the market. The forces of supply and demand tend to move the price toward the equilibrium price, but when the market price hits the ceiling, it can rise no further. Thus, the market price equals the price ceiling. At this price, the quantity of ice cream demanded (125 cones in the figure) exceeds the quantity supplied (75 cones). There is a shortage of ice cream; 50 people who want to buy ice cream at the going price are unable to.

In response to this shortage, some mechanism for rationing ice cream will naturally develop. The mechanism could be long lines: Buyers who are willing to

FIGURE 6.1

A Market with a Price Ceiling

In panel (a), the government imposes a price ceiling of $4. Because the price ceiling is above the equilibrium price of $3, the price ceiling has no effect, and the market can reach the equilibrium of supply and demand. In this equilibrium, quantity supplied and quantity demanded both equal 100 cones. In panel (b), the government imposes a price ceiling of $2. Because the price ceiling is below the equilibrium price of $3, the market price equals $2. At this price, 125 cones are demanded and only 75 are supplied, so there is a shortage of 50 cones.

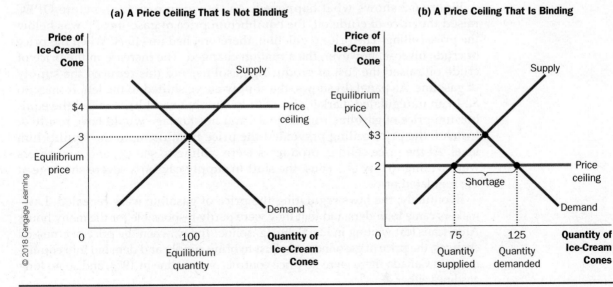

(a) A Price Ceiling That Is Not Binding

(b) A Price Ceiling That Is Binding

arrive early and wait in line get a cone, while those unwilling to wait do not. Alternatively, sellers could ration ice-cream cones according to their own personal biases, selling them only to friends, relatives, or members of their own racial or ethnic group. Notice that even though the price ceiling was motivated by a desire to help buyers of ice cream, not all buyers benefit from the policy. Some buyers do get to pay a lower price, although they may have to wait in line to do so, but other buyers cannot get any ice cream at all.

This example in the market for ice cream shows a general result: When the government imposes a binding price ceiling on a competitive market, a shortage of the good arises, and sellers must ration the scarce goods among the large number of potential buyers. The rationing mechanisms that develop under price ceilings are rarely desirable. Long lines are inefficient because they waste buyers' time. Discrimination according to seller bias is both inefficient (because the good does not necessarily go to the buyer who values it most highly) and potentially unfair. By contrast, the rationing mechanism in a free, competitive market is both efficient and impersonal. When the market for ice cream reaches its equilibrium, anyone who wants to pay the market price can get a cone. Free markets ration goods with prices.

case study Lines at the Gas Pump

As we discussed in the preceding chapter, in 1973 the Organization of the Petroleum Exporting Countries (OPEC) raised the price of crude oil in world oil markets. Because crude oil is the major input used to make gasoline, the higher oil prices reduced the supply of gasoline. In Canada the price of gas increased, but there were very few shortages. In the United States, it was very different. Long lines at gas stations became commonplace, and American motorists often had to wait for hours to buy only a few litres of gas.

What was responsible for the long gas lines? Most people blame OPEC. Surely, if OPEC had not raised the price of crude oil, the shortage of gasoline would not have occurred. Yet economists blame U.S. government regulations that limited the price that oil companies could charge for gasoline.

Figure 6.2 shows what happened. As shown in panel (a), before OPEC raised the price of crude oil, the equilibrium price of gasoline, P_1, was below the price ceiling. The price regulation, therefore, had no effect. When the price of crude oil rose, however, the situation changed. The increase in the price of crude oil raised the cost of producing gasoline, and this reduced the supply of gasoline. As panel (b) shows, the supply curve shifted to the left, from S_1 to S_2. In an unregulated market, this shift in supply would have raised the equilibrium price of gasoline from P_1 to P_2, and no shortage would have resulted. Instead, the price ceiling prevented the price from rising to the equilibrium level. At the price ceiling, producers were willing to sell Q_S, and consumers were willing to buy Q_D. Thus, the shift in supply caused a severe shortage at the regulated price.

Eventually, the laws regulating the price of gasoline were repealed. Lawmakers came to understand that they were partly responsible for the many hours Americans lost waiting in line to buy gasoline. Today, when the price of crude oil changes, the price of gasoline can adjust to bring supply and demand into equilibrium. In Canada there were no price controls on gasoline in 1973, and so no long gas lines either. ■

FIGURE 6.2

The Market for Gasoline with a Price Ceiling

Panel (a) shows the gasoline market when the price ceiling is not binding because the equilibrium price, P_1, is below the ceiling. Panel (b) shows the gasoline market after an increase in the price of crude oil (an input into making gasoline) shifts the supply curve to the left from S_1 to S_2. In an unregulated market the price would have risen from P_1 to P_2. The price ceiling, however, prevents this from happening. At the binding price ceiling, consumers are willing to buy Q_D, but producers of gasoline are willing to sell only Q_S. The difference between quantity demanded and quantity supplied, $Q_D - Q_S$, measures the gasoline shortage.

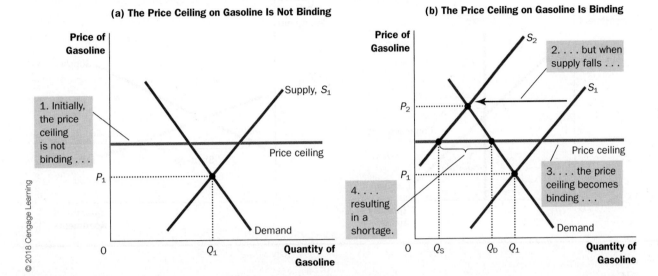

(a) The Price Ceiling on Gasoline Is Not Binding

(b) The Price Ceiling on Gasoline Is Binding

© 2018 Cengage Learning

Rent Control in the Short Run and the Long Run

case study One common example of a price ceiling is rent control. In some provinces, the provincial government places a ceiling on rents that landlords may charge their tenants. For example, in Canada, some form of rent control exists in the provinces of Ontario, Quebec, British Columbia, Manitoba, and Prince Edward Island. For example, landlords in Ontario cannot increase the rent for most private rental units each year by more than the amount set by the Government of Ontario's rent increase guidelines. The guidelines set the maximum percentage that rent can be increased in the following calendar year. In 2017 the maximum amount that rent could be increased was 1.5 percent, and in 2018 it was 1.8 percent. The goal of this policy is to help the poor by making housing more affordable. Economists often criticize rent control, arguing that it is a highly inefficient way to help the poor raise their standard of living. One economist has called rent control "the best way to destroy a city, other than bombing."

The adverse effects of rent control are less apparent to the general population because these effects occur over many years. In the short run, landlords have a fixed number of apartments to rent, and they cannot adjust this number quickly as market conditions change. Moreover, the number of people searching for housing in a city may not be highly responsive to rents in the short run because people take time to adjust their housing arrangements. Therefore, the short-run supply and demand for housing are relatively inelastic.

FIGURE 6.3

Rent Control in the Short Run and in the Long Run

Panel (a) shows the short-run effects of rent control: Because the supply and demand for apartments are relatively inelastic, the price ceiling imposed by a rent-control law causes only a small shortage of housing. Panel (b) shows the long-run effects of rent control: Because the supply and demand for apartments are more elastic, rent control causes a large shortage.

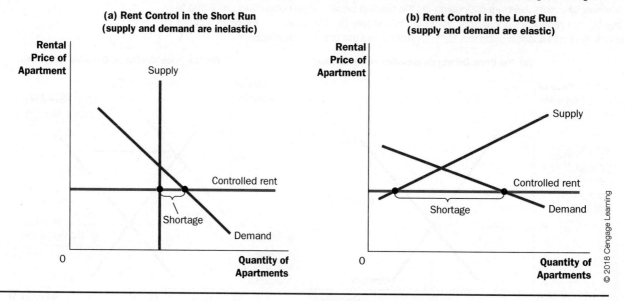

Panel (a) of Figure 6.3 shows the short-run effects of rent control on the housing market. As with any binding price ceiling, rent control causes a shortage. Yet because supply and demand are inelastic in the short run, the initial shortage caused by rent control is small. The primary effect in the short run is to reduce rents.

The long-run story is very different because the buyers and sellers of rental housing respond more to market conditions as time passes. On the supply side, landlords respond to low rents by not building new apartments and by failing to maintain existing ones. On the demand side, low rents encourage people to find their own apartments (rather than living with their parents or sharing apartments with roommates) and induce more people to move into a city. Therefore, both supply and demand are more elastic in the long run.

Panel (b) of Figure 6.3 illustrates the housing market in the long run. When rent control depresses rents below the equilibrium level, the quantity of apartments supplied falls substantially, and the quantity of apartments demanded rises substantially. The result is a large shortage of housing.

In provinces with rent control, landlords use various mechanisms to ration housing. Some landlords keep long waiting lists. Others give a preference to tenants without children. Still others discriminate on the basis of race. Sometimes, apartments are allocated to those willing to offer under-the-table payments to building superintendents. In essence, these bribes bring the total price of an apartment (including the bribe) closer to the equilibrium price.

To understand fully the effects of rent control, we have to remember one of the ten principles of economics from Chapter 1: People respond to incentives.

In free markets, landlords try to keep their buildings clean and safe because desirable apartments command higher prices. By contrast, when rent control creates shortages and waiting lists, landlords lose their incentive to respond to tenants' concerns. Why should a landlord spend his money to maintain and improve his property when people are waiting to get in as it is? In the end, tenants get lower rents, but they also get lower-quality housing.

Policymakers often react to the effects of rent control by imposing additional regulations. For example, there are laws that make racial discrimination in housing illegal and require landlords to provide minimally adequate living conditions. These laws, however, are difficult and costly to enforce. By contrast, when rent control is eliminated and a market for housing is regulated by the forces of competition, such laws are less necessary. In a free market, the price of housing adjusts to eliminate the shortages that give rise to undesirable landlord behaviour. ■

Ask the Experts

Rent Control

"Local ordinances that limit rent increases for some rental housing units have had a positive impact over the past three decades on the amount and quality of broadly affordable rental housing in cities that have used them."

What do economists say?

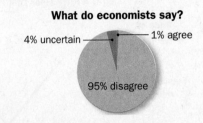

4% uncertain — 1% agree

95% disagree

Source: IGM Economic Experts Panel, February 7, 2012.
Figure © 2018 Cengage Learning.

6-1b How Price Floors Affect Market Outcomes

To examine the effects of another kind of government price control, let's return to the market for ice cream. Imagine now that the government is persuaded by the pleas of the Canadian Organization of Ice-Cream Makers, whose members feel that the $3 equilibrium price is too low. In this case, the government might institute a price floor. Price floors, like price ceilings, are an attempt by the government to maintain prices at other than equilibrium levels. Whereas a price ceiling places a legal maximum on prices, a price floor places a legal minimum.

When the government imposes a price floor on the ice-cream market, two outcomes are possible. If the government imposes a price floor of $2 per cone when the equilibrium price is $3, we obtain the outcome in panel (a) of Figure 6.4. In this case, because the equilibrium price is above the floor, the price floor is not binding. Market forces naturally move the economy to the equilibrium, and the price floor has no effect.

Panel (b) of Figure 6.4 shows what happens when the government imposes a price floor of $4 per cone. In this case, because the equilibrium price of $3 is below the floor, the price floor is a binding constraint on the market. The forces of supply and demand tend to move the price toward the equilibrium price, but when the market price hits the floor, it can fall no further. The market price equals the price floor. At this floor, the quantity of ice cream supplied (120 cones) exceeds the quantity demanded (80 cones). Because of this excess supply of 40 cones, some people who want to sell ice cream at the going price are unable to. *Thus, a binding price floor causes a surplus.*

Just as shortages resulting from price ceilings can lead to undesirable rationing mechanisms, so can the surpluses resulting from price floors. The sellers who appeal to the personal biases of the buyers, perhaps due to racial or familial ties, may be better able to sell their goods than those who do not. By contrast, in a free market, the price serves as the rationing mechanism, and sellers can sell all they want at the equilibrium price.

FIGURE 6.4

A Market with a Price Floor

In panel (a), the government imposes a price floor of $2. Because this is below the equilibrium price of $3, the price floor has no effect. The market price adjusts to balance supply and demand. At the equilibrium, quantity supplied and quantity demanded both equal 100 cones. In panel (b), the government imposes a price floor of $4, which is above the equilibrium price of $3. Therefore, the market price equals $4. Because 120 cones are supplied at this price and only 80 are demanded, there is a surplus of 40 cones.

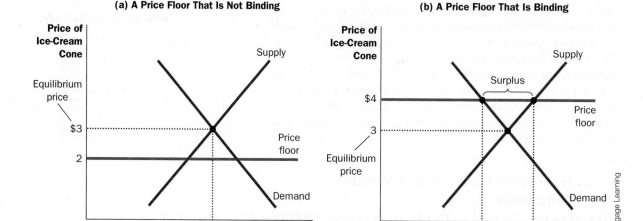

The Minimum Wage

case study   An important example of a price floor is the minimum wage. Minimum-wage laws dictate the lowest price for labour that any employer may pay. Minimum-wage rates differ by province and territory, as shown in Table 6.1. As of July 1, 2019, minimum wages ranged from a low of $10.96 per hour in Saskatchewan to a high of $15 in Alberta. In some provinces, lower rates apply for inexperienced workers and for restaurant and bar staff, who can earn tips to supplement their wages. For example, in Alberta the minimum wage is $13 per hour for teenagers 17 years of age and younger. Many other countries have minimum-wage laws as well. For example, in the United States the federally mandated minimum wage is $7.25. (Some states mandate minimum wages above the federal level.)

To examine the effects of a minimum wage, we must consider the market for labour. Panel (a) of Figure 6.5 shows the labour market, which, like all markets, is subject to the forces of supply and demand. Workers determine the supply of labour, and firms determine the demand. If the government doesn't intervene, the wage normally adjusts to balance labour supply and labour demand.

Panel (b) of Figure 6.5 shows the labour market with a minimum wage. If the minimum wage is above the equilibrium level, as it is here, the quantity of labour supplied exceeds the quantity demanded. The result is unemployment. Thus, the minimum wage raises the incomes of those workers who have jobs, but it lowers the incomes of those workers who cannot find jobs.

To fully understand the minimum wage, keep in mind that the economy contains not a single labour market but many labour markets for different types of

TABLE 6.1

Minimum-Wage Rates across
Canada, October 1, 2018

Province or Territory	Minimum Hourly Wage
Alberta	$15.00
British Columbia[a]	$11.35
Manitoba	$11.15
New Brunswick[b]	$11.25
Newfoundland and Labrador	$11.15
Northwest Territories	$13.46
Nova Scotia[b]	$11.00
Nunavut	$13.00
Ontario	$14.00
Prince Edward Island	$11.55
Quebec	$12.00
Saskatchewan[b]	$10.96
Yukon	$11.51

Source: Provincial government websites.
a. To rise to $15.20 by June 1, 2020.
b. Adjusted annually for inflation.

FIGURE 6.5

How the Minimum Wage
Affects the Labour
Market

Panel (a) shows a labour market in which the wage adjusts to balance labour supply and
labour demand. Panel (b) shows the impact of a binding minimum wage. Because the
minimum wage is a price floor, it causes a surplus: The quantity of labour supplied exceeds
the quantity demanded. The result is unemployment.

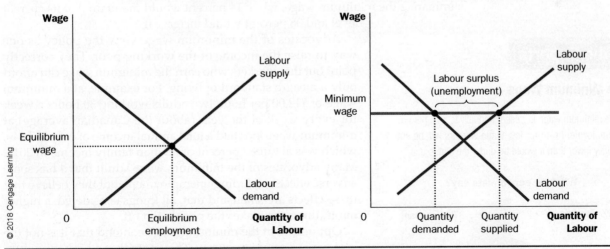

workers. The impact of the minimum wage depends on the skill and experience
of the worker. Highly skilled and experienced workers are not affected because
their equilibrium wages are well above the minimum. For these workers, the minimum wage is not binding.

The minimum wage has its greatest impact on the market for teenage labour. The equilibrium wages of teenagers are low because teenagers are among the least skilled and least experienced members of the labour force. In addition, teenagers are often willing to accept a lower wage in exchange for on-the-job training. (Some teenagers are willing to work as "interns" for no pay at all. Because internships pay nothing, however, the minimum wage does not apply to them. If it did, these jobs might not exist.) As a result, the minimum wage is more often binding for teenagers than for other members of the labour force.

Many economists have studied how minimum-wage laws affect the teenage labour market. These researchers compare the changes in the minimum wage over time with the changes in teenage employment. Although there is some debate about how much the minimum wage affects employment, the typical study finds that a 10-percent increase in the minimum wage depresses teenage employment between 1 and 3 percent. In interpreting this estimate, note that a 10-percent increase in the minimum wage does not raise the average wage of teenagers by 10 percent. A change in the law does not directly affect those teenagers who are already paid above the minimum, and enforcement of minimum-wage laws is not perfect. Moreover, the estimates of the impact of minimum wages on the employment of adults are smaller: for young adults aged 20 to 25 a 10-percent increase in the minimum wage would lead to a decline in employment of about 0.5 percent, and for older adults essentially zero.

In addition to altering the quantity of labour demanded, the minimum wage alters the quantity supplied. Because the minimum wage raises the wage that teenagers can earn, it increases the number of teenagers who choose to look for jobs. Studies have found that a higher minimum wage influences which teenagers are employed. When the minimum wage rises, some teenagers who are still attending school choose to drop out and take jobs. These new dropouts displace other teenagers who had already dropped out of school and who now become unemployed.

The minimum wage is a frequent topic of debate. Economists are about evenly divided on the issue. In a 2006 survey of Ph.D. economists, 47 percent favoured eliminating the minimum wage, while 14 percent would maintain it at its current level and 38 percent would increase it.

Advocates of the minimum wage view the policy as one way to raise the income of the working poor. They correctly point out that workers who earn the minimum wage can afford only a meagre standard of living. For example, at a minimum wage of $12.00 per hour, two adults working 30 hours a week for every week of the year (about the Canadian average) at minimum-wage jobs had a total annual income of only $37 440, which was about 53 percent of median family income in 2015. Many advocates of the minimum wage admit that it has some adverse effects, including unemployment, but they believe that these effects are small and that, all things considered, a higher minimum wage makes the poor better off.

Opponents of the minimum wage contend that it is not the best way to combat poverty. They note that a high minimum wage causes unemployment, encourages teenagers to drop out of school, and prevents some unskilled workers from getting the on-the-job training they need. Moreover, opponents of the minimum wage point out that the minimum wage is a poorly targeted policy. Not all minimum-wage workers are

Ask the Experts

The Minimum Wage

"If the minimum wage is raised gradually to $15 per hour, the employment rate for low-wage workers will be substantially lower than it would be under the status quo."

What do economists say?

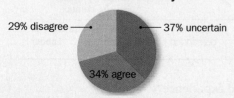

29% disagree

37% uncertain

34% agree

Source: IGM Economic Experts Panel, September 22, 2015.
Figure © 2018 Cengage Learning.

heads of households trying to help their families escape poverty. In fact, fewer than a third of minimum-wage earners are in families with incomes below the poverty line. Some are teenagers from middle-class homes working at part-time jobs for extra spending money. ■

Minimum Wage in Alberta and Ontario

Minimum wages are a matter of some controversy and disagreement. This article by two leading labour economists in Canada discusses a study of their impact, noting that local labour market conditions should be taken into account.

Is a $15 Minimum Wage Worth It? Here's What the Numbers Say

By Joseph Marchand and David Green

On Tuesday, Sept. 25, there were three provinces that had a $15 minimum wage scheduled to come into effect: Alberta (by 2018), Ontario (by 2019), and British Columbia (by 2021). By Wednesday, Sept. 26, there were only two, Alberta and British Columbia, as Ontario decided to halt its scheduled minimum wage increases one dollar short of that goal.

As two labour economists, each with an independent policy piece on the possible effects of the $15 minimum wage in our provinces (British Columbia for David Green, published by the Canadian Centre for Policy Alternatives in April, 2015, and Alberta for Joseph Marchand, published by the C.D. Howe Institute in September, 2017), we represent the two remaining cases.

We each analyzed the effects of virtually the same nominal increase of 46 per cent and 47 per cent, as British Columbia's proposed plan in 2015 was a move from $10.25 to $15 an hour and Alberta's plan enacted in 2015 was a move from $10.20 to $15 an hour by Oct. 1, 2018. B.C. has since made the goal of a $15 minimum wage a reality (rising in September, 2017, to $11.25 and going to $15.20 by 2021).

We then agreed as to the average potential employment loss from these wage increases. Our calculations show a 7.6-per-cent to 8-per-cent loss among affected workers (that is, those initially working below $15 or those of younger

ages) and a 0.98-per-cent to 1.04-per-cent loss in total employment. This translates to about 23,000 to 26,000 jobs lost in each province, with similarly sized labour forces.

Ontario, with its smaller minimum wage increase of 31 per cent ($11.40 in 2016 to $15 by 2019), would have been expecting a smaller percentage loss in employment. But with a labour force more than three times the size of Alberta or B.C., this would have translated to a larger job loss count. By stopping $1 short of its $15 goal, Ontario presumably shielded itself from some of that loss.

So, was the postponement of Ontario's $15 minimum wage the right or wrong thing to do? Was its policy decision a good or bad one? We discuss a few broader points to help answer that.

First, sound methodology should be a point of agreement regardless of any policy conclusions. Methodological questions should be kept separate from policy discussions that follow in order to provide a sound basis for those discussions. For Alberta and B.C., we agree on methodology and the implied employment conclusions. Ontario's job projections should be similarly viewed.

That said, both of our studies went beyond a job-loss calculation. For B.C., Mr. Green highlighted the benefits of reduced employee turnover and a more equitable distribution. For Alberta, Mr. Marchand highlighted the concerns of poor timing owing to the energy bust and the prioritization of wages while employment was a pressing issue. Those wider scopes help to set up our next point.

Second, any policy comes with costs. The prediction that minimum wage increases will have employment effects is not a sufficient

argument in itself not to implement the increases. There are many factors to consider. Whether the wage increases should be implemented depends on analyses of accompanying costs and benefits and, potentially, on the state of the economy.

For example, from April, 2015 (prior to Alberta's policy), to mid-2018, the total employment rate has gone up by two percentage points in B.C. and dropped by two percentage points in Alberta. For young workers (between the ages of 15 to 24), their employment rate has gone up five percentage points in B.C. and gone down by five percentage points in Alberta. Given these opposite trends, actual job loss may occur in Alberta and only shave off growth in B.C.

Third, reasonable people can disagree on some of the factors that determine the ultimate advisability of a minimum wage increase. And the same person might see it as advisable in some cases, but not in others. However, it is important not to politicize the main empirical findings themselves in order to permit a mature discussion, which we believe is achievable.

Given the different focus of each of our studies and the state of the economy in each province, Mr. Green's outlook for B.C. was somewhat more optimistic and Mr. Marchand's outlook for Alberta was somewhat more pessimistic. So again, was Ontario right or wrong in pressing the brakes on their minimum wage at $14? Our simple answer would have to be neither—it's both.

Source: Joseph Marchand and David Green, "Is a $15 Minimum Wage Worth It? Here's What the Numbers Say," Special to *The Globe and Mail*, Published October 15, 2018. https://www.theglobeandmail.com/business/commentary/article-is-a-15-minimum-wage-worth-it-heres-what-the-numbers-say/. Reproduced by permission of the authors.

6-1c Evaluating Price Controls

One of the ten principles of economics discussed in Chapter 1 is that markets are usually a good way to organize economic activity. This principle explains why economists usually oppose price ceilings and price floors. To economists, prices are not the outcome of some haphazard process. Prices, they contend, are the result of the millions of business and consumer decisions that lie behind the supply and demand curves. Prices have the crucial job of balancing supply and demand and, thereby, coordinating economic activity. When policymakers set prices by legal decree, they obscure the signals that normally guide the allocation of society's resources.

Another one of the ten principles of economics is that governments can sometimes improve market outcomes. Indeed, policymakers are led to control prices because they view the market's outcome as unfair. Price controls are often aimed at helping the poor. For instance, rent-control laws try to make housing affordable for everyone, and minimum-wage laws try to help people escape poverty.

Yet price controls often hurt those they are trying to help. Rent control may keep rents low, but it also discourages landlords from maintaining their buildings and makes housing hard to find. Minimum-wage laws may raise the incomes of some workers, but they also cause other workers to be unemployed.

Helping those in need can be accomplished in ways other than controlling prices. For instance, the government can make housing more affordable by paying a fraction of the rent for poor families. Unlike rent control, such rent subsidies do not reduce the quantity of housing supplied and, therefore, do not lead to housing shortages. Similarly, wage subsidies raise the living standards of the working poor without discouraging firms from hiring them.

Although these alternative policies are often better than price controls, they are not perfect. Rent and wage subsidies cost the government money and, therefore, require higher taxes. As we see in the next section, taxation has costs of its own.

QUICK Quiz   *Define price ceiling and price floor, and give an example of each. Which leads to a shortage? Which leads to a surplus? Why?*

6-2 Taxes

All governments—from the federal government in Ottawa to the local governments in small towns—use taxes to raise revenue for public projects, such as roads, schools, and national defence. Because taxes are such an important policy instrument, and affect our lives in many ways, we return to the study of taxes several times throughout this book. In this section, we begin our study of how taxes affect the economy.

To set the stage for our analysis, imagine that a local government decides to hold an annual ice-cream celebration—with a parade, fireworks, and speeches by town officials. To raise revenue to pay for the event, the town decides to place a $0.50 tax on the sale of ice-cream cones. When the plan is announced, our two lobbying groups swing into action. The Canadian Association of Ice-Cream Eaters claims that consumers of ice cream are having trouble making ends meet, and it argues that *sellers* of ice cream should pay the tax. The Canadian Organization of Ice-Cream Makers claims that its members are struggling to survive in a competitive market, and it argues that *buyers* of ice cream should have to pay the tax. The town mayor, hoping to reach a compromise, suggests that half the tax be paid by the buyers and half be paid by the sellers.

To analyze these proposals, we need to address a simple but subtle question: When the government levies a tax on a good, who actually bears the burden of the tax? The people buying the good? The people selling the good? Or, if buyers and sellers share the tax burden, what determines how the burden is divided? Can the government simply legislate the division of the burden, as the mayor is suggesting, or is the division determined by more fundamental market forces? The term **tax incidence** refers to how the burden of a tax is distributed among the various people who make up the economy. As we will see, some surprising lessons about tax incidence arise just by applying the tools of supply and demand.

tax incidence
the manner in which the burden of a tax is shared among participants in a market

6-2a How Taxes on Buyers Affect Market Outcomes

We begin by considering a tax levied on buyers of a good. Suppose, for instance, that our local government passes a law requiring buyers of ice-cream cones to send $0.50 to the government for each ice-cream cone they buy. How does this law affect the buyers and sellers of ice cream? To answer this question, we can follow the three steps in Chapter 4 for analyzing supply and demand: (1) We decide whether the law affects the supply curve or demand curve (or perhaps both). (2) We decide which way the curve shifts. (3) We examine how the shift affects the equilibrium.

Step One The immediate impact of the tax is on the demand for ice cream. The supply curve is not affected because, for any given price of ice cream, sellers have the same incentive to provide ice cream to the market. By contrast, buyers now have to pay a tax to the government (as well as the price to the sellers) whenever they buy ice cream. Thus, the tax shifts the demand curve for ice cream.

Step Two We next determine the direction of the shift. Because the tax on buyers makes buying ice cream less attractive, buyers demand a smaller quantity of ice cream at every price. As a result, the demand curve shifts to the left (or, equivalently, downward), as shown in Figure 6.6.

FIGURE 6.6

A Tax on Buyers

When a tax of $0.50 is levied on buyers, the demand curve shifts down by $0.50 from D_1 to D_2. The equilibrium quantity falls from 100 to 90 cones. The price that sellers receive falls from $3.00 to $2.80. The price that buyers pay (including the tax) rises from $3.00 to $3.30. Even though the tax is levied on buyers, buyers and sellers share the burden of the tax.

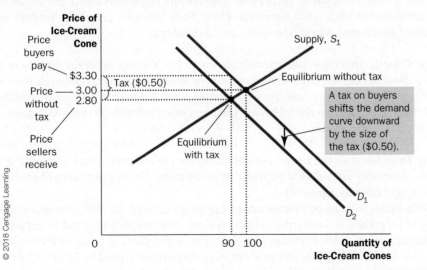

© 2018 Cengage Learning

We can, in this case, be precise about how much the curve shifts. Because of the $0.50 tax levied on buyers, the effective price to buyers is now $0.50 higher than the market price (whatever the market price happens to be). For example, if the market price of a cone happened to be $2.00, the effective price to buyers would be $2.50. Because buyers look at their total cost including the tax, they demand a quantity of ice cream as if the market price were $0.50 higher than it actually is. In other words, to induce buyers to demand any given quantity, the market price must now be $0.50 lower to make up for the effect of the tax. Thus, the tax shifts the demand curve *downward* from D_1 to D_2 by exactly the size of the tax ($0.50).

Step Three Having determined how the demand curve shifts, we can now see the effect of the tax by comparing the initial equilibrium and the new equilibrium. You can see in Figure 6.6 that the equilibrium price of ice cream falls from $3.00 to $2.80 and the equilibrium quantity falls from 100 to 90 cones. Because sellers sell less and buyers buy less in the new equilibrium, the tax on ice cream reduces the size of the ice-cream market.

Implications We can now return to the question of tax incidence: Who pays the tax? Although buyers send the entire tax to the government, buyers and sellers share the burden. Because the market price falls from $3.00 to $2.80 when the tax is introduced, sellers receive $0.20 less for each ice-cream cone than they did without the tax. Thus, the tax makes sellers worse off. Buyers pay sellers a lower price ($2.80), but the effective price including the tax rises from $3.00 before the tax to $3.30 with the tax ($2.80 + $0.50 = $3.30). Thus, the tax also makes buyers worse off.

To sum up, the analysis yields two lessons:

- Taxes discourage market activity. When a good is taxed, the quantity of the good sold is smaller in the new equilibrium.
- Buyers and sellers share the burden of taxes. In the new equilibrium, buyers pay more for the good, and sellers receive less.

6-2b How Taxes on Sellers Affect Market Outcomes

Now consider a tax levied on sellers of a good. Suppose the local government passes a law requiring sellers of ice-cream cones to send $0.50 to the government for each cone they sell. How does this law affect the buyers and sellers of ice cream? Again, we apply our three steps.

Step One In this case, the immediate impact of the tax is on the sellers of ice cream. Because the tax is not levied on buyers, the quantity of ice cream demanded at any given price is the same; thus, the demand curve does not change. By contrast, the tax on sellers makes the ice-cream business less profitable at any given price, so it shifts the supply curve.

Step Two Because the tax on sellers raises the cost of producing and selling ice cream, it reduces the quantity supplied at every price. The supply curve shifts to the left (or, equivalently, upward).

Once again, we can be precise about the magnitude of the shift. For any market price of ice cream, the effective price to sellers—the amount they get to keep after paying the tax—is $0.50 lower. For example, if the market price of a cone happened to be $2.00, the effective price received by sellers would be $1.50. Whatever the market price, sellers will supply a quantity of ice cream as if the price were

FIGURE 6.7

A Tax on Sellers

When a tax of $0.50 is levied on sellers, the supply curve shifts up by $0.50 from S_1 to S_2. The equilibrium quantity falls from 100 to 90 cones. The price that buyers pay rises from $3.00 to $3.30. The price that sellers receive (after paying the tax) falls from $3.00 to $2.80. Even though the tax is levied on sellers, buyers and sellers share the burden of the tax.

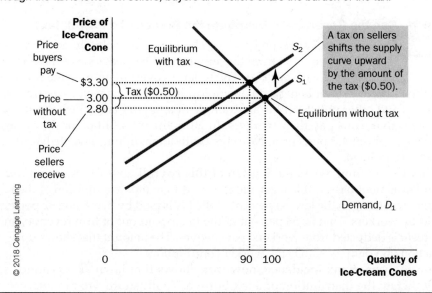

$0.50 lower than it is. Put differently, to induce sellers to supply any given quantity, the market price must now be $0.50 higher to compensate for the effect of the tax. Thus, as shown in Figure 6.7, the supply curve shifts *upward* from S_1 to S_2 by exactly the size of the tax ($0.50).

Step Three Having determined how the supply curve shifts, we can now compare the initial and the new equilibrium. The figure shows that the equilibrium price of ice cream rises from $3.00 to $3.30, and the equilibrium quantity falls from 100 to 90 cones. Once again, the tax reduces the size of the ice-cream market. And once again, buyers and sellers share the burden of the tax. Because the market price rises, buyers pay $0.30 more for each cone than they did before the tax was enacted. Sellers receive a higher price than they did without the tax, but the effective price (after paying the tax) falls from $3.00 to $2.80.

Implications If you compare Figures 6.6 and 6.7, you will notice a surprising conclusion: *Taxes on buyers and taxes on sellers are equivalent*. In both cases, the tax places a wedge between the price that buyers pay and the price that sellers receive. The wedge between the buyers' price and the sellers' price is the same, regardless of whether the tax is levied on buyers or sellers. In either case, the wedge shifts the relative position of the supply and demand curves. In the new equilibrium, buyers and sellers share the burden of the tax. The only difference between taxes on buyers and taxes on sellers is who sends the money to the government.

The equivalence of these two taxes is easy to understand if we imagine that the government collects the $0.50 ice-cream tax in a bowl on the counter of each ice-cream store. When the government levies the tax on buyers, the buyer is required to place $0.50 in the bowl every time a cone is bought. When the government levies the tax on sellers, the seller is required to place $0.50 in the bowl after the sale of each cone. Whether the $0.50 goes directly from the buyer's pocket into the bowl, or indirectly from the buyer's pocket into the seller's hand and then into the bowl, does not matter. Once the market reaches its new equilibrium, buyers and sellers share the burden, regardless of how the tax is levied.

case study   Can the Government Distribute the Burden of a Payroll Tax?

If you have ever received a paycheque, you probably noticed that taxes were deducted from the amount you earned. One of these taxes is called Employment Insurance (EI). The federal government uses the revenue from the EI tax to pay for benefits to unemployed workers, as well as for training programs and other policies. EI is an example of a payroll tax, which is a tax on the wages that firms pay their workers. In 2015, the total EI tax for the typical worker was about 4.5 percent of earnings (with a maximum payable based on $49 500 in earnings).

Who do you think bears the burden of this payroll tax—firms or workers? When Parliament passed this legislation, it tried to mandate a division of the tax burden. According to the law, 58 percent of the tax is paid by firms, and 42 percent is paid by workers. That is, 58 percent of the tax is paid out of firm revenue, and 42 percent is deducted from workers' paycheques. The amount that shows up as a deduction on your pay stub is the worker contribution.

Our analysis of tax incidence, however, shows that lawmakers cannot so easily dictate the distribution of a tax burden. To illustrate, we can analyze a payroll tax as merely a tax on a good, where the good is labour and the price is the wage. The key feature of the payroll tax is that it places a wedge between the wage that firms pay and the wage that workers receive. Figure 6.8 shows the outcome. When a payroll tax is enacted, the wage received by workers falls, and the wage paid by firms rises. In the end, workers and firms share the burden of the tax, much as the legislation requires. Yet this division of the tax burden between workers and firms has nothing to do with the legislated division: The division of the burden in Figure 6.8 is not necessarily 58−42 percent, and the same outcome would prevail if the law levied the entire tax on workers or if it levied the entire tax on firms.

This example shows that the most basic lesson of tax incidence is often overlooked in public debate. Lawmakers can decide whether a tax comes from the buyer's pocket or from the seller's, but they cannot legislate the true burden of a tax. Rather, tax incidence depends on the forces of supply and demand. ∎

6-2c Elasticity and Tax Incidence

When a good is taxed, buyers and sellers of the good share the burden of the tax. But how exactly is the tax burden divided? Only rarely will it be shared equally. To see how the burden is divided, consider the impact of taxation in the two markets in Figure 6.9. In both cases, the figure shows the initial demand curve, the initial supply curve, and a tax that drives a wedge between the amount paid by buyers and the amount received by sellers. (Not drawn in either panel of the figure is the new supply or demand curve. Which curve shifts depends on whether the tax is levied on buyers or sellers. As we have seen, this is irrelevant for the incidence of the tax.) The difference in the two panels is the relative elasticity of supply and demand.

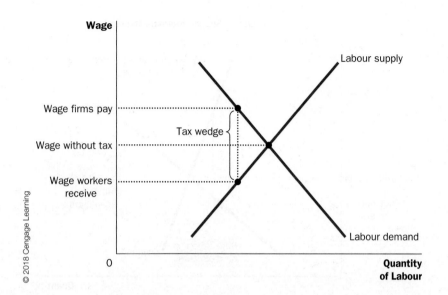

© 2018 Cengage Learning

FIGURE 6.8

A Payroll Tax

A payroll tax places a wedge between the wage that workers receive and the wage that firms pay. Comparing wages with and without the tax, you can see that workers and firms share the tax burden. This division of the tax burden between workers and firms does not depend on whether the government levies the tax on workers, levies the tax on firms, or divides the tax equally between the two groups.

Panel (a) of Figure 6.9 shows a tax in a market with very elastic supply and relatively inelastic demand. That is, sellers are very responsive to changes in the price of the good (so the supply curve is relatively flat), whereas buyers are not very responsive (so the demand curve is relatively steep). When a tax is imposed on a market with these elasticities, the price received by sellers does not fall much, so sellers bear only a small burden. By contrast, the price paid by buyers rises substantially, indicating that buyers bear most of the burden of the tax.

Panel (b) of Figure 6.9 shows a tax in a market with relatively inelastic supply and very elastic demand. In this case, sellers are not very responsive to changes in the price (so the supply curve is steeper), while buyers are very responsive (so the demand curve is flatter). The figure shows that when a tax is imposed, the price paid by buyers does not rise much, while the price received by sellers falls substantially. Thus, sellers bear most of the burden of the tax.

The two panels of Figure 6.9 show a general lesson about how the burden of a tax is divided: *A tax burden falls more heavily on the side of the market that is less elastic.* Why is this true? In essence, the elasticity measures the willingness of buyers or sellers to leave the market when conditions become unfavourable. A small elasticity of demand means that buyers do not have good alternatives to consuming this particular good. A small elasticity of supply means that sellers do not have good alternatives to producing this particular good. When the good is taxed, the side of the market with fewer good alternatives is less willing to leave the market and must, therefore, bear more of the burden of the tax.

We can apply this logic to the payroll tax discussed in the previous case study. Most labour economists believe that the supply of labour is much less elastic than the demand. This means that workers, rather than firms, bear most of the burden of the payroll tax. In other words, the distribution of the tax burden is not at all close to the 58–42 split that lawmakers intended.

FIGURE 6.9

How the Burden of a Tax Is Divided

In panel (a), the supply curve is elastic, and the demand curve is inelastic. In this case, the price received by sellers falls only slightly, while the price paid by buyers rises substantially. Thus, buyers bear most of the burden of the tax. In panel (b), the supply curve is inelastic, and the demand curve is elastic. In this case, the price received by sellers falls substantially, while the price paid by buyers rises only slightly. Thus, sellers bear most of the burden of the tax.

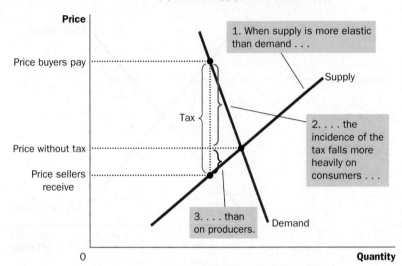

(a) Elastic Supply, Inelastic Demand

1. When supply is more elastic than demand . . .
2. . . . the incidence of the tax falls more heavily on consumers . . .
3. . . . than on producers.

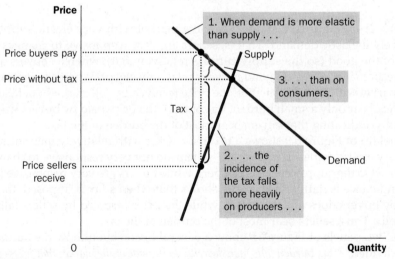

(b) Inelastic Supply, Elastic Demand

1. When demand is more elastic than supply . . .
2. . . . the incidence of the tax falls more heavily on producers . . .
3. . . . than on consumers.

© 2018 Cengage Learning

QUICK Quiz *Assume you are to levy a tax on yachts. Should you impose it on yacht buyers or yacht producers? Explain.*

QUICK Quiz *In a supply-and-demand diagram, show how a tax on car buyers of $1000 per car affects the quantity of cars sold and the price of cars. In another diagram, show how a tax on car sellers of $1000 per car affects the quantity of cars sold and the price of cars. In both of your diagrams, show the change in the price paid by car buyers and the change in price received by car sellers.*

6-3 Conclusion

The economy is governed by two kinds of laws: the laws of supply and demand and the laws enacted by governments. In this chapter, we have begun to see how these laws interact. Price controls and taxes are common in various markets in the economy, and their effects are frequently debated in the press and among policy-makers. Even a little bit of economic knowledge can go a long way toward understanding and evaluating these policies.

In subsequent chapters, we analyze many government policies in greater detail. We examine the effects of taxation more fully, and consider a broader range of policies than we considered here. Yet the basic lessons of this chapter will not change: When analyzing government policies, supply and demand are the first and most useful tools of analysis.

summary

- A price ceiling is a legal maximum on the price of a good or service. An example is rent control. If the price ceiling is below the equilibrium price, so the price ceiling is binding, the quantity demanded exceeds the quantity supplied. Because of the resulting shortage, sellers must in some way ration the good or service among buyers.

- A price floor is a legal minimum on the price of a good or service. An example is the minimum wage. If the price floor is above the equilibrium price, so the price floor is binding, the quantity supplied exceeds the quantity demanded. Because of the resulting surplus, buyers' demands for the good or service must in some way be rationed among sellers.

- When the government levies a tax on a good, the equilibrium quantity of the good falls. That is, a tax on a market shrinks the size of the market.

- A tax on a good places a wedge between the price paid by buyers and the price received by sellers. When the market moves to the new equilibrium, buyers pay more for the good and sellers receive less for it. In this sense, buyers and sellers share the tax burden. The incidence of a tax (that is, the division of the tax burden) does not depend on whether the tax is levied on buyers or sellers.

- The incidence of a tax depends on the price elasticities of supply and demand. The burden tends to fall on the side of the market that is less elastic because that side of the market can respond less easily to the tax by changing the quantity bought or sold.

KEY concepts

price ceiling, *p. 122*   price floor, *p. 122*   tax incidence, *p. 133*

QUESTIONS FOR review

1. Give an example of a price ceiling and an example of a price floor.

2. Which causes a shortage of a good—a price ceiling or a price floor? Which causes a surplus?

3. What mechanisms allocate resources when the price of a good is not allowed to bring supply and demand into equilibrium?

4. Explain why economists usually oppose controls on prices.

5. Suppose the government removes a tax on buyers of a good and levies a tax of the same size on sellers of

the good. How does this change in tax policy affect the price that buyers pay sellers for this good, the amount buyers are out of pocket (including any tax payments they make), the amount sellers receive (net of any tax payments they make), and the quantity of the good sold?

6. How does a tax on a good affect the price paid by buyers, the price received by sellers, and the quantity sold?

7. What determines how the burden of a tax is divided between buyers and sellers? Why?

QUICK CHECK **multiple choice**

1. When the government imposes a binding price floor, it causes which of the following to occur?
   a. the supply curve to shift to the left
   b. the demand curve to shift to the right
   c. a shortage of the good to develop
   d. a surplus of the good to develop

2. In a market with a binding price ceiling, an increase in the ceiling will _____ the quantity supplied, _____ the quantity demanded, and reduce the _____.
   a. increase, decrease, surplus
   b. decrease, increase, surplus
   c. increase, decrease, shortage
   d. decrease, increase, shortage

3. A $1 per unit tax levied on consumers of a good is equivalent to which of the following?
   a. a $1 per unit tax levied on producers of the good
   b. a $1 per unit subsidy paid to producers of the good
   c. a price floor that raises the good's price by $1 per unit
   d. a price ceiling that raises the good's price by $1 per unit

4. Which of the following would increase quantity supplied, decrease quantity demanded, and increase the price that consumers pay?
   a. the imposition of a binding price floor
   b. the removal of a binding price floor
   c. the passage of a tax levied on producers
   d. the repeal of a tax levied on producers

5. Which of the following would increase quantity supplied, increase quantity demanded, and decrease the price that consumers pay?
   a. the imposition of a binding price floor
   b. the removal of a binding price floor
   c. the passage of a tax levied on producers
   d. the repeal of a tax levied on producers

6. When a good is taxed, in which scenario does the burden of the tax fall mainly on consumers?
   a. when the tax is levied on consumers
   b. when the tax is levied on producers
   c. when supply is inelastic and demand is elastic
   d. when supply is elastic and demand is inelastic

PROBLEMS AND **applications**

1. Lovers of classical music persuade Parliament to impose a price ceiling of $40 per concert ticket. As a result of this policy, do more or fewer people attend classical music concerts? Explain.

2. The government has decided that the free-market price of cheese is too low.
   a. Suppose the government imposes a binding price floor in the cheese market. Use a supply-and-demand diagram to show the effect of this policy on the price of cheese and the quantity of cheese sold. Is there a shortage or surplus of cheese?
   b. Farmers complain that the price floor has reduced their total revenue. Is this possible? Explain.
   c. In response to farmers' complaints, the government agrees to purchase all of the surplus cheese at the price floor. Compared to the basic price floor, who benefits from this new policy? Who loses?

3. A recent study found that the demand and supply schedules for Frisbees are as follows:

Price per Frisbee	Quantity Demanded	Quantity Supplied
$11	1 million	15 million
10	2	12
9	4	9
8	6	6
7	8	3
6	10	1

a. What are the equilibrium price and quantity of Frisbees?
b. Frisbee manufacturers persuade the government that Frisbee production improves scientists' understanding of aerodynamics and thus is important for national security. A concerned Parliament votes to impose a price floor $2 above the equilibrium price. What is the new market price? How many Frisbees are sold?
c. Irate students march on Ottawa and demand a reduction in the price of Frisbees. An even more concerned Parliament votes to repeal the price floor and impose a price ceiling $1 below the former price floor. What is the new market price? How many Frisbees are sold?

4. Suppose the provincial government requires beer drinkers to pay a $2 tax on each case of beer purchased.
   a. Draw a supply-and-demand diagram of the market for beer without the tax. Show the price paid by consumers, the price received by producers, and the quantity of beer sold. What is the difference between the price paid by consumers and the price received by producers?
   b. Now draw a supply-and-demand diagram for the beer market with the tax. Show the price paid by consumers, the price received by producers, and the quantity of beer sold. What is the difference between the price paid by consumers and the price received by producers? Has the quantity of beer sold increased or decreased?

5. An MP wants to raise tax revenue and make workers better off. A staff member proposes raising the payroll tax paid by firms and using part of the extra revenue to reduce the payroll tax paid by workers. Would this accomplish the MP's goal?

6. If the government places a $500 tax on luxury cars, will the price paid by consumers rise by more than $500, less than $500, or exactly $500? Explain.

7. Parliament decides that Canada should reduce air pollution by reducing its use of gasoline. It imposes a $0.50 tax for each litre of gasoline sold.
   a. Should it impose this tax on producers or consumers? Explain carefully, using a supply-and-demand diagram.
   b. If the demand for gasoline were more elastic, would this tax be more effective or less effective in reducing the quantity of gasoline consumed? Explain with both words and a diagram.
   c. Are consumers of gasoline helped or hurt by this tax? Why?
   d. Are workers in the oil industry helped or hurt by this tax? Why?

8. A case study in this chapter discusses the minimum-wage law.
   a. Suppose the minimum wage is above the equilibrium wage in the market for unskilled labour. Using a supply-and-demand diagram of the market for unskilled labour, show the market wage, the number of workers who are employed, and the number of workers who are unemployed. Also show the total wage payments to unskilled workers.
   b. Now suppose the provincial government proposes an increase in the minimum wage. What effect would this increase have on employment? Does the change in employment depend on the elasticity of demand, the elasticity of supply, both elasticities, or neither?
   c. What effect would this increase in the minimum wage have on unemployment? Does the change in unemployment depend on the elasticity of demand, the elasticity of supply, both elasticities, or neither?
   d. If the demand for unskilled labour were inelastic, would the proposed increase in the minimum

wage raise or lower total wage payments to unskilled workers? Would your answer change if the demand for unskilled labour were elastic?

9. The Canadian government administers two programs that affect the market for cigarettes. Health Canada media campaigns and labelling requirements are aimed at making the public aware of the dangers of cigarette smoking. At the same time, Agriculture and Agri-Food Canada imposes production quotas on tobacco farmers, which raise the price of tobacco above the equilibrium price.
   a. How do these two programs affect cigarette consumption? Use a graph of the cigarette market in your answer.
   b. What is the combined effect of these two programs on the price of cigarettes?
   c. Cigarettes are also heavily taxed. What effect does this tax have on cigarette consumption?

10. A subsidy is the opposite of a tax. With a $0.50 tax on the buyers of ice-cream cones, the government collects $0.50 for each cone purchased; with a $0.50 subsidy for the buyers of ice-cream cones, the government pays buyers $0.50 for each cone purchased.
    a. Show the effect of a $0.50 per cone subsidy on the demand curve for ice-cream cones, the effective price paid by consumers, the effective price received by sellers, and the quantity of cones sold.
    b. Do consumers gain or lose from this policy? Do producers gain or lose? Does the government gain or lose?

11. At the Scotiabank Arena, home of the Raptors and the Maple Leafs, seating is limited to about 19 000. Hence, the number of tickets issued is fixed at that figure. (Assume that all seats are equally desirable and are sold at the same price.) Seeing a golden opportunity to raise revenue, the City of Toronto levies a per-ticket tax of $5 to be paid by the ticket buyer. Toronto sports fans, a famously civic-minded lot, dutifully send in the $5 per ticket. Draw a well-labelled graph showing the impact of the tax. On whom does the tax burden fall—each team's owners, the fans, or both? Why?

The Mathematics of Market Equilibrium with Taxes

In the appendix to Chapter 4, we showed you how to solve algebraically for the equilibrium price in a competitive market characterized by linear demand and supply curves. We saw in this chapter that when a tax is imposed on a good, there are, in effect, two types of prices in equilibrium because the tax places a wedge between the price that buyers pay and the price that sellers receive. In this appendix, we show you how to adapt the approach explained in the appendix to Chapter 4 to account for taxes.

We again proceed by way of an example. Recall from the linear demand and supply curves from the appendix to Chapter 4:

$$Q^D = 56 - 4P$$
$$Q^S = -4 + 2P$$

Now consider a tax imposed on the sale of the good. Say the tax is equal to T per unit of the good purchased. The tax drives a wedge between the price paid by consumers and the price received by sellers, that wedge being equal to the tax paid to the government. It is therefore useful to distinguish between the price paid by the buyers of the good, denoted P_B, and the price received by the sellers, denoted P_S. Rewriting the demand and supply curves using this notation gives:

$$Q^D = 56 - 4P_B$$
$$Q^S = -4 + 2P_S$$

as the price paid by buyers determines demand and the price received by sellers determines supply. Now assume that the tax is levied on the demand side of the market, and paid by the buyers. This means that $P_B = P_S + T$, and we see that the tax T drives a wedge between the price paid by consumers (P_B) and the price received by sellers (P_S). Substituting this into the equation for the demand curve gives:

$$Q^D = 56 - 4(P_S + T)$$

Rewrite this as $Q^D = (56 - 4T) - 4P_S$, and for concreteness assume that the tax is $T = \$1.50$ per unit, which gives $Q^D = (56 - 6) - 4P_S = 50 - 4P_S$. We can see that the tax acts just like a downward shift in the demand curve, as the x-intercept is now 50 (rather than 56) and the y-intercept is 12.5 (rather than 14).

We can then proceed exactly as in the appendix to Chapter 4 and set the quantity demanded equal to quantity supplied to determine the equilibrium prices in the presence of the tax:

$$50 - 4P_S = -4 + 2P_S$$

Using simple algebra to gather terms, with P_S on the left-hand side and the other terms on the right-hand side:

$$2P_S + 4P_S = 50 + 4$$
$$6P_S = 54$$
$$P_S = 9$$

which is the equilibrium price received by the sellers in the presence of the $1.50 tax levied on the buyers. We thus see that the price received by sellers in the presence of the tax, $9, is $1 lower than the price without the tax determined in the appendix to Chapter 4, $10. So we see that, despite the fact that the tax is levied on the buyers of the good, the sellers share in the burden of the tax by receiving a lower price.

To determine the price paid by buyers, inclusive of the tax, we note that it is simply the price received by sellers plus the tax, or $P_B = P_S + T = \$9 + \$1.50 = \$10.50$, and we see that the tax increases the price paid by buyers by $0.50. Buyers also share in the burden of the tax by having to pay a higher price. This is all illustrated in Figure 6A.1.

Substituting the price paid by buyers, P_B, into the demand curve gives the equilibrium quantity demanded in the presence of the tax: $Q^D = 56 - 4P_B = 56 - 4(10.50) = 14$. Alternatively, the equilibrium quantity supplied is given by substituting the price received by sellers, P_S, into the supply curve: $Q^S = -4 + 2P_S = -4 + 2(9) = -4 + 18 = 14$. Of course, they are equal in equilibrium. The tax therefore shrinks the size of the market by 2 units, from 16 to 14.

Notice in this example that the imposition of a tax of $1.50 per unit causes the price received by the sellers to decrease by $1 and the price paid by the buyers to increase by $0.50. Thus, the share of the $1.50 tax borne by buyers is 1/3 and the share borne by sellers is 2/3. In this example, the sellers bear a larger share of the burden of the tax than the buyers. As discussed previously in this chapter, the burden of a tax falls more heavily on the side of the market that is less elastic. In this case, the supply side of the market is less elastic than the demand side, and therefore bears more of the burden. This can be seen by comparing the absolute

---

FIGURE 6A.1

Market Equilibrium with Linear Demand and Supply Curves and a Tax on Buyers

This figure illustrates the market equilibrium for linear demand and supply curves given by the equations $Q^D = 56 - 4P$ and $Q^S = 4 + 2P$. In the absence of the tax, the equilibrium price is determined by setting $Q^D = Q^S$ and solving for $P = \$10$. When a tax of $1.50 per unit is imposed on buyers of the good, a wedge is driven between the price paid by buyers (P_B) and the price paid by sellers (P_S), $P_B = P_S + \$1.50$. The demand curve becomes $Q^D = 50 - 4P_S$. Again setting $Q^D = Q^S$ and solving for $P_S = \$9$ gives the seller's price of the good. The "buyer's price" is $P_B = P_S + \$1.50 = \$9 + \$1.50 = \$10.50$, and the equilibrium quantity drops from 16 to 14.

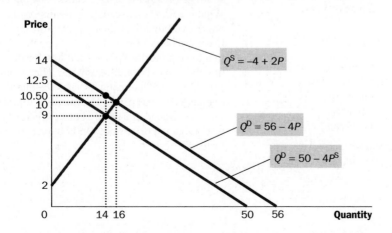

value of the slopes of the demand and supply curves. As shown in the appendix to Chapter 4, the absolute value of the slope of the demand curve in this example is 1/4, while the slope of the supply curve is 1/2. The demand curve is flatter—more elastic—than the supply curve, and therefore the demand side bears less of the burden of the tax.

So far we have assumed that the tax is imposed on the buyers of the good. If the tax were imposed on the sellers, the demand and supply curves would look like this:

$$Q^D = 56 - 4P_B$$
$$Q^S = -4 + 2(P_B - T)$$

where we have used the fact that if the tax is paid by the sellers then $P_S = P_B - T$ is now the effective price received by sellers. Proceeding exactly as above with a tax of $T = \$1.50$, we find that the price paid by buyers (\$10.50) and the price received by sellers (\$9) are exactly the same as when the tax is imposed on the buyers, which confirms that taxes on buyers and taxes on sellers are equivalent in terms of their economic impact.

PROBLEMS AND **applications**

A1. The demand and supply functions for hockey sticks are given by

$$Q^D = 286 - 20P$$
$$Q^S = 88 + 40P$$

In order to raise revenue to finance minor hockey so that Canada can continue its gold medal streak at the Olympics, the federal government decides to impose a tax of \$2 per hockey stick sold, to be paid by the buyers of hockey sticks.
  a. Determine the equilibrium price and quantity of hockey sticks both before and after the tax. How is the burden of the tax shared between buyers and sellers?
  b. How many hockey sticks would be sold before the tax is imposed? After the tax?
  c. Graph the supply and the demand curves for hockey sticks both before and after the tax, clearly showing the intercepts and equilibrium outcomes.
  d. What would happen if the tax were paid by the sellers of hockey sticks instead of the buyers?

A2. Say the demand schedule for ice-cream cones can be represented by the equation $Q^D = 160 - 3P$, where

Q^D is the quantity demanded and P is the price. The supply schedule can be represented by $Q^S = 140 + 7P$, where Q^S is the quantity supplied.
  a. Calculate the equilibrium price and quantity in the market for ice-cream cones.
  b. Say the Canadian Association of Ice-Cream Eaters complains that the equilibrium price calculated in part (a) is too high, and their members cannot eat enough ice-cream cones at this price. They lobby the government to impose a price ceiling on ice-cream cones of \$1. What is the quantity demanded at this price? The quantity supplied? Is there a shortage or surplus of ice cream? How big is it? What if a \$2.50 price ceiling were imposed instead?
  c. Say instead that the Canadian Organization of Ice-Cream Makers lobbies the government, arguing that the equilibrium price is too low for their members to make a decent living. They want a price floor of \$3 per cone. What is the quantity demanded at this price? The quantity supplied? Is there a shortage or a surplus of ice cream? What is it? What if a price floor of \$1.50 were imposed instead?

CHAPTER

7

LEARNING
objectives

Consumers, Producers, and the Efficiency of Markets

In this chapter, you will ...

1   Examine the link between buyers' willingness to pay for a good and the demand curve

2   Learn how to define and measure consumer surplus

3   Examine the link between sellers' cost of producing a good and the supply curve

4   Learn how to define and measure producer surplus

5   See that the equilibrium of supply and demand maximizes total surplus in a market

When consumers go to grocery stores to buy their turkeys for a holiday dinner, they may be disappointed that the price of turkey is as high as it is. At the same time, when farmers bring to market the turkeys they have raised, they wish the price of turkey was even higher. These views are not surprising: Buyers always want to pay less, and sellers always want to be paid more. But is there a "right price" for turkey from the standpoint of society as a whole?

In previous chapters we saw how, in market economies, the forces of supply and demand determine the prices of goods and services and the quantities sold. So far, however, we have described the way markets allocate scarce resources without directly addressing the question of whether these market allocations are desirable. In other words, our analysis has been *positive* (what is) rather than *normative* (what should be). We know that the price of turkey adjusts to ensure that the quantity of turkey supplied equals the quantity of turkey demanded. But, at this equilibrium, is the quantity of turkey produced and consumed too small, too large, or just right?

welfare economics

the study of how the allocation of resources affects economic well-being

In this chapter, we take up the topic of **welfare economics**, the study of how the allocation of resources affects economic well-being. We begin by examining the benefits that buyers and sellers receive from engaging in market transactions in any perfectly competitive market. We then examine how society can make these benefits as large as possible. This analysis leads to a profound conclusion: In any market, the equilibrium of supply and demand maximizes the total benefits received by buyers and sellers combined.

As you may recall from Chapter 1, one of the ten principles of economics is that markets are usually a good way to organize economic activity. The study of welfare economics explains this principle more fully. It also answers our question about the right price of turkey: The price that balances the supply and demand for turkey is, in a particular sense, the best one because it maximizes the total welfare of turkey consumers and turkey producers. No consumer or producer of turkeys aims to achieve this goal, but their joint action directed by market prices moves them toward a welfare-maximizing outcome, as if led by an invisible hand.

7-1 Consumer Surplus

We begin our study of welfare economics by looking at the benefits buyers receive from participating in a market.

7-1a Willingness to Pay

Imagine that you own a mint-condition recording of Elvis Presley's first album. Because you are not an Elvis Presley fan, you decide to sell it. One way to do so is to hold an auction.

Four Elvis fans show up for your auction: Taylor, Carrie, Rihanna, and Gaga. They would all like to own the album, but each of them has a limit on the amount she is willing to pay for it. Table 7.1 shows the maximum price that each of the four possible buyers would pay. Each buyer's maximum is called her **willingness to pay**, and it measures how much that buyer values the good. This limit may come from differences in tastes and preferences, as well as income. Each buyer would be eager to buy the album at a price less than her willingness to pay, and she would refuse to buy the album at a price more than her willingness to pay. At a price equal to her willingness to pay, the buyer would be indifferent about buying the good: If the price is exactly the same as the value she places on the album, she would be equally happy buying it or keeping her money.

willingness to pay

the maximum amount that a buyer will pay for a good

TABLE 7.1

Four Possible Buyers' Willingness to Pay

Buyer	Willingness to Pay
Taylor	$100
Carrie	80
Rihanna	70
Gaga	50

To sell your album, you begin the bidding process at a low price, say $10. Because all four buyers are willing to pay much more, the price rises quickly. The bidding stops when Taylor bids $80 (or slightly more). At this point, Carrie, Rihanna, and Gaga have all dropped out of the bidding because they are unwilling to bid any more than $80. Taylor pays you $80 and gets the album. Note that the album has gone to the buyer who values the album most highly.

What benefit does Taylor receive from buying the Elvis Presley album? In a sense, Taylor has found a real bargain: She is willing to pay $100 for the album but pays only $80 for it. We say that Taylor receives *consumer surplus* of $20. **Consumer surplus** is the amount a buyer is willing to pay for a good minus the amount the buyer actually pays for it.

Consumer surplus measures the benefit buyers receive from participating in a market. In this example, Taylor receives a $20 benefit from participating in the auction because she pays only $80 for a good she values at $100. Carrie, Rihanna, and Gaga get no consumer surplus from participating in the auction because they left without the album and without paying anything.

Now consider a somewhat different example. Suppose that you had two identical Elvis Presley albums to sell. Again, you auction them off to the four possible buyers. To keep things simple, we assume that both albums are to be sold for the same price and that no buyer is interested in buying more than one album. Therefore, the price rises until two buyers are left.

In this case, the bidding stops when Taylor and Carrie bid $70 (or slightly higher). At this price, Taylor and Carrie are each happy to buy an album, and Rihanna and Gaga are not willing to bid any higher. Taylor and Carrie each receive consumer surplus equal to her willingness to pay minus the price. Taylor's consumer surplus is $30, and Carrie's is $10. Taylor's consumer surplus is higher now than in the previous examples because she gets the same album but pays less for it. The total consumer surplus in the market is $40.

7-1b Using the Demand Curve to Measure Consumer Surplus

Consumer surplus is closely related to the demand curve for a product. To see how they are related, let's continue our example and consider the demand curve for this rare Elvis Presley album.

We begin by using the willingness to pay of the four possible buyers to find the demand schedule for the album. The table in Figure 7.1 shows the demand schedule that corresponds to Table 7.1. If the price is above $100, the quantity demanded in the market is 0 because no buyer is willing to pay that much. If the price is between $80 and $100, the quantity demanded is 1 because only Taylor is willing to pay such a high price. If the price is between $70 and $80, the quantity

consumer surplus
a buyer's willingness to pay minus the amount the buyer actually pays

FIGURE 7.1

The Demand Schedule and the Demand Curve

The table shows the demand schedule for the buyers in Table 7.1. The graph shows the corresponding demand curve. Note that the height of the demand curve reflects buyers' willingness to pay.

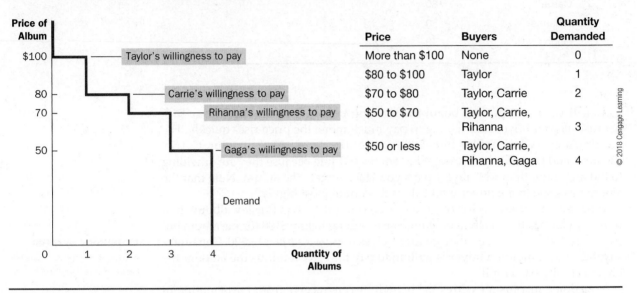

Price	Buyers	Quantity Demanded
More than $100	None	0
$80 to $100	Taylor	1
$70 to $80	Taylor, Carrie	2
$50 to $70	Taylor, Carrie, Rihanna	3
$50 or less	Taylor, Carrie, Rihanna, Gaga	4

© 2018 Cengage Learning

demanded is 2 because both Taylor and Carrie are willing to pay the price. We can continue this analysis for other prices as well. In this way, the demand schedule is derived from the willingness to pay of the four possible buyers.

The graph in Figure 7.1 shows the demand curve that corresponds to this demand schedule. Note the relationship between the height of the demand curve and the buyers' willingness to pay. At any quantity, the price given by the demand curve shows the willingness to pay of the *marginal buyer,* the buyer who would leave the market first if the price was any higher. At a quantity of 4 albums, for instance, the demand curve has a height of $50, the price that Gaga (the marginal buyer) is willing to pay for an album. At a quantity of 3 albums, the demand curve has a height of $70, the price that Gaga (who is now the marginal buyer) is willing to pay. As such, we can actually think of the demand curve as a *marginal willingness to pay curve,* representing the willingness to pay of the marginal buyer at each quantity.

Because the demand curve reflects buyers' willingness to pay, we can also use it to measure consumer surplus. Figure 7.2 uses the demand curve to compute consumer surplus in our two examples. In panel (a), the price is $80 (or slightly above), and the quantity demanded is 1. Note that the area above the price and below the demand curve equals $20. This amount is exactly the consumer surplus we computed earlier when only 1 album is sold.

Panel (b) of Figure 7.2 shows consumer surplus when the price is $70 (or slightly above). In this case, the area above the price and below the demand curve equals the total area of the two rectangles: Taylor's consumer surplus at this price is $30 and Carrie's is $10. This area equals a total of $40. Once again, this amount is the consumer surplus we computed earlier.

FIGURE 7.2

**Measuring Consumer
Surplus with the
Demand Curve**

In panel (a), the price of the good is $80, and the consumer surplus is $20. In panel (b), the
price of the good is $70, and the consumer surplus is $40.

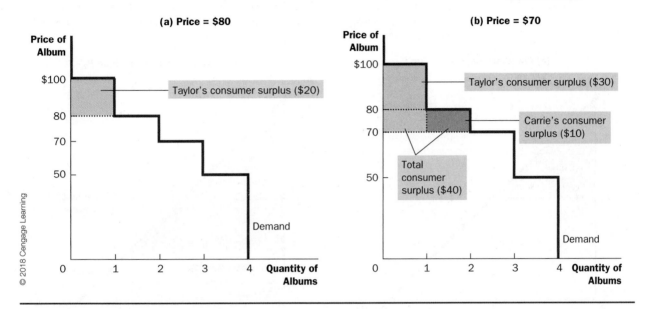

(a) Price = $80

(b) Price = $70

The lesson from this example holds for all demand curves: *The area below the
demand curve and above the price measures the consumer surplus in a market.* The
reason is that the height of the demand curve measures the value buyers place on
the good, as measured by their willingness to pay for it. The difference between
this willingness to pay and the market price is each buyer's consumer surplus.
Thus, the total area below the demand curve and above the price is the sum of the
consumer surplus of all buyers in the market for a good or service.

7-1c How a Lower Price Raises Consumer Surplus

Because buyers always want to pay less for the goods they buy, a lower price
makes buyers of a good better off. But how much does buyers' well-being rise in
response to a lower price? We can use the concept of consumer surplus to answer
this question precisely.

Figure 7.3 shows a typical demand curve. You may notice that this curve gradually slopes downward instead of taking discrete steps as in the previous two figures. In a market with many buyers, the resulting steps from each buyer dropping
out are so small that they form, in essence, a smooth curve. Although this curve
has a different shape, the ideas we have just developed still apply: Consumer surplus is the area above the price and below the demand curve. In panel (a), consumer surplus at a price of P_1 is the area of triangle ABC.

Now suppose that the price falls from P_1 to P_2, as shown in panel (b). The consumer surplus now equals area ADF. The increase in consumer surplus attributable to the lower price is the area BCFD.

This increase in consumer surplus is composed of two parts. First, those
buyers who were already buying Q_1 of the good at the higher price P_1 are better

FIGURE 7.3

How the Price Affects Consumer Surplus

In panel (a), the price is P_1, the quantity demanded is Q_1, and consumer surplus equals the area of the triangle ABC. When the price falls from P_1 to P_2, as in panel (b), the quantity demanded rises from Q_1 to Q_2, and the consumer surplus rises to the area of the triangle ADF. The increase in consumer surplus (area BCFD) occurs in part because existing consumers now pay less (area BCED) and in part because new consumers enter the market at the lower price (area CEF).

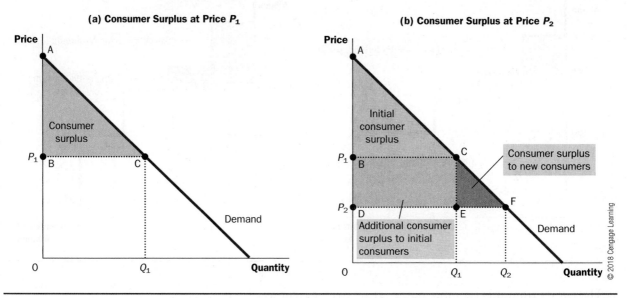

(a) Consumer Surplus at Price P_1 (b) Consumer Surplus at Price P_2

off because now they pay less. The increase in consumer surplus of existing buyers is the reduction in the amount they pay; it equals the area of the rectangle BCED. Second, some new buyers enter the market because they are willing to buy the good at the lower price. As a result, the quantity demanded in the market increases from Q_1 to Q_2. The consumer surplus these newcomers receive is the area of the triangle CEF.

7-1d What Does Consumer Surplus Measure?

Our goal in developing the concept of consumer surplus is to make judgments about the desirability of market outcomes. Now that you have seen what consumer surplus is, let's consider whether it is a good measure of economic well-being.

Imagine that you are a policymaker trying to design a good economic system. Would you care about the amount of consumer surplus? Consumer surplus, the amount that buyers are willing to pay for a good minus the amount they actually pay for it, measures the benefit that buyers receive from a good *as the buyers themselves perceive it.* Thus, consumer surplus is a good measure of economic well-being if policymakers want to satisfy the preferences of buyers.

In some circumstances, policymakers might choose to disregard consumer surplus because they do not respect the preferences that drive buyer behaviour. For example, drug addicts are willing to pay a high price for heroin. Yet we would not say that addicts get a large benefit from being able to buy heroin at a low price (even though addicts might say they do). From the standpoint of society, willingness to pay in this instance is not a good measure of the buyers' benefit, and consumer surplus is not a good measure of economic well-being, because addicts are not looking after their own best interests.

In most markets, however, consumer surplus does reflect economic well-being. Economists normally assume that buyers are rational when they make decisions. Rational people do the best they can to achieve their objectives, given their opportunities. Economists also normally assume that people's preferences should be respected. In this case, consumers are the best judges of how much benefit they receive from the goods they buy.

 Draw a demand curve for turkey. In your diagram, show a price of turkey and the consumer surplus that results from that price. Explain in words what this consumer surplus measures.

7-2 Producer Surplus

We now turn to the other side of the market and consider the benefits sellers receive from participating in a market. As you will see, our analysis of sellers' welfare is similar to our analysis of buyers' welfare.

7-2a Cost and the Willingness to Sell

Imagine now that you are a homeowner and you want to get your house painted. You turn to four sellers of painting services: Vincent, Claude, Pablo, and Andy. Each painter is willing to do the work for you if the price is right. You decide to take bids from the four painters and auction off the job to the painter who will do the work for the lowest price.

Each painter is willing to take the job if the price he would receive exceeds his cost of doing the work. Here the term **cost** should be interpreted as the painters' opportunity cost: It includes the painters' out-of-pocket expenses (for paint, brushes, and so on) as well as the value that the painters place on their own time. Table 7.2 shows each painter's cost. Because a painter's cost is the lowest price he would accept for his work, cost is a measure of his willingness to sell his services. Each painter would be eager to sell his services at a price greater than his cost and would refuse to sell his services at a price less than his cost. At a price exactly equal to his cost, he would be indifferent about selling his services: He would be equally happy getting the job or using his time, energy, supplies, etc. for another purpose.

When you take bids from the painters, the price might start off high, but it quickly falls as the painters compete for the job. Once Andy has bid $600

cost
the value of everything a seller must give up to produce a good

TABLE 7.2

The Costs of Four Possible Sellers

Seller	Cost
Vincent	$900
Claude	800
Pablo	600
Andy	500

(or slightly less), he is the sole remaining bidder. Andy is happy to do the job for this price because his cost is only $500. Vincent, Claude, and Pablo are unwilling to do the job for less than $600. Note that the job goes to the painter who can do the work at the lowest cost.

What benefit does Andy receive from getting the job? Because he is willing to do the work for $500 but gets $600 for doing it, we say that he receives *producer surplus* of $100. **Producer surplus** is the amount a seller is paid minus the cost of production. Producer surplus measures the benefit to sellers of participating in a market.

Now consider a somewhat different example. Suppose that you have two houses that need painting. Again, you auction off the jobs to the four painters. To keep things simple, let's assume that no painter is able to paint both houses, that all paint jobs are of the same quality, and that you will pay the same amount to paint each house. Therefore, the price falls until two painters are left.

In this case, the bidding stops when Andy and Pablo each offer to do the job for a price of $800 (or slightly less). Andy and Pablo are willing to do the work at this price, while Vincent and Claude are not willing to bid a lower price. At a price of $800, Andy receives producer surplus of $300 and Pablo receives producer surplus of $200. The total producer surplus in the market is $500.

producer surplus

the amount a seller is paid for a good minus the seller's cost

7-2b Using the Supply Curve to Measure Producer Surplus

Just as consumer surplus is closely related to the demand curve, producer surplus is closely related to the supply curve. To see how, let's continue our example.

We begin by using the costs of the four painters to find the supply schedule for painting services. The table in Figure 7.4 shows the supply schedule that corresponds to the costs in Table 7.2. If the price is below $500, none of the four painters is willing to do the job, so the quantity supplied is zero. If the price is between

FIGURE 7.4

The Supply Schedule and the Supply Curve

The table shows the supply schedule for the sellers in Table 7.2. The graph shows the corresponding supply curve. Note that the height of the supply curve reflects sellers' costs.

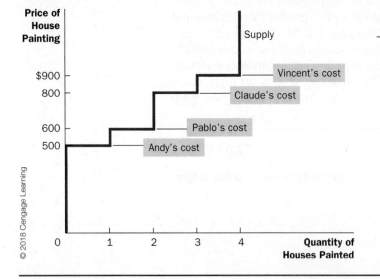

Price	Sellers	Quantity Supplied
$900 or more	Vincent, Claude, Pablo, Andy	4
$800 to $900	Claude, Pablo, Andy	3
$600 to $800	Pablo, Andy	2
$500 to $600	Andy	1
Less than $500	None	0

$500 and $600, only Andy is willing to do the job, so the quantity supplied is 1. If the price is between $600 and $800, Andy and Pablo are willing to do the job, so the quantity supplied is 2, and so on. Thus, the supply schedule is derived from the costs of the four painters.

The graph in Figure 7.4 shows the supply curve that corresponds to this supply schedule. Note that the height of the supply curve is related to the sellers' costs. At any quantity, the price given by the supply curve shows the cost of the *marginal seller*, the seller who would leave the market first if the price was any lower. At a quantity of 4 houses, for instance, the supply curve has a height of $900, the cost that Vincent (the marginal seller) incurs to provide his painting services. At a quantity of 3 houses, the supply curve has a height of $800, the cost that Claude (who is now the marginal seller) incurs. As such, we can actually think of the supply curve as a *marginal cost curve*, representing the cost of the marginal seller at each quantity.

Because the supply curve reflects sellers' costs, we can use it to measure producer surplus. Figure 7.5 uses the supply curve to compute producer surplus in our two examples. In panel (a), we assume that the price is $600 (or slightly less). In this case, the quantity supplied is 1. Note that the area below the price and above the supply curve equals $100. This amount is exactly the producer surplus we computed earlier for Andy.

Panel (b) of Figure 7.5 shows producer surplus at a price of $800 (or slightly less). In this case, the area below the price and above the supply curve equals the total area of the two rectangles. This area equals $500, the producer surplus we computed earlier for Pablo and Andy when two houses needed painting.

FIGURE 7.5

In panel (a), the price of the good is $600, and the producer surplus is $100. In panel (b), the price of the good is $800, and the producer surplus is $500.

Measuring Producer Surplus with the Supply Curve

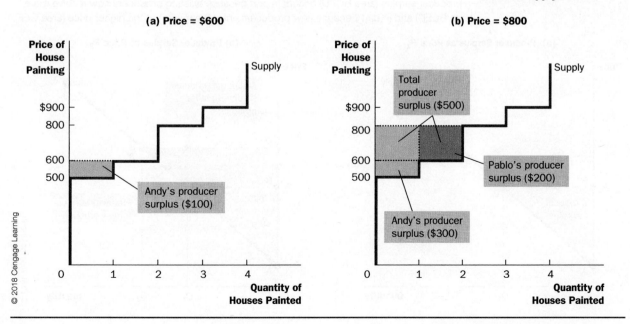

The lesson from this example applies to all supply curves: *The area below the price and above the supply curve measures the producer surplus in a market.* The logic is straightforward: The height of the supply curve measures sellers' costs, and the difference between the price and the cost of production is each seller's producer surplus. Thus, the total area is the sum of the producer surplus of all sellers.

7-2c How a Higher Price Raises Producer Surplus

You will not be surprised to hear that sellers always want to receive a higher price for the goods they sell. But how much does sellers' well-being rise in response to a higher price? The concept of producer surplus offers a precise answer to this question.

Figure 7.6 shows a typical upward-sloping supply curve that would arise in a market with many sellers. Although this supply curve differs in shape from the previous figure, we measure producer surplus in the same way: Producer surplus is the area below the price and above the supply curve. In panel (a), the price is P_1, and producer surplus is the area of triangle ABC.

Panel (b) shows what happens when the price rises from P_1 to P_2. Producer surplus now equals area ADF. This increase in producer surplus has two parts. First, those sellers who were already selling Q_1 of the good at the lower price P_1 are better off because they now get more for what they sell. The increase in producer surplus for existing sellers equals the area of the rectangle BCED. Second, some new sellers enter the market because they are willing to produce the good at the higher price, resulting in an increase in the quantity supplied from Q_1 to Q_2. The producer surplus of these newcomers is the area of the triangle CEF.

FIGURE 7.6

How the Price Affects Producer Surplus

In panel (a), the price is P_1, the quantity supplied is Q_1, and producer surplus equals the area of the triangle ABC. When the price rises from P_1 to P_2, as in panel (b), the quantity supplied rises from Q_1 to Q_2, and the producer surplus rises to the area of the triangle ADF. The increase in producer surplus (area BCFD) occurs in part because existing producers now receive more (area BCED) and in part because new producers enter the market at the higher price (area CEF).

(a) Producer Surplus at Price P_1

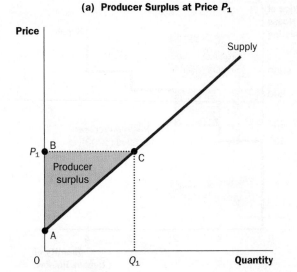

(b) Producer Surplus at Price P_2

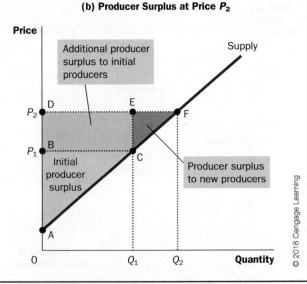

© 2018 Cengage Learning

As this analysis shows, we use producer surplus to measure the well-being of sellers in much the same way as we use consumer surplus to measure the well-being of buyers. Because these two measures of economic welfare are so similar, it is natural to use them together. And, indeed, that is exactly what we do in the next section.

 QUICK Quiz *Draw a supply curve for turkey. In your diagram, show a price of turkey and the producer surplus that results from that price. Explain in words what this producer surplus measures.*

7-3 Market Efficiency

Consumer surplus and producer surplus are the basic tools that economists use to study the welfare of buyers and sellers in a market. These tools can help us address a fundamental economic question: Is the allocation of resources determined by free markets in any way desirable?

7-3a The Benevolent Social Planner

To evaluate market outcomes, we introduce into our analysis a new, hypothetical character called the *benevolent social planner.* The benevolent social planner is an all-knowing, all-powerful, well-intentioned dictator. This planner wants to maximize the economic well-being of everyone in society. What should this planner do? Should she just leave buyers and sellers at the equilibrium that they reach naturally on their own? Or can she increase economic well-being by altering the market outcome in some way?

To answer this question, the planner must first decide how to measure the economic well-being of a society. One possible measure is the sum of consumer and producer surplus, which we call *total surplus.* Consumer surplus is the benefit that buyers receive from participating in a market, and producer surplus is the benefit that sellers receive. It is, therefore, natural to use total surplus as a measure of society's economic well-being.

To better understand this measure of economic well-being, recall how we measure consumer and producer surplus. We define consumer surplus as

$$\text{Consumer surplus} = \text{Value to buyers} - \text{Amount paid by buyers}$$

Similarly, we define producer surplus as

$$\text{Producer surplus} = \text{Amount received by sellers} - \text{Cost to sellers}$$

When we add consumer and producer surplus together, we obtain

$$\text{Total surplus} = (\text{Value to buyers} - \text{Amount paid by buyers})$$
$$+ (\text{Amount received by sellers} - \text{Cost to sellers})$$

The amount paid by buyers equals the amount received by sellers, so the middle two terms in this expression cancel each other. As a result, we can write total surplus as

$$\text{Total surplus} = \text{Value to buyers} - \text{Cost to sellers}$$

Total surplus in a market is the total value to buyers of the goods, as measured by their willingness to pay, minus the total cost to sellers of providing those goods.

efficiency

the property of a resource allocation of maximizing the total surplus received by all members of society

equity

the fairness of the distribution of well-being among the members of society

If an allocation of resources maximizes total surplus, we say that the allocation exhibits **efficiency**. If an allocation is not efficient, then some of the potential gains from trade among buyers and sellers are not being realized. For example, an allocation is inefficient if a good is not being produced by the sellers with lowest cost. In this case, moving production from a high-cost producer to a low-cost producer will lower the total cost to sellers and raise total surplus. Similarly, an allocation is inefficient if a good is not being consumed by the buyers who value it most highly. In this case, moving consumption of the good from a buyer with a low valuation to a buyer with a high valuation will raise total surplus.

In addition to efficiency, the social planner might also care about **equity**—the fairness of the distribution of well-being among the various buyers and sellers. In essence, the gains from trade in a market are like a pie to be distributed among the market participants. The question of efficiency is whether the pie is as big as possible. The question of equality concerns how the pie is sliced and how the portions are distributed among members of society. In this chapter we concentrate on efficiency as the social planner's goal. Keep in mind, however, that policymakers often care about equity as well. That is, they care about both the size of the economic pie and how the pie gets sliced and distributed among members of society. This will be discussed in more detail at various points in the book.

7-3b Evaluating the Market Equilibrium

Figure 7.7 shows consumer and producer surplus when a market reaches the equilibrium of supply and demand. Recall that consumer surplus equals the area above the price and under the demand curve, and producer surplus equals the area below the price and above the supply curve. Thus, the total area between the supply and demand curves up to the point of equilibrium represents the total surplus in this market.

FIGURE 7.7

Consumer and Producer Surplus in the Market Equilibrium

Total surplus—the sum of consumer and producer surplus—is the area between the supply and demand curves up to the equilibrium quantity.

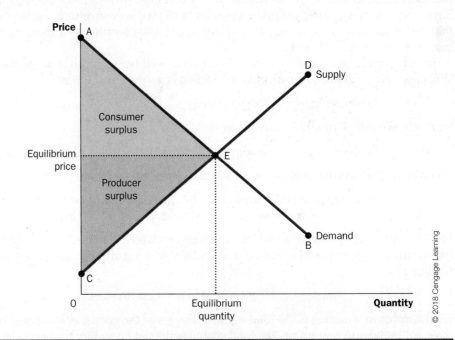

Is this equilibrium allocation of resources efficient? That is, does it maximize total surplus? To answer these questions, recall that when a market is in equilibrium, the price determines which buyers and sellers participate in the market. Those buyers who value the good more than the price (represented by the segment AE on the demand curve) choose to buy the good; those buyers who value it less than the price (represented by the segment EB) do not. Similarly, those sellers whose costs are less than the price (represented by the segment CE on the supply curve) choose to produce and sell the good; sellers whose costs are greater than the price (represented by the segment ED) do not.

These observations lead to two insights about market outcomes:

1. Free markets allocate the supply of goods to the buyers who value them most highly, as measured by their willingness to pay.
2. Free markets allocate the demand for goods to the sellers who can produce them at the lowest cost.

Thus, given the quantity produced and sold in a market equilibrium, the social planner cannot increase economic well-being by changing the allocation of consumption among buyers or the allocation of production among sellers.

But can the social planner raise total economic well-being by increasing or decreasing the quantity of the good? The answer is no, as stated in this third insight about market outcomes:

3. Free markets produce the quantity of goods that maximizes the sum of consumer and producer surplus.

Figure 7.8 illustrates why this is true. To interpret this figure, keep in mind that the demand curve reflects the value to buyers and the supply curve reflects

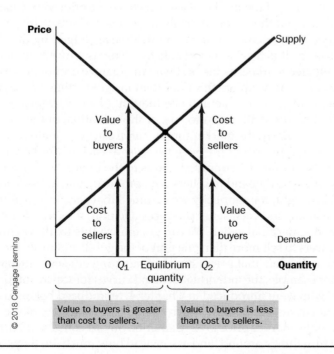

FIGURE 7.8

The Efficiency of the Equilibrium Quantity

At quantities less than the equilibrium quantity, such as Q_1, the value to buyers exceeds the cost to sellers. At quantities greater than the equilibrium quantity, such as Q_2, the cost to sellers exceeds the value to buyers. Therefore, the market equilibrium maximizes the sum of producer and consumer surplus.

the cost to sellers. At any quantity below the equilibrium level, such as Q_1, the value to the marginal buyer exceeds the cost to the marginal seller. As a result, increasing the quantity produced and consumed raises total surplus. This continues to be true until the quantity reaches the equilibrium level. Similarly, at any quantity beyond the equilibrium level, such as Q_2, the value to the marginal buyer is less than the cost to the marginal seller. In this case, decreasing the quantity raises total surplus, and this continues to be true until quantity falls to the equilibrium level. To maximize total surplus, the social planner would choose the quantity where the supply and demand curves intersect.

Together, these three insights tell us that the market outcome makes the sum of consumer and producer surplus as large as it can be. In other words, the equilibrium outcome is an efficient allocation of resources. The benevolent social planner can, therefore, leave the market outcome just as she finds it. This policy of leaving well enough alone goes by the French expression *laissez faire,* which literally translates to "leave to do" but is more broadly interpreted as "let people do as they will."

Society is lucky that the social planner doesn't need to intervene. Although it has been a useful exercise imagining what an all-knowing, all-powerful, well-intentioned dictator would do, let's face it: Such characters are hard to come by. Dictators are rarely benevolent, and even if we found someone so virtuous, she would lack crucial information.

Suppose our social planner tried to choose an efficient allocation of resources on her own, instead of relying on market forces. To do so, she would need to know the value of a particular good to every potential consumer in the market and the cost of every potential producer. And she would need this information not only for this market but for every one of the many thousands of markets in the economy. The task is practically impossible, which explains why centrally planned economies never work very well.

The planner's job becomes easy, however, once he takes on a partner: Adam Smith's invisible hand of the marketplace, which we introduced in Chapter 1. The invisible hand takes all the information about buyers and sellers into account and guides everyone in the market to the best outcome as judged by the standard of economic efficiency. It is truly a remarkable feat. That is why economists so often advocate largely free markets as the best way to organize economic activity.

We can generalize and explore this important insight further. We have seen that the market demand curve can actually be thought of as a *marginal willingness to pay curve*, reflecting the willingness to pay, or the valuation, of the *marginal buyer* at each quantity. Similarly, the market supply curve can be thought of as a *marginal cost curve*, reflecting the cost of the *marginal seller* at each quantity. We have seen that free markets allocate the supply of goods to the buyers who value them the most, and allocates the demand to sellers who produce them at the lowest cost. In developing this insight, for simplicity we assumed that each buyer purchases just one unit of the good, and each seller produces one unit; thus the notion of a marginal buyer and a marginal seller. We can generalize this to allow consumers to buy and producers to sell more than one unit of the good, and in so doing develop more insight into the role that prices play in generating efficient outcomes.

Consider, for example, the individual demand curves for ice-cream for Catherine and Nicholas, who were introduced in Chapter 4, reproduced below in Figure 7.9. These demand curves tell us how much each of them will consume at a given price. That is, if the market price is $2, Catherine buys 4 cones and Nicholas buys 3 cones. Now turn things around, and ask instead how much are they each willing

FIGURE 7.9

The quantity demanded in a market is the sum of the quantities demanded by all the buyers at each price. Thus, the market demand curve is found by adding horizontally the individual demand curves. At a price of $2, Catherine demands 4 ice-cream cones, and Nicholas demands 3 ice-cream cones, for a market demand of 7 cones. Equivalently, the marginal benefit of consuming the last of 4 cones by Catherine is equal to the marginal benefit of consuming the last of 3 cones by Nicholas, which is equal to the market price of $2. Catherine's consumer surplus is A, Nicholas's consumer surplus is B, and total consumer surplus is C = A + B.

Individual and Market Demand

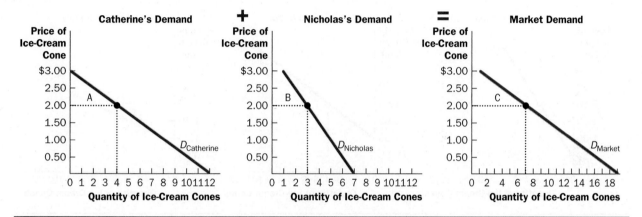

to pay for one more cone at any given quantity? Here we see that Catherine is willing to pay $2 for the last of 4 cones she consumes, while Nicholas is willing to pay $2 for the last of 3 cones that he consumes.

Now say that the market price of ice-cream is $2. As indicated, we see that at that price Catherine consumes 4 cones and Nicholas consumes 3 cones. Note that at the market price of $2, although Catherine and Nicholas consume different quantities of ice-cream cones, their *marginal willingness to pay* for the last cone that they consume—or, equivalently, the *marginal benefit* they receive from the last cone consumed—is exactly the same, and is equal to the market price of $2. Although they have different preferences for ice-cream cones, as reflected by their different demand curves, at the given market price Catherine and Nicholas receive exactly the same marginal benefit from the last ice-cream cone that they consume.

We showed in Chapter 4 that the market demand curve is the horizontal sum of all of the individual demand curves, which we show in the last panel of Figure 7.9. At the market price of $2 total demand in our illustration is 7 cones, 4 for Catherine and 3 for Nicholas. Catherine's consumer surplus is given by area A in the first panel, Nicholas's by area B in the second panel, and total consumer surplus in the market by area C = A + B in the third panel. Generalizing this to a market with perhaps thousands of consumers, we see that although all of these consumers may have different preferences, and therefore receive very different consumer surplus from buying ice-cream, the marginal benefit that they receive from the very last ice-cream cone that they consume is exactly the same for all consumers, and is equal to the market price.

Similarly, recall Ben and Jerry from Chapter 4, who supply ice-cream cones. Their individual supply curves for ice-cream cones are replicated in Figure 7.10.

FIGURE 7.10

Individual and Market Supply

The quantity supplied in a market is the sum of the quantities supplied by all the sellers at each price. Thus, the market supply curve is found by adding horizontally the individual supply curves. At a price of $2, Ben supplies 3 ice-cream cones, and Jerry supplies 4 ice-cream cones, for a market supply of 7 cones. Equivalently, the marginal cost of supplying the last of 3 cones by Ben is equal to the marginal cost of supplying the last of 4 cones by Jerry, which is equal to the market price of $2. Ben earns producer surplus of D, Jerry earns producer surplus of E, and total producer surplus is F = D + E.

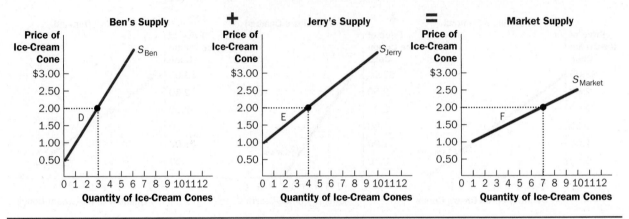

These supply curves tell us how much each of them will supply at a given price. So, if the market price is $2 Ben supplies 3 cones and Jerry supplies 4 cones. Now turn things around, and ask what is the minimum amount they must receive to produce one more cone at any given quantity. This amount will equal the *marginal cost* of producing one more cone. Here we see that the marginal cost of producing the last of 3 cones for Ben is $2, while the marginal cost of producing the last of 4 cones for Jerry is $2. Now say the market price of ice-cream cones is $2. As indicated above, we see that Ben supplies 3 cones and Jerry supplies 4 cones.

At the market price of $2, although Ben and Jerry supply different quantities of ice-cream cones, the marginal cost of the last cone that they produce is exactly the same, and is equal to the market price of $2. Although they may have different cost schedules, as reflected in their different supply curves, at the given market price Ben and Jerry incur exactly the same marginal cost on the last ice-cream cone that they supply.

We showed in Chapter 4 that the market supply curve is the horizontal sum of all of the individual supply curves, as shown in the last panel of Figure 7.10. At the market price of $2 total supply in our illustration is 7 cones, 3 for Ben and 4 for Jerry. Ben earns producer surplus given by area D in the first panel, Jerry by area E in the second panel, and total producer surplus in the market by area F = D + E in the third panel. Generalizing this to a market with perhaps thousands of producers, we see that although all of these producers may have different cost schedules, and earn very different producer surplus from selling ice cream, the marginal cost of producing the very last ice-cream cone that they sell is exactly the same for all producers, and is equal to the market price.

Bringing this all together we get a rather profound and remarkable insight. At the market equilibrium, given by the intersection of the market demand and supply curves, the marginal benefit received from the last ice-cream cone that they consume is exactly the same for all buyers, which is equal to the marginal cost of producing the last ice-cream cone that they produce for all sellers, both of which are equal to the market price. The market price thus plays a key coordinating role in drawing together, and equating, the marginal benefits of the buyers and the marginal costs of the sellers. Because the marginal benefits of all of the buyers in the market are the same at the market equilibrium, as are the marginal costs of all of the sellers, there is no way to reallocate demand and supply amongst them so as to increase total surplus. Similarly, because the marginal benefit of all of the buyers is equal to the marginal cost of all of the sellers, there is no way to change the overall size of the market and increase total surplus.

A useful way to remember this is that the equilibrium in our perfectly competitive market is described by the following relationships:

$$\text{Price} = \text{Marginal benefit to Catherine} = \text{Marginal benefit to Nicholas}$$

$$= \text{Marginal cost to Ben} = \text{Marginal cost to Jerry}$$

Which is precisely what is required for the outcome to be efficient, thereby maximizing total surplus. This is another way of seeing how competitive markets generate an efficient outcome which emphasizes the key role that market prices play in coordinating Adam Smith's invisible hand of the market place.

FYI   Adam Smith and the Invisible Hand

Why do decentralized market economies work so well? Is it because people can be counted on to treat one another with love and kindness? Not at all. Here is Adam Smith's description of how people interact in a market economy:

Man has almost constant occasion for the help of his brethren, and it is in vain for him to expect it from their benevolence only.

He will be more likely to prevail if he can interest their self-love in his favour, and show them that it is for their own advantage to do for him what he requires of them…. Give me that which I want, and you shall have this which you want, is the meaning of every such offer; and it is in this manner that we obtain from one another the far greater part of those good offices which we stand in need of.

Adam Smith

It is not from the benevolence of the butcher, the brewer, or the baker that we expect our dinner, but from their regard to their own interest. We address ourselves, not to their humanity but to their self-love, and never talk to them of our own necessities but of their advantages. Nobody but a beggar chooses to depend chiefly upon the benevolence of his fellow-citizens….

Every individual … neither intends to promote the public interest, nor knows how much he is promoting it…. He intends only his own gain, and he is in this, as in many other cases, led by an invisible hand to promote an end which was no part of his intention. Nor is it always the worse for the society that it was no part of it. By pursuing his own interest he frequently promotes that of the society more effectually than when he really intends to promote it.

Smith is saying that participants in the economy are motivated by self-interest and that the "invisible hand" of the marketplace guides this self-interest into promoting general economic well-being, operationalized and made more precise by the notion of total surplus.

case study **Uber's Surge Pricing Makes Economists Giddy—A Reprise**

We first touched upon Uber's surge pricing in Chapter 1, observing that Adam Smith himself would no doubt have the Uber app on his phone. With an understanding of demand and supply, market equilibrium, and consumer surplus in hand we can investigate the efficiency implications of Uber's surge pricing in more detail.

In the normal taxi market fares are regulated: they are the same at all times of the day regardless of demand. This means that when the demand for taxis surges—when bars close, when concerts or hockey games finish, or during snow or rain storms—there may be a shortage of taxis.

Consider, for example, Figure 7.11. Say the taxi market is originally in equilibrium at the regulated price, P_0. For some reason demand surges, perhaps due to a rain storm or a concert finishing at the Scotiabank Arena. The demand curve shifts out from D_0 to D_1. If the regulated price were allowed to adjust in response to this higher demand, prices would rise, more taxis would hit the streets, and a new equilibrium would be attained at a price of P^* and a quantity Q^*. However, because the regulated price does not change, there is a shortage of taxis—quantity supplied at the regulated price of P_0 stays at Q_0 and quantity demanded is higher at Q_1.

Enter Uber and surge pricing. A recent paper by Uber economists Jonathan Hall and Cory Kendrick and university economist Chris Nosko illustrates surge pricing in action using a sold-out March 2015 concert by pop superstar Ariana Grande at Madison Square Garden in New York City. Thousands of concertgoers seeking to get home at the end of the show opened up the Uber app, which caused Uber's surge pricing algorithm to kick in; Uber fares surged by up to 1.8 times the base fare in response to the increase in demand. This rise in price attracted more Uber drivers into the area, up to twice as many from the pre-surge baseline. The increase in Uber drivers matched supply with demand, and allowed riders who otherwise wouldn't get a ride (or who would have to wait a long time) to get one; 100 percent of the ride requests were fulfilled within 15 minutes.

FIGURE 7.11

Taxi Shortages in a Regulated Market

At the regulated fare the taxi market is in equilibrium at P_0 and Q_0. As the demand for taxis surges, the demand curve shifts from D_0 to D_1. If the price is allowed to adjust, supply equals demand at the new equilibrium P^* and Q^*. However, if the regulated fare does not change, and the price stays at P_0, quantity supplied is Q_0 and quantity demanded is Q_1; there is a shortage of taxis.

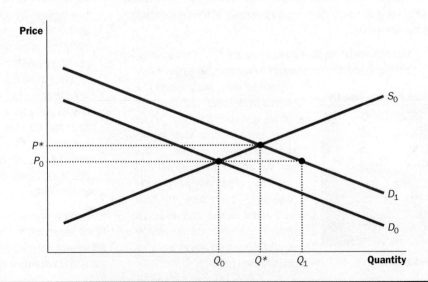

Moreover, and importantly, while the number of app openings increased significantly after the concert, the number of actual ride requests didn't increase by as much. This is because some riders who opened the app and saw that surge pricing was in effect decided not to request a ride—they weren't willing to pay the higher price. This means that surge pricing allocated Uber rides to individuals who valued them the most— those who had the highest willingness to pay. As we have discussed, from an economic efficiency standpoint this is a desirable outcome.

The authors consider another example, again in New York City. New Year's Eve is a particularly challenging time to get a taxi because the demand is very high and it's a time when many drivers do not like to work. On New Year's Eve 2014/15, Uber's surge pricing algorithm in New York City went down for 26 minutes just after midnight because of a technical glitch. Just prior to the outage, the surge multiplier had increased to 2.7 times the standard fare. During the 26-minute outage period, prices fell back to the standard rate—and as a result, the supply of drivers fell significantly. A handful of lucky riders took up all of the available Uber cars on the road, and got a great deal at one times the normal price. Many riders, however, did not get a ride at all, despite the fact that they were willing to pay more than the standard rate; the ride completion rate fell dramatically, to less than 20 percent. Unlike the Ariana Grande example, in this case driver supply failed to match rider demand, and a low number of rides were completed even though many riders were willing to pay more than the standard price.

So we see that surge pricing, and indeed any form of dynamic pricing that involves prices adjusting to changes in demand and supply, generates efficiency gains by matching the quantity demanded to the quantity supplied, and by allocating that supply to those who value it the most.

How big are those gains? As we have discussed, economists use the concepts of consumer and producer surplus to quantify the gains from trade in a market. Uber economists Jonathan Hall and Peter Cohen partnered with university economists Steven Levitt (of *Freakonomics* fame), Robert Hahn, and Robert Metcalfe to investigate this in a paper entitled "Using Big Data to Estimate Consumer Surplus: The Case of Uber."

They used nearly 50 million individual-level observations (that's the Big Data part) from the four largest Uber markets in the United States in 2015 (Chicago, Los Angeles, New York, and San Francisco) to estimate the consumer surplus generated by UberX (the most popular and lowest-cost service).

Surge pricing, and the response of riders to it, allowed the economists to estimate the demand curve for UberX services. The techniques they used to do this are quite technical, but conceptually relatively straightforward. Because Uber's surge system changes prices to match supply and demand, the authors were able to determine both when individuals accepted a ride at a given surge price and *when they rejected a ride at that price.* They were then able to create a demand curve by tracing out the share of users who still bought rides as the price rose. By drilling down into individual ride completion rates, they were able to measure the percent increase in price associated with the drop in ride acceptance at every point on the demand curve. For example, say 80 percent of users requested a ride at a base price of $10, but only 70 percent accepted a surge price of $11—then the authors knew that a 10-percent increase in the price resulted in a 10-percent drop in the share of people who took rides. Making these comparisons all along the demand curve allowed them to estimate how many customers were willing to pay more and, importantly, *how much more they were willing to pay,* at every price point. In other words, they were able to estimate the consumer surplus generated by UberX.

So, how much consumer surplus is generated by UberX? They calculate that for every dollar spent by consumers on UberX about $1.60 in consumer surplus is generated. Adding this up over the four big cities they studied, and extrapolating to the entire U.S., they calculate that the overall consumer surplus generated by UberX in the U.S. in 2015 was $6.9 billion. If we use the standard assumption that the Canadian market is about 10 percent of the U.S. market, and using the average Canada–U.S. exchange rate in 2015 of US$1 = CDN$1.28, this equates to $883 million in Canada.

While there are other issues that arise in connection with ride sharing services—for example driver screening and the application of regulations and other business requirements—Uber's surge pricing makes economists downright giddy! ∎

Draw the supply and demand for turkey. In the equilibrium, show producer and consumer surplus. Explain why producing more turkey would lower total surplus.

IN THE news

Uber's Watching You . . .

A lot of attention has been given recently to the way tech companies such as Facebook and Google use data to target content, advertising, and other messaging to users. This article explains how Uber can potentially use the battery life on your phone to target pricing.

Uber Users with Low Phone Batteries More Likely to Accept Surge Pricing

It's no secret that Uber uses surge pricing at peak periods, such as New Year's Eve, when demand is high. But what many may not know is that when you download the Uber app, the company can track your smartphone battery life—and it's studying how that influences your price point. The company has determined that customers are more willing to accept surge pricing if they know their phone is about to lose power.

The ride-hailing service is alerted when a customer's phone battery is running low because the app switches into power-saving mode.

In a recent NPR podcast titled "This Is Your Brain on Uber," Keith Chen, the company's head of economic research, said people with fading batteries are less inclined to wait "10 to 15 minutes" to see if demand for drivers drops, along with pricing, because with a low battery, they may not get a ride at all.

The behavioural economist at UCLA said users are willing to accept surge pricing increases as high as 9.9 times the normal price of a ride if their smartphone's battery is close to dying.

Chen said it's just "an interesting kind of psychological fact of human behaviour." He stressed the company is not going to act on the information to set fares.

Uber says it uses "dynamic pricing" to meet its goal of getting a car to anyone who wants one within minutes in a busy city and provide an incentive for drivers to go where they're most needed. People who have time to wait longer usually pay a cheaper fare.

Chen also said people are getting used to the surge and Uber has seen demand during peak periods drop by a much smaller amount than when it introduced the system.

The Uber app will always ask a potential passenger to confirm the higher fare first before requesting a car. "In many major cities in the United States, we're up to 60 per cent cheaper than taxi fares when we're not surging. What that means is you can surge 2.1 (times) and still come out even [compared to] if you had just taken a taxi," Chen told NPR.

7-4 Conclusion: Market Efficiency and Market Failure

This chapter introduced the basic tools of welfare economics—consumer and producer surplus—and used them to evaluate the efficiency of free markets. We showed that the forces of supply and demand allocate resources efficiently. That is, even though each buyer and seller in a market is concerned only about his or her own welfare, together they are led by an invisible hand to an equilibrium that maximizes the total benefits to buyers and sellers.

A word of warning is in order. To conclude that markets are efficient, we made several assumptions about how markets work. When these assumptions do not hold, our conclusion that the market equilibrium is efficient may no longer be true. As we close this chapter, let's consider briefly two of the most important of these assumptions.

First, our analysis assumed that markets are perfectly competitive. In actual economies, however, competition is sometimes far from perfect. In some markets, a single buyer or seller (or a small group of them) may be able to control market prices. This ability to influence prices is called *market power.* Market power can cause markets to be inefficient because it keeps the price and quantity away from the levels determined by the equilibrium of supply and demand.

Second, our analysis assumed that the outcome in a market matters only to the buyers and sellers who participate in that market. Yet sometimes the decisions of buyers and sellers affect people who are not participants in the market at all. Pollution is the classic example. The use of agricultural pesticides, for instance, affects not only the manufacturers who make them and the farmers who use them, but also many others who breathe air or drink water that has been polluted with these pesticides. When a market exhibits such side effects, called *externalities,* the welfare implications of market activity depend on more than just the value obtained by the buyers and the cost incurred by the sellers. Because buyers and sellers may ignore these side effects when deciding how much to consume and produce, the equilibrium in a market can be inefficient from the standpoint of society as a whole.

Market power and externalities are examples of a general phenomenon called *market failure*—the inability of some unregulated markets to allocate resources efficiently. When markets fail, public policy can potentially remedy the problem and increase economic efficiency. Microeconomists devote much effort to studying when market failure is likely and what sorts of policies are best at correcting market failures. As you continue your study of economics, you will see that the tools of welfare economics developed here are readily adapted to that endeavour.

Despite the possibility of market failure, the invisible hand of the marketplace is extraordinarily important. In many markets, the assumptions we made in this chapter work well, and the conclusion of market efficiency applies directly. Moreover, we can use our analysis of welfare economics and market efficiency to shed light on the effects of various government policies. In the next two chapters we apply the tools we have just developed to study two important policy issues—the welfare effects of taxation and of international trade.

IN THE news

Rockon-omics

As the following article shows, everyone can profit by thinking a little like an economist. In this case Taylor Swift shows how to grab a little producer surplus.

Look What Scalpers Made Her Do: The New Way Taylor Swift Is Selling Concert Tickets Could Be a Game Changer

By Scott Duke Kominers

Taylor Swift made sparks fly last week when she announced a new approach to selling concert tickets. Instead of "first come, first served"—which invites predation by bots—Swift's upcoming tour will sell tickets first to the people who engage the most with Swift's website.

Swift is using Ticketmaster's Verified Fan program. Users register and then undertake "boost activities" like buying Swift's new album, sharing links on social media and watching videos. When tickets go on sale, they'll be offered to fans in order, according to who did the most "boosting."

The goal, as Swift explains in an animated cat video, is to make sure that tickets get to superfans instead of scalpers. The public reaction has been mixed. Some have praised Swift's entrepreneurship. But others think her approach is exploitative of fans and downright mean.

Let's set the PR aside and think through the economics: Effectively, Swift is selling her tickets in an auction. Even though the tickets themselves will be sold at fixed prices, they'll go to the people who are willing to "pay" the most through buying merchandise, generating social media buzz, and watching Swift's music videos over and over again. Potential buyers are competing with one another, just like in a traditional auction.

Concert ticket auctions have been tried on Ticketmaster before. They worked out well for artists, and badly for scalpers.

My economist colleagues Aditya Bhave and Eric Budish studied a series of auctions that Ticketmaster ran in 2007. In each case, some tickets were sold by auction, and others were sold at fixed prices, so Bhave and Budish could compare artist revenue across the two pricing strategies. By checking resale prices on eBay, they could measure the scalper rates, as well.

Bhave and Budish found that using auctions roughly doubled artists' revenues. Meanwhile, the auctions substantially cut the profits associated to reselling tickets—even though some ticket brokers did bid in the auctions, their average profits were an order of magnitude lower than the return to scalping tickets they bought at a fixed face value.

Getting money to artists instead of scalpers is something we can all get behind. We can probably also agree that auctions are an imperfect approach.

There's inequality when you run an auction: Wealthier people are more able to afford tickets. But some of that same inequality is already present in the fixed-price system; it's just harder to see. With brokers and bots buying up tickets and reselling them, many of the fans who make it to concerts are the ones who can pay premium prices to scalpers.

Swift's auction is special because its currency is user engagement, meaning that the "wealth" favoured is not strictly financial. Engagement costs much less to true fans—which the internet informs me are called "Swifties"—than it does to ticket brokers. If you're already watching Swift's videos 22 times per day, and post about

her on social media every 15 minutes, then you jump ahead in line without having to adjust your behavior at all.

But if you're a scalper, everything has changed: Now to get to the front of the line, you have to buy a large number of copies of Swift's albums.

A bigger concern about Swift's auction is that even the people who don't win still end up paying. And remember also: Nobody's bidding for tickets directly; they're just bidding for chances to buy them.

Bhave and Budish found evidence that less experienced bidders in Ticketmaster auctions sometimes made substantial bidding mistakes, paying far more for tickets than they actually needed to. Swift is providing some transparency by giving bidders a meter that indicates how well they're doing. But even so, it's quite likely that some people will over- or under-bid, and be left disappointed.

In particular, some fans may invest a lot of time and money boosting Swift, and still not receive a chance to buy tickets. At least when people pay too much in more standard auctions, they still end up with tickets. Here, they might end up paying for blank space. That's not good, and could perhaps be fixed by using different auction mechanisms in the future.

Nevertheless, we should thank Swift for trying out this new approach. It's a worthy experiment in pricing, despite any initial bad blood.

summary

- Consumer surplus equals buyers' willingness to pay for a good minus the amount they actually pay, and it measures the benefit that buyers receive from participating in a market. Consumer surplus can be computed by finding the area below the demand curve and above the price.

- Producer surplus equals the amount that sellers receive for their goods minus their costs of production, and it measures the benefit that sellers receive from participating in a market. Producer surplus can be computed by finding the area below the price and above the supply curve.

- An allocation of resources that maximizes the sum of consumer and producer surplus is said to be efficient. Policymakers are often concerned with the efficiency, as well as the equity, of economic outcomes.

- The equilibrium of supply and demand maximizes the sum of consumer and producer surplus. That is, the invisible hand of the marketplace leads buyers and sellers to allocate resources efficiently.

- Markets do not allocate resources efficiently in the presence of market failures such as market power or externalities.

KEY concepts

welfare economics, *p. 146*
willingness to pay, *p. 146*
consumer surplus, *p. 147*

cost, *p. 151*
producer surplus, *p. 152*

efficiency, *p. 156*
equity, *p. 156*

QUESTIONS FOR review

1. Explain how buyers' willingness to pay, consumer surplus, and the demand curve are related.

2. Explain how sellers' costs, producer surplus, and the supply curve are related.

3. In a supply-and-demand diagram, show producer and consumer surplus in the market equilibrium.

4. What is efficiency? Is it the only goal of economic policymakers?

5. Name two types of market failure. Explain why each may cause market outcomes to be inefficient.

QUICK CHECK multiple choice

1. Jen values her time at $60 an hour. She spends 2 hours giving Colleen a massage. Colleen was willing to pay as much as $300 for the massage, but they negotiate a price of $200. Which of the following is true regarding this transaction?
   a. consumer surplus is $20 larger than producer surplus
   b. consumer surplus is $40 larger than producer surplus
   c. producer surplus is $20 larger than consumer surplus
   d. producer surplus is $40 larger than consumer surplus

2. The demand curve for cookies is downward sloping. When the price of cookies is $2, the quantity demanded is 100. If the price rises to $3, what happens to consumer surplus?
   a. It falls by less than $100.
   b. It falls by more than $100.

   c. It rises by less than $100.
   d. It rises by more than $100.

3. John has been working as a tutor for $300 a semester. When the university raises the price it pays tutors to $400, Emily enters the market and begins tutoring as well. How much does producer surplus rise as a result of this price increase?
   a. by less than $100
   b. between $100 and $200
   c. between $200 and $300
   d. by more than $300

4. Which of the following is maximized by an efficient allocation of resources?
   a. consumer surplus
   b. producer surplus
   c. consumer surplus plus producer surplus
   d. consumer surplus minus producer surplus

5. When a market is in equilibrium, the buyers are those with the ___ willingness to pay and the sellers are those with the ___ costs.
   a. highest, highest
   b. highest, lowest
   c. lowest, highest
   d. lowest, lowest

6. Producing a quantity larger than the equilibrium of supply and demand is inefficient when the marginal buyer's willingness to pay can be described as which of the following?
   a. negative
   b. zero
   c. positive but less than the marginal seller's cost
   d. positive and greater than the marginal seller's cost

PROBLEMS AND **applications**

1. A drought in Nova Scotia reduces the apple harvest. Explain what happens to consumer surplus in the market for apples. What happens to consumer surplus in the market for apple juice? Illustrate your answers with diagrams.

2. Suppose the demand for French bread rises. What happens to producer surplus in the market for French bread? What happens to producer surplus in the market for flour? Illustrate your answer with diagrams.

3. It is a hot day, and Bert is thirsty. Here is the value he places on a bottle of water:

Value of first bottle	$7
Value of second bottle	5
Value of third bottle	3
Value of fourth bottle	1

   a. From this information, derive Bert's demand schedule. Graph his demand curve for bottled water.
   b. If the price of a bottle of water is $4, how many bottles does Bert buy? How much consumer surplus does Bert get from his purchases? Show Bert's consumer surplus in your graph.
   c. If the price falls to $2, how does quantity demanded change? How does Bert's consumer surplus change? Show these changes in your graph.

4. Ernie owns a water pump. Because pumping large amounts of water is harder than pumping small amounts, the cost of producing a bottle of water rises as he pumps more. Here is the cost he incurs to produce each bottle of water:

Cost of first bottle	$1
Cost of second bottle	3
Cost of third bottle	5
Cost of fourth bottle	7

   a. From this information, derive Ernie's supply schedule. Graph his supply curve for bottled water.
   b. If the price of a bottle of water is $4, how many bottles does Ernie produce and sell? How much producer surplus does Ernie get from these sales? Show Ernie's producer surplus in your graph.
   c. If the price rises to $6, how does quantity supplied change? How does Ernie's producer surplus change? Show these changes in your graph.

5. Consider a market in which Bert from problem 3 is the buyer and Ernie from problem 4 is the seller.
   a. Use Ernie's supply schedule and Bert's demand schedule to find the quantity supplied and quantity demanded at prices of $2, $4, and $6. Which of these prices brings supply and demand into equilibrium?
   b. What are consumer surplus, producer surplus, and total surplus in this equilibrium?
   c. If Ernie produced and Bert consumed one fewer bottle of water, what would happen to total surplus?
   d. If Ernie produced and Bert consumed one additional bottle of water, what would happen to total surplus?

6. The cost of producing flat-screen TVs has fallen over the past decade. Let's consider some implications of this fact.
   a. Use a supply-and-demand diagram to show the effect of falling production costs on the price and quantity of flat-screen TVs sold.
   b. In your diagram, show what happens to consumer surplus and producer surplus.
   c. Suppose the supply of flat-screen TVs is very elastic. Who benefits most from falling production costs—consumers or producers of these TVs?

7. There are four consumers willing to pay the following amounts for haircuts:

   Gloria: $35   Jay: $10   Claire: $40   Phil: $25

There are four haircutting businesses with the following costs:

Firm A: $15   Firm B: $30   Firm C: $20   Firm D: $10

Each firm has the capacity to produce only one haircut. For efficiency, how many haircuts should be given? Which businesses should cut hair, and which consumers should have their hair cut? How large is the maximum possible total surplus?

8. One of the largest changes in the economy over the past several decades is that technological advances have reduced the cost of making computers.
   a. Draw a supply-and-demand diagram to show what happened to price, quantity, consumer surplus, and producer surplus in the market for computers.
   b. Several decades ago, students used typewriters to prepare papers for their classes; today they use computers. Does that make computers and typewriters complements or substitutes? Use a supply-and-demand diagram to show what happens to price, quantity, consumer surplus, and producer surplus in the market for typewriters. Describe what has happened to producer surplus in the typewriter market over the last several decades.
   c. Are computers and software complements or substitutes? Draw a supply-and-demand diagram to show what happened to price, quantity, consumer surplus, and producer surplus in the market for software. Describe what has happened to producer surplus for software producers.
   d. Does this analysis help explain why software producer Bill Gates is one of the world's richest men?

9. Melissa buys an iPhone for $240 and gets consumer surplus of $160.
   a. What is her willingness to pay?
   b. If she had bought the iPhone on sale for $180, what would her consumer surplus have been?
   c. If the price of an iPhone was $500, what would her consumer surplus have been?

The Mathematics of Consumer and Producer Surplus

In the appendix to Chapter 4, we showed you how to use simple mathematics to determine equilibrium prices and quantities for linear supply and demand curves. Here we show you how to calculate consumer and producer surplus for linear supply and demand curves.

The demand and supply curves from the appendix to Chapter 4:

$$Q^D = 56 - 4P$$
$$Q^S = -4 + 2P$$

Recall from Chapter 4 that the y-intercept of the demand curve occurs at $P = \$14$, the y-intercept for the supply curve occurs at $P = \$2$, the equilibrium price is $P = \$10$, and the equilibrium quantity is $Q = 16$. These curves, and the equilibrium outcome, are graphed in Figure 7A.1.

As discussed in this chapter, consumer surplus is the area below the demand curve and above the equilibrium price. In this case this is equal to the area of the triangle given by ABC. Recall that the area of a triangle is equal to one-half the base times the height, or $(1/2) \times$ base $\times$ height. The base of the triangle ABC is given by the equilibrium quantity $Q = 16$, therefore base $= 16$. The height of the triangle is given by the difference between the y-intercept of the demand curve at $P = \$14$ and the equilibrium price at $P = \$10$, therefore height $= \$14 - \$10 = \$4$.

FIGURE 7A.1

Consumer and Producer Surplus with Linear Demand and Supply Curves

This diagram illustrates a linear demand curve given by $Q^D = 56 - 4P$ and a linear supply curve given by $Q^S = -4 + 2P$. Consumer surplus is given by the area of the triangle ABC, which is equal to \$32. Producer surplus is given by the area of the triangle CBD, which is \$64. Total surplus is the sum of consumer and producer surplus, which is the area of the triangle ABD, or \$96.

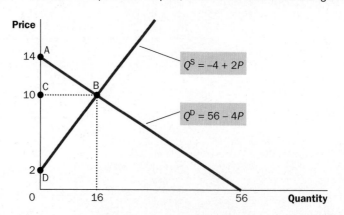

Consumer surplus at the equilibrium is therefore:

$$\text{Consumer surplus} = \text{Area ABC} = (1/2) \times \text{Base} \times \text{Height}$$
$$= (1/2) \times 16 \times \$4$$
$$= \$32$$

Similarly, producer surplus is the area below the equilibrium price and above the supply curve; the area of the triangle given by CBD in Figure 7A.1. The base of this triangle is, again, the equilibrium quantity of $Q = 16$, therefore base $= 16$. The height is the difference between the equilibrium price of $P = \$10$ and the y-intercept of the supply curve at $P = \$2$, therefore height $= \$10 - 2 = \$8$. Using the formula for the area of a triangle, producer surplus at the equilibrium is:

$$\text{Producer surplus} = \text{Area CBD} = (1/2) \times \text{Base} \times \text{Height}$$
$$= (1/2) \times 16 \times \$8$$
$$= \$64$$

So, in this case the excess of what sellers in aggregate receive for their goods over their costs of production is also $64.

Total surplus, which is the sum of consumer and producer surplus, is given by the area of the triangle ABD, which in this case is simply:

$$\text{Total surplus} = \text{Consumer surplus} + \text{Producer surplus} = \text{Area ABD} = \$32 + \$64 = \$96$$

For this example, total surplus—which is the total value to buyers measured by their willingness to pay less the total cost to sellers of providing the good—is therefore $96.

PROBLEMS AND **applications**

A1. The supply and demand for broccoli are described by the following equations:

$$\text{Supply: } Q^S = 4P - 80$$
$$\text{Demand: } Q^D = 100 - 2P$$

Q is in tonnes, and P is in dollars per bushel.
   a. Graph the supply curve and the demand curve. What is the equilibrium price and quantity?
   b. Calculate consumer surplus, producer surplus, and total surplus at the equilibrium.
   c. If a dictator who hated broccoli were to ban the vegetable, who would bear the larger burden—the buyers or sellers of broccoli?

A2. A friend of yours is considering two providers of cell-phone services. Provider A charges $120 per month for the service, regardless of the number of phone calls made. Provider B does not have a fixed service fee but instead charges $1 per minute for calls. Your friend's monthly demand for minutes of calling is given by the equation $Q^D = 150 - 50P$, where P is the price of a minute.
   a. With each provider, what is the cost to your friend of an extra minute on the phone?

b. In light of your answer to (a), how many minutes would your friend spend on the phone with each provider?
   c. How much would he end up paying each provider every month?
   d. How much consumer surplus would he obtain with each provider? (Hint: Graph the demand curve and recall the formula for the area of a triangle.)
   e. Which provider would you recommend that your friend choose? Why?

A3. The demand for broccoli in the Kingdom of Vegan is described by a linear demand curve: $Q^D = 100 - 2P$. Say the price of broccoli is set by the ruler of the kingdom, Mr. Potato Head. Say initially that the price is $5 per bunch of broccoli.
   a. What is the equilibrium quantity demanded at this price and the consumer surplus?
   b. Now say that in order to encourage people to consume more broccoli, Mr. Potato Head decrees that the price of broccoli will decline to $4. What is the new equilibrium quantity? The change in consumer surplus?

CHAPTER

8

LEARNING
objectives

Application: The Costs of Taxation

In this chapter, you will ...

1   Examine how taxes reduce consumer and producer surplus

2   Learn the meaning and causes of the deadweight loss of a tax

3   Consider why some taxes have larger deadweight losses than others

4   Examine how tax revenue and deadweight loss vary with the size of a tax

Taxes are often the source of heated debate. Political parties in Canada often debate the proper size and configuration of the tax system. Yet few would deny that some level of taxation is necessary. As the noted American jurist Oliver Wendell Holmes, Jr., once said, "Taxes are what we pay for civilized society."

Because taxation has such a major impact on the modern economy, we return to the topic several times throughout this book as we expand the set of tools we have at our disposal. We began our study of taxes in Chapter 6. There we saw how a tax on a good affects its price and the quantity sold and how the forces of supply and demand divide the burden of a tax between buyers and sellers. In this chapter we extend this analysis and look at how taxes affect welfare, the economic well-being of participants in a market. In other words, we see how high the price of a civilized society can be.

The effects of taxes on welfare might at first seem obvious. The government enacts taxes to raise revenue, and that revenue must come out of someone's pocket. As we saw in Chapter 6, both buyers and sellers are worse off when a good is taxed: A tax raises the price buyers pay and lowers the price sellers receive. Yet to fully understand how taxes affect economic well-being, we must compare the reduced welfare of buyers and sellers to the amount of revenue the government raises. The tools of consumer and producer surplus allow us to make this comparison. The analysis will show that the cost of taxes to buyers and sellers exceeds the revenue raised by the government.

While this chapter is devoted to discussing the costs of taxation, it is important to remember that taxes give rise to important benefits as well. One of the ten principles of economics in Chapter 1 is that governments can sometimes improve market outcomes. Taxes are one of the ways that governments can do this.

For example, governments must often provide goods and services such as roads, parks, police, and national defence, which are not well provided by the market; they need revenue to do this. We will discuss this in detail in Chapter 11. Also, sometimes governments can impose taxes to achieve a more efficient outcome when markets don't function properly, as in the case of so-called "corrective taxes," which will be discussed in Chapter 10. Finally, governments are also concerned with the distribution of income in society, and the tax system can play an important role in achieving equity objectives; we will pay some attention to this in Chapter 20. We discuss the implications of the costs associated with taxes for the size of government spending in general terms at the end of this chapter.

8-1 The Deadweight Loss of Taxation

We begin by recalling one of the surprising lessons from Chapter 6: The impact of a tax on a market outcome is the same whether the tax is levied on buyers or sellers of a good. When a tax is levied on buyers, the demand curve shifts downward by the size of the tax; when it is levied on sellers, the supply curve shifts upward by that amount. In either case, when the tax is enacted, the price paid by buyers rises, and the price received by sellers falls. In the end, the relative elasticities of supply and demand determine how the tax burden is distributed between producers and consumers. The distribution is the same regardless of how it is levied.

Figure 8.1 shows these effects. To simplify our discussion, this figure does not show a shift in either the supply or demand curve, although one curve must shift.

FIGURE 8.1

The Effects of a Tax

A tax on a good places a wedge between the price that buyers pay and the price that sellers receive. The quantity of the good sold falls.

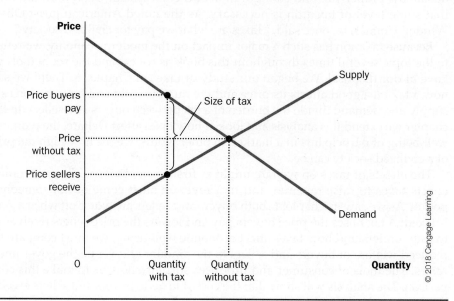

Which curve shifts depends on whether the tax is levied on sellers (the supply curve shifts) or buyers (the demand curve shifts). In this chapter, we keep the analysis general and simplify the graphs by not showing the shift. For our purposes here, the key result is that the tax places a wedge between the price buyers pay and the price sellers receive. Because of this tax wedge, the quantity sold falls below the level that would be sold without a tax. In other words, a tax on a good causes the size of the market for the good to shrink. These results should be familiar from Chapter 6.

8-1a How a Tax Affects Market Participants

Let's use the tools of welfare economics to measure the gains and losses from a tax on a good. To do this, we must take into account how the tax affects buyers, sellers, and the government. The benefit received by buyers in a market is measured by consumer surplus—the amount buyers are willing to pay for the good minus the amount they actually pay for it. The benefit received by sellers in a market is measured by producer surplus—the amount sellers receive for the good minus their costs. These are precisely the measures of economic welfare we used in Chapter 7.

What about the third interested party, the government? If T is the size of the tax and Q is the quantity of the good sold, then the government gets total tax revenue of $T \times Q$. It can use this tax revenue to provide services, such as roads, police, and public education, or to help the needy. Therefore, to analyze how taxes affect economic well-being, we use the government's tax revenue to measure the public benefit from the tax. Keep in mind, however, that this benefit actually accrues not to the government but to those on whom the revenue is spent.

Figure 8.2 shows that the government's tax revenue is represented by the rectangle between the supply and demand curves. The height of this rectangle is the size of the tax, T, and the width of the rectangle is the quantity of the good sold, Q.

FIGURE 8.2

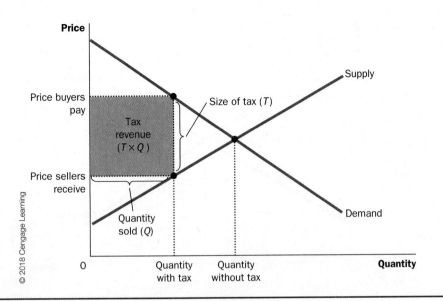

Tax Revenue
The tax revenue that the government collects equals $T \times Q$, the size of the tax T times the quantity sold Q. Thus, tax revenue equals the area of the rectangle between the supply and demand curves.

Because a rectangle's area is its height times its width, this rectangle's area is $T \times Q$, which equals the tax revenue.

Welfare without a Tax To see how a tax affects welfare, we begin by considering welfare before the government imposes a tax. Figure 8.3 shows the supply-and-demand diagram and marks the key areas marked by the letters A through F.

Without a tax, the equilibrium price and quantity are found at the intersection of the supply and demand curves. The price is P_1, and the quantity sold is Q_1. Because the demand curve reflects buyers' willingness to pay, consumer surplus is the area between the demand curve and the price, A + B + C. Similarly, because the supply curve reflects sellers' costs, producer surplus is the area between the supply curve and the price, D + E + F. In this case, because there is no tax, tax revenue equals zero.

Total surplus, the sum of consumer and producer surplus, equals the area A + B + C + D + E + F. In other words, as we saw in Chapter 7, total surplus is the area between the supply and demand curves up to the equilibrium quantity. The first column of the table in Figure 8.3 summarizes these conclusions.

Welfare with a Tax Now consider welfare after the tax is enacted. The price paid by buyers rises from P_1 to P_B, so consumer surplus now equals only area A (the area below the demand curve and above the buyer's price). The price received by sellers falls from P_1 to P_S, so producer surplus now equals only area F (the area above the supply curve and below the seller's price). The quantity sold falls from Q_1 to Q_2, and the government collects tax revenue equal to the area B + D.

To compute total surplus with the tax, we add consumer surplus, producer surplus, and tax revenue. Thus, we find that total surplus is area A + B + D + F. The second column of the table provides a summary of these results.

FIGURE 8.3

How a Tax Affects Welfare

A tax on a good reduces consumer surplus (by the area B + C) and producer surplus (by the area D + E). Because the fall in producer and consumer surplus exceeds tax revenue (area B + D), the tax is said to impose a deadweight loss (area C + E).

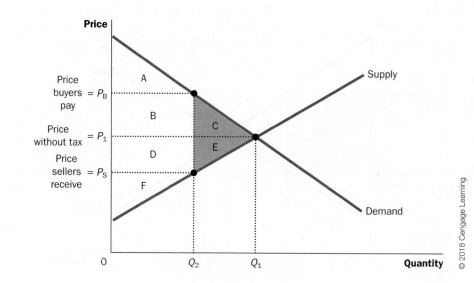

	Without Tax	With Tax	Change
Consumer Surplus	A + B + C	A	−(B + C)
Producer Surplus	D + E + F	F	−(D + E)
Tax Revenue	None	B + D	+(B + D)
Total Surplus	A + B + C + D + E + F	A + B + D + F	−(C + E)

The area C + E shows the fall in total surplus and is the deadweight loss of the tax.

deadweight loss

the fall in total surplus that results from a market distortion, such as a tax

Changes in Welfare We can now see the effects of the tax by comparing welfare before and after the tax is enacted. The last column in the table in Figure 8.3 shows the changes. Consumer surplus falls by the area B + C, and producer surplus falls by the area D + E. Tax revenue rises by the area B + D. Not surprisingly, the tax makes buyers and sellers worse off and the government better off.

The change in total welfare includes the change in consumer surplus (which is negative), the change in producer surplus (which is also negative), and the change in tax revenue (which is positive). When we add these three pieces together, we find that total surplus in the market falls by the area C + E. *Thus, the losses to buyers and sellers from a tax exceed the revenue raised by the government.* The fall in total surplus that results when a tax (or some other policy) distorts a market outcome is called a **deadweight loss**. The area C + E measures the size of the deadweight loss. By convention we often measure the deadweight loss of taxes as a positive number.

To understand why taxes impose deadweight losses, recall one of the ten principles of economics discussed in Chapter 1: People respond to incentives. In Chapter 7 we saw that free markets normally allocate scarce resources efficiently.

That is, in the absence of any tax, the equilibrium of supply and demand maximizes the total surplus of buyers and sellers in a market. When the government imposes a tax, it raises the price buyers pay and lowers the price sellers receive, giving buyers an incentive to consume less and sellers an incentive to produce less. As buyers and sellers respond to these incentives, the equilibrium size of the market shrinks below its optimum (as shown in the figure by the movement from Q_1 to Q_2). In other words, the size of the tax base—what the tax is applied to—shrinks because of the behavioural responses of buyers and sellers to the tax. Thus, because taxes distort incentives, they cause markets to allocate resources inefficiently.

8-1b Deadweight Losses and the Gains from Trade

To better understand why taxes cause deadweight losses, consider an example. Imagine that Mike cleans Mei's house each week for $100. The opportunity cost of Mike's time is $80, and the value of a clean house to Mei is $120. Thus, Mike and Mei each receive a $20 benefit from their deal. The total surplus of $40 measures the gains from trade in this particular transaction.

Now suppose that the government levies a $50 tax on the providers of cleaning services. There is now no price that Mei can pay Mike that will leave both of them better off. The most Mei would be willing to pay is $120, but then Mike would be left with only $70 after paying the tax, which is less than his $80 opportunity cost. Conversely, for Mike to receive his opportunity cost of $80, Mei would need to pay $130, which is above the $120 value she places on a clean house. As a result, Mei and Mike cancel their arrangement. Mike goes without the income, and Mei lives in a dirtier house.

The tax has made Mike and Mei worse off by a total of $40 because they have each lost $20 of surplus. But note that the government collects no revenue from Mike and Mei because they decide to cancel their arrangement. The $40 is pure deadweight loss: It is a loss to buyers and sellers in a market not offset by an increase in government revenue. From this example, we can see the ultimate source of deadweight losses: *Taxes cause deadweight losses because they prevent buyers and sellers from realizing some of the gains from trade.*

The area of the triangle between the supply and demand curves created by the tax wedge (area C + E in Figure 8.3) measures these losses. This conclusion can be seen more easily in Figure 8.4 by recalling that the demand curve reflects the value of the good to consumers and that the supply curve reflects the costs of producers. When the tax raises the price buyers pay to P_B and lowers the price sellers receive to P_S, the marginal buyers and sellers leave the market, so the quantity sold falls from Q_1 to Q_2. Yet, as the figure shows, the value of the good to these buyers still exceeds the cost to these sellers. At every quantity between Q_1 and Q_2, the situation is the same as in our example with Mike and Mei. The gains from trade—the difference between buyers' value and sellers' cost—are less than the tax. As a result, these trades are not made once the tax is imposed. The deadweight loss is the surplus lost because the tax discourages these mutually advantageous trades.

Draw the supply and demand curves for cookies. If the government imposes a tax on cookies, show what happens to the quantity sold, the price paid by buyers, and the price paid by sellers. In your diagram, show the deadweight loss from the tax. Explain the meaning of the deadweight loss.

FIGURE 8.4

The Deadweight Loss
When the government imposes a
tax on a good, the quantity sold
falls from Q_1 to Q_2. As a result,
some of the potential gains from
trade among buyers and sellers
do not get realized. These lost
gains from trade create the
deadweight loss.

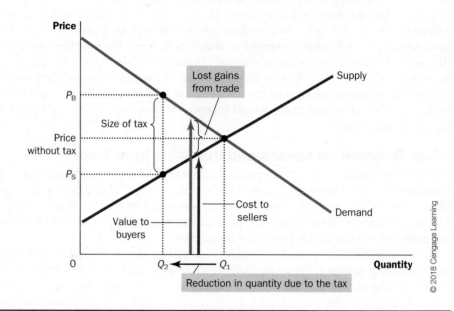

8-2 The Determinants of the Deadweight Loss

What determines whether the deadweight loss from a tax is large or small? The answer is the price elasticities of supply and demand, which measure how much the quantity supplied and quantity demanded respond to changes in the price.

Let's consider first how the elasticity of supply affects the size of the deadweight loss. In the top two panels of Figure 8.5, the demand curve and the size of the tax are the same. The only difference in these figures is the elasticity of the supply curve. In panel (a), the supply curve is relatively inelastic: Quantity supplied responds only slightly to changes in the price. In panel (b), the supply curve is relatively elastic: Quantity supplied responds substantially to changes in the price. Notice that the deadweight loss, the area of the triangle between the supply and demand curves, is larger when the supply curve is more elastic.

Similarly, the bottom two panels of Figure 8.5 show how the elasticity of demand affects the size of the deadweight loss. Here the supply curve and the size of the tax are held constant. In panel (c), the demand curve is relatively inelastic, and the deadweight loss is small. In panel (d), the demand curve is more elastic, and the deadweight loss from the tax is larger.

The lesson from this figure is apparent. A tax has a deadweight loss because it induces buyers and sellers to change their behaviour. The tax raises the price paid by buyers, so they consume less. At the same time, the tax lowers the price received by sellers, so they produce less. Because of these changes in behaviour, the equilibrium quantity in the market shrinks below the optimal quantity. The more responsive buyers and sellers are to changes in the price, the more the equilibrium quantity shrinks. Hence, *the greater the elasticities of supply and demand, the greater the deadweight loss of a tax.*

You will notice from Figure 8.5 that a high deadweight loss is associated with a large reduction in the equilibrium size of the market due to the tax. Another way of stating this is that the deadweight loss of a tax is greater the greater is the

FIGURE 8.5

Tax Distortions and Elasticities

In panels (a) and (b), the demand curve and the size of the tax are the same, but the price elasticity of supply is different. Notice that the more elastic the supply curve, the larger the deadweight loss of the tax. In panels (c) and (d), the supply curve and the size of the tax are the same, but the price elasticity of demand is different. Notice that the more elastic the demand curve, the larger the deadweight loss of the tax.

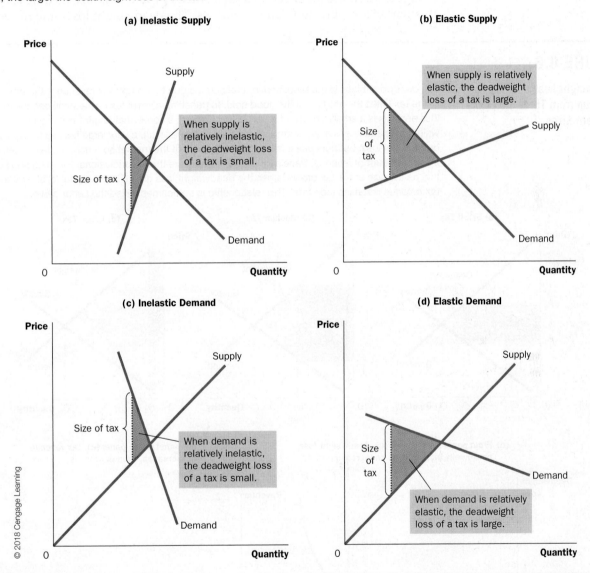

elasticity of the tax base with respect to the tax, which in this case is the equilibrium quantity of the good. And, in turn, the elasticity of the tax base is greater the greater the elasticities of demand and supply.

elasticity of the tax base
the sensitivity of the tax base to changes in the tax rate

The demand for beer is more elastic than the demand for milk. Would a tax on beer or a tax on milk have a larger deadweight loss? Why?

8-3 Deadweight Loss and Tax Revenue as Taxes Vary

Taxes rarely stay the same for long periods of time. Policymakers in local, provincial, territorial, and federal governments are always considering raising one tax or lowering another. Here we consider what happens to the deadweight loss and tax revenue when the size of a tax changes.

Figure 8.6 shows the effects of a small, medium, and large tax, holding constant the market's supply and demand curves. The deadweight loss—the reduction

---

FIGURE 8.6

Deadweight Loss and Tax Revenue from Three Taxes of Different Sizes

The deadweight loss is the reduction in total surplus due to the tax. Tax revenue is the amount of the tax times the amount of the good sold. In panel (a), a small tax has a small deadweight loss and raises a small amount of revenue. In panel (b), a somewhat larger tax has a larger deadweight loss and raises a larger amount of revenue. In panel (c), a very large tax has a very large deadweight loss, but because it has reduced the size of the market so much, the tax raises only a small amount of revenue. Panels (d) and (e) summarize these conclusions. Panel (d) shows that as the size of the tax grows larger, the deadweight loss grows larger. Panel (e) shows that tax revenue first rises then falls. This relationship is sometimes called the *Laffer curve*.

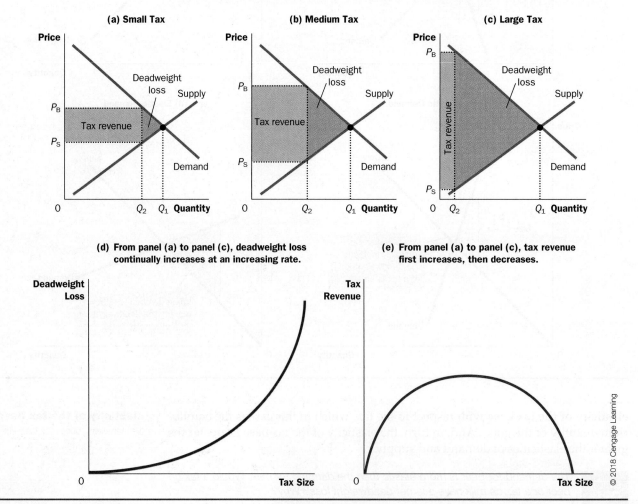

(d) From panel (a) to panel (c), deadweight loss continually increases at an increasing rate.

(e) From panel (a) to panel (c), tax revenue first increases, then decreases.

© 2018 Cengage Learning

in total surplus that results when the tax reduces the size of a market below the optimum—equals the area of the triangle between the supply and demand curves. For the small tax in panel (a), the area of the deadweight loss triangle is quite small. But as the size of a tax rises in panels (b) and (c), the deadweight loss grows larger and larger.

Indeed, the deadweight loss of a tax rises even more rapidly than the size of the tax. This occurs because the deadweight loss is an area of a triangle, and an area of a triangle depends on the *square* of its size. If we double the size of a tax, for instance, the base and height of the triangle double, so the deadweight loss rises by a factor of 4. If we triple the size of a tax, the base and height triple, so the deadweight loss rises by a factor of 9.

The government's tax revenue is the size of the tax times the amount of the good sold. As the first three panels of Figure 8.6 show, tax revenue equals the area of the rectangle between the supply and demand curves. For the small tax in panel (a), tax revenue is small. As the size of a tax rises from panel (a) to panel (b), tax revenue grows. But as the size of the tax rises further from panel (b) to panel (c), tax revenue falls because the higher tax drastically reduces the size of the market. For a very large tax, no revenue would be raised, because people would stop buying and selling the good altogether.

The last two panels of Figure 8.6 summarize these results. In panel (d), we see that as the size of a tax increases, its deadweight loss quickly gets larger. By contrast, panel (e) shows that tax revenue first rises with the size of the tax, but then, as the tax gets larger, the market shrinks so much that tax revenue starts to fall.

The curve in panel (e) of Figure 8.6 is sometimes called the Laffer curve, after economist Arthur Laffer. One day in 1974, Laffer sat in a Washington restaurant with some prominent journalists and politicians. Famously, he took out a napkin and drew a figure on it to show how tax rates affect tax revenue. It looked much like panel (e) of our Figure 8.6. Laffer then suggested that the United States was on the downward-sloping side (the "wrong side") of this curve. Tax rates were so high, he argued, that reducing them would actually raise tax revenue.

Most economists were skeptical of Laffer's suggestion. There was, and is, no doubt that the idea that a cut in tax rates could increase tax revenue was correct as a matter of economic theory, but there was considerable doubt about whether it would do so in practice. And indeed, broad-based tax cuts in the U.S. implemented by President Ronald Reagan in the 1980s, which were in part inspired by the Laffer curve, resulted in a substantial drop in government revenue. However, as we will see below, while it is very unlikely that broad-based tax cuts will lead to an increase in revenue, there is evidence that some taxes, in specific circumstances, may be on the "wrong" side of the Laffer curve.

We have seen that economists measure the efficiency costs of a tax by its deadweight loss. A related concept that economists find useful is the marginal cost of public funds. To get the idea behind the marginal cost of public funds, consider Figure 8.7. It shows the deadweight loss generated by an existing tax of T_1 on the good, given by the area of triangle A; it also shows the revenue generated by the tax, the area of rectangle E + C.

Now consider a small increase in the size of the tax from T_1 to T_2. In Figure 8.7 we illustrate a large increase in the tax so we can see it clearly on the graph, but you should be thinking in terms of a very small increase in the tax. The higher tax increases the size of the deadweight loss to the area of triangle A + B + C + D.

FIGURE 8.7

The Effect of a Tax Increase
At the initial tax of T_1 the dead-weight loss is A and revenue is C + E. At the higher tax rate T_2, the deadweight loss is A + B + C + D and revenue is F + E + G. The change in the deadweight loss from increasing the tax is ΔDWL = A + B + C + D − A = B + C + D, and the change in revenue is ΔR = F + E + G − (E + C) = F + G − C

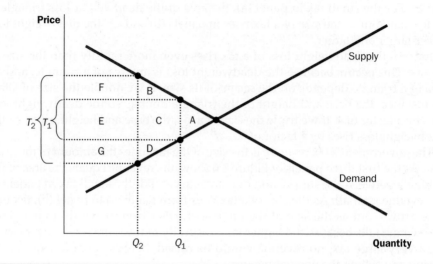

The increase in the deadweight loss due to the increase in the tax is therefore A + B + C + D − A = B + C + D, which we denote as ΔDWL, recalling that the Δ symbol means "change in"; thus ΔDWL = B + C + D is the "change in the deadweight loss" resulting from the increase in the tax. Similarly tax revenue under the higher tax is given by the area of the rectangle F + E + G, and there-fore the change in tax revenue is area F + E + G − (E + C) = F + G − C, which we denote as ΔR = F + G − C, for the "change in revenue." In principle, ΔR could be either positive (if F + G > C) or negative (if F + G < C) depending on where we are on the Laffer curve; we will assume that tax revenue increases in response to the higher tax (we are on the upward-sloping side of the Laffer curve), and therefore that ΔR is positive.

We can think of the total cost to society of a tax as consisting of the sum of the revenue generated by the tax plus the deadweight loss; denote this as C = R + DWL. The change in the total cost to society associated with an increase in the tax is then ΔC = ΔR + ΔDWL. As mentioned, although we draw a large increase in the size of the tax in Figure 8.7 for illustrative purposes, we have in mind a very small (marginal) increase, so small that tax revenue increases by just $1; thus set ΔR = F + G − C = 1. The **marginal cost of public funds** of a tax is defined as the change in the total cost to society of raising one more dollar in tax revenue, or MCF = ΔC = 1 + ΔDWL = 1 + (B + D + C). The marginal cost of public funds of a tax is therefore equal to the incremental $1 in revenue raised plus the associated increase in deadweight loss, which means that the marginal cost of public funds will generally be greater than $1.

Recall that a tax generates deadweight loss because of the behavioural responses of the market participants to the tax, which manifests itself in a shrinkage in the tax base. In Figure 8.7 the increase in the size of the tax causes the tax base to shrink from Q_1 to Q_2. As an example, say an existing tax is levied at $1 per unit, and the tax increases by 10 percent to $1.10 per unit. Say that the

marginal cost of public funds

the total cost to society of raising one more dollar in tax revenue equilibrium size of the market (the tax base) shrinks by 2 percent in response to the tax increase. This means that government revenue from the higher tax will increase by only 8 percent. Because a 10 percent increase in the tax generates only an 8 percent increase in tax revenue, the marginal cost of public funds of the tax is (approximately) 10/8, or $1.25. Thus, the total cost of raising one more dollar in revenue from this tax is $1.25, which consists of the $1 raised plus 25 cents in increased deadweight loss.

The marginal cost of public funds depends on the sensitivity of the tax base to the tax. If the tax base was more sensitive to an increase in the tax—the elasticity of the tax base was higher—the marginal cost of public funds would be higher. For example, say that instead the equilibrium size of the market shrinks by 3 percent in response to the tax increase. In this case the marginal cost of public funds would be 10/7, or about $1.43.

It is also useful to note that the higher is the size of the tax, and the more revenue generated by it (assuming we are not on the "wrong" side of the Laffer curve), the higher will be the marginal cost of public funds. This is because, as indicated in panel (d) of Figure 8.6, the deadweight loss of a tax increases at an increasing rate as the size of the tax increases.

case study

The Marginal Cost of Public Funds in Canada: The Laffer Curve Is No Laughing Matter

Economists have attempted to measure the marginal cost of public funds associated with different types of taxes. A recent study by university economists Bev Dahlby and Ergete Ferede provides estimates of the marginal cost of public funds for the three biggest sources of tax revenue in Canada for each of the provinces: the Personal Income Tax (PIT), the Corporate Income Tax (CIT), and the Provincial Sales Tax (PST); for the PIT the estimate is for an increase in the tax rate levied on the top income earners. (The structure of Canada's tax system is discussed in more detail in Chapter 12.)

Their estimates, shown in Table 8.1, reflect long-run behavioural responses to these taxes over time. It should also be noted that this is just one study of the marginal cost of public funds in Canada. Other studies will present different numbers.

Note that the marginal cost of public funds varies for a given tax across the provinces. For example, Dahlby and Ferede estimate the marginal cost of public funds of the PIT in British Columbia to be $2.86. Thus, raising one more dollar in tax revenue from increasing the PIT rate on the top income earners costs society $2.86, comprising the $1 plus $1.86 in incremental deadweight loss due to the tax. In Alberta the marginal cost of public funds of the PIT is much lower, at $1.41, suggesting that the PIT is less distortionary in Alberta than British Columbia. This variation reflects differences in the size of the different taxes across the provinces.

The marginal cost of public funds also varies across different types of taxes within a province. For example, for Manitoba the marginal cost of public funds for the PIT is $2.42, for the PST it is $1.34, and for the CIT it is $4.70. The variations in the marginal cost of public funds across different sources of revenue reflect differences in the behavioural responses of market participants to the taxes, as reflected in the elasticity of the underlying tax bases. Importantly, they suggest that from a pure efficiency perspective, the economic cost of the CIT is much higher than the PIT

TABLE 8.1

The Marginal Cost of Public Funds for the Major Taxes in Canadian Provinces

N/A Means the marginal cost of public funds could not be estimated.

*** Means the marginal cost of public funds could not be computed because a tax rate increase would reduce the long-run total tax revenue.

	Personal Income Tax	Provincial Sales Tax	Corporate Income Tax
British Columbia	2.86	N/A	3.19
Alberta	1.41	1.00	2.91
Saskatchewan	2.38	1.41	***
Manitoba	2.42	1.34	4.70
Ontario	6.76	N/A	5.21
Quebec	3.05	1.92	3.62
New Brunswick	1.91	1.42	***
Nova Scotia	N/A	1.62	***
Prince Edward Island	2.80	2.44	***
Newfoundland and Labrador	2.16	1.57	***

Source: Bev Dahlby and Ergete Ferede (2016), "The Costliest Tax of All: Raising Revenue Through Corporate Tax Hikes Can be Counter-Productive for Provinces". SPP Research Paper Vol. 9(11), School of Public Policy, University of Calgary. Table 2, p. 16. Retrieved from https://www.policyschool.ca/wp-content/uploads/2016/05/estimating-tax-base-ferede-dahlby.pdf

and the PST (we will discuss the asterisked entries (***) for some of the provinces for the CIT momentarily). This pattern holds across most provinces, suggesting that the CIT is a costly way to raise revenue from an economic efficiency perspective.

Differences in the marginal cost of public funds across different types of taxes suggests scope for revenue-neutral efficiency-enhancing changes to the tax system. Again using the example of Manitoba, imagine lowering the CIT rate so as to reduce tax revenue by $1 and raising the PST rate so as to increase tax revenue by $1. This tax change is revenue neutral as it generates the same amount of total tax revenue. However, the change is not neutral from an efficiency perspective. The reduction in CIT lowers the total cost to society by $4.70, while the increase in PST increases the total cost by $1.34. The net efficiency gain from this revenue-neutral change is $4.70 − $1.34 = $3.36, which suggests that reducing corporate income taxes and increasing provincial sales taxes in a revenue-neutral manner would be efficiency enhancing.

Now what about the entries with *** for the CIT in five provinces in Table 8.1? It turns out that Dahlby and Ferede determine that these provinces are actually on the "wrong" side of the Laffer curve (the downward-sloping side) for the CIT. In these provinces their estimates suggest that an increase in the CIT rate would actually generate a reduction in tax revenue (ΔR is negative). When this is the case the marginal cost of public funds cannot be determined. For example, Figure 8.8 shows the CIT Laffer curve for Saskatchewan as estimated by Dahlby and Ferede. It shows that the existing provincial CIT rate in Saskatchewan of 12.0 percent is higher than their estimate of the revenue-maximizing tax rate of 5.7 percent. Thus, according to their estimates, Saskatchewan could increase tax revenue by decreasing its CIT rate; the same is true for New Brunswick, Nova Scotia, Prince Edward Island, and Newfoundland and Labrador. For these provinces, the Laffer curve is no laughing matter. ■

FIGURE 8.8

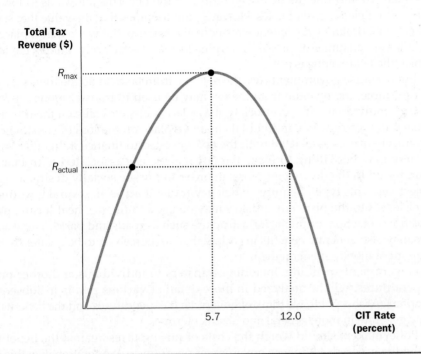

The CIT Laffer Curve for Saskatchewan
This figure shows the CIT Laffer curve for Saskatchewan estimated by Dahlby and Ferede. It indicates that the current CIT rate of 12.0 percent is higher than the revenue-maximizing tax rate of 5.7 percent.

QUICK Quiz *If the government doubles the tax on gasoline, can you be sure that revenue from the gasoline tax will rise? Can you be sure that the deadweight loss from the gasoline tax will rise? Explain.*

8-4 The Cost of Taxes and the Size of Government

Supply, demand, elasticity, deadweight loss, marginal cost of public funds—all of this economic theory is enough to make your head spin. But believe it or not, these ideas go to the heart of a profound political question: How big should the government be? The debate hinges on these concepts because the larger the deadweight loss of taxation, the larger the cost of any government program. If taxation entails large deadweight losses, then these losses are an argument for a leaner government that does less and taxes less. But if taxes impose small deadweight losses, then government programs are less costly than they otherwise might be.

While our intention in this chapter is to focus primarily on the costs associated with taxes, the tools that we have developed allow us to think about the issue of the size of government in a useful way. To do this we need to think about the uses to which tax revenue is put, at least in general terms. In this regard, up to this point we have made an important assumption that it is now time to address. In determining the deadweight loss of a tax (and the associated concept of the marginal cost of public funds) we have treated a dollar of tax revenue as being equivalent to a dollar of consumer and producer surplus. When this is the case we can simply subtract tax revenue from the change in consumer and producer surplus to determine the deadweight loss of the tax. This allows us to focus on the pure efficiency cost of taxes. However, this assumes that the value that society places on a dollar of tax revenue raised is the same as the value that it places on a dollar of consumer or producer surplus lost, and effectively ignores the use to which the tax revenue is put.

But of course governments use the revenue from taxes to do the things they do. For example, the revenue from the tax may be used to transfer money to lower income individuals. We, as a society, may place a greater value on the transfer of money to lower income individuals than we place on the loss of consumer and producer surplus associated with the taxes needed to finance it. In other words, society may be willing to incur the efficiency costs associated with taxes, as manifested in the deadweight loss, in order to pursue socially desirable equity objectives. This type of equity–efficiency tradeoff arises in several government decisions. Or, the proceeds of taxes may be used to finance health care, police and fire protection, or public infrastructure such as roads and parks. These activities may also generate benefits to society that are perceived to be greater than the amount of money spent on them.

Government spending, including transfers to individuals and other public expenditures, will be analyzed in more detail at various points in subsequent chapters. At this point, we think of government expenditures and the benefits that they generate in more general and abstract terms.

Policymakers should weigh the costs of raising taxes against the benefits of using the proceeds to finance government programs. We operationalize this idea in Figure 8.9. The figure graphs the marginal cost of public funds (MCF) associated with raising one more dollar in tax revenue against the revenue collected. Recall that the marginal cost of public funds is equal to the $1 raised in incremental revenue plus the associated increase in the deadweight loss. The MCF curve is upward sloping, reflecting the idea discussed previously that the deadweight loss of a tax increases at an increasing rate with the size of the tax (and the

FIGURE 8.9

The Marginal Cost and Benefit of Public Funds

The figure shows the marginal cost of public funds (MCF), which is the total cost to society of raising one more dollar of revenue, and the marginal benefit of public funds (MBF), which is the total benefit to society of spending one more dollar on a government program. Social welfare is maximized at R^*, where the marginal cost of financing a government program (MCF) is equal to the marginal benefit (MBF).

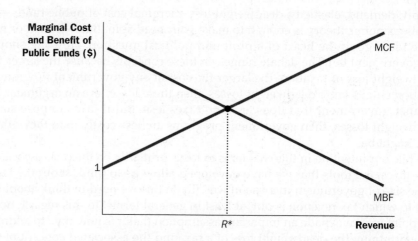

amount of revenue generated). This means that the marginal cost of public funds increases with the size of the tax, and the amount of revenue raised. Note that when no revenue is collected from the tax (the tax rate is zero) the marginal cost of public funds is simply $1, as reflected by the intersection of the MCF curve with $1 on the vertical axis.

Now let's introduce a similar notion for the use of the tax revenue, which we refer to as the **marginal benefit of public funds** (MBF). The marginal benefit of public funds is the benefit that society places on one more dollar of expenditure on government programs financed by the tax. Up to this point we have implicitly treated the marginal benefit of public funds as being equal to $1. However, as discussed, society may place a value on an additional dollar of program expenditure that is greater than $1, as might be the case, for example, if the proceeds of the tax are used to finance transfers to low income individuals. This is represented by the MBF curve in Figure 8.9, which is drawn as downward sloping, reflecting the idea that marginal benefit that society perceives from an incremental dollar of government spending declines as more is spent, which seems reasonable.

Now recall two of our principles of economics—Principle #1: People Face Tradeoffs, and Principle #3: Rational People Think at the Margin. Well, policymakers in government are rational people too (for the most part). An incremental dollar should be spent on a government program only if the perceived marginal benefit to society exceeds the marginal cost. For example, if the marginal cost of public funds is $1.25, an incremental dollar spent on a government program must generate a perceived benefit that is at least as big as $1.25 in order for it to make sense from an economic welfare point of view; if the marginal cost of public funds is $5 then the marginal benefit must exceed $5.

Indeed, the government should continue to increase expenditures on the program, and increase the taxes to finance it, up to the point where MCF = MBF. Thus, the amount of revenue-generated taxes that maximizes "social welfare," which reflects the valuation of the perceived costs and benefits of taxation, is such that the marginal benefit of an additional dollar spent on a program is just equal to the marginal cost of the taxes needed to finance it, which occurs at R^* in Figure 8.9. If the government collects (and spends) less than R^*, MBF > MCF and it could increase social welfare by increasing taxes and expenditures; if it collects more than R^*, MBF < MCF and it can increase welfare by lowering taxes and expenditures. The optimal amount of revenue collected by a tax (and implicitly the underlying size of the tax) thus reflects the tradeoff that society makes between the efficiency cost of taxes and the perceived benefits of the programs they finance.

While quantifying the marginal cost of public funds for various taxes is not straightforward, as illustrated above economists have produced studies that attempt to do so. It is more difficult to quantify the marginal benefit that society may place on an incremental expenditure for a given government program, be it transfers to low income individuals, health care, or public roads. This often requires a subjective value judgment regarding the benefits of government spending, including the value of income redistribution. And indeed, members of society may well differ in their views on this. However, this is the essence of policymaking, and when designing a tax and expenditure system policymakers must implicitly make this type of value judgment. Our analysis here emphasizes that whatever that value judgment is, the marginal benefit perceived from spending an additional dollar on a government program must at least exceed the marginal cost of public funds used to finance it.

marginal benefit of public funds
the value that society places on one more dollar of expenditure on a government program

An important point in this regard is that because the marginal cost of public funds is greater than $1, this raises the "cost–benefit bar" when assessing government programs, and the overall size of the government. Indeed, whenever you see two policy analysts debating whether the government should provide more services or reduce the tax burden, part of the disagreement may rest on different views about the marginal cost of public funds (and the underlying elasticity of the tax base).

We began this chapter with a quote from Oliver Wendell Holmes Jr.: "Taxes are what we pay for civilized society." We have introduced tools in this chapter that allow us to think about this in useful way.

8-5 Conclusion

In this chapter, we have used the tools developed in the previous chapter to further our understanding of taxes. One of the ten principles of economics discussed in Chapter 1 is that markets are usually a good way to organize economic activity. In Chapter 7, we used the concepts of producer and consumer surplus to make this principle more precise. Here, we have seen that when the government imposes taxes on buyers or sellers of a good, society loses some of the benefits of market efficiency. Taxes are costly to market participants, not only because taxes transfer resources from those participants to the government, but also because they alter incentives and distort market outcomes. We have also seen that taxes are used to finance expenditures that society views as beneficial. Good government policy should measure the benefits of these expenditures against the costs of the taxes used to finance them.

The analysis presented here and in Chapter 6 should give you a good basis for understanding the economic impact of taxes, but this is not the end of the story. We touched briefly on the equity–efficiency tradeoff that underlies some government policies. Microeconomists study in more detail how best to design a tax and expenditure system, including how to strike the right balance between equality and efficiency. Macroeconomists study how taxes influence the overall economy and how policymakers can use the tax system to stabilize economic activity and to achieve more rapid economic growth. So as you continue your study of economics, don't be surprised when the subject of taxation comes up yet again.

summary

- A tax on a good reduces the welfare of buyers and sellers of the good, and the reduction in consumer and producer surplus usually exceeds the revenue raised by the government. The fall in total surplus—the sum of consumer surplus, producer surplus, and tax revenue—is called the *deadweight loss of the tax*.

- Taxes have deadweight losses because they cause buyers to consume less and sellers to produce less, and this change in behaviour shrinks the size of the market below the level that maximizes total surplus.

Because the elasticities of supply and demand measure how much market participants respond to market conditions, larger elasticities imply larger deadweight losses.

- As a tax grows larger, it distorts incentives more, and its deadweight loss grows larger. Because a tax reduces the size of the market, however, tax revenue does not continually increase. It first rises with the size of a tax, but if the tax gets large enough, tax revenue starts to fall.

KEY **concepts**

deadweight loss, *p. 176*
elasticity of the tax base, *p. 179*

marginal cost of public
funds, *p. 182*

marginal benefit of public
funds, *p. 187*

QUESTIONS FOR **review**

1. What happens to consumer and producer surplus
   when the sale of a good is taxed? How does the
   change in consumer and producer surplus compare to
   the tax revenue? Explain.

2. Draw a supply-and-demand diagram with a tax on
   the sale of the good. Show the deadweight loss. Show
   the tax revenue.

3. How do the elasticities of supply and demand affect
   the deadweight loss of a tax? Why do they have this
   effect?

4. Why do experts disagree about whether labour taxes
   have small or large deadweight losses?

5. What happens to the deadweight loss and tax revenue
   when a tax is increased?

QUICK CHECK **multiple choice**

1. In which of the following circumstances does a tax
   on a good have a deadweight loss?
   a. the reduction in consumer and producer surplus is
      greater than the tax revenue
   b. the tax revenue is greater than the reduction in con-
      sumer and producer surplus
   c. the reduction in consumer surplus is greater than
      the reduction in producer surplus
   d. the reduction in producer surplus is greater than
      the reduction in consumer surplus

2. Jane pays Chuck $50 to mow her lawn every week.
   When the government levies a mowing tax of $10
   on Chuck, he raises his price to $60. Jane continues
   to hire him at the higher price. What is the change in
   producer surplus, change in consumer surplus, and
   deadweight loss?
   a. $0, $0, $10
   b. $0, −$10, $0
   c. +$10, −$10, $10
   d. +$10, −$10, $0

3. Eggs have a supply curve that is linear and upward
   sloping and a demand curve that is linear and downward sloping. If a tax of 2 cents per egg is increased to
   3 cents, what happens to the deadweight loss of the tax?
   a. it increases by less than 50 percent and may even
      decline
   b. it increases by exactly 50 percent

   c. it increases by more than 50 percent
   d. The answer depends on whether supply or
      demand is more elastic.

4. Peanut butter has an upward-sloping supply curve
   and a downward-sloping demand curve. If a tax of
   10 cents per kilogram is increased to 15 cents, what
   happens to the government's tax revenue?
   a. it increases by less than 50 percent and may even decline
   b. it increases by exactly 50 percent
   c. it increases by more than 50 percent
   d. The answer depends on whether supply or
      demand is more elastic.

5. The Laffer curve illustrates that, in some circumstances, the government can reduce a tax on a good
   and increase which of the following?
   a. deadweight loss
   b. government's tax revenue
   c. equilibrium quantity
   d. price paid by consumers

6. If a policymaker wants to raise revenue by taxing
   goods while minimizing the deadweight losses, he
   should look for goods with ___ elasticities of demand
   and ___ elasticities of supply.
   a. small, small
   b. small, large
   c. large, small
   d. large, large

PROBLEMS AND **applications**

1. The market for pizza is characterized by a downward-
   sloping demand curve and an upward-sloping supply
   curve.

   a. Draw the competitive market equilibrium. Label
      the price, quantity, consumer surplus, and producer
      surplus. Is there any deadweight loss? Explain.

b. Suppose that the government forces each pizzeria to pay a $1 tax on each pizza sold. Illustrate the effect of this tax on the pizza market, being sure to label the consumer surplus, producer surplus, government revenue, and deadweight loss. How does each area compare to the pre-tax case?

c. If the tax were removed, pizza eaters and sellers would be better off but the government would lose tax revenue. Suppose that consumers and producers voluntarily transferred some of their gains to the government. Could all parties (including the government) be better off than they were with a tax? Explain using the labelled areas in your graph.

2. Evaluate the following two statements. Do you agree? Why or why not?

a. "A tax that has no deadweight loss cannot raise any revenue for the government."

b. "A tax that raises no revenue for the government cannot have any deadweight loss."

3. Consider the market for rubber bands.

a. If this market has very elastic supply and very inelastic demand, how would the burden of a tax on rubber bands be shared between consumers and producers? Use the tools of consumer surplus and producer surplus in your answer.

b. If this market has very inelastic supply and very elastic demand, how would the burden of a tax on rubber bands be shared between consumers and producers? Contrast your answer with your answer to part (a).

4. Suppose that the government imposes a tax on heating oil.

a. Would the deadweight loss from this tax likely be greater in the first year after it is imposed or in the fifth year? Explain.

b. Would the revenue collected from this tax likely be greater in the first year after it is imposed or in the fifth year? Explain.

5. After economics class one day, your friend suggests that taxing food would be a good way to raise revenue because the demand for food is quite inelastic. In what sense is taxing food a "good" way to raise revenue? In what sense is it not a "good" way to raise revenue?

6. U.S. Senator Daniel Patrick Moynihan once introduced a bill that would levy a 10 000-percent tax on certain hollow-tipped bullets.

a. Do you expect that this tax would raise much revenue? Why or why not?

b. Even if the tax would raise no revenue, what might be Senator Moynihan's reason for proposing it?

7. The government places a tax on the purchase of socks.

a. Illustrate the effect of this tax on equilibrium price and quantity in the sock market. Identify the following areas both before and after the imposition of the tax: total spending by consumers,

total revenue for producers, and government tax revenue.

b. Does the price received by producers rise or fall? Can you tell whether total receipts for producers rise or fall? Explain.

c. Does the price paid by consumers rise or fall? Can you tell whether total spending by consumers rises or falls? Explain carefully. (*Hint:* Think about elasticity.) If total consumer spending falls, does consumer surplus rise? Explain.

8. Suppose the government currently raises $100 million through a $0.01 tax on widgets, and another $100 million through a $0.10 tax on gadgets. If the government doubled the tax rate on widgets and eliminated the tax on gadgets, would it raise more tax revenue than it does today, less tax revenue, or the same amount? Explain.

9. Suppose the Canadian government decides that it needs to raise an additional $100 million in tax revenues. One Cabinet minister argues for a tax on all soft drinks. A second Cabinet minister argues for a tax on cola only, since this would give consumers a choice of paying the tax (by drinking cola) or avoiding it (by switching to another soft drink).

a. Which market has the more elastic supply and demand curves: the market for cola, or the market for all soft drinks?

b. To raise the same $100 million in revenue, which would require a higher rate: a tax on cola, or a tax on all soft drinks?

c. Which would cause a larger deadweight loss: a tax on cola, or a tax on all soft drinks?

d. Which would be the better tax? Explain.

10. Hotel rooms in Smalltown go for $100, and 1000 rooms are rented on a typical day.

a. To raise revenue, the mayor decides to charge hotels a tax of $10 per rented room. After the tax is imposed, the going rate for hotel rooms rises to $108, and the number of rooms rented falls to 900. Calculate the amount of revenue this tax raises for Smalltown and the deadweight loss of the tax. (*Hint:* The area of a triangle is ½ × base × height.)

b. The mayor now doubles the tax to $20. The price rises to $116, and the number of rooms rented falls to 800. Calculate tax revenue and deadweight loss with this larger tax. Do they double, more than double, or less than double? Explain.

11. This chapter analyzed the welfare effects of a tax on a good. Consider now the opposite policy. Suppose that the government *subsidizes* a good: For each unit of the good sold, the government pays $2 to the buyer. How does the subsidy affect consumer surplus, producer surplus, tax revenue, and total surplus? Does a subsidy lead to a deadweight loss? Explain.

The Mathematics of Deadweight Loss

In previous appendixes, we have used mathematics and linear demand and supply curves to allow us to be more precise about some important economic relationships. We use a similar approach here to be more precise about the concept of deadweight loss.

Figure 8.3 in this chapter shows how the various areas between the supply and demand curves can be used to determine how taxes affect welfare. In this diagram, and in the subsequent discussion about Figure 8.4, it was shown that the area C + E in Figure 8.3 is the deadweight loss of the tax. In the case of linear supply and demand curves, this is the area of a triangle that, using a similar technique to that used in the appendix to Chapter 7, can be calculated as one-half of the height times the base. The height of the triangle in this case is the wedge driven between the price paid by buyers and the price paid by sellers, which is the amount of the tax, T, per unit, and the base is the change in equilibrium quantity demanded due to the increase in the price that buyers pay because of the tax, $Q_1 - Q_2$. Thus, the deadweight loss of a tax imposed at T per unit is simply

$$\text{Deadweight loss} = \left(\frac{1}{2}\right)T(Q_1 - Q_2)$$

As an example, we can use the linear supply and demand curves employed in the previous chapter appendixes. Recall from the appendix to Chapter 6 that in the presence of a tax the demand and supply curves were:

$$Q^D = 56 - 4P_B$$
$$Q^s = -4 + 2P_S$$

where P_B is the price paid by buyers of the good, P_S is the price received by sellers, and $P_B = P_S + T$. In that appendix we showed that for a tax of $T = \$1.50$ per unit, the equilibrium quantity demanded fell from 16 to 14. The equilibrium for this example is shown in Figure 8A.1. Using our deadweight loss formula, the deadweight loss of the tax in this example is therefore:

$$\text{Deadweight loss} = \left(\frac{1}{2}\right)\$1.50(16 - 14) = \$1.50$$

This is the amount by which the losses of the buyers and sellers of the good due to the tax exceed the revenue raised by the tax. The deadweight loss of a tax is often expressed as a percentage of the revenue raised by the tax. In this case the revenue raised is the amount of the per-unit tax times the number of units sold, or $\$1.50 \times 14 = \$21$. So deadweight loss as a percentage of tax revenue raised is $\$1.50/\$21$ or just over 7 percent.

FIGURE 8A.1

Deadweight Loss of a Tax

This figure illustrates the revenue raised and the deadweight loss associated with a tax in the case of a demand curve $Q_D = 56 - 4P_B$ and supply curve $Q_S = -4 + 2P_S$. The deadweight loss of the tax is given by the area of the identified triangle ($1.50) and the revenue raised is given by the area of the rectangle.

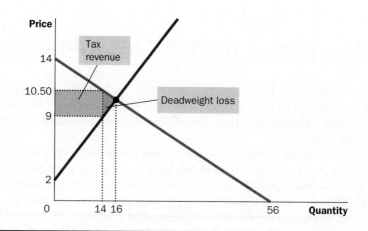

PROBLEMS AND **applications**

A1. Suppose that a market is described by the following supply and demand equations:

$$Q^s = 2P$$
$$Q^D = 300 - P$$

a. Solve for the equilibrium price and the equilibrium quantity.

b. Suppose that a tax of T is placed on buyers, so the new demand equation is

$$Q^D = 300 - (P + T)$$

Solve for the new equilibrium. What happens to the price received by sellers, the price paid by buyers, and the quantity sold?

c. Tax revenue is $T \times Q$. Use your answer to part (b) to solve for tax revenue as a function of T. Graph this relationship for T between 0 and 300.

d. The deadweight loss of a tax is the area of the triangle between the supply and demand curves. Recalling that the area of a triangle is ½ × base × height, solve for deadweight loss as a function of T. Graph this relationship for T between 0 and 300. (*Hint:* Looking sideways, the base of the deadweight loss triangle is T, and the height is the difference between the quantity sold with the tax and the quantity sold without the tax.)

e. The government now levies a tax on this good of $200 per unit. Is this a good policy? Why or why not? Can you propose a better policy?

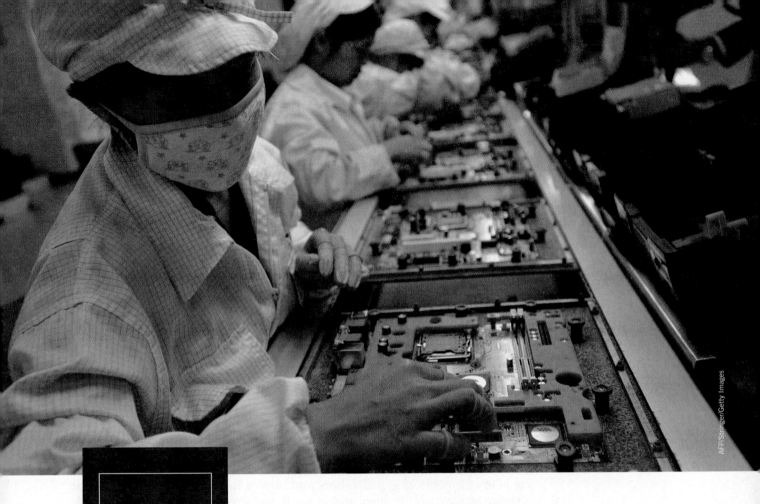

Application: International Trade

In this chapter, you will ...

1 Consider what determines whether a country imports or exports a good

2 Examine who wins and who loses from international trade

3 Learn that the gains to winners from international trade exceed the losses to losers

4 Analyze the welfare effects of tariffs and import quotas

5 Examine the arguments people use to advocate trade restrictions

If you check the labels on the clothes you are wearing, you will probably find that some were made in another country. A century ago the textiles and clothing industry was a major part of the Canadian economy, but that is no longer the case. Faced with foreign competitors that could produce quality goods at low cost, many Canadian firms found it increasingly difficult to produce and sell textiles and clothing at a profit. As a result, they laid off their workers and shut down their factories. Today, much of the textiles and clothing that Canadians consume are imported from abroad.

The story of the textiles industry raises important questions for economic policy: How does international trade affect economic well-being? Who gains and who loses from free trade among countries, and how do the gains compare to the losses?

Chapter 3 introduced the study of international trade by applying the principle of comparative advantage. According to this principle, all countries can benefit from trading with one another because trade allows each country to specialize in doing what it does best. But the analysis in Chapter 3 was incomplete. It did not explain how the international marketplace achieves these gains from trade or how the gains are distributed among various economic participants.

In this chapter we return to the study of international trade to tackle these questions. Over the past several chapters, we have developed many tools for analyzing how markets work: supply, demand, equilibrium, consumer surplus, producer surplus, and so on. With these tools, we can learn more about how international trade affects economic well-being.

Before beginning our analysis, it is useful to briefly discuss the notion of "globalization" in a Canadian context. There has been a great deal of attention in political and policy discourse over the last several years regarding the extent of globalization, and the subsequent emergence of anti-globalism sentiment. There are many elements of globalization, and indeed it is not clear precisely what is meant by the concept—there are economic, social, cultural, and political aspects of globalization. Here we view globalization through an economic lens, and focus on the worldwide movement toward economic, financial, and trade integration.

Trade is the cornerstone of Canada's economy, and indeed the country was conceived in large part as a way to reduce interprovincial trade barriers and create a nation to facilitate exports and attract foreign investment. Today, virtually every aspect of our daily living, and most of what we eat, drink, wear, and consume, is made possible by trade. One way to see this is to measure total trade, which is the sum of imports and exports, as a percentage of gross domestic product (GDP), which is a measure of total value of everything produced in a country. Figure 9.1 shows the trade to GDP ratio for Canada, the United States, and the aggregate of all 35 OECD (Organisation of Economic Co-operation and Development) countries, from 1960 to 2016. It shows that trade is a big part of the Canadian economy, more so than the OECD average and significantly more so than the United States: in 2016 trade as a percentage of GDP was about 64 percent in Canada, 55 percent in the OECD, and 27 percent in the U.S. Indeed, in the early 2000s, the trade to GDP ratio in Canada was above 80 percent. The significant drop since then is due in large part to the collapse of oil prices, which lowered the value of oil exports from Canada. Notwithstanding that reduction, the general trend over the last several decades has been one of increasing trade relative to the size of the economy, which is consistent with the globalization narrative.

In what follows we focus for illustrative purposes on trade in final goods, like textiles. However, it turns out that the bulk of international trade actually takes place in intermediate goods, which are inputs traded between firms. Only about 20 percent of total world trade is accounted for by final consumption goods.

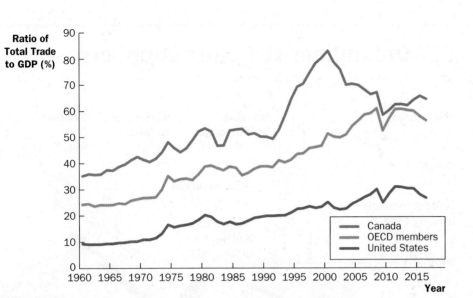

FIGURE 9.1

Trade and Globalization, 1960–2016

This figure shows the ratio of total trade (imports plus exports) to gross domestic product (GDP) in Canada, the OECD, and the U.S. Trade is an important part of the Canadian economy and has generally been growing over the past several decades.

Source: The World Bank: "Trade (% of GDP)" https://data.worldbank.org/indicator/NE.TRD.GNFS.ZS

The prevalence of offshoring and global supply chains is illustrated in Figure 9.2, which shows the origin of some of the major parts in the Boeing 787 Dreamliner aircraft. While the aircraft is assembled in the U.S., at Boeing's plants in Washington state and South Carolina, the parts are imported from around the world, from France, to Japan, to India and, yes, even Canada; who knew that Canada has a comparative advantage in the production of "movable trailing edges"?

9-1 The Determinants of Trade

While international trade can be complicated, we focus here on a relatively simply market in order to illustrate ideas. Consider the market for textiles. The textile market is well suited to examining the gains and losses from international trade: Textiles are made in many countries around the world, and there is much world trade in textiles. Moreover, the textile market is one in which policymakers often consider (and sometimes implement) trade restrictions to protect domestic producers from foreign competitors. We examine here the textile market in the imaginary country of Isoland.

9-1a The Equilibrium without Trade

As our story begins, the Isolandian textile market is isolated from the rest of the world. By government decree, no one in Isoland is allowed to import or export textiles, and the penalty for violating the decree is so large that no one dares try.

Because there is no international trade, the market for textiles in Isoland consists solely of Isolandian buyers and sellers. As Figure 9.3 shows, the domestic price adjusts to balance the quantity supplied by domestic sellers and the quantity demanded by domestic buyers. The figure shows the consumer and producer surplus in the equilibrium without trade. The sum of consumer and producer surplus measures the total benefits that buyers and sellers receive from participating in the textile market.

FIGURE 9.2

The Global Origins of the Boeing Dreamliner

This figure illustrates the prevalence of offshoring and global supply chains using the origin of some of the parts used in the Boeing 787 Dreamliner.

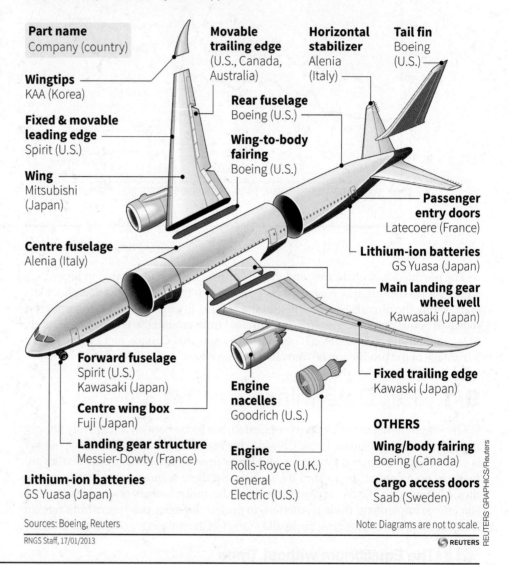

787 Dreamliner structure suppliers

Selected component and system suppliers.

Part name
Company (country)

Wingtips
KAA (Korea)

Fixed & movable leading edge
Spirit (U.S.)

Wing
Mitsubishi (Japan)

Centre fuselage
Alenia (Italy)

Forward fuselage
Spirit (U.S.)
Kawasaki (Japan)

Centre wing box
Fuji (Japan)

Landing gear structure
Messier-Dowty (France)

Lithium-ion batteries
GS Yuasa (Japan)

Movable trailing edge
(U.S., Canada, Australia)

Rear fuselage
Boeing (U.S.)

Wing-to-body fairing
Boeing (U.S.)

Horizontal stabilizer
Alenia (Italy)

Tail fin
Boeing (U.S.)

Passenger entry doors
Latecoere (France)

Lithium-ion batteries
GS Yuasa (Japan)

Main landing gear wheel well
Kawasaki (Japan)

Engine nacelles
Goodrich (U.S.)

Engine
Rolls-Royce (U.K.)
General Electric (U.S.)

Fixed trailing edge
Kawaski (Japan)

OTHERS

Wing/body fairing
Boeing (Canada)

Cargo access doors
Saab (Sweden)

Sources: Boeing, Reuters

Note: Diagrams are not to scale.

RNGS Staff, 17/01/2013

REUTERS

REUTERS GRAPHICS/Reuters

Now suppose that, in an election upset, Isoland elects a new president. The president campaigned on a platform of "change" and promised the voters bold new ideas. Her first act is to assemble a team of economists to evaluate Isolandian trade policy. She asks them to report back on three questions:

1. If the government allowed Isolandians to import and export textiles, what would happen to the price of textiles and the quantity of textiles sold in the domestic textile market?

Canada Must Step Up to Defend a Globalized World

Recent events in several countries seem to reflect pushback against globalization, writ large. The difficulties surrounding the renegotiation of NAFTA in 2018, which culminated in the new United States–Mexico–Canada Agreement (USMCA), and issues arising in connection with Brexit in the U.K. are just two examples of this. Canada is in a position to step up to defend globalization on the world stage.

Canada Advances with Globalization

The worldwide economic recession has decelerated the pace of globalization, but not as profoundly as initially forecast. Canada has weathered the storm well. And this is welcome; the more globalized a nation's economy, the happier and wealthier its citizens. It also correlates with a higher GDP per capita, and a higher percentage of the work force in professional, knowledge-based and creative jobs.

Canada ranked 13th overall on a list of 100 countries on the just-released Globalization Index, produced by the KOF Swiss Economic Institute. Measuring trade and investment volume, and the extent to which countries apply trade and capital movement restrictions to protect their own economies, the index showed that overall globalization has slowed as a result of the 2008 financial crisis. It also measured social globalization—the extent of the free flow of information and ideas—and political globalization, the degree of political co-operation between countries.

Belgium, Austria, the Netherlands, Sweden, and Switzerland took the top five spots on the overall globalization index, while Canada ranked fourth in social globalization. The U.S. ranked 50th overall. As the world's largest economy, it can afford to be more inward-looking because it relies on internal trade and production. But in general, globalization is closely associated with a higher level of economic development, notes Richard Florida, author and director of the Martin Prosperity Institute.

As a mid-sized country, Canada is perfectly positioned to become even more globalized, which in turn will lead to greater prosperity and influence. Canada must continue to eliminate trade barriers, diversify trade, innovate and assume a greater role on the world stage.

Source: Fred Lum, "Canada Advances with Globalization," *The Globe and Mail*, March 27, 2011, updated March 25, 2018. https://www.theglobeandmail.com/opinion/editorials/canada-advances-with-globalization/article574213/. © The Globe and Mail Inc. All Rights Reserved.

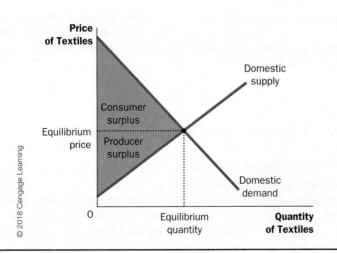

FIGURE 9.3

The Equilibrium without International Trade

When an economy cannot trade in world markets, the price adjusts to balance domestic supply and demand. This figure shows consumer and producer surplus in an equilibrium without international trade for the textile market in the imaginary country of Isoland.

2. Who would gain from free trade in textiles and who would lose, and would the gains exceed the losses?
3. Should a tariff (a tax on textile imports) or an import quota (a limit on textile imports) be part of the new trade policy?

After reviewing supply and demand in their favourite textbook (this one, of course), the Isolandian economics team begins its analysis.

9-1b The World Price and Comparative Advantage

The first issue our economists take up is whether Isoland is likely to become a textile importer or a textile exporter. In other words, if free trade is allowed, will Isolandians end up buying or selling textiles in world markets?

To answer this question, the economists compare the current Isolandian price of textiles to the price of textiles in other countries. We call the price prevailing in world markets the **world price**. If the world price of textiles is higher than the domestic price, then Isoland will export textiles once trade is permitted. Isolandian textile producers will be eager to receive the higher prices available abroad and will start selling their textiles to buyers in other countries. Conversely, if the world price of textiles is lower than the domestic price, then Isoland will import textiles. Because foreign sellers offer a better price, Isolandian textile consumers will quickly start buying textiles from other countries.

In essence, comparing the world price with the domestic price before trade reveals whether Isoland has a comparative advantage in producing textiles. The domestic price reflects the opportunity cost of textiles: It tells us how much an Isolandian must give up to get one unit of textiles. If the domestic price is low, the cost of producing textiles in Isoland is low, suggesting that Isoland has a comparative advantage in producing textiles relative to the rest of the world. If the domestic price is high, then the cost of producing textiles in Isoland is high, suggesting that foreign countries have a comparative advantage in producing textiles.

As we saw in Chapter 3, trade among nations is ultimately based on comparative advantage. That is, trade is beneficial because it allows each nation to specialize in doing what it does best. By comparing the world price and the domestic price before trade, we can determine whether Isoland is better or worse than the rest of the world at producing textiles.

world price
the price of a good that prevails in the world market for that good

 QUICK Quiz *The country Autarka does not allow international trade. In Autarka, you can buy a wool suit for 100 grams of gold. Meanwhile, in neighbouring countries, you can buy the same suit for 60 grams of gold. If Autarka were to allow free trade, would it import or export suits? Why?*

9-2 The Winners and Losers from Trade

To analyze the welfare effects of free trade, the Isolandian economists begin with the assumption that Isoland is a small economy compared to the rest of the world. This small-economy assumption means that Isoland's actions have little effect on world markets. Specifically, any change in Isoland's trade policy will not affect the world price of textiles. The Isolandians are said to be *price takers* in the world economy. That is, they take the world price of textiles as given. Isoland can be an exporting country by selling textiles at this price or an importing country by buying textiles at this price.

The small-economy assumption is not necessary to analyze the gains and losses from international trade. But the Isolandian economists know from experience (and from reading Chapter 2 of this book) that making simplifying assumptions is a key part of building a useful economic model. The assumption that Isoland is a small economy simplifies the analysis, and the basic lessons do not change in the more complicated case of a large economy. It turns out to be a pretty accurate characterization of the Canadian economy, which accounts for under 2 percent of world GDP.

9-2a The Gains and Losses of an Exporting Country

Figure 9.4 shows the Isolandian textile market when the domestic equilibrium price before trade is below the world price. Once free trade is allowed, the domestic price rises to equal the world price. No seller of textiles would accept less than the world price, and no buyer would pay more than the world price.

After the domestic price has risen to equal the world price, the domestic quantity supplied differs from the domestic quantity demanded. The supply curve shows the quantity of textiles supplied by Isolandian sellers. The demand curve shows the quantity of textiles demanded by Isolandian buyers. Because the domestic quantity supplied is greater than the domestic quantity demanded, Isoland sells textiles to other countries. Thus, Isoland becomes a textile exporter.

FIGURE 9.4

International Trade in an Exporting Country

Once trade is allowed, the domestic price rises to equal the world price. The supply curve shows the quantity of textiles produced domestically, and the demand curve shows the quantity consumed domestically. Exports from Isoland equal the difference between the domestic quantity supplied and the domestic quantity demanded at the world price. Sellers are better off (producer surplus rises from C to B + C + D), and buyers are worse off (consumer surplus falls from A + B to A). Total surplus rises by an amount equal to area D, indicating that trade raises the economic well-being of the country as a whole.

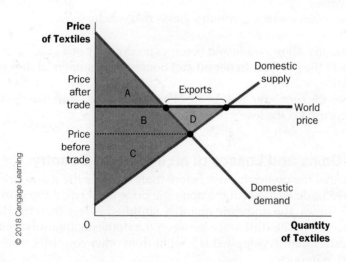

© 2018 Cengage Learning

	Before Trade	After Trade	Change
Consumer Surplus	A + B	A	−B
Producer Surplus	C	B + C + D	+(B + D)
Total Surplus	A + B + C	A + B + C + D	= D

The area D shows the increase in total surplus and represents the gains from trade.

Although domestic quantity supplied and domestic quantity demanded differ, the textile market is still in equilibrium because there is now another participant in the market: the rest of the world. One can view the horizontal line at the world price as representing the rest of the world's demand for textiles. This demand curve is perfectly elastic because Isoland, as a small economy, can sell as many textiles as it wants at the world price.

Consider the gains and losses from opening up trade. Clearly, not everyone benefits. Trade forces the domestic price to rise to the world price. Domestic producers of textiles are better off because they can now sell textiles at a higher price, but domestic consumers of textiles are worse off because they now have to buy textiles at a higher price.

To measure these gains and losses, we look at the changes in consumer and producer surplus. Before trade is allowed, the price of textiles adjusts to balance domestic supply and domestic demand. Consumer surplus, the area between the demand curve and the before-trade price, is area A + B. Producer surplus, the area between the supply curve and the before-trade price, is area C. Total surplus before trade, the sum of consumer and producer surplus, is area A + B + C.

After trade is allowed, the domestic price rises to the world price. Consumer surplus is reduced to area A (the area between the demand curve and the world price). Producer surplus is increased to area B + C + D (the area between the supply curve and the world price). Thus, total surplus with trade is area A + B + C + D.

These welfare calculations show who wins and who loses from trade in an exporting country. Sellers benefit because producer surplus increases by the area B + D. Buyers are worse off because consumer surplus decreases by the area B. Because the gains of sellers exceed the losses of buyers by the area D, total surplus in Isoland increases.

This analysis of an exporting country yields two conclusions:

1. When a country allows trade and becomes an exporter of a good, domestic producers of the good are better off and domestic consumers of the good are worse off.
2. Trade raises the economic well-being of a nation in the sense that the gains of the winners exceed the losses of the losers.

9-2b The Gains and Losses of an Importing Country

Now suppose that the domestic price before trade is above the world price. Once again, after free trade is allowed, the domestic price must equal the world price. As Figure 9.5 shows, the domestic quantity supplied is less than the domestic quantity demanded. The difference between the domestic quantity demanded and the domestic quantity supplied is bought from other countries, and Isoland becomes a textile importer.

In this case, the horizontal line at the world price represents the supply of the rest of the world. This supply curve is perfectly elastic because Isoland is a small economy and, therefore, can buy as many textiles as it wants at the world price.

Now consider the gains and losses from trade. As in the previous case, not everyone benefits, but here the winners and losers are reversed. When trade forces the domestic price to fall, domestic consumers are better off (they can now buy textiles at a lower price), and domestic producers are worse off (they now have to sell textiles at a lower price). Changes in consumer and producer surplus measure

FIGURE 9.5

International Trade in an Importing Country

Once trade is allowed, the domestic price falls to equal the world price. The supply curve shows the amount produced domestically, and the demand curve shows the amount consumed domestically. Imports equal the difference between the domestic quantity demanded and the domestic quantity supplied at the world price. Buyers are better off (consumer surplus rises from A to A + B + D), and sellers are worse off (producer surplus falls from B + C to C). Total surplus rises by an amount equal to area D, indicating that trade raises the economic well-being of the country as a whole.

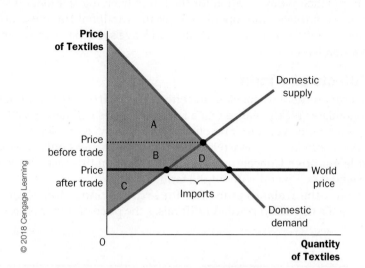

© 2018 Cengage Learning

	Before Trade	After Trade	Change
Consumer Surplus	A	A + B + D	+(B + D)
Producer Surplus	B + C	C	−B
Total Surplus	A + B + C	A + B + C + D	+D

The area D shows the increase in total surplus and represents the gains from trade.

the size of the gains and losses. Before trade, consumer surplus is area A, producer surplus is area B + C, and total surplus is area A + B + C. After trade is allowed, consumer surplus is area A + B + D, producer surplus is area C, and total surplus is area A + B + C + D.

These welfare calculations show who wins and who loses from trade in an importing country. Buyers benefit because consumer surplus increases by the area B + D. Sellers are worse off because producer surplus falls by the area B. The gains of buyers exceed the losses of sellers, and total surplus increases by the area D.

This analysis of an importing country yields two conclusions parallel to those for an exporting country:

1. When a country allows trade and becomes an importer of a good, domestic consumers of the good are better off, and domestic producers of the good are worse off.
2. Trade raises the economic well-being of a nation in the sense that the gains of the winners exceed the losses of the losers.

Having completed our analysis of trade, we can better understand one of the ten principles of economics in Chapter 1: Trade can make everyone better off. If Isoland opens up its textile market to international trade, that change will create winners and losers, regardless of whether Isoland ends up exporting or importing textiles. In either case, however, the gains of the winners exceed the losses of the losers, so the winners could compensate the losers and still be better off. In this sense, trade *can* make everyone better off. But *will* trade make everyone better off? Probably not. In practice, compensation for the losers from international trade is rare. Without such compensation, opening up to international trade is a policy that expands the size of the economic pie, but it can leave some participants in the economy with a smaller slice.

9-2c The Effects of a Tariff

tariff

a tax on goods produced abroad and sold domestically

The Isolandian economists next consider the effects of a **tariff**—a tax on imported goods. The economists quickly realize that a tariff on textiles will have no effect if Isoland becomes a textile exporter. If no one in Isoland is interested in importing textiles, a tax on textile imports is irrelevant. The tariff matters only if Isoland becomes a textile importer. Concentrating their attention on this case, the economists compare welfare with and without the tariff.

Figure 9.6 shows the Isolandian market for textiles. Under free trade, the domestic price equals the world price. A tariff raises the price of imported textiles

---

FIGURE 9.6

The Effects of a Tariff

A tariff reduces the quantity of imports and moves a market closer to the equilibrium that would exist without trade. Total surplus falls by an amount equal to area D + F. These two triangles represent the dead-weight loss from the tariff.

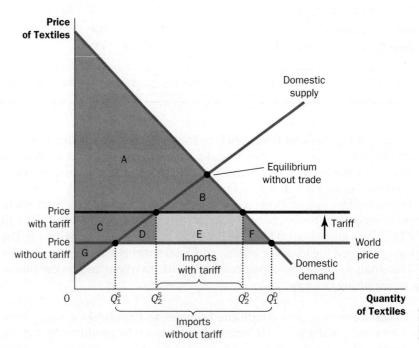

© 2018 Cengage Learning

	Before Trade	After Trade	Change
Consumer Surplus	A + B + C + D + E + F	A + B	−(C + D + E + F)
Producer Surplus	G	C + G	+C
Government Revenue	None	E	+E
Total Surplus	A + B + C + D + E + F + G	A + B + C + E + G	−(D + F)

The area D + F shows the fall in total surplus and represents the deadweight loss of the tariff.

above the world price by the amount of the tariff. Domestic suppliers of textiles, who compete with suppliers of imported textiles, can now sell their textiles for the world price plus the amount of the tariff. Thus, the price of textiles—both imported and domestic—rises by the amount of the tariff and is, therefore, closer to the price that would prevail without trade.

The change in price affects the behaviour of domestic buyers and sellers. Because the tariff raises the price of textiles, it reduces the domestic quantity demanded from Q_1^D to Q_2^D and raises the domestic quantity supplied from Q_1^S to Q_2^S. Thus, *the tariff reduces the quantity of imports and moves the domestic market closer to its equilibrium without trade.*

Now consider the gains and losses from the tariff. Because the tariff raises the domestic price, domestic sellers are better off and domestic buyers are worse off. In addition, the government raises revenue. To measure these gains and losses, we look at the changes in consumer surplus, producer surplus, and government revenue. These changes are summarized in the table in Figure 9.6.

Before the tariff, the domestic price equals the world price. Consumer surplus, the area between the demand curve and the world price, is area A + B + C + D + E + F. Producer surplus, the area between the supply curve and the world price, is area G. Government revenue equals zero. Total surplus—the sum of consumer surplus, producer surplus, and government revenue—is area A + B + C + D + E + F + G.

Once the government imposes a tariff, the domestic price exceeds the world price by the amount of the tariff. Consumer surplus is now area A + B. Producer surplus is area C + G. Government revenue, which is the size of the tariff multiplied by the quantity of after-tariff imports, is area E. Thus, total surplus with the tariff is area A + B + C + E + G.

To determine the total welfare effects of the tariff, we add the change in consumer surplus (which is negative), the change in producer surplus (positive), and the change in government revenue (positive). We find that total surplus in the market decreases by the area D + F. This fall in total surplus is called the *deadweight loss* of the tariff.

A tariff causes a deadweight loss because a tariff is a type of tax. Like most taxes, it distorts incentives and pushes the allocation of scarce resources away from the optimum. In this case, we can identify two effects. First, when the tariff raises the domestic price of textiles above the world price, it encourages domestic producers to increase production from Q_1^S to Q_2^S. Even though the cost of making these incremental units exceeds the cost of buying them at the world price, the tariff makes it profitable for domestic producers to manufacture them nonetheless. Second, when the tariff raises the price that domestic textile consumers have to pay, it encourages them to reduce consumption of textiles from Q_1^D to Q_2^D. Even though domestic consumers value these incremental units at more than the world price, the tariff induces them to cut back their purchases. Area D represents the deadweight loss from the overproduction of textiles, and area F represents the deadweight loss from the underconsumption of textiles. The total deadweight loss of the tariff is the sum of these two triangles.

9-2d Import Quotas: Another Way to Restrict Trade

Beyond tariffs, another way that nations sometimes restrict international trade is by putting limits on how much of a good can be imported. In this book, we will not analyze such a policy, other than to point out the conclusion: Import quotas are much like tariffs. Both tariffs and import quotas reduce the quantity of imports, raise the domestic price of the good, decrease the welfare of domestic consumers, increase the welfare of domestic producers, and cause deadweight losses.

There is only one difference between these two types of trade restriction: A tariff raises revenue for the government, whereas an import quota creates surplus for those who obtain the licences to import. The profit for the holder of an import licence is the difference between the domestic price (at which the licence holder sells the imported good) and the world price (at which the licence holder buys it).

Tariffs and import quotas are even more similar if the government charges a fee for the import licences. Suppose the government sets the licence fee equal to the difference between the domestic price and the world price. In this case, all of the profit of licence holders is paid to the government in licence fees, and the import quota works exactly like a tariff. Consumer surplus, producer surplus, and government revenue are precisely the same under the two policies.

9-2e The Lessons for Trade Policy

The team of Isolandian economists can now write to the new president:

Dear Madam President,

You asked us three questions about opening up trade. After much hard work, we have the answers.

Question: If the government allowed Isolandians to import and export textiles, what will happen to the price of textiles and the quantity of textiles in the domestic textile market?

Answer: Once trade is allowed, the Isolandian price of textiles will be driven to equal the price prevailing around the world.

If the world price is now higher than the Isolandian price, our price will rise. The higher price will reduce the amount of textiles Isolandians consume and raise the amount of textiles that Isolandians produce. Isoland will, therefore, become a textile exporter. This occurs because, in this case, Isoland has a comparative advantage in producing textiles.

Conversely, if the world price is now lower than the Isolandian price, our price will fall. The lower price will raise the amount of textiles that Isolandians consume and lower the amount of textiles that Isolandians produce. Isoland will, therefore, become a textile importer. This occurs because, in this case, other countries have a comparative advantage in producing textiles.

Question: Who will gain from free trade in textiles and who will lose, and will the gains exceed the losses?

Answer: The answer depends on whether the price rises or falls when trade is allowed. If the price rises, producers of textiles gain, and consumers of textiles lose. If the price falls, consumers gain, and producers lose. In both cases, the gains are larger than the losses. Thus, ignoring distributional considerations, free trade raises the total welfare of Isolandians.

Question: Should a tariff or an import quota be part of the new trade policy?

Answer: A tariff has an impact only if Isoland becomes a textile importer. In this case, a tariff moves the economy closer to its no-trade equilibrium and, like most taxes, has deadweight losses. A tariff improves the welfare of domestic producers and raises revenue for the government, but these gains are more than offset by the losses suffered by consumers. An import quota works much like a tariff and would cause similar deadweight losses. The best policy, from the standpoint of pure economic efficiency, would be to allow trade without a tariff or an import quota. There may be distributional considerations which bear upon this issue which we do not address here.

We hope you find these answers helpful as you decide on your new policy.

Your faithful servants,
Isolandian Economics Team

The letter written by the Isolandian Economics Team emphasizes that there are winners and losers from implementing a tariff on textiles and departing from the free trade equilibrium in a small open economy. Consumers are losers because the price of textiles increases, which leads to a reduction in consumer surplus. Producers are winners because they are able to sell more textiles domestically at a higher price, which increases producer surplus. And indeed, it is even more complicated than this. Some of the producer surplus may in turn be shared with the workers employed by textile firms, due to higher wages and more jobs. Other suppliers to textile firms may also benefit. The government is also a winner because it has revenue at its disposal, which it can use to provide goods and services or income transfers that are perceived to be beneficial to the recipients.

As we first discussed in Chapter 8 in our analysis of the costs of taxation, from a pure efficiency perspective we treat the value a dollar accruing to the losers as being the same as a dollar accruing to winners. When this is the case, as pointed out by the Isolandian Economics Team, the losses of the losers due to a tariff on textiles exceeds the gains of the winners, which produces a deadweight loss. They conclude that from the standpoint of economic efficiency, the best policy would be to allow free trade in textiles. This is the typical efficiency argument against tariffs, or for any policy that impinges upon free trade. And it is a compelling argument.

However, the Isolandian economists also allude to distributional considerations that need to be kept in mind when analyzing the benefits and costs of tariffs, and indeed any government policy. Society may subjectively value the gains and losses of the various market participants differently. For example, notwithstanding the possibility that free trade may well generate new jobs (as we discuss below), society may place a greater value on the gains accruing to textile workers by protecting their jobs through tariffs than on the losses imposed on consumers due to higher prices. This sort of value judgment is subjective and is difficult to quantify, and indeed is very much a political decision, which is why the Isolandian Economics Team focused on economic efficiency. However, it is nonetheless important to understand, and underlies virtually every policy choice a government must make.

As in Chapter 8 where we consider the marginal costs and benefits of public funds when discussing the tradeoffs that governments must make when deciding tax and expenditure policy, a similar tradeoff exists in trade policy. In this regard, there is a marginal cost of public funds associated with increasing tariff revenue by one dollar, which is equal to the $1 in revenue raised plus the associated increase in the deadweight loss triangles D + F in Figure 9.6. There will also be a marginal benefit associated with a one-dollar increase in the tariff. In this case the marginal benefit not only could reflect the benefit arising from a higher valuation that society may place on the possible uses of the tariff revenue, but also could reflect the higher valuation that society may place on the increase in surplus accruing to textile producers and their workers relative to consumers. As such, there may be a type of equity–efficiency policy tradeoff in play. The government should weigh the marginal cost of a tariff on textiles, including the increase in the deadweight loss, against the marginal benefit, which reflect differences in the valuation of the welfare changes imposed on the different market participants. For example, Isolandians in general may be willing to pay extra for their clothing and incur an increase in deadweight loss in the interests of employing more domestic textile workers. The optimal tariff on textiles should reflect these tradeoffs and be set such that the marginal benefit of increasing the tariff equals the marginal cost. This is illustrated in Figure 9.7, where the optimal tariff that trades off the marginal benefits against the marginal costs is given by T^*.

Evaluating this type of policy tradeoff clearly requires a value judgment reflecting the weight that society places on the relative welfare of the various market participants. While this is subjective and difficult to quantify, it reflects the essence of many government policies. It also emphasizes that we must look beyond the size of the monetary flows when evaluating government policies. In particular, we must recognize that the deadweight losses associated with the distortions caused by those policies raises the "cost–benefit bar." We must then trade that cost off against the perceived distributional implications for different market participants. Policy choices inevitably involve tradeoffs that require these types of subjective value judgments, and it is better to recognize and confront them head on.

This framework also helps us see why the debate over trade policy is often contentious. Whenever a policy creates winners and losers, there may be legitimate differences of opinion on the part of policy analysts regarding the size of the associated deadweight losses and on the valuation of the gains of the winners and the losses of the losers. These differences can in turn set the stage for political battles. For example, nations may sometimes fail to enjoy the gains from trade liberalization because the losers from freer trade are better organized than the winners. This can arise in trade policy because the gains of trade

FIGURE 9.7

Marginal Benefit and Cost of Public Funds for a Tariff

This figure shows the marginal cost and benefit of public funds for a tariff. The optimal tariff T^* equates the MCF to the MBF.

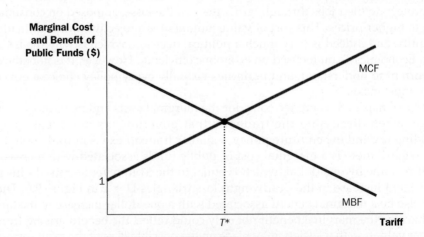

liberalization are often quite diffuse, spread across a large number of consumers, while the losses are concentrated in a small number of producers. The losers may be able to better organize because of their smaller numbers, and turn their cohesiveness into political clout and lobby for trade restrictions such as tariffs and import quotas. In terms of our analysis, they may be able to use the political process to alter (shift to the right) the marginal benefit curve perceived by politicians.

Draw the supply and demand curves for wool suits in the country of Autarka. When trade is allowed, the price of a suit falls from 100 to 60 grams of gold. In your diagram, what is the change in consumer surplus, the change in producer surplus, and the change in total surplus? How would a tariff on suit imports alter these effects?

9-2f Other Benefits of International Trade

The conclusions of the Isolandian economics team are based on the standard analysis of international trade. Their analysis uses the most fundamental tools in the economist's toolbox: supply, demand, and producer and consumer surplus. It shows that there are winners and losers when a nation opens itself up to trade, but the gains to the winners exceed the losses of the losers.

The case for free trade can be made even stronger, however, because there are several other economic benefits of trade beyond those emphasized in the standard analysis. Here, in a nutshell, are some of these other benefits:

- **Increased variety of goods.** Goods produced in different countries are not exactly the same. German beer, for instance, is not the same as Canadian beer. Free trade gives consumers in all countries greater variety from which to choose.
- **Lower costs through economies of scale.** Some goods can be produced at low cost only if they are produced in large quantities—a phenomenon called *economies of scale*. A firm in a small country cannot take full advantage of economies of scale if it can sell only in a small domestic market. Free trade gives firms access to larger world markets and allows them to realize economies of scale more fully.
- **Increased competition.** A company shielded from foreign competitors is more likely to have market power, which in turn gives it the ability to raise prices above competitive levels. This is a type of market failure. Opening up trade fosters competition and gives the invisible hand a better chance to work its magic.
- **Enhanced flow of ideas.** The transfer of technological advances around the world is often thought to be linked to the trading of the goods that embody those advances. The best way for a poor agricultural nation to learn about the computer revolution, for instance, is to buy some computers from abroad rather than trying to make them domestically.

Thus, free international trade increases variety for consumers, allows firms to take advantage of economies of scale, makes markets more competitive, and facilitates the spread of technology. If the Isolandian economists also took these effects into account, their advice to their president would be even more forceful.

9-3 The Arguments for Restricting Trade

The letter from the economics team persuades the new president of Isoland to consider opening up trade in textiles. She notes that the domestic price is now high compared to the world price. Free trade would, therefore, cause the price of textiles to fall and hurt domestic textile producers. Before implementing the new policy, she asks Isolandian textile companies to comment on the economists' advice.

Not surprisingly, the textile companies are opposed to free trade in textiles. They believe that the government should protect the domestic textile industry from foreign competition. Let's consider some of the arguments they might give to support their position and how the economics team would respond.

9-3a The Jobs Argument

Opponents of free trade often argue that trade with other countries destroys domestic jobs. In our example, free trade in textiles would cause the price of textiles to fall, reducing the quantity of textiles produced in Isoland and thus reducing employment in the Isolandian textile industry. Some Isolandian textile workers would lose their jobs.

Yet free trade creates jobs at the same time that it destroys them. When Isolandians buy textiles from other countries, those countries obtain the resources to buy other goods from Isoland. Isolandian workers would move from the textile industry to those industries in which Isoland has a comparative advantage. The transition may impose hardship on some workers in the short run, but it allows Isolandians as a whole to enjoy a higher standard of living.

Opponents of trade are often skeptical that trade creates jobs. They might respond that *everything* can be produced more cheaply abroad. Under free trade, they might argue, Isolandians could not be profitably employed in any industry. As Chapter 3 explains, however, the gains from trade are based on comparative advantage, not absolute advantage. Even if one country is better than another country at producing everything, each country can still gain from trading with the other. Workers in each country will eventually find jobs in the industry in which that country has a comparative advantage. While many trade economists argue that in the long run trade liberalization is largely job neutral—in the sense that as many new jobs are created as old jobs are eliminated—the transition may take some time. As such, government policies to facilitate the transition to new jobs are sometimes advocated.

9-3b The National-Security Argument

When an industry is threatened with competition from other countries, opponents of free trade often argue that the industry is vital to national security. For example, if Isoland were considering free trade in steel, domestic steel companies might point out that steel is used to make guns and tanks. Free trade would allow Isoland to become dependent on foreign countries to supply steel. If a war later broke out and the foreign supply was interrupted, Isoland might be unable to produce enough steel and weapons to defend itself.

Economists acknowledge that protecting key industries may be appropriate when there are legitimate concerns over national security. Yet they fear that this argument may be used too quickly by producers eager to gain at consumers' expense. Indeed, in 2018 the Trump administration in the U.S. invoked national security arguments to impose new tariffs on steel and aluminum. These tariffs were widely recognized, and condemned, as having being motivated by considerations that had little to do with national security.

One should be wary of the national-security argument when it is made by representatives of industry rather than the defence establishment. Companies have an incentive to exaggerate their role in national defence to obtain protection from foreign competition. A nation's generals may see things very differently. Indeed, when the military is a consumer of an industry's output, it would benefit from imports. Cheaper steel in Isoland, for example, would allow the Isolandian military to accumulate a stockpile of weapons at lower cost.

9-3c The Infant-Industry Argument

New industries sometimes argue for temporary trade restrictions to help them get started. After a period of protection, the argument goes, these industries will mature and be able to compete with foreign firms.

Similarly, older industries sometimes argue that they need temporary protection to help them adjust to new conditions. Canada's "National Policy," started by Sir John A. Macdonald in 1878, could be seen as an attempt to protect the infant Canadian manufacturing sector from foreign (especially U.S.) competition. This protection from foreign competition lasted for 110 years, until the Canada–U.S. Free Trade Agreement of 1989.

Economists are often skeptical about such claims, largely because the infant-industry argument is difficult to implement in practice. To apply protection successfully, the government would need to decide which industries will eventually be profitable and decide whether the benefits of establishing these industries exceed the costs of this protection to consumers. Yet "picking winners" is extraordinarily difficult. It is made even more difficult by the political process, which often awards protection to those industries that are politically powerful. And once a powerful industry is protected from foreign competition, the "temporary" policy is hard to remove.

In addition, many economists are skeptical about the infant-industry argument in principle. Suppose, for instance, that an industry is young and unable to compete profitably against foreign rivals, but there is reason to believe that the industry can be profitable in the long run. In this case, firm owners should be willing to incur temporary losses to obtain the eventual profits. Protection is not necessary for an infant industry to grow. History shows that start-up firms often incur temporary losses and succeed in the long run, even without protection from foreign competition.

9-3d The Unfair-Competition Argument

A common argument is that free trade is desirable only if all countries play by the same rules. If firms in different countries are subject to different laws and regulations, then it is unfair (the argument goes) to expect the firms to compete in the international marketplace. For instance, suppose that the government of Neighbourland subsidizes its textile industry by giving textile companies large tax breaks. The Isolandian textile industry might argue that it should be protected from this foreign competition because Neighbourland is not competing fairly.

Would it, in fact, hurt Isoland to buy textiles from another country at a subsidized price? Certainly, Isolandian textile producers would suffer, but Isolandian textile consumers would benefit from the low price. The case for free trade is the same as before: The gains of the consumers from buying at the low price would exceed the losses of the producers. Neighbourland's subsidy to its textile industry may be a bad policy, but it is the taxpayers of Neighbourland who bear the burden. Isoland can benefit from the opportunity to buy textiles at a subsidized price. Rather than objecting to the foreign subsidies, perhaps Isoland should send Neighbourland a thank-you note.

9-3e The Protection-as-a-Bargaining-Chip Argument

Another argument for trade restrictions concerns the strategy of bargaining. Many policymakers claim to support free trade but, at the same time, argue that trade restrictions can be useful when we bargain with our trading partners. They claim that the threat of a trade restriction can help remove a trade restriction already imposed by a foreign government. For example, Isoland might threaten to impose a tariff on textiles unless Neighbourland removes its tariff on wheat. If Neighbourland responds to this threat by removing its tariff, the result can be freer trade.

The problem with this bargaining strategy is that the threat may not work. If it doesn't work, the country faces a choice between two bad options. It can carry out its threat and implement the trade restriction, which would reduce its own economic welfare. Or it can back down from its threat, which would cause it to lose prestige in international affairs. Faced with this choice, the country would probably wish that it had never made the threat in the first place.

case study   **Canadian Trade Agreements**

A country can take one of two approaches to achieving free trade. It can take a *unilateral* approach and remove its trade restrictions on its own. This is the approach that Great Britain took in the nineteenth century and that Chile and South Korea have taken in recent years. Alternatively, a country can take a *multilateral* approach and reduce its trade restrictions while other countries do the same. In other words, it can bargain with its trading partners in an attempt to reduce trade restrictions around the world.

Canada has signed or is in negotiations on more than 30 multilateral free trade agreements. The most important of these is the United States–Mexico–Canada Agreement (USMCA), negotiations over which concluded in October 2018. The USMCA, which as of the writing of this book still needed to be ratified by the three governments, replaced the North American Free Trade Agreement (NAFTA), which in 1993 lowered trade barriers among the United States, Mexico, and Canada. The U.S. is Canada's largest trading partner, accounting for over three-quarters of our total trade. Moreover, Canada is America's second largest trading partner (behind China).

Two other important free trade agreements for Canada are the Comprehensive and Progressive Agreement for Trans-Pacific Partnership (CPTPP) and the Canada–European Union Comprehensive Economic and Trade Agreement (CETA). CPTPP came into force at the beginning of 2019 and CETA in September 2017.

Free trade agreements are often dissected in terms of "winners and losers." While there can be winners and losers associated with free trade agreements, and some agreements are certainly better than others, it is important to understand that in many cases the losses, such as lost jobs, are short term in nature. Moreover, trade liberalization need not be a "zero sum game," where one country's "win" is another country's "loss." As discussed, trade can be mutually beneficial. Moreover, and importantly, one key winner in most free trade agreements is often ignored—the consumers who are able to access a wider array of goods at lower prices.

Another important multilateral agreement that Canada is party to is the General Agreement on Tariffs and Trade (GATT), which is a continuing series of negotiations among many of the world's countries with the goal of promoting free trade. Canada helped to found GATT after World War II in response to the high tariffs imposed during the Great Depression of the 1930s. Many economists believe that the high tariffs contributed to the economic hardship during that period. GATT has successfully reduced the average tariff among member countries from about 40 percent after World War II to about 5 percent today.

The rules established under GATT are now enforced by an international institution called the World Trade Organization (WTO). The WTO was established in 1995 and has its headquarters in Geneva, Switzerland. As of November 2018, 164 countries had joined the organization, accounting for 97 percent of world trade. The functions of the WTO are to administer trade agreements, provide a forum for negotiations, and handle disputes that arise among member countries.

What are the pros and cons of the multilateral approach to free trade? One advantage is that the multilateral approach has the potential to result in freer trade than a unilateral approach because it can reduce trade restrictions abroad as well as at home. If international negotiations fail, however, the result could be more restricted trade than under a unilateral approach.

In addition, the multilateral approach may have a political advantage. In most markets, producers are fewer and better organized than consumers—and thus wield greater political influence. Reducing the Isolandian tariff on textiles, for example, may be politically difficult if considered by itself. The textile companies would oppose free trade, and the buyers of textiles who would benefit are so numerous that organizing their support would be difficult. Yet suppose that Neighbourland promises to reduce its tariff on wheat at the same time that Isoland reduces its tariff on textiles. In this case, the Isolandian wheat farmers, who are also politically powerful, would back the agreement. Thus, the multilateral approach to free trade can sometimes win political support when a unilateral reduction cannot. ∎

Ask the Experts

Trade Deals

"We have benefitted from past major trade deals."

What do economists say?

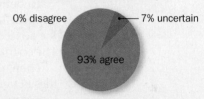

0% disagree   7% uncertain

93% agree

"Refusing to liberalize trade unless partner countries adopt new labor or environmental rules is a bad policy, because even if the new standards would reduce distortions on some dimensions, such a policy involves threatening to maintain large distortions in the form of restricted trade."

What do economists say?

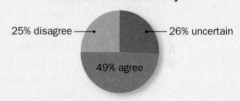

25% disagree   26% uncertain

49% agree

Source: IGM Economic Experts Panel, November 11, 2014 and March 27, 2013. Figures © 2018 Cengage Learning.

QUICK Quiz *The textile industry of Autarka advocates a ban on the import of wool suits. Describe five arguments its lobbyists might make. Give a response to each of these arguments.*

9-4 Conclusion

Economists and the general public often disagree about free trade. In 1988, for example, Canada faced the question of whether to sign the Canada–U.S. Free Trade Agreement, which reduced trade restrictions between Canada and the United States. Opinion polls showed the general public in Canada to be about evenly split on the issue. Prime Minister Brian Mulroney campaigned for the free trade agreement and won re-election, but with a minority of the popular vote.

Opponents viewed free trade as a threat to job security and the Canadian standard of living. By contrast, economists overwhelmingly supported the agreement. They viewed free trade as a way of allocating production efficiently and raising living standards in both countries.

Economists see the benefits of trade between countries in the same way that they see the benefits of trade between provinces, or between cities, or between people. Individuals would have a much lower standard of living if they had to produce all their own food, clothing, and housing. So would a city. So would a province. The United States has always had unrestricted trade among the states, and the country as a whole has benefited from the specialization that trade allows in such a large market. With a few exceptions, Canada, too, has free trade among the provinces and territories: Ontario builds cars, Alberta pumps oil, British Columbia saws lumber, and so on. The world could similarly benefit from free trade among countries.

To better understand economists' view of trade, let's continue our parable. Suppose that the president of Isoland, after reading the latest poll results, ignores the advice of her economics team and decides not to allow free trade in textiles. The country remains in the equilibrium without international trade.

Then, one day, some Isolandian inventor discovers a new way to make textiles at very low cost. The process is quite mysterious, however, and the inventor insists on keeping it a secret. What is odd is that the inventor doesn't need traditional inputs such as cotton or wool. The only material input he needs is wheat. And even more oddly, to manufacture textiles from wheat, he hardly needs any labour input at all.

The inventor is hailed as a genius. Because everyone buys clothing, the lower cost of textiles allows all Isolandians to enjoy a higher standard of living. Workers who had previously produced textiles experience some hardship when their factories close, but eventually they find work in other industries. Some become farmers and grow the wheat that the inventor turns into textiles. Others enter new industries that emerge as a result of higher Isolandian living standards. Everyone understands that the displacement of workers in outmoded industries is an inevitable part of technological progress and economic growth.

After several years, a newspaper reporter decides to investigate this mysterious new textile process. She sneaks into the inventor's factory and learns that the inventor is a fraud. The inventor has not been making textiles at all. Instead, he has been smuggling wheat abroad in exchange for textiles from other countries. The only thing that the inventor had discovered was the gains from international trade.

When the truth is revealed, the government shuts down the inventor's operation. The price of textiles rises, and workers return to jobs in textile factories. Living standards in Isoland fall back to their former levels. The inventor is jailed and held up to public ridicule. After all, he was no inventor. He was just an economist.

summary

- The effects of free trade can be determined by comparing the domestic price without trade to the world price. A low domestic price indicates that the country has a comparative advantage in producing the good and that the country will become an exporter. A high domestic price indicates that the rest of the world has a comparative advantage in producing the good and that the country will become an importer.

- When a country allows trade and becomes an exporter of a good, producers of the good are better off, and consumers of the good are worse off. When a country allows trade and becomes an importer of a good, consumers are better off, and producers are worse off. In both cases, the gains from trade exceed the losses.

- A tariff—a tax on imports—moves a market closer to the equilibrium that would exist without trade and, therefore, reduces the gains from trade. Although domestic producers are better off and the government raises revenue, the losses to consumers exceed these gains.

- There are various arguments for restricting trade: protecting jobs, defending national security, helping infant industries, preventing unfair competition, and responding to foreign trade restrictions. Although some of these arguments have merit in some cases, economists believe that free trade is usually the better policy.

KEY **concepts**

world price, *p. 198*

tariff, *p. 202*

QUESTIONS FOR **review**

1. What does the domestic price that prevails without international trade tell us about a nation's comparative advantage?

2. When does a country become an exporter of a good? An importer?

3. Draw the supply-and-demand diagram for an importing country. What is consumer surplus and producer surplus before trade is allowed? What is consumer surplus and producer surplus with free trade? What is the change in total surplus?

4. Describe what a tariff is, and describe its economic effects.

5. List five arguments often given to support trade restrictions. How do economists respond to these arguments?

6. What is the difference between the unilateral and multilateral approaches to achieving free trade? Give an example of each.

QUICK CHECK **multiple choice**

1. What would be the result if a nation that does not allow international trade in steel has a domestic price of steel lower than the world price?
   a. The nation has a comparative advantage in producing steel and would become a steel exporter if it opened up trade.
   b. The nation has a comparative advantage in producing steel and would become a steel importer if it opened up trade.
   c. The nation does not have a comparative advantage in producing steel and would become a steel exporter if it opened up trade.
   d. The nation does not have a comparative advantage in producing steel and would become a steel importer if it opened up trade.

2. When the nation of Ectenia opens itself to world trade in coffee beans, the domestic price of coffee beans falls. Which of the following describes the situation?
   a. Domestic production of coffee rises, and Ectenia becomes a coffee importer.
   b. Domestic production of coffee rises, and Ectenia becomes a coffee exporter.
   c. Domestic production of coffee falls, and Ectenia becomes a coffee importer.
   d. Domestic production of coffee falls, and Ectenia becomes a coffee exporter.

3. What is the result when a nation opens itself to trade in a good and becomes an importer?
   a. producer surplus decreases, but consumer surplus and total surplus both increase
   b. producer surplus decreases, consumer surplus increases, and so the impact on total surplus is ambiguous
   c. producer surplus and total surplus increase, but consumer surplus decreases
   d. producer surplus, consumer surplus, and total surplus all increase

4. If a nation that imports a good imposes a tariff, it will increase which of the following?
   a. the domestic quantity demanded
   b. the domestic quantity supplied
   c. the quantity imported from abroad
   d. the quantity exported abroad

5. Which of the following trade policies would benefit producers, hurt consumers, and increase the amount of trade?
   a. the increase of a tariff in an importing country
   b. the reduction of a tariff in an importing country
   c. starting to allow trade when the world price is greater than the domestic price
   d. starting to allow trade when the world price is less than the domestic price

6. The main difference between imposing a tariff and handing out licences under an import quota is that a tariff increases which of the following?
   a. consumer surplus
   b. producer surplus
   c. international trade
   d. government revenue

PROBLEMS AND **applications**

1. When China's clothing industry expands, the increase in world supply lowers the world price of clothing.
   a. Draw an appropriate diagram to analyze how this change in price affects consumer surplus, producer surplus, and total surplus in a nation that imports clothing, such as the United States.
   b. Now draw an appropriate diagram to show how this change in price affects consumer surplus, producer surplus, and total surplus in a nation that exports clothing, such as the Dominican Republic.
   c. Compare your answers to parts (a) and (b). What are the similarities and what are the differences? Which country should be concerned about the expansion of the Chinese textile industry? Which country should be applauding it? Explain.

2. The world price of wine is below the price that would prevail in Canada in the absence of trade.
   a. Assuming that Canadian imports of wine are a small part of total world wine production, draw a graph for the Canadian market for wine under free trade. Identify consumer surplus, producer surplus, and total surplus in an appropriate table.
   b. Now suppose that an unusual shift of the Gulf Stream leads to an unseasonably cold summer in Europe, destroying much of the grape harvest there. What effect does this shock have on the world price of wine? Using your graph and table from part (a), show the effect on consumer surplus, producer surplus, and total surplus in Canada. Who are the winners and losers? Is Canada as a whole better off or worse off?

3. Suppose that Parliament imposes a tariff on imported clothes to protect the Canadian clothing industry from foreign competition. Assuming that Canada is a price taker in the world clothing market, show the following on a diagram: (a) the change in the quantity of imports, (b) the loss to Canadian consumers, (c) the gain to Canadian manufacturers, (d) government revenue, and (e) the deadweight loss associated with the tariff. The loss to consumers can be decomposed into three pieces: a transfer to domestic producers, a transfer to the government, and a deadweight loss. Use your diagram to identify these three pieces.

4. Most Canadian dairy farmers oppose free trade, and most Canadian lumber producers support it. For simplicity, assume that Canada is a small country in the markets for both milk and lumber, and that without free trade Canada would not trade these goods internationally. (Both of these assumptions are false, but they do not affect the qualitative responses to the following questions.)
   a. Based on who opposes and who supports free trade, do you think the world milk price is above or below the Canadian no-trade milk price? Do you think the world lumber price is above or below the Canadian no-trade lumber price? Now analyze the welfare consequences of free trade for both markets.
   b. Considering both markets together, would free trade make Canadian producers as a group better off or worse off? Would it make Canadian consumers as a group better off or worse off? Does it make Canada as a whole better off or worse off?

5. Imagine that winemakers in British Columbia petitioned the provincial government to tax wines imported from Ontario. They argue that this tax would both raise tax revenue for the provincial government and raise employment in the British Columbia wine industry. Do you agree with these claims? Is it a good policy?

6. The nation of Textilia does not allow imports of clothing. In its equilibrium without trade, a T-shirt costs $20 and the equilibrium quantity is 3 million T-shirts. One day, after reading Adam Smith's *The Wealth of Nations* while on vacation, the president decides to open the Textilian market to international trade. The market price of a T-shirt falls to the world price of $16. The number of T-shirts consumed in Textilia rises to 4 million, while the number of T-shirts produced declines to 1 million.
   a. Illustrate in a graph the situation just described. Your graph should show all of the numbers.

b. Calculate the change in consumer surplus, producer surplus, and total surplus that results from opening up trade. (*Hint:* Recall that the area of a triangle is ½ × base × height.)

7. Consider a small country that exports steel. Suppose that a "pro-trade" government decides to subsidize the export of steel by paying a certain amount for each tonne sold abroad. How does this export subsidy affect the domestic price of steel, the quantity of steel produced, the quantity of steel consumed, and the quantity of steel exported? How does it affect consumer surplus, producer surplus, government revenue, and total surplus? (*Hint:* The analysis of an export subsidy is similar to the analysis of a tariff.)

8. Consider the arguments for restricting trade.
   a. Assume you are a lobbyist for timber, an established industry suffering from low-priced foreign competition. Which two or three of the five arguments do you think would be most persuasive to the average member of Parliament as to why he or she should support trade restrictions? Explain your reasoning.
   b. Now assume you are an astute student of economics (hopefully not a hard assumption). Although all the arguments for restricting trade have their shortcomings, name the two or three arguments that seem to make the most economic sense to you. For each, describe the economic rationale for and against these arguments for trade restrictions.

9. China is a major producer of grains, such as wheat, corn, and rice. In 2008, the Chinese government, concerned that grain exports were driving up food prices for domestic consumers, imposed a tax on grain exports. Draw the graph that describes the market for grain in an exporting country. Use this graph as the starting point to answer the following questions.
   a. How does an export tax affect domestic grain prices?
   b. How does it affect the welfare of domestic consumers, the welfare of domestic producers, and government revenue?
   c. What happens to total welfare in China, as measured by the sum of consumer surplus, producer surplus, and tax revenue?

10. Consider a country that imports a good from abroad. For each of the following statements, say whether it is true or false. Explain your answer.
    a. "The greater the elasticity of demand, the greater the gains from trade."
    b. "If demand is perfectly inelastic, there are no gains from trade."
    c. "If demand is perfectly inelastic, consumers do not benefit from trade."

11. Having rejected a tariff on textiles (a tax on imports), the president of Isoland is now considering the same-sized tax on textile consumption (including both imported and domestically produced textiles).
    a. Using Figure 9.6, identify the quantity consumed and the quantity produced in Isoland under a textile consumption tax.
    b. Construct a table similar to that in Figure 9.6 for the textile consumption tax.
    c. Which raises more revenue for the government—the consumption tax or the tariff? Which has a smaller deadweight loss? Explain.

The Mathematics of Tariffs

Following on our previous appendixes, here we show you how to compute the deadweight loss of a tariff. Recall our example demand and supply curves introduced in the appendix to Chapter 4:

$$Q^D = 56 - 4P$$

$$Q^S = -4 + 2P$$

where we should now interpret these as domestic demand and supply curves.

Figure 9A.1 replicates parts of Figure 9.6 for these demand and supply curves, assuming that the world price of the good is $8. Recall from the appendix to Chapter 4 that in the absence of international trade the equilibrium price in the domestic market was $10 and the quantity was 16. In the presence of free trade, the domestic quantity supplied is determined by substituting the world price of $8 into the domestic supply curve: $Q_1^S = -4 + 2(8) = -4 + 16 = 12$. Similarly the domestic quantity demanded is determined by substituting the world price into the domestic demand curve: $Q_1^D = 56 - 4(8) = 56 - 32 = 24$. Thus, in the presence of free trade and a world price of $8, domestic demand is 24 units of the good, domestic firms supply 12 units, and the remainder, $24 - 12 = 12$, is made up of imports.

Now consider a tariff of $1 per unit imposed on the good. This increases the world price of the good to $9, as shown in Figure 9A.1. At this price, domestic supply is given by $Q_2^S = -4 + 2(9) = 4 + 18 = 14$ domestic demand is given by $Q_2^D = 56 - 4(9) = 56 - 36 = 20$, and imports are $20 - 14 = 6$. We see that the tariff increases domestic supply by 2 units, reduces domestic demand by 4 units, and lowers imports by 6 units.

Figure 9.6 in the text identified, among other things, the amount of revenue raised by the tariff and the deadweight loss of the tariff. In Figure 9A.1, the

FIGURE 9A.1

Tariff with Linear Demand and Supply Curves

This diagram illustrates the impact of a $1 tariff imposed on the world price of $8 for our linear supply and demand curves. Area E is the revenue raised from the tariff; area D plus area F is the deadweight loss associated with the tariff.

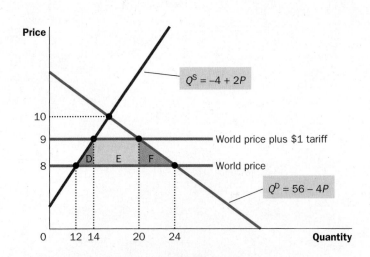

revenue raised by the tariff is given by the tariff rate times the amount of imports under the tariff, which is the area of rectangle E. The area of a rectangle is given by its base × height. The base of rectangle E is the amount of imports after the tariff is imposed (6), and the height is the size of the tariff imposed on those imports ($1), giving area E = 6 × $1 = $6.

The deadweight loss of the tariff is given by the sum of the areas of the triangles D and F. Recall that the area of a triangle is (½) × base × height. For triangle D the height is the amount of the tariff ($1), and the base is the increase in domestic supply due to the tariff (2); therefore area D = (½) × (2) × ($1) = $1. For the triangle F the height is again the amount of the tariff ($1) and the base is the reduction in domestic demand due to the tariff (4), giving area F = (½) × (4) × ($1) = $2. Thus, the deadweight loss of the tariff is area (D + F) = $1 + $2 = $3. Expressing the deadweight loss as a percentage of the revenue raised from the tariff gives $3/$6 = .5, or 50 percent.

PROBLEMS AND **applications**

A1. Assume that Canada is an importer of televisions and that there are no trade restrictions. Canadian consumers buy 1 million televisions per year, of which 400 000 are produced domestically and 600 000 are imported.

a. Suppose that a technological advance among Japanese television manufacturers causes the world price of televisions to fall by $100. Draw a graph to show how this change affects the welfare of Canadian consumers and Canadian producers and how it affects total surplus in Canada.

b. After the fall in price, consumers buy 1.2 million televisions, of which 200 000 are produced domestically and 1 million are imported. Calculate the change in consumer surplus, producer surplus, and total surplus from the price reduction.

c. If the government responded by putting a $100 tariff on imported televisions, what would this do? Calculate the revenue that would be raised and the deadweight loss. Would it be a good policy from the standpoint of Canadian welfare? Who might support the policy? Who might oppose it?

d. Suppose that the fall in price is attributable not to technological advance but to a $100 per television subsidy from the Japanese government to Japanese industry. How would this affect your analysis?

A2. Kawmin is a small country that produces and consumes jelly beans. The world price of jelly beans is $1 per bag, and Kawmin's domestic demand and supply for jelly beans are governed by the following equations:

$$\text{Demand: } Q^D = 8 - P$$
$$\text{Supply: } Q^S = P$$

where P is in dollars per bag and Q is in bags of jelly beans.

a. Draw a well-labelled graph of the situation in Kawmin if the nation does not allow trade. Calculate the following (recalling that the area of a triangle is ½ × base × height): the equilibrium price and quantity, consumer surplus, producer surplus, and total surplus.

b. Kawmin then opens the market to trade. Draw another graph to describe the new situation in the jelly bean market. Calculate the equilibrium price, quantities of consumption and production, imports, consumer surplus, producer surplus, and total surplus.

c. After a while, the czar of Kawmin responds to the pleas of jelly bean producers by placing a $1 per bag tariff on jelly bean imports. On a graph, show the effects of this tariff. Calculate the equilibrium price, quantities of consumption and production, imports, consumer surplus, producer surplus, government revenue, and total surplus.

d. What are the gains from opening up trade? What are the deadweight losses from restricting trade with the tariff? Give numerical answers.

Jeff Zehnder/Shutterstock.com

CHAPTER

10

LEARNING
objectives

Externalities

In this chapter, you will ...

1 Learn the nature of an externality

2 See why externalities can make market outcomes inefficient

3 Examine the various government policies aimed at solving the problem of externalities

4 Examine how people can sometimes solve the problem of externalities on their own

5 Consider why private solutions to externalities sometimes do not work

Firms that make and sell paper also create, as a by-product of the manufacturing process, a chemical called *dioxin*. Scientists believe that once dioxin enters the environment, it raises the population's risk of cancer, birth defects, and other health problems.

Is the production and release of dioxin a problem for society? In Chapters 4 through 9, we examined how markets allocate scarce resources with the forces of supply and demand, and we saw that the equilibrium of supply and demand is typically an efficient allocation of resources. To use Adam Smith's famous metaphor, the invisible hand of the marketplace leads self-interested buyers and sellers in a market to maximize the total benefit that society derives from that market. This insight is the basis for one of the ten principles of economics in Chapter 1: Markets are usually a good way to organize economic activity. Should we conclude, therefore, that the invisible hand prevents firms in the paper market from emitting too much dioxin?

Markets do many things well, but they do not do everything well. In this chapter we begin our study of another of the ten principles of economics: Government action can sometimes improve upon market outcomes. We examine why markets sometimes fail to allocate resources efficiently, how government policies can potentially improve the market's allocation, and what kinds of policies are likely to work best.

The market failures examined in this chapter fall under a general category called *externalities.* An **externality** arises when a person engages in an activity that influences the well-being of a bystander but neither pays nor receives compensation for that effect. If the impact on the bystander is adverse, it is called a *negative externality*. If it is beneficial, it is called a *positive externality*. In the presence of externalities, society's interest in a market outcome extends beyond the well-being of buyers and sellers who participate in the market; it also includes the well-being of bystanders who are affected indirectly. Because buyers and sellers neglect the external effects of their actions when deciding how much to demand or supply, the market equilibrium is not efficient when there are externalities. That is, the equilibrium fails to maximize the total benefit to society as a whole. The release of dioxin into the environment, for instance, is a negative externality. Self-interested paper firms will not consider the full cost of the pollution they create in their production process, and consumers of paper will not consider the full cost of the pollution they contribute to as a result of their purchasing decisions. Therefore, the firms will emit too much pollution unless the government prevents or discourages them from doing so.

externality
the uncompensated impact of one person's actions on the well-being of a bystander

Externalities come in many varieties, as do the policy responses that try to deal with the market failure. Here are some examples:

- The exhaust from automobiles is a negative externality because it creates smog that other people have to breathe. Because drivers may ignore this externality when deciding what cars to buy and how much to use them, they tend to pollute too much. The federal government addresses this problem by setting emission standards for cars. It also taxes gasoline to reduce the amount that people drive.
- Restored historic buildings convey a positive externality because people who walk or ride by them can enjoy their beauty and the sense of history that these buildings provide. Building owners do not get the full benefit of restoration and, therefore, tend to discard older buildings too quickly. Many local governments respond to this problem by regulating the destruction of historic buildings and by providing tax breaks to owners who restore them.

- Barking dogs create a negative externality because neighbours are disturbed by the noise. Dog owners do not bear the full cost of the noise and, therefore, tend to take too few precautions to prevent their dogs from barking. Local governments address this problem by making it illegal to "disturb the peace."
- Research into new technologies provides a positive externality because it creates knowledge that other people can use. Because inventors cannot capture the full benefits of their inventions, they tend to devote too few resources to research. The federal government addresses this problem partially through the patent system, which gives inventors exclusive rights to their inventions for a period of time.
- A large body of scientific research suggests that carbon dioxide and other greenhouse gas emissions associated with the use of fossil fuels contributes to global warming. This in turn is thought to be associated with changes in ocean levels, weather patterns, and other climate-related changes. Individuals do not take full account of these externalities when consuming energy and therefore tend to consume too much. Governments around the world have addressed this by imposing taxes on carbon emissions as well as by implementing cap-and-trade systems with tradable permits.

In each of these cases, some decision maker fails to take account of the external effects of his behaviour. The government responds by trying to influence this behaviour to protect the interests of bystanders.

10-1   Externalities and Market Inefficiency

In this section we use the tools of welfare economics developed in Chapter 7 to examine how externalities affect economic well-being. The analysis shows precisely why externalities cause markets to allocate resources inefficiently. Later in the chapter, we examine various ways in which private individuals and public policymakers may remedy this type of market failure.

10-1a Welfare Economics: A Recap

We begin by recalling the key lessons of welfare economics from Chapter 7. To make our analysis concrete, we will consider a specific market—the market for aluminum. Figure 10.1 shows the supply and demand curves in the market for aluminum.

Recall from Chapter 7 that the supply and demand curves contain important information about costs and benefits. The demand curve for aluminum reflects the value of aluminum to consumers, as measured by the prices they are willing to pay. At any given quantity, the height of the demand curve shows the willingness to pay of the marginal buyer. In other words, it shows the value to the consumer of the last unit of aluminum bought. Similarly, the supply curve reflects the costs of producing aluminum. At any given quantity, the height of the supply curve shows the cost to the marginal seller. In other words, it shows the cost to the producer of the last unit of aluminum sold.

In the absence of government intervention, the price adjusts to balance the supply and demand for aluminum. The quantity produced and consumed in the market equilibrium, shown as Q_{MARKET} in Figure 10.1, is efficient in the sense that it maximizes the sum of producer and consumer surplus. That is, the market

FIGURE 10.1

The Market for Aluminum

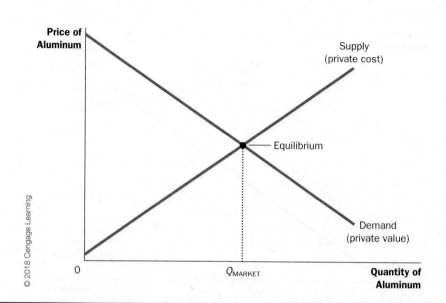

The demand curve reflects the value to buyers, and the supply curve reflects the costs of sellers. The equilibrium quantity, Q_{MARKET}, maximizes the total value to buyers minus the total costs of sellers. In the absence of externalities, therefore, the market equilibrium is efficient.

© 2018 Cengage Learning

allocates resources in a way that maximizes the total value to the consumers who buy and use aluminum minus the total costs to the producers who make and sell aluminum.

10-1b Negative Externalities

Now let's suppose that aluminum factories emit pollution: For each unit of aluminum produced, a certain amount of smoke enters the atmosphere. Because this smoke creates a health risk for those who breathe the air, it is a negative externality. How does this externality affect the efficiency of the market outcome?

Because of the externality, the cost to *society* of producing aluminum is larger than the cost to the aluminum producers. For each unit of aluminum produced, the *social cost* includes the private costs of the aluminum producers plus the external cost imposed on the bystanders affected adversely by the pollution. Figure 10.2 shows the social cost of producing aluminum. The social-cost curve is above the supply curve because it includes the external costs imposed on society by aluminum production. For example, if the external cost imposed on bystanders due to pollution is T per unit of aluminum produced, the vertical distance between the social-cost curve and the supply curve is T.

What quantity of aluminum should be produced? To answer this question, we once again consider what a benevolent social planner would do. The planner wants to maximize the total surplus derived from the market. This includes the value to consumers of aluminum minus the private cost of producing aluminum. The planner understands, however, that there is a third party involved—the bystanders negatively affected by the pollution created by producing aluminum. The cost to society, therefore, includes the external costs of the pollution imposed on bystanders.

The planner would choose the level of aluminum production at which the demand curve crosses the social-cost curve. This intersection determines the

FIGURE 10.2

Pollution and the Social Optimum

In the presence of a negative externality, such as pollution, the social cost of the good exceeds the private cost. The optimal quantity, $Q_{OPTIMUM}$, is therefore smaller than the equilibrium quantity, Q_{MARKET}.

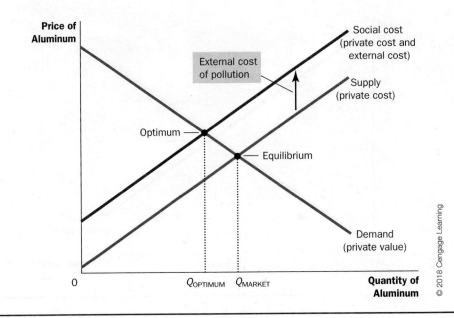

optimal amount of aluminum from the standpoint of society as a whole. Below this level of production, the value of the aluminum to consumers (as measured by the height of the demand curve) exceeds the social cost of producing it (as measured by the height of the social-cost curve). Above this level of production, the social cost of producing additional aluminum exceeds the value to consumers.

Note that the equilibrium quantity of aluminum, Q_{MARKET}, is larger than the socially optimal quantity, $Q_{OPTIMUM}$. This inefficiency occurs because the market equilibrium reflects only the private costs of production. In the market equilibrium, the marginal consumer values aluminum at less than the social cost of producing it. That is, at Q_{MARKET} the demand curve lies below the social-cost curve. Thus, reducing aluminum production and consumption below the market equilibrium level raises total economic well-being.

We can measure the value of this increase in economic well-being using the concept of *deadweight loss* introduced in Chapters 8 and 9. In those chapters the deadweight loss was the reduction in total surplus that resulted from the imposition of a tax or tariff. The same approach can be used to measure the reduction in total surplus associated with the inefficient allocation of resources due to the presence of an externality.

Figure 10.3 shows how we use the concepts of consumer and producer surplus to determine the deadweight loss of the externality caused by the aluminum factory emitting pollution. The equilibrium is determined by the intersection of the supply curve, which reflects the private cost of producing aluminum, and the demand curve. The equilibrium quantity is Q_{MARKET} and the price is P_{MARKET}.

At the equilibrium level of aluminum production, Q_{MARKET}, and the corresponding market price, P_{MARKET}, consumer surplus is measured in the usual way as the area between the demand curve and the equilibrium price, A + B + C + D.

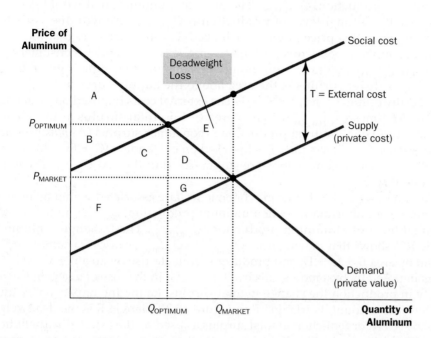

FIGURE 10.3

Deadweight Loss of a Negative Externality

A negative externality means that the social-cost curve lies above the demand curve at the market equilibrium quantity, Q_{MARKET}. Compared with the social optimum, $Q_{OPTIMUM}$, consumer surplus at the market equilibrium is higher by area B + C + D, producer surplus is lower by B + C − G, and bystanders are worse off by D + E + G. The net effect is a reduction in total surplus, shown by deadweight loss triangle E.

Producer surplus is similarly measured in the usual way as the area above the supply curve at Q_{MARKET} up the equilibrium price, F + G.

Aside from consumers and producers there is now a third party involved— the bystanders negatively affected by the production of aluminum. As discussed above, the external cost imposed on the bystanders is T per unit of aluminum produced, which is the vertical distance between the social cost curve and the supply curve. The cost imposed on the bystanders from the production of aluminum is therefore T times Q_{MARKET}, which is the area C + D + E + F + G in Figure 10.3.

Total surplus at the market equilibrium level of aluminum production then consists of consumer surplus (A + B + C + D) *plus* producer surplus (F + G) *less* the costs imposed on bystanders (C + D + E + F + G), which is the area A + B − E. The "At Q_{MARKET}" column of Table 10.1 summarizes these conclusions.

TABLE 10.1

Deadweight Loss of a Negative Production Externality

This table refers to the areas marked in Figure 10.3 to show how a negative externality generates a deadweight loss in the economy.

	At Q_{MARKET}	At $Q_{OPTIMUM}$	Change
Consumer surplus	A + B + C + D	A	−(B + C + D)
Producer surplus	F + G	B + C + F	B + C − G
External cost	C + D + E + F + G	C + F	−(D + E + G)
Total surplus	A + B − E	A + B	E

Does your neighbour's lawn have the socially optimal number of dandelions?

Now consider economic welfare measured at the socially optimal level of aluminum production, $Q_{OPTIMUM}$. The price of aluminum that would generate this socially optimal level of production is $P_{OPTIMUM}$. We will discuss below ways in which this price might be achieved. For now, let's say that the social planner simply imposes this price on the market. At this price, consumers will demand $Q_{OPTIMUM}$ units of aluminum, and consumer surplus is given by the area A. Producer surplus is the area above the supply curve at $Q_{OPTIMUM}$ up the socially optimal price, B + C + F. The external costs imposed on bystanders is now $T times $Q_{OPTIMUM}$, which is area C + F. Total surplus at the socially optimal level of aluminum production is consumer surplus (A) *plus* producer surplus (B + C + F) *less* the costs imposed on bystanders (C + F), which is the area A + B. These conclusions are summarized in the "At $Q_{OPTIMUM}$" column of Table 10.1.

We can now see the change in economic welfare associated with moving from the market equilibrium level of aluminum production, Q_{MARKET}, to the socially optimal level of aluminum production, $Q_{OPTIMUM}$. The "Change" column of Table 10.1 shows that moving from Q_{MARKET} to $Q_{OPTIMUM}$ causes consumer surplus to fall by area B + C + D, and producer surplus to rise by area B + C − G. The costs imposed by bystanders falls by D + E + G. In the case of a negative externality in production the change in total surplus, taking the impact on all three parties into account, is triangle E in Figure 10.3. Triangle E is the deadweight loss to society, or reduction in total surplus, caused by the externality (pollution) associated with producing aluminum.

10-1c Positive Externalities

Although some activities impose costs on third parties, others yield benefits. Consider education, for example. To a large extent, the benefit of education is private: The consumer of education becomes a more productive worker and thus reaps much of the benefit in the form of higher wages. Beyond these private benefits, however, education also yields positive externalities. One externality is that a more educated population leads to more informed voters, which means better government for everyone. Another externality is that a more educated population tends to mean lower crime rates. A third externality is that a more educated population may encourage the development and dissemination of technological advances, leading to higher productivity and wages for everyone. Because of these three positive externalities, a person may prefer to have neighbours who are well educated.

The analysis of positive externalities is similar to the analysis of negative externalities. As Figure 10.4 shows, the demand curve does not reflect the value to society of the good. Because the social value is greater than the private value, the social-value curve lies above the demand curve. The optimal quantity is found where the social-value curve and the supply curve (which represents costs) intersect. Hence, the socially optimal quantity is greater than the quantity the private market would naturally reach on its own. As is the case with a negative externality, the equilibrium outcome is inefficient and gives rise to a deadweight loss equal to the triangle shown in Figure 10.4.

To summarize: Negative externalities lead markets to produce a larger quantity than is socially desirable. Positive externalities lead markets to produce a smaller quantity than is socially desirable. In both cases if left to its own devices the market will generate an inefficient outcome, giving rise to deadweight losses.

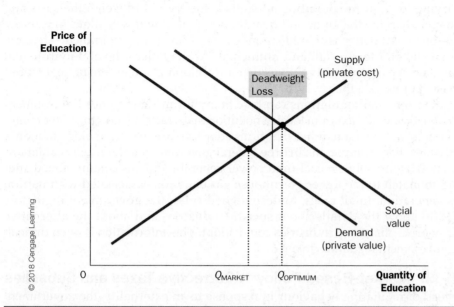

FIGURE 10.4

Education and the Social Optimum

In the presence of a positive externality, the social value of the good exceeds the private value. The optimal quantity, Q_{OPTIMUM}, is therefore larger than the equilibrium quantity, Q_{MARKET}.

QUICK Quiz *Give an example of a negative externality and a positive externality. • Explain why market outcomes are inefficient in the presence of externalities.*

10-2 Public Policies toward Externalities

We have discussed why externalities lead markets to allocate resources inefficiently but have not discussed how this inefficiency can be remedied. In practice, both public policymakers and private individuals can respond to externalities in various ways. All of the remedies share the goal of moving the allocation of resources closer to the social optimum. This section considers governmental solutions. Later we consider the scope for private solutions.

As a general matter, the government can respond to externalities in one of two ways. *Command-and-control policies* regulate behaviour directly. *Market-based policies* provide incentives so that private decision makers will choose to solve the problem on their own.

10-2a Command-and-Control Policies: Regulation

The government can remedy an externality by making certain behaviours either required or forbidden. For example, it is a crime to dump poisonous chemicals into the water supply. In this case, the external costs to society far exceed the benefits to the polluter. The government therefore institutes a command-and-control policy that prohibits this act altogether.

In most cases of pollution, however, the situation is not this simple. Despite the stated goals of some environmentalists, it would be impossible to prohibit all polluting activity. For example, virtually all forms of transportation—even the horse—produce some undesirable polluting by-products. But it would not be sensible for the government to ban all transportation. As a result, instead of trying to eradicate pollution altogether, society has to weigh the costs and benefits to decide the kinds and quantities of pollution it will allow. In Canada, environmental policy is shared among all three levels of government—federal, provincial and territorial, and municipal. At the federal level, Environment Canada is the department responsible for developing and enforcing regulations aimed at protecting the environment.

Environmental regulations can take many forms. Sometimes Environment Canada dictates a maximum level of pollution that a factory may emit. Other times Environment Canada requires that firms adopt a particular technology to reduce emissions. For example, in 2011 the federal government announced regulations that will require all new coal-fired power generation plants commissioned after 2015 to match to the lower greenhouse gas emissions associated with natural gas generation. In all cases, to design good rules, the government regulators need to know the details about specific industries and about the alternative technologies that those industries could adopt. This information is often difficult for government regulators to obtain.

10-2b Market-Based Policy 1: Corrective Taxes and Subsidies

Instead of regulating behaviour in response to an externality, the government can use market-based policies to align private incentives with social efficiency. One approach is to impose taxes on activities that have negative externalities and subsidies on activities that have positive externalities. Taxes enacted to deal with the effects of negative externalities are called **corrective taxes**. They are also called *Pigovian taxes* after economist Arthur Pigou (1877–1959), an early advocate of their use.

corrective taxes
taxes enacted to correct the effects of negative externalities

Reconsidering the aluminum example discussed above, this would involve imposing a tax on aluminum producers for each tonne of aluminum sold. The tax would shift the supply curve for aluminum up by the size of the tax. The ideal corrective tax would equal the external cost associated with activity that generates the negative externality. In Figure 10.3, the ideal corrective tax is the difference between the social-cost curve and the private-supply curve associated with the production of aluminum, which is equal to the size of the external cost imposed on bystanders per unit of production, or T. If the tax accurately reflects the external cost of the pollution, the new tax inclusive supply curve coincides with the social-cost curve. In the new market equilibrium, aluminum producers would produce the socially optimum quantity of aluminum.

internalizing the externality
alter incentives so that people take account of the external effects of their actions

The use of such a tax is called **internalizing the externality** because it gives buyers and sellers in the market an incentive to take into account the external effects of their actions. Aluminum producers would, in essence, take the costs of pollution into account when deciding how much aluminum to supply because the tax would make them pay for these external costs. And, because the market price would reflect the tax on producers, consumers of aluminum would have an incentive to use a smaller quantity. The policy is based on one of the ten principles of economics: People respond to incentives.

The appropriate response in the case of positive externalities is exactly the opposite to the case of negative externalities. To move the market equilibrium closer to the social optimum, a positive externality requires a subsidy. For example, in the case of positive externalities associated with education discussed above, the government could subsidize the costs of education. And in fact, that is exactly the policy that many governments follow: Education is heavily subsidized through public schools and government scholarships.

Economists usually prefer corrective taxes over regulations as a way to deal with pollution because such taxes can reduce pollution at a lower cost to society. To see why, let us consider an example.

Suppose that two factories—a paper mill and a steel mill—are each dumping 500 tonnes of glop into a river every year. Environment Canada decides that it wants to reduce the amount of pollution. It considers two solutions:

1. *Regulation*: Environment Canada could tell each factory to reduce its pollution to 300 tonnes of glop per year.
2. *Corrective tax*: Environment Canada could levy a tax on each factory of $50 000 for each tonne of glop it emits.

Notice that in this case the corrective tax is imposed directly on the emission of glop rather than on the production of paper and steel, the goods that generate the pollution, as was the case with the aluminum example. The idea is precisely the same, however, and taxing the externality directly is typically preferred to taxing the production of goods as it is simpler and applies equally to all factories that emit glop regardless of what they produce.

The regulation would dictate a level of pollution, whereas the tax would give factory owners an economic incentive to reduce pollution. Which solution do you think is better? Most economists prefer the tax. To explain this preference, they would first point out that a tax is just as effective as a regulation in reducing the overall level of pollution. Environment Canada can achieve whatever level of pollution it wants by setting the tax at the appropriate level. The higher the tax, the larger the reduction in pollution. Indeed, if the tax is high enough, the factories will close down altogether, reducing pollution to zero.

Although regulation and corrective taxes are both capable of reducing pollution, the tax accomplishes this goal more efficiently. The regulation requires each factory to reduce pollution by the same amount. An equal reduction, however, is not necessarily the least expensive way to clean up the water. It is possible that the paper mill can reduce pollution at lower cost than the steel mill. If so, the paper mill would respond to the tax by reducing pollution substantially to avoid the tax, whereas the steel mill would respond by reducing pollution less and paying the tax.

In essence, the corrective tax places a price on the right to pollute. Just as markets allocate goods to those buyers who value them most highly, a corrective tax allocates pollution to those factories that face the highest cost of reducing it. Whatever the level of pollution Environment Canada chooses, it can achieve this goal at the lowest total cost using a tax.

Economists also argue that corrective taxes are better for the environment. Under the command-and-control policy of regulation, the factories have no reason to reduce emission further once they have reached the target of 300 tonnes of glop. By contrast, the tax gives the factories an incentive to develop cleaner technologies because a cleaner technology would reduce the amount of tax the factory has to pay.

Corrective taxes are unlike most other taxes. As we discussed in Chapter 8, most taxes distort incentives and move the allocation of resources away from the social optimum. The reduction in economic well-being—that is, in consumer and producer surplus—exceeds the amount of revenue the government raises, resulting in a deadweight loss. By contrast, when externalities are present, society also cares about the well-being of the affected bystanders. Corrective taxes alter incentives that market participants face to account for the presence of externalities and thereby move the allocation of resources closer to the social optimum. Thus, while corrective taxes raise revenue for the government, they also enhance economic efficiency.

10-2c   Market-Based Policy 2: Tradable Pollution Permits

Returning to our example of the paper mill and the steel mill, let us suppose that, despite the advice of its economists, Environment Canada adopts the regulation and requires each factory to reduce its pollution to 300 tonnes of glop per year. Then one day, after the regulation is in place and both mills have complied, the two firms go to Environment Canada with a proposal. The steel mill wants to increase its emission of glop by 100 tonnes. The paper mill has agreed to reduce its emission by the same amount if the steel mill pays it $5 million. Should Environment Canada allow the two factories to make this deal?

From the standpoint of economic efficiency, allowing the deal is good policy. The deal must make the owners of the two factories better off because they are voluntarily agreeing to it. Moreover, the deal does not have any external effects because the total amount of pollution remains the same. Thus, social welfare is enhanced by allowing the paper mill to sell its right to pollute to the steel mill.

The same logic applies to any voluntary transfer of the right to pollute from one firm to another. If Environment Canada allows firms to make these deals, it will, in essence, have created a new scarce resource: pollution permits. A market to trade these permits will eventually develop, and that market will be governed by the forces of supply and demand. The invisible hand will ensure that this new market efficiently allocates the right to pollute. That is, the permits will end up in the hands of those firms that value them most highly, as judged by their willingness to pay. A firm's willingness to pay for the right to pollute, in turn, will depend on its cost of reducing pollution: The more costly it is for a firm to cut back on pollution, the more it will be willing to pay for a permit.

An advantage of allowing a market for pollution permits is that the initial allocation of pollution permits among firms does not matter from the standpoint of economic efficiency. Those firms that can reduce pollution at a low cost will sell whatever permits they get, while firms that can reduce pollution only at high cost will buy whatever permits they need. As long as there is a free market for the pollution rights, the final allocation will be efficient whatever the initial allocation.

Reducing pollution using pollution permits may seem very different from using corrective taxes, but the two policies have much in common. In both cases, firms pay for their pollution. With corrective taxes, polluting firms must pay a tax to the government. With pollution permits, polluting firms must pay to buy the permit. (Even firms that already own permits must pay to pollute: The opportunity cost of polluting is what they could have received by selling their permits on the open market.) Both corrective taxes and pollution permits internalize the externality of pollution by making it costly for firms to pollute.

FIGURE 10.5

The Equivalence of Corrective Taxes and Pollution Permits

In panel (a), Environment Canada sets a price on pollution by levying a corrective tax, and the demand curve determines the quantity of pollution. In panel (b), Environment Canada limits the quantity of pollution by limiting the number of pollution permits, and the demand curve determines the price of pollution. The price and quantity of pollution are the same in the two cases.

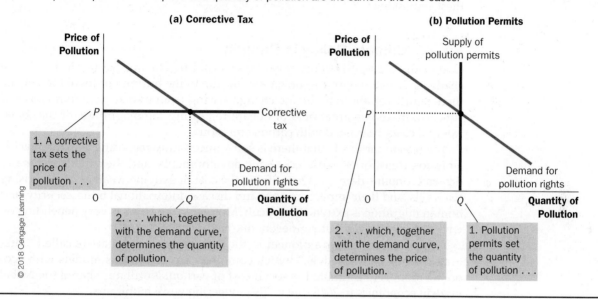

(a) Corrective Tax

Price of Pollution

P — Corrective tax

Demand for pollution rights

0   Q   Quantity of Pollution

1. A corrective tax sets the price of pollution . . .

2. . . . which, together with the demand curve, determines the quantity of pollution.

(b) Pollution Permits

Price of Pollution

Supply of pollution permits

P

Demand for pollution rights

0   Q   Quantity of Pollution

1. Pollution permits set the quantity of pollution . . .

2. . . . which, together with the demand curve, determines the price of pollution.

© 2018 Cengage Learning

The similarity of the two policies can be seen by considering the market for pollution. Both panels in Figure 10.5 show the demand curve for the right to pollute. This curve shows that the lower the price of polluting, the more firms will choose to pollute. In panel (a), Environment Canada uses a corrective tax to set a price for pollution. In this case, the supply curve for pollution rights is perfectly elastic (because firms can pollute as much as they want by paying the tax), and the position of the demand curve determines the quantity of pollution. In panel (b), Environment Canada sets a quantity of pollution by issuing pollution permits. In this case, the supply curve for pollution rights is perfectly inelastic (because the quantity of pollution is fixed by the number of permits), and the position of the demand curve determines the price of pollution. Hence, for any given demand curve for pollution, Environment Canada can achieve any point on the demand curve either by setting a price with a corrective tax or by setting a quantity with pollution permits.

In some circumstances, however, selling pollution permits may be better than levying a corrective tax. Suppose Environment Canada wants no more than 600 tonnes of glop to be dumped into the river. But, because Environment Canada does not know the demand curve for pollution, it is not sure what size tax would achieve that goal. In this case, it can simply auction off 600 pollution permits. The auction price would yield the appropriate size of the corrective tax.

The idea of the government auctioning off the right to pollute may at first sound like a figment of some economist's imagination. And in fact, that is how the idea began. But increasingly pollution permits, like corrective taxes, are now widely viewed as a cost-effective way to keep the environment clean.

Emission permit trading systems (also known as *cap and trade*) are common throughout the world. For example, the European Union Emission Trading Scheme for greenhouse gas emissions is the largest emissions trading scheme in the world. Also, since 1990 Canada and the United States have had in place a cap and trade market for sulphur and nitrous oxides, produced primarily by power plants and which lead to acid rain, leading to a significant reduction in these emissions.

10-2d Climate Policy in Canada

One of the most important negative externalities facing the world is climate change associated with carbon emissions due to the burning of fossil fuel. While there is little doubt that climate change arising from human activities is of real concern, there is a great deal of debate regarding the magnitude of the social external costs associated with carbon emissions.

The reason for this is that there is some uncertainty regarding climate physics, emission trajectories, socio-economic developments, and the extent of climate-driven economic damage. Quantifying the cost of extreme weather events, rising sea levels, and their impact on crops and disease, international trade, security, and human migration is extremely difficult. Moreover, the impacts vary depending on where you live and what your economic circumstances are.

William Nordhaus is a pioneer in the development of what are called "integrated assessment models," which combine climate physics models with economic models to estimate the social cost of carbon. Nordhaus shared the Nobel Prize in economics in 2018 due to his pioneering work in this area.

The central estimate of the social cost of carbon by the Government of Canada, based largely on work done by the U.S. government, is about $45 per tonne in 2019, rising to $75 by 2050. However, considerable uncertainty exists regarding these numbers, and some estimates are much higher—think $200 per tonne or more. One of the most important issues involves placing a value today on costs imposed far into the future, several decades or more. There is some disagreement on how to value (discount) these costs, which can generate sizable differences in estimates of the social cost of carbon. Climate policies are often the subject of considerable political debate. However, notwithstanding the difficulties in estimating the social cost of carbon, economists agree widely on the nature of the appropriate approach—pricing carbon emissions, either through a carbon tax or cap and trade, is overwhelmingly viewed as the best approach.

Climate policy in Canada is a hodgepodge, to put it lightly, as both the provinces and the federal government have jurisdiction in the area. Both federal and provincial regulations abound. In terms of carbon pricing the provinces have been leaders, with B.C. implementing a broad-based carbon tax in 2008 at $10 per tonne of CO_2 emissions. In 2018 the tax was levied at $40 per tonne, and will increase by $5 per year until 2021. Alberta imposed a broad-based carbon tax in 2017; the rate in 2018 was $30 per tonne, with no further increases scheduled until 2021.

Other Canadian provinces have adopted a cap and trade approach. Quebec implemented a cap and trade system in 2012. Ontario briefly joined the Quebec system in 2018, but has since withdrawn and eliminated carbon pricing. Nova Scotia implemented its own cap and trade system in 2019.

For its part, the federal government has indicated that it is willing to leave carbon pricing to the provinces. However, it provides a "backstop," called the

Pan-Canadian Framework on Clean Growth and Climate Change. The way this backstop works is that the provinces can choose whatever type of carbon pricing system they want as long as it applies to a broad range of emissions and meets certain guidelines. Provinces that choose the carbon tax route must levy a tax at a minimum of $20 per tonne starting in 2019, and increase the tax by $10 per year to $50 per tonne in 2022. Provinces adopting a cap and trade approach must implement declining emission caps that correspond, at a minimum, to the projected emission reductions that would have resulted from applying the direct carbon tax.

If provinces do not adopt their own carbon pricing policies, the federal government will impose a tax meeting the benchmark requirements, with the revenue returned to the provinces on an equal per capita basis based on provincial emissions. As it currently stands all but four provinces are compliant with the federal rules—the federal backstop will apply only to Ontario, Saskatchewan, Manitoba, and New Brunswick.

Carbon pricing is a hot political topic (pardon the pun), and the landscape is constantly changing. For example, in June of 2019 the newly elected government in Alberta eliminated the provincial carbon levy. As you are reading this, it may well be that the policies described above have changed.

Canada's Ecofiscal Commission is a group of experienced, independent, policy-minded economists from across the country, seeking to broaden the discussion of ecofiscal policy reform beyond the academic sphere and into the realm of practical policy application. The Commission has come to a strong and overwhelming conclusion: carbon pricing works. Their analysis of the B.C. carbon tax, for example, indicates that the fuel efficiency of the entire vehicle fleet in B.C. improved by 4 percent more than it would have in the absence of the tax, that per capita gasoline consumption would have been between 7 and 17 percent higher without the tax, and that overall annual emissions would have been between 5 and 15 percent higher without a carbon tax in place.

While carbon pricing is an effective way to deal with emissions, it does not come without costs. Depending on what is done with the revenues, the Ecofiscal Commission estimates that carbon prices at the above levels will lead to a reduction in annual gross domestic product (GDP) growth by from 0.02 percent to 0.12 percent. However, as discussed above, the net benefit to society of internalizing the externalities is positive.

case study: And So, Pipelines

And so we come to pipelines, a perennial source of controversy and disagreement in Canada and elsewhere. Pipelines involve many issues—spill risks, Indigenous land issues, NIMBYism (not in my backyard), and so on. However, much of the opposition to pipelines is climate related, focusing on the implications for carbon emissions; in a Canadian context, this means oil sands. It is often argued that allowing new pipelines to proceed is inconsistent with and contradictory to other policies designed to address climate change. Let's examine this claim from an economic perspective.

A ban on new pipelines can be considered a type of command and control approach to climate policy, whereby the government imposes (or bans) a particular approach or technology in order to lower emissions. A key question is whether banning new pipelines is a cost-effective way to lower carbon emissions.

Immunization

Canada could look at the lead of Australia, which is jabbing deeper at parents who don't vaccinate their children by cutting child tax benefits, says a Canadian vaccine specialist—though he would prefer parents be rewarded for vaccinating rather than penalized for not.

Australia Fines Parents Who Don't Vaccinate Kids. Should Canada?

By Meredith MacLeod

The Australian government is jabbing deeper at the wallets of parents who don't vaccinate their children.

The country already has a "No Jab, No Pay" policy but a tougher version took effect July 1. It cuts child benefit payments by AUD$28 every two weeks for each child who isn't immunized.

The only exemptions are those approved by medical practitioners for health reasons. There are no conscientious or ideological opt-outs, which Canadian provinces allow.

Canada doesn't have federal rules around vaccinations. Some provinces, including Ontario and New Brunswick, require proof of vaccination for school registration but many provinces only check for immunization, says Dr. Scott Halperin, a pediatric infectious specialist and director of the Canadian Center for Vaccinology at Dalhousie University.

"Parents who don't immunize their children are putting their own kids at risk as well as the children of other people," said Dan Tehan, Australia's Minister for Social Services, in a statement.

Previously, parents with a taxable income of AUD$80,000 lost an end-of-year supplement for not vaccinating their children. But now, the penalty is taken out of each payment of roughly AUD$400, meant to serve as a "constant reminder for parents to keep their children's immunization up to date."

The rules make vaccines mandatory for school-aged children and allow for fines against child-care centres that admit unvaccinated children.

According to the Australian government, the policy introduced by Prime Minister Malcolm Turnbull in 2016 has resulted in 246,000 children being vaccinated. That has boosted the country's overall rate from 90 per cent to 93 per cent.

But critics say "No Jab, No Pay" unfairly targets lower-income families who need help, not penalty.

Australia joins Italy and France in making a number of vaccines mandatory for children. Germany requires schools to report parents who haven't vaccinated their children. States in the U.S. require up-to-date vaccinations for enrollment in schools.

There are no jurisdictions in the world which force vaccinations through the involvement of courts or child-welfare agencies, Halperin said, since there is no imminent risk to a child who is not vaccinated.

But Halperin says there is a case for tying vaccines to social welfare programs.

"Why do governments give social benefits? It's part of a social contract where we say we are responsible for each other and we provide benefits based on that. Vaccines protect individuals but are also part of the social contract to protect others become some people don't respond to vaccines or can't have them for medical reasons or can't get them when they're too young," he said.

"So, on that basis, vaccinations and social benefits are tied together."

But Halperin says he prefers a "carrot" approach that rewards parents who do vaccinate with a bonus to their benefits payments, rather than penalizing those who don't. He also would like to see improved education around vaccination, easier access for parents and a much improved tracking system.

If provinces were to tie vaccination to social benefits, Halperin says those programs must be

Trevor Tombe, an economics professor at the University of Calgary, argues no, not by a long shot.

Without new pipelines, more oil will be shipped by rail. This is expensive, not to mention less safe and more emission intensive than pipelines, and so oil production will be lower than it otherwise would be. Moreover, without pipelines that access tidewater in Canada, prices are lower for Alberta oil due to shipping constraints. Estimates vary, but Tombe suggests that a $10 per barrel discount on Alberta oil due to pipeline constraints is a very conservative estimate. In fact, in 2018 the discount increased well above this. These lower prices will also reduce oil production in Alberta.

carefully evaluated to make sure they resulted in increased immunization rates.

Some Canadian research has found that immunization is challenging in remote areas or among immigrant populations. As well, there is no electronic record of immunization in Canada and vaccine scheduling is complicated in early childhood. There are 14 immunizations recommended for children, some requiring boosters, and each province has its own recommended schedule.

According to UNICEF, Canada has the second-lowest rate of childhood vaccination among developed countries. While the exact rate is unclear, it's generally accepted to be around 85 per cent for childhood vaccines in Canada. The World Health Organisation has a target of 90 to 95 per cent.

Halperin says he doesn't believe rates are as low as international organizations suggest because they often rely on federal statistics when provincial ones are more accurate. He says vaccinations for infants and children are quite high but they tend to drop in adolescence when boosters are required.

There are concerns worldwide about vaccination rates, especially given outbreaks of measles, mumps and whooping cough that have been reported across North America and Europe, prompting health officials to issue warnings.

Halperin says vaccine complacency means diseases will return. Diphtheria, for example, had been virtually eliminated, but when the Soviet Union dissolved, vaccinations fell apart in the new independent states. The disease made a swift comeback, with more than 100,000 cases that also spread to neighbouring countries. Several thousand people died.

"It's easy to get complacent when we haven't seen the disease. But remember, parents were lining up for the polio vaccine when it first came out. Whenever there is a scare of any kind, people are clamouring for a vaccine. The problem is that otherwise, prevention is not sexy."

A report by the C.D. Howe Institute last year said only a tiny portion of Canadians—perhaps two per cent—hold anti-vaccine views. The researchers said complacency, costs associated with taking time off work, and difficulties in finding a healthcare provider, are among many reasons parents aren't fully immunizing their kids.

"In addition, there appear to be significant misconceptions about the costs and benefits of immunization. Despite scientific evidence to the contrary, more and more parents are concerned about the risks of immunization than in the past."

But the researchers said making immunization compulsory would be misguided and lead to further entrenched positions among parents with safety concerns. Instead, stricter voluntary policy measures, more reliance on public health nurses, electronic registries tracking vaccinations from birth to adulthood, and targeted interventions, including phone calls or emails to "fence-sitting parents" would have better results in raising vaccination rates, they said.

Halperin agrees that anti-vaxxers are a very small group and are "lost causes." Instead, health authorities should focus on parents who simply forget, don't get around to it, don't have easy access or who need some further education.

Health Canada surveyed 1,029 Canadians and found that only five per cent of parents had "low trust" in vaccinations. In the results released in March, 48 per cent of Canadian parents and expecting parents said they have no doubts or concerns about vaccination. One in three said they have minor doubts or concerns, while six per cent said they have many doubts but still get their kids vaccinated. One in 10 said they had "refused or delayed" some vaccines for their kids.

Those who expressed concerns said they worried about possible allergic reactions, side effects or toxic ingredients, and that they felt there was a lack of testing of vaccines.

According to the Public Health Agency of Canada (PHAC), coverage rates for vaccine-preventable diseases at age two vary from 72 per cent for Haemophilus influenza type B (hib) and 73 per cent for varicella (chicken pox) to 91 per cent for polio and 89 per cent for meningococcal C.

Source: Meredith MacLeod, "Australia Fines Parents Who Don't Vaccinate Kids. Should Canada?" CTVNews.ca, July 12, 2018. https://www.ctvnews.ca/health/australia-fines-parents-who -don-t-vaccinate-kids-should-canada-1.4010595. Reproduced by permission of Bell Media.

But, of course, for those who oppose pipelines this is exactly the point—lower production means lower emissions. However this comes with a cost. A key issue here is the extent to which the unproduced oil in Alberta due to a ban on new pipelines is replaced by oil produced elsewhere. Tombe considers two scenarios. At one extreme he assumes that each barrel of Alberta oil forgone by not constructing new pipelines is not replaced at all, in which case global oil production falls barrel for barrel. Credible estimates suggest that each barrel of oil from the Alberta oil sands creates about 600 kg of "well-to-wheels" carbon emissions on average. In the (highly implausible) case where the reduced Alberta production is not replaced at all, he calculates that the

Ask the Experts

Vaccines

"Declining to be vaccinated against contagious diseases such as measles imposes costs on other people, which is a negative externality."

What do economists say?

0% disagree   0% uncertain

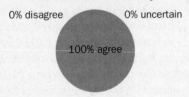

100% agree

"Considering the costs of restricting free choice, and the share of people who choose not to vaccinate their children for measles, the social benefit of mandating measles vaccines for all citizens (except those with compelling medical reasons) would exceed the social cost."

What do economists say?

6% disagree ——— 5% uncertain

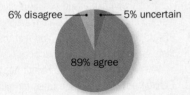

89% agree

Source: IGM Economic Experts Panel, March 10, 2015. Figures © 2018 Cengage Learning.

cost of reducing carbon emissions by banning new pipelines is about $200 per tonne. In the more likely case that the reduction in oil production in Alberta is replaced elsewhere, say by increased production in Saudi Arabia, global carbon emissions decline by only 110 kg per barrel (Saudi oil has a lower "well-to-wheels" carbon footprint than Alberta oil sands), in which case he calculates the cost of reducing carbon emissions by banning new pipelines is about $1000 per tonne.

So, the economic cost of reducing carbon emissions by banning new pipelines is somewhere between $200 and $1000 per tonne, and could be much higher if the discount on Alberta oil increases even more. This is well in excess of the central estimates of the social cost of carbon used by the Government of Canada, which range from about $45 per tonne currently to $75 by 2050. Moreover, compare this to the cost of reducing carbon emissions using a carbon tax or cap and trade scheme, which Tombe calculates is just over $50 per tonne, and we see that reducing emissions by blocking pipelines costs substantially more than carbon pricing.

Climate change is real, and we need sensible policies to deal with it. Internalizing the externalities by pricing carbon, through either taxes or cap and trade, is the least costly and most effective way to lower global emissions; command and control policies such as banning pipelines are not. Approving pipelines, subject to reasonable regulations regarding spill prevention and remediation and with due consideration to Indigenous land issues, while at the same time imposing appropriate carbon prices is a consistent and logical policy from an economic perspective, resulting in emission reductions in the least costly manner. ■

10-2e Objections to the Economic Analysis of Pollution

Some people object to the use of pollution permits and other market-based solutions to pollution on the grounds that it is simply not right to allow someone to pollute for a fee. Clean air and clean water, they argue, are fundamental human rights that should not be debased by considering them in economic terms. How can you put a price on clean air and clean water? The environment is so important, they claim, that we should protect it as much as possible, regardless of the cost.

Economists have little sympathy for this type of argument. To economists, good environmental policy begins by acknowledging the first of the ten principles of economics mentioned in Chapter 1: People face tradeoffs. Certainly, clean air and clean water have value. But their value must be compared to their opportunity cost—that is, to what one must give up to obtain them. Eliminating all pollution is impossible. Trying to eliminate all pollution would reverse many of the technological advances that allow us to enjoy a high standard of living. Few people would be willing to accept poor nutrition, inadequate medical care, or shoddy housing to make the environment as clean as possible.

Economists argue that some environmental activists hurt their own cause by not thinking in economic terms. A clean environment can be viewed as simply another good. Like all normal goods, it has a positive income elasticity: Rich countries can afford a cleaner environment than poor ones and, therefore, usually have more rigorous environmental protection. In addition, like most other goods, clean air and clean water obey the law of demand: The lower the price of environmental protection, the more the public will want. The economic approach of using pollution permits and corrective taxes reduces the cost of environmental protection and should, therefore, increase the public's demand for a clean environment.

 QUICK Quiz *A glue factory and a steel mill emit smoke containing a chemical that is harmful if inhaled in large amounts. Describe three ways the town government might respond to this externality. What are the pros and cons of each of your solutions?*

10-3 Private Solutions to Externalities

Although externalities tend to cause markets to be inefficient, government action is not always needed to solve the problem. In some circumstances, people can develop private solutions.

10-3a The Types of Private Solutions

Sometimes, the problem of externalities is solved with moral codes and social sanctions. Consider, for instance, why most people do not litter. Although there are laws against littering, these laws are not vigorously enforced. Most people choose not to litter just because it is the wrong thing to do. The Golden Rule taught to most children says, "Do unto others as you would have them do unto you." This moral injunction tells us to take account of how our actions affect other people. In economic terms, it tells us to internalize externalities.

Another private solution to externalities is charities, many of which are established to deal with externalities. For example, Greenpeace, whose goal is to protect the environment, is a nonprofit organization funded with private donations. As another example, colleges and universities receive gifts from alumni, corporations, and foundations in part because education has positive externalities for society. The government encourages this private solution to externalities through the tax system by allowing an income tax deduction for charitable donations.

The private market can sometimes solve the problem of externalities by relying on the self-interest of the relevant parties. Sometimes the solution takes the form of integrating different types of businesses. For example, consider an apple grower and a beekeeper who are located next to each other. Each business confers a positive externality on the other: By pollinating the flowers on the trees, the bees help the orchard produce apples. At the same time, the bees use the nectar they get from the apple trees to produce honey. Nonetheless, when the apple grower is deciding how many trees to plant and the beekeeper is deciding how many bees to keep, they neglect the positive externality. As a result, the apple grower plants too few trees and the beekeeper keeps too few bees. These externalities could be internalized if the beekeeper bought the apple orchard or if the apple grower bought the beehives: Both activities would then take place within the same firm, and this single firm could choose the optimal number of trees and bees.

Internalizing externalities is one reason that some firms are involved in multiple types of business.

Another way for the private market to deal with external effects is for the interested parties to enter into a contract. In the foregoing example, a contract between the apple grower and the beekeeper can solve the problem of too few trees and too few bees. The contract can specify the number of trees, the number of bees, and perhaps a payment from one party to the other. By setting the right number of trees and bees, the contract can solve the inefficiency that normally arises from these externalities and make both parties better off.

10-3b The Coase Theorem

Coase theorem

the proposition that if private parties can bargain without cost over the allocation of resources, they can solve the problem of externalities on their own

How effective is the private market in dealing with externalities? A famous result, called the **Coase theorem** after economist Ronald Coase, suggests that it can be very effective in some circumstances. According to the Coase theorem, if private parties can bargain over the allocation of resources at no cost, then the private market will always solve the problem of externalities and allocate resources efficiently.

To see how the Coase theorem works, consider an example. Suppose that Dick owns a dog named Spot. Spot barks and disturbs Jane, Dick's neighbour. Dick gets a benefit from owning the dog, but the dog confers a negative externality on Jane. Should Dick be forced to send Spot to the pound, or should Jane have to suffer sleepless nights because of Spot's barking?

Consider first what outcome is socially efficient. A social planner, considering the two alternatives, would compare the benefit that Dick gets from the dog to the cost that Jane bears from the barking. If the benefit exceeds the cost, it is efficient for Dick to keep the dog and for Jane to live with the barking. Yet if the cost exceeds the benefit, then Dick should get rid of the dog.

According to the Coase theorem, the private market will reach the efficient outcome on its own. How? Jane can simply offer to pay Dick to get rid of the dog. Dick will accept the deal if the amount of money Jane offers is greater than the benefit of keeping the dog.

By bargaining over the price, Dick and Jane can always reach the efficient outcome. For instance, suppose that Dick gets a $500 benefit from the dog and Jane bears an $800 cost from the barking. In this case, Jane can offer Dick $600 to get rid of the dog, and Dick will gladly accept. Both parties are better off than they were before, and the efficient outcome is reached.

It is possible, of course, that Jane would not be willing to offer any price that Dick would accept. For instance, suppose that Dick gets a $1000 benefit from the dog and Jane bears an $800 cost from the barking. In this case, Dick would turn down any offer below $1000, while Jane would not offer any amount above $800. Therefore, Dick ends up keeping the dog. Given these costs and benefits, however, this outcome is efficient.

So far, we have assumed that Dick has the legal right to keep a barking dog. In other words, we have assumed that Dick can keep Spot unless Jane pays him enough to induce him to give up the dog voluntarily. How different would the outcome be, on the other hand, if Jane had the legal right to peace and quiet?

According to the Coase theorem, the initial distribution of rights does not matter for the market's ability to reach the efficient outcome. For instance, suppose that Jane can legally compel Dick to get rid of the dog. Although having this right works to Jane's advantage, it probably will not change the outcome. In this case, Dick can offer to pay Jane to allow him to keep the dog. If the benefit of the dog to Dick exceeds the cost of the barking to Jane, then Dick and Jane will strike a bargain in which Dick keeps the dog.

Although Dick and Jane can reach the efficient outcome regardless of how rights are initially distributed, the distribution of rights is not irrelevant: It determines the distribution of economic well-being. Whether Dick has the right to a barking dog or Jane the right to peace and quiet determines who pays whom in the final bargain. But, in either case, the two parties can bargain with each other and solve the externality problem. Dick will end up keeping the dog only if the benefit exceeds the cost.

To sum up: *The Coase theorem says that private economic actors can potentially solve the problem of externalities among themselves. Whatever the initial distribution of rights, the interested parties can reach a bargain in which everyone is better off and the outcome is efficient.*

10-3c Why Private Solutions Do Not Always Work

Despite the appealing logic of the Coase theorem, private individuals on their own often fail to resolve the problems caused by externalities. The Coase theorem applies only when the interested parties have no trouble reaching and enforcing an agreement. In the real world, however, bargaining does not always work, even when a mutually beneficial agreement is possible.

Sometimes the interested parties fail to solve an externality problem because of **transaction costs**, the costs that parties incur in the process of agreeing to and following through on a bargain. In our example, imagine that Dick and Jane speak different languages so that, to reach an agreement, they will need to hire a translator. If the benefit of solving the barking problem is less than the cost of the translator, Dick and Jane might choose to leave the problem unsolved. In more realistic examples, the transaction costs are the expenses not of translators but of lawyers required to draft and enforce contracts.

At other times, bargaining simply breaks down. The recurrence of wars and labour strikes shows that reaching agreement can be difficult and that failing to reach agreement can be costly. The problem is often that each party tries to hold out for a better deal. For example, suppose that Dick gets a $500 benefit from having the dog and Jane bears an $800 cost from the barking. Although it is efficient for Jane to pay Dick to find another home for the dog, there are many prices that could lead to this outcome. Dick might demand $750, and Jane might offer only $550. As they haggle over the price, the inefficient outcome with the barking dog persists.

Reaching an efficient bargain is especially difficult when the number of interested parties is large because coordinating everyone is costly. For example, consider a factory that pollutes the water of a nearby lake. The pollution confers a negative externality on the local fishermen. According to the Coase theorem, if the pollution is inefficient, then the factory and the fishermen could reach a bargain in which the fishermen pay the factory not to pollute. If there are many fishermen, however, trying to coordinate them all to bargain with the factory may be almost impossible.

When private bargaining does not work, the government can sometimes play a role. The government is an institution designed for collective action. In this example, the government can act on behalf of the fishermen, even when it is impractical for the fishermen to act for themselves.

transaction costs
the costs that parties incur in the process of agreeing to and following through on a bargain

Give an example of a private solution to an externality. • *What is the Coase theorem?* • *Why are private economic actors sometimes unable to solve the problems caused by an externality?*

10-4 Conclusion

The invisible hand is powerful but not omnipotent. A market's equilibrium maximizes the sum of producer and consumer surplus. When the buyers and sellers in the market are the only interested parties, this outcome is efficient from the standpoint of society as a whole. But when there are external effects, such as pollution, evaluating a market outcome requires taking into account the well-being of third parties as well. In this case, the invisible hand of the marketplace may fail to allocate resources efficiently.

In some cases, people can solve the problem of externalities on their own. The Coase theorem suggests that the interested parties can bargain among themselves and agree on an efficient solution. Sometimes, however, an efficient outcome cannot be reached, perhaps because the large number of interested parties makes bargaining difficult.

When people cannot solve the problem of externalities privately, the government often steps in. Yet even with government intervention, society should not abandon market forces entirely. Rather, the government can address the problem by requiring decision makers to bear the full costs of their actions. Corrective taxes on emissions and pollution permits, for instance, are designed to internalize the externality of pollution. More and more, they are the policy of choice for those interested in protecting the environment. Market forces, properly redirected, are often the best remedy for market failure.

summary

- When a transaction between a buyer and a seller directly affects a third party, the effect is called an *externality*. If an activity yields negative externalities, such as pollution, the socially optimal quantity in a market is less than the equilibrium quantity. If an activity yields positive externalities, such as technology spillovers, the socially optimal quantity is greater than the equilibrium quantity.

- Governments pursue various policies to remedy the inefficiencies caused by externalities. Sometimes the government prevents socially inefficient activity by regulating behaviour. Other times it internalizes an externality using corrective taxes. Another public policy is to issue permits. For instance, the government could protect the environment by issuing a limited number of pollution permits. The result of this policy is largely the same as imposing corrective taxes on polluters.

- Those affected by externalities can sometimes solve the problem privately. For instance, when one business confers an externality on another business, the two businesses can internalize the externality by merging. Alternatively, the interested parties can solve the problem by negotiating a contract. According to the Coase theorem, if people can bargain without cost, then they can always reach an agreement in which resources are allocated efficiently. In many cases, however, reaching a bargain among the many interested parties is difficult, so the Coase theorem does not apply.

KEY **concepts**

externality, *p. 219*
corrective taxes, *p. 226*

internalizing the externality, *p. 226*
Coase theorem, *p. 236*

transaction costs, *p. 237*

QUESTIONS FOR **review**

1. Give an example of a negative externality and an example of a positive externality.

2. Draw a supply-and-demand diagram to explain the effect of a negative externality in production.

3. In what way does the patent system help society solve an externality problem?

4. List some of the ways that the problems caused by externalities can be solved without government intervention.

5. Imagine that you are a nonsmoker sharing a room with a smoker. According to the Coase theorem, what determines whether your roommate smokes in the room? Is this outcome efficient? How do you and your roommate reach this solution?

6. Even if the externality issue is resolved using a private solution (Coase), can you think of other issues or problems that would stem from the situation? (For example, how do you determine to whom to give rights?)

7. What are corrective taxes? Why do economists prefer them over regulations as a way to protect the environment from pollution?

QUICK CHECK **multiple choice**

1. Which of the following is an example of a positive externality?
   a. Dev mows Hillary's lawn and is paid $100 for performing the service.
   b. While mowing the lawn, Dev's lawnmower spews out smoke that Hillary's neighbour Kristen has to breathe.
   c. Hillary's newly cut lawn makes her neighbourhood more attractive.
   d. Hillary's neighbours pay her if she promises to get her lawn cut on a regular basis.

2. If the production of a good yields a negative externality, then the social-cost curve lies _____ the supply curve, and the socially optimal quantity is _____ than the equilibrium quantity.
   a. above, greater
   b. above, less
   c. below, greater
   d. below, less

3. When the government levies a tax on a good equal to the external cost associated with the good's production, it _____ the price paid by consumers and makes the market outcome _____ efficient.
   a. increases, more
   b. increases, less
   c. decreases, more
   d. decreases, less

4. Which of the following statements about corrective taxes is NOT true?
   a. Economists prefer them to command-and-control regulation.
   b. They raise government revenue.
   c. They cause deadweight losses.
   d. They reduce the quantity sold in a market.

5. The government auctions off 500 units of pollution rights. They sell for $50 per unit, raising total revenue of $25 000. This policy is equivalent to a corrective tax of what amount per unit of pollution?
   a. $10
   b. $50
   c. $450
   d. $500

6. The Coase theorem does NOT apply in which of the following scenarios?
   a. a significant externality exists between two parties
   b. the court system vigorously enforces all contracts
   c. transaction costs make negotiating difficult
   d. both parties understand the externality fully

PROBLEMS AND **applications**

1. Consider two ways to protect your car from theft. The Club (a car steering wheel lock) makes it difficult for a car thief to take your car. LoJack (a car tracking and recovery system) makes it easier for the police to catch a car thief. Which of these types of protection conveys a negative externality on other car owners? Which conveys a positive externality? Do you think there are any policy implications of your analysis?

2. Do you agree with the following statements? Why or why not?
   a. "The benefits of corrective taxes as a way to reduce pollution have to be weighed against the deadweight losses that these taxes cause."
   b. "When deciding whether to levy a corrective tax on consumers or producers, the government should be careful to levy the tax on the side of the market generating the externality."

3. Consider the market for fire extinguishers.
   a. Why might fire extinguishers exhibit positive externalities?
   b. Draw a graph of the market for fire extinguishers, labelling the demand curve, the social-value curve, the supply curve, and the social-cost curve.
   c. Indicate the market equilibrium level of output and the efficient level of output. Give an intuitive explanation for why these quantities differ.
   d. If the external benefit is $10 per extinguisher, describe a government policy that would result in the efficient outcome.

4. Ringo loves playing rock-and-roll music at high volume. Luciano loves opera and hates rock and roll. Unfortunately, they are next-door neighbours in an apartment building with paper-thin walls.
   a. What is the externality here?
   b. What command-and-control policy might the landlord impose? Could such a policy lead to an inefficient outcome?
   c. Suppose the landlord lets the tenants do whatever they want. According to the Coase theorem, how might Ringo and Luciano reach an efficient outcome on their own? What might prevent them from reaching an efficient outcome?

5. Greater consumption of alcohol leads to more motor vehicle accidents and, thus, imposes costs on people who do not drink and drive.
   a. Illustrate the market for alcohol, labelling the demand curve, the social-value curve, the supply curve, the social-cost curve, the market equilibrium level of output, and the efficient level of output.
   b. On your graph, shade the area corresponding to the deadweight loss of the market equilibrium. (*Hint:* The deadweight loss occurs because some units of alcohol are consumed for which the social cost exceeds the social value.) Explain.

6. Many observers believe that the levels of pollution in our society are too high.
   a. If society wishes to reduce overall pollution by a certain amount, why is it efficient to have different amounts of reduction at different firms?
   b. Command-and-control approaches often rely on uniform reductions among firms. Why are these approaches generally unable to target the firms that should undertake larger reductions?
   c. Economists argue that appropriate corrective taxes or tradable pollution rights will result in efficient pollution reduction. How do these approaches target the firms that should undertake larger reductions?

7. The many identical residents of Whoville love drinking Zlurp. Each resident has the following willingness to pay for the tasty refreshment:

First bottle	$5	Fourth bottle	2
Second bottle	4	Fifth bottle	1
Third bottle	3	Further bottles	0

   a. The cost of producing Zlurp is $1.50, and the competitive suppliers sell it at this price. (The supply curve is horizontal.) How many bottles will each Whovillian consume? What is each person's consumer surplus?
   b. Producing Zlurp creates pollution. Each bottle has an external cost of $1. Taking this additional cost into account, what is total surplus per person in the allocation you described in part (a)?
   c. Cindy Lou Who, one of the residents of Whoville, decides on her own to reduce her consumption of Zlurp by one bottle. What happens to Cindy's welfare (her consumer surplus minus the cost of pollution she experiences)? How does Cindy's decision affect total surplus in Whoville?
   d. Mayor Grinch imposes a $1 tax on Zlurp. What is consumption per person now? Calculate consumer surplus, the external cost, government revenue, and total surplus per person.
   e. Based on your calculations, would you support the mayor's policy? Why or why not?

8. Figure 10.5 shows that for any given demand curve for the right to pollute, the government can achieve the same outcome either by setting a price with a corrective tax or by setting a quantity with pollution permits. Suppose there is a sharp improvement in the technology for controlling pollution.
   a. Using graphs similar to those in Figure 10.5, illustrate the effect of this development on the demand for pollution rights.
   b. What is the effect on the price and quantity of pollution under each regulatory system? Explain.

9. Suppose that the government decides to issue tradable permits for a certain form of pollution.
   a. Does it matter for economic efficiency whether the government distributes or auctions the permits? Why or why not?
   b. If the government chooses to distribute the permits, does the allocation of permits among firms matter for efficiency? Explain.

10. A local drama company proposes a new neighbour-hood theatre in Vancouver. Before approving the building permit, the city planner completes a study of the theatre's impact on the surrounding community.
  a. One finding of the study is that theatres attract traffic, which adversely affects the community. The city planner estimates that the cost to the community from the extra traffic is $5 per ticket. What kind of an externality is this? Why?
  b. Graph the market for theatre tickets, labelling the demand curve, the social-value curve, the supply curve, the social-cost curve, the market equilibrium level of output, and the efficient level of output. Also show the per-unit amount of the externality.
  c. On further review, the city planner uncovers a second externality. Rehearsals for the plays tend to run until late at night, with actors, stagehands, and other theatre members coming and going at various hours. The planner has found that the increased foot traffic improves the safety of the surrounding streets, an estimated benefit to the community of $2 per ticket. What kind of externality is this? Why?
  d. On a new graph, illustrate the market for theatre tickets in the case of these two externalities. Again, label the demand curve, the social-value curve, the supply curve, the social-cost curve, the market equilibrium level of output, the efficient level of output, and the per-unit amount of both externalities.
  e. Describe a government policy that would result in an efficient outcome.

11. There are three industrial firms in Happy Valley.

Firm	Initial Pollution Level	Cost of Reducing Pollution by 1 Unit
A	70 units	$20
B	80	25
C	50	10

The government wants to reduce pollution to 120 units, so it gives each firm 40 tradable pollution permits.
  a. Who sells permits and how many do they sell? Who buys permits and how many do they buy?

Briefly explain why the sellers and buyers are each willing to do so. What is the total cost of pollution reduction in this situation?
  b. How much higher would the costs of pollution reduction be if the permits could not be traded?

12. The market for a particular chemical, called Negext, is described by the following equations.

Demand is given by

$$Q^D = 100 - 5P$$

Supply is given by

$$Q^S = 5P$$

where Q is measured as units of Negext and P is price in dollars per unit.
  a. Find the equilibrium price and quantity. Compute consumer surplus, producer surplus, and total surplus in the market equilibrium.
  b. For each unit of Negext produced, 4 units of pollution are emitted, and each unit of pollution imposes a cost on society of $1. Compute the total cost of pollution when the market for Negext is in equilibrium. What is total surplus from this market after taking into account the cost of pollution?
  c. Would banning Negext increase or decrease welfare? Why?
  d. Suppose that the government restricts emissions to 100 units of pollution. Graph the Negext market under this constraint. Find the new equilibrium price and quantity and show them on your graph. Compute how this policy affects consumer surplus, producer surplus, and the cost of pollution. Would you recommend this policy? Why?
  e. Suppose that instead of restricting pollution, the government imposes a tax on producers equal to $4 for each unit of chemical produced. Calculate the new equilibrium price and quantity, as well as consumer surplus, producer surplus, tax revenue, and the cost of pollution. What is total surplus now? Would you recommend this policy? Why?
  f. New research finds the social cost of pollution is actually higher than $1. How would that change the optimal policy response? Is there some cost of pollution that would make it sensible to ban Negext? If so, what is it?

CHAPTER
11

LEARNING
objectives

Public Goods and Common Resources

In this chapter, you will ...

1 Learn the defining characteristics of public goods and common resources

2 Examine why private markets fail to provide public goods

3 Consider some of the important public goods in our economy

4 See why the cost–benefit analysis of public goods is both necessary and difficult

5 Examine why people tend to use common resources too much

6 Consider some of the important common resources in our economy

An old song lyric maintains that "the best things in life are free." A moment's thought reveals a long list of goods that the songwriter could have had in mind. Nature provides some of them, such as rivers, mountains, beaches, lakes, and oceans. The government provides others, such as playgrounds, parks, and parades. In each case, people often do not pay a fee when they choose to enjoy the benefit of the good.

Goods without prices provide a special challenge for economic analysis. Most goods in our economy are allocated through markets, in which buyers pay for what they receive and sellers are paid for what they provide. For these goods, prices are the signals that guide the decisions of buyers and sellers, and these decisions lead to an efficient allocation of resources. When goods are available free of charge, however, the market forces that normally allocate resources in our economy are absent.

In this chapter, we examine the problems that arise for the allocation of resources when there are goods without market prices. Our analysis will shed light on one of the ten principles of economics discussed in Chapter 1: Governments can sometimes improve market outcomes. When a good does not have a price attached to it, private markets cannot ensure that the good is produced and consumed in the proper amounts. In such cases, government policy can potentially remedy the market failure and raise economic well being.

11-1 The Different Kinds of Goods

How well do markets work in providing the goods that people want? The answer to this question depends on the good being considered. As we discussed in Chapter 7, a market can provide the efficient number of ice-cream cones: The price of ice-cream cones adjusts to balance supply and demand, and this equilibrium maximizes the sum of producer and consumer surplus. Yet, as we discussed in Chapter 10, the market cannot be counted to prevent aluminum manufacturers from polluting the air we breathe: Buyers and sellers in a market typically do not take account of the external effects of their decisions. Thus, markets work well if the good is ice cream, but they don't if the good is clean air.

In thinking about the various goods in the economy, it is useful to group them according to two characteristics:

1. Is the good **excludable**? Can people be prevented from using the good?
2. Is the good **rival in consumption**? Does one person's use of the good diminish another person's ability to use it?

Using these two characteristics, Figure 11.1 divides goods into four categories:

1. **Private goods** are both excludable and rival in consumption. Consider an ice-cream cone, for example. An ice-cream cone is excludable because it is possible to prevent someone from eating one—you just don't give it to her. An ice cream cone is rival in consumption because if one person eats an ice-cream cone, another person cannot eat the same cone. Most goods in the economy are private goods like ice cream cones: You don't get one unless you pay for it, and once you have it, you are the only person who benefits. When we analyzed supply and demand in Chapters 4, 5, and 6 and the efficiency of markets in Chapters 7, 8, and 9, we implicitly assumed that goods were both excludable and rival in consumption.

excludability
the property of a good whereby a person can be prevented from using it

rival in consumption
the property of a good whereby one person's use diminishes other people's use

private goods
goods that are both excludable and rival

public goods

goods that are neither excludable nor rival

common resources

goods that are rival but not excludable

club goods

goods that are excludable but not rival

2. **Public goods** are neither excludable nor rival in consumption. That is, people cannot be prevented from using a public good, and one person's use of a public good does not reduce another person's ability to use it. For example, a tornado siren in a small town is a public good. Once the siren sounds, it is impossible to prevent any single person from hearing it (so it is not excludable). Moreover, when one person gets the benefit of the warning, she does not reduce the benefit to anyone else (so it is not rival in consumption).

3. **Common resources** are rival in consumption but not excludable. For example, fish in the ocean are rival in consumption: When one person catches fish, there are fewer fish for the next person to catch. Yet these fish are not an excludable good because it is difficult to stop fishermen from taking fish out of a vast ocean.

4. **Club goods** are excludable but not rival in consumption. For instance, consider fire protection in a small town. It is easy to exclude someone from using this good: The fire department can just let her house burn down. But fire protection is not rival in consumption: Once a town has paid for the fire department, the additional cost of protecting one more house is small. (We discuss club goods again in Chapter 15, where we see that they are one type of a *natural monopoly*.)

Although Figure 11.1 offers a clean separation of goods into four categories, the boundaries between the categories are sometimes fuzzy. Whether goods are excludable or rival in consumption is often a matter of degree. Fish in an ocean may not be excludable because monitoring fishing is so difficult, but a large enough Coast Guard could make fish at least partly excludable. Similarly, although fish are generally rival in consumption, this would be less true if the population of fishermen was small relative to the population of fish. (Think of North American fishing waters before the arrival of European settlers.) For purposes of our analysis, however, it will be helpful to group goods into these four categories.

In this chapter, we examine goods that are not excludable: public goods and common resources. Because people cannot be prevented from using these goods,

FIGURE 11.1

Four Types of Goods

Goods can be grouped into four categories according to two characteristics: (1) A good is *excludable* if people can be prevented from using it; (2) a good is *rival in consumption* if one person's use of the good diminishes other people's use of it. This diagram gives examples of goods in each category.

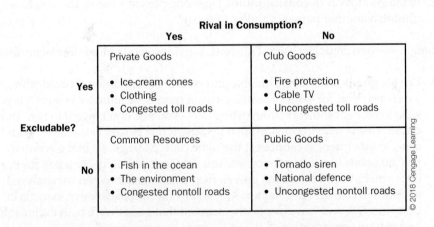

		Rival in Consumption?	
		Yes	**No**
Excludable?	**Yes**	Private Goods • Ice-cream cones • Clothing • Congested toll roads	Club Goods • Fire protection • Cable TV • Uncongested toll roads
	No	Common Resources • Fish in the ocean • The environment • Congested nontoll roads	Public Goods • Tornado siren • National defence • Uncongested nontoll roads

they are available to everyone free of charge. The study of public goods and common resources is closely related to the study of externalities. For both of these types of goods, externalities arise because something of value has no price attached to it. If one person were to provide a public good, such as a tornado siren, other people would be better off. They would receive a benefit without paying for it—a positive externality. Similarly, when one person uses a common resource such as the fish in the ocean, other people are worse off because there are fewer fish to catch. They suffer a loss but are not compensated for it—a negative externality. Because of these external effects, private decisions about consumption and production can lead to an inefficient allocation of resources, and government intervention can potentially raise economic well-being.

 QUICK Quiz *Define public goods and common resources, and give an example of each.*

11-2 Public Goods

To understand how public goods differ from other goods and why they present problems for society, let's consider an example: a fireworks display. This good is not excludable because it is impossible to prevent someone from seeing fireworks, and it is not rival in consumption because one person's enjoyment of fireworks does not reduce anyone else's enjoyment of them.

11-2a The Free-Rider Problem

The citizens of Smalltown, Canada, like seeing fireworks on Canada Day. Each of the town's 500 residents places a $10 value on the experience for a total benefit of $5000. The cost of putting on a fireworks display is $1000. Because the $5000 of benefits exceed the $1000 of costs, it is efficient for Smalltown residents to have a fireworks display on Canada Day.

Would the private market produce the efficient outcome? Probably not. Imagine that Ellen, a Smalltown entrepreneur, decided to put on a fireworks display. Ellen would surely have trouble selling tickets to the event because her potential customers would quickly figure out that they could see the fireworks even without a ticket. Because fireworks are not excludable, people have an incentive to be free riders. A **free rider** is a person who receives the benefit of a good but avoids paying for it. Because people would have an incentive to be free riders rather than ticket buyers, the market would fail to produce an efficient outcome.

One way to view this market failure is that it arises because of an externality. If Ellen puts on the fireworks display, she confers an external benefit on those who see the display without paying for it. When deciding whether to put on the display, however, Ellen does not take the external benefits into account. Even though a fireworks display is socially desirable, it is not privately profitable. As a result, Ellen makes the privately rational but socially inefficient decision not to put on the display.

Although the private market fails to supply the fireworks display demanded by Smalltown residents, the solution to Smalltown's problem is obvious: The local government can sponsor a Canada Day celebration. The town council can raise everyone's taxes by $2 and use the revenue to hire Ellen to produce the fireworks. Everyone in Smalltown is better off by $8—the $10 at which residents value the fireworks minus the $2 tax bill. Ellen can help Smalltown reach the efficient

free rider

a person who receives the benefit of a good but avoids paying for it

outcome as a public employee even though she could not do so as a private entrepreneur.

The story of Smalltown is simplified, but it is also realistic. In fact, many local governments in Canada do pay for fireworks on Canada Day. Moreover, the story shows a general lesson about public goods: Because public goods are not excludable, the free-rider problem prevents the private market from supplying them. The government, however, can potentially remedy the problem. If the government decides that the total benefits exceed the costs, it can provide the public good and pay for it with tax revenue, making everyone better off.

To investigate this further consider another simplified economy consisting of two neighbours (call them Bob and Doug). The good in question is street lights installed in front of their houses. The first panel in Figure 11.2 shows their individual demand curves for street lights, D_B and D_D, which we know from Chapter 7 can be thought of as marginal willingness to pay, or marginal benefit, curves. Assume for a moment, and inappropriately, that street lights are a pure private good. In this case, as we discussed in Chapters 4 and 7, we determine the market demand curve by *horizontally summing* the individual demand curves, which gives $D_{PRIVATE}$ in the second panel of the figure. To simplify the supply side, assume that street lights can be purchased at a market price of \$4, which is equal to the constant marginal cost of producing them; this gives a horizontal market supply curve at \$4, which is also shown in the second panel of the figure. It is evident that neither Bob nor Doug will purchase street lights, as the market price of \$4 exceeds their individual marginal benefits—and indeed we see that the market supply and demand curves treating street lights as a private good intersect at an equilibrium quantity of zero. And if street lights were a private good this would in fact be the efficient outcome as the social marginal cost of installing a street light exceeds the social marginal benefit.

But of course street lights are not a private good. They are not excludable—neither Bob nor Doug can prevent the other from benefiting from the lights if they

FIGURE 11.2

Demand Curves for Street Lights

Panel (a) shows the individual demand curves for Bob and Doug for street lights. Panel (b) treats streetlights as a private good, horizontally summing the individual curves to get the aggregate demand $D_{PRIVATE}$. Neither Bob nor Doug purchase street lights if the marginal cost is \$4. Panel (c) treats street lights more appropriately as a public good, vertically summing the individual curves to get the appropriate aggregate demand D_{PUBLIC}. The socially optimal number of street lights is two, determined by the intersection of the MC curve with the appropriate demand curve D_{PUBLIC}.

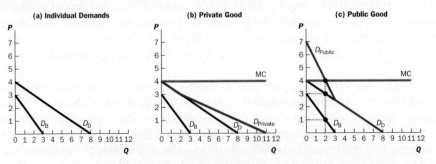

are installed—and they are not rival in consumption—Bob's use of a street light does not diminish Doug's use, and vice versa. Street lights are therefore a public good. Unlike a private good, where individual demand curves are horizontally summed to obtain the market demand curve, for a public good individual demand curves should be *vertically summed* to get the appropriate market demand curve. This is because Bob and Doug both benefit when street lights are installed, unlike the case of a private good where only the individual who purchases the good benefits. This vertical summation is shown in the third panel of Figure 11.2, which gives D_{PUBLIC}. The socially optimal number of street lights is determined by the intersection of the horizontal marginal cost curve with the *social marginal benefit curve* D_{PUBLIC}, which is the vertical summation of the individual marginal benefit curves. We see that if two street lights are installed, Bob receives a marginal benefit of \$1 and Doug receives a marginal benefit of \$3, for a total social marginal benefit of \$4. This is equal to the marginal cost of street lights of \$4, and is therefore the socially efficient outcome.

In the case of a public good like street lights, the socially efficient outcome will not occur naturally if the private sector is left to its own devices because the individual marginal benefit of the lights for both Bob and Doug is less than the marginal cost of \$4, and neither has an incentive to take the benefit received by the other into account. As noted earlier, it is in this sense in which a public good is like an externality.

Recall from Chapter 7 that in the case of a private good like ice cream we had the following set of relationships:

Price = Marginal benefit to Catherine = Marginal benefit to Nicholas

= Marginal cost to Ben = Marginal cost to Jerry

and the market equilibrium outcome is efficient due to the coordinating role played by prices in equating marginal benefits and marginal costs. In the case of a public good, prices do not provide the proper signal for the invisible hand to achieve an efficient outcome, which now requires:

Marginal cost = Marginal social benefit = Marginal benefit to Bob + Marginal benefit to Doug

and the market fails to provide the efficient amount of lighting.

The solution to this market failure is for the government to install the street lights. It is worth reiterating in this regard that the government will need to use tax revenue to finance the street lights, and the social marginal cost of the lights should take account of the marginal cost of public funds to account for the distortions associated with those taxes, as discussed in Chapter 8.

11-2b Some Important Public Goods

There are many examples of public goods. Here we consider three of the most important.

National Defence The defence of a country from foreign aggressors is a classic example of a public good. Once the country is defended, it is impossible to prevent any single person from enjoying the benefit of this defence. And when one person enjoys the benefit of national defence, she does not reduce the benefit of anyone else. Thus, national defence is neither excludable nor rival in consumption.

National defence in Canada falls under the control of the federal government. In 2014 the federal government spent about \$21.5 billion on national defence, or around

$605 per person. While this is a lot of money, other countries spend even more. In 2014 the U.S. federal government spent a total of US$748 billion, or about US$2346 per person, on national defence. People disagree about whether this amount is too small or too large, but almost no one doubts that some government spending for national defence is necessary. Even economists who advocate for small government agree that national defence is a public good that government should provide.

Basic Research   Knowledge is created through research. In evaluating the appropriate public policy toward knowledge creation, it is important to distinguish general knowledge from specific technological knowledge. Specific technological knowledge, such as the invention of a longer-lasting battery, a smaller microchip, or a better digital music player, can be patented. The patent gives the inventor the exclusive right to the knowledge she has created for a period of time. Anyone else who wants to use the patented information must pay the inventor for the right to do so. In other words, the patent makes the knowledge created by the inventor excludable.

By contrast, general knowledge is a public good. For example, a mathematician cannot patent a theorem. Once a theorem is proved, the knowledge is not excludable: The theorem enters society's general pool of knowledge that anyone can use without charge. The theorem is also not rival in consumption: One person's use of the theorem does not prevent any other person from using the theorem.

Profit-seeking firms spend a lot on research trying to develop new products that they can patent and sell, but they do not spend much on basic research. Their incentive, instead, is to free-ride on the general knowledge created by others. As a result, in the absence of any public policy, society would devote too few resources to creating new knowledge.

The government tries to provide the public good of general knowledge in various ways. Federal government agencies, such as the Natural Sciences and Engineering Research Council of Canada and the Social Sciences and Humanities Research Council of Canada, subsidize basic research in medicine, mathematics, physics, chemistry, biology, and even economics. Determining the appropriate level of governmental support for basic research is difficult because the benefits are hard to measure. Moreover, members of Parliament who determine the funding for these sorts of programs have little expertise in science and, therefore, are not in the best position to judge what lines of research will produce the largest benefits. So, while basic research is surely a public good, we should not be surprised if the public sector fails to pay for the right amount and the right kinds.

Fighting Poverty   Many government programs are aimed at helping the poor. The welfare programs administered by the provinces and territories provide some income for low-income individuals. Many municipalities provide subsidized housing for low-income families. Other benefits to low-income individuals are delivered through the tax system by means of refundable tax credits, the value of which declines as a person's income increases.

Economists disagree among themselves about what role the government should play in fighting poverty. We discuss this debate more fully in Chapter 20, but here we note one important argument: Advocates of antipoverty programs claim that fighting poverty is a public good. Even if everyone prefers living in a society without poverty, fighting poverty is not a "good" that private actions will adequately provide.

To see why, suppose someone tried to organize a group of wealthy individuals to try to eliminate poverty. They would be providing a public good. This good would not be rival in consumption: One person's enjoyment of living in a society without poverty would not reduce anyone else's enjoyment of it. The good would not be excludable: Once poverty is eliminated, no one can be prevented from taking pleasure in this fact. As a result, there would be a tendency for people to free-ride on the generosity of others, enjoying the benefits of poverty elimination without contributing to the cause.

Because of the free-rider problem, eliminating poverty through private charity will probably not work. Yet government action can solve this problem. Taxing the wealthy to raise the living standards of the poor can potentially make everyone better off. The poor are better off because they now enjoy a higher standard of living, and those paying the taxes are better off because they enjoy living in a society with less poverty.

case study **Are Lighthouses Public Goods?**

Some goods can switch between being public goods and being private goods depending on the circumstances. For example, a fireworks display is a public good if performed in a town with many residents. Yet if performed at a private amusement park such as Canada's Wonderland, a fireworks display is more like a private good because visitors to the park pay for admission.

Another example is a lighthouse. Economists have long used lighthouses as an example of a public good. Lighthouses mark specific locations along the coast so that passing ships can avoid treacherous waters. The benefit that the lighthouse provides to the ship captain is neither excludable nor rival in consumption, so each captain has an incentive to free-ride by using the lighthouse to navigate without paying for the service. Because of this free-rider problem, private markets usually fail to provide the lighthouses that ship captains need. As a result, most lighthouses today are operated by the government.

In some cases, however, lighthouses may be closer to private goods. On the coast of England in the nineteenth century, some lighthouses were privately owned and operated. Instead of trying to charge ship captains for the service, however, the owner of the lighthouse charged the owner of the nearby port. If the port owner did not pay, the lighthouse owner turned off the light, and ships avoided that port.

In deciding whether something is a public good, one must determine the number of beneficiaries and whether these beneficiaries can be excluded from using the good. A free-rider problem arises when the number of beneficiaries is large and exclusion of any one of them is impossible. If a lighthouse benefits many ship captains, it is a public good. Yet if it primarily benefits a single port owner, it is more like a private good. ■

Cape Bonavista Lighthouse in Newfoundland is what kind of good?

11-2c The Difficult Job of Cost–Benefit Analysis

So far we have seen that the government provides public goods because the private market on its own will not produce an efficient quantity. Yet deciding that the government must play a role is only the first step. The government must then determine what kinds of public goods to provide and in what quantities.

cost–benefit analysis
a study that compares the costs and benefits to society of providing a public good

Suppose that the government is considering a public project, such as building a new highway. To judge whether to build the highway, it must compare the total benefits for all those who would use it to the costs of building and maintaining it. To make this decision, the government might hire a team of economists and engineers to conduct a study, called a **cost–benefit analysis**, to estimate the total costs and benefits of the project to society as a whole.

Cost–benefit analysts have a tough job. Because the highway will be available to everyone free of charge, there is no price with which to judge the value of the highway. Simply asking people how much they would value the highway is not reliable: Quantifying benefits is difficult using the results from a questionnaire, and respondents have little incentive to tell the truth. Those who would use the highway have an incentive to exaggerate the benefit they receive to get the highway built. Those who would be harmed by the highway have an incentive to exaggerate the costs to them to prevent the highway from being built.

The efficient provision of public goods is, therefore, intrinsically more difficult than the efficient provision of private goods. When buyers of private goods enter a market, they reveal the value they place on it through the prices they are willing to pay. At the same time, sellers reveal their costs with the prices they are willing to accept. The equilibrium is an efficient allocation of resources because it reflects all this information. By contrast, cost–benefit analysts do not have any price signals to observe when evaluating whether the government should provide a public good and how much to provide. Their findings on the costs and benefits of public projects are, therefore, rough approximations at best.

case study ### How Much Is a Life Worth?

Imagine that you have been elected to serve as a member of your local town council. The town engineer comes to you with a proposal: The town can spend $20 000 to build and operate a traffic light at a town intersection that now has only a stop sign. The benefit of the traffic light is increased safety. The engineer estimates, based on data from similar intersections, that the traffic light would reduce the risk of a fatal traffic accident over the lifetime of the traffic light from 1.6 to 1.1 percent. Should you spend the money for the new light?

To answer this question, you turn to cost–benefit analysis. But you quickly run into an obstacle: The costs and benefits must be measured in the same units if you are to compare them meaningfully. The cost is measured in dollars, but the benefit—the possibility of saving a person's life—is not directly monetary. To make your decision, you have to put a dollar value on a human life.

At first, you may be tempted to conclude that a human life is priceless. After all, there is probably no amount of money that you could be paid to voluntarily give up your life or that of a loved one. This suggests that a human life has an infinite dollar value.

For the purposes of cost–benefit analysis, however, this answer leads to nonsensical results. If we truly placed an infinite value on human life, we should place traffic lights on every street corner, and we should all drive large cars loaded with all the latest safety features. Yet traffic lights are not at every corner, and people sometimes choose to pay less for smaller cars without safety options such as side-impact air bags or antilock brakes. In both our public and private decisions, we are at times willing to risk our lives to save some money.

Once we have accepted the idea that a person's life has an implicit dollar value, how can we determine what that value is? One approach, sometimes used by courts

Tomasz Bidermann/Shutterstock.com

to award damages in wrongful-death suits, is to look at the total amount of money a person would have earned if he or she had lived. Economists are often critical of this approach because it ignores other opportunity costs of losing one's life. It thus has the bizarre implication that the life of a retired or disabled person has no value.

A better way to value human life is to look at the risks that people are voluntarily willing to take and how much they must be paid for taking them. Mortality risk varies across jobs, for example. Construction workers in high-rise buildings face greater risk of death on the job than office workers do. By comparing wages in risky and less risky occupations, controlling for education, experience, and other determinants of wages, economists can get some sense about what value people put on their own lives.

Economists have made estimates of the "value of a statistical life" (VSL), a phrase only an economist would love, which governments use to undertake cost–benefit analysis. Transport Canada uses a VSL of $8.98 million to assess the value of avoided traffic fatalities.

We can now return to our original example and respond to the town engineer. The traffic light reduces the risk of fatality by 0.5 percentage points. Using Transport Canada's VSL of $8.98 million the expected benefit from having the traffic light is $44 900 (.005 × $8.98 million). This easily exceeds the cost of $20 000, so you should approve the project. ■

 QUICK Quiz *What is the free-rider problem? • Why does the free-rider problem induce the government to provide public goods? • How should the government decide whether to provide a public good?*

11-3 Common Resources

Common resources, like public goods, are not excludable: They are available free of charge to anyone who wants to use them. Common resources are, however, rival in consumption: One person's use of the common resource reduces other people's ability to use it. Thus, common resources give rise to a new problem. Once the good is provided, policymakers need to be concerned about how much it is used. This problem is best understood from the classic parable called the **Tragedy of the Commons**.

11-3a The Tragedy of the Commons

Consider life in a small medieval town. Of the many economic activities that take place in the town, one of the most important is raising sheep. Many of the town's families own flocks of sheep and support themselves by selling the sheep's wool, which is used to make clothing.

As our story begins, the sheep spend much of their time grazing on the land surrounding the town, called the Town Common. No family owns the land. Instead, the town residents own the land collectively, and all the residents are allowed to graze their sheep on it. Collective ownership works well because land is plentiful. As long as everyone can get all the good grazing land they want, the Town Common is not rival in consumption, and allowing residents' sheep to graze for free causes no problems. Everyone in the town is happy.

As the years pass, the population of the town grows, and so does the number of sheep grazing on the Town Common. With a growing number of sheep and a fixed amount of land, the land starts to lose its ability to replenish itself.

Tragedy of the Commons
a parable that illustrates why common resources get used more than is desirable from the standpoint of society as a whole

Eventually, the land is grazed so heavily that it becomes barren. With no grass left on the Town Common, raising sheep is impossible, and the town's once prosperous wool industry disappears. Many families lose their source of livelihood.

What causes the tragedy? Why do the shepherds allow the sheep population to grow so large that it destroys the Town Common? The reason is that social and private incentives differ. Avoiding the destruction of the grazing land depends on the collective action of the shepherds. If the shepherds acted together, they could reduce the sheep population to a size that the Town Common can support. Yet no single family has an incentive to reduce the size of its own flock because each flock represents only a small part of the problem.

In essence, the Tragedy of the Commons arises because of an externality. When one family's flock grazes on the common land, it reduces the quality of the land available for other families. Because people neglect this negative externality when deciding how many sheep to own, the result is an excessive number of sheep.

If the tragedy had been foreseen, the town could have solved the problem in various ways. It could have regulated the number of sheep in each family's flock, internalized the externality by taxing sheep, or auctioned off a limited number of sheep-grazing permits. That is, the medieval town could have dealt with the problem of overgrazing in the way that modern society deals with the problem of pollution.

In the case of land, however, there is a simpler solution. The town can divide the land among town families. Each family can enclose its parcel of land with a fence and then protect it from excessive grazing. In this way, the land becomes a private good rather than a common resource. This outcome in fact occurred during the enclosure movement in England in the seventeenth century.

The Tragedy of the Commons is a story with a general lesson: When one person uses a common resource, she diminishes other people's enjoyment of it. Because of this negative externality, common resources tend to be used excessively. The government can solve the problem by using regulation or taxes to reduce consumption of the common resource. Alternatively, the government can sometimes turn the common resource into a private good.

This lesson has been known for thousands of years. The ancient Greek philosopher Aristotle pointed out the problem with common resources: "What is common to many is taken least care of, for all men have greater regard for what is their own than for what they possess in common with others."

11-3b Some Important Common Resources

There are many examples of common resources. In almost all cases, the same problem arises as in the Tragedy of the Commons: Private decision makers use the common resource too much. Governments often regulate behaviour or impose fees to mitigate the problem of overuse.

Clean Air and Water As we discussed in Chapter 10, markets do not adequately protect the environment. Pollution is a negative externality that can be remedied with regulations or with corrective taxes on polluting activities. One can view this market failure as an example of a common-resource problem. Clean air and clean water are common resources like open grazing land, and excessive pollution is like excessive grazing. Environmental degradation is a modern Tragedy of the Commons.

Congested Roads Roads can be either public goods or common resources. If a road is not congested, then one person's use does not affect anyone else. In this case, use is not rival in consumption, and the road is a public good. Yet if a road is congested, then use of that road yields a negative externality. When one additional person drives on the road, it becomes more crowded, and other people must drive more slowly. In this case, the road is a common resource.

One way for the government to address the problem of road congestion is to charge drivers a toll. A toll is, in essence, a corrective tax on the externality of congestion. Sometimes, as in the case of local roads, tolls are not a practical solution because the cost of collecting them is too high. However, technological innovations have lowered the cost of collecting tolls. For example, the 407 Express Toll Route is a privately operated highway just north of Toronto. It uses a system of cameras and transponders to toll vehicles automatically; there are no toll booths.

Sometimes congestion is a problem only at certain times of day. If a bridge is heavily travelled only during rush hour, for instance, the congestion externality is larger during this time. The efficient way to deal with these externalities is to charge higher tolls during rush hour. This toll would provide an incentive for drivers to alter their schedules, reducing traffic when congestion is greatest.

Another policy that responds to the problem of road congestion is a tax on gasoline. Gasoline is a complementary good to driving: An increase in the price of gasoline tends to reduce the quantity of driving demanded. Therefore, a gasoline tax reduces road congestion. A gasoline tax, however, is an imperfect solution, because it affects other decisions besides the amount of driving on congested roads. For example, the gasoline tax discourages driving on noncongested roads, even though there is no congestion externality for these roads.

Ask the Experts

Congestion Pricing

"In general, using more congestion charges in crowded transportation networks—such as higher tolls during peak travel times in cities, and peak fees for airplane takeoff and landing slots—and using the proceeds to lower other taxes would make citizens on average better off."

What do economists say?

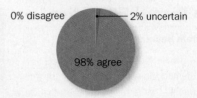

0% disagree — 2% uncertain

98% agree

Source: IGM Economic Experts Panel, January 11, 2012.
Figure © 2018 Cengage Learning.

case study Do Bridge Tolls Affect Behaviour?

Economists expound the benefits of tolls to deal with congested roads and bridges. However, politicians are typically not keen on making drivers pay for access to roads that they traditionally view as being "free"; good politics is not always consistent with good economics.

A case in point is the Port Mann Bridge, a major bridge over the Fraser River on the TransCanada highway entering Vancouver (actually Coquitlam) from Surrey. The new Port Mann Bridge replaced the old bridge in 2012. In order to recover construction and operating costs the bridge was electronically tolled. The toll per crossing ranged from $3.15 for cars to $9.45 for large trucks. In 2017 the newly elected NDP government decided to eliminate the tolls on the Port Mann Bridge (and the Golden Ears Bridge), effective September 1, 2017. The elimination of the tolls provides an interesting opportunity to examine the impact of tolls on behaviour and to determine the extent to which drivers respond to prices.

Figure 11.3 shows the monthly average weekday traffic on the Port Mann Bridge from 2013 to the first three months in 2018. A marked seasonal pattern exists, with traffic volume peaking in the summer and then falling in the winter. There was also a sizable increase in traffic volume in 2016. But what really stands out in the figure is the impact of the elimination of the toll on September 1, 2017. There was a substantial increase in traffic volume in September and for

Are Economics Students Grinches?

This article describes some research that examines the extent to which students contribute to a public good. It finds that economics students tend to contribute less to public goods than other students. The author concludes that "we" could do a better job of providing "balance" in economics education. An alternative conclusion is that students who choose to major in economics better understand the underlying incentives.

The Dismal Education

By Yoram Bauman

The stereotypes about economists are well known: that we're selfish Grinches; that we don't read human interest stories because they don't interest us; that the only reason we don't sell our children is that we think they'll be worth more later.

But are the stereotypes true? And if so is the cause nature or nurture? In other words, are selfish people disproportionately likely to become economists? Or is there something about being an economist (or being on the receiving end of economics education) that *makes* people selfish?

Illumination/Universal/Kobal/Shutterstock

Academic research suggests that there's a good deal of truth to the stereotype. Many studies have looked at how economists behave in what are called public goods situations. A key feature of these situations is that you can benefit from public goods even if you don't contribute to them. You can watch PBS without making a donation; you can enjoy clean air even if you drive a car that pollutes. Such goods, however,

give rise to the so-called free-rider problem: acting selfishly makes sense for each individual (why sacrifice if you don't have to?) but as more and more people choose to act selfishly, the good disappears and everyone loses.

Public goods run counter to Adam Smith's "invisible hand" theory in that self-interested behavior by individuals does not, as the theory would have it, lead to good outcomes for society as a whole. These situations flummox just about everybody—look at all the trouble that nations and individuals are having in dealing with climate change—but economists and economics students appear to be especially likely to free-ride and act in ways that are "anti-social" rather than "pro-social."

FIGURE 11.3

Monthly Average Weekday Traffic on the Port Mann Bridge

The figure shows the monthly average weekday traffic on the Port Mann Bridge in Vancouver from 2013 to the first three months in 2018. Bridge tolls were eliminated on September 1, 2017, which has led to a substantial increase in traffic volume.

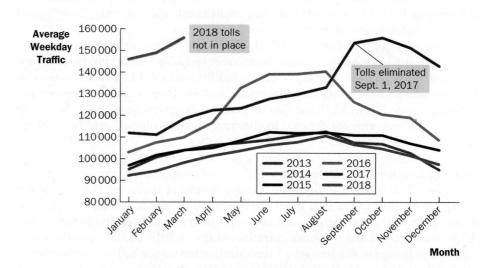

My research with the economist Elaina Rose, published in August in the *Journal of Economic Behavior and Organization,* has looked at a real-life public goods situation faced by students at the University of Washington. During our study period (1999 to 2002), when students went online to register for classes each quarter, they were asked if they wanted to donate $3 to support Wash PIRG, a left-leaning activist group. Students were also asked if they wanted to donate $3 to Affordable Tuition Now (ATN), a group that lobbied for "sensible tuition rates, quality financial aid and adequate funding."

You may question whether these groups actually serve the common good, but that's mostly beside the point. Regardless of the groups' actual social value, a purely self-interested individual would choose to free-ride rather than contribute; after all, a single $3 donation is not going to make a noticeable difference in tuition rates.

Our data showed that each group received donations from about 10 percent of the students each quarter. Although students remained anonymous, we could look at all of the 8,743 members of our data set and determine what their majors were, when they took economics classes (if at all) and whether or not they donated to ATN or Wash PIRG during each quarter of our study period.

In line with previous research, what we found supported the Grinch stereotype. About 5 percent of economics majors donated to Wash PIRG in a given quarter, compared with 8 percent for other arts and sciences majors. A similar divide— 10 percent versus almost 15 percent—occurred with respect to donations to ATN.

We also found evidence that the giving behavior of students who became economics majors was driven by nature, not nurture: taking economics classes did not have a significant negative effect on later giving by economics majors.

But taking economics classes *did* have a significant negative effect on later giving by students who *did not* become economics majors.

One interpretation of these results is that students who were not economics majors suffered a "loss of innocence" after taking an economics class, presumably because of exposure to certain ideas (like the invisible hand) or certain people (like economics teachers).

In contrast, students who became economics majors did not suffer a loss of innocence. This may be because they lost their innocence in high school—other research suggests that pre-university exposure to economics reduces giving— or perhaps even because economics majors were "born guilty."

Our research suggests that economics education could do a better job of providing balance. Learning about the shortcomings as well as the successes of free markets is at the heart of any good economics education, and students— especially those who are not destined to major in the field—deserve to hear both sides of the story.

the rest of 2017, and continuing into 2018, relative to previous years when the toll was in place. Indeed, compared to the same months over 2016, which was already a historically high year in terms of volume, traffic over the Port Mann Bridge increased by almost 30 percent on average after the toll was eliminated. This is a sizable increase, suggesting that even relatively modest tolls can have a big impact on drivers. ∎

Fish, Whales, and Other Wildlife Many species of animals are common resources. Fish and whales, for instance, have commercial value, and anyone can go to the ocean and catch whatever is available. Each person has little incentive to maintain the species for the next year. Just as excessive grazing can destroy the Town Common, excessive fishing and whaling can destroy commercially valuable marine populations.

Oceans remain one of the least regulated common resources. Two problems prevent an easy solution. First, many countries have access to the oceans, so any solution would require international cooperation among countries that hold different values. Second, because the oceans are so vast, enforcing any agreement is difficult. As a result, fishing rights have been a frequent source of international tension among normally friendly countries.

In Canada, various laws aim to protect fish and other wildlife. For example, the government charges for fishing and hunting licences, and it restricts the lengths of the fishing and hunting seasons. Fishermen are often required to throw back small fish, and hunters can kill only a limited number of animals. All these laws reduce the use of a common resource and help maintain animal populations.

How did the collapse of the Atlantic cod fishery affect the people living in Rose Blanche, Newfoundland?

case study
The Collapse of the Atlantic Cod Fishery

The Atlantic Ocean off the shores of Newfoundland was once so full of cod that in 1497 explorer John Cabot marvelled that they actually blocked his ship. In the centuries to follow, boats from fishing nations around the world flocked to Canada's east coast to exploit the abundance of northern cod. Five hundred years later, the cod are virtually gone. What happened?

The population of northern cod had yielded an overall annual catch of about 250 000 tonnes for more than a century prior to the mid-1950s. Until then, most of the fishing took place mainly in small craft in waters relatively close to shore, using traditional techniques that involved fishing from dories or small trawlers.

In the mid-1950s, Newfoundland's dories were displaced by a new breed of factory fishing vessel. These new "factory trawlers," or "draggers," came from Germany, Great Britain, Spain, Portugal, Poland, the Soviet Union, Cuba, and even East Asia, and legally fished to within 20 kilometres of the eastern Canadian coast. They set and hauled enormous baglike nets that plowed and scraped the ocean bottom, quickly processing and deep-freezing the fish on board. Catches of northern cod increased substantially throughout the late 1950s and early 1960s as fishing vessels from around the world enjoyed essentially unencumbered access to the north Atlantic fishery off Canada's east coast. With no meaningful regulation of the resource, the catch peaked at just over 800 000 tonnes in the late 1960s.

The distant-water fleet, new technology, and virtually unlimited access to the common property resource subjected the northern cod to intense pressure, and by 1975 the declining northern cod population was yielding just 300 000 tonnes annually. Concerned that stocks were being reduced to almost nothing, Canada passed legislation in 1976 to extend their national jurisdictions over marine resources to 370 kilometres, prohibiting foreign boats from fishing within this limit.

In recognition of the overfishing that resulted from unregulated access to the fish stocks, Canada also initiated a quota system for fishing the northern cod, by implementing total allowable catch (TAC) limits based on the concept of maximum sustainable yield (MSY)—the maximum amount of fish that could be taken from a stock without depleting it. Unfortunately, when setting TAC limits the government considered short-term economic and political factors as well as biological ones in establishing its quota, which meant that TAC figures were set too high.

Although the 370-kilometre limit and a new regulatory regime were intended to conserve and restore fish stocks, they actually resulted in a larger Canadian fishing fleet to replace foreign fishers, as throughout the 1980s the Canadian government promoted more and more investment in the Atlantic fishery. In the mid-1980s, scientists began warning that the stock was declining and recommended the TAC limits be cut in half. Instead of acting immediately and reducing catch quotas at the first signs of overfishing, the federal government delayed conservation action and implemented only moderate reductions in the TAC limits, fearing the massive unemployment that would have resulted from shutting down the industry.

In 1992, the biomass estimate for northern cod was the lowest ever measured and the Canadian minister of Fisheries and Oceans had no choice but to declare a ban on fishing northern cod. Over 40 000 people lost their jobs, and the marine ecosystem is still in a state of collapse.

The collapse of the cod fishery is a prototypical example of what can go wrong with a common property resource, even in the presence of the government's attempt to manage the resource. While Canada finally introduced measures that in principle could have preserved the fish stocks and protected them from the Tragedy of the Commons, the government acted too slowly and based quotas on short-term political and economic considerations. This provides an example of how ill-conceived government intervention might not ultimately address market failures and improve market outcomes. ■

QUICK Quiz *Why do governments try to limit the use of common resources?*

11-4 Conclusion: The Importance of Property Rights

In this and the previous chapter, we have seen there are some "goods" that the market does not provide adequately. Markets do not ensure that the air we breathe is clean or that our country is defended from foreign aggressors. Instead, societies rely on the government to protect the environment and to provide for national defence.

The problems we considered in these chapters arise in many different markets, but they share a common theme. In all cases, the market fails to allocate resources efficiently because *property rights* are not well established. That is, some item of value does not have an owner with the legal authority to control it. For example, although no one doubts that the "good" of clean air or national defence is valuable, no one has the right to attach a price to it and profit from its use. A factory pollutes too much because no one charges the factory for the pollution it emits. The market does not provide for national defence because no one can charge those who are defended for the benefit they receive.

When the absence of property rights causes a market failure, the government can potentially solve the problem. Sometimes, as in the sale of pollution permits, the solution is for the government to help define property rights and thereby unleash market forces. Other times, as in the restriction on hunting seasons, the solution is for the government to regulate private behaviour. Still other times, as in the provision of national defence, the solution is for the government to use tax revenue to supply a good that the market fails to supply. In all cases, if the policy is well planned and well run, it can make the allocation of resources more efficient and thus raise economic well-being.

summary

- Goods differ in whether they are excludable and whether they are rival in consumption. A good is excludable if it is possible to prevent someone from using it. A good is rival in consumption if one person's use of the good reduces other's ability to use the same unit of the good. Markets work best for private goods, which are both excludable and rival in consumption. Markets do not work as well for other types of goods.

- Public goods are neither rival in consumption nor excludable. Examples of public goods include fireworks displays, national defence, and the creation of fundamental knowledge. Because people are not charged for their use of the public good, they have an incentive to free-ride, making the private provision of the good untenable. Therefore, governments provide public goods, making their decision about the quantity based on cost–benefit analysis.

- Common resources are rival in consumption but not excludable. Examples include common grazing land, clean air, and congested roads. Because people are not charged for their use of common resources, they tend to use them excessively. Therefore, governments try to limit the use of common resources.

KEY **concepts**

excludability, *p. 243*
rival in consumption, *p. 243*
private goods, *p. 243*

public goods, *p. 244*
common resources, *p. 244*
club goods, *p. 244*

free rider, *p. 245*
cost–benefit analysis, *p. 250*
Tragedy of the Commons, *p. 251*

QUESTIONS FOR **review**

1. Explain what is meant by a good being "excludable." Explain what is meant by a good being "rival in consumption." Is a slice of pizza excludable? Is it rival in consumption?

2. Define and give an example of a public good. Can the private market provide this good on its own? Explain.

3. What is cost–benefit analysis of public goods? Why is it important? Why is it hard?

4. Define and give an example of a common resource. Without government intervention, will people use this good too much or too little? Why?

QUICK CHECK **multiple choice**

1. Which categories of goods are excludable?
   a. private goods and club goods
   b. private goods and common resources
   c. public goods and club goods
   d. public goods and common resources

2. Which categories of goods are rival in consumption?
   a. private goods and club goods
   b. private goods and common resources
   c. public goods and club goods
   d. public goods and common resources

3. Which of the following is an example of a public good?
   a. residential housing
   b. national defence
   c. restaurant meals
   d. fish in the ocean

4. Which of the following is an example of a common resource?
   a. residential housing
   b. national defence
   c. restaurant meals
   d. fish in the ocean

5. Which of the following describes public goods?
   a. efficiently provided by market forces
   b. underprovided in the absence of government
   c. overused in the absence of government
   d. a type of natural monopoly

6. Which of the following describes common resources?
   a. efficiently provided by market forces
   b. underprovided in the absence of government
   c. overused in the absence of government
   d. a type of natural monopoly

PROBLEMS AND **applications**

1. Both public goods and common resources involve externalities.
   a. Are the externalities associated with public goods generally positive or negative? Use examples in your answer. Is the free-market quantity of public goods generally greater or less than the efficient quantity?

   b. Are the externalities associated with common resources generally positive or negative? Use examples in your answer. Is the free-market use of common resources generally greater or less than the efficient use?

2. Think about the goods and services provided by your local government.
   a. Using the classification in Figure 11.1, explain into which category each of the following goods falls:
      • police protection
      • snowplowing
      • education
      • rural roads
      • city streets
   b. Why do you think the government provides items that are not public goods?

3. Charlie loves watching *Downton Abbey* on his local public TV station, but he never sends any money to support the station during its fundraising drives.
   a. What name do economists have for people like Charlie?
   b. How can the government solve the problem caused by people like Charlie?
   c. Can you think of ways the private market can solve this problem? How does the existence of cable TV alter the situation?

4. Some economists argue that private firms will not undertake the efficient amount of basic scientific research.
   a. Explain why this is so. In your answer, classify basic research in one of the categories shown in Figure 11.1.
   b. What sort of policy has Canada adopted in response to this problem?
   c. It is often argued that this policy increases the technological capability of Canadian producers relative to that of foreign firms. Is this argument consistent with your classification of basic research in part (a)? (*Hint:* Can excludability apply to some potential beneficiaries of a public good and not others?)

5. Why is there often litter along most highways but rarely in people's yards?

6. High-income people are willing to pay more than lower-income people to avoid the risk of death. For example, they are more likely to pay for safety features on cars. Do you think cost–benefit analysts should take this fact into account when evaluating public projects? Consider, for instance, a rich town and a poor town, both of which are considering the installation of a traffic light. Should the rich town use a higher dollar value for a human life in making this decision? Why or why not?

7. Four roommates are planning to spend the weekend in their dorm room watching old movies, and they are debating how many to watch. The following table shows their willingness to pay for each film.

	Orson	Alfred	Woody	Ingmar
First film	$7	$5	$3	$2
Second film	6	4	2	1
Third film	5	3	1	0
Fourth film	4	2	0	0
Fifth film	3	1	0	0

   a. Within the dorm room, is the showing of a movie a public good? Why or why not?
   b. If it costs $8 to rent a movie, how many movies should the roommates rent to maximize total surplus?
   c. If they choose the optimal number from part (b) and then split the cost of renting the movies equally, how much surplus does each person obtain from watching the movies?
   d. Is there any way to split the cost to ensure that everyone benefits? What practical problems does this solution raise?
   e. Suppose they agree in advance to choose the efficient number and to split the cost of the movies equally. When Orson is asked his willingness to pay, will he have an incentive to tell the truth? If so, why? If not, what will he be tempted to say?
   f. What does this example teach you about the optimal provision of public goods?

8. Wireless, high-speed Internet is provided for free in the airport of the city of Communityville.
   a. At first, only a few people use the service. What type of a good is this and why?
   b. Eventually, as more people find out about the service and start using it, the speed of the connection begins to fall. Now what type of a good is the wireless Internet service?
   c. What problem might result and why? What is one possible way to correct this problem?

9. Two towns, each with three members, are deciding whether to put on a fireworks display to celebrate the New Year. Fireworks cost $360. In each town, some people enjoy fireworks more than others.
   a. In the town of Bayport, each of the residents values the public good as follows:

Frank	$50
Joe	$100
Callie	$300

   Would fireworks pass a cost–benefit analysis? Explain.
   b. The mayor of Bayport proposes to decide by majority rule and, if the fireworks referendum

passes, to split the cost equally among all residents. Who would vote in favour, and who would vote against? Would the vote yield the same answer as the cost–benefit analysis?

c. In the town of River Heights, each of the residents values the public good as follows:

Nancy	$20
Bess	$140
Ned	$160

Would fireworks pass a cost–benefit analysis? Explain.

d. The mayor of River Heights also proposes to decide by majority rule and, if the fireworks referendum passes, to split the cost equally among all residents. Who would vote in favour, and who would vote against? Would the vote yield the same answer as the cost–benefit analysis?

e. What do you think these examples say about the optimal provision of public goods?

10. The nation of Wiknam has 5 million residents, whose only activity is producing and consuming fish. They produce fish in two ways. Each person who works on a fish farm raises 2 fish per day. Each person who goes fishing in one of the nation's many lakes catches X fish per day. X depends on N, the number of residents (in millions) fishing in the lakes. In particular, if N million people fish in the lakes, each catches $X = 6 - N$ fish. Each resident is attracted to the job that pays more fish, so in equilibrium the two jobs must offer equal pay.

a. Why do you suppose that X, the productivity of each fisherman, falls as N, the number of fishermen, rises? What economic term would you use to describe the fish in the country's lakes? Would the same description apply to the fish from the farms? Explain.

b. The country's Freedom Party thinks every individual should have the right to choose between fishing in the lakes and farming without government interference. Under its policy, how many of the residents would fish in the lakes and how many would work on fish farms? How many fish are produced?

c. The country's Efficiency Party thinks Wiknam should produce as many fish as it can. To achieve this goal, how many of the residents should fish in the lakes and how many should work on the farms? (*Hint:* Create a table that shows the number of fish produced—on farms, from the lakes, and in total—for each N from 0 to 5.)

d. The Efficiency Party proposes achieving its goal by taxing each person fishing in the lakes by an amount equal to T fish per day. It will then distribute the proceeds equally among all Wiknam residents. (Fish are assumed to be divisible, so these rebates need not be whole numbers.) Calculate the value of T that would yield the outcome you derived in part (c). Compared with the Freedom Party's hands-off policy, who benefits and who loses from the imposition of the Efficiency Party's fishing tax?

**Canada Customs
and Revenue Agency**

**Agence des douanes
et du revenu du Canada**

**National
Headquarters**

**Administration
centrale**

**Connaught
Building**

**Édifice
Connaught**

**Deliveries
Sussex Drive**

**Livraisons
Entrée de la promenade Sussex**

Canada

The Design of the Tax System

In this chapter, you will ...

1 Gain an overview of how Canadian governments raise and spend money

2 Examine the efficiency costs of taxes

3 Learn alternative ways to judge the equity of a tax system

4 See why studying tax incidence is crucial for evaluating tax equity

5 Consider the tradeoff between efficiency and equity in the design of a tax system

As Benjamin Franklin said, "In this world nothing is certain but death and taxes." Taxes are inevitable because we as citizens expect the government to provide us with various goods and services. The previous two chapters have started to shed light on one of the ten principles of economics from Chapter 1: The government can sometimes improve market outcomes. When the government remedies an externality (such as air pollution), provides a public good (such as national defence), or regulates the use of a common resource (such as fish in a public lake), it can raise economic well-being. Yet the benefits of government come with costs. For the government to perform these and its many other functions, it needs to raise revenue through taxation.

We began our study of taxation in earlier chapters, where we saw how a tax on a good affects supply and demand for that good. In Chapter 6, we saw that a tax reduces the quantity sold in a market, and we examined how the burden of a tax is shared by buyers and sellers, depending on the elasticities of supply and demand. In Chapter 8, we examined how taxes affect economic well-being. We learned that taxes cause *deadweight losses:* The reduction in consumer and producer surplus resulting from a tax exceeds the revenue raised by the government.

In this chapter we build on these lessons to discuss the design of a tax system. We begin with a financial overview of Canadian governments. When thinking about the tax system, it is useful to know some basic facts about how Canadian governments raise and spend money. We then consider the fundamental principles of taxation. Most people agree that taxes should impose as small a cost on society as possible and that the burden of taxes should be distributed fairly. That is, the tax system should be both *efficient* and *equitable.* As we will see, however, stating these goals is easier than achieving them.

12-1 A Financial Overview of Canadian Governments

How much of the nation's income do governments take as taxes? Figure 12.1 shows government revenue, including federal, provincial and territorial, and local governments, as a percentage of total income for the Canadian economy

FIGURE 12.1

Government Revenue as a Percentage of GDP
This figure shows the combined revenue of all levels of government in Canada from 1980 to 2018 as a percentage of GDP.

Source: International Monetary Fund, World Economic Outlook Database, 2018.

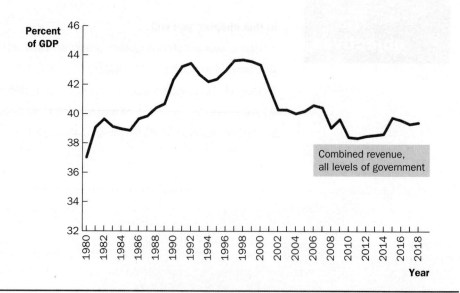

TABLE 12.1

Total Government Tax Revenue as a Percentage of GDP: G7 Countries, 2018

Source: International Monetary Fund, World Economic Outlook Database, 2018.

Country	Tax Revenue as % of GDP
France	53.5%
Italy	46.7
Germany	45.4
United Kingdom	36.7
Canada	39.4
United States	30.7
Japan	33.1
G7 Average	40.8

from 1980 to 2018. In the 1980s, governments collected about 40 percent of the income of the economy in taxes. This rose to about 45 percent in the 1990s, and has since fallen to about 39 percent.

The overall size of government tells only part of the story. Behind the total dollar figures lie thousands of individual decisions about taxes and spending. To understand the governments' finances more fully, let's look at how the total breaks down into some broad categories.

Table 12.1 compares the tax burden for the G7 countries, which consist of seven of the world's major developed economies, as measured by total government tax revenue (federal, provincial and territorial, and local) as a percentage of the nation's total income. Canada's tax burden is slightly below the G7 average, but it is quite a bit higher than the United States'. Before examining government revenue in more detail, it is useful to know a few things about the structure of the government sector in Canada.

Canada has a *federalist* structure, which means political power is divided between the federal government and the provincial and territorial governments. The third level of government, local or municipal, is granted powers by the provincial and territorial governments. The British North America (BNA) Act of 1867, Canada's Constitution, sets out the responsibilities of the federal and provincial and territorial governments. The BNA Act has been amended several times, most recently in 1982; however, the federalist structure has remained intact. In fact, it is one of the defining features of our country.

The federal government is responsible for matters of national interest, including national defence and foreign policy, international trade, competition policy, criminal law, and money and banking. The federal government is also responsible for delivering some of Canada's national social programs, such as Employment Insurance and the Canada Pension Plan. This level of government has essentially unlimited taxing powers.

The provinces and territories are responsible for the areas of health care, education, welfare, natural resources within their boundaries, and civil law. The provinces and territories have extensive taxing powers, although they are less extensive than the federal government's. Compared with provincial/territorial and state governments in most other federations, including the United States, Canadian provinces and territories have a great deal of power, accounting for more than half of the activities undertaken by the public sector in Canada. Local governments—cities, towns, and municipalities—are creatures of the provinces and territories, from which they receive their spending and taxing authority.

An important aspect of our federalist government structure is the role of *transfers* from the federal government to the provinces and territories. Although the federal government is not directly responsible for programs related to health, education, and welfare, it has been able to exercise influence in these areas through the "power of the purse." The most important transfer programs in Canada are the Canada Social Transfer (CST) and the Canada Health Transfer (CHT). The CST is funding for programs in postsecondary education, social services (welfare), and early childhood development, while the CHT is intended to finance health programs. However, both the CST and the CHT are largely unconditional per capita grants that simply enter general provincial and territorial government revenues and may be used as these governments see fit.

Another important feature of the Canadian federation is the role of *equalization payments*. Under this system, the federal government provides general-purpose transfers to the "have-not" provinces so that they can provide services that are roughly comparable in quality to those provided by the "have" provinces. In 2017–18, the "have" provinces—the ones that do not receive equalization payments—are Alberta, British Columbia, Saskatchewan, and Newfoundland and Labrador. The remaining provinces receive various amounts of equalization payments, depending on their need. Yukon, Northwest Territories, and Nunavut receive similar payments under a separate system.

12-1a The Federal Government

The federal government collects about 46 percent of the taxes in our economy. It raises this money in a number of ways, and it finds even more ways to spend it.

Receipts Table 12.2 shows total federal government revenue from different sources in the 2016–17 fiscal year ended March 31. Total revenue in this year was $293 billion. To bring this huge number down to Earth, we can divide it by the Canadian population. We then find that the average Canadian paid about $8324 to the federal government.

TABLE 12.2

Federal Government Revenue, 2016–17

Note: Numbers may not add up due to rounding.

Revenue Source	Amount (in billions)	Amount per Person	% of Revenue
Personal income taxes	$144	$4091	49
Corporate income taxes	42	1193	14
Goods and Services tax	34	966	12
Excise taxes and duties	17	483	6
Employment Insurance payroll taxes	22	625	8
Other	34	966	12
Total	$293	$8324	100

Source: Adapted from Department of Finance Canada, Fiscal Reference Tables—2017. https://www.fin.gc.ca/frt-trf/2017/frt-trf-17-eng.asp.

TABLE 12.3

Federal Personal Income Tax Rates, 2018

On Taxable Income...	The Tax Rate Is
Up to $46 605	15%
From $46 606 to $93 208	20.5
From $93 209 to $144 489	26
From $144 490 to $205 842	29
Over $205 843	33

Source: Data from the Canada Revenue Agency, Federal Tax Rates for 2018, https://www.canada.ca/en/revenue-agency/services/tax/individuals/frequently-asked-questions-individuals/canadian-income-tax-rates-individuals-current-previous-years.html#federal.

The biggest source of revenue for the federal government is the personal income tax, which accounts for almost half of total federal revenue. In 2017, over 26 million Canadian taxpayers filled out tax returns to determine how much income tax they owed. Taxpayers are required to report their income from all sources: employment income, interest on savings, dividends from corporations in which they own shares, and so on. An individual's *tax liability* (how much the person owes in taxes) is then based on that person's total income.

A person's tax liability is not simply proportional to the person's income. Instead, the law requires a more complicated calculation. Taxable income is computed by subtracting from total income various deductions for things such as contributions to registered pension plans and registered retirement savings plans—both of which will be discussed later—child-care expenses, and so on. The person's basic tax liability is then calculated from taxable income using the schedule shown in Table 12.3.

Table 12.3 presents the *marginal tax rate*—the rate of tax applied to each additional dollar of income. For 2018 there are five federal *tax brackets* in Canada (six if you count people who don't pay taxes at all because they don't earn enough income). Because the marginal tax rate rises as people enter higher tax brackets, higher-income individuals pay a larger percentage of their income in taxes than do lower-income individuals. (We will discuss the concept of the marginal tax rate more fully later in this chapter.) Note that the tax rates in Table 12.3 are federal tax rates only; provinces and territories also levy personal income taxes, as will be discussed later in the chapter. From this basic tax liability are deducted various tax credits in order to determine the individual's final tax liability. There are many credits, including a basic individual credit that everyone receives, a spousal credit, a child tax credit for dependent children, a credit for charitable donations, and other credits for low-income individuals. After all of this, the average Canadian paid about $4091 in federal personal income taxes in 2017.

Another important source of federal revenue is the Goods and Services Tax (GST), which accounts for about 12 percent of federal government revenue. The GST is levied at a 5 percent rate on the sales of most goods in Canada, with some notable exceptions such as most food. The average Canadian paid $966 in GST in 2017. Excise and customs duties brought in an additional $483 per person, or 6 percent of federal revenue. Excise taxes are sales taxes on specific goods, such as gasoline, cigarettes, and alcohol. Customs duties are taxes applied to goods imported into the country. Total taxes on the sale of goods and services, consisting of the GST plus excise taxes and customs duties, account for 18 percent of federal revenue, or $1449 per person.

The corporate income tax accounts for 14 percent of federal revenue, or about $1193 per person. A corporation is a business that is set up as a separate legal entity. The government taxes each corporation on the basis of its profits—the amount the corporation receives for its goods or services minus the cost of producing them.

Another important revenue source for the federal government is payroll taxes used to finance the Employment Insurance (EI) program. A *payroll tax* is a tax on the wages that a firm pays its workers. In Canada, EI payroll taxes are paid by both employees and employers. Table 12.2 shows that the average Canadian paid about $625 in EI payroll taxes in 2017. Another program that is financed by payroll taxes is the Canada Pension Plan (CPP), which provides pensions to all retired Canadians. CPP payroll taxes are not included in Table 12.2 because the program operates under a separate budget.

Spending Table 12.4 shows federal government spending in 2016–17. Total spending was $311 billion, or about $8835 per person. Approximately 8 percent of this went to pay the interest on the federal government's debt. The remaining 92 percent, or $8153 per person, was devoted to *program spending*—that is, all government expenditures that are not debt payments.

One of the largest categories of federal government expenditures, aside from debt payments, is payments to elderly people under the Old Age Security program, which in 2017 accounted for 15 percent of total spending. Payments to senior citizens are likely to grow in importance as increases in life expectancy and decreases in birthrates cause this population to grow more rapidly than the total population. Another important source of government-provided income for seniors is the CPP. As mentioned above, payments made under the CPP are accounted for separately.

Transfers to the provinces under the CHT and CST together account for 16 percent of program expenditures; equalization payments account for an additional

TABLE 12.4

Federal Government Spending, 2016–17

Category	Amount (in billions)	Amount per Person	% of Spending
Old Age Security	$48	$1364	15
Canada Health Transfer	37	1051	12
Canada Social Transfer	14	398	4
Equalization	18	511	6
Employment Insurance	21	597	7
National defence	26	739	8
Other	123	3494	40
Total program spending	287	8153	92
Debt service	24	682	8
Total spending	$311	$8835	100

Source: Adapted from Department of Finance Canada, Fiscal Reference Tables—2017.
https://www.fin.gc.ca/frt-trf/2017/frt-trf-17-eng.asp.

6 percent. Total transfers to the provinces and territories thus make up 22 percent of federal government expenditures.

Payments under the EI program in 2017 amounted to $21 billion, or about 7 percent of total federal spending. It is interesting to note that the federal government collected $22 billion in EI payroll taxes in the same year (see Table 12.2). That is, EI revenue exceeded EI spending by $1 billion, meaning that the government used some of the EI revenues to finance other spending.

In 2017, spending on national defence accounted for 8 percent of total federal expenditures. Canada spends substantially less in this area than the United States, which devotes roughly 20 percent of federal government expenditures to national defence.

You may have noticed that total federal revenue, shown in Table 12.2, falls short of total spending in Table 12.4. This excess of spending over revenue is called a **budget deficit** (if revenue exceeds spending, a **budget surplus** results). In 2016–17, the federal budget deficit was $18 billion.

12-1b Provincial/Territorial Governments

Provincial/territorial governments collect about 54 percent of taxes in the economy. Let's look at how they obtain tax revenue and how they spend it.

Receipts Table 12.5 shows the total revenue of provincial/territorial governments in 2016–17: $347 billion, or $9853 per person. However, $71 billion of total provincial/territorial revenue (20 percent) came from transfers from the federal government. Provincial/territorial own-source revenues therefore amounted to $276 billion, or $7834 per person.

The single most important source of revenue for the provinces and territories, as for the federal government, is personal income taxes. In 2017, personal income taxes accounted for 25 percent of total provincial/territorial revenue, or about $2442 per person. The provinces and territories levy personal taxes on the same taxable income base as the federal government, but determine their own tax rates and brackets on top of the federal taxes. All provinces and territories have several tax brackets.

The next-largest revenue source for the provinces is provincial sales taxes (PST), which account for 16 percent of total provincial revenue. All of the provinces

budget deficit
an excess of government spending over government receipts

budget surplus
an excess of government receipts over government spending

TABLE 12.5

Provincial/Territorial Government Revenue, 2016–17

Category	Amount (in billions)	Amount per Person	% of Revenue
Personal income taxes	$86	$2442	25%
Corporate income taxes	36	1029	10
Provincial sales taxes	57	1624	16
Natural resource revenue	8	227	2
Federal government transfers	71	2019	20
Other	88	2512	25
Total	347	9853	100

Source: Adapted from Canadian Provincial Government Budget Data, 1980–81 to 2013–14, Ron Kneebone and Margarita Wilkins, *Canadian Public Policy*, Vol. 42(1), pages 1–19, March 2016. Data updated at https://www.policyschool.ca/publication-category/research-data/.

TABLE 12.6

Provincial Sales Tax (PST) Rates, 2018

Province/Territory	PST Rate
British Columbia	7%
Alberta	No PST
Saskatchewan	6%
Manitoba	8%
Ontario*	8%
Quebec*	9.975%
Newfoundland and Labrador*	10%
Nova Scotia*	10%
New Brunswick*	10%
Prince Edward Island*	10%
Northwest Territories	No PST
Nunavut	No PST
Yukon	No PST

Source: Data from the Canada Revenue Agency, GST/HST Rates, 2018. Provinces with a
* levy an HST, the others levy a retail sales tax.

except Alberta levy sales taxes. None of the territories levy this tax. Newfoundland and Labrador, Prince Edward Island, Nova Scotia, New Brunswick, Quebec, and Ontario have all harmonized their sales taxes with the federal GST, called the harmonized sales tax (HST); the other provinces levy a PST at the retail level. As seen in Table 12.6, the provincial sales tax rates range from 6 percent to 10 percent.

The provinces also levy their own taxes on corporations. The most important of these is the corporate income tax, which accounts for 10 percent of provincial revenues.

Finally, the ownership of natural resources, such as oil and gas, minerals, and so on, lies with provincial governments. They collect various taxes on those natural resources in the form of royalties, mining taxes, and so on. Revenue from natural resources is most important in B.C., Alberta, Saskatchewan, and Newfoundland. Collectively, they account for about 2 percent of total provincial revenue.

Spending   Table 12.7 shows total provincial/territorial government spending in 2016–17 and how it breaks down. Spending on health, education, and social services (the "big three") account for the lion's share of provincial spending—75 percent of total spending in 2017, or $7700 per person. Health is the biggest single component, followed by education and social services. Education includes spending on primary, secondary, and postsecondary schools. Health includes expenditures on hospital care, medical care, and preventive care. Social services primarily consist of welfare programs for low-income people. Debt service charges accounted for 7 percent.

Notice that total provincial/territorial government spending exceeds total provincial/territorial government revenue in Table 12.5—the aggregate provincial/territorial budget in 2017 was in a $14-billion deficit situation.

TABLE 12.7

Provincial/Territorial Government Spending, 2016–17

Note: Numbers may not add up due to rounding.

Category	Amount (in billions)	Amount per Person	% of Spending
Health	$150	$4266	42%
Education	83	2369	23
Social services	37	1065	10
Debt service	26	735	7
Other	64	1821	18
Total	361	10256	100

Source: Adapted from Canadian Provincial Government Budget Data, 1980–81 to 2013–14, Ron Kneebone and Margarita Wilkins, *Canadian Public Policy*, Vol. 42(1), pages 1–19, March 2016. Data updated at https://www.policyschool.ca/publication-category/research-data/.

 QUICK **Quiz**   *What are the two most important sources of tax revenue for the federal government? • What are the two most important sources of tax revenue for provincial and territorial governments?*

12-2 Taxes and Efficiency

Now that we have seen how Canadian governments at various levels raise and spend money, let's consider how one might evaluate their tax policy. The primary aim of a tax system is to raise revenue for the governments. But there are many ways to raise any given amount of money. In designing a tax system, policymakers have two objectives: efficiency and equity.

One tax system is more efficient than another if it raises the same amount of revenue at a smaller cost to taxpayers. What are the costs of taxes to taxpayers? The most obvious cost is the tax payment itself. This transfer of money from the taxpayer to the government is an inevitable feature of any tax system. Yet taxes also impose two other costs, which a well-designed tax policy tries to avoid or, at least, minimize:

1. The deadweight losses that result when taxes distort the decisions that people make
2. The administrative burdens that taxpayers bear as they comply with the tax laws

An efficient tax system is one that imposes small deadweight losses and small administrative burdens.

12-2a Deadweight Losses

One of the ten principles of economics discussed in Chapter 1 is that people respond to incentives, and this includes incentives provided by the tax system. If the government taxes ice cream, people eat less ice cream and more frozen yogurt. If the government taxes housing, people live in smaller houses and spend more of their income on other things. If the government taxes labour earnings, people work less and enjoy more leisure.

Because taxes distort incentives, they entail deadweight losses. As we first discussed in Chapter 8, the deadweight loss of a tax is the reduction in economic well-being of taxpayers in excess of the amount of revenue raised by the government. The deadweight loss is the inefficiency that a tax creates as people allocate resources according to the tax incentive rather than the true costs and benefits of the goods and services that they buy and sell.

To recall how taxes cause deadweight losses, consider an example. Suppose that Joe places an $8 value on a pizza, and Jane places a $6 value on it. If there is no tax on pizza, the price of pizza will reflect the cost of making it. Let's suppose that the price of pizza is $5, so both Joe and Jane choose to buy one. Both consumers get some surplus of value over the amount paid. Joe gets consumer surplus of $3, and Jane gets consumer surplus of $1. Total surplus is $4.

Now suppose that the government levies a $2 tax on pizza and the price of pizza rises to $7. Joe still buys a pizza, but now he has consumer surplus of only $1. Jane now decides not to buy a pizza because its price is higher than its value to her. The government collects tax revenue of $2 on Joe's pizza. Total consumer surplus has fallen by $3 (from $4 to $1). Because total surplus has fallen by more than the tax revenue, the tax has a deadweight loss. In this case, the deadweight loss is $1.

Notice that the deadweight loss comes not from Joe, the person who pays the tax, but from Jane, the person who doesn't. The reduction of $2 in Joe's surplus exactly offsets the amount of revenue the government collects. The deadweight loss arises because the tax causes Jane to alter her behaviour. When the tax raises the price of pizza, Jane is worse off, and yet there is no offsetting revenue to the government. This reduction in Jane's welfare is the deadweight loss of the tax.

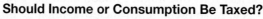

case study ### Should Income or Consumption Be Taxed?

When taxes induce people to change their behaviour—such as inducing Jane to buy less pizza—the taxes cause deadweight losses and make the allocation of resources less efficient. As we have already seen, much government revenue comes from the individual income tax. In a case study in Chapter 8, we discussed how this tax discourages people from working as hard as they otherwise might. Another inefficiency caused by this tax is that it discourages people from saving.

Consider a person 25 years old who is considering saving $1000. If he puts this money into a savings account that earns 8 percent and leaves it there, he would have $21 720 when he retires at age 65. Yet if the government taxes one-fourth of his interest income each year, the effective interest rate is only 6 percent. After 40 years of earning 6 percent, the $1000 grows to only $10 290, less than half of what it would have been without taxation. Thus, because interest income is taxed, saving is much less attractive.

Some economists advocate eliminating the current tax system's disincentive toward saving by changing the basis of taxation. Rather than taxing the amount of income that people *earn*, the government could tax the amount that people *spend*. Under this proposal, all income that is saved would not be taxed until the saving is later spent. This alternative system, called a *consumption tax*, would not distort people's saving decisions.

A tax on consumption can be implemented in several ways. The approach that most people are familiar with is a sales tax on goods and services purchased by consumers. Examples include provincial sales taxes and the federal government's GST.

Some economists have suggested another approach to taxing consumption. People can do two basic things with their income: They can spend (consume) it, or they can save it. This gives rise to the model: Income = Consumption + Savings (or I = C + S). Rearranging this model, an individual's consumption can be defined simply as income minus savings (or C = I − S). This suggests that the tax system could be used to tax consumption in the following way. The individual's total income (I) could be determined and savings (S) could be allowed as a deduction. The interest (or dividends or capital gains) earned on the amount saved would then accumulate tax-free. When, some time later, the individual withdraws the savings in order to consume, the amount withdrawn would be fully taxable.

In fact, Canada's personal income tax system works in a very similar way. All contributions to registered retirement savings plans (RRSPs) and registered pension plans (RPPs), up to a maximum amount per year, are fully deductible from income. Moreover, interest earned in these plans accumulates tax-free, and withdrawals may be made at any time, at which point they are fully taxable. RRSPs and RPPs are vehicles intended to encourage people to save for their retirement. For people who do most of their saving through RRSPs and RPPs—and figures show that very few Canadians contribute up to the allowed limits—Canada's personal income tax functions like a tax on consumption.

Combined with provincial sales taxes and the GST, the tax treatment of RPPs and RRSPs suggests that Canada's tax system as a whole raises most of its revenue by taxing consumption rather than income. ∎

12-2b Administrative Burden

If you ask the typical person on April 30 for an opinion about the tax system, you might hear about the headache of filling out tax forms. The administrative burden of any tax system is part of the inefficiency it creates. This burden includes not only the time spent in April filling out forms but also the time spent throughout the year keeping records for tax purposes and the resources the government has to use to enforce the tax laws.

Many taxpayers—especially those in higher tax brackets—hire tax lawyers and accountants to help them with their taxes. These experts in the complex tax laws fill out the tax forms for their clients and help clients arrange their affairs in a way that reduces the amount of taxes owed. This behaviour is legal tax avoidance, which is different from illegal tax evasion.

Critics of our tax system say that these advisers help their clients avoid taxes by abusing some of the detailed provisions of the tax laws, often dubbed "loopholes." In some cases, loopholes are government mistakes: They arise from ambiguities or omissions in the tax laws. More often, they arise because the government has chosen to give special treatment to specific types of behaviour. An example of this is the special provision for contributions to RRSPs and RPPs discussed earlier.

The resources devoted to complying with the tax laws are a type of deadweight loss. The government gets only the amount of taxes paid. By contrast, the taxpayer loses not only this amount but also the time and money spent documenting, computing, and avoiding taxes.

The administrative burden of the tax system could be reduced by simplifying the tax laws. Yet simplification is often politically difficult. Most people are ready to simplify the tax laws by eliminating the loopholes that benefit others, yet few are eager to give up the loopholes that they use. In the end, the complexity of the tax laws results from the political process as various taxpayers with their own special interests lobby for their causes.

12-2c Average Tax Rates versus Marginal Tax Rates

average tax rate

total taxes paid divided by total income

marginal tax rate

the extra taxes paid on an additional dollar of income

When discussing the efficiency and equity of income taxes, economists distinguish between two notions of the tax rate: the average and the marginal. The **average tax rate** is total taxes paid divided by total income. The **marginal tax rate** is the extra taxes paid on an additional dollar of income.

For example, suppose that the government taxes 20 percent of the first $50 000 of income and 50 percent of all income above $50 000. Under this tax, a person who makes $60 000 pays a tax of $15 000: 20 percent of the first $50 000 (0.20 × $50 000 = $10 000) plus 50 percent of the next $10 000 (0.50 × $10 000 = $5000). For this person, the average tax rate is $15 000/$60 000, or 25 percent. But the marginal tax rate is 50 percent. If the taxpayer earned an additional dollar of income, that dollar would be subject to the 50 percent tax rate, so the amount the taxpayer would owe to the government would rise by $0.50.

The marginal and average tax rates each contain a useful piece of information. If we are trying to gauge the sacrifice made by a taxpayer, the average tax rate is more appropriate because it measures the fraction of income paid in taxes. By contrast, if we are trying to gauge how much the tax system distorts incentives, the marginal tax rate is more meaningful. One of the ten principles of economics discussed in Chapter 1 is that rational people think at the margin. A corollary to this principle is that the marginal tax rate measures how much the tax system discourages people from working. If you are thinking of working an extra few hours, the marginal tax rate determines how much the government takes of your additional earnings. It is the marginal tax rate, therefore, that determines the deadweight loss of an income tax.

12-2d Lump-Sum Taxes

Suppose the government imposes a tax of $4000 on everyone. That is, everyone owes the same amount, regardless of earnings or any actions that a person might take. Such a tax is called a **lump-sum tax**.

lump-sum tax

a tax that is the same amount for every person

A lump-sum tax shows clearly the difference between average and marginal tax rates. For a taxpayer with income of $20 000, the average tax rate of a $4000 lump-sum tax is 20 percent; for a taxpayer with income of $40 000, the average tax rate is 10 percent. For both taxpayers, the marginal tax rate is zero because no tax is owed on an additional dollar of income.

A lump-sum tax is the most efficient tax possible. Because a person's decisions do not alter the amount owed, the tax does not distort incentives and, therefore, does not cause deadweight losses. Because everyone can easily compute the amount owed and because there is no benefit to hiring tax lawyers and accountants, the lump-sum tax imposes a minimal administrative burden on taxpayers.

If lump-sum taxes are so efficient, why do we rarely observe them in the real world? The reason is that efficiency is only one goal of the tax system. A lump-sum tax would take the same amount from the poor and the rich, an outcome most people would view as unfair. To understand the tax systems that we observe, in the next section we consider the other major goal of tax policy: equity.

What is meant by the efficiency of a tax system? • What can make a tax system inefficient?

12-3 Taxes and Equity

Although economists tend to focus on the efficiency aspects of the tax system, Canadian policy debates about taxes tend to be dominated by discussions about the fairness of the tax system—in particular, whether its burden is distributed fairly. Of course, if we are to rely on the government to provide some of the goods and services we want, taxes must fall on someone. In this section we consider the equity of a tax system. How should the burden of taxes be divided among the population? How do we evaluate whether a tax system is fair? Everyone agrees that the tax system should be equitable, but there is much disagreement about what equity means and how the equity of a tax system can be judged.

12-3a The Benefits Principle

One principle of taxation, called the **benefits principle**, states that people should pay taxes based on the benefits they receive from government services. This principle tries to make public goods similar to private goods. It seems fair that a person who often goes to the movies pays more in total for movie tickets than a person who rarely goes. Similarly, a person who gets great benefit from a public good should pay more for it than a person who gets little benefit.

The gasoline tax, for instance, is sometimes justified using the benefits principle. In some provinces and territories, revenues from the gasoline tax are used to build and maintain roads. Because those who buy gasoline are the same people who use the roads, the gasoline tax might be viewed as a fair way to pay for this government service.

The benefits principle can also be used to argue that wealthy citizens should pay higher taxes than poorer ones. Why? Simply because the wealthy benefit more from public services. Consider, for example, the benefits of police protection from theft. Citizens with much to protect benefit more from police than do those with less to protect. Therefore, according to the benefits principle, the wealthy should contribute more than the poor to the cost of maintaining the police force. The same argument can be used for many other public services, such as fire protection, national defence, and the court system.

It is even possible to use the benefits principle to argue for antipoverty programs funded by taxes on the wealthy. As we discussed in Chapter 11, people may prefer living in a society without poverty, suggesting that antipoverty programs are a public good. If the wealthy place a greater dollar value on this public good than members of the middle class do, perhaps just because the wealthy have more to spend, then, according to the benefits principle, they should be taxed more heavily to pay for these programs.

benefits principle
the idea that people should pay taxes based on the benefits they receive from government services

12-3b The Ability-to-Pay Principle

Another way to evaluate the equity of a tax system is called the **ability-to-pay principle**, which states that taxes should be levied on a person according to how well that person can shoulder the burden. This principle is sometimes justified by the claim that all citizens should make an "equal sacrifice" to support the government. The magnitude of a person's sacrifice, however, depends not only on the size of the person's tax payment but also on that person's income and other circumstances. A $1000 tax paid by a poor person may require a larger sacrifice than a $10 000 tax paid by a rich one.

ability-to-pay principle
the idea that taxes should be levied on a person according to how well that person can shoulder the burden

TABLE 12.8

Three Tax Systems

Income	Proportional Tax		Regressive Tax		Progressive Tax	
	Amount of Tax	% of Income	Amount of Tax	% of Income	Amount of Tax	% of Income
$50 000	$12 500	25%	$15 000	30%	$10 000	20%
100 000	25 000	25	25 000	25	25 000	25
200 000	50 000	25	40 000	20	60 000	30

vertical equity
the idea that taxpayers with a greater ability to pay taxes should pay larger amounts

horizontal equity
the idea that taxpayers with similar abilities to pay taxes should pay the same amount

proportional tax
a tax for which high-income and low-income taxpayers pay the same fraction of income

regressive tax
a tax for which high-income taxpayers pay a smaller fraction of their income than do low-income taxpayers

progressive tax
a tax for which high-income taxpayers pay a larger fraction of their income than do low-income taxpayers

The ability-to-pay principle leads to two corollary notions of equity: vertical equity and horizontal equity. **Vertical equity** states that taxpayers with a greater ability to pay taxes should contribute a larger amount. **Horizontal equity** states that taxpayers with similar abilities to pay should contribute the same amount. Although these notions of equity are widely accepted, applying them to evaluate a tax system is rarely straightforward.

Vertical Equity If taxes are based on ability to pay, then richer taxpayers should pay more than poorer taxpayers. But how much more should the rich pay? Much of the debate over tax policy concerns this question.

Consider the three tax systems in Table 12.8. In each case, taxpayers with higher incomes pay more. Yet the systems differ in how quickly taxes rise with income. The first system is called **proportional** because all taxpayers pay the same fraction of income. The second system is called **regressive** because high-income taxpayers pay a smaller fraction of their income, even though they pay a larger amount. The third system is called **progressive** because high-income taxpayers pay a larger fraction of their income.

Which of these three tax systems is most fair? There is no obvious answer, and economic theory does not offer much help in trying to find one. Equity, like beauty, is in the eye of the beholder.

case study | **How the Tax Burden Is Distributed**

Much of the debate over tax policy relates to whether the wealthy pay their fair share of taxes. There is no objective way to make this judgment. However, when evaluating this issue for yourself, it is useful to know how the burden of the current tax system is distributed among families with different incomes.

Table 12.9 presents some data on how income taxes are distributed among income groups in Canada. To construct this table, families are ranked according to their income and placed into five groups of equal size, called *quintiles*.

Column (2) shows the average market income of each group. The poorest one-fifth of families had average income of $6800, and the richest one-fifth had average income of $120 700.

Column (3) of the table shows total income taxes paid as a percentage of income for each group. As you can see, the Canadian income tax system is progressive, as the share of income paid in taxes paid by each group increases with income, with the poorest fifth of families paying an average of 8 percent of their income in taxes, and the richest fifth paying 23 percent.

(1) Group	(2) Average Market Income	(3) Income Taxes as a % of Market Income	(4) % of Income Taxes	(5) Transfers as a % of Income	(6) % of Transfers
Bottom fifth	$6 800	8%	1%	180%	33%
Second fifth	26 650	11	6	35	25
Middle fifth	44 350	14	13	16	19
Fourth fifth	65 250	17	23	8	13
Top fifth	120 700	23	58	3	9

Source: Author calculations adapted from Statistics Canada CANSIM Tables 206-0032.

Column (4) gives the distribution of taxes across income groups. The poorest quintile accounts for 1 percent of all income taxes, the richest quintile pays 58 percent.

Column (5) shows that the transfer system is even more progressive. The poorest fifth of families receives 180 percent of their market income in transfers. This means that they receive almost double their average income in government transfers. The richest fifth receives just 3 percent of their average income in transfers. Column (6) reinforces this, as we see that the poorest fifth of the population receives 33 percent of all transfers and the richest fifth 9 percent.

The analysis here looks at just income taxes and cash transfers, which are shown to be progressive. A more complete study would incorporate other taxes, including the GST, provincial sales taxes, excise taxes, corporate taxes, and property taxes. ■

Horizontal Equity If taxes are based on ability to pay, then similar taxpayers should pay similar amounts of taxes. But what determines if two taxpayers are similar? Families differ in many ways. To evaluate whether tax laws are horizontally equitable, one must determine which differences are relevant for a family's ability to pay and which differences are not.

Suppose the Smith and Jones families each have income of $100 000. The Smiths have no children, but Mr. Smith has an illness that causes medical expenses of $40 000. The Joneses are in good health, but they have four children. Two of the Jones children are in university, generating tuition bills of $60 000. Would it be fair for these two families to pay the same tax because they have the same income? Would it be more fair to give the Smiths a tax break to help them offset their high medical expenses? Would it be more fair to give the Joneses a tax break to help them with their tuition expenses?

There are no easy answers to these questions. In practice, the Canadian income tax is filled with special provisions that alter a family's tax based on its specific circumstances.

12-3c Tax Incidence and Tax Equity

Tax incidence—the study of who bears the burden of taxes—is central to evaluating tax equity. As we first saw in Chapter 6, the person who bears the burden of a tax is not always the person who gets the tax bill from the government. Because taxes alter supply and demand, they alter equilibrium prices. As a result, they affect people beyond those who, according to statute, actually pay the tax. When evaluating the vertical and horizontal equity of any tax, it is important to take account of these indirect effects.

Many discussions of tax equity ignore the indirect effects of taxes and are based on what economists mockingly call the *flypaper theory* of tax incidence. According to this theory, the burden of a tax, like a fly on flypaper, sticks wherever it first lands. This assumption, however, is rarely valid.

For example, a person not trained in economics might argue that a tax on expensive fur coats is vertically equitable because most buyers of furs are wealthy. Yet if these buyers can easily substitute other luxuries for furs, then a tax on furs might only reduce the sale of furs. In the end, the burden of the tax will fall more on those who make and sell furs than on those who buy them. Because most workers who make furs are not wealthy, the equity of a fur tax could be quite different from what the flypaper theory indicates.

This worker pays part of the corporate income tax.

case study

Who Pays the Corporate Income Tax?

The corporate income tax provides a good example of the importance of tax incidence for tax policy. The corporate tax is popular among voters. After all, corporations are not people. Voters are always eager to have their taxes reduced and have some impersonal corporation pick up the tab.

But before deciding that the corporate income tax is a good way for the government to raise revenue, we should consider who bears the burden of the corporate tax. This is a difficult question on which economists disagree, but one thing is certain: *People pay all taxes.* When the government levies a tax on a corporation, the corporation is more like a tax collector than a taxpayer. The burden of the tax ultimately falls on people—the owners, customers, or workers of the corporation.

Many economists believe that workers and customers bear much of the burden of the corporate income tax. To see why, consider an example. Suppose that the government decides to raise the tax on the income earned by car companies. At first, this tax hurts the owners of the car companies, who receive less profit. But, over time, these owners will respond to the tax. Because producing cars is less profitable, they invest less in building new car factories. Instead, they invest their wealth in other ways—for example, by buying larger houses or by building factories in other industries or other countries. With fewer car factories, the supply of cars declines, as does the demand for autoworkers. Thus, a tax on corporations making cars causes the price of cars to rise and the wages of autoworkers to fall.

A recent study by one of the authors of this book, Ken McKenzie, and his co-author Ergete Ferede considers the impact of increases in provincial corporate income taxes on wages in Canada. They estimate that a 10-percent increase in the provincial corporate tax rate (say from 10 percent to 11 percent) leads to a reduction in real average hourly wages of about 1 percent (that is, the elasticity of the wage rate with respect to the corporate income tax rate is −0.10).

They use this estimate to calculate the reduction in wages per worker for every dollar in additional corporate income tax revenue per worker raised from an increase in the corporate tax rate. They present two sets of calculations, shown in Table 12.10. The first assumes that there is no reduction in corporate taxable income in response to an increase in the tax rate, shown in column (1) of the table. Here we see that even if there is no behavioural response on the part of corporations to the

TABLE 12.10

Reduction in Wages per Dollar of Revenue Generated by an Increase in the Corporate Tax Rate

	(1) No Change in Corporate Behaviour	(2) Change in Corporate Behaviour
British Columbia	1.34	1.93
Alberta	0.96	1.39
Saskatchewan	1.12	1.86
Manitoba	1.52	1.98
Ontario	1.14	1.89
Quebec	0.98	1.25
New Brunswick	1.74	2.38
Nova Scotia	1.18	1.96
Prince Edward Island	1.59	2.51
Newfoundland and Labrador	0.95	1.43

Source: McKenzie, Kenneth and Ferede, Ergete, The Incidence of the Corporate Income Tax on Wages: Evidence from Canadian Provinces (April 20, 2017). SPP Research Paper, Volume 10, Issue 7, April 2017. Available at SSRN: https://ssrn.com/abstract=2957893

increase in the tax rate, the reduction in wages per worker for every dollar in additional revenue generated by an increase in the corporate tax rate wage income per worker ranges from 95 cents in Newfoundland to $1.74 in New Brunswick.

As discussed above, however, we know that corporations will react to an increase in the tax rate by investing less and perhaps shifting corporate income to other jurisdictions. Column (2) of the table takes this into account, and shows that in this case for every dollar in additional revenue generated by an increase in the corporate tax rate wage income per worker falls by even more, from $1.25 in Quebec to $2.51 in PEI. These estimates suggest that a good deal of the burden of the corporate income tax falls on workers in Canada through lower wages.

The corporate income tax shows how dangerous the flypaper theory of tax incidence can be. The corporate income tax is popular in part because it appears to be paid by rich corporations. Yet those who bear the ultimate burden of the tax—the customers and workers of corporations—are often not rich. If the true incidence of the corporate tax were more widely known, this tax might be less popular among voters. ■

Explain the benefits principle and the ability-to-pay principle. • What are vertical equity and horizontal equity? • Why is studying tax incidence important for determining the equity of a tax system?

12-4 Conclusion: The Tradeoff between Equity and Efficiency

Almost everyone agrees that equity and efficiency are the two most important goals of the tax system. But often these two goals conflict. Many proposed changes in the tax laws increase efficiency while reducing equity, or increase equity while reducing efficiency. People disagree about tax policy often because they attach different weights to these two goals. As a result, tax policy is often the subject of heated political debate. Indeed, elections may be won and lost on the basis of the weights the political parties attach to the conflicting goals of efficiency and equity.

Economics alone cannot determine the best way to balance the goals of efficiency and equity. This issue involves political philosophy as well as economics. But economists do have an important role in the political debate over tax policy: They can shed light on the tradeoffs that society faces and can help us avoid policies that sacrifice efficiency without any benefit in terms of equity.

summary

- Canadian governments raise revenue using various taxes. The most important tax for the federal and the provincial/territorial governments is the personal income tax.

- The efficiency of a tax system refers to the costs it imposes on taxpayers. There are two costs of taxes beyond the transfer of resources from the taxpayer to the government. The first is the distortion in the allocation of resources that arises as taxes alter incentives and behaviour. The second is the administrative burden of complying with the tax laws.

- The equity of a tax system concerns whether the tax burden is distributed fairly among the population.

- According to the benefits principle, it is fair for people to pay taxes based on the benefits they receive from the government. According to the ability-to-pay principle, it is fair for people to pay taxes based on their capability to handle the financial burden. When evaluating the equity of a tax system, it is important to remember a lesson from the study of tax incidence: The distribution of tax burdens is not the same as the distribution of tax bills.

- When considering changes in the tax laws, policymakers often face a tradeoff between efficiency and equity. Much of the debate over tax policy arises because people give different weights to these two goals.

KEY **concepts**

budget deficit, *p. 267*
budget surplus, *p. 267*
average tax rate, *p. 272*
marginal tax rate, *p. 272*

lump-sum tax, *p. 272*
benefits principle, *p. 273*
ability-to-pay principle, *p. 273*
vertical equity, *p. 274*

horizontal equity, *p. 274*
proportional tax, *p. 274*
regressive tax, *p. 274*
progressive tax, *p. 274*

QUESTIONS FOR **review**

1. Over the past several decades, has government grown more or less slowly than the rest of the economy?

2. What are the two most important sources of revenue for the federal government?

3. Why is the burden of a tax to taxpayers greater than the revenue received by the government?

4. Why do some economists advocate taxing consumption rather than income?

5. Give two arguments why wealthy taxpayers should pay more taxes than poor taxpayers.

6. What is the concept of horizontal equity, and why is it hard to apply?

QUICK CHECK **multiple choice**

1. What are the two largest sources of tax revenue for the Canadian federal government?
   a. individual and corporate income taxes
   b. individual income taxes and payroll taxes for social insurance
   c. corporate income taxes and payroll taxes for social insurance
   d. payroll taxes for social insurance and property taxes

2. Andy gives piano lessons. He has an opportunity cost of $50 per lesson and charges $60. He has two students: Bob, who has a willingness to pay of $70, and Carl, who has a willingness to pay of $90. When the government puts a $20 tax on piano lessons and Andy raises his price to $80, the deadweight loss is ___ and the tax revenue is ___.
   a. $10, $20
   b. $10, $40
   c. $20, $20
   d. $20, $40

3. If the tax code exempts the first $20 000 of income from taxation and then taxes 25 percent of all income above that level, then a person who earns $50 000 has an average tax rate of ___ percent and a marginal tax rate of ___ percent.
   a. 15, 25
   b. 25, 15
   c. 25, 30
   d. 30, 25

4. A toll is a tax on those citizens who use toll roads. This policy can be viewed as an application of which of the following?
   a. the benefits principle
   b. horizontal equity
   c. vertical equity
   d. tax progressivity

5. If the corporate income tax induces businesses to reduce their capital investment, then which of the following is true?
   a. the tax does not have any deadweight loss
   b. corporate shareholders benefit from the tax
   c. workers bear some of the burden of the tax
   d. the tax achieves the goal of vertical equity

PROBLEMS AND **applications**

1. Government spending in Canada has grown as a share of national income over time. What changes in our economy and our society might explain this trend? Do you expect the trend to continue?

2. In a published source or on the Internet, find out whether the Canadian federal government had a budget deficit or surplus last year. What do policy-makers expect to happen over the next few years?

3. Explain how individuals' behaviour is affected by the following features of the federal tax laws.
   a. Contributions to charity are tax deductible.
   b. Sales of beer are taxed.
   c. Realized capital gains are taxed, but accrued gains are not. (When someone owns a share of stock that rises in value, she has an "accrued" capital gain. If she sells the share, she has a "realized" gain.)

4. Suppose that your province raises its sales tax from 5 percent to 6 percent. The government forecasts a 20-percent increase in sales tax revenue. Is this plausible? Explain.

5. Categorize each of the following funding schemes as examples of the benefits principle or the ability-to-pay principle.
   a. Visitors to many national parks pay an entrance fee.
   b. Local property taxes support elementary and secondary schools.
   c. An airport trust fund collects a tax on each plane ticket sold and uses the money to improve airports and the air traffic control system.

6. Any income tax schedule embodies two types of tax rates—average tax rates and marginal tax rates.
   a. The average tax rate is defined as total taxes paid divided by income. For the proportional tax system presented in Table 12.8, what are the average tax rates for people earning $50 000, $100 000, and $200 000? What are the corresponding average tax rates in the regressive and progressive tax systems?
   b. The marginal tax rate is defined as the extra taxes paid on additional income divided by the increase in income. Calculate the marginal tax rate for the proportional tax system as income rises from $50 000 to $100 000. Calculate the marginal tax rate as income rises from $100 000 to $200 000. Calculate the corresponding marginal tax rates for the regressive and progressive tax systems.

c. Describe the relationship between average tax rates and marginal tax rates for each of these three systems. In general, which rate is relevant for someone deciding whether to accept a job that pays slightly more than her current job? Which rate is relevant for judging the vertical equity of a tax system?

7. If a salesperson takes a client to lunch, part of the cost of the lunch is a deductible business expense for his/her company. Some MPs have argued that this feature of the tax laws benefits relatively wealthy businesspeople and should be eliminated. Yet their arguments have been met with greater opposition from eating and drinking establishments than from companies themselves. Explain.

8. Provincial/territorial welfare programs have very high "clawback" rates. For example, when a person receiving welfare earns money from employment, that person's welfare payments decline by as much as 75 cents for each dollar earned. What do you think is the effect of this feature of welfare programs on the labour supply of low-income individuals? Explain.

9. Federal payroll taxes to fund the EI program are levied at a combined rate of 3.89 percent up to an income ceiling of $53 100.

a. If there was no limit on the income level at which these taxes apply, would they be proportional, progressive, or regressive? With the limit, are the taxes proportional, progressive, or regressive?

b. The amount of EI benefits that people receive depends on the amount of payroll taxes they paid. Relative to people who had low earnings, people who had higher earnings and paid more in taxes receive more benefits, but not proportionally more. Does this feature of the EI system make EI a progressive or a regressive payroll tax?

10. What is the efficiency justification for taxing consumption rather than income? Suppose that Ottawa reduced personal tax rates and, to raise the same amount of revenue, increased the GST rate. Would this make the Canadian tax system more or less progressive? Explain.

11. Payroll taxes to fund the EI system are paid by both employees and employers. Does this legal division of responsibility indicate the true incidence of these taxes? Explain.

CHAPTER
13

LEARNING objectives

The Costs of Production

In this chapter, you will ...

1 Examine what items are included in a firm's costs of production

2 Analyze the link between a firm's production process and its total costs

3 Learn the meaning of average total cost and marginal cost and how they are related

4 Consider the shape of a typical firm's cost curves

5 Examine the relationship between short-run and long-run costs

The economy is made up of thousands of firms that produce the goods and services you enjoy every day: General Motors produces automobiles, General Electric produces lightbulbs, and General Mills produces breakfast cereals. Some firms, such as these three, are large; they employ thousands of workers and have thousands of shareholders who share the firms' profits. Other firms, such as the local barbershop or café, are small; they employ only a few workers and are owned by a single person or family.

In previous chapters, we used the supply curve to summarize firms' production decisions. According to the law of supply, firms are willing to produce and sell a greater quantity of a good when the price of the good is higher. This response leads to a supply curve that slopes upward. For analyzing many questions, the law of supply is all you need to know about firm behaviour.

In this chapter and the ones that follow, we examine firm behaviour in more detail. This topic will give you a better understanding of the decisions behind the supply curve. In addition, it will introduce you to a part of economics called *industrial organization*—the study of how firms' decisions regarding prices and quantities depend on the market conditions they face. The town in which you live, for instance, may have several pizzerias but only one cable television company. This raises a key question: How does the number of firms affect the prices in a market and the efficiency of the market outcome? The field of industrial organization addresses exactly this question.

Before we turn to these issues we need to discuss the costs of production. All firms, from Air Canada to your local deli, incur costs as they produce the goods and carry out the services that they sell. As we will see in the coming chapters, a firm's costs are a key determinant of its production and pricing decisions. In this chapter, we define some of the variables that economists use to measure a firm's costs, and we consider the relationships among them.

A word of warning: This topic can seem dry and technical. To be honest, one might even call it boring. But this material provides a crucial foundation for the fascinating topics that follow.

13-1 What Are Costs?

We begin our discussion of costs at Caroline's Cookie Factory. Caroline, the owner of the firm, buys flour, sugar, chocolate chips, and other cookie ingredients. She also buys the mixers and ovens, and hires workers to run this equipment. She then sells the cookies to consumers. By examining some of the issues that Caroline faces in her business, we can learn some lessons about costs that apply to all firms in the economy.

13-1a Total Revenue, Total Cost, and Profit

We begin with the firm's objective. To understand what decisions a firm makes, we must understand what it is trying to do. Although it is conceivable that Caroline started her firm because of an altruistic desire to provide the world with cookies or, perhaps, out of love for the cookie business. More likely, Caroline started her business to make money. Economists normally assume that the goal of a firm is to maximize profit, and they find that this assumption works well in most cases.

What is a firm's profit? The amount that the firm receives for the sale of its output (cookies) is called its **total revenue**. The amount that the firm pays to buy inputs (flour, sugar, workers, ovens, and so forth) is called **total cost**. Caroline

total revenue (for a firm)
the amount a firm receives for the sale of its output

total cost
the market value of the inputs a firm uses in production

gets to keep any revenue that is not needed to cover costs. **Profit** is a firm's total revenue minus its total cost:

$$\text{Profit} = \text{Total revenue} - \text{Total cost}$$

Caroline's objective is to make her firm's profit as large as possible.

To see how a firm goes about maximizing profit, we must consider fully how to measure its total revenue and its total cost. Total revenue is the easy part: It equals the quantity of output the firm produces multiplied by the price at which it sells its output. If Caroline produces 10 000 cookies and sells them at $2 a cookie, her total revenue is $20 000. By contrast, the measurement of a firm's total cost is more subtle.

13-1b Costs as Opportunity Costs

When measuring costs at Caroline's Cookie Factory or any other firm, it is important to keep in mind one of the ten principles of economics from Chapter 1: The cost of something is what you give up to get it. Recall that the *opportunity cost* of an item refers to all those things that must be forgone to acquire that item. When economists speak of a firm's cost of production, they include all the opportunity costs of making its output of goods and services.

While some of a firm's opportunity costs of production are obvious, others are less so. When Caroline pays $1000 for flour, that $1000 is an opportunity cost because Caroline can no longer use that $1000 to buy something else. Similarly, when Caroline hires workers to make the cookies, the wages she pays are part of the firm's costs. Because these opportunity costs require the firm to pay out some money, they are called **explicit costs**. By contrast, some of a firm's opportunity costs, called **implicit costs**, do not require a cash outlay. Imagine that Caroline is skilled with computers and could earn $100 per hour working as a programmer. For every hour that Caroline works at her cookie factory, she gives up $100 in income, and this forgone income is also part of her costs. The total cost of Caroline's business is the sum of her explicit and implicit costs.

This distinction between explicit and implicit costs highlights an important difference between how economists and accountants analyze a business. Economists are interested in studying how firms make production and pricing decisions. Because these decisions are based on both explicit and implicit costs, economists include both when measuring a firm's costs. By contrast, accountants have the job of keeping track of the money that flows into and out of firms. As a result, they measure the explicit costs but usually ignore the implicit costs.

The difference between the methods of economists and accountants is easy to see in the case of Caroline's Cookie Factory. When Caroline gives up the opportunity to earn money as a computer programmer, her accountant will not count this as a cost of her cookie business. Because no money flows out of the business to pay for this cost, it never shows up on the accountant's financial statements. An economist, however, will count the forgone income as a cost because it will affect the decisions that Caroline makes in her cookie business. For example, if Caroline's wage as a computer programmer rises from $100 to $500 per hour, she might decide that running her cookie business is too costly and choose to shut down the factory to become a full-time computer programmer.

13-1c The Cost of Capital as an Opportunity Cost

An important implicit cost of almost every business is the opportunity cost of the financial capital that has been invested in the business. Suppose, for instance, that Caroline used $300 000 of her savings to buy her cookie factory from its previous owner. If Caroline had instead left this money in a savings account that pays an interest rate of 5 percent, she would have earned $15 000 per year. To own her cookie factory, therefore, Caroline has given up $15 000 a year in interest income. This forgone $15 000 is one of the implicit opportunity costs of Caroline's business.

As we have already noted, economists and accountants treat costs differently, and this is especially true in their treatment of the cost of capital. An economist views the $15 000 in interest income that Caroline gives up every year as an implicit cost of her business. Caroline's accountant, however, will not show this $15 000 as a cost because no money flows out of the business to pay for it.

To further explore the difference between the methods of economists and accountants, let's change the example slightly. Suppose now that Caroline did not have the entire $300 000 to buy the factory but, instead, used $100 000 of her own savings and borrowed $200 000 from a bank at an interest rate of 5 percent. Caroline's accountant, who measures only explicit costs, will now count the $10 000 interest paid on the bank loan every year as a cost because this amount of money now flows out of the firm. By contrast, according to an economist, the opportunity cost of owning the business is still $15 000. The opportunity cost equals the interest on the bank loan (an explicit cost of $10 000) plus the forgone interest on savings (an implicit cost of $5000).

13-1d Economic Profit versus Accounting Profit

Now let's return to the firm's objective—profit. Because economists and accountants measure costs differently, they also measure profit differently. An economist measures a firm's **economic profit** as the firm's total revenue minus all the opportunity costs (explicit and implicit) of producing the goods and services sold. An accountant measures the firm's **accounting profit** as the firm's total revenue minus only the firm's explicit costs.

Figure 13.1 summarizes this difference. Notice that because the accountant ignores the implicit costs, accounting profit is usually larger than economic profit. For a business to be profitable from an economist's standpoint, total revenue must cover all the opportunity costs, both explicit and implicit.

economic profit
total revenue minus total cost, including both explicit and implicit costs

accounting profit
total revenue minus total explicit cost

FIGURE 13.1

Economists versus Accountants

Economists include all opportunity costs when analyzing a firm, whereas accountants measure only explicit costs. Therefore, economic profit is smaller than accounting profit.

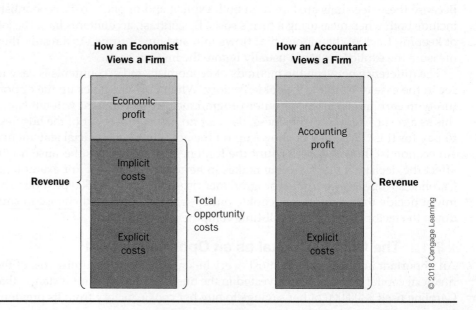

© 2018 Cengage Learning

Economic profit is an important concept because it is what motivates the firms that supply goods and services. As we will see, a firm making positive economic profit will stay in business. It is covering all its opportunity costs and has some revenue left to reward the firm owners. When a firm is making economic losses (that is, when economic profits are negative), the business owners are failing to make enough to cover all the costs of production. Unless conditions change, the firm owners will eventually close the business down and exit the industry. To understand how industries evolve, we need to keep an eye on economic profit.

QUICK Quiz *Farmer McDonald gives banjo lessons for $20 an hour. One day, he spends 10 hours planting $100 worth of seeds on his farm. What opportunity cost has he incurred? What cost would his accountant measure? If these seeds will yield $200 worth of crops, does McDonald earn an accounting profit? Does he earn an economic profit?*

13-2 Production and Costs

Firms incur costs when they buy inputs to produce the goods and services that they plan to sell. In this section we examine the link between a firm's production process and its total cost. Once again, we consider Caroline's Cookie Factory.

In the analysis that follows, we make an important simplifying assumption: We assume that the size of Caroline's factory is fixed and that Caroline can vary the quantity of cookies produced only by changing the number of workers she employs. This assumption is realistic in the short run, but not in the long run. That is, Caroline cannot build a larger factory overnight, but she can do so over the next year or two. This analysis, therefore, describes the production decisions that Caroline faces in the short run. We examine the relationship between costs and time horizon more fully later in the chapter.

13-2a The Production Function

Table 13.1 shows how the quantity of cookies Caroline's factory produces per hour depends on the number of workers. As you see in the first two columns, if there are

TABLE 13.1

A Production Function and Total Cost: Caroline's Cookie Factory

(1) Number of Workers	(2) Output (quantity of cookies produced per hour)	(3) Marginal Product of Labour	(4) Cost of Factory	(5) Cost of Workers	(6) Total Cost of Inputs (cost of factory + cost of workers)
0	0		$30	$0	$30
		50			
1	50		30	10	40
		40			
2	90		30	20	50
		30			
3	120		30	30	60
		20			
4	140		30	40	70
		10			
5	150		30	50	80

no workers in the factory, Caroline produces no cookies. When there is 1 worker, she produces 50 cookies. When there are 2 workers, she produces 90 cookies, and so on. Panel (a) of Figure 13.2 presents a graph of these two columns of numbers. The number of workers is on the horizontal axis, and the number of cookies produced is on the vertical axis. This relationship between the quantity of inputs (workers) and quantity of output (cookies) is called the **production function**.

One of the ten principles of economics introduced in Chapter 1 is that rational people think at the margin. As we will see in future chapters, this idea is the key to understanding the decision a firm makes about how many workers to hire and how much output to produce. To take a step toward understanding these decisions, column (3) in the table gives the marginal product of a worker. The **marginal product** of any input in the production process is the increase in the quantity of output obtained from one additional unit of that input. When the number of workers goes from 1 to 2, cookie production increases from 50 to 90, so the marginal product of the second worker is 40 cookies. And when the number of workers goes from 2 to 3, cookie production increases from 90 to 120, so the

production function

the relationship between quantity of inputs used to make a good and the quantity of output of that good

marginal product

the increase in output that arises from an additional unit of input

---

FIGURE 13.2

Caroline's Production Function and Total-Cost Curve

The production function in panel (a) shows the relationship between the number of workers hired and the quantity of output produced. Here the number of workers hired (on the horizontal axis) is from column (1) in Table 13.1, and the quantity of output produced (on the vertical axis) is from column (2). The production function gets flatter as the number of workers increases, which reflects diminishing marginal product. The total-cost curve in panel (b) shows the relationship between the quantity of output produced and total cost of production. Here the quantity of output produced (on the horizontal axis) is from column (2) in Table 13.1, and the total cost (on the vertical axis) is from column (6). The total-cost curve gets steeper as the quantity of output increases because of diminishing marginal product.

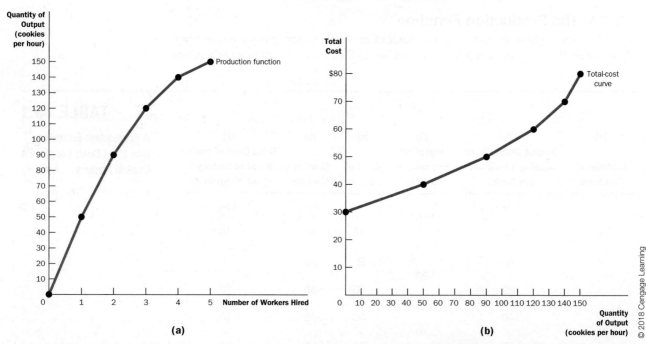

marginal product of the third worker is 30 cookies. In the table, the marginal product is shown halfway between two rows because it represents the change in output as the number of workers increases from one level to another.

Notice that as the number of workers increases, the marginal product declines. The second worker has a marginal product of 40 cookies, the third worker has a marginal product of 30 cookies, and the fourth worker has a marginal product of 20 cookies. This property is called **diminishing marginal product**. At first, when only a few workers are hired, they have easy access to Caroline's kitchen equipment. As the number of workers increases, additional workers have to share equipment and work in more crowded conditions. Eventually, the kitchen becomes so overcrowded that workers often get in each other's way. Hence, as more workers are hired, each additional worker contributes fewer additional cookies to total production.

Diminishing marginal product is also apparent in Figure 13.2. The production function's slope ("rise over run") tells us the change in Caroline's output of cookies ("rise") for each additional input of labour ("run"). That is, the slope of the production function measures the marginal product of a worker. As the number of workers increases, the marginal product declines, and the production function becomes flatter.

diminishing marginal product

the property whereby the marginal product of an input declines as the quantity of the input increases

13-2b From the Production Function to the Total-Cost Curve

Columns (4), (5), and (6) in Table 13.1 show Caroline's cost of producing cookies. In this example, the cost of Caroline's factory is $30 per hour, and the cost of a worker is $10 per hour. If she hires 1 worker, her total cost is $40 per hour. If she hires 2 workers, her total cost is $50 per hour, and so on. With this information, the table now shows how the number of workers Caroline hires is related to the quantity of cookies she produces and to her total cost of production.

Our goal in the next several chapters is to study firms' production and pricing decisions. For this purpose, the most important relationship in Table 13.1 is between quantity produced (in column (2)) and total costs (in column (6)). Panel (b) of Figure 13.2 graphs these two columns of data with the quantity produced on the horizontal axis and total cost on the vertical axis. This graph is called the *total-cost curve.*

Now compare the total-cost curve in panel (b) with the production function in panel (a). These two curves are opposite sides of the same coin. The total-cost curve gets steeper as the amount produced rises, whereas the production function gets flatter as production rises. These changes in slope occur for the same reason. High production of cookies means that Caroline's kitchen is crowded with many workers. Because the kitchen is crowded, each additional worker adds less to production, reflecting diminishing marginal product. Therefore, the production function is relatively flat. But now turn this logic around: When the kitchen is crowded, producing an additional cookie requires a lot of additional labour and is thus very costly. Therefore, when the quantity produced is large, the total-cost curve is relatively steep.

QUICK **Quiz** *If Farmer Jones plants no seeds on his farm, he gets no harvest. If he plants 1 bag of seeds, he gets 3 bushels of wheat. If he plants 2 bags, he gets 5 bushels. If he plants 3 bags, he gets 6 bushels. A bag of seeds costs $100, and seeds are his only cost. Use these data to graph the farmer's production function and total-cost curve. Explain their shapes.*

13-3 The Various Measures of Cost

Our analysis of Caroline's Cookie Factory demonstrated how a firm's total cost reflects its production function. From data on a firm's total cost, we can derive several related measures of cost, which will turn out to be useful when we analyze production and pricing decisions in future chapters. To see how these related measures are derived, we consider the example in Table 13.2. This table presents cost data on Caroline's neighbour: Conrad's Coffee Shop.

Column (1) of the table shows the number of cups of coffee that Conrad might produce, ranging from 0 to 10 cups per hour. Column (2) shows Conrad's total cost of producing coffee. Figure 13.3 plots Conrad's total-cost curve. The quantity of coffee (from column (1)) is on the horizontal axis, and total cost (from column (2)) is on the vertical axis. Conrad's total-cost curve has a shape similar to Caroline's. In particular, it becomes steeper as the quantity produced rises, which (as we have discussed) reflects diminishing marginal product.

TABLE 13.2

The Various Measures of Cost: Conrad's Coffee Shop

(1) Quantity of Coffee (cups per hour)	(2) Total Cost	(3) Fixed Cost	(4) Variable Cost	(5) Average Fixed Cost	(6) Average Variable Cost	(7) Average Total Cost	(8) Marginal Cost
0	$3.00	$3.00	$0.00	—	—	—	
							$0.30
1	3.30	3.00	0.30	$3.00	$0.30	$3.30	
							0.50
2	3.80	3.00	0.80	1.50	0.40	1.90	
							0.70
3	4.50	3.00	1.50	1.00	0.50	1.50	
							0.90
4	5.40	3.00	2.40	0.75	0.60	1.35	
							1.10
5	6.50	3.00	3.50	0.60	0.70	1.30	
							1.30
6	7.80	3.00	4.80	0.50	0.80	1.30	
							1.50
7	9.30	3.00	6.30	0.43	0.90	1.33	
							1.70
8	11.00	3.00	8.00	0.38	1.00	1.38	
							1.90
9	12.90	3.00	9.90	0.33	1.10	1.43	
							2.10
10	15.00	3.00	12.00	0.30	1.20	1.50	

FIGURE 13.3

Conrad's Total-Cost Curve

Here the quantity of output produced (on the horizontal axis) is from column (1) in Table 13.2, and the total cost (on the vertical axis) is from column (2). As in Figure 13.2, the total-cost curve gets steeper as the quantity of output increases because of diminishing marginal product.

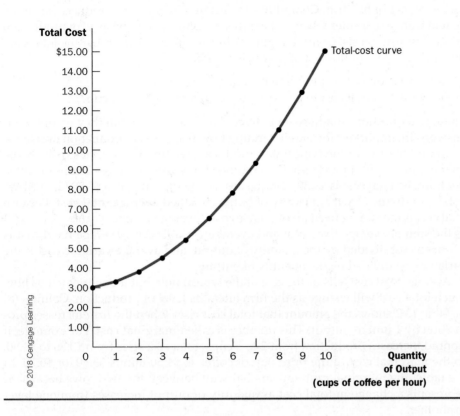

© 2018 Cengage Learning

13-3a Fixed and Variable Costs

Conrad's total cost can be divided into two types. Some costs, called **fixed costs**, do not vary with the quantity of output produced. They are incurred even if the firm produces nothing at all. Conrad's fixed costs include any rent he pays because this cost is the same regardless of how much coffee he produces. Similarly, if Conrad needs to hire a full-time bookkeeper to pay bills, regardless of the quantity of coffee produced, the bookkeeper's salary is a fixed cost. The third column in Table 13.2 shows Conrad's fixed cost, which in this example is $3.00.

Some of the firm's costs, called **variable costs**, change as the firm alters the quantity of output produced. Conrad's variable costs include the cost of coffee beans, milk, sugar, and paper cups: The more cups of coffee Conrad makes, the more of these items he needs to buy. Similarly, if Conrad has to hire more workers to make more cups of coffee, the salaries of these workers are variable costs. Column (4) of the table shows Conrad's variable cost. The variable cost is 0 if he produces nothing, $0.30 if he produces 1 cup of coffee, $0.80 if he produces 2 cups, and so on.

A firm's total cost is the sum of fixed and variable costs. In Table 13.2, total cost in the second column equals fixed cost in the third column plus variable cost in the fourth column.

fixed costs
costs that do not vary with the quantity of output produced

variable costs
costs that do vary with the quantity of output produced

13-3b Average and Marginal Costs

As the owner of his firm, Conrad has to decide how much to produce. One issue he will want to consider when making this decision is how the level of production affects his firm's costs. Conrad might ask his production supervisor the following two questions about the cost of producing coffee:

- How much does it cost to make the typical cup of coffee?
- How much does it cost to increase production of coffee by 1 cup?

These two questions might seem to have the same answer, but they do not. Both answers are important for understanding how firms make production decisions.

To find the cost of the typical unit produced, we divide the firm's costs by the quantity of output it produces. For example, if the firm produces 2 cups of coffee per hour, its total cost is $3.80, and the cost of the typical cup is $3.80/2, or $1.90. Total cost divided by the quantity of output is called **average total cost**. Because total cost is the sum of fixed and variable costs, average total cost can be expressed as the sum of average fixed cost and average variable cost. **Average fixed cost** is the fixed cost divided by the quantity of output, and **average variable cost** is the variable cost divided by the quantity of output.

Average total cost tells us the cost of the typical unit, but it does not tell us how much total cost will change as the firm alters its level of production. Column (8) in Table 13.2 shows the amount that total cost rises when the firm increases production by 1 unit of output. This number is called **marginal cost**. For example, if Conrad increases production from 2 to 3 cups, total cost rises from $3.80 to $4.50, so the marginal cost of the third cup of coffee is $4.50 minus $3.80, or $0.70. In the table, the marginal cost appears halfway between the two rows because it represents a change in total cost as quantity of output increases from one level to another.

It may be helpful to express these definitions mathematically:

$$\text{Average total cost} = \text{Total cost/Quantity}$$
$$ATC = TC/Q$$

and

$$\text{Marginal cost} = \text{Change in total cost/Change in quantity}$$
$$MC = \Delta TC/\Delta Q$$

Here Δ, the Greek letter *delta*, represents the change in a variable. These equations show how average total cost and marginal cost are derived from total cost. *Average total cost tells us the cost of a typical unit of output if total cost is divided evenly over all the units produced. Marginal cost tells us the increase in total cost that arises from producing an additional unit of output.* As we will see more fully in the next chapter, business managers like Conrad need to keep in mind the concepts of average total cost and marginal cost when deciding how much of their product to supply to the market.

13-3c Cost Curves and Their Shapes

Just as we found graphs of supply and demand useful when analyzing the behaviour of markets in previous chapters, we will find graphs of average and marginal cost useful when analyzing the behaviour of firms. Figure 13.4 graphs Conrad's costs using the data from Table 13.2. The horizontal axis measures the quantity

average total cost
total cost divided by the quantity of output

average fixed cost
fixed cost divided by the quantity of output

average variable cost
variable cost divided by the quantity of output

marginal cost
the increase in total cost that arises from an extra unit of production

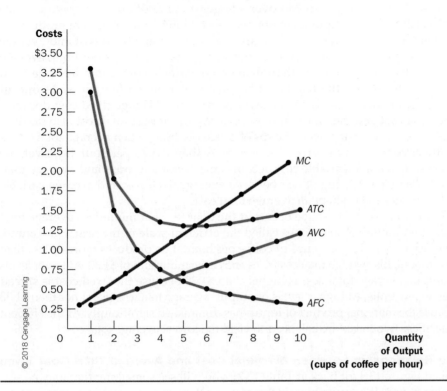

© 2018 Cengage Learning

FIGURE 13.4

Conrad's Average-Cost and Marginal-Cost Curves

This figure shows the average total cost (*ATC*), average fixed cost (*AFC*), average variable cost (*AVC*), and marginal cost (*MC*) for Conrad's Coffee Shop. All of these curves are obtained by graphing the data in Table 13.2. These cost curves show three features: (1) Marginal cost rises with the quantity of output. (2) The average-total-cost curve is U-shaped. (3) The marginal-cost curve crosses the average-total-cost curve at the minimum of average total cost.

the firm produces, and the vertical axis measures marginal and average costs. The graph shows four curves: average total cost (*ATC*), average fixed cost (*AFC*), average variable cost (*AVC*), and marginal cost (*MC*).

The cost curves shown here for Conrad's Coffee Shop have some features that are common to the cost curves of many firms in the economy. Let's examine three features in particular: the shape of the marginal-cost curve, the shape of the average-total-cost curve, and the relationship between marginal and average total cost.

Rising Marginal Cost Conrad's marginal cost rises as the quantity of output produced increases. This upward slope reflects the property of diminishing marginal product. When Conrad produces a small quantity of coffee, he has few workers, and much of his equipment is not used. Because he can easily put these idle resources to use, the marginal product of an extra worker is large, and the marginal cost of an extra cup of coffee is small. By contrast, when Conrad produces a large quantity of coffee, his shop is crowded with workers and most of his equipment is fully utilized. Conrad can produce more coffee by adding workers, but these new workers have to work in crowded conditions and may have to wait to use the equipment. Therefore, when the quantity of coffee produced is already high, the marginal product of an extra worker is low, and the marginal cost of an extra cup of coffee is large.

U-Shaped Average Total Cost Conrad's average-total-cost curve is U-shaped. To understand why, remember that average total cost is the sum of average fixed cost and average variable cost. Average fixed cost always declines as output rises because the fixed cost is spread over a larger number of units. Average variable cost usually rises as output increases because of diminishing marginal product.

Average total cost reflects the shapes of both average fixed cost and average variable cost. At very low levels of output, such as 1 or 2 cups per hour, average total cost is very high. Even though average variable cost is low, average fixed cost is high because the fixed cost is spread over only a few units. As output increases, the fixed cost is spread over more units. Average fixed cost declines, rapidly at first and then more slowly. As a result, average total cost also declines until Conrad's output reaches 5 cups of coffee per hour, when average total cost is $1.30 per cup. When the firm produces more than 6 cups per hour, however, the increase in average variable cost becomes the dominant force, and average total cost starts rising. The tug of war between average fixed cost and average variable cost generates the U-shape in average total cost.

efficient scale
the quantity of output that
minimizes average total cost

The bottom of the U-shape occurs at the quantity that minimizes average total cost. This quantity is sometimes called the **efficient scale** of the firm. For Conrad, the efficient scale is 5 or 6 cups of coffee per hour. If he produces more or less than this amount, his average total cost rises above the minimum of $1.30. At lower levels of output, average total cost is higher than $1.30 because the fixed cost is spread over so few units. At higher levels of output, average total cost is higher than $1.30 because the marginal product of inputs has diminished significantly. At the efficient scale, these two forces are balanced to yield the lowest average total cost.

The Relationship between Marginal Cost and Average Total Cost If you look at Figure 13.4 (or back at Table 13.2), you will see something that may be surprising at first. Whenever marginal cost is less than average total cost, average total cost is falling. Whenever marginal cost is greater than average total cost, average total cost is rising. This feature of Conrad's cost curves is not a coincidence from the particular numbers used in the example: It is true for all firms.

To see why, consider an analogy. Average total cost is like your cumulative grade point average. Marginal cost is like the grade in the next course you will take. If your grade in your next course is less than your grade point average, your grade point average will fall. If your grade in your next course is higher than your grade point average, your grade point average will rise. The mathematics of average and marginal costs is exactly the same as the mathematics of average and marginal grades.

This relationship between average total cost and marginal cost has an important corollary: *The marginal-cost curve crosses the average-total-cost curve at its minimum.* Why? At low levels of output, marginal cost is below average total cost, so average total cost is falling. But after the two curves cross, marginal cost rises above average total cost. As a result, average total cost must start to rise at this level of output. Hence, this point of intersection is the minimum of average total cost. As you will see in the next chapter, minimum average total cost plays a key role in the analysis of competitive firms.

13-3d Typical Cost Curves

In the examples we have studied so far, the firms have exhibited diminishing marginal product and, therefore, rising marginal cost at all levels of output. This simplifying assumption was useful because it allowed us to focus on the key features of cost curves that are useful in analyzing firm behaviour. Yet actual firms are usually more complicated than this. In many firms, marginal product does not

FIGURE 13.5

Cost Curves for a Typical Firm

Many firms experience increasing marginal product before diminishing marginal product. As a result, they have cost curves shaped like those in this figure. Notice that marginal cost and average variable cost fall for a while before starting to rise.

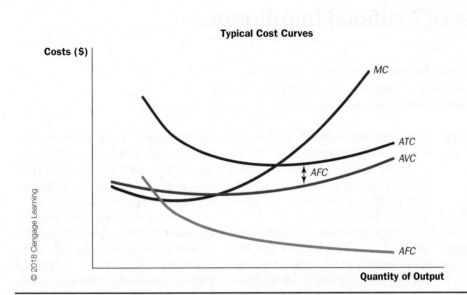

Typical Cost Curves

start to fall immediately after the first worker is hired. Depending on the production process, the second or third worker might have higher marginal product than the first because a team of workers can divide tasks and work more productively than a single worker. Firms exhibiting this pattern would experience increasing marginal product for a while before diminishing marginal product set in.

Figure 13.5 shows the cost curves for such a firm, including average total cost (*ATC*), average fixed cost (*AFC*), average variable cost (*AVC*), and marginal cost (*MC*). At low levels of output, the firm experiences increasing marginal product, and the marginal-cost curve falls. Eventually, the firm starts to experience diminishing marginal product, and the marginal-cost curve starts to rise. This combination of increasing and then diminishing marginal product also makes the average-variable-cost curve U-shaped.

Despite these differences from the Conrad example, the cost curves shown here share the three properties that are most important to remember:

1. Marginal cost eventually rises with the quantity of output.
2. The average-total-cost curve is U-shaped.
3. The marginal-cost curve crosses the average-total-cost curve at the minimum of average total cost.

QUICK Quiz *Suppose Honda's total cost of producing 4 cars is $225 000 and its total cost of producing 5 cars is $250 000. What is the average total cost of producing 5 cars? What is the marginal cost of the fifth car? • Draw the marginal-cost curve and the average-total-cost curve for a typical firm, and explain why these curves cross where they do.*

13-4 Costs in the Short Run and in the Long Run

We noted earlier in this chapter that a firm's costs might depend on the time horizon being examined. Let's examine more precisely why this might be the case.

The Rise of Artificial Intelligence

Will the rise of artificial intelligence make you more or less likely to find your dream job? Firms seeking to lower the cost of production using robotics are changing the nature of work, with profound social, economic, and legal implications.

Robot Revolution: AI and the Future of Work

By Doug Gray

Predictions of how we will work in the decades to come and how artificial intelligence (AI) will transform our daily lives have been notoriously imprecise ever since AI research began in the 1950s.

But as developments have gathered pace and slowly been applied in the workplace, the huge impact that AI is sure to have has become clearer—even if its exact social and legal implications are only gradually making themselves known.

The acceleration of AI research in recent years can be traced directly to the enormous resources of the computer giants leading the race, the dynamism and inventiveness of the

startups they consume, and the size of the prize at the end of the AI rainbow.

Venture capitalist database CB Insights shows that tech giants such as Google, Intel, Apple and IBM have made almost 140 acquisitions in the area since 2011.

One of the most striking was Google's 2014 purchase of Deep Mind, the British artificial intelligence company behind AlphaGo, a computer capable of playing the ancient Chinese board game Go that mimics the way the human brain functions.

Could such a machine also learn to do our jobs? Where do we now stand on the timeline of AI and how far it will impact on humankind?

Jeff Bezos, CEO of Amazon, one of the first companies to effectively deploy robots alongside humans in its warehouses, has talked at length about the world being on the cusp of a golden age of AI. Will this also mean the dawn of a new age of

leisure for humans? This year Finland will become the first European country to trial the introduction of an unconditional income, giving 2,000 unemployed people a universal basic wage in anticipation of a future when machines do most of the legwork.

Internet pioneer and Google Vice President Vint Cerf believes a balance will need to be struck that will see humans enhanced, rather than replaced by AI, at least in the short term. As Google scientists go on developing their robots' algorithms, the world will also need to be learning about AI.

"On the whole, robots and intelligent software seem destined to be used in cooperative and collaborative ways with humans," says Mr Cerf. Augmenting human capacity with machine intelligence seems to be the most fruitful way forward in the near term. Ingestion and analysis of large quantities of information and pattern recognition are all ways in which

13-4a The Relationship between Short-Run and Long-Run Average Total Cost

For many firms, the division of total costs between fixed and variable costs depends on the time horizon. Consider, for instance, a car manufacturer, such as Ford Motor Company. Over a period of only a few months, Ford cannot adjust the number or sizes of its car factories. The only way it can produce additional cars is to hire more workers at the factories it already has. The cost of these factories is, therefore, a fixed cost in the short run. By contrast, over a period of several years, Ford can expand the size of its factories, build new factories, or close old ones. Thus, the cost of its factories is a variable cost in the long run.

Because many decisions are fixed in the short run but variable in the long run, a firm's long-run cost curves differ from its short-run cost curves. Figure 13.6 shows an example. The figure presents three short-run average-total-cost curves—for a small, medium, and large factory. It also presents the long-run average-total-cost curve. As the firm moves along the long-run curve, it is adjusting the size of the factory to the quantity of production.

This graph shows how short-run and long-run costs are related. The long-run average-total-cost curve is a much flatter U-shape than the short-run average-total-cost curve. In addition, all the short-run curves lie on or above the long-run

robotic systems and software can be used to assist human endeavour.

Assisting is one thing, but numerous applications are being developed to enable machines to learn to do the jobs of humans. A 2014 joint study between Oxford University and Deloitte revealed that around 35% of jobs in the UK are at "high risk" of computation over the next 20 years, particularly in the retail, transport and storage sectors. Research by the same university a year earlier put that figure at 47% for the US.

"The search for affordable and useful robotics continues," says Mr Cerf. "Among the more interesting experiments is using machine learning to train a robot and to transfer that training to an unlimited number of copies of the robot. Just as the successful AlphaGo program was trained in part by playing against itself, it seems possible that mechanical robots can learn from each other in cooperative training exercises."

A 2016 Deloitte report found that 2.1 million jobs had a high chance of succumbing to automation in the UK wholesale and retail industry (59% of the total sector workforce). This was followed by transport and storage (1.5 million jobs) and human health and social work (1.3 million).

Professional, scientific and technical roles were also at high risk, but the impact would be offset by the creation of some 650,000 jobs in the field as a direct result of the move to automation.

If computers could be used in hospitals to monitor patients more effectively, rather than reduce the number of nurses, it could free up staff to spend more valuable time with patients assessing their individual needs. Social and cognitive skills would become more highly valued in order to make the essential judgement calls that would still be necessary in a more automated and sanitised workplace.

It is this brighter hope of job creation outstripping loss that AI disciples and those emerging from higher education must cling to. While, for instance, the prospect of machines 'learning' and sharing thousands of pages of legal documents could disrupt the world of law as it stands, the flip-side would be the vast amount of expertise required in the areas of legal responsibility and patents to oversee the implementation of AI in the workplace. If you have an accident in a self-driving car, who would be responsible—the user, system developer, or the manufacturer? Robots will force us all to change the way we *live*, not just how most of us work.

But Professor Bart Verheij, vice-president of the International Association for Artificial Intelligence and Law, says it will first be necessary to develop ethical systems before machines can start telling us what is right and what isn't—"systems with norms and values embedded in them and an understanding of our complex world that allows for sensible deliberation about doing the right thing.

"For now, I do not fear for the jobs of lawyers. First, we need a revolution in AI: bridging knowledge and data technology. Only once such bridges are well understood from a technological perspective will the job market of lawyers and other people with high education levels change beyond recognition."

The revolution is coming, but it will not happen overnight. Deloitte's research shows advances will naturally gravitate towards relevant sectors, starting with the more predictable and repetitive tasks and allowing room for society to adapt. The amount of social and political change that results—such as whether governments might be forced to pay us a basic income to do nothing—depends precisely on the speed of that introduction, and just how much humankind is prepared to let robots do the work.

Source: Article originally written by The Report Company for IE University, and appeared in economist.com.

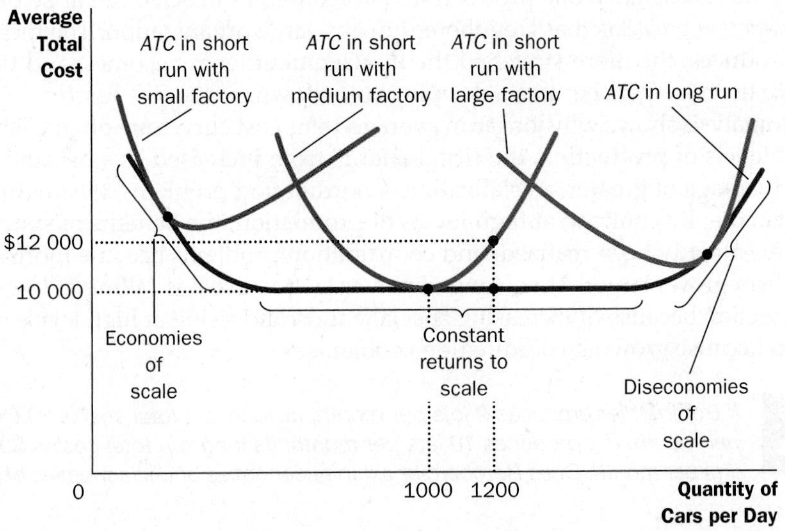

FIGURE 13.6

Average Total Cost in the Short and Long Runs

Because fixed costs are variable in the long run, the average-total-cost curve in the short run differs from the average-total-cost curve in the long run.

curve. These properties arise because firms have greater flexibility in the long run. In essence, in the long run, the firm gets to choose which short-run curve it wants to use. But in the short run, it has to use whatever short-run curve it has, based on decisions it has made in the past.

The figure shows an example of how a change in production alters costs over different time horizons. When Ford wants to increase production from 1000 to 1200 cars per day, it has no choice in the short run but to hire more workers at its existing medium-sized factory. Because of diminishing marginal product, average total cost rises from $10 000 to $12 000 per car. In the long run, however, Ford can expand both the size of the factory and its workforce, and average total cost returns to $10 000.

How long does it take a firm to get to the long run? The answer depends on the firm. It can take a year or more for a major manufacturing firm, such as a car company, to build a larger factory. By contrast, a person running a coffee shop can buy another coffee maker within a few days. There is, therefore, no single answer to the question of how long it takes a firm to adjust its production facilities.

13-4b Economies and Diseconomies of Scale

The shape of the long-run average-total-cost curve conveys important information about the production processes that a firm has available for manufacturing a good. In particular, it tells us how costs vary with the scale—that is, the size—of a firm's operations. When long-run average total cost declines as output increases, there are said to be **economies of scale**. When long-run average total cost rises as output increases, there are said to be **diseconomies of scale**. When long-run average total cost does not vary with the level of output, there are said to be **constant returns to scale**. As we can see in Figure 13.6, Ford has economies of scale at low levels of output, constant returns to scale at intermediate levels of output, and diseconomies of scale at high levels of output.

What might cause economies or diseconomies of scale? Economies of scale often arise because higher production levels allow *specialization* among workers, which permits each worker to become better at a specific task. For instance, if Ford hires a large number of workers and produces a large number of cars, it can reduce costs with modern assembly-line production. Diseconomies of scale can arise because of *coordination problems* that are inherent in any large organization. The more cars Ford produces, the more stretched the management team becomes, and the less effective the managers become at keeping costs down.

This analysis shows why long-run average-total-cost curves are often U-shaped. At low levels of production, the firm benefits from increased size because it can take advantage of greater specialization. Coordination problems, meanwhile, are not yet acute. By contrast, at high levels of production, the benefits of specialization have already been realized, and coordination problems become more severe as the firm grows larger. Thus, long-run average total cost is falling at low levels of production because of increasing specialization and rising at high levels of production because growing coordination problems.

economies of scale
the property whereby long-run average total cost falls as the quantity of output increases

diseconomies of scale
the property whereby long-run average total cost rises as the quantity of output increases

constant returns to scale
the property whereby long-run average total cost stays the same as the quantity of output changes

 QUICK **Quiz**　*If Bombardier produces 9 jets per month, its long-run total cost is $9.0 million per month. If it produces 10 jets per month, its long-run total cost is $9.5 million per month. Does Bombardier exhibit economies or diseconomies of scale?*

13-5 Conclusion

The purpose of this chapter has been to develop some tools to study how firms make production and pricing decisions. You should now understand what economists mean by the term *costs* and how costs vary with the quantity of output a firm produces. To refresh your memory, Table 13.3 summarizes some of the definitions we have encountered.

By themselves, of course, a firm's cost curves do not tell us what decisions the firm will make. But they are an important component of that decision, as we will begin to see in the next chapter.

TABLE 13.3

The Many Types of Cost: A Summary

Term	Definition	Mathematical Description
Explicit costs	Costs that require an outlay of money by the firm	—
Implicit costs	Costs that do not require an outlay of money by the firm	—
Fixed costs	Costs that do not vary with the quantity of output produced	FC
Variable costs	Costs that do vary with the quantity of output produced	VC
Total cost	The market value of all the inputs that a firm uses in production	$TC = FC + VC$
Average fixed cost	Fixed costs divided by the quantity of output	$AFC = FC/Q$
Average variable cost	Variable costs divided by the quantity of output	$AVC = VC/Q$
Average total cost	Total cost divided by the quantity of output	$ATC = TC/Q$
Marginal cost	The increase in total cost that arises from an extra unit of production	$MC = \Delta TC/\Delta Q$

summary

- The goal of firms is to maximize profit, which equals total revenue minus total cost.

- When analyzing a firm's behaviour, it is important to include all the opportunity costs of production. Some of the opportunity costs, such as the wages a firm pays its workers, are explicit. Other opportunity costs, such as the wages the firm owner gives up by working in the firm rather than taking another job, are implicit. Economic profit takes both explicit and implicit costs into account, whereas accounting profit considers only explicit costs.

- A firm's costs reflect its production process. A typical firm's production function gets flatter as the quantity of an input increases, displaying the property of diminishing marginal product. As a result, a firm's total-cost curve gets steeper as the quantity produced rises.

- A firm's total costs can be divided between fixed costs and variable costs. Fixed costs are costs that do not change when the firm alters the quantity of output produced. Variable costs are costs that do change when the firm alters the quantity of output produced.

- From a firm's total cost, two related measures of cost are derived. Average total cost is total cost divided by the quantity of output. Marginal cost is the amount by which total cost rises if output increases by 1 unit.

- When analyzing firm behaviour, it is often useful to graph average total cost and marginal cost. For a typical firm, marginal cost rises with the quantity of output. Average total cost first falls as output increases and then rises as output increases further. The marginal-cost curve always crosses the average-total-cost curve at the minimum of average total cost.

- A firm's costs often depend on the time horizon being considered. In particular, many costs are fixed in the short run but variable in the long run. As a result, when the firm changes its level of production, average total cost may rise more in the short run than in the long run.

KEY **concepts**

total revenue (for a firm), *p. 282*	production function, *p. 286*	average variable cost, *p. 290*
total cost, *p. 282*	marginal product, *p. 286*	marginal cost, *p. 290*
profit, *p. 283*	diminishing marginal product, *p. 287*	efficient scale, *p. 292*
explicit costs, *p. 283*	fixed costs, *p. 289*	economies of scale, *p. 296*
implicit costs, *p. 283*	variable costs, *p. 289*	diseconomies of scale, *p. 296*
economic profit, *p. 284*	average total cost, *p. 290*	constant returns to scale, *p. 296*
accounting profit, *p. 284*	average fixed cost, *p. 290*	

QUESTIONS FOR **review**

1. What is the relationship between a firm's total revenue, profit, and total cost?

2. Give an example of an opportunity cost that an accountant might not count as a cost. Why would the accountant ignore this cost?

3. What is marginal product, and what does it mean if it is diminishing?

4. Draw a production function that exhibits diminishing marginal product of labour. Draw the associated total-cost curve. (In both cases, be sure to label the axes.) Explain the shapes of the two curves you have drawn.

5. Define total cost, average total cost, and marginal cost. How are they related?

6. Draw the marginal-cost and average-total-cost curves for a typical firm. Explain why the curves have the shapes that they do and why they cross where they do.

7. How and why does a firm's average-total-cost curve differ in the short run compared with the long run?

8. Define *economies of scale* and explain why they might arise. Define *diseconomies of scale* and explain why they might arise.

QUICK CHECK **multiple choice**

1. Raj opens up a lemonade stand for two hours. He spends $10 for ingredients and sells $60 worth of lemonade. In the same two hours, he could have mowed his neighbour's lawn for $40. Raj has an accounting profit of _____ and an economic profit of _____ .
   a. $50, $10
   b. $90, $50
   c. $10, $50
   d. $50, $90

2. Diminishing marginal product explains why, as a firm's output increases, which of the following is likely to occur?
   a. the production function and total-cost curve both get steeper
   b. the production function and total-cost curve both get flatter
   c. the production function gets steeper, while the total-cost curve gets flatter
   d. the production function gets flatter, while the total-cost curve gets steeper

3. A firm is producing 1000 units at a total cost of $5000. If it were to increase production to 1001 units, its total cost would rise to $5008. What does this information tell you about the firm?
   a. Marginal cost is $5, and average variable cost is $8.
   b. Marginal cost is $8, and average variable cost is $5.
   c. Marginal cost is $5, and average total cost is $8.
   d. Marginal cost is $8, and average total cost is $5.

4. A firm is producing 20 units with an average total cost of $25 and marginal cost of $15. If it were to increase production to 21 units, which of the following must occur?
   a. Marginal cost would decrease.
   b. Marginal cost would increase.
   c. Average total cost would decrease.
   d. Average total cost would increase.

5. The government imposes a $1000-per-year licence fee on all pizza restaurants. Which cost curves shift as a result?
   a. average total cost and marginal cost
   b. average total cost and average fixed cost
   c. average variable cost and marginal cost
   d. average variable cost and average fixed cost

6. If a higher level of production allows workers to specialize in particular tasks, a firm will likely exhibit _____ of scale and _____ average total cost.
   a. economies, falling
   b. economies, rising
   c. diseconomies, falling
   d. diseconomies, rising

PROBLEMS AND **applications**

1. This chapter discusses many types of costs: opportunity cost, total cost, fixed cost, variable cost, average total cost, and marginal cost. Fill in the type of cost that best completes each phrase below:
   a. The true cost of taking some action is its _____.
   b. _____ is falling when marginal cost is below it, and rising when marginal cost is above it.
   c. A cost that does not depend on the quantity produced is a(n) _____.
   d. In the ice-cream industry in the short run, _____ includes the cost of cream and sugar, but not the cost of the factory.
   e. Profits equal total revenue less _____.
   f. The cost of producing an extra unit of output is the _____.

2. Your aunt is thinking about opening a hardware store. She estimates that it would cost $500 000 per year to rent the location and buy the stock. In addition, she would have to quit her $50 000 per year job as an accountant.
   a. Define opportunity cost.
   b. What is your aunt's opportunity cost of running a hardware store for a year? If your aunt thought she could sell $510 000 worth of merchandise in a year, should she open the store? Explain.

3. The city government is considering two tax proposals:
   • a lump-sum tax of $300 on each producer of hamburgers
   • a tax of $1 per burger, paid by producers of hamburgers
   a. Which of the following curves—average fixed cost, average variable cost, average total cost, and marginal cost—would shift as a result of the lump-sum tax? Why? Show this in a graph. Label the graph as precisely as possible.
   b. Which of these same four curves would shift as a result of the per-burger tax? Why? Show this in a new graph. Label the graph as precisely as possible.

4. A commercial fisherman notices the following relationship between hours spent fishing and the quantity of fish caught:

Hours	Quantity of Fish (in kilograms)
0	0
1	10
2	18
3	24
4	28
5	30

   a. What is the marginal product of each hour spent fishing?
   b. Use these data to graph the fisherman's production function. Explain its shape.
   c. The fisherman has a fixed cost of $10 (his pole). The opportunity cost of his time is $5 per hour. Graph the fisherman's total-cost curve. Explain its shape.

5. Nimbus Ltd. makes brooms and then sells them door to door. Here is the relationship between the number of workers and Nimbus's output in a given day:

Workers	Output	Marginal Product	Total Cost	Average Total Cost	Marginal Cost
0	0		—	—	
		—			—
1	20		—	—	
		—			—
2	50		—	—	
		—			—
3	90		—	—	
		—			—
4	120		—	—	
		—			—
5	140		—	—	
		—			—
6	150		—	—	
		—			—
7	155		—	—	

a. Fill in the column of marginal products. What pattern do you see? How might you explain it?
b. A worker costs $100 per day, and the firm has fixed costs of $200. Use this information to fill in the column for total cost.
c. Fill in the column for average total cost. (Recall that $ATC = TC/Q$.) What pattern do you see?
d. Now fill in the column for marginal cost. (Recall that $MC = \Delta TC/\Delta Q$.) What pattern do you see?
e. Compare the column for marginal product and the column for marginal cost. Explain the relationship.
f. Compare the column for average total cost and the column for marginal cost. Explain the relationship.

6. A firm uses two inputs in production: capital and labour. In the short run, the firm cannot adjust the amount of capital it is using, but it can adjust the size of its workforce. What happens to the firm's average-total-cost curve, the average-variable-cost curve, and the marginal-cost curve when
a. the cost of renting capital increases?
b. the cost of hiring labour increases?

7. Consider the following cost information for a pizzeria:

Q (dozens)	Total Cost	Variable Cost
0	$300	$0
1	350	50
2	390	90
3	420	120
4	450	150
5	490	190
6	540	240

a. What is the pizzeria's fixed cost?
b. Construct a table in which you calculate the marginal cost per dozen pizzas using the information on total cost. Also calculate the marginal cost per dozen pizzas using the information on variable cost. What is the relationship between these sets of numbers? Comment.

8. You are thinking about setting up a coffee stand. The stand itself costs $200. The ingredients for each cup of coffee cost $0.50.
a. What is your fixed cost of doing business? What is your variable cost per cup?
b. Construct a table showing your total cost, average total cost, and marginal cost for output levels varying from 0 to 40 L. (*Hint:* There are 4 cups in a litre.) Draw the three cost curves.

9. Your cousin Vinnie owns a painting company with fixed costs of $200 and the following schedule for variable costs:

Quantity of Houses Painted per Month	1	2	3	4	5	6	7
Variable Costs	$10	$20	$40	$80	$160	$320	$640

Calculate average fixed cost, average variable cost, and average total cost for each quantity. What is the efficient scale of the painting company?

10. Jane's Juice Bar has the following cost schedules:

Q (vats)	Variable Cost	Total Cost
0	$0	$30
1	10	40
2	25	55
3	45	75
4	70	100
5	100	130
6	135	165

a. Calculate average variable cost, average total cost, and marginal cost for each quantity.
b. Graph all three curves. What is the relationship between the marginal-cost curve and the average-total-cost curve? Between the marginal-cost curve and the average-variable-cost curve? Explain.

11. Consider the following table of long-run total cost for three different firms:

Quantity	1	2	3	4	5	6	7
Firm A	$60	$70	$80	$90	$100	$110	$120
Firm B	11	24	39	56	75	96	119
Firm C	21	34	49	66	85	106	129

Does each of these firms experience economies of scale or diseconomies of scale?

12. You are the chief financial officer for a firm that sells digital music players. Your firm has the following average total cost schedule:

Quantity	Average Total Cost
600 players	$300
601 players	301

Your current level of production is 600 devices, all of which have been sold. Someone calls, desperate to buy one of your music players. The caller offers you $550 for it. Should you accept the offer? Why or why not?

Firms in Competitive Markets

In this chapter, you will ...

1   Learn what characteristics make a market competitive

2   Examine how competitive firms decide how much output to produce

3   Examine how competitive firms decide when to shut down production temporarily

4   Examine how competitive firms decide whether to exit or enter a market

5   See how firm behaviour determines a market's short-run and long-run supply curves

If your local gas station raised its price for gasoline by 20 percent, it would see a large drop in the amount of gasoline it sold. Its customers would quickly switch to buying their gasoline at other gas stations. By contrast, if your local water company raised the price of water by 20 percent, it would see only a small decrease in the amount of water it sold. People might water their lawns less often and buy more water-efficient showerheads, but they would be hard-pressed to reduce water consumption greatly or to find another supplier. The difference between the gasoline market and the water market is that many firms supply gasoline to the local market, but only one firm supplies water. As you might expect, this difference in market structure shapes the pricing and production decisions of the firms that operate in these markets.

In this chapter we examine the behaviour of competitive firms, such as your local gas station. You may recall that a market is competitive if each buyer and seller is small compared to the size of the market and, therefore, has little ability to influence market prices. By contrast, if a firm can influence the market price of the good it sells, it is said to have *market power*. Later in the book, we examine the behaviour of firms with market power, such as your local water company.

Our analysis of competitive firms in this chapter sheds light on the decisions that lie behind the supply curve in a competitive market. As we have already discussed in previous chapters, not surprisingly, we find that a market supply curve is tightly linked to firms' costs of production. In this chapter we explore this idea more closely. Moreover, we discuss which among a firm's various costs—fixed, variable, average, and marginal—are most relevant for its supply decision. We see that all these measures of cost play important and interrelated roles.

14-1 What Is a Competitive Market?

Our goal in this chapter is to examine how firms make production decisions in competitive markets. As a background for this analysis, we begin by considering what a competitive market is.

14-1a The Meaning of Competition

A **competitive market**, sometimes called a *perfectly competitive market*, has two characteristics:

1. There are many buyers and many sellers in the market.
2. The goods offered by the various sellers are largely the same.

competitive market
a market in which there are many buyers and many sellers so that each has a negligible impact on the market price

As a result of these conditions, the actions of any single buyer or seller in the market have a negligible impact on the market price. Each buyer and seller takes the market price as given.

As an example, consider the market for milk. No single consumer of milk can influence the price of milk because each buys a small amount relative to the size of the market. Similarly, each seller of milk has limited control over the price because many other sellers are offering milk that is essentially identical. Because each seller can sell all he wants to at the going price, he has little reason to charge less, and if he charges more, buyers will go elsewhere. Buyers and sellers in competitive markets must accept the price the market determines and, therefore, are said to be *price takers*.

In addition to the foregoing two conditions for competition, there is a third condition sometimes thought to characterize perfectly competitive markets:

3. Firms can freely enter or exit the market.

If, for instance, anyone can start a dairy farm, and if any existing dairy farmer can leave the dairy business, then the dairy industry satisfies this condition. Much of the analysis of competitive firms does not need the assumption of free entry and exit because this condition is not necessary for firms to be price takers. Yet, as we see later in this chapter, when there is free entry and exit in a competitive market it is a powerful force in shaping the long-run equilibrium.

14-1b The Revenue of a Competitive Firm

A firm in a competitive market, like most other firms in the economy, tries to maximize profit (total revenue minus total cost). To see how it does this, we first consider the revenue of a competitive firm. To keep matters concrete, let's consider a specific firm: the Smith Family Dairy Farm.

The Smith farm produces a quantity of milk, Q, and sells each unit at the market price, P. The farm's total revenue is $P \times Q$. For example, if a 4-L jug of milk sells for $6 and the farm sells 1000 jugs, its total revenue is $6000.

Because the Smith farm is small compared to the world market for milk, it takes the price as given by market conditions. This means, in particular, that the price of milk does not depend on the quantity of output that the Smith farm produces and sells. If the Smiths double the amount of milk they produce to 2000 jugs, the price of milk remains the same, and their total revenue doubles to $12 000. As a result, total revenue is proportional to the amount of output.

Table 14.1 shows the revenue for the Smith Family Dairy Farm. Columns (1) and (2) show the amount of output the farm produces and the price at which it sells its output. Column (3) is the farm's total revenue. The table assumes that the price of milk is $6 per jug, so total revenue is simply $6 times the number of jugs.

TABLE 14.1

Total, Average, and Marginal Revenue for a Competitive Firm

(1) Quantity	(2) Price	(3) Total Revenue	(4) Average Revenue	(5) Marginal Revenue
(Q)	(P)	$(TR = P \times Q)$	$(AR = TR/Q)$	$(MR = \Delta TR/\Delta Q)$
1 jug	$6	$6	$6	$6
2	6	12	6	6
3	6	18	6	6
4	6	24	6	6
5	6	30	6	6
6	6	36	6	6
7	6	42	6	6
8	6	48	6	6

Just as the concepts of average and marginal were useful in the preceding chapter when analyzing costs, they are also useful when analyzing revenue. To see what these concepts tell us, consider these two questions:

1. How much revenue does the farm receive for the typical jug of milk?
2. How much additional revenue does the farm receive if it increases production of milk by 1 jug?

Columns (4) and (5) in Table 14.1 answer these questions.

average revenue
total revenue divided by the quantity sold

Column (4) in the table shows **average revenue**, which is total revenue (from column (3)) divided by the amount of output (from column (1)). Average revenue tells us how much revenue a firm receives for the typical unit sold. In Table 14.1, you can see that average revenue equals $6, the price of a jug of milk. This illustrates a general lesson that applies not only to competitive firms but to other firms as well. Average revenue is total revenue ($P \times Q$) divided by the quantity (Q). Therefore, *for all firms, average revenue equals the price of the good.*

marginal revenue
the change in total revenue from an additional unit sold

Column (5) shows **marginal revenue**, which is the change in total revenue from the sale of each additional unit of output. In Table 14.1, marginal revenue equals $6, the price of a jug of milk. This result illustrates a lesson that applies only to competitive firms. Total revenue is $P \times Q$, and P is fixed for a competitive firm. Therefore, when Q rises by 1 unit, total revenue rises by P dollars. *For competitive firms, marginal revenue equals the price of the good.*

 QUICK **Quiz** *When a competitive firm doubles the amount it sells, what happens to the price of its output and its total revenue?*

14-2 Profit Maximization and the Competitive Firm's Supply Curve

The goal of a firm is to maximize profit, which equals total revenue minus total cost. We have just discussed the competitive firm's revenue, and in the preceding chapter, we discussed the firm's costs. We are now ready to examine how a competitive firm maximizes profit and how that decision determines its supply curve.

14-2a A Simple Example of Profit Maximization

Let's begin our analysis of the firm's supply decision with the example in Table 14.2. In Column (1) in the table is the number of 4-L jugs of milk the Smith Family Dairy Farm produces. Column (2) shows the farm's total revenue, which is $6 times the number of jugs. Column (3) shows the farm's total cost. Total cost includes fixed costs, which are $3 in this example, and variable costs, which depend on the quantity produced.

Column (4) shows the farm's profit, which is computed by subtracting total cost from total revenue. If the farm produces nothing, it has a loss of $3 (its fixed cost). If it produces 1 jug, it has a profit of $1. If it produces 2 jugs, it has a profit of $4, and so on. Because the Smith family's goal is to maximize profit, it chooses to produce the quantity of milk that makes profit as large as possible. In this example, profit is maximized when the farm produces 4 or 5 jugs of milk, when the profit is $7.

There is another way to look at the Smith farm's decision: The Smiths can find the profit-maximizing quantity by comparing the marginal revenue and marginal

TABLE 14.2

Profit Maximization: A Numerical Example

(1) Quantity	(2) Total Revenue	(3) Total Cost	(4) Profit	(5) Marginal Revenue	(6) Marginal Cost	(7) Change in Profit
(Q)	(TR)	(TC)	(TR − TC)	(MR = ΔTR/ΔQ)	(MC = ΔTC/ΔQ)	(MR − MC)
0 jugs	$0	$3	−$3			
				$6	$2	$4
1	6	5	1			
				6	3	3
2	12	8	4			
				6	4	2
3	18	12	6			
				6	5	1
4	24	17	7			
				6	6	0
5	30	23	7			
				6	7	−1
6	36	30	6			
				6	8	−2
7	42	38	4			
				6	9	−3
8	48	47	1			

cost from each unit produced. Columns (5) and (6) in Table 14.2 compute marginal revenue and marginal cost from the changes in total revenue and total cost, and column (7) shows the change in profit for each additional 4-L jug of milk produced. The first jug of milk the farm produces has a marginal revenue of $6 and a marginal cost of $2; hence, producing that jug increases profit by $4 (from −$3 to $1). The second jug produced has a marginal revenue of $6 and a marginal cost of $3, so that jug increases profit by $3 (from $1 to $4). As long as marginal revenue exceeds marginal cost, increasing the quantity produced raises profit. Once the Smith farm has reached five 4-L jugs of milk, however, the situation changes. The sixth jug would have marginal revenue of $6 and marginal cost of $7, so producing it would reduce profit by $1 (from $7 to $6). As a result, the Smiths would not produce beyond 5 jugs of milk.

One of the ten principles of economics in Chapter 1 is that rational people think at the margin. We now see how the Smith Family Dairy Farm can apply this principle. If marginal revenue is greater than marginal cost—as it is at 1, 2, or 3 jugs—the Smiths should increase the production of milk because it will put more money in their pockets (marginal revenue) than it takes out (marginal cost). If marginal revenue is less than marginal cost—as it is at 6, 7, or 8 jugs—the Smiths should decrease production. If the Smiths think at the margin and make incremental adjustments to the level of production, they end up producing the profit-maximizing quantity.

14-2b The Marginal-Cost Curve and the Firm's Supply Decision

To extend this analysis of profit maximization, consider the cost curves in Figure 14.1. These cost curves have the three features that, as we discussed in the previous chapter, are thought to describe most firms: The marginal-cost curve (*MC*) is upward sloping. The average-total-cost curve (*ATC*) is U-shaped. And the marginal-cost curve crosses the average-total-cost curve at the minimum of average total cost. The figure also shows a horizontal line at the market price (*P*). The price line is horizontal because a competitive firm is a price taker: The price of the firm's output is the same regardless of the quantity that the firm decides to produce. Keep in mind that, for a competitive firm, the price equals both its average revenue (*AR*) and its marginal revenue (*MR*).

We can use Figure 14.1 to find the quantity of output that maximizes profit. Imagine that the firm is producing at Q_1. At this level of output, marginal revenue is greater than marginal cost. This means that if the firm were to raise its production by 1 unit, the additional revenue (MR_1) would exceed the additional costs (MC_1). Profit, which equals total revenue minus total cost, would increase. Hence, if marginal revenue is greater than marginal cost, as it is at Q_1, the firm can increase profit by increasing production.

A similar argument applies when output is at Q_2. In this case, the marginal-cost curve is above the marginal-revenue curve, showing that marginal cost is greater

FIGURE 14.1

Profit Maximization for a Competitive Firm

This figure shows the marginal-cost curve (*MC*), the average-total-cost curve (*ATC*), and the average-variable-cost curve (*AVC*). It also shows the market price (*P*), which equals marginal revenue (*MR*) and average revenue (*AR*). At the quantity Q_1, marginal revenue MR_1 exceeds marginal cost MC_1, so raising production increases profit. At the quantity Q_2, marginal cost MC_2 is above marginal revenue MR_2, so reducing production increases profit. The profit-maximizing quantity Q_{MAX} is found where the horizontal price line intersects the marginal-cost curve.

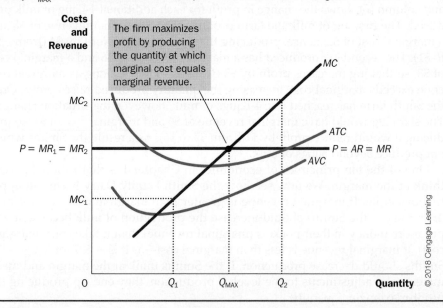

than marginal revenue. If the firm were to reduce production by 1 unit, the costs saved (MC_2) would exceed the revenue lost (MR_2). Therefore, if marginal revenue is less than marginal cost, as it is at Q_2, the firm can increase profit by reducing production.

Where do these marginal adjustments to production end? Regardless of whether the firm begins with production at a low level (such as Q_1) or at a high level (such as Q_2), the firm will eventually adjust production until the quantity produced reaches Q_{MAX}. This analysis yields three general rules for profit maximization:

1. If marginal revenue is greater than marginal cost, the firm should increase its output.
2. If marginal cost is greater than marginal revenue, the firm should decrease its output.
3. At the profit-maximizing level of output, marginal revenue and marginal cost are exactly equal.

These rules are the key to rational decision making by any profit-maximizing firm. They apply not only to competitive firms but, as we will see in the next few chapters, to other types of firms as well.

We can now see how the competitive firm decides the quantity of its good to supply to the market. Because a competitive firm is a price taker, its marginal revenue equals the market price. For any given price, the competitive firm's profit-maximizing quantity of output is found by looking at the intersection of the price with the marginal-cost curve. In Figure 14.1, that quantity of output is Q_{MAX}.

Suppose the price prevailing in this market rises, perhaps because of an increase in market demand. Figure 14.2 shows how a competitive firm responds to an increase in the price. When the price is P_1, the firm produces quantity Q_1, the quantity that equates marginal cost to the price. When the price rises to P_2, the firm finds that marginal revenue is now higher than marginal cost at the previous level of output, so the firm increases production. The new profit-maximizing

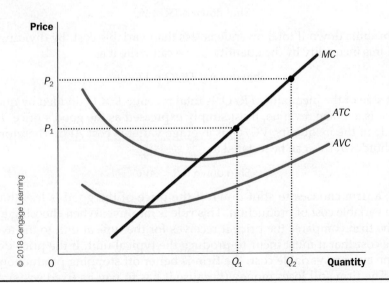

FIGURE 14.2

Marginal Cost as the Competitive Firm's Supply Curve

An increase in the price from P_1 to P_2 leads to an increase in the firm's profit-maximizing quantity from Q_1 to Q_2. Because the marginal-cost curve shows the quantity supplied by the firm at any given price, it is the firm's supply curve (see Figure 14.3).

© 2018 Cengage Learning

quantity is Q_2, at which marginal cost equals the new higher price. *In essence, because the firm's marginal-cost curve determines the quantity of the good the firm is willing to supply at any price, it is the competitive firm's supply curve.* There are, however, some caveats to this conclusion, which we examine next.

14-2c The Firm's Short-Run Decision to Shut Down

So far we have been analyzing the question of how much a competitive firm will produce. In some circumstances, however, the firm will decide to shut down and not produce anything at all.

Here we need to distinguish between a temporary shutdown of a firm and the permanent exit of a firm from the market. A *shutdown* refers to a short-run decision not to produce anything during a specific period of time because of current market conditions. *Exit* refers to a long-run decision to leave the market. The short-run and long-run decisions differ because most firms cannot avoid their fixed costs in the short run but can do so in the long run. That is, a firm that shuts down temporarily still has to pay its fixed costs, whereas a firm that exits the market does not have to pay any costs at all, fixed or variable.

For example, consider the production decision that a farmer faces. The cost of the land is one of the farmer's fixed costs. If the farmer decides not to produce any crops one season, the land lies fallow and he cannot recover this cost. When making the short-run decision whether to shut down for a season, the fixed cost of land is said to be a *sunk cost.* By contrast, if the farmer decides to leave farming altogether, he can sell the land. When making the long-run decision whether to exit the market, the cost of land is not sunk. (We return to the issue of sunk costs shortly.)

Now let's consider what determines a firm's shutdown decision. If the firm shuts down, it loses all revenue from the sale of its product. At the same time, it saves the variable costs of making its product (but must still pay the fixed costs). Thus, *the firm shuts down if the revenue that it would earn from producing is less than its variable costs of production.*

A bit of mathematics can make this shutdown rule more useful. If *TR* stands for total revenue, and *VC* stands for variable costs, then the firm's decision can be written as

$$\text{Shut down if } TR < VC$$

The firm shuts down if total revenue is less than variable cost. By dividing both sides of this inequality by the quantity Q, we can write it as

$$\text{Shut down if } TR/Q < VC/Q$$

The left side of the inequality, TR/Q, is total revenue $P \times Q$ divided by quantity Q, which is average revenue, most simply expressed as the good's price, P. The right side of the inequality, VC/Q, is average variable cost AVC. Therefore, the firm's shutdown rule can be restated as

$$\text{Shut down if } P < AVC$$

That is, a firm chooses to shut down if the price of the good is less than the average variable cost of production. This rule is intuitive: When choosing to produce, the firm compares the price it receives for the typical unit to the average variable cost that it must incur to produce the typical unit. If the price doesn't cover the average variable cost, the firm is better off stopping production altogether. The firm still loses money (because it has to pay its fixed costs), but it would lose even more money by staying open. Thus, the price that coincides with the minimum point on the average-*variable*-cost curve is sometimes referred to as the *shutdown price.* If the market price is less than the shutdown price, the firm shuts down and ceases production. If conditions change in the future so that the price exceeds the shutdown price, the firm can reopen. Of course we could just as easily refer to it as the *start-up price.*

We now have a full description of a competitive firm's profit-maximizing strategy. If the firm produces anything, it produces the quantity at which marginal cost equals the good's price, which the firm takes as given. Yet if the price is less than average variable cost at that quantity, the firm is better off shutting down temporarily and not producing anything. These results are illustrated in Figure 14.3. *The competitive firm's short-run supply curve is the portion of its marginal-cost curve that lies above average variable cost.*

14-2d Spilt Milk and Other Sunk Costs

Sometime in your life you have probably been told, "Don't cry over spilt milk," or "Let bygones be bygones." These adages hold a deep truth about rational decision making. Economists say that a cost is a **sunk cost** when it has already been committed and cannot be recovered. Because nothing can be done about sunk costs, you should ignore them when making decisions about various aspects of life, including business strategy.

Our analysis of the firm's shutdown decision is one example of the irrelevance of sunk costs. We assume that the firm cannot recover its fixed costs by temporarily stopping production. That is, regardless of the quantity of output supplied (even if it is zero), the firm still has to pay its fixed costs. As a result, the fixed costs are sunk in the short run, and the firm should ignore them when deciding how much to produce. The firm's short-run supply curve is the part of the marginal-cost curve that lies above average variable cost, and the size of the fixed cost does not matter for this supply decision.

sunk cost
a cost that has already been committed and cannot be recovered

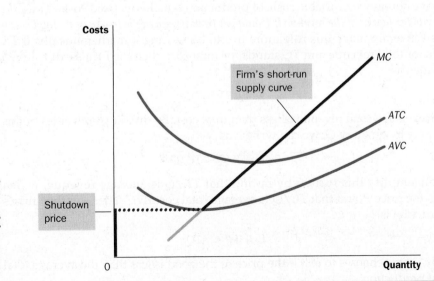

FIGURE 14.3

The Competitive Firm's Short-Run Supply Curve

In the short run, the competitive firm's supply curve is its marginal-cost curve (*MC*) above average variable cost (*AVC*). If the price falls below average variable cost, the firm is better off shutting down.

© 2018 Cengage Learning

The irrelevance of sunk costs is also important when making personal decisions. Imagine, for instance, that you place a $15 value on seeing a newly released movie. You buy a ticket for $10, but before entering the theatre, you lose the ticket. Should you buy another ticket? Or should you now go home and refuse to pay a total of $20 to see the movie? The answer is that you should buy another ticket. The benefit of seeing the movie ($15) still exceeds the opportunity cost (the $10 for the second ticket). The $10 you paid for the lost ticket is a sunk cost. As with spilt milk, there is no point in crying about it.

Staying open can be profitable, even when facilities are empty.

case study

Near-Empty Restaurants and Off-Season Miniature Golf

Have you ever walked into a restaurant for lunch and found it almost empty? Why, you might have asked, does the restaurant even bother to stay open? It might seem that the revenue from so few customers could not possibly cover the cost of running the restaurant.

In making the decision whether to open for lunch, a restaurant owner must keep in mind the distinction between fixed and variable costs. Many of a restaurant's costs—the rent, kitchen equipment, tables, plates, silverware, and so on—are fixed. Shutting down during lunch would not reduce these costs. In other words, these costs are sunk in the short run. When the owner is deciding whether to serve lunch, only the variable costs—the price of the additional food and the wages of the extra staff—are relevant. The owner shuts down the restaurant at lunchtime only if the revenue from the few lunchtime customers fails to cover the restaurant's variable costs.

An operator of a miniature-golf course in a summer resort community faces a similar decision. Because revenue varies substantially from season to season, the firm must decide when to open and when to close. Once again, the fixed costs—the costs of buying the land and building the course—are irrelevant. The miniature-golf course should be open for business only during those times of year when its revenue exceeds its variable costs. ■

14-2e The Firm's Long-Run Decision to Exit or Enter a Market

A firm's long-run decision to exit a market is similar to its shutdown decision. If the firm exits, it again will lose all revenue from the sale of its product, but now it will save not only its variable costs of production but also its fixed costs. Thus, *the firm exits the market if the revenue it would get from producing is less than its total costs.*

We can again make this rule more useful by writing it mathematically. If *TR* stands for total revenue and *TC* stands for total cost, then the firm's exit rule can be written as

$$\text{Exit if } TR < TC$$

The firm exits if total revenue is less than total cost. By dividing both sides of this inequality by quantity *Q*, we can write it as

$$\text{Exit if } TR/Q < TC/Q$$

We can simplify this further by noting that TR/Q is average revenue, which equals the price *P*, and that TC/Q is average total cost *ATC*. Therefore, the firm's exit criterion is

$$\text{Exit if } P < ATC$$

That is, a firm chooses to exit if the price of the good is less than the average total cost of production.

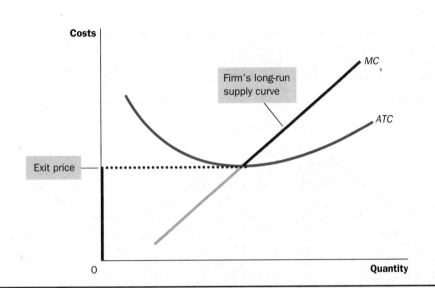

FIGURE 14.4

The Competitive Firm's Long-Run Supply Curve

In the long run, the competitive firm's supply curve is its marginal-cost curve (*MC*) above average total cost (*ATC*). If the price falls below average total cost, the firm is better off exiting the market.

A parallel analysis applies to an entrepreneur who is considering starting a firm. He will enter the market if starting a firm would be profitable, which occurs if the price of the good exceeds the average total cost of production. The entry rule is

$$\text{Enter if } P > ATC$$

The rule for entry is exactly the opposite of the rule for exit.

We can now describe a competitive firm's long-run profit-maximizing strategy. If the firm produces anything, it chooses the quantity at which marginal cost equals the price of the good. Yet if the price is less than the average total cost at that quantity, the firm chooses to exit (or not enter) the market. These results are illustrated in Figure 14.4. *The competitive firm's long-run supply curve is the portion of its marginal-cost curve that lies above average total cost.*

14-2f Measuring Profit in Our Graph for the Competitive Firm

As we study exit and entry, it is useful to analyze the firm's profit in more detail. Recall that profit equals total revenue (*TR*) minus total cost (*TC*):

$$\text{Profit} = TR - TC$$

We can rewrite this definition by multiplying and dividing the right-hand side by *Q*:

$$\text{Profit} = (TR/Q - TC/Q) \times Q$$

But note that TR/Q is average revenue, which is the price *P*, and TC/Q is average total cost *ATC*. Therefore,

$$\text{Profit} = (P - ATC) \times Q$$

This way of expressing the firm's profit allows us to measure profit in our graphs.

Panel (a) of Figure 14.5 shows a firm earning positive profit. As we have already discussed, the firm maximizes profit by producing the quantity at which

FIGURE 14.5

Profit as the Area between Price and Average Total Cost

The area of the shaded box between price and average total cost represents the firm's profit. The height of this box is price minus average total cost ($P - ATC$), and the width of the box is the quantity of output (Q). In panel (a), price is above average total cost, so the firm has positive profit. In panel (b), price is less than average total cost, so the firm has losses.

(a) A Firm with Profits

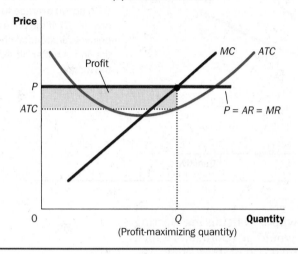

(b) A Firm with Losses

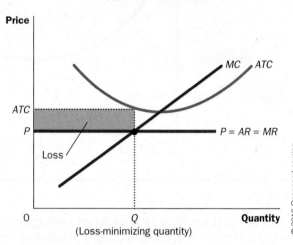

price equals marginal cost. Now look at the shaded rectangle. The height of the rectangle is $P - ATC$, the difference between price and average total cost. The width of the rectangle is Q, the quantity produced. Therefore, the area of the rectangle is $(P - ATC) \times Q$, which is the firm's profit.

Similarly, panel (b) of this figure shows a firm with losses (negative profit). In this case, maximizing profit means minimizing losses, a task accomplished once again by producing the quantity at which price equals marginal cost. Now consider the shaded rectangle. The height of the rectangle is $ATC - P$, and the width is Q. The area is $(ATC - P) \times Q$, which is the firm's loss. Because a firm in this situation is not making enough revenue on each unit to cover its average total cost, it would choose to exit the market in the long run.

QUICK Quiz   *How does the price faced by a profit-maximizing competitive firm compare to its marginal cost? Explain.* • *When does a profit-maximizing competitive firm decide to shut down? When does a profit-maximizing competitive firm decide to exit a market?*

14-3 The Supply Curve in a Competitive Market

Now that we have examined the supply decision of a single firm, we can discuss the supply curve for a market. There are two cases to consider. First, we examine a market with a fixed number of firms. Second, we examine a market in which the number of firms can change as old firms exit the market and new firms enter. Both cases are important, for each applies over a specific time horizon. Over short periods of time, it is often difficult for firms to enter and exit, so the assumption of a fixed number of firms is appropriate. But over long periods of time, the number of firms can adjust to changing market conditions.

14-3a The Short Run: Market Supply with a Fixed Number of Firms

Consider a market with 1000 identical firms. For any given price, each firm supplies a quantity of output so that its marginal cost equals the price, as shown in panel (a) of Figure 14.6. That is, as long as price is above average variable cost, each firm's marginal-cost curve is its supply curve. The quantity of output supplied to the market equals the sum of the quantities supplied by each of the 1000 individual firms. Thus, to derive the market supply curve, we add the quantity supplied by each firm in the market. As panel (b) of Figure 14.6 shows, because the firms are identical, the quantity supplied to the market is 1000 times the quantity supplied by each firm.

14-3b The Long Run: Market Supply with Entry and Exit

Now consider what happens if firms are able to enter or exit the market. Let's suppose that everyone has access to the same technology for producing the good and access to the same markets to buy the inputs into production. Therefore, all current and potential firms have the same cost curves.

Decisions about entry and exit in a market of this type depend on the incentives facing the owners of existing firms and the entrepreneurs who could start new firms. If firms already in the market are profitable, then new firms will have an incentive to enter the market. This entry will expand the number of firms, increase the quantity of the good supplied, and drive down prices and profits. Conversely, if firms in the market are making losses, then some existing firms will

FIGURE 14.6

Market Supply with a Fixed Number of Firms

In the short run, the number of firms in the market is fixed. As a result, the market supply curve, shown in panel (b), reflects the individual firms' marginal-cost curves, shown in panel (a). Here, in a market of 1000 firms, the quantity of output supplied to the market is 1000 times the quantity supplied by each firm.

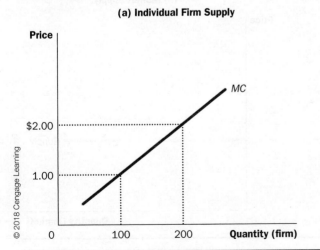

(a) Individual Firm Supply

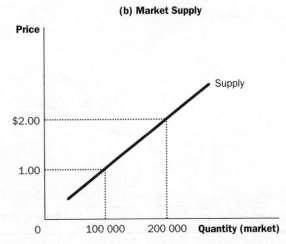

(b) Market Supply

© 2018 Cengage Learning

exit the market. Their exit will reduce the number of firms, decrease the quantity of the good supplied, and drive up prices and profits. *At the end of this process of entry and exit, firms that remain in the market must be making zero economic profit.*

Recall that we can write a firm's profits as

$$\text{Profit} = (P - ATC) \times Q$$

This equation shows that an operating firm has zero profit if and only if the price of the good equals the average total cost of producing that good. If price is above average total cost, profit is positive, which encourages new firms to enter. If price is less than average total cost, profit is negative, which encourages some firms to exit. *The process of entry and exit ends only when price and average total cost are driven to equality.*

This analysis has a surprising implication. We noted earlier in the chapter that competitive firms maximize profits by choosing a quantity at which price equals marginal cost. We just noted that free entry and exit forces price to equal average total cost. But if price is to equal both marginal cost and average total cost, these two measures of cost must equal each other. Marginal cost and average total cost are equal, however, only when the firm is operating at the minimum of average total cost. Recall from the preceding chapter that the level of production with lowest average total cost is called the firm's *efficient scale*. Therefore, *the long-run equilibrium of a competitive market with free entry and exit must have firms operating at their efficient scale.*

Panel (a) of Figure 14.7 shows a firm in such a long-run equilibrium. In this figure, price *P* equals marginal cost *MC*, so the firm is maximizing profits. Price also equals average total cost *ATC*, so profits are zero. New firms have no incentive to enter the market, and existing firms have no incentive to leave the market.

FIGURE 14.7

Market Supply with Entry and Exit

Firms will enter or exit the market until profit is driven to zero. Thus, in the long run, price equals the minimum of average total cost, as shown in panel (a). The number of firms adjusts to ensure that all demand is satisfied at this price. The long-run market supply curve is horizontal at this price, as shown in panel (b).

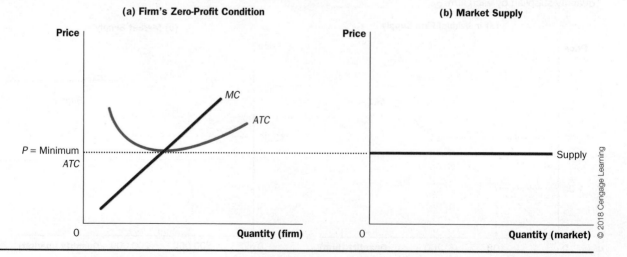

(a) Firm's Zero-Profit Condition

(b) Market Supply

© 2018 Cengage Learning

From this analysis of firm behaviour, we can determine the long-run supply curve for the market. In a market with free entry and exit, there is only one price consistent with zero profit—the minimum of average total cost. As a result, the long-run market supply curve must be horizontal at this price, as illustrated by the perfectly elastic supply curve in panel (b) of Figure 14.7. Any price above this level would generate profit, leading to entry and an increase in the total quantity supplied. Any price below this level would generate losses, leading to exit and a decrease in the total quantity supplied. Eventually, the number of firms in the market adjusts so that price equals the minimum of average total cost, and there are enough firms to satisfy all the demand at this price.

14-3c Why Do Competitive Firms Stay in Business If They Make Zero Profit?

At first, it might seem odd that competitive firms earn zero profit in the long run. After all, people start businesses to make a profit. If entry eventually drives profit to zero, there might seem to be little reason to stay in business.

To understand the zero-profit condition more fully, recall that profit equals total revenue minus total cost, and that total cost includes all the opportunity costs of the firm. In particular, total cost includes the time and money that the firm owners devote to the business. In the zero-profit equilibrium, the firm's revenue must compensate the owners for these opportunity costs.

Consider an example. Suppose that, to start his farm, a farmer had to invest $1 million, which otherwise he could have deposited in a bank and earned $50 000 a year in interest. In addition, he had to give up another job that would have paid him $30 000 a year. Then the farmer's opportunity cost of farming includes both the interest he could have earned and the forgone wages—a total of $80 000. Even if his profit is driven to zero, his revenue from farming compensates him for these opportunity costs.

Keep in mind that accountants and economists measure costs differently. As we discussed in the previous chapter, accountants keep track of explicit costs but not implicit costs. That is, they measure costs that require an outflow of money from the firm, but they do not include opportunity costs of production that do not involve an outflow of money. As a result, in the zero-profit equilibrium, economic profit is zero, but accounting profit is positive. Our farmer's accountant, for instance, would conclude that the farmer earned an accounting profit of $80 000, which is enough to keep the farmer in business.

14-3d A Shift in Demand in the Short Run and the Long Run

Now that we have a more complete understanding of how firms make supply decisions, we can better explain how markets respond to changes in demand. Because firms can enter and exit in the long run but not in the short run, the response of a market to a change in demand depends on the time horizon. To see this, let's trace the effects of a shift in demand over time.

Suppose the market for milk begins in long-run equilibrium. Firms are earning zero profit, so price equals the minimum of average total cost. Panel (a) of Figure 14.8 shows this situation. The long-run equilibrium is point A, the quantity sold in the market is Q_1, and the price is P_1.

Now suppose scientists discover that milk has miraculous health benefits. As a result, the quantity of milk demanded at every price increases, and the demand curve for milk shifts outward from D_1 to D_2, as in panel (b). The short-run

FIGURE 14.8

An Increase in Demand in the Short Run and Long Run

The market starts in a long-run equilibrium, shown as point A in panel (a). In this equilibrium, each firm makes zero profit, and the price equals the minimum average total cost. Panel (b) shows what happens in the short run when demand rises from D_1 to D_2. The equilibrium goes from point A to point B, price rises from P_1 to P_2, and the quantity sold in the market rises from Q_1 to Q_2. Because price now exceeds average total cost, firms make profits, which over time encourages new firms to enter the market. This entry shifts the short-run supply curve to the right from S_1 to S_2, as shown in panel (c). In the new long-run equilibrium, point C, price has returned to P_1 but the quantity sold has increased to Q_3. Profits are again zero, price is back to the minimum of average total cost, but the market has more firms to satisfy the greater demand.

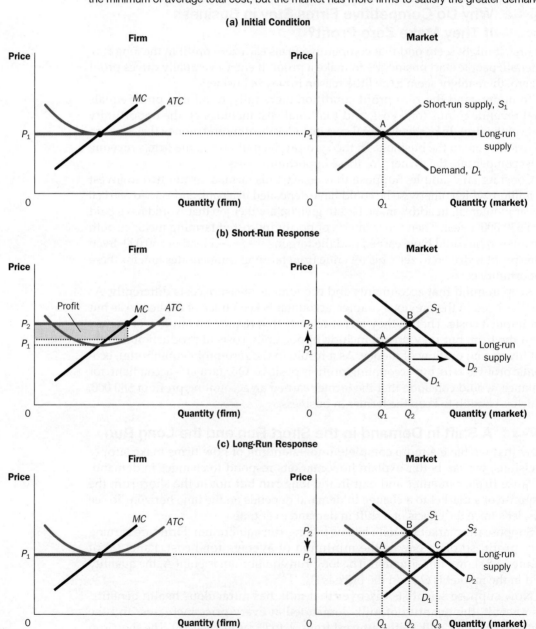

(a) Initial Condition

(b) Short-Run Response

(c) Long-Run Response

equilibrium moves from point A to point B; as a result, the quantity rises from Q_1 to Q_2, and the price rises from P_1 to P_2. All of the existing firms respond to the higher price by raising the amount produced. Because each firm's supply curve reflects its marginal-cost curve, how much each firm increases production is determined by the marginal-cost curve. In the new short-run equilibrium, the price of milk exceeds average total cost, so the firms are making positive profit.

Over time, the profit generated in this market encourages new firms to enter. Some farmers may switch to producing milk instead of other farm products, for example. As the number of firms grows, the quantity supplied at every price increases, the short-run supply curve shifts to the right from S_1 to S_2, as in panel (c), and this shift causes the price of milk to fall. Eventually, the price is driven back down to the minimum of average total cost, profits are zero, and firms stop entering. Thus, the market reaches a new long-run equilibrium, point C. The price of milk has returned to P_1, but the quantity produced has risen to Q_3. Each firm is again producing at its efficient scale, but because more firms are in the dairy business, the quantity of milk produced and sold is higher.

14-3e Why the Long-Run Supply Curve Might Slope Upward

So far we have seen that entry and exit can cause the long-run market supply curve to be perfectly elastic. The essence of our analysis is that there are a large number of potential entrants, each of which faces the same costs. As a result, the long-run market supply curve is horizontal at the minimum of average total cost. When the demand for the good increases, the long-run result is an increase in the number of firms and in the total quantity supplied, without any change in the price.

There are, however, two reasons why the long-run market supply curve might slope upward. The first is that some resources used in production may be available only in limited quantities. For example, consider the market for farm products. Anyone can choose to buy land and start a farm, but the quantity of land is limited. As more people become farmers, the price of farmland is bid up, which raises the costs of all farmers in the market. Thus, an increase in demand for farm products cannot induce an increase in quantity supplied without also inducing a rise in farmers' costs, which in turn means a rise in price. The result is a long-run market supply curve that is upward sloping, even with free entry into farming.

This case is illustrated in Figure 14.9. The initial equilibrium is at point A in both panels. In panel (a) at point A, each firm is maximizing profits by choosing a quantity where price equals marginal cost, and we are in a long-run equilibrium with the price P_1 equal to minimum average total cost and economic profits are zero. In panel (b) at point A, market demand equals short-run market supply. Now consider an increase in demand as discussed above, to D_2. As before, the new short-run equilibrium is at point B, with a price of P_2 and each firm earns short-run economic profits because this price is greater than average total cost. As firms enter the market in response to the existence of these positive profits, the short-run market supply curve begins to shift to the right.

Now, however, imagine that as new firms enter the market, the price of an input, say farmland, increases because entering firms demand land. This increase in the price of land shifts up the average total cost curve for all firms. The new long-run equilibrium occurs at point C at a price of P_3, where each firm is again maximizing profits by choosing a quantity where price equals marginal cost. Economic profits are again zero—and there is no further entry—because the equilibrium price is equal to the minimum of the new average-total-cost curve, ATC_2.

FIGURE 14.9

An Upward Sloping Long-Run Supply Curve

The market starts in long-run equilibrium at point A in both panels. In panel (a) at point A, each firm is maximizing profits by choosing a quantity where price equals marginal cost, and we are in a long-run equilibrium, with the price P_1 equal to average total cost and economic profits are zero. In panel (b) at point A, market demand equals short-run market supply. Panel (b) shows what happens in the short run as demand increases from D_1 to D_2. The short-run equilibrium goes from point A to point B, and the price rises from P_1 to P_2. Because the price exceeds average total costs, firms make profits, which over time attract entrants into the market. This entry shifts the short-run supply curve to the right. It also bids up the price of an input to the production of the good, say land, which shifts up the average total cost curve. In the new long-run equilibrium the price is P_3, which is equal to the minimum of the new long-run average-cost curve, ATC_2. Profits are again zero and there are more firms to satisfy the greater demand, but the new equilibrium price P_3 is higher than the original price P_1 because of the increase in average total costs associated with entry. This generates an upward sloping long-run supply curve, as shown in panel (b).

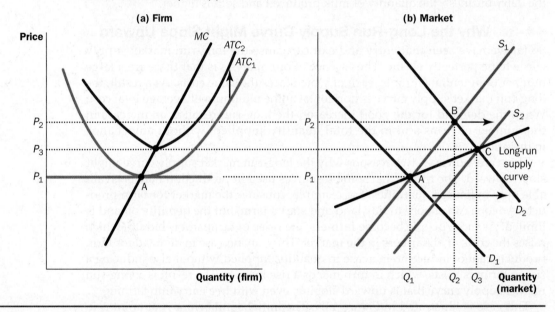

The new short-run supply curve is S_2. Because the entry of firms into the market drives up the price of land, shifting up the average-total-cost curve, the new long-run equilibrium price of P_3 is higher than original price of P_1, and the long-run supply curve is upward sloping, as illustrated in panel (b).

A second reason for an upward-sloping supply curve is that firms may have different costs. For example, consider the market for painters. Anyone can enter the market for painting services, but not everyone has the same costs. Costs vary in part because some people work faster than others and in part because some people have better alternative uses of their time than others. For any given price, those with lower costs are more likely to enter than those with higher costs. To increase the quantity of painting services supplied, additional entrants must be encouraged to enter the market. Because these new entrants have higher costs, the price must rise to make entry profitable for them. Thus, the long-run market supply curve for painting services slopes upward even with free entry into the market.

Notice that if firms have different costs, some firms earn profit even in the long run. In this case, the price in the market reflects the average total cost of the *marginal firm*—the firm that would exit the market if the price were any lower. This firm earns zero profit, but firms with lower costs earn positive profit. Entry does not eliminate this profit because would-be entrants have higher costs than firms already in the market. Higher-cost firms will enter only if the price rises, making the market profitable for them.

Thus, for these two reasons, the long-run supply curve in a market may be upward sloping rather than horizontal, indicating that a higher price is necessary to induce a larger quantity supplied. Nonetheless, the basic lesson about entry and exit remains true: *Because firms can enter and exit more easily in the long run than in the short run, the long-run supply curve is typically more elastic than the short-run supply curve.*

 QUICK Quiz *In the long run with free entry and exit, is the price in a market equal to marginal cost, average total cost, both, or neither? Explain with a diagram.*

14-4 Conclusion: Behind the Supply Curve

We have been discussing the behaviour of profit-maximizing firms that supply goods in perfectly competitive markets. You may recall from Chapter 1 that one of the ten principles of economics is that rational people think at the margin. This chapter has applied this idea to the competitive firm. Marginal analysis has given us a theory of the supply curve in a competitive market and, as a result, a deeper understanding of market outcomes.

We have learned that when you buy a good from a firm in a competitive market, you can be assured that the price you pay is close to the cost of producing that good. In particular, if firms are competitive and profit maximizing, the price of a good equals the marginal cost of making that good. In addition, if firms can freely enter and exit the market, the price also equals the lowest possible average total cost of production.

Although we have assumed throughout this chapter that firms are price takers, many of the tools developed here are also useful for studying firms in less competitive markets. In the next few chapters we will examine the behaviour of firms with market power. Marginal analysis will again be useful in analyzing these firms, but it will have quite different implications.

summary

- Because a competitive firm is a price taker, its revenue is proportional to the amount of output it produces. The price of the good equals both the firm's average revenue and its marginal revenue.

- To maximize profit, a firm chooses a quantity of output such that marginal revenue equals marginal cost. Because marginal revenue for a competitive firm equals the market price, the firm chooses quantity so that price equals marginal cost. Thus, the firm's marginal-cost curve is its supply curve.

- In the short run when a firm cannot recover its fixed costs, the firm will choose to shut down temporarily if the price of the good is less than average variable cost. In the long run when the firm can recover both fixed and variable costs, it will choose to exit if the price is less than average total cost.

- In a market with free entry and exit, profits are driven to zero in the long run. In this long-run equilibrium, all firms produce at the efficient scale, price equals the minimum of average total cost, and the number of firms adjusts to satisfy the quantity demanded at this price.

- Changes in demand have different effects over different time horizons. In the short run, an increase in demand raises prices and leads to profits, and a decrease in demand lowers prices and leads to losses. But if firms can freely enter and exit the market, then in the long run the number of firms adjusts to drive the market back to the zero-profit equilibrium.

KEY **concepts**

competitive market, *p. 302*
average revenue, *p. 304*

marginal revenue, *p. 304*

sunk cost, *p. 309*

QUESTIONS FOR **review**

1. What are the main characteristics of a competitive firm?

2. Explain the difference between a firm's revenue and its profit. Which do firms maximize?

3. Draw the cost curves for a typical firm. For a given price, explain how the firm chooses the level of output that maximizes profit. At that level of output, show on your graph the firm's total revenue and total costs.

4. Under what conditions will a firm shut down temporarily? Explain.

5. Under what conditions will a firm exit a market? Explain.

6. Does a firm's price equal marginal cost in the short run, in the long run, or both? Explain.

7. Does a firm's price equal the minimum of average total cost in the short run, in the long run, or both? Explain.

8. Are market supply curves typically more elastic in the short run or in the long run? Explain.

QUICK CHECK **multiple choice**

1. Which of the following occurs in the case of a perfectly competitive firm?
   a. chooses its price to maximize profits
   b. sets its price to undercut other firms selling similar products
   c. takes its price as given by market conditions
   d. picks the price that yields the largest market share

2. A competitive firm maximizes profit by choosing the quantity where which condition occurs?
   a. average total cost is at its minimum
   b. marginal cost equals the price
   c. average total cost equals the price
   d. marginal cost equals average total cost

3. A competitive firm's short-run supply curve is its _____ cost curve above its _____ cost curve.
   a. average total, marginal
   b. average variable, marginal
   c. marginal, average total
   d. marginal, average variable

4. If a profit-maximizing, competitive firm is producing a quantity at which marginal cost is between average variable cost and average total cost, it will do which of the following?
   a. keep producing in the short run but exit the market in the long run

   b. shut down in the short run but return to production in the long run
   c. shut down in the short run and exit the market in the long run
   d. keep producing both in the short run and in the long run

5. In the long-run equilibrium of a competitive market with identical firms, what is the relationship between price P, marginal cost MC, and average total cost ATC?
   a. $P > MC$ and $P > ATC$
   b. $P > MC$ and $P = ATC$
   c. $P = MC$ and $P > ATC$
   d. $P = MC$ and $P = ATC$

6. Pretzel stands in Ottawa are a perfectly competitive industry in long-run equilibrium. One day, the city starts imposing a $100 per month tax on each stand. How does this policy affect the number of pretzels consumed in the short run and in the long run?
   a. down in the short run, no change in the long run
   b. up in the short run, no change in the long run
   c. no change in the short run, down in the long run
   d. no change in the short run, up in the long run

PROBLEMS AND **applications**

1. You go out to the best restaurant in town and order a lobster dinner for $40. After eating half of the lobster, you realize that you are quite full. Your date wants you to finish your dinner, because you can't take it home and because "you've already paid for it." What should you do? Relate your answer to the material in this chapter.

2. When going to the supermarket, check out how many different companies produce toilet paper/eggs/cereals/milk. Which of these goods are more likely to exhibit the characteristics of competitive market?

3. Bob's lawn-mowing service is a profit-maximizing, competitive firm. Bob mows lawns for $27 each. His total cost each day is $280, of which $30 is a fixed cost. He mows 10 lawns a day. What can you say about Bob's short-run decision regarding shutdown and his long-run decision regarding exit?

4. Consider total cost and total revenue given in the table below:

Quantity	0	1	2	3	4	5	6	7
Total Cost	$8	$9	$10	$11	$13	$19	$27	$37
Total Revenue	0	8	16	24	32	40	48	56

a. Calculate profit for each quantity. How much should the firm produce to maximize profit?

b. Calculate marginal revenue and marginal cost for each quantity. Graph them. (*Hint:* Put the points between whole numbers. For example, the marginal cost between 2 and 3 should be graphed at 2.5.) At what quantity do these curves cross? How does this relate to your answer to part (a)?

c. Can you tell whether this firm is in a competitive industry? If so, can you tell whether the industry is in a long-run equilibrium?

5. In 2003, a single case in Alberta of bovine spongiform encephalopathy, also known as mad cow disease, temporarily shut down export markets for Canadian beef.

a. Using firm and industry diagrams, show the short-run effect of declining demand for Canadian beef due to the shutdown of its export markets. Label the diagram carefully and write out in words all of the changes that you can identify.

b. Although export markets eventually began to open up later that same year, the demand for Canadian beef remained low. On a new diagram, show the long-run effect of the declining demand. Explain in words.

6. Suppose the book-printing industry is competitive and begins in a long-run equilibrium.

a. Draw a diagram describing the typical firm in the industry.

b. Hi-Tech Printing Company invents a new process that sharply reduces the cost of printing books. What happens to Hi-Tech's profits and the price of books in the short run when Hi-Tech's patent prevents other firms from using the new technology?

c. What happens in the long run when the patent expires and other firms are free to use the technology?

7. Many small boats are made of fibreglass, which is derived from crude oil. Suppose that the price of oil rises.

a. Using diagrams, show what happens to the cost curves of an individual boat-making firm and to the market supply curve.

b. What happens to the profits of boat makers in the short run? What happens to the number of boat makers in the long run?

8. Suppose that the Canadian textile industry is competitive, and there is no international trade in textiles. In long-run equilibrium, the price per unit of cloth is $30.

a. Describe the equilibrium using graphs for the entire market and for an individual producer.

b. Now suppose that textile producers in other countries are willing to sell large quantities of cloth in Canada for only $25 per unit. Assuming that Canadian textile producers have large fixed costs, what is the short-run effect of these imports on the quantity produced by an individual producer? What is the short-run effect on profits? Illustrate your answer with a graph.

c. What is the long-run effect on the number of Canadian firms in the industry?

9. Suppose there are 1000 hot-pretzel stands operating in Toronto. Each stand has the usual U-shaped average-total-cost curve. The market demand curve for pretzels slopes downward, and the market for pretzels is in long-run competitive equilibrium.

a. Draw the current equilibrium, using graphs for the entire market and for an individual pretzel stand.

b. Now the city decides to restrict the number of pretzel-stand licences, reducing the number of stands to only 800. What effect will this action have on the market and on an individual stand that is still operating? Use graphs to illustrate your answer.

c. Suppose that the city decides to charge a licence fee for the 800 licences. How will this affect the number of pretzels sold by an individual stand, and the stand's profit? The city wants to raise as much revenue as possible and also wants to ensure that 800 pretzel stands remain in the city. By how much should the city increase the licence fee? Show the answer on your graph.

10. The market for apple pies in the city of Ectenia is competitive and has the following demand schedule:

Price	Quantity Demanded
$1	1200 pies
2	1100
3	1000
4	900
5	800
6	700
7	600
8	500
9	400
10	300
11	200
12	100
13	0

Each producer in the market has fixed costs of $9 and the following marginal cost:

Quantity	Marginal Cost
1 pie	$2
2	4
3	6
4	8
5	10
6	12

a. Compute each producer's total cost and average total cost for 1 to 6 pies.
b. The price of a pie is now $11. How many pies are sold? How many pies does each producer make? How many producers are there? How much profit does each producer earn?
c. Is the situation described in part (b) a long-run equilibrium? Why or why not?
d. Suppose that in the long run there is free entry and exit. How much profit does each producer earn in the long-run equilibrium? What is the market price and number of pies each producer makes? How many pies are sold? How many pie producers are operating?

11. Ball Bearings Inc. faces costs of production as follows:

Quantity	Total Fixed Costs	Total Variable Costs
0	$100	$0
1	100	50
2	100	70
3	100	90
4	100	140
5	100	200
6	100	360

a. Calculate the company's average fixed costs, average variable costs, average total costs, and marginal costs.
b. The price of a case of ball bearings is $50. Seeing that she can't make a profit, the chief executive officer (CEO) decides to shut down operations. What are the firm's profits/losses? Was this a wise decision? Explain.
c. Vaguely remembering his introductory economics course, the chief financial officer tells the CEO it is better to produce one case of ball bearings because marginal revenue equals marginal cost at that quantity. What are the firm's profits/losses at that level of production? Was this the best decision? Explain.

12. An industry currently has 100 firms, each of which has fixed costs of $16 and average variable costs as follows:

Quantity	Average Variable Cost
1	$1
2	2
3	3
4	4
5	5
6	6

a. Compute a firm's marginal cost and average total cost for each quantity from 1 to 6.
b. The equilibrium price is currently $10. How much does each firm produce? What is the total quantity supplied in the market?
c. In the long run, firms can enter and exit the market, and all entrants have the same costs as above. As this market makes the transition to its long-run equilibrium, will the price rise or fall? Will the quantity demanded rise or fall? Will the

quantity supplied by each firm rise or fall? Explain your answers.

d. Graph the long-run supply curve for this market, with specific numbers on the axes as relevant.

13. A profit-maximizing firm in a competitive market is currently producing 100 units of output. It has average revenue of $10, average total cost of $8, and fixed costs of $200.
   a. What is profit?
   b. What is marginal cost?
   c. What is average variable cost?
   d. Is the efficient scale of the firm more than, less than, or exactly 100 units?

14. The market for fertilizer is perfectly competitive. Firms in the market are producing output, but are currently experiencing economic losses.
   a. How does the price of fertilizer compare to the average total cost, the average variable cost, and the marginal cost of producing fertilizer?
   b. Draw two graphs, side by side, illustrating the present situation for the typical firm and in the market.
   c. Assuming there is no change in demand or in the firms' cost curves, explain what will happen in the long run to the price of fertilizer, marginal cost, average total cost, the quantity supplied by each firm, and the total quantity supplied to the market.

15. Analyze the two following scenarios for firms in competitive markets:
   a. Suppose that $TC = 100 + 15Q$, where TC is total cost and Q is the quantity produced. What is the minimum price necessary for this firm to produce any output in the short run?
   b. Suppose that $MC = 4Q$, where MC is marginal cost. The perfectly competitive firm maximizes profits by producing 10 units of output. At what price does it sell these units?

16. There is a single production technology available to firms that might choose to operate in the market for hammers. Suppose all firms have access to a technology that gives the following total cost (TC) for producing a quantity (Q) of hammers: $TC = 3 + 3Q^2$, for any $Q > 0$, but the costs of production are equal to zero if $Q = 0$. The marginal cost of producing hammers is $MC = 6Q$.
   a. What is the equation for the average variable cost (AVC) and the average total cost (ATC)?
   b. If the price of hammers is P, find the supply curve of a single firm, for all possible prices $P > 0$. For the following two parts suppose that there is free entry into the hammer market, and the cost functions of firms don't change. The market demand for hammers is given by $Q^D = 600 - 50P$.
   c. The market demand for hammers is given by $Q^D = 600 - 50P$. What is the long-run equilibrium price in the market and how much does each firm produce at this price?
   d. How many firms in total are in the market?

Monopoly

In this chapter, you will ...

1 Learn why some markets have only one seller

2 Analyze how a monopoly determines the quantity to produce and the price to charge

3 See how the monopoly's decisions affect economic well-being

4 See why monopolies try to charge different prices to different customers

5 Consider the various public policies aimed at solving the problem of monopoly

If you own a personal computer, it probably uses some version of Windows, the operating system sold by Microsoft Corporation. When Microsoft first designed Windows many years ago, it applied for and received a copyright from the government. The copyright gives Microsoft the exclusive right to make and sell copies of the Windows operating system. So if a person wants to buy a copy of Windows, she has little choice but to give Microsoft the approximately $100 that the firm has decided to charge for its product. Microsoft is said to have a *monopoly* in the market for Windows.

Microsoft's business decisions are not well described by the model of firm behaviour we developed in the previous chapter. In that chapter we analyzed competitive markets, in which many firms offer essentially identical products, so each firm has little influence over the price it receives. By contrast, a monopoly such as Microsoft has no close competitors and, therefore, has the power to influence the market price of its product. While a competitive firm is a *price taker,* a monopoly firm is a *price maker.*

In this chapter, we examine the implications of this market power. We will see that market power alters the relationship between a firm's costs and the price at which it sells its product. A competitive firm takes the price of its output as given by the market and then chooses the quantity it will supply so that price equals marginal cost. By contrast, a monopoly charges a price that exceeds marginal cost. Sure enough, we observe this practice in the case of Microsoft's Windows. The marginal cost of Windows—the extra cost that Microsoft would incur by allowing another user—is minuscule. The market price of Windows is many times its marginal cost.

It is not surprising that monopolies charge high prices for their products. Customers of monopolies might seem to have little choice but to pay whatever the monopoly charges. But, if so, why does a copy of Windows not cost $1000? Or $10 000? The reason is that if Microsoft were to set the price that high, fewer people would buy the product. People would buy fewer computers, switch to other operating systems, or make illegal copies. A monopoly firm can control the price of the good it sells, but because a high price reduces the quantity that its customers buy, the monopoly's profits are not unlimited.

As we examine the production and pricing decisions of monopolies, we also consider the implications of monopoly for society as a whole. Monopoly firms, like competitive firms, aim to maximize profit. But this goal has very different ramifications for competitive and monopoly firms. As we first saw in Chapter 7, self-interested buyers and sellers in competitive markets are unwittingly led by an invisible hand to promote general economic well-being. By contrast, because monopoly firms are unchecked by competition, the outcome in a market with a monopoly is often not in the best interest of society.

One of the ten principles of economics discussed in Chapter 1 is that governments can sometimes improve market outcomes. The analysis in this chapter will shed more light on this principle. As we examine the problems that monopolies raise for society, we discuss the various ways in which government policymakers might respond to these problems. The U.S. government, for example, keeps a close eye on Microsoft's business decisions. In 1994, it prevented Microsoft from buying Intuit, a leading seller of personal finance software, on the grounds that combining the two firms would concentrate too much market power in one firm. Similarly, in 1998 the U.S. Justice Department objected when Microsoft started integrating its Internet browser into its Windows operating system, claiming that this addition would extend the firm's market power into new areas. In recent years, regulators in the United States and abroad have shifted their focus to firms with growing market power, such as Google and Samsung, but continue to monitor Microsoft's compliance with the antitrust laws.

15-1 Why Monopolies Arise

monopoly
a firm that is the sole seller of a product without close substitutes

A firm is a **monopoly** if it is the sole seller of its product and if its product does not have any close substitutes. The fundamental cause of monopoly is *barriers to entry*: A monopoly remains the only seller in its market because other firms cannot enter the market and compete with it. Barriers to entry, in turn, have three main sources:

1. *Monopoly resources:* A key resource is owned by a single firm.
2. *Government regulation:* The government gives a single firm the exclusive right to produce some good or service.
3. *The production process:* A single firm can produce output at a lower cost than can a large number of producers.

Let's briefly discuss each of these.

15-1a Monopoly Resources

The simplest way for a monopoly to arise is for a single firm to own a key resource. For example, consider the market for water in an early Canadian small town. If dozens of town residents have working wells, the competitive model discussed in the preceding chapter describes the behaviour of sellers. As a result of competition among water suppliers, the price of a litre of water is driven to equal the marginal cost of pumping an extra litre. But if there is only one well in town and it is impossible to get water from anywhere else, then the owner of the well has a monopoly on water. Not surprisingly, the monopolist has much greater market power than any single firm in a competitive market. In the case of a necessity like water, the monopolist could command quite a high price, even if the marginal cost is low.

The tsunami that hit Japan in 2011 revealed how important monopoly ownership of key resources can be in the integrated global supply chain network. Just as some financial institutions proved "too big to fail" in the 2008 financial crisis, some Japanese suppliers were shown to be too crucial to do without. Two firms, Mitsubishi Gas Chemical Company and Hitachi Chemical Company, control about 90 percent of the market for a specialty resin used to bond parts of microchips that go into smartphones and other devices. The compact battery in Apple's iPhones relies on a polymer made by Kureha Corporation, which holds 70 percent of the market. These firms exhibit substantial market power over key inputs into important consumer devices, which is reflected in their high prices. Moreover, all three suffered significant damage in the tsunami, throwing the worldwide supply chain into disarray.

Although exclusive ownership of a key resource is a potential cause of monopoly, in practice monopolies rarely arise for this reason. Economies are large, and resources are owned by many people. The natural scope of many markets is worldwide, because goods are often traded internationally. There are, therefore, few examples of firms that own a resource for which there are no close substitutes.

15-1b Government-Created Monopolies

In many cases, monopolies arise because the government has given one person or firm the exclusive right to sell some good or service. Sometimes the monopoly arises from the sheer political clout of the would-be monopolist. Kings, for example, once granted exclusive business licences to their friends and allies. At other times, the government grants a monopoly because doing so is viewed to be in the public interest.

The patent and copyright laws are two important examples. When a pharmaceutical company discovers a new drug, it can apply to the government for a patent. If the government deems the drug to be truly original, it approves the patent, which gives the company the exclusive right to manufacture and sell the drug for 20 years. Similarly, when a novelist finishes a book, she can copyright it. The copyright is a government guarantee that no one can print and sell the work without the author's permission. The copyright makes the novelist a monopolist in the sale of her novel.

The effects of patent and copyright laws are easy to see. Because these laws give one producer a monopoly, they lead to higher prices than would occur under competition. But by allowing these monopoly producers to charge higher prices and earn higher profits, the laws also encourage some desirable behaviour. Drug companies are allowed to be monopolists in the drugs they discover to encourage research. Authors are allowed to be monopolists in the sale of their books to encourage them to write more and better books.

Thus, the laws governing patents and copyrights have benefits and costs. The benefits of the patent and copyright laws are the increased incentive for creative activity. This benefits are offset, to some extent, by the costs of monopoly pricing, which we examine fully later in this chapter.

15-1c Natural Monopolies

An industry is a **natural monopoly** when a single firm can supply a good or service to an entire market at a lower cost than could two or more firms. A natural monopoly arises when there are economies of scale over the relevant range of output. Figure 15.1 shows the average total costs of a firm with economies of scale. In this case, a single firm can produce any amount of output at least cost. That is, for any given amount of output, a larger number of firms lead to less output per firm and higher average total cost.

An example of a natural monopoly is the distribution of water. To provide water to residents of a town, a firm must build a network of pipes throughout the

natural monopoly
a monopoly that arises because a single firm can supply a good or service to an entire market at a smaller cost than could two or more firms

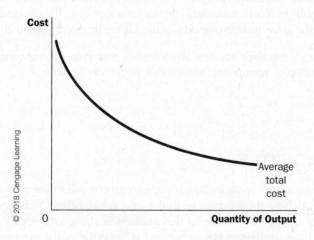

FIGURE 15.1

Economies of Scale as a Cause of Monopoly

When a firm's average-total-cost curve continually declines, the firm has what is called a *natural monopoly*. In this case, when production is divided among more firms, each firm produces less, and average total cost rises. As a result, a single firm can produce any given amount at the smallest cost.

© 2018 Cengage Learning

town. If two or more firms were to compete in the provision of this service, each firm would have to pay the fixed cost of building a network. Thus, the average total cost of water is lowest if a single firm serves the entire market.

We saw other examples of natural monopolies when we discussed public goods and common resources in Chapter 11. We noted that *club goods* are excludable but not rival in consumption. An example is a bridge used so infrequently that it is never congested. The bridge is excludable because a toll collector can prevent someone from using it. The bridge is not rival in consumption because use of the bridge by one person does not diminish the ability of others to use it. Because there is a large fixed cost of building the bridge and a negligible marginal cost of additional users, the average total cost of a trip across the bridge (the total cost divided by the number of trips) falls as the number of trips rises. Hence, the bridge is a natural monopoly.

When a firm is a natural monopoly, it is less concerned about new entrants eroding its monopoly power. Normally, a firm has trouble maintaining a monopoly position without ownership of a key resource or protection from government. The monopolist's profit attracts entrants into the market, and these entrants make the market more competitive. By contrast, entering a market in which another firm has a natural monopoly is unattractive. Would-be entrants know that they cannot achieve the same low costs that the monopolist enjoys because, after entry, each firm would have a smaller piece of the market.

In some cases, the size of the market is one determinant of whether an industry is a natural monopoly. Again, consider a bridge across a river. When the population is small, the bridge may be a natural monopoly. A single bridge can satisfy the entire demand for trips across the river at lowest cost. Yet as the population grows and the bridge becomes congested, satisfying the entire demand may require two or more bridges across the same river. Thus, as a market expands, a natural monopoly can evolve into a competitive market.

An example of a near-monopoly bridge relevant to Canada is the Ambassador Bridge between Windsor, Ontario, and Detroit, Michigan. It is the busiest international border crossing in North America, accounting for over 20 percent of the trade flow between Canada and the United States, and it is owned and operated by a private U.S. company, Detroit International Bridge Company. While there is some competition for border crossing in the area (for example, the Detroit–Windsor Tunnel, which is jointly owned by the two cities), the high volume of traffic and the relative lack of competition has allowed the owner of the Ambassador Bridge to charge the highest bridge tolls in North America. The near monopoly of the Ambassador Bridge will end when the government-owned Gordie Howe Bridge opens in 2020.

 What are the three reasons why a market might have a monopoly? • Give two examples of monopolies, and explain the reason for each.

15-2 How Monopolies Make Production and Pricing Decisions

Now that we know how monopolies arise, we can consider how a monopoly firm decides how much of its product to make and what price to charge for it. The analysis of monopoly behaviour in this section is the starting point for evaluating whether monopolies are desirable and what policies the government might pursue in monopoly markets.

15-2a Monopoly versus Competition

The key difference between a competitive firm and a monopoly is the monopoly's ability to influence the price of its output. A competitive firm is small relative to the market in which it operates and, therefore, has no power to influence the price of its output. It takes the price as given by market conditions. By contrast, because a monopoly is the sole producer in its market, it can alter the price of its good by adjusting the quantity it supplies to the market.

One way to view this difference between a competitive firm and a monopoly is to consider the demand curve that each firm faces. When we analyzed profit maximization by competitive firms in the preceding chapter, we drew the market price as a horizontal line. Because a competitive firm can sell as much or as little as it wants at this price, the competitive firm faces a horizontal demand curve, as in panel (a) of Figure 15.2. In effect, because the competitive firm sells a product with many perfect substitutes (the products of all the other firms in its market), the demand curve that any one firm faces is perfectly elastic.

By contrast, because a monopoly is the sole producer in its market, its demand curve is the market demand curve. Thus, the monopolist's demand curve slopes downward for all the usual reasons, as in panel (b) of Figure 15.2. If the monopolist raises the price of its good, consumers buy less of it. Looked at another way, if the monopolist reduces the quantity of output it sells, the price of its output increases.

The market demand curve provides a constraint on a monopoly's ability to profit from its market power. A monopolist would prefer, if it were possible, to charge a high price and sell a large quantity at that high price. The market demand curve makes that outcome impossible. In particular, the market demand curve describes the combinations of price and quantity that are available to a monopoly

---

FIGURE 15.2

Demand Curves for Competitive and Monopoly Firms

Because competitive firms are price takers, they in effect face horizontal demand curves, as in panel (a). Because a monopoly firm is the sole producer in its market, it faces the downward-sloping market demand curve, as in panel (b). As a result, the monopoly has to accept a lower price if it wants to sell more output.

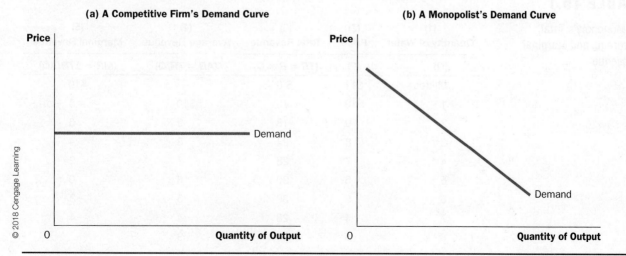

© 2018 Cengage Learning

firm. By adjusting the quantity produced (or equivalently, the price charged), the monopolist can choose any point on the demand curve, but it cannot choose a point off the demand curve.

What price and quantity of output will the monopolist choose? As with competitive firms, we assume that the monopolist's goal is to maximize profit. Because the firm's profit is total revenue minus total costs, our next task in explaining monopoly behaviour is to examine a monopolist's revenue.

15-2b A Monopoly's Revenue

Consider a town with a single producer of water. Table 15.1 shows how the monopoly's revenue might depend on the amount of water produced.

Columns (1) and (2) show the monopolist's demand schedule. If the monopolist produces 1 L of water, it can sell that litre for $10. If it produces 2 L, it must lower the price to $9 in order to sell both litres. And if it produces 3 L, it must lower the price to $8. And so on. If you graphed these two columns of numbers, you would get a typical downward-sloping demand curve.

Column (3) of the table presents the monopolist's *total revenue*. It equals the quantity sold (from column (1)) times the price (from column (2)). Column (4) computes the firm's *average revenue*, the amount of revenue the firm receives per unit sold. We compute average revenue by taking the number for total revenue in column (3) and dividing it by the quantity of output in column (1). As we discussed in the previous chapter, average revenue always equals the price of the good. This is true for monopolists as well as for competitive firms.

Column (5) of Table 15.1 computes the firm's *marginal revenue*, the amount of revenue that the firm receives for each additional unit of output. We compute marginal revenue by taking the change in total revenue when output increases by 1 unit. For example, when the firm is producing 3 L of water, it receives total revenue of $24. Raising production to 4 L increases total revenue to $28. Thus, marginal revenue is $28 minus $24, or $4.

Table 15.1 shows a result that is important for understanding monopoly behaviour: *A monopolist's marginal revenue is always less than the price of its good.*

TABLE 15.1

A Monopoly's Total, Average, and Marginal Revenue

(1) Quantity of Water	(2) Price	(3) Total Revenue	(4) Average Revenue	(5) Marginal Revenue
(Q)	(P)	(TR = P × Q)	(AR = TR/Q)	(MR = ΔTR/ΔQ)
0 litres	$11	$ 0	–	$10
1	10	10	$10	8
2	9	18	9	6
3	8	24	8	4
4	7	28	7	2
5	6	30	6	0
6	5	30	5	−2
7	4	28	4	−4
8	3	24	3	

For example, if the firm raises production of water from 3 to 4 L, it will increase total revenue by only $4, even though it will be able to sell each litre for $7. For a monopoly, marginal revenue is lower than price because a monopoly faces a downward-sloping demand curve. To increase the amount sold, a monopoly firm must lower the price of its good. Hence, to sell the fourth litre of water, the monopolist must get $1 less revenue for each of the first three litres. This $3 loss accounts for the difference between the price of the fourth litre ($7) and the marginal revenue of that fourth litre ($4).

Marginal revenue for monopolies is very different from marginal revenue for competitive firms. When a monopoly increases the amount it sells, it has two effects on total revenue ($P \times Q$):

1. *The output effect:* More output is sold, so Q is higher, which tends to increase total revenue.
2. *The price effect:* The price falls, so P is lower, which tends to decrease total revenue.

Because a competitive firm can sell all it wants at the market price, there is no price effect. When it increases production by 1 unit, it receives the market price for that unit, and it does not receive any less for the units it was already selling. That is, because the competitive firm is a price taker, its marginal revenue equals the price of its good. By contrast, when a monopoly increases production by 1 unit, it must reduce the price it charges for every unit it sells, and this cut in price reduces revenue on the units it was already selling. As a result, a monopoly's marginal revenue is less than its price.

Figure 15.3 graphs the demand curve and the marginal-revenue curve for a monopoly firm. (Because the firm's price equals its average revenue, the demand curve is also the average-revenue curve.) These two curves always start at the same point on the vertical axis because the marginal revenue of the first unit sold equals the price of the good. But for the reason we just discussed, the monopolist's marginal revenue on all units after the first is less than the price of the good. Thus, a monopoly's marginal-revenue curve lies below its demand curve.

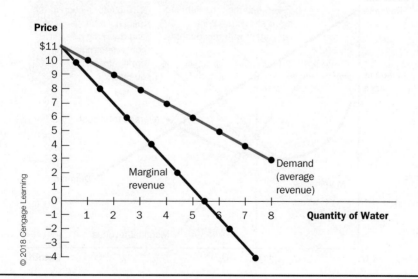

FIGURE 15.3

Demand and Marginal-Revenue Curves for a Monopoly

The demand curve shows how the quantity affects the price of the good. The marginal-revenue curve shows how the firm's revenue changes when the quantity increases by 1 unit. Because the price on *all* units sold must fall if the monopoly increases production, marginal revenue is always less than the price.

© 2018 Cengage Learning

You can see in the figure (as well as in Table 15.1) that marginal revenue can even become negative. Marginal revenue is negative when the price effect on revenue is greater than the output effect. In this case, when the firm produces an extra unit of output, the price falls by enough to cause the firm's total revenue to decline, even though the firm is selling more units.

15-2c Profit Maximization

Now that we have considered the revenue of a monopoly firm, we are ready to examine how such a firm maximizes profit. Recall from Chapter 1 that one of the ten principles of economics is that rational people think at the margin. This lesson is as true for monopolists as it is for competitive firms. Here we apply the logic of marginal analysis to the monopolist's decision about how much to produce.

Figure 15.4 graphs the demand curve, the marginal-revenue curve, and the cost curves for a monopoly firm. All these curves should seem familiar: The demand and marginal-revenue curves are like those in Figure 15.3, and the cost curves are like those we encountered in the last two chapters. These curves contain all the information we need to determine the level of output that a profit-maximizing monopolist will choose.

Suppose, first, that the firm is producing at a low level of output, such as Q_1. In this case, marginal cost is less than marginal revenue. If the firm increased production by 1 unit, the additional revenue would exceed the additional costs, and profit would rise. Thus, when marginal cost is less than marginal revenue, the firm can increase profit by producing more units.

A similar argument applies at high levels of output, such as Q_2. In this case, marginal cost is greater than marginal revenue. If the firm reduced production by 1 unit, the costs saved would exceed the revenue lost. Thus, if marginal cost is greater than marginal revenue, the firm can raise profit by reducing production.

In the end, the firm adjusts its level of production until the quantity reaches Q_{MAX}, at which marginal revenue equals marginal cost. *Thus, the monopolist's profit-maximizing*

FIGURE 15.4

Profit Maximization for a Monopoly

A monopoly maximizes profit by choosing the quantity at which marginal revenue equals marginal cost (point A). It then uses the demand curve to find the price that will induce consumers to buy that quantity (point B).

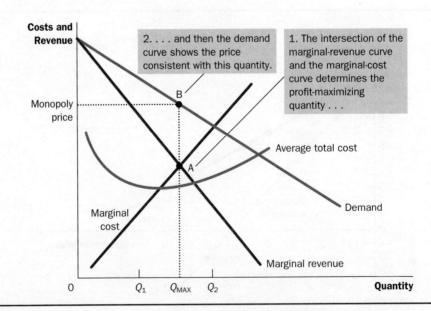

FYI Why a Monopoly Does Not Have a Supply Curve

You may have noticed that we have analyzed the price in a monopoly market using the market demand curve and the firm's cost curves. We have not made any mention of the market supply curve. By contrast, when we analyzed prices in competitive markets beginning in Chapter 4, the two most important words were always *supply* and *demand*.

What happened to the supply curve? Although monopoly firms make decisions about what quantity to supply (in the way described in this chapter), a monopoly does not have a supply curve. A supply curve tells us the quantity that firms choose to supply at any given price. This concept makes sense when we are analyzing competitive firms, which are price takers. But a monopoly firm is a price maker, not a price taker. It is not meaningful to ask what amount such a firm would produce at any price because the firm sets the price at the same time as it chooses the quantity to supply.

Indeed, the monopolist's decision about how much to supply is impossible to separate from the demand curve it faces. The shape of the demand curve determines the shape of the marginal-revenue curve, which in turn determines the monopolist's profit-maximizing quantity. In a competitive market, supply decisions can be analyzed without knowing the demand curve, but that is not true in a monopoly market. Therefore, we never talk about a monopoly's supply curve.

quantity of output is determined by the intersection of the marginal-revenue curve and the marginal-cost curve. In Figure 15.4, this intersection occurs at point A.

You might recall from the previous chapter that competitive firms also choose the quantity of output at which marginal revenue equals marginal cost. In following this rule for profit maximization, competitive firms and monopolies are alike. But there is also an important difference between these types of firms: The marginal revenue of a competitive firm equals its price, whereas the marginal revenue of a monopoly is less than its price. That is,

$$\text{For a competitive firm: } P = MR = MC$$
$$\text{For a monopoly firm: } \quad P > MR = MC$$

The equality of marginal revenue and marginal cost determines the profit-maximizing quantity for both types of firms. What differs is how the price is related to marginal revenue and marginal cost.

How does the monopoly find the profit-maximizing price for its product? The demand curve answers this question because the demand curve relates the amount that customers are willing to pay to the quantity sold. Thus, after the monopoly firm chooses the quantity of output that equates marginal revenue and marginal cost, it uses the demand curve to find the highest price it can charge for that quantity. In Figure 15.4, the profit-maximizing price is found at point B.

We can now see a key difference between markets with competitive firms and markets with a monopoly firm: *In competitive markets, price equals marginal cost. In monopolized markets, price exceeds marginal cost.* As we will see in a moment, this finding is crucial to understanding the social cost of monopoly.

15-2d A Monopoly's Profit

How much profit does the monopoly make? To see the monopoly's profit, recall that profit equals total revenue (*TR*) minus total costs (*TC*):

$$\text{Profit} = TR - TC$$

FIGURE 15.5

The Monopolist's Profit

The area of the box BCDE equals the profit of the monopoly firm. The height of the box (BC) is price minus average total cost, which equals profit per unit sold. The width of the box (DC) is the number of units sold.

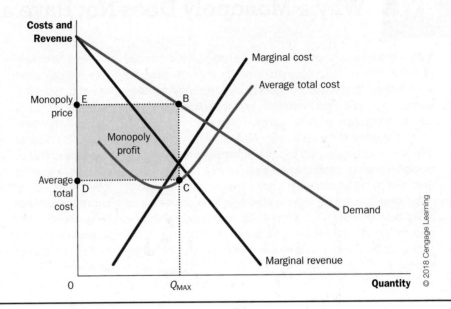

We can rewrite this as

$$\text{Profit} = (TR/Q - TC/Q) \times Q$$

TR/Q is average revenue, which equals the price P, and TC/Q is average total cost ATC. Therefore,

$$\text{Profit} = (P - ATC) \times Q$$

This equation for profit (which also holds for competitive firms) allows us to measure the monopolist's profit in our graph.

Consider the shaded box in Figure 15.5. The height of the box (the segment BC) is price minus average total cost, $P - ATC$, which is the profit on the typical unit sold. The width of the box (the segment DC) is the quantity sold, Q_{MAX}. Therefore, the area of this box is the monopoly firm's total profit.

case study Monopoly Drugs versus Generic Drugs

According to our analysis, prices are determined differently in monopolized markets and competitive markets. A natural place to test this theory is the market for pharmaceutical drugs because this market takes on both market structures. When a firm discovers a new drug, patent laws give the firm a monopoly on the sale of that drug. But eventually the firm's patent runs out, and any company can make and sell the drug. At that time, the market switches from being monopolistic to being competitive.

What should happen to the price of a drug when the patent runs out? Figure 15.6 shows the market for a typical drug. In this figure, the marginal cost of producing the drug is constant. (This is approximately true for many drugs.) During the life of the patent, the monopoly firm maximizes profit by producing the quantity at which marginal revenue equals marginal cost and charging a price

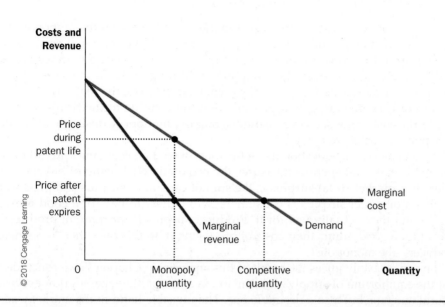

FIGURE 15.6

The Market for Drugs

When a patent gives a firm a monopoly over the sale of a drug, the firm charges the monopoly price, which is well above the marginal cost of making the drug. When the patent on a drug runs out, new firms enter the market, making it more competitive. As a result, the price falls from the monopoly price to marginal cost.

well above marginal cost. But when the patent runs out, the profit from making the drug should encourage new firms to enter the market. As the market becomes more competitive, the price should fall to equal marginal cost.

Experience is, in fact, consistent with our theory. When the patent on a drug expires, other companies quickly enter and begin selling generic products that are chemically identical to the former monopolist's brand-name product. Just as our analysis predicts, the price of the competitively produced generic drug is well below the price that the monopolist was charging.

The expiration of a patent, however, does not cause the monopolist to lose all of its market power. Some consumers remain loyal to the brand-name drug, perhaps out of fear that the new generic drugs are not actually the same as the drug they have been using for years. As a result, the former monopolist can continue to charge a price above the price charged by its new competitors.

For example, one of the top-selling brand-name prescription drugs on the market in Canada is the cholesterol-lowering drug Lipitor. Although the price varies by province, a one-month supply costs about $85. The generic equivalent, Atorvastatin, which is the same medicine, sells for about $46. This price differential can persist because some consumers are not convinced that the two pills are perfect substitutes. While it is clear that the generic equivalent is much cheaper, many analysts have found that generic drug prices in Canada are much higher than they are in other countries. This is because several factors, including some government policies, have restricted the amount of competition between generic drug manufacturers in Canada, where the market is dominated by two large companies, Apotex and Teva (formerly Teva Novopharm). ■

Explain how a monopolist chooses the quantity of output to produce and the price to charge.

15-3 The Welfare Cost of Monopoly

Is monopoly a good way to organize a market? We have seen that a monopoly, in contrast to a competitive firm, charges a price above marginal cost. From the standpoint of consumers, this high price makes monopoly undesirable. At the same time, however, the monopoly is earning profit from charging this high price. From the standpoint of the owners of the firm, the high price makes monopoly very desirable. Is it possible that the benefits to the firm's owners exceed the costs imposed on consumers, making monopoly desirable from the standpoint of society as a whole?

We can answer this question using the tools of welfare economics. Recall from Chapter 7 that total surplus measures the economic well-being of buyers and sellers in a market. Total surplus is the sum of consumer surplus and producer surplus. Consumer surplus is consumers' willingness to pay for a good minus the amount they actually pay for it. Producer surplus is the amount producers receive for a good minus their costs of producing it. In this case, there is a single producer—the monopolist.

You can probably guess the result of this analysis. In Chapter 7, we concluded that the equilibrium of supply and demand in a competitive market is not only a natural outcome but also a desirable one. The invisible hand of the market leads to an allocation of resources that makes total surplus as large as it can be. Because a monopoly leads to an allocation of resources different from that in a competitive market, the outcome must, in some way, fail to maximize total economic well-being.

15-3a The Deadweight Loss

We begin by considering what the monopoly firm would do if it were run by a benevolent social planner. The social planner cares not only about the profit earned by the firm's owners but also about the benefits received by the firm's consumers. The planner tries to maximize total surplus, which equals producer surplus (profit) plus consumer surplus. Keep in mind that total surplus equals the value of the good to consumers minus the costs of making the good incurred by the monopoly producer.

Figure 15.7 analyzes how a benevolent social planner would choose the monopoly's level of output. The demand curve reflects the value of the good to consumers, as measured by their willingness to pay for it. The marginal-cost curve reflects the costs of the monopolist. *Thus, the socially efficient quantity is found where the demand curve and the marginal-cost curve intersect.* Below this quantity, the value to consumers exceeds the marginal cost of providing the good, so increasing output would raise total surplus. Above this quantity, the marginal cost exceeds the value to consumers, so decreasing output would raise total surplus. At the optimal quantity, the value of an extra unit to consumers exactly equals the marginal cost of production.

If the social planner were running the monopoly, the firm could achieve this efficient outcome by charging the price found at the intersection of the demand and marginal-cost curves. Thus, like a competitive firm and unlike a profit-maximizing monopoly, a social planner would charge a price equal to marginal cost. Because this price would give consumers an accurate signal about the cost of producing the good, consumers would buy the efficient quantity.

We can evaluate the welfare effects of monopoly by comparing the level of output that the monopolist chooses to the level of output that a social planner

FIGURE 15.7

The Efficient Level of Output

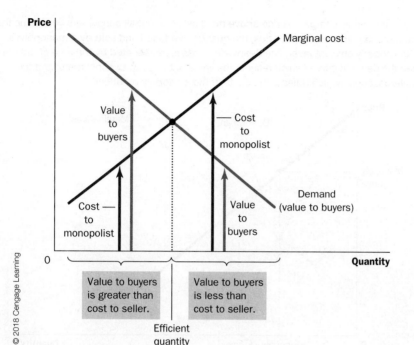

A benevolent social planner who wanted to maximize total surplus in the market would choose the level of output where the demand curve and marginal-cost curve intersect. Below this level, the value of the good to the marginal buyer (as reflected in the demand curve) exceeds the marginal cost of making the good. Above this level, the value to the marginal buyer is less than marginal cost.

would choose. As we have seen, the monopolist chooses to produce and sell the quantity of output at which the marginal-revenue and marginal-cost curves intersect; the social planner would choose the quantity at which the demand and marginal-cost curves intersect. Figure 15.8 shows the comparison. *The monopolist produces less than the socially efficient quantity of output.*

We can also view the inefficiency of monopoly in terms of the monopolist's price. Because the market demand curve describes a negative relationship between the price and quantity of the good, a quantity that is inefficiently low is equivalent to a price that is inefficiently high. When a monopolist charges a price above marginal cost, some potential consumers value the good at more than its marginal cost but less than the monopolist's price. These consumers do not buy the good. Because the value these consumers place on the good is greater than the cost of providing it to them, this result is inefficient. Thus, monopoly pricing prevents some mutually beneficial trades from taking place.

The inefficiency of monopoly can be measured with a deadweight loss triangle, as illustrated in Figure 15.8. Because the demand curve reflects the value to consumers and the marginal-cost curve reflects the costs to the monopoly producer, the area of the deadweight loss triangle between the demand curve and the marginal-cost curve equals the total surplus lost because of monopoly pricing. It is the reduction in economic well-being that results from the monopoly's use of its market power.

The deadweight loss caused by a monopoly is similar to the deadweight loss caused by a tax. Indeed, a monopolist is like a private tax collector. As we saw in Chapter 8, a tax on a good places a wedge between consumers' willingness to pay (as reflected by the demand curve) and producers' costs (as reflected by the

FIGURE 15.8

The Inefficiency of Monopoly

Because a monopoly charges a price above marginal cost, not all consumers who value the good at more than its cost buy it. Thus, the quantity produced and sold by a monopoly is below the socially efficient level. The deadweight loss is represented by the area of the triangle between the demand curve (which reflects the value of the good to consumers) and the marginal-cost curve (which reflects the costs of the monopoly producer).

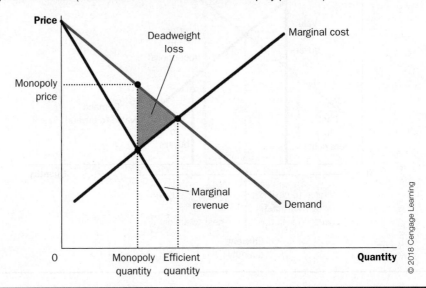

supply curve). Because a monopoly exerts its market power by charging a price above marginal cost, it creates a similar wedge. In both cases, the wedge causes the quantity sold to fall short of the social optimum. The difference between the two cases is that the government gets the revenue from a tax, whereas a private firm gets the monopoly profit.

15-3b The Monopoly's Profit: A Social Cost?

It is tempting to decry monopolies for "profiteering" at the expense of the public. And, indeed, a monopoly firm does earn a profit by virtue of its market power. According to the economic analysis of monopoly, however, the firm's profit is not in itself necessarily a problem for society.

Welfare in a monopolized market, like all markets, includes the welfare of both consumers and producers. Whenever a consumer pays an extra dollar to a producer because of a monopoly price, the consumer is worse off by a dollar, and the producer is better off by the same amount. This transfer from the consumers of the good to the owners of the monopoly does not affect the market's total surplus—the sum of consumer and producer surplus. In other words, the monopoly profit itself does not represent a reduction in the size of the economic pie but merely a bigger slice for producers and a smaller slice for consumers. Unless consumers are for some reason more deserving than producers—a normative judgment about equity that goes beyond the realm of economic efficiency—the monopoly profit is not a social problem.

The problem in a monopolized market arises because the firm produces and sells a quantity of output below the level that maximizes total surplus.

The deadweight loss measures how much the economic pie shrinks as a result. This inefficiency is connected to the monopoly's high price: Consumers buy fewer units when the firm raises its price above marginal cost. But keep in mind that the profit earned on the units that continue to be sold is not the problem. The problem stems from the inefficiently low quantity of output. Put differently, if the high monopoly price did not discourage some consumers from buying the good, it would raise producer surplus by exactly the amount it reduced consumer surplus, leaving total surplus the same as could be achieved by a benevolent social planner.

There is, however, a possible exception to this conclusion. Suppose that a monopoly firm has to incur additional costs to maintain its monopoly position. For example, a firm with a government-created monopoly might need to hire lobbyists to convince lawmakers to continue its monopoly. In this case, the monopoly may use up some of its monopoly profits paying for these additional costs. If so, the social loss from monopoly includes both these costs and the deadweight loss resulting from a price above marginal cost.

For example, earlier in the chapter we discussed the near monopoly Windsor–Detroit Ambassador Bridge. In response to a proposed government-owned bridge, the owners of the Ambassador Bridge have spent millions on advertising opposing the second bridge and sponsored a petition calling for a plebiscite. These costs can be viewed as social costs incurred to protect its monopoly position.

 How does a monopolist's quantity of output compare to the quantity of output that maximizes total surplus?

15-4 Price Discrimination

So far we have been assuming that the monopoly firm charges the same price to all customers. Yet in many cases firms try to sell the same good to different customers for different prices, even though the costs of producing for the two customers are the same. This practice is called **price discrimination**.

Before discussing the behaviour of a price-discriminating monopolist, we should note that price discrimination is not possible when a good is sold in a competitive market. In a competitive market, many firms are selling the same good at the market price. No firm is willing to charge a lower price to any customer because the firm can sell all it wants at the market price. And if any firm tried to charge a higher price to a customer, that customer would buy from another firm. For a firm to price-discriminate, it must have some market power.

price discrimination
the business practice of selling the same good at different prices to different customers

15-4a A Parable about Pricing

To understand why a monopolist would price-discriminate, let's consider an example. Imagine that you are the president of Readalot Publishing Company. Readalot's best-selling author has just written a new novel. To keep things simple, let's imagine that you pay the author a flat $2 million for the exclusive rights to publish the book. Let's also assume that the cost of printing the book is zero (as it would be, for example, for an e-book). Readalot's profit, therefore, is the revenue from selling the book minus the $2 million it has paid to the author. Given these assumptions, how would you, as Readalot's president, decide the book's price?

Your first step is to estimate the demand for the book. Readalot's marketing department tells you that the book will attract two types of readers. The book will appeal to the author's 100 000 die-hard fans who are willing to pay as much as $30. In addition, it will appeal to about 400 000 less enthusiastic readers who are willing to pay $5 or less.

If Readalot charges a single price to all consumers, what price maximizes profit? There are two natural prices to consider: $30 is the highest price Readalot can charge and still get the 100 000 die-hard fans, and $5 is the highest price it can charge and still get the entire market of 500 000 potential readers. Solving Readalot's problem is a matter of simple arithmetic. At a price of $30, Readalot sells 100 000 copies, has revenue of $3 million, and makes profit of $1 million. At a price of $5, it sells 500 000 copies, has revenue of $2.5 million, and makes a profit of $500 000. Thus, Readalot maximizes profit by charging $30 and forgoing the opportunity to sell to the 400 000 less enthusiastic readers.

Notice that Readalot's decision causes a deadweight loss. There are 400 000 readers willing to pay $5 for the book, and the marginal cost of providing it to them is zero. Thus, $2 million of total surplus is lost when Readalot charges the higher price. This deadweight loss is the usual inefficiency that arises whenever a monopolist charges a price above marginal cost.

Now suppose that Readalot's marketing department makes a discovery: These two groups of readers are in separate markets. The die-hard fans live in Australia, and the other readers live in Canada. Moreover, it is difficult for readers in one country to buy books in the other.

In response to this discovery, Readalot can change its marketing strategy and increase profits. To the 100 000 Australian readers, it can charge $30 for the book. To the 400 000 Canadian readers, it can charge $5 for the book. In this case, revenue is $3 million in Australia and $2 million in Canada, for a total of $5 million. Profit is then $3 million, which is substantially greater than the $1 million the company could earn charging the same $30 price to all customers. Not surprisingly, Readalot chooses to follow this strategy of price discrimination.

The story of Readalot Publishing is hypothetical, but it describes accurately the business practice of many publishing companies. Textbooks, for example, are often sold at a lower price in Europe than in Canada. Even more important is the price differential between hardcover books and paperbacks. When a publisher has a new novel, it initially releases an expensive hardcover edition and later releases a cheaper paperback edition. The difference in price between these two editions far exceeds the difference in printing costs. The publisher's goal is just as in our example. By selling the hardcover to die-hard fans and the paperback to less enthusiastic readers, the publisher price-discriminates and raises its profit.

15-4b The Moral of the Story

Like any parable, the story of Readalot Publishing is stylized. Yet also like any parable, it teaches some general lessons. In this case, three lessons can be learned about price discrimination.

The first and most obvious lesson is that price discrimination is a rational strategy for a profit-maximizing monopolist. That is, by charging different prices to different customers, a monopolist can increase its profit. In essence, a price-discriminating monopolist charges each customer a price closer to her willingness to pay than is possible with a single price.

The second lesson is that price discrimination requires the ability to separate customers according to their willingness to pay. In our example, customers were separated geographically. But sometimes monopolists choose other differences, such as age or income, to distinguish among customers.

A corollary to this second lesson is that certain market forces can prevent firms from price-discriminating. In particular, one such force is *arbitrage,* the process of buying a good in one market at a low price and selling it in another market at a higher price to profit from the price difference. In our example, if Australian bookstores could buy the book in Canada and resell it to Australian readers, the arbitrage would prevent Readalot from price-discriminating because no Australian would buy the book at the higher price.

The third lesson from our parable is the most surprising: Price discrimination can raise economic welfare. Recall that a deadweight loss arises when Readalot charges a single $30 price because the 400 000 less enthusiastic readers do not end up with the book, even though they value it at more than its marginal cost of production. By contrast, when Readalot price-discriminates, all readers get the book and the outcome is efficient. Thus, price discrimination can eliminate the inefficiency inherent in monopoly pricing.

Note that in this example the increase in welfare from price discrimination shows up as higher producer surplus rather than higher consumer surplus. Consumers are no better off for having bought the book: The price they pay exactly equals the value they place on the book, so they receive no consumer surplus. The entire increase in total surplus from price discrimination accrues to Readalot Publishing in the form of higher profit.

15-4c The Analytics of Price Discrimination

Let's consider a bit more formally how price discrimination affects economic welfare. We begin by assuming that the monopolist can price-discriminate perfectly. *Perfect price discrimination* describes a situation in which the monopolist knows exactly each customer's willingness to pay and can charge each customer a different price. In this case, the monopolist charges each customer exactly her willingness to pay, and the monopolist gets the entire surplus in every transaction. Perfect price discrimination is sometimes referred to as first-degree price discrimination.

Figure 15.9 illustrates producer and consumer surplus with and without price discrimination. To keep things simple, this figure is drawn assuming constant per unit costs—that is, marginal and average cost are constant and equal. Without price discrimination, the firm charges a single price above marginal cost, as shown in panel (a). Because some potential customers who value the good at more than marginal cost do not buy it at this high price, the monopoly causes a deadweight loss. Yet when a firm can perfectly price-discriminate, as shown in panel (b), each customer who values the good at more than marginal cost buys the good and is charged his willingness to pay. All mutually beneficial trades take place, there is no deadweight loss, and the entire surplus derived from the market goes to the monopoly producer in the form of profit.

In reality, of course, price discrimination is not perfect. Customers do not walk into stores with signs displaying their willingness to pay. Instead, firms price-discriminate by dividing customers into groups: young versus old, weekday versus weekend shoppers, Canadians versus Australians, and so on. Unlike those in our parable of Readalot Publishing, customers within each group differ in their willingness to pay for the product, making perfect price discrimination impossible.

Imperfect price discrimination comes in two forms, referred to as second- and third-degree price discrimination. Second-degree price discrimination involves charging different prices to the same customer for different units that the customer buys. For example, many firms offer lower prices to customers who buy

FIGURE 15.9

Welfare with and without Price Discrimination

Panel (a) shows a monopolist that charges the same price to all customers. Total surplus in this market equals the sum of profit (producer surplus) and consumer surplus. Panel (b) shows a monopolist that can perfectly price-discriminate. Because consumer surplus equals zero, total surplus now equals the firm's profit. Comparing these two panels, you can see that perfect price discrimination raises profit, raises total surplus, and lowers consumer surplus.

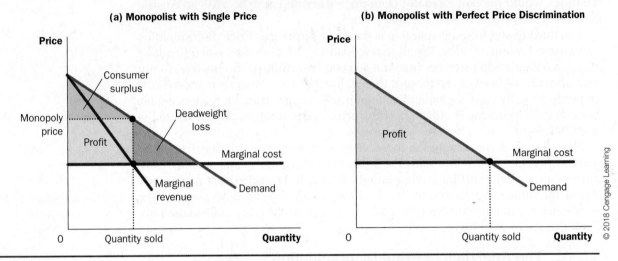

large quantities. A bakery might charge $0.50 for each donut but $5 for a dozen. This is a form of price discrimination because the customer pays a higher price for the first unit bought than for the twelfth. Quantity discounts are often a successful way of price-discriminating because a customer's willingness to pay for an additional unit declines as the customer buys more units.

Third-degree price discrimination can be achieved when the market can be segmented and when the segments have different elasticities of demand. A good example of third-degree price discrimination is movie tickets. Many movie theatres charge a lower price for children and senior citizens than for other patrons. This fact is hard to explain in a competitive market. In a competitive market, price equals marginal cost, and the marginal cost of providing a seat for a child or senior citizen is the same as the marginal cost of providing a seat for anyone else. Yet this fact is easily explained if movie theatres have some local monopoly power and if children and senior citizens have a lower willingness to pay for a ticket. In this case, movie theatres raise their profit by price-discriminating.

This is illustrated in Figure 15.10 for the case of two market segments—adults and children. The total market demand in panel (a) is the sum of the demand of the two market segments, given in panels (b) and (c). It is assumed that the adult demand curve is less elastic than the child demand curve, and that the price at which the demand of children is equal to zero is lower than the equivalent price for adults. This means that there is a kink in the total market-demand curve at the point where the children's demand curve kicks in. This kink is translated into the marginal-revenue curve as well.

The movie theatre decides on the total number of tickets to sell by equating *MC* with *MR* in panel (a). However, there is not just one price. Drawing a horizontal line through the *MC* = *MR* point until it intersects with the *MR* curves for adults

FIGURE 15.10

Third-Degree Price Discrimination

Panels (b) and (c) show the demand and marginal-revenue curves for the adult and child segment of the market for movie tickets. Panel (a) sums these curves to give the demand and marginal-revenue curves for the total market. The monopolist maximizes profits by setting $MC = MR$ and selling a total quantity of Q_T [panel (a)], but this involves charging different prices in each market: P_A in the adult market [panel (b)] and P_C in the child market [panel (c)], with Q_A tickets sold to adults and Q_C tickets sold to children. The adult price is higher than the child price because the adult demand is less elastic.

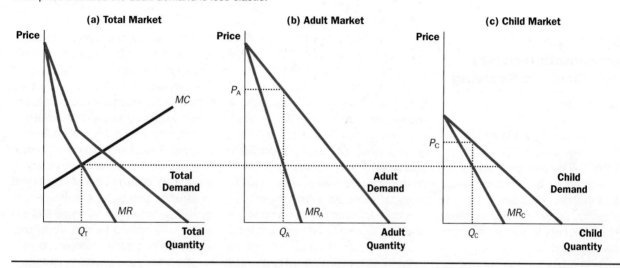

(a) Total Market

(b) Adult Market

(c) Child Market

(MR_A) and children (MR_C) and then reading the price off the respective demand curves determines the price in each market segment, P_A and P_C, as well as the number of tickets sold in each market, Q_A and Q_C. Not surprisingly the price in the adult market is higher because the demand curve is less elastic.

How does imperfect price discrimination affect welfare? The analysis of these pricing schemes is quite complicated, and it turns out that there is no general answer to this question. Compared to the monopoly outcome with a single price, imperfect price discrimination can raise, lower, or leave unchanged total surplus in a market. The only certain conclusion is that price discrimination raises the monopoly's profit; otherwise, the firm would choose to charge all customers the same price.

15-4d Examples of Price Discrimination

Firms in our economy use various business strategies aimed at charging different prices to different customers. We have considered the example of quantity discounts and movie tickets. Now that we understand the economics of price discrimination, let's consider some other examples.

Airline Prices Seats on airplanes are sold at many different prices. Most airlines charge a lower price for a round-trip ticket between two cities if the traveller stays over a Saturday night. At first this seems odd. Why should it matter to the airline whether a passenger stays over a Saturday night? The reason is that this rule provides a way to separate business travellers and leisure travellers. A passenger on a business trip has a high willingness to pay and, most likely, does not want to stay over a Saturday night. By contrast, a passenger travelling for personal reasons has

Price Discrimination

*The ability of tech companies to determine personal characteristics and prefer-
ences from online behaviour has led to increasing concerns about privacy. It has
also allowed companies to engage in a sophisticated form of personalized price
discrimination.*

Online Price Discrimination Exists. Here's How It's Evolving

By Daniel Herman

Recently the awareness of price discrimination rose as a result of a phenomenon
called "Pink Tax". This phenomenon refers to the
price difference of similar products for men and
women. A recent study by a data-mining company, ParseHub, unveiled that Canadian women
pay 43 percent more for their personal care
products than men pay for comparable items. In
addition, in 2015, New York City's Department of
Consumer Affairs found that women pay about
7 percent more than men for similar products.

The Telegraph also reported that ticket prices
to see Calvin Harris in Las Vegas are 150 more
expensive for men than for women.

The economic term which captures these
cases is "third degree price discrimination". This
discrimination occurs when sellers charge different prices for similar products to different
groups of consumers. This price discrimination
exists across different industries and products. For
example, movie tickets are generally cheaper for
seniors and students due to their cost-sensitivity.

A more advanced price discrimination is
called "first degree price discrimination". In this
pricing method, the seller is able to identify the
customers' willingness to pay and can therefore
personalize the price of the product to the elasticity of the demand.

Just try to imagine a merchant in a bazaar
who sells a product for a higher price tag to a
person that is dressed nicer and looks "richer".
The computer indeed can't see what we are
wearing, but it is nonetheless capable of extracting
a much deeper understanding of the consumer.

As targeting and clustering capabilities are
progressing, personalized pricing will become
more and more evident and common among
online sellers. Building a profile of a client based
on variables such as: location, device type,
gender, age and interest will enable sellers to
provide to the customer the most relevant price
according to the customers' willingness to pay.

Sellers now could provide the customer a
price that will fit his preferences and willingness to pay. If in the past sellers were capable of

a lower willingness to pay and is more likely to be willing to stay over a Saturday
night. Thus, the airlines can successfully price-discriminate by charging a lower
price for passengers who stay over a Saturday night.

Discount Coupons Many companies offer discount coupons to the public in
newspapers and magazines. More recently, these coupons are available online via
websites such as Groupon. Buyers have to clip coupons—or, in Groupon's case,
click a daily deal—in order to buy the good at a lower price. Why do companies
offer these coupons? Why don't they just cut the price of the product to begin with?

The answer is that coupons allow companies to price-discriminate. Companies
know that not all customers are willing to spend time to clip out coupons or sign
up for Groupon and check on daily deals. Moreover, the willingness to use coupons is related to the consumer's willingness to pay. A rich and busy executive
is unlikely to spend her time clipping discount coupons out of the newspaper,
and she is probably willing to pay a higher price for many goods. A person who
is unemployed is more likely to clip coupons and to have a lower willingness
to pay. Younger people who not only are more tech-savvy but also may have a
lower willingness to pay are more likely to use sites like Groupon. So, by charging
a lower price only to those customers who use coupons, firms can successfully
price-discriminate.

differentiating between different groups, now, they could potentially differentiate between individuals and thus provide the customer a price that will fit his preferences and willingness to pay. The same mechanism that works in online advertising will now be adjusted to personalized pricing.

The most advanced implementation of personalized pricing is evident in the travel sector, where prices of flights are dynamic and changing constantly according to your intent to fly to a certain location. Currently the flight change in pricing is being affected by components such as number of searches and the day of the search (weekends can be more expensive). But imagine that in the future, flight providers will be able to provide the most relevant price for the client according to their "customer profile". For example, the system will identify that the customer is a student in his twenties and will provide him a lower price than a high net income individual in his forties for the same flight.

Another form of personalized pricing could be personalized discounts. Machine learning algorithms that can identify clients that have a high probability of leaving the seller's website or app without purchase are not science fiction anymore. Marketing automation technology companies fill this void, and they now offer personalized discounts and messages according to the user's profile. A new report by Coupons.com and research firm Boyitz supports this claim. They have found that millennials long for personalized coupons and are willing to provide information about themselves in exchange for it.

The public opinion towards price discrimination is usually negative and can harm the company's reputation. Hence, a company that will use this method might increase their revenue and profits in the short term, but in the long term, a viral shaming campaign might harm the company's reputation and future sales. The fact that the media was vexed with gender price discrimination is an example of the potential downsides that may loom in the future for personalized pricing.

In addition, crunching massive datasets into real time insights is a quite a challenge. A company that wants to use first degree price discrimination will need to invest high amounts of resources in order to make it happen. Moreover, gathering the relevant data for building the profile of the user is a challenging task by itself.

There are few ways how consumers can fight against their "profile building".

First, consumers can use a VPN service that will camouflage their online activities. Second, comparing the price of products with your friends and family could help the consumers to come up with a solid benchmark. Third, erasing cookies can disrupt the user profiling building.

It seems then that personalized pricing is inevitable, as the infrastructure is already here.

Currently, public acceptance is the main obstacle for a broad implementation. Although fixed pricing is not dead yet, consumers will need to adapt to this new idea in the future. Regulation over this pricing model might be needed in order to protect the interests of consumers and their privacy. It will also require responsibility and transparency from the seller's side in order to prevent mistrust between them and the consumer.

The question is not whether personalized pricing will occur, but a question of when and how.

Source: Daniel Herman, "Online Price Discrimination Exists. Here's How It's Evolving." *Tech in Asia*, May 19, 2016, https://www.techinasia.com/talk/online-price-discrimination-exists-evolving. Reproduced by permission of the author.

Financial Aid Many colleges and universities give financial aid to students who have lower incomes. One can view this policy as a type of price discrimination. Wealthier students have greater financial resources and, therefore, a higher willingness to pay than students who have less resources. By charging high tuition and selectively offering financial aid, schools in effect charge prices to customers based on the value they place on going to that school. This behaviour is like that of any price-discriminating monopolist.

QUICK Quiz *Give two examples of price discrimination. • How does perfect price discrimination affect consumer surplus, producer surplus, and total surplus?*

15-5 Public Policy toward Monopolies

We have seen that monopolies, in contrast to competitive markets, fail to allocate resources efficiently. Monopolies produce less than the socially desirable quantity of output and charge prices above marginal cost. Policymakers in the government can respond to the problem of monopoly in one of four ways:

1. By trying to make monopolized industries more competitive
2. By regulating the behaviour of the monopolies

3. By turning some private monopolies into public enterprises
4. By doing nothing at all

15-5a Increasing Competition with Competition Law

One way that the government can respond to the inefficiencies resulting from market power in general, and monopoly in particular, is through legislation designed to encourage competition and discourage the use of monopoly practices. For example, if a merger between two companies would make the industry less competitive and, as a result, reduce the economic well-being of the country as a whole, the government could pass laws that prevent such mergers.

Competition law in Canada is enforced by the federal government's Competition Bureau. Lawyers and economists in the bureau investigate anticompetitive practices that fall within the scope of the act. When appropriate, cases may be referred for criminal prosecution to the attorney general of Canada. In other instances, a case may be referred to the Competition Tribunal for review and adjudication.

The tribunal is a quasi-judicial body that is similar to a court. It consists of judges and lay members who are experts from the business, academic, and civil service communities. In most of the cases it deals with, the tribunal must determine whether a particular practice or action has an adverse effect on competition. If it concludes that there is an anticompetitive effect, the tribunal can issue an order to prohibit the practice or action. For example, the tribunal can block a merger or require that a firm divest itself of assets. In 2005, the Competition Bureau ruled that the merger of two of Canada's largest movie theatre companies, Cineplex Galaxy and Famous Players, would have substantial anticompetitive effects. Although the merger was allowed to proceed, the Bureau ordered Cineplex Galaxy to sell 35 theatres in 17 cities with total annual box-office revenues of about $100 million.

Competition law in Canada prevents other kinds of anticompetitive practices, some of which we will discuss in Chapter 16.

Competition laws have costs as well as benefits. Sometimes companies merge not to reduce competition but to lower costs through more efficient joint production. The benefits of greater efficiency as a result of mergers are called *synergies*. These considerations are particularly important in a global context because some Canadian companies are large and dominant in the domestic market but small in the international market. For example, although the banking market in Canada is dominated by the "Big Five," these banks are small players on the international banking scene. Some bankers have argued that Canadian banks can compete in international markets only by realizing the synergies that would result when operations are combined. Using this argument, four of Canada's largest banks sought permission to merge in 1998: the Royal Bank with the Bank of Montreal, and the Canadian Imperial Bank of Commerce with TD Canada Trust. Both merger deals were rejected by the federal government.

If competition laws are to raise social welfare, the government must be able to determine which mergers are desirable and which are not. That is, it must be able to measure and compare the social benefit from synergies with the social cost of reduced competition. However, critics of competition laws are skeptical that the government can perform the necessary cost–benefit analysis with sufficient accuracy.

15-5b Regulation

Another way the government deals with the problem of monopoly is by regulating the behaviour of monopolists. This solution is common in the case of natural monopolies, such as water and electric companies. These companies are not allowed to charge any price they want. Instead, government agencies regulate their prices.

What price should the government set for a natural monopoly? This question is not as easy as it might at first appear. One might conclude that the price should equal the monopolist's marginal cost. If price equals marginal cost, customers will buy the quantity of the monopolist's output that maximizes total surplus, and the allocation of resources will be efficient.

There are, however, two practical problems with marginal-cost pricing as a regulatory system. The first arises from the logic of cost curves. By definition, natural monopolies have declining average total cost. As we first discussed in Chapter 13, when average total cost is declining, marginal cost is less than average total cost. This situation is illustrated in Figure 15.11, which shows a firm with a large fixed cost and then constant marginal cost thereafter. If regulators are to set price equal to marginal cost, that price will be less than the firm's average total cost, and the firm will lose money. Instead of charging such a low price, the monopoly firm would just exit the industry.

Regulators can respond to this problem in various ways, none of which is perfect. One way is to subsidize the monopolist. In essence, the government picks up the losses inherent in marginal-cost pricing. Yet to pay for the subsidy, the government needs to raise money through taxation, which involves its own deadweight losses. Alternatively, the regulators can allow the monopolist to charge a price higher than marginal cost. If the regulated price equals average total cost, the monopolist earns exactly zero economic profit. Yet average-cost pricing leads to deadweight losses because the monopolist's price no longer reflects the marginal cost of producing the good. In essence, average-cost pricing is like a tax on the good the monopolist is selling.

The second problem with marginal-cost pricing as a regulatory system (and with average-cost pricing as well) is that it gives the monopolist no incentive to reduce costs. Each firm in a competitive market tries to reduce its costs because lower costs mean higher profits. But if a regulated monopolist knows that

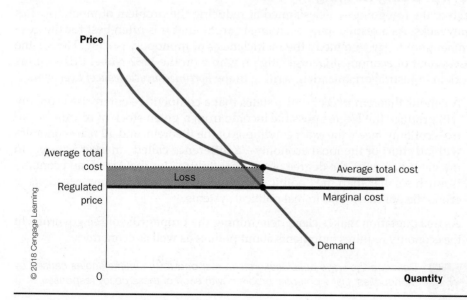

FIGURE 15.11

Marginal-Cost Pricing for a Natural Monopoly

Because a natural monopoly has declining average total cost, marginal cost is less than average total cost. Therefore, if regulators require a natural monopoly to charge a price equal to marginal cost, price will be below average total cost, and the monopoly will lose money.

regulators will reduce prices whenever costs fall, the monopolist will not benefit from lower costs. In practice, regulators deal with this problem by allowing monopolists to keep some of the benefits from lower costs in the form of higher profit, a practice that requires some departure from marginal-cost pricing.

15-5c Public Ownership

The third policy used by the government to deal with monopoly is public ownership. That is, rather than regulating a natural monopoly that is run by a private firm, the government can run the monopoly itself. In contrast to the United States, where there is very little public ownership, this solution is common in many European countries. It is also relatively common in Canada, although somewhat less so in recent years.

In Canada, government ownership occurs at both the federal and the provincial/territorial levels. Government-owned firms are known as Crown corporations. Federal Crown corporations include Canada Post, the Canadian Broadcasting Corporation, and VIA Rail. In the past, the federal government has privatized some of its Crown corporations, including Petro-Canada, Air Canada, and Canadian National Railway.

At the provincial/territorial level, Crown corporations exist in insurance (Saskatchewan Government Insurance), hydroelectricity (Manitoba Hydro and Hydro-Québec), and telecommunications (Saskatchewan Tel). Gas and water utilities are also publicly owned in most provinces/territories.

Economists usually prefer private to public ownership of natural monopolies. The key issue is how the ownership of the firm affects the costs of production. Private owners have an incentive to minimize costs as long as they reap part of the benefit in the form of higher profit. If the firm's managers are doing a bad job of keeping costs down, the firm's owners will fire them. By contrast, if the government bureaucrats who run a monopoly do a bad job, the losers are the customers and taxpayers, whose only recourse is the political system. The bureaucrats may become a special-interest group and attempt to block cost-reducing reforms. Put simply, as a way of ensuring that firms are well run, the voting booth is less reliable than the profit motive.

15-5d Doing Nothing

Each of the foregoing policies aimed at reducing the problem of monopoly has drawbacks. As a result, some economists argue that it is often best for the government not to try to remedy the inefficiencies of monopoly pricing. Here is the assessment of economist George Stigler, who won the 1982 Nobel Prize for his work in industrial organization, writing in the *Fortune Encyclopedia of Economics*:

> A famous theorem in economics states that a competitive enterprise economy will produce the largest possible income from a given stock of resources. No real economy meets the exact conditions of the theorem, and all real economies will fall short of the ideal economy—a difference called "market failure." In my view, however, the degree of "market failure" for the American economy is much smaller than the "political failure" arising from the imperfections of economic policies found in real political systems.

As this quotation makes clear, determining the proper role of the government in the economy requires judgments about politics as well as economics.

QUICK
Quiz

Describe the ways policymakers can respond to the inefficiencies caused by monopolies. List a potential problem with each of these policy responses.

15-6 Conclusion: The Prevalence of Monopoly

This chapter has discussed the behaviour of firms that have control over the prices they charge. We have seen that these firms behave very differently from the competitive firms studied in the previous chapter. Table 15.2 summarizes some of the key similarities and differences between competitive and monopoly markets.

From the standpoint of public policy, a crucial result is that monopolists produce less than the socially efficient quantity and charge prices above marginal cost. As a result, they cause deadweight losses. In some cases, these inefficiencies can be mitigated through price discrimination by the monopolist, but other times they call for policymakers to take an active role.

How prevalent are the problems of monopoly? There are two answers to this question.

In one sense, monopolies are common. Most firms have some control over the prices they charge. They are not forced to charge the market price for their goods because their goods are not exactly the same as those offered by other firms. A Ford Taurus is not the same as a Toyota Camry. Ben & Jerry's ice cream is not the same as Breyers'. Each of these goods has a downward-sloping demand curve, which gives each producer some degree of monopoly power.

Yet firms with substantial monopoly power are rare. Few goods are truly unique. Most have substitutes that, even if not exactly the same, are similar. Ben and Jerry can raise the price of their ice cream a little without losing all its sales, but if they raise it a lot, sales will fall substantially as its customers switch to another brand.

In the end, monopoly power is a matter of degree. It is true that many firms have some monopoly power. It is also true that their monopoly power is usually limited. In these cases, we will not go far wrong assuming that firms operate in competitive markets, even if that is not precisely the case.

TABLE 15.2

Competition versus Monopoly: A Summary Comparison

	Competition	Monopoly
Similarities		
Goal of firms	Maximize profits	Maximize profits
Rule for maximizing	$MR = MC$	$MR = MC$
Can earn economic profits in the short run?	Yes	Yes
Differences		
Number of firms	Many	One
Marginal revenue	$MR = P$	$MR < P$
Price	$P = MC$	$P > MC$
Produces welfare-maximizing level of output?	Yes	No
Entry in long run?	Yes	No
Can earn economic profits in long run?	No	Yes
Price discrimination possible?	No	Yes

summary

- A monopoly is a firm that is the sole seller in its market. A monopoly arises when a single firm owns a key resource, when the government gives a firm the exclusive right to produce a good, or when a single firm can supply the entire market at a lower cost than many firms could.

- Because a monopoly is the sole producer in its market, it faces a downward-sloping demand curve for its product. When a monopoly increases production by 1 unit, it causes the price of its good to fall, which reduces the amount of revenue earned on all units produced. As a result, a monopoly's marginal revenue is always below the price of its good.

- Like a competitive firm, a monopoly firm maximizes profit by producing the quantity at which marginal revenue equals marginal cost. The monopoly then chooses the price at which that quantity is demanded. Unlike a competitive firm, a monopoly firm's price exceeds its marginal revenue, so its price exceeds marginal cost.

- A monopolist's profit-maximizing level of output is below the level that maximizes the sum of consumer and producer surplus. That is, when the monopoly charges a price above marginal cost, some consumers who value the good more than its cost of production do not buy it. As a result, monopoly causes deadweight losses similar to those caused by taxes.

- A monopolist often increases profits by charging different prices for the same good based on a buyer's willingness to pay. This practice of price discrimination can raise economic welfare by getting the good to some consumers who otherwise would not buy it. In the extreme case of perfect price discrimination, the deadweight losses of monopoly are completely eliminated. More generally, when price discrimination is imperfect, it can either raise or lower welfare compared to the outcome with a single monopoly price.

- Policymakers can respond to the inefficiency of monopoly behaviour in four ways. (1) They can use the antitrust laws to try to make the industry more competitive. (2) They can regulate the prices that the monopoly charges. (3) They can turn the monopolist into a government-run enterprise. (4) Or, if the market failure is deemed small compared to the inevitable imperfections of policies, they can do nothing at all.

KEY **concepts**

monopoly, *p. 326*   natural monopoly, *p. 327*   price discrimination, *p. 339*

QUESTIONS FOR **review**

1. Give an example of a government-created monopoly. Is creating this monopoly necessarily bad public policy? Explain.

2. Define *natural monopoly*. What does the size of a market have to do with whether an industry is a natural monopoly?

3. Why is a monopolist's marginal revenue less than the price of its good? Can marginal revenue ever be negative? Explain.

4. Draw the demand, marginal-revenue, and marginal-cost curves for a monopolist. Show the profit-maximizing level of output. Show the profit-maximizing price.

5. In your diagram from the previous question, show the level of output that maximizes total surplus. Show

the deadweight loss from the monopoly. Explain your answer.

6. What gives the government the power to regulate mergers between firms? From the standpoint of the welfare of society, give a good reason and a bad reason why two firms might want to merge.

7. Describe the two problems that arise when regulators tell a natural monopoly that it must set a price equal to marginal cost.

8. Give two examples of price discrimination. In each case, explain why the monopolist chooses to follow this business strategy.

QUICK CHECK **multiple choice**

1. A firm is a natural monopoly if it exhibits which of the following as its output increases?
   a. decreasing marginal revenue
   b. increasing marginal cost
   c. decreasing average revenue
   d. decreasing average total cost

2. For a profit-maximizing monopoly that charges the same price to all consumers, what is the relationship between price P, marginal revenue MR, and marginal cost MC?
   a. $P = MR$ and $MR = MC$
   b. $P > MR$ and $MR = MC$
   c. $P = MR$ and $MR > MC$
   d. $P > MR$ and $MR > MC$

3. If a monopoly's fixed costs increase, its price will _____ and its profit will _____ .
   a. increase, decrease
   b. decrease, increase
   c. increase, stay the same
   d. stay the same, decrease

4. Compared to the social optimum, a monopoly firm chooses which of the following?
   a. a quantity that is too low and a price that is too high
   b. a quantity that is too high and a price that is too low
   c. a quantity and a price that are both too high
   d. a quantity and a price that are both too low

5. Why does the deadweight loss from monopoly arise?
   a. the monopoly firm makes higher profits than a competitive firm would
   b. some potential consumers who forgo buying the good value it more than its marginal cost
   c. consumers who buy the good have to pay more than marginal cost, reducing their consumer surplus
   d. the monopoly firm chooses a quantity that fails to equate price and average revenue

6. What is reduced when a monopolist switches from charging a single price to perfect price discrimination?
   a. the quantity produced
   b. the firm's profit
   c. consumer surplus
   d. total surplus

PROBLEMS AND **applications**

1. A publisher faces the following demand schedule for the next novel from one of its popular authors:

Price	Quantity Demanded
$100	0
90	100 000
80	200 000
70	300 000
60	400 000
50	500 000
40	600 000
30	700 000
20	800 000
10	900 000
0	1 000 000

The author is paid $2 million to write the book, and the marginal cost of publishing the book is a constant $10 per book.
   a. Compute total revenue, total cost, and profit at each quantity. What quantity would a profit-maximizing publisher choose? What price would it charge?
   b. Compute marginal revenue. (Recall that $MR = \Delta TR/\Delta Q$.) How does marginal revenue compare to the price? Explain.
   c. Graph the marginal-revenue, marginal-cost, and demand curves. At what quantity do the marginal-revenue and marginal-cost curves cross? What does this signify?
   d. In your graph, shade in the deadweight loss. Explain in words what this means.
   e. If the author was paid $3 million instead of $2 million to write the book, how would this affect the publisher's decision regarding the price to charge? Explain.
   f. Suppose the publisher was not profit-maximizing but was concerned with maximizing economic efficiency. What price would it charge for the book? How much profit would it make at this price?

2. A small town is served by many competing supermarkets, which have constant marginal cost.
   a. Using a diagram of the market for groceries, show the consumer surplus, producer surplus, and total surplus.
   b. Now suppose that the independent supermarkets combine into one chain. Using a new diagram, show the new consumer surplus, producer surplus, and total surplus. Relative to the competitive market, what is the transfer from consumers to producers? What is the deadweight loss?

3. Johnny Rockabilly has just finished recording his latest CD. His record company's marketing department determines that the demand for the CD is as follows:

Price	Number of CDs
$24	10 000
22	20 000
20	30 000
18	40 000
16	50 000
14	60 000

The company can produce the CD with no fixed cost and a variable cost of $5 per CD.
a. Find total revenue for quantity equal to 10 000, 20 000, and so on. What is the marginal revenue for each 10 000 increase in the quantity sold?
b. What quantity of CDs would maximize profit? What would be the price? What would be the profit?
c. If you were Johnny's agent, what recording fee would you advise Johnny to demand from the record company? Why?

4. A company is considering building a bridge across a river. The bridge would cost $2 million to build and nothing to maintain. The following table shows the company's anticipated demand over the lifetime of the bridge.

Price per Crossing	Number of Crossings (in thousands)
$8	0
7	100
6	200
5	300
4	400
3	500
2	600
1	700
0	800

a. If the company were to build the bridge, what would be its profit-maximizing price? Would that be the efficient level of output? Why or why not?
b. If the company is interested in maximizing profit, should it build the bridge? What would be its profit or loss?
c. If the government were to build the bridge, what price should it charge?
d. Should the government build the bridge? Explain.

5. Larry, Curly, and Moe run the only saloon in town. Larry wants to sell as many drinks as possible without losing money. Curly wants the saloon to bring in as much revenue as possible. Moe wants to make the largest possible profits. Using a single diagram of the saloon's demand curve and its cost curves, show the price and quantity combinations favoured by each of the three partners. Explain.

6. For many years, both local and long-distance phone services have been provided by provincially owned or regulated monopolies.
a. Explain why long-distance phone service was originally a natural monopoly.
b. Over the past several decades, technological developments have allowed companies to launch communications satellites that can transmit a limited number of calls. How did the growing role of satellites change the cost structure of long-distance phone service?
c. In response to these technological developments, some provinces/territories have deregulated the long-distance market in Canada. Local phone service has remained regulated. Why might it be efficient to have competition in long-distance phone service and regulated monopolies in local phone service?

7. Many schemes for price-discriminating involve some cost. For example, discount coupons take up the time and resources of both the buyer and the seller. This question considers the implications of costly price discrimination. To keep things simple, let's assume that our monopolist's production costs are simply proportional to output, so that average total cost and marginal cost are constant and equal to each other.
a. Draw the cost, demand, and marginal-revenue curves for the monopolist. Show the price the monopolist would charge without price discrimination.
b. In your diagram, mark the area equal to the monopolist's profit and call it X. Mark the area equal to consumer surplus and call it Y. Mark the area equal to the deadweight loss and call it Z.
c. Now suppose that the monopolist can perfectly price-discriminate. What is the monopolist's profit? (Give your answer in terms of X, Y, and Z.)
d. What is the change in the monopolist's profit from price discrimination? What is the change in total surplus from price discrimination? Which change is larger? Explain. (Give your answers in terms of X, Y, and Z.)
e. Now suppose that there is some cost of price discrimination. To model this cost, let's assume that the monopolist has to pay a fixed cost C in order to price-discriminate. How would a monopolist make

the decision whether to pay this fixed cost? (Give your answer in terms of X, Y, Z, and C.)

f. How would a benevolent social planner, who cares about total surplus, decide whether the monopolist should price-discriminate? (Give your answer in terms of X, Y, Z, and C.)

g. Compare your answers to parts (e) and (f). How does the monopolist's incentive to price-discriminate differ from the social planner's? Is it possible that the monopolist will price-discriminate even though it is not socially desirable?

8. Consider the relationship between monopoly pricing and price elasticity of demand.

a. Explain why a monopolist will never produce a quantity at which the demand curve is inelastic. (*Hint:* If demand is inelastic and the firm raises its price, what happens to total revenue and total costs?)

b. Draw a diagram for a monopolist, precisely labelling the portion of the demand curve that is inelastic. (*Hint:* The answer is related to the marginal-revenue curve.)

c. On your diagram, show the quantity and price that maximizes total revenue.

9. If the government wanted to encourage a monopoly to produce the socially efficient quantity, should it use a per-unit tax or a per-unit subsidy? Explain how this tax or subsidy would achieve the socially efficient level of output. Among the various interested parties—the monopoly firm, the monopoly's consumers, and other taxpayers—who would support the policy and who would oppose it?

10. You live in a town with 300 adults and 200 children, and you are thinking about putting on a play to entertain your neighbours and make some money. This type of play has a fixed cost of $2000, but selling an extra ticket has zero marginal cost. Here are the demand schedules for your two types of customer:

Price	Adults	Children
$10	0	0
9	100	0
8	200	0
7	300	0
6	300	0
5	300	100
4	300	200
3	300	200
2	300	200
1	300	200
0	300	200

a. To maximize profit, what price would you charge for an adult ticket? For a child's ticket? How much profit do you make?

b. The town council passes a law prohibiting you from charging different prices to different customers. What price do you set for a ticket now? How much profit do you make?

c. Who is worse off because of the law prohibiting price discrimination? Who is better off? (If you can, quantify the changes in welfare.)

d. If the fixed cost of the play was $3000 rather than $2000, how would your answers to parts (a), (b), and (c) change?

11. The residents of the town Ectenia all love economics, and the mayor proposes building an economics museum. The museum has a fixed cost of $2 400 000 and no variable costs. There are 100 000 town residents, and each has the same demand for museum visits: $Q^D = 10 - P$, where P is the price of admission.

a. Graph the museum's average-total-cost curve and its marginal-cost curve. What kind of market would describe the museum?

b. The mayor proposes financing the museum with a lump-sum tax of $24 and then opening the museum free to the public. How many times would each person visit? Calculate the benefit each person would get from the museum, measured as consumer surplus minus the new tax.

c. The mayor's anti-tax opponent says the museum should finance itself by charging an admission fee. What is the lowest price the museum can charge without incurring losses? (*Hint:* Find the number of visits and museum profits for prices of $2, $3, $4, and $5.)

d. For the break-even price you found in part (c), calculate each resident's consumer surplus. Compared with the mayor's plan, who is better off with this admission fee, and who is worse off? Explain.

e. What real-world considerations absent in the above problem might argue in favour of an admission fee?

12. Only one firm produces and sells soccer balls in the country of Wiknam, and as the story begins, international trade in soccer balls is prohibited. The following equations describe the monopolist's demand, marginal revenue, total cost, and marginal cost:

$$\begin{aligned} \text{Demand:} \quad & P = 10 - Q \\ \text{Marginal Revenue:} \quad & MR = 10 - 2Q \\ \text{Total Cost:} \quad & TC = 3 + Q + 0.5Q^2 \\ \text{Marginal Cost:} \quad & MC = 1 + Q \end{aligned}$$

where Q is quantity and P is the price measured in Wiknamian dollars.

a. How many soccer balls does the monopolist produce? At what price are they sold? What is the monopolist's profit?

b. One day, the king of Wiknam decrees that henceforth there will be free trade—either imports or exports—of soccer balls at the world price of $6. The firm is now a price taker in a competitive market. What happens to domestic production of soccer balls? To domestic consumption? Does Wiknam export or import soccer balls?

c. In our analysis of international trade in Chapter 9, a country becomes an exporter when the price without trade is below the world price and an importer when the price without trade is above the world price. Does that conclusion hold in your answers to parts (a) and (b)? Explain.

d. Suppose that the world price was not $6 but, instead, happened to be exactly the same as the domestic price without trade as determined in part (a). Would allowing trade have changed anything in the Wiknamian economy? Explain. How does the result here compare with the analysis in Chapter 9?

13. Based on market research, a film production company obtains the following information about the demand and production costs of its new DVD:

$$\text{Price} = 1000 - 10Q$$
$$\text{Total Revenue} = 1000Q - 10Q^2$$
$$\text{Marginal Revenue} = 1000 - 20Q$$
$$\text{Marginal Cost} = 100 + 10Q$$

where Q indicates the number of copies sold and P is the price in cents.

a. Find the price and quantity that maximizes the company's profit.

b. Find the price and quantity that would maximize social welfare.

c. Calculate the deadweight loss from monopoly.

d. Suppose, in addition to the costs above, the director of the film has to be paid. The company is considering four options:

   i. A flat fee of 2000 cents
   ii. 50 percent of the profits
   iii. 150 cents per unit sold
   iv. 50 percent of the revenue

   For each option, calculate the profit-maximizing price and quantity. Which, if any, of these compensation schemes would alter the deadweight loss from monopoly? Explain.

Monopolistic Competition

In this chapter, you will ...

1 Analyze competition among firms that sell differentiated products

2 Compare the outcome under monopolistic competition and under perfect competition

3 Consider the desirability of outcomes in monopolistically competitive markets

4 Examine the debate over the effects of advertising

5 Review the debate over the role of brand names

You walk into a bookstore to buy a book to read during your vacation. On the store's shelves you find a Kathy Reichs mystery, novels by Michael Ondaatje and Margaret Atwood, and many other choices. When you pick out a book and buy it, what kind of market are you participating in?

On the one hand, the market for books seems competitive. As you look over the shelves at the bookstore, you find many authors and many publishers vying for your attention. A buyer in this market has thousands of competing products from which to choose. And because anyone can enter the industry by writing and publishing a book, the book business is not very profitable. For every highly paid novelist, there are hundreds of struggling ones.

On the other hand, the market for books seems monopolistic. Because each book is unique, publishers have some latitude in choosing what price to charge. The sellers in this market are price makers rather than price takers. And indeed, the price of books greatly exceeds marginal cost. The price of a typical hardcover novel, for instance, is about $25, whereas the cost of printing one additional copy of the novel is less than $5.

The market for novels fits neither the competitive nor the monopoly model. Instead, it is best described by the model of monopolistic competition, the subject of this chapter. The term "monopolistic competition" might at first seem to be an oxymoron, like "jumbo shrimp." But as we will see, monopolistically competitive industries are like monopolies in some ways and like competitive firms in others. The model describes not only the publishing industry but also the market for many other goods and services.

16-1 Between Monopoly and Perfect Competition

The previous two chapters analyzed markets with many competitive firms and markets with a single monopoly firm. In Chapter 14, we saw that the price in a perfectly competitive market always equals the marginal cost of production. We also saw that, in the long run, entry and exit drive economic profit to zero, so the price also equals average total cost. In Chapter 15, we saw how monopoly firms can use their market power to keep prices above marginal cost, leading to a positive economic profit for the firm and a deadweight loss for society. Competition and monopoly are extreme forms of market structure. Competition occurs when there are many firms in a market offering essentially identical products; monopoly occurs when there is only one firm in a market.

Although the cases of perfect competition and monopoly illustrate some important ideas about how markets work, most markets in the economy include elements of both these cases and, therefore, are not completely described by either of them. The typical firm in the economy faces competition, but the competition is not so rigorous that it makes the firm a price taker like the firms analyzed in Chapter 14. The typical firm also has some degree of market power, but its market power is not so great that the firm can be described exactly by the monopoly model presented in Chapter 15. In other words, many industries fall somewhere between the polar cases of perfect competition and monopoly. Economists call this situation *imperfect competition*.

oligopoly

a market structure in which only a few sellers offer similar or identical products

One type of imperfectly competitive market is an **oligopoly**, a market with only a few sellers, each offering a product that is similar or identical to the products offered by other sellers in the market. Economists measure a market's domination by a small number of firms with a statistic called the *concentration ratio*, which is the percentage of total output in the market supplied by the four largest firms. In the Canadian economy, most industries have a four-firm concentration ratio under 50 percent, but in some industries, the biggest firms play a more dominant role. Highly concentrated industries include breakfast cereal (which has a concentration ratio of 78 percent), aircraft manufacturing (81 percent), electric lamp bulbs (89 percent), household laundry equipment (93 percent), and cigarettes (95 percent). These industries are best described as oligopolies. In the next chapter we see that the small number of firms in oligopolies makes strategic interactions among them a key part of the analysis. That is, in choosing how much to produce and what price to charge, each firm in an oligopoly is concerned not only with what its competitors are doing but also with how its competitors would react to what it might do.

A second type of imperfectly competitive market is called **monopolistic competition**. This describes a market structure in which there are many firms selling products that are similar but not identical. In a monopolistically competitive market, each firm has a monopoly over the product it makes, but many other firms make similar products that compete for the same customers.

> **monopolistic competition**
> a market structure in which many firms sell products that are similar but not identical

To be more precise, monopolistic competition describes a market with the following attributes:

- *Many sellers:* There are many firms competing for the same group of customers.
- *Product differentiation:* Each firm produces a product that is at least slightly different from those of other firms. Thus, rather than being a price taker, each firm faces a downward-sloping demand curve.
- *Free entry and exit:* Firms can enter or exit the market without restriction. Thus, the number of firms in the market adjusts until economic profits are driven to zero.

A moment's thought reveals a long list of markets with these attributes: books, DVDs, computer games, restaurants, piano lessons, cookies, clothing, and so on.

Monopolistic competition, like oligopoly, is a market structure that lies between the extreme cases of perfect competition and monopoly. But oligopoly and monopolistic competition are quite different. Oligopoly departs from the perfectly competitive ideal of Chapter 14 because there are only a few sellers in the market. The small number of sellers makes rigorous competition less likely and strategic interactions among them vitally important. By contrast, a monopolistically competitive market has many sellers, each of which is small compared to the market. It departs from the perfectly competitive ideal because each of the sellers offers a somewhat different product.

Figure 16.1 summarizes the four types of market structure. The first question to ask about any market is how many firms there are. If there is only one firm, the market is a monopoly. If there are only a few firms, the market is an oligopoly. If there are many firms, we need to ask another question: Do the firms sell identical or differentiated products? If the many firms sell identical products, the market is perfectly competitive. But if the many firms sell differentiated products, the market is monopolistically competitive.

Because reality is never as clear-cut as theory, at times you may find it hard to decide what structure best describes a market. There is, for instance, no magic number that separates "few" from "many" when counting the number of firms. (Do the approximately one dozen companies that now sell cars in Canada make this market an oligopoly or more competitive? The answer is open to debate.)

FIGURE 16.1

The Four Types of Market Structure

Economists who study industrial organization divide markets into four types—monopoly, oligopoly, monopolistic competition, and perfect competition.

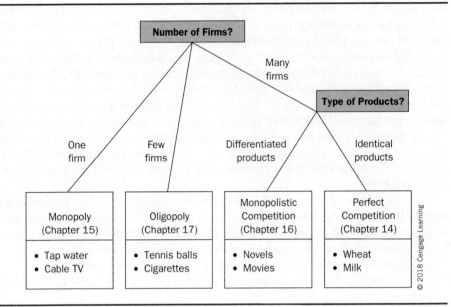

© 2018 Cengage Learning

Similarly, there is no sure way to determine when products are differentiated and when they are identical. (Are different brands of milk really the same? Again, the answer is debatable.) When analyzing actual markets, economists have to keep in mind the lessons learned from studying all types of market structure and then apply each lesson as it seems appropriate.

Now that we understand how economists define the various types of market structure, we can continue our analysis of each of them. In this chapter we examine monopolistic competition. In the next chapter, we analyze oligopoly.

 Define oligopoly and monopolistic competition and give an example of each.

QUICK **Quiz**

16-2 Competition with Differentiated Products

To understand monopolistically competitive markets, we first consider the decisions facing an individual firm. We then examine what happens in the long run as firms enter and exit the industry. Next, we compare the equilibrium under monopolistic competition to the equilibrium under perfect competition that we examined in Chapter 14. Finally, we consider whether the outcome in a monopolistically competitive market is desirable from the standpoint of society as a whole.

16-2a The Monopolistically Competitive Firm in the Short Run

Each firm in a monopolistically competitive market is, in many ways, like a monopoly. Because its product is different from those offered by other firms, it faces a downward-sloping demand curve. (By contrast, a perfectly competitive firm faces a horizontal demand curve at the market price.) Thus, the monopolistically competitive firm follows a monopolist's rule for profit maximization: It chooses to produce the quantity at which marginal revenue equals marginal cost and then uses its demand curve to find the price at which it can sell that quantity.

FIGURE 16.2

Monopolistic Competitors
in the Short Run

Monopolistic competitors, like monopolists, maximize profit by producing the quantity at which marginal revenue equals marginal cost. The firm in panel (a) makes a profit because, at this quantity, price is above average total cost. The firm in panel (b) experiences losses because, at this quantity, price is less than average total cost.

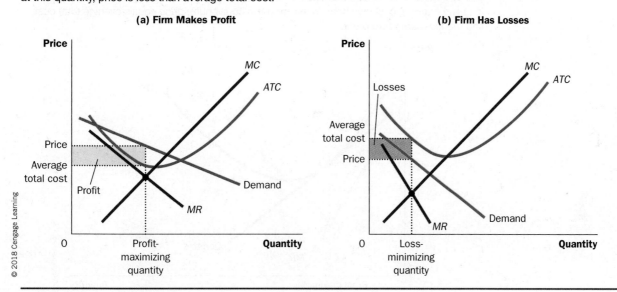

Figure 16.2 shows the cost, demand, and marginal-revenue curves for two typical firms, each in a different monopolistically competitive industry. In both panels of this figure, the profit-maximizing quantity is found at the intersection of the marginal-revenue and marginal-cost curves. The two panels show different outcomes for the firm's profit. In panel (a), price exceeds average total cost, so the firm makes a profit. In panel (b), price is below average total cost. In this case, the firm is unable to make a positive profit, so the best the firm can do is to minimize its losses.

All this should seem familiar. A monopolistically competitive firm chooses its quantity and price just as a monopoly does. In the short run, these two types of market structure are similar.

16-2b The Long-Run Equilibrium

The situations depicted in Figure 16.2 do not last long. When firms are making profits, as in panel (a), new firms have an incentive to enter the market. This entry increases the number of products from which customers can choose and, therefore, reduces the demand faced by each firm already in the market. In other words, profit encourages entry, and entry shifts the demand curves faced by the incumbent firms to the left. As the demand for incumbent firms' products fall, these firms experience declining profit.

Conversely, when firms are making losses, as in panel (b), firms in the market have an incentive to exit. As firms exit, customers have fewer products from which to choose. This decrease in the number of firms expands the demand faced by those firms that stay in the market. In other words, losses encourage exit, and exit shifts the demand curves of the remaining firms to the right. As the demand for the remaining firms' products rises, these firms experience rising profit (that is, declining losses).

FIGURE 16.3

A Monopolistic Competitor in the Long Run

In a monopolistically competitive market, if firms are making profit new firms enter and the demand curves for the incumbent firms shift to the left. Similarly, if firms are experiencing losses, old firms exit, and the demand curves of the remaining firms shift to the right. Because of these shifts in demand, a monopolistically competitive firm eventually finds itself in the long-run equilibrium shown here. In this long-run equilibrium, price equals average total cost, and the firm earns zero profit.

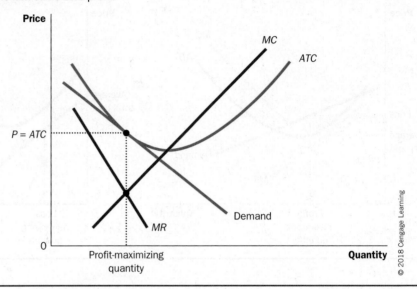

This process of entry and exit continues until the firms in the market are making exactly zero economic profit. Figure 16.3 depicts the long-run equilibrium. Once the market reaches this equilibrium, new firms have no incentive to enter, and existing firms have no incentive to exit.

Notice that the demand curve in this figure just barely touches the average-total-cost curve. Mathematically, we say the two curves are *tangent* to each other. These two curves must be tangent once entry and exit have driven profit to zero. Because profit per unit sold is the difference between price (found on the demand curve) and average total cost, the maximum profit is zero only if these two curves touch each other without crossing. Also note that this point of tangency occurs at the same quantity where marginal revenue equals marginal cost. That these two points line up is not a coincidence: It is required because this particular quantity maximizes profit and the maximum profit is exactly zero in the long run.

To sum up, two characteristics describe the long-run equilibrium in a monopolistically competitive market:

1. As in a monopoly market, price exceeds marginal cost. This conclusion arises because profit maximization requires marginal revenue to equal marginal cost and because the downward-sloping demand curve makes marginal revenue less than the price.
2. As in a competitive market, price equals average total cost. This conclusion arises because free entry and exit drive economic profit to zero.

The second characteristic shows how monopolistic competition differs from monopoly. Because a monopoly is the sole seller of a product without close substitutes, it can earn positive economic profit, even in the long run. By contrast, because there is free entry into a monopolistically competitive market, the economic profit of a firm in this type of market is driven to zero.

16-2c Monopolistic versus Perfect Competition

Figure 16.4 compares the long-run equilibrium under monopolistic competition to the long-run equilibrium under perfect competition. (Chapter 14 discussed the equilibrium with perfect competition.) There are two noteworthy differences between monopolistic and perfect competition—excess capacity and the markup.

Excess Capacity As we have just seen, entry and exit drive each firm in a monopolistically competitive market to a point of tangency between its demand and average-total-cost curves. Panel (a) of Figure 16.4 shows that the quantity of output at this point is smaller than the quantity that minimizes average total cost. Thus, under monopolistic competition, firms produce on the downward-sloping portion of their average-total-cost curves. In this way, monopolistic competition contrasts starkly with perfect competition. As panel (b) of Figure 16.4 shows, free entry in competitive markets drives firms to produce at the minimum of average total cost.

FIGURE 16.4

Monopolistic versus Perfect Competition

Panel (a) shows the long-run equilibrium in a monopolistically competitive market, and panel (b) shows the long-run equilibrium in a perfectly competitive market. Two differences are notable: (1) The perfectly competitive firm produces at the efficient scale, where average total cost is minimized. By contrast, the monopolistically competitive firm produces at less than the efficient scale. (2) Price equals marginal cost under perfect competition, but price is above marginal cost under monopolistic competition.

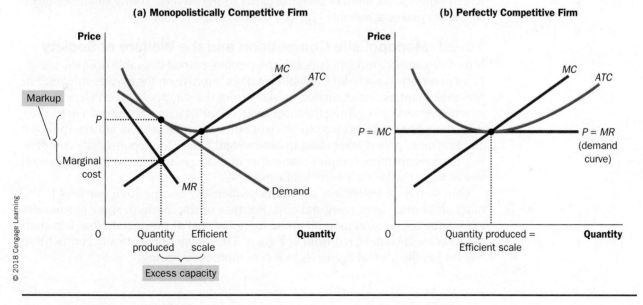

© 2018 Cengage Learning

The quantity that minimizes average total cost is called the *efficient scale* of the firm. In the long run, perfectly competitive firms produce at the efficient scale, whereas monopolistically competitive firms produce below this level. Firms are said to have *excess capacity* under monopolistic competition. In other words, a monopolistically competitive firm, unlike a perfectly competitive firm, could increase the quantity it produces and lower the average total cost of production. The firm forgoes this opportunity because it would need to cut its price to sell the additional output. It is more profitable for a monopolistic competitor to continue operating with excess capacity.

Markup over Marginal Cost A second difference between perfect competition and monopolistic competition is the relationship between price and marginal cost. For a competitive firm, such as that shown in panel (b) of Figure 16.4, price equals marginal cost. For a monopolistically competitive firm, such as that shown in panel (a), price exceeds marginal cost because the firm always has some market power.

How is this markup over marginal cost consistent with free entry and zero profit? The zero-profit condition ensures only that price equals average total cost. It does *not* ensure that price equals marginal cost. Indeed, in the long-run equilibrium, monopolistically competitive firms operate on the declining portion of their average-total-cost curves, so marginal cost is below average total cost. Thus, for price to equal average total cost, price must be above marginal cost.

In this relationship between price and marginal cost, we see a key behavioural difference between perfect competitors and monopolistic competitors. Imagine that you were to ask a firm the following question: "Would you like to see another customer come through your door ready to buy from you at your current price?" A perfectly competitive firm would answer that it didn't care. Because price exactly equals marginal cost, the profit from an extra unit sold is zero. By contrast, a monopolistically competitive firm is always eager to get another customer. Because its price exceeds marginal cost, an extra unit sold at the posted price means more profit.

According to an old quip, monopolistically competitive markets are those in which sellers send holiday greeting cards to the buyers. Trying to attract more customers makes sense only if price exceeds marginal cost.

16-2d Monopolistic Competition and the Welfare of Society

Is the outcome in a monopolistically competitive market desirable from the standpoint of society as a whole? Can policymakers improve on the market outcome? In previous chapters, we evaluated markets from the standpoint of efficiency—that is, whether society is getting the most it can out of its scarce resources. We learned that competitive markets lead to efficient outcomes, unless there are externalities, and that monopoly markets lead to deadweight losses. Monopolistically competitive markets are more complex than either of these polar cases, so evaluating welfare in these markets is a more subtle exercise.

One source of inefficiency in monopolistically competitive markets is the markup of price over marginal cost. Because of the markup, some consumers who value the good at more than the marginal cost of production (but less than the price) will be deterred from buying it. Thus, a monopolistically competitive market has the normal deadweight loss of monopoly pricing.

This outcome is undesirable compared with the efficient quantity that arises when price equals marginal cost, but there is no easy way for policymakers to fix the problem. To enforce marginal-cost pricing, they would need to regulate all firms that produce differentiated products. Because such products are so common in the economy, the administrative burden of such regulation would be overwhelming.

Moreover, regulating monopolistic competitors would entail all the problems of regulating natural monopolies. In particular, because monopolistic competitors are making zero profits already, requiring them to lower their prices to equal marginal cost would cause them to make losses. To keep these firms in business, the government would need to help them cover these losses. Rather than raising taxes to pay for these subsidies, policymakers may decide it is better to live with the inefficiency of monopolistic pricing.

Another source of inefficiency under monopolistic competition is that the number of firms in the market may not be "ideal." That is, there may be too much or too little entry. One way to think about this problem is in terms of the externalities associated with entry. Whenever a new firm considers entering the market with a new product, it takes into account only the profit it would make. Yet its entry would also have the following two effects that are external to the firm:

1. *The product-variety externality:* Because consumers get some consumer surplus from the introduction of a new product, entry of a new firm conveys a positive externality on consumers.
2. *The business-stealing externality:* Because other firms lose customers and profits from the entry of a new competitor, entry of a new firm imposes a negative externality on existing firms.

Thus, in a monopolistically competitive market, there are both positive and negative externalities associated with the entry of new firms. Depending on which externality is larger, a monopolistically competitive market could have either too few or too many products.

Both of these externalities are closely related to the conditions for monopolistic competition. The product-variety externality arises because new firms offer products that differ from those of the existing firms. The business-stealing externality arises because firms post a price above marginal cost and, therefore, are always eager to sell additional units. Conversely, because perfectly competitive firms produce identical goods and charge a price equal to marginal cost, neither of these externalities exists under perfect competition.

In the end, we can conclude only that monopolistically competitive markets do not have all the desirable welfare properties of perfectly competitive markets. That is, the invisible hand does not ensure that total surplus is maximized under monopolistic competition. Yet because the inefficiencies are subtle, hard to measure, and hard to fix, there is no easy way for public policy to improve the market outcome.

QUICK Quiz *List the three key attributes of monopolistic competition. • Draw a diagram and explain the long-run equilibrium in a monopolistically competitive market. How does this equilibrium differ from that in a perfectly competitive market?*

16-3 Advertising

It is nearly impossible to go through a typical day in a modern economy without being bombarded with advertising. Whether you are surfing the Internet, posting on Facebook, reading a newspaper, watching television, or driving down the highway, some firm will try to convince you to buy its product. Such behaviour is a natural feature of monopolistic competition (as well as some oligopolistic industries). When firms sell differentiated products and charge prices above marginal cost, each firm has an incentive to advertise to attract more buyers to its particular product.

The amount of advertising varies substantially across products. Firms that sell highly differentiated consumer goods, such as over-the-counter drugs, perfumes, soft drinks, razor blades, breakfast cereals, and dog food, typically spend between 10 and 20 percent of their revenue on advertising. Firms that sell industrial products, such as drill presses and communications satellites, typically spend very little on advertising. And firms that sell homogeneous products, such as wheat, peanuts, or crude oil, spend nothing at all.

For the economy as a whole, about 2 percent of total firm revenue is spent on advertising. This spending takes many forms, including ads on websites, social media, television, radio, and billboards and in newspapers, magazines, and direct mail.

Less Produce Variety and Higher Prices in Canada Due to Lack of Competition

In a 2014 study, University of Toronto economist Nicholas Li argues that the price gap between Canada and U.S. goods is due in large part to lower competition in Canada. He also finds that product variety in Canada is much lower than in the United States.

Ottawa Could Act to Reduce U.S.–Canada Price Gap, Study Says

By Barrie McKenna

The federal government likes to cast itself as the champion of consumers in combatting the frustratingly large gap between Canadian and U.S. prices. But a new report from the Toronto-based C.D. Howe Institute says Ottawa could fix much of the problem by putting its own house in order first—starting by slashing import tariffs and getting rid of the supply management regime that artificially inflates prices for dairy products, chickens and eggs.

"The easiest thing Canadian governments can do if they want to reduce the Canada–U.S. wholesale price gap is to eliminate existing tariffs and supply management policies that are responsible for the largest price gaps," University of Toronto economist Nicholas Li concludes in the 15-page report, *Sticker Shock: The Causes and Consequences of the Canada–U.S. Price Differential*.

The federal government should also raise duty-free exemptions for Canadians who buy goods outside the country, Mr. Li said.

The report, being released Tuesday, similarly questions whether Ottawa's plan to direct competition authorities to pursue companies that overcharge will work. "It is not obvious how the

Niki Love/Shutterstock.com

government can increase the extent of competition in sectors … that already have relatively free entry," the report said.

In its 2014 budget, Ottawa proposed beefing up the powers of the Competition Bureau to

16-3a The Debate over Advertising

Is society wasting the resources it devotes to advertising? Or does advertising serve a valuable purpose? Assessing the social value of advertising is difficult and often generates heated argument among economists. Let's consider both sides of the debate.

The Critique of Advertising Critics of advertising argue that firms advertise to manipulate people's tastes. Much advertising is psychological rather than informational. Consider, for example, the typical television commercial for some brand of soft drink. The commercial most likely does not tell the viewer about the product's price or quality. Instead, it might show a group of happy people at a party on a beach on a beautiful sunny day. In their hands are cans of the soft drink. The goal of the commercial is to convey a subconscious (if not subtle) message: "You too can have many friends and be happy, if only you drink our product." Critics of advertising argue that such a commercial creates a desire that otherwise might not exist.

Critics also argue that advertising impedes competition. Advertising often tries to convince consumers that products are more different than they truly are. By increasing the perception of product differentiation and fostering brand loyalty, advertising makes buyers less concerned with price differences among similar goods, thereby making the demand for a particular brand less elastic. When a firm faces a less elastic demand curve, it can increase its profits by charging a larger markup over marginal cost.

pursue manufacturers that engage in illegitimate country-specific pricing.

But Mr. Li argued that the practice of companies using their market power to impose country pricing—where manufacturers sometimes charge retailers and distributors higher prices in Canada—is ubiquitous in most market economies.

Several other factors also contribute to higher Canadian prices, including less competition, higher costs of doing business and added distribution costs due to Canada's sparser population density, according to the report.

In a recent letter to Industry Minister James Moore, a coalition of Canadian manufacturing groups similarly urged Ottawa not "intervene in setting prices," pointing out that federal government policies contribute to the cross-border gap through such things as outdated regulations. "It is critical to note

that the government itself plays a major role in the retail price consumers pay for goods in Canada," said the letter, signed by the heads of nine organization, including Canadian Manufacturers & Exporters.

The C.D. Howe report found that a large wholesale price gap emerged in the 2000s, exacerbated by a runup in the Canadian dollar. In 2002, a typical basket of goods that consumers buy regularly was 22 per cent lower in Canada than the U.S.—a trend that was the norm from the mid-1990s to the early 2000s. By 2012, the trend had reversed and the same goods had become 27 per cent more expensive in Canada.

An even larger swing hit food prices, which were 57 per cent more expensive in Canada in 2012, compared to 9 per cent cheaper a decade earlier. The widest price discrepancy of all, at 76 per cent in 2012, was for milk, eggs

and cheese—products governed by supply management, according to the report. And the Canada–U.S. price difference for these products widened more than for other food items over the decade. Under supply management, Ottawa allows farmers to fix their own prices, while imposing tariffs of up to 300 per cent to keep most imports out.

The report also found that Canadian consumers enjoy much less product variety than Americans—10,000 products at an average store versus 14,000 in the U.S.—the result of a less competitive manufacturing and retail environment.

U.S. supermarkets chains, for example, have larger stores than Canadian grocers (an average of 49,000 square feet versus 41,000), and outlets are served by fewer and larger distribution centres.

The Defence of Advertising Defenders of advertising argue that firms use advertising to provide information to customers. Advertising conveys the prices of the goods offered for sale, the existence of new products, and the locations of retail outlets. This information allows customers to make better choices about what to buy and, thus, enhances the ability of markets to allocate resources efficiently.

Defenders also argue that advertising fosters competition. Because advertising allows customers to be more fully informed about all the firms in the market, customers can more easily take advantage of price differences. Thus, each firm has less market power. In addition, advertising allows new firms to enter more easily, because it gives entrants a means to attract customers from existing firms.

Over time, policymakers have come to accept the view that advertising can make markets more competitive. One important example is the regulation of advertising for certain professions, such as lawyers, doctors, and pharmacists. In the past, these groups succeeded in getting governments to prohibit advertising in their fields on the grounds that advertising was "unprofessional." In recent years, however, the courts have concluded that the primary effect of these restrictions on advertising was to curtail competition. They have, therefore, overturned many of the laws that prohibit advertising by members of these professions.

case study **Canada Goose Flying High**

Marketing campaigns can help differentiate a product from the competition. An example of such a product is the distinctive Canadian goose down–filled parkas made by Canada Goose, the Canadian maker of outdoor apparel. The likes of Emma Watson, Matt Damon, Hayden Christensen, Maggie Gyllenhaal, and Hilary Duff have all been seen sporting the company's jackets. They've also shown up onscreen: Nicolas Cage wore a Canada Goose parka in *National Treasure* (2004), Jessica Alba appeared in one in *Good Luck Chuck* (2007), and Kate Beckinsale donned one in *Whiteout* (2009).

The parkas were originally designed for hard-core outdoor use—Canada Goose claims they can withstand temperatures as low as –70°C. From the beginning, the company aspired to make its name synonymous with quality, especially the quality of its goose down, which is obtained from Hutterite farmers across Canada. Hutterite farmers keep small flocks of geese and allow them to mature before being plucked. This means the down is larger, creating more pockets in which warm air is trapped. It also means Hutterite down is more expensive, which is what makes Canada Goose jackets so expensive and feeds into their "elite" perception.

While temperatures as low as –70°C are not likely to occur in Hollywood, the company has turned Canada Goose parkas into the latest "must-have" fashion accessory through the use of a savvy marketing campaign designed to emphasize the elite nature of the product. The company's approach has not been to stage a high-cost advertising campaign, but rather to use product placement and so-called "guerrilla marketing" tactics. This involves not only appearances in Hollywood movies, but placing the product with security personnel and ushers at outdoor winter sporting events and bouncers, valets, and doormen at Fairmont hotels—anyone who operates in a cold environment. These "human billboards" have served as effective ambassadors for the product. These advertising tactics are particularly effective and important in the social media age, where a picture of Emma Watson wearing a Canada Goose parka can go viral on the Internet.

The fashion market is notoriously fickle. Whether Canada Goose continues to fly high or goes the way of other must-have products of the past remains to be seen. But the recent success of the company shows how important product differentiation supported by innovative marketing geared toward social media can be. ∎

16-3b Advertising as a Signal of Quality

Many types of advertising contain little apparent information about the product being advertised. Consider a firm introducing a new breakfast cereal. The firm might saturate the airwaves with advertisements showing some actor eating the cereal and exclaiming how wonderful it tastes. How much information does the advertisement really provide?

The answer is: more than you might think. Defenders of advertising argue that even advertising that appears to contain little hard information may in fact tell consumers something about product quality. The willingness of the firm to spend a large amount of money on advertising can itself be a *signal* to consumers about the quality of the product being offered.

Consider the problem facing two firms—Post and Kellogg. Each company has just come up with a recipe for a new cereal that it would sell for $3 a box. To keep things simple, let's assume that the marginal cost of making cereal is zero, so the $3 is all profit. Each company knows that if it spends $10 million on advertising, it will get 1 million consumers to try its new cereal. And each company knows that if consumers like the cereal, they will buy it not once but many times.

First consider Post's decision. Based on market research, Post knows that its cereal tastes like shredded newspaper with sugar on top. Advertising would sell one box to each of 1 million consumers, but consumers would quickly learn that the cereal is not very good and stop buying it. Post decides it is not worth paying $10 million in advertising to get only $3 million in sales. So it does not bother to advertise. It sends its cooks back to the test kitchen to develop another recipe.

Kellogg, on the other hand, knows that its cereal is great. Each person who tries it will buy a box a month for the next year. Thus, the $10 million in advertising will bring in $36 million in sales. Advertising is profitable here because Kellogg has a good product that consumers will buy repeatedly. Thus, Kellogg chooses to advertise.

Now that we have considered the behaviour of the two firms, let's consider the behaviour of consumers. We began by asserting that consumers are inclined to try a new cereal that they see advertised. But is this behaviour rational? Should a consumer try a new cereal just because the seller has chosen to advertise it?

In fact, it may be completely rational for consumers to try new products that they see advertised. In our story, consumers decide to try Kellogg's new cereal because Kellogg advertises. Kellogg chooses to advertise because it knows that its cereal is quite good, while Post chooses not to advertise because it knows that its cereal is only mediocre. By its willingness to spend money on advertising, Kellogg signals to consumers the quality of its cereal. Each consumer thinks, quite sensibly, "Boy, if Kellogg Company is willing to spend so much money advertising this new cereal, it must be really good."

What is most surprising about this theory of advertising is that the content of the advertisement is irrelevant. Kellogg signals the quality of its product by its willingness to spend money on advertising. What the advertisements say is not as important as the fact that consumers know ads are expensive. By contrast, cheap advertising cannot be effective at signalling quality to consumers. In our example, if an advertising campaign cost less than $3 million, both Post and Kellogg would use it to market their new cereals. Because both good and mediocre cereals would be advertised, consumers could not infer the quality of a new cereal from the fact that it is advertised. Over time, consumers would learn to ignore such cheap advertising.

This theory can explain why firms pay famous actors large amounts of money to make advertisements that, on the surface, appear to convey no information at all. The information is not in the advertisement's content, but simply in its existence and expense.

16-3c Brand Names

Advertising is closely related to the existence of brand names. In many markets, there are two types of firms. Some firms sell products with widely recognized brand names, while other firms sell generic substitutes. For example, in a typical drugstore, you can find Bayer aspirin on the shelf next to generic aspirin. In a typical grocery store, you can find Pepsi next to less familiar colas. Most often, the firm with the brand name spends more on advertising and charges a higher price for its product.

Just as there is disagreement about the economics of advertising, there is disagreement about the economics of brand names. Let's consider both sides of the debate.

Critics argue that brand names cause consumers to perceive differences that do not really exist. In many cases, the generic good is almost indistinguishable from the brand-name good. Consumers' willingness to pay more for the brand-name good, these critics assert, is a form of irrationality fostered by advertising. Economist Edward Chamberlin, one of the early developers of the theory of monopolistic competition, concluded from this argument that brand names were bad for the economy. He proposed that the government discourage their use by refusing to enforce the exclusive trademarks that companies use to identify their products.

More recently, economists have defended brand names as a useful way for consumers to ensure that the goods they buy are of high quality. There are two related arguments. First, brand names provide consumers with *information* about quality when quality cannot be easily judged in advance of purchase. Second, brand names give firms an *incentive* to maintain high quality, because firms have a financial stake in maintaining the reputation of their brand names.

To see how these arguments work in practice, consider a famous brand name: McDonald's. Imagine that you are driving through an unfamiliar town and want to stop for lunch. You see a McDonald's and a local restaurant next to it. Which do you choose? The local restaurant may in fact offer better food at lower prices, but you have no way of knowing that. By contrast, McDonald's offers a consistent product across many cities. Its brand name is useful to you as a way of judging the quality of what you are about to buy.

The McDonald's brand name also ensures that the company has an incentive to maintain quality. For example, if some customers were to become ill from spoiled food sold at a McDonald's, the news would be disastrous for the company. McDonald's would lose much of the valuable reputation that it has built up with years of expensive advertising. As a result, it would lose sales and profit not just in the outlet that sold the bad food but also in many other McDonald's outlets throughout the country. By contrast, if some customers were to become ill from bad food at a local restaurant, that restaurant might have to close down, but the lost profits would be much smaller. Hence, McDonald's has a greater incentive to ensure that its food is safe.

The debate over brand names thus centres on the question of whether consumers are rational in preferring brand names to generic substitutes. Critics argue that brand names are the result of an irrational consumer response to advertising. Defenders argue that consumers have good reason to pay more for brand-name products because they can be more confident about the quality of these products.

 How might advertising make markets less competitive? How might it make markets more competitive? • Give the arguments for and against brand names.

16-4 Conclusion

Monopolistic competition is true to its name: It is a hybrid of monopoly and competition. Like a monopoly, each monopolistic competitor faces a downward-sloping demand curve and, as a result, charges a price above marginal cost. As in a perfectly competitive market, there are many firms, and entry and exit drive the profit of each monopolistic competitor toward zero in the long run. Table 16.1 summarizes these lessons.

TABLE 16.1

Monopolistic Competition: Between Perfect Competition and Monopoly

	Market Structure		
	Perfect Competition	Monopolistic Competition	Monopoly
Features that all three market structures share			
Goal of firms	Maximize profits	Maximize profits	Maximize profits
Rule for maximizing	$MR = MC$	$MR = MC$	$MR = MC$
Can earn economic profits in the short run?	Yes	Yes	Yes
Features that monopoly and monopolistic competition share			
Price taker?	Yes	No	No
Price	$P = MC$	$P > MC$	$P > MC$
Produces welfare-maximizing level of output?	Yes	No	No
Features that perfect competition and monopolistic competition share			
Number of firms	Many	Many	One
Entry in long run?	Yes	Yes	No
Can earn economic profits in long run?	No	No	Yes

Because monopolistically competitive firms produce differentiated products, each firm advertises in order to attract customers to its own brand. To some extent, advertising manipulates consumers' tastes, promotes irrational brand loyalty, and impedes competition. To a larger extent, advertising provides information, establishes brand names of reliable quality, and fosters competition.

The theory of monopolistic competition seems to describe many markets in the economy. It is somewhat disappointing, therefore, that the theory does not yield simple and compelling advice for public policy. From the standpoint of the economic theorist, the allocation of resources in monopolistically competitive markets is not perfect. Yet, from the standpoint of a practical policymaker, there may be little that can be done to improve it.

summary

- A monopolistically competitive market is characterized by three attributes: many firms, differentiated products, and free entry.

- The equilibrium in a monopolistically competitive market differs from that in a perfectly competitive market in two related ways. First, each firm in a monopolistically competitive market has excess capacity. That is, it operates on the downward-sloping portion of the average-total-cost curve. Second, each firm charges a price above marginal cost.

- Monopolistic competition does not have all the desirable properties of perfect competition. There is the standard deadweight loss of monopoly caused by the markup of price over marginal cost. In addition, the number of firms (and thus the variety of products) can be too large or too small. In practice, the ability of policymakers to correct these inefficiencies is limited.

- The product differentiation inherent in monopolistic competition leads to the use of advertising and brand names. Critics of advertising and brand names argue that firms use them to take advantage of consumer irrationality and to reduce competition. Defenders of advertising and brand names argue that firms use them to inform consumers and to compete more vigorously on price and product quality.

KEY concepts

oligopoly, *p. 356*

monopolistic competition, *p. 357*

QUESTIONS FOR review

1. Describe the three attributes of monopolistic competition. How is monopolistic competition like monopoly? How is it like perfect competition?

2. Draw a diagram depicting a firm in a monopolistically competitive market that is making profits. Now show what happens to this firm as new firms enter the industry.

3. Draw a diagram of the long-run equilibrium in a monopolistically competitive market. How is price related to average total cost? How is price related to marginal cost?

4. Does a monopolistic competitor produce too much or too little output compared to the most efficient level? What practical considerations make it difficult for policymakers to solve this problem?

5. How might advertising reduce economic well-being? How might advertising increase economic well-being?

6. How might advertising with no apparent informational content in fact convey information to consumers?

7. Explain two benefits that might arise from the existence of brand names.

QUICK CHECK **multiple choice**

1. Which of the following conditions does NOT describe a firm in a monopolistically competitive market?
   a. It makes a product different from its competitors.
   b. It takes its price as given by market conditions.
   c. It maximizes profit both in the short run and in the long run.
   d. It has the freedom to enter or exit in the long run.

2. Which of the following goods best fits the definition of monopolistic competition?
   a. wheat
   b. tap water
   c. crude oil
   d. restaurants

3. A monopolistically competitive firm will increase its production in which of the following circumstances?
   a. marginal revenue is greater than marginal cost
   b. marginal revenue is greater than average total cost
   c. price is greater than marginal cost
   d. price is greater than average total cost

4. New firms will enter a monopolistically competitive market in which of the following circumstances?
   a. marginal revenue is greater than marginal cost
   b. marginal revenue is greater than average total cost
   c. price is greater than marginal cost
   d. price is greater than average total cost

5. Which of the following is true of a monopolistically competitive market in long-run equilibrium?
   a. Price is greater than marginal cost.
   b. Price is equal to marginal revenue.
   c. Firms make positive economic profits.
   d. Firms produce at the minimum of average total cost.

6. If advertising makes consumers more loyal to particular brands, it could _____ the elasticity of demand and _____ the markup of price over marginal cost.
   a. increase, increase
   b. increase, decrease
   c. decrease, increase
   d. decrease, decrease

PROBLEMS AND **applications**

1. Classify the following markets as perfectly competitive, monopolistic, or monopolistically competitive, and explain your answers.
   a. wooden #2 pencils
   b. bottled water
   c. copper
   d. local telephone service
   e. peanut butter
   f. lipstick
   g. cola
   h. beer

2. For each of the following characteristics, say whether it describes a perfectly competitive firm, a monopolistically competitive firm, both, or neither.
   a. sells a differentiated product from its competitors
   b. has marginal revenue less than price
   c. earns economic profit in the long run
   d. produces at minimum of average total cost in the long run
   e. equates marginal revenue and marginal cost
   f. charges a price above marginal cost

3. For each of the following characteristics, say whether it describes a monopoly firm, a monopolistically competitive firm, both, or neither.
   a. faces a downward-sloping demand curve
   b. has marginal revenue less than price
   c. faces the entry of new firms selling similar products
   d. earns economic profit in the long run

   e. equates marginal revenue and marginal cost
   f. produces the socially efficient quantity of output

4. Sparkle is one firm of many in the market for toothpaste, which is in long-run equilibrium.
   a. Draw a diagram showing Sparkle's demand curve, marginal-revenue curve, average-total-cost curve, and marginal-cost curve. Label Sparkle's profit-maximizing output and price.
   b. What is Sparkle's profit? Explain.
   c. On your diagram, show the consumer surplus derived from the purchase of Sparkle toothpaste. Also show the deadweight loss relative to the efficient level of output.
   d. If the government forced Sparkle to produce the efficient level of output, what would happen to the firm? What would happen to Sparkle's customers?

5. You are hired as the consultant to a monopolistically competitive firm. The firm reports the following information about its price, marginal cost, and average total cost. Can the firm possibly be maximizing profit? If not, what should it do to increase profit? If the firm is profit-maximizing, is the firm in a long-run equilibrium? If not, what will happen to restore long-run equilibrium?
   a. $P < MC, P < ATC$
   b. $P > MC, P < ATC$
   c. $P = MC, P > ATC$
   d. $P > MC, P = ATC$

6. For each of the following pairs of firms, explain which firm would be more likely to engage in advertising:
   a. a family-owned farm or a family-owned restaurant
   b. a manufacturer of forklifts or a manufacturer of cars
   c. a company that invented a very reliable watch or a company that invented a less reliable watch that costs the same amount to make

7. The makers of Tylenol pain reliever do a lot of advertising and have very loyal customers. In contrast, the makers of generic acetaminophen do no advertising, and their customers shop only for the lowest price. Assume that the marginal costs of Tylenol and generic acetaminophen are the same and constant.
   a. Draw a diagram showing Tylenol's demand, marginal-revenue, and marginal-cost curves. Label Tylenol's price and markup over marginal cost.
   b. Repeat part (a) for a producer of generic acetaminophen. How do the diagrams differ? Which company has the bigger markup? Explain.
   c. Which company has the greater incentive for careful quality control? Why?

8. Sleek Sneakers Co. is one of many firms in the market for shoes.
   a. Assume that Sleek is currently earning short-run economic profits. On a correctly labelled diagram, show Sleek's profit-maximizing output and price, as well as the area representing profit.
   b. What happens to Sleek's price, output, and profit in the long run? Explain this change in words, and show it on a new diagram.
   c. Suppose that over time, consumers become more focused on stylistic differences among shoe brands. How would this change in attitude affect each firm's price elasticity of demand? In the long run, how will this change in demand affect Sleek's price, output, and profits?
   d. At the profit-maximizing price you identified in part (c), is Sleek's demand curve elastic or inelastic? Explain.

9. The market for peanut butter in Nutville is monopolistically competitive and in long-run equilibrium. One day, consumer advocate Skippy Jif discovers that all brands of peanut butter in Nutville are identical. Thereafter, the market becomes perfectly competitive and again reaches its long-run equilibrium. Using an appropriate diagram, explain whether each of the following variables increases, decreases, or stays the same for the typical firm in the market:
   - price
   - quantity
   - average total cost
   - marginal cost
   - profit

10. Consider a monopolistically competitive market with N firms. Each firm's business opportunities are described by the following equations:

Demand:	$Q = 100/N - P$
Marginal Revenue:	$MR = 100/N - 2Q$
Total Cost:	$TC = 50 + Q^2$
Marginal Cost:	$MC = 2Q$

   a. How does N, the number of firms in the market, affect each firm's demand curve? Why?
   b. How many units does each firm produce? (The answer to this question and the next two depend on N.)
   c. What price does each firm charge?
   d. How much profit does each firm make?
   e. In the long run, how many firms will exist in this market?

Adrian Brown/Bloomberg/Getty Images

CHAPTER

17

LEARNING
objectives

Oligopoly

In this chapter, you will ...

1 See what market structures lie between monopoly and competition

2 Examine what outcomes are possible when a market is an oligopoly

3 Learn about the prisoners' dilemma and how it applies to oligopoly and other issues

4 Consider how competition laws try to foster competition in oligopolistic markets

If you play hockey, it is likely that your skates are one of two brands: Nike–Bauer or Reebok–CCM. These two companies make almost all of the skates sold in Canada. Together these firms determine the quantity of skates produced and, given the market demand curve, the price at which skates are sold. Similarly, if you fly within Canada you probably have to choose between WestJet and Air Canada, who between them account for about 70 percent of the domestic airline market.

oligopoly

a market structure in which only a few sellers offer similar or identical products

The markets for hockey skates and air travel are examples of an **oligopoly**. The essence of an oligopolistic market is that there are only a few sellers. As a result, the actions of any one seller in the market can have a large impact on the profits of all the other sellers. Oligopolistic firms are interdependent in a way that competitive firms are not. Our goal in this chapter is to see how this interdependence shapes the firms' behaviour and what problems it raises for public policy.

game theory

the study of how people behave in strategic situations

The analysis of oligopoly offers an opportunity to introduce **game theory**, the study of how people behave in strategic situations. By "strategic," we mean a situation in which a person, when choosing among alternative courses of action, must consider how others might respond to the action she takes. Strategic thinking is crucial not only in checkers, chess, and tic-tac-toe but also in many business decisions. Because oligopolistic markets have only a small number of firms, each firm must act strategically. Each firm knows that its profit depends on both how much it produces and how much the other firms produce. In making its production decision, each firm in an oligopoly should consider how its decision might affect the production decisions of the other firms in the market.

Game theory is not necessary for understanding competitive, monopolistically competitive, or monopoly markets. In a market that is either perfectly competitive or monopolistically competitive, each firm is so small compared to the market that strategic interactions with other firms are not important. In a monopolized market, strategic interactions are absent because the market has only one firm. But, as we will see, game theory is useful for understanding oligopolies and many other situations in which a small number of players interact with one another. Game theory helps explain the strategies that people choose, whether they are playing hockey or selling hockey skates.

17-1 Markets with Only a Few Sellers

Because an oligopolistic market has only a small group of sellers, a key feature of oligopoly is the tension between cooperation and self-interest. Oligopolists are best off when they cooperate and act like a monopolist—producing a small quantity of output and charging a price above marginal cost. Yet because each oligopolist cares about only its own profit, there are powerful incentives at work that hinder a group of firms from maintaining the cooperative outcome.

17-1a A Duopoly Example

To understand the behaviour of oligopolies, let's consider an oligopoly with only two members, called a *duopoly*. Duopoly is the simplest type of oligopoly. Oligopolies with three or more members face the same problems as duopolies, so we do not lose much by starting with the simpler case.

TABLE 17.1

The Demand Schedule for Water

Quantity (in litres)	Price	Total Revenue (and total profit)
0	$120	$ 0
10	110	1100
20	100	2000
30	90	2700
40	80	3200
50	70	3500
60	60	3600
70	50	3500
80	40	3200
90	30	2700
100	20	2000
110	10	1100
120	0	0

Imagine a town in which only two residents—Jack and Jill—own wells that produce water safe for drinking. Each Saturday, Jack and Jill decide how many litres of water to pump, bring the water to town, and sell it for whatever price the market will bear. To keep things simple, suppose that Jack and Jill can pump as much water as they want without cost. That is, the marginal cost of water equals zero.

Table 17.1 shows the town's demand schedule for water. The first column shows the total quantity demanded, and the second column shows the price. If the two well owners sell a total of 10 L of water, water goes for $110 per litre. If they sell a total of 20 L, the price falls to $100 per litre. And so on. If you graphed these two columns of numbers, you would get a standard downward-sloping demand curve.

The last column in Table 17.1 shows the total revenue from the sale of water. It equals the quantity sold times the price. Because there is assumed to be no cost to pumping water, the total revenue of the two producers equals their total profit.

Let's now consider how the organization of the town's water industry affects the price of water and the quantity of water sold.

17-1b Competition, Monopolies, and Cartels

Before considering the price and quantity of water that results from the duopoly of Jack and Jill, let's discuss briefly what the outcome would be if the water market were either perfectly competitive or monopolistic. These two polar cases are natural benchmarks.

If the market for water were perfectly competitive, the production decisions of each firm would drive price to equal marginal cost. Because we have assumed that the marginal cost of pumping additional water is zero, the equilibrium price of water under perfect competition would be zero as well. The equilibrium quantity would be 120 L. The price of water would reflect the cost of producing it, and the efficient quantity of water would be produced and consumed.

Now consider how a monopoly would behave. Table 17.1 shows that total profit is maximized at a quantity of 60 L and a price of $60 per litre. A profit-maximizing monopolist, therefore, would produce this quantity and charge this price. As is standard for monopolies, price would exceed marginal cost. The result would be inefficient, because the quantity of water produced and consumed would fall short of the socially efficient level of 120 L.

What outcome should we expect from our duopolists? One possibility is that Jack and Jill get together and agree on the quantity of water to produce and the price to charge for it. Such an agreement among firms over production and price is called **collusion**, and the group of firms acting in unison is called a **cartel**. Once a cartel is formed, the market is in effect served by a monopoly and we can apply our analysis from Chapter 15. That is, if Jack and Jill collude, they will agree on the monopoly outcome because that outcome maximizes their total profit. Our two producers would produce a total of 60 L, which sell at a price of $60 per litre. Once again, price exceeds marginal cost, and the outcome is socially inefficient.

A cartel must agree not only on the total level of production but also on the amount produced by each member. In our case, Jack and Jill must agree on how to split the monopoly production of 60 L. Each member of the cartel will want a larger share of the market because a larger market share means larger profit. If Jack and Jill agreed to split the market equally, each would produce 30 L, the price would be $60 per litre, and each would get a profit of $1800.

17-1c The Equilibrium for an Oligopoly

Oligopolists would like to form cartels and earn monopoly profits, but that is often impossible. Squabbling among cartel members over how to divide the profit in the market can make agreement among members difficult. In addition, as we discuss later in this chapter, competition laws prohibit explicit agreements among oligopolists as a matter of public policy. Let's therefore consider what happens if Jack and Jill decide separately how much water to produce.

At first, one might expect Jack and Jill to reach the monopoly outcome on their own, because this outcome maximizes their joint profit. In the absence of a binding agreement, however, the monopoly outcome is unlikely. To see why, imagine that Jack expects Jill to produce only 30 L (half of the monopoly quantity). Jack would reason as follows:

"I could produce 30 L as well. In this case, a total of 60 L of water would be sold at a price of $60 per litre. My profit would be $1800 (30 L × $60 per litre). Alternatively, I could produce 40 L. In this case, a total of 70 L of water would be sold at a price of $50 per litre. My profit would be $2000 (40 L × $50 per litre). Even though total profit in the market would fall, my profit would be higher, because I would have a larger share of the market."

Of course, Jill might reason the same way. If so, Jack and Jill would each bring 40 L to town. Total sales would be 80 L, and the price would fall to $40. Thus, if the duopolists individually pursue their own self-interest when deciding how much to produce, they produce a total quantity greater than the monopoly quantity, charge a price lower than the monopoly price, and earn total profit less than the monopoly profit.

Although the logic of self-interest increases the duopoly's output above the monopoly level, it does not push the duopolists to reach the competitive allocation. Consider what happens when each duopolist is producing 40 L. The price is $40, and each duopolist makes a profit of $1600. In this case, Jack's self-interested logic leads to a different conclusion:

collusion

an agreement among firms in a market about quantities to produce or prices to charge

cartel

a group of firms acting in unison

"Right now, my profit is $1600. Suppose I increase my production to 50 L. In this case, a total of 90 L of water would be sold, and the price would be $30 per litre. Then my profit would be only $1500. Rather than increasing production and driving down the price, I am better off keeping my production at 40 L."

The outcome in which Jack and Jill each produce 40 L looks like some sort of equilibrium. In fact, this outcome is called a *Nash equilibrium*. (It is named after Nobel winning economic theorist John Nash, whose life was portrayed in the book and movie *A Beautiful Mind*.) A **Nash equilibrium** is a situation in which economic actors interacting with one another each choose their best strategy given the strategies the others have chosen. In this case, given that Jill is producing 40 L, the best strategy for Jack is to produce 40 L. Similarly, given that Jack is producing 40 L, the best strategy for Jill is to produce 40 L. Once they reach this Nash equilibrium, neither Jack nor Jill has an incentive to make a different decision.

This example illustrates the tension between cooperation and self-interest. Oligopolists would be better off cooperating and reaching the monopoly outcome. Yet because they each pursue their own self-interest, they do not end up reaching the monopoly outcome and, thus, fail to maximize their joint profit. Each oligopolist is tempted to raise production and capture a larger share of the market. As each of them tries to do this, total production rises and the price falls.

At the same time, self-interest does not drive the market all the way to the competitive outcome. Like monopolists, oligopolists are aware that increasing the amount they produce reduces the price of their product, which in turn affects profits. Therefore, they stop short of following the competitive firm's rule of producing up to the point where price equals marginal cost.

In summary, when firms in an oligopoly individually choose production to maximize profit, they produce a quantity of output greater than the level produced by monopoly and less than the level produced by competition. The oligopoly price is less than the monopoly price but greater than the competitive price (which equals marginal cost).

17-1d How the Size of an Oligopoly Affects the Market Outcome

We can use the insights from this analysis of duopoly to discuss how the size of an oligopoly is likely to affect the outcome in a market. Suppose, for instance, that John and Joan suddenly discover water sources on their property and join Jack and Jill in the water oligopoly. The demand schedule in Table 17.1 remains the same, but now more producers are available to satisfy this demand. How would an increase in the number of sellers from two to four affect the price and quantity of water in the town?

If the sellers of water could form a cartel, they would once again try to maximize total profit by producing the monopoly quantity and charging the monopoly price. Just as when there were only two sellers, the members of the cartel would need to agree on production levels for each member and find some way to enforce the agreement. As the cartel grows larger, however, this outcome is less likely. Reaching and enforcing an agreement becomes more difficult as the size of the group increases.

Nash equilibrium
a situation in which economic actors interacting with one another each choose their best strategy given the strategies that all the other actors have chosen

Ask the Experts

Nash Equilibrium

"Behavior in many complex and seemingly intractable strategic settings can be understood more clearly by working out what each party in the game will choose to do if they realize that the other parties will be solving the same problem. This insight has helped us understand behavior as diverse as military conflicts, price setting by competing firms and penalty kicking in soccer."

What do economists say?

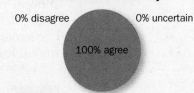

0% disagree   0% uncertain

100% agree

Source: IGM Economic Experts Panel, June 2, 2015.
Figure © 2018 Cengage Learning.

If the oligopolists do not form a cartel—perhaps because the competition laws prohibit it—they must each decide on their own how much water to produce. To see how the increase in the number of sellers affects the outcome, consider the decision facing each seller. At any time, each well owner has the option to raise production by 1 litre. In making this decision, the well owner weighs two effects:

1. *The output effect:* Because price is above marginal cost, selling 1 more litre of water at the going price will raise profit.
2. *The price effect:* Raising production will increase the total amount sold, which will lower the price of water and lower the profit on all the other litres sold.

If the output effect is larger than the price effect, the well owner will increase production. If the price effect is larger than the output effect, the owner will not raise production. (In fact, in this case, it is profitable to reduce production.) Each oligopolist continues to increase production until these two marginal effects exactly balance, taking the other firms' production as given.

Now consider how the number of firms in the industry affects the marginal analysis of each oligopolist. The larger the number of sellers, the less each seller is concerned about her own impact on the market price. That is, as the oligopoly grows in size, the magnitude of the price effect falls. When the oligopoly grows very large, the price effect disappears altogether. In this extreme case, the production decision of an individual firm no longer affects the market price. Each firm takes the market price as given when deciding how much to produce and, therefore increases production as long as price is above marginal cost.

We can now see that a large oligopoly is essentially a group of competitive firms. A competitive firm considers only the output effect when deciding how much to produce: Because a competitive firm is a price taker, the price effect is absent. Thus, *as the number of sellers in an oligopoly grows larger, an oligopolistic market looks more and more like a competitive market. The price approaches marginal cost, and the quantity produced approaches the socially efficient level.*

This analysis of oligopoly offers a new perspective on the effects of international trade. Imagine that Toyota and Honda are the only automakers in Japan, Volkswagen and BMW are the only automakers in Germany, and Ford and General Motors are the only automakers in Canada. If these nations prohibited international trade in autos, each would have an auto oligopoly with only two members, and the market outcome would likely depart substantially from the competitive ideal. With international trade, however, the car market is a world market, and the oligopoly in this example has six members. Allowing free trade increases the number of producers from which each consumer can choose, and this increased competition keeps prices closer to marginal cost. Thus, the theory of oligopoly provides another reason, in addition to the theory of comparative advantage discussed in Chapter 3, why all countries can benefit from free trade.

QUICK Quiz *If the members of an oligopoly could agree on a total quantity to produce, what quantity would they choose? • If the oligopolists do not act together but instead make production decisions individually, do they produce a total quantity more or less than in your answer to the previous question? Why?*

17-2 The Economics of Cooperation

As we have seen, oligopolies would like to reach the monopoly outcome. Doing so, however, requires cooperation, which at times is difficult to establish and maintain. In this section we look more closely at the problems that arise when cooperation among actors is desirable but difficult. To analyze the economics of cooperation, we need to learn a little about game theory.

In particular, we focus on a "game" called the **prisoners' dilemma**, which provides insight into why cooperation is difficult. Many times in life, people fail to cooperate with one another even when cooperation would make them all better off. An oligopoly is just one example. The story of the prisoners' dilemma contains a general lesson that applies to any group trying to maintain cooperation among its members.

prisoners' dilemma
a particular "game" between two captured prisoners that illustrates why cooperation is difficult to maintain even when it is mutually beneficial

17-2a The Prisoners' Dilemma

The prisoners' dilemma is a story about two criminals who have been captured by the police. Let's call them Bonnie and Clyde. The police have enough evidence to convict Bonnie and Clyde of the minor crime of carrying an unregistered gun, so that each would spend a year in jail. The police also suspect that the two criminals have committed a bank robbery together, but they lack hard evidence to convict them of this major crime. The police question Bonnie and Clyde in separate rooms and offer each of them the following deal:

"Right now, we can lock you up for 1 year. If you confess to the bank robbery and implicate your partner, however, we'll give you immunity and you can go free. Your partner will get 20 years in jail. But if you both confess to the crime, we won't need your testimony and we can avoid the cost of a trial, so you will each get an intermediate sentence of 8 years."

If Bonnie and Clyde, heartless bank robbers that they are, care only about their own sentences, what would you expect them to do? Figure 17.1 shows their choices. Each prisoner has two strategies: confess or remain silent. The sentence each prisoner gets depends on the strategy he or she chooses and the strategy chosen by his or her partner in crime.

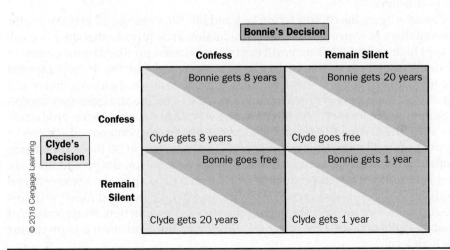

FIGURE 17.1

The Prisoners' Dilemma

In this game between two criminals suspected of committing a crime, the sentence that each receives depends both on his or her decision whether to confess or remain silent and on the decision made by the other.

Consider first Bonnie's decision. She reasons as follows: "I don't know what Clyde is going to do. If he remains silent, my best strategy is to confess, because then I'll go free rather than spending a year in jail. If he confesses, my best strategy is still to confess, because then I'll spend 8 years in jail rather than 20. So, regardless of what Clyde does, I am better off confessing."

dominant strategy
a strategy that is best for a player in a game regardless of the strategies chosen by the other players

In the language of game theory, a strategy is called a **dominant strategy** if it is the best strategy for a player to follow regardless of the strategies pursued by other players. In this case, confessing is a dominant strategy for Bonnie. She spends less time in jail if she confesses, regardless of whether Clyde confesses or remains silent.

Now consider Clyde's decision. He faces the same choices as Bonnie, and he reasons in much the same way. Regardless of what Bonnie does, Clyde can reduce his time in jail by confessing. In other words, confessing is also a dominant strategy for Clyde.

In the end, both Bonnie and Clyde confess, and both spend eight years in jail. This outcome is a Nash equilibrium: Each criminal is choosing the best strategy available, given the strategy the other is following. Yet, from their standpoint, the outcome is terrible. If they had *both* remained silent, both of them would have been better off, spending only 1 year in jail on the gun charge. By each pursuing his or her own interests, the two prisoners together reach an outcome that is worse for each of them.

You might have thought that Bonnie and Clyde would have foreseen this situation and planned ahead. But even with advance planning, they would still run into problems. Imagine that, before the police captured Bonnie and Clyde, the two criminals had made a pact not to confess. Clearly, this agreement would make them both better off *if* they both live up to it, because they would each spend only one year in jail. But would the two criminals in fact remain silent, simply because they had agreed to? Once they are being questioned separately, the logic of self-interest takes over and leads them to confess. Cooperation between the two prisoners is difficult to maintain, because cooperation is individually irrational.

17-2b Oligopolies as a Prisoners' Dilemma

What does the prisoners' dilemma have to do with markets and imperfect competition? It turns out that the game oligopolists play in trying to reach the monopoly outcome is similar to the game that the two prisoners play in the prisoners' dilemma.

Consider again the choices facing Jack and Jill. After prolonged negotiation, the two suppliers of water agree to keep production at 30 litres so that the price will be kept high and together they will earn the maximum profit. After they agree on production levels, however, each of them must decide whether to cooperate and live up to this agreement or to ignore it and produce at a higher level. Figure 17.2 shows how the profits of the two producers depend on the strategies they choose.

Suppose you are Jack. You might reason as follows: "I could keep production low at 30 litres as we agreed, or I could raise my production and sell 40 litres. If Jill lives up to the agreement and keeps her production at 30 litres, then I earn profit of $2000 with high production and $1800 with low production. In this case, I am better off with high production. If Jill fails to live up to the agreement and produces 40 litres, then I earn $1600 with high production and $1500 with low production. Once again, I am better off with high production. So regardless of what Jill chooses to do, I am better off reneging on our agreement and producing at a high level."

FIGURE 17.2

Jack and Jill's Oligopoly Game

In this game between Jack and Jill, the profit that each earns from selling water depends on both the quantity he or she chooses to sell and the quantity the other chooses to sell.

Jack's Decision

	Sell 40 L	Sell 30 L
Jill's Decision Sell 40 L	Jack gets $1600 profit / Jill gets $1600 profit	Jack gets $1500 profit / Jill gets $2000 profit
Sell 30 L	Jack gets $2000 profit / Jill gets $1500 profit	Jack gets $1800 profit / Jill gets $1800 profit

© 2018 Cengage Learning

Producing 40 litres is a dominant strategy for Jack. Of course, Jill reasons in exactly the same way, and the Nash equilibrium is for both to produce at the higher level of 40 litres. The result is the inferior outcome (from Jack's and Jill's standpoints) with low profits for each of the two producers.

This example illustrates why oligopolies have trouble maintaining monopoly profits. The monopoly outcome is jointly rational for the oligopoly, but each oligopolist has an incentive to cheat. Just as self-interest drives the prisoners in the prisoners' dilemma to confess, self-interest makes it difficult for the oligopoly to maintain the cooperative outcome with low production, high prices, and monopoly profits.

case study | **OPEC and the World Oil Market**

Our story about the town's market for water is fictional, but if we change water to crude oil, and Jack and Jill to Iran and Iraq, the story is quite close to being true. Much of the world's oil is produced by a few countries, mostly in the Middle East. These countries together make up an oligopoly. Their decisions about how much oil to pump are much the same as Jack and Jill's decisions about how much water to pump.

The countries that produce most of the world's oil have formed a cartel, called the Organization of the Petroleum Exporting Countries (OPEC). As originally formed in 1960, OPEC included Iran, Iraq, Kuwait, Saudi Arabia, and Venezuela. In 2010, Qatar, Indonesia, Libya, the United Arab Emirates, Algeria, Nigeria, Ecuador, and Angola were also members. These countries control more than three-fourths of the world's oil reserves. Like any cartel, OPEC tries to raise the price of its product through a coordinated reduction in quantity produced. OPEC tries to set production levels for each of the member countries.

The problem that OPEC faces is much the same as the problem that Jack and Jill face in our story. The OPEC countries would like to maintain a high price of oil. But each member of the cartel is tempted to increase its production to get a larger share of the total profit. OPEC members frequently agree to reduce production but then cheat on their agreements.

OPEC was most successful at maintaining cooperation and high prices in the period from 1973 to 1985. The price of crude oil rose from US$3 per barrel in 1972 to US$11 in 1974 and then to US$35 in 1981. But in the early 1980s member countries began arguing about production levels, and OPEC became ineffective at maintaining cooperation. By 1986 the price of crude oil had fallen back to US$13 per barrel.

The members of OPEC have continued to meet regularly, but the cartel has been far less successful at reaching and enforcing agreements. Although the price of oil rose significantly in 2007 and 2008, to in excess of US$100 per barrel, the primary cause was increased demand in the world oil market, in part from a booming Chinese economy, rather than restricted supply.

More recently, OPEC has taken a different approach. The increase in the price of oil in 2007 caused a great deal of new production to come on to the market. This is particularly the case in the United States where new technologies, such as fracking, have allowed new reserves to be exploited. In Alberta the oil sands industry also reacted to these high prices by increasing production and investment in new projects. This increased production, coupled with now waning demand from China, has caused the price of oil to fall drastically, to below US$50 per barrel. Rather than attempting to increase prices by decreasing production, OPEC has opted instead to maintain, and even increase, production. The apparent strategy is to keep prices low in order to make the new production in North America and elsewhere uneconomic, thereby driving them out of the market. The problem, of course, is that OPEC producers are also suffering due to very low prices. It remains to be seen whether OPEC's strategy of suffering "short term pain for long term gain" will be successful. ∎

17-2c Other Examples of the Prisoners' Dilemma

We have seen how the prisoners' dilemma can be used to understand the problem facing oligopolies. The same logic applies to many other situations as well. Here we consider two examples in which self-interest prevents cooperation and leads to an inferior outcome for the parties involved.

Advertising When two firms advertise to attract the same customers, they face a problem similar to the prisoners' dilemma. For example, consider the decisions facing two beer companies, Molson and Labatt. If neither company advertises, the two companies split the market. If both advertise, they again split the market, but profits are lower, since each company must bear the cost of advertising. Yet if one company advertises while the other does not, the one that advertises attracts customers from the other.

Figure 17.3 shows how the profits of the two companies depend on their actions. You can see that advertising is a dominant strategy for each firm. Thus, both firms choose to advertise, even though both firms would be better off if neither firm advertised.

An interesting example of this is cigarette advertising. In 1971 the U.S. banned cigarette advertising on television and radio. Similar restrictions exist in Canada. As a result of this ban cigarette companies spent less on advertising, but there is little evidence of a marked reduction in aggregate sales. This suggests that cigarette advertising is motivated more by gaining market share than by expanding the overall market. As a result, the restriction on advertising may have actually helped the industry avoid the prisoners' dilemma.

Common Resources In Chapter 11 we saw that people tend to overuse common resources. One can view this problem as an example of the prisoners' dilemma.

FIGURE 17.3

An Advertising Game

In this game between firms selling similar products, the profit that each earns depends on both its own advertising decision and the advertising decision of the other firm.

	Molson's Decision	
	Advertise	**Don't Advertise**
Advertise	Molson gets $3 billion profit / Labatt gets $3 billion profit	Molson gets $2 billion profit / Labatt gets $5 billion profit
Don't Advertise	Molson gets $5 billion profit / Labatt gets $2 billion profit	Molson gets $4 billion profit / Labatt gets $4 billion profit

Labatt's Decision

Imagine that two oil companies—Shell and Esso (Imperial Oil)—own adjacent oil fields. Under the fields is a common pool of oil worth $12 million. Drilling a well to recover the oil costs $1 million. If each company drills one well, each will get half of the oil and earn a $5-million profit ($6 million in revenue minus $1 million in costs).

Because the pool of oil is a common resource, the companies will not use it efficiently. Suppose that either company could drill a second well. If one company has two of the three wells, that company gets two-thirds of the oil, which yields a profit of $6 million. The other company gets one-third of the oil, for a profit of $3 million. Yet if each company drills a second well, the two companies again split the oil. In this case, each bears the cost of a second well, so profit is only $4 million for each company.

Figure 17.4 shows the game. Drilling two wells is a dominant strategy for each company. Once again, the self-interest of the two players leads them to an inferior outcome.

FIGURE 17.4

A Common-Resources Game

In this game between firms pumping oil from a common pool, the profit that each earns depends on both the number of wells it drills and the number of wells drilled by the other firm.

	Shell's Decision	
	Drill Two Wells	**Drill One Well**
Drill Two Wells	Shell gets $4 million profit / Esso gets $4 million profit	Shell gets $3 million profit / Esso gets $6 million profit
Drill One Well	Shell gets $6 million profit / Esso gets $3 million profit	Shell gets $5 million profit / Esso gets $5 million profit

Esso's Decision

17-2d The Prisoners' Dilemma and the Welfare of Society

The prisoners' dilemma describes many of life's situations, and it shows that cooperation can be difficult to maintain, even when cooperation would make both players in the game better off. Clearly, this lack of cooperation is a problem for those involved in these situations. But is lack of cooperation a problem from the standpoint of society as a whole? The answer depends on the circumstances.

In some cases, the noncooperative equilibrium is bad for society as well as the players. For example, in the common-resources game in Figure 17.4, the extra wells dug by Shell and Esso are pure waste. Society would be better off if the two players could reach the cooperative outcome.

By contrast, in the case of oligopolists trying to maintain monopoly profits, lack of cooperation is desirable from the standpoint of society as a whole. The monopoly outcome is good for the oligopolists, but it is bad for the consumers of the product. As we first saw in Chapter 7, the competitive outcome is best for society because it maximizes total surplus. When oligopolists fail to cooperate, the quantity they produce is closer to this optimal level. Put differently, the invisible hand guides markets to allocate resources efficiently only when markets are competitive, and markets are competitive only when firms in the market fail to cooperate with one another.

Similarly, consider the case of the police questioning two suspects. Lack of cooperation between the suspects is desirable because it allows the police to convict more criminals. The prisoners' dilemma is a dilemma for the prisoners, but it can be a boon to everyone else.

17-2e Why People Sometimes Cooperate

The prisoners' dilemma shows that cooperation is difficult. But is it impossible? Not all prisoners, when questioned by the police, decide to turn in their partners in crime. Cartels sometimes do manage to maintain collusive arrangements, despite the incentive for individual members to defect. Very often, players can solve the prisoners' dilemma because they play the game not once but many times.

To see why cooperation is easier to enforce in repeated games, let's return to our duopolists, Jack and Jill, whose choices were given in Figure 17.2. Jack and Jill would like to agree to maintain the monopoly outcome in which each produces 30 L. Yet if Jack and Jill are to play this game only once, neither has any incentive to live up to this agreement. Self-interest drives each to renege and choose the dominant strategy of 40 L.

Now suppose that Jack and Jill know that they will play the same game every week. When they make their initial agreement to keep production low, they can also specify what happens if one party reneges. They might agree, for instance, that once one of them reneges and produces 40 L, both of them will produce 40 L forever after. This penalty is easy to enforce because if one party is producing at a high level, the other has every reason to do the same.

The threat of this penalty may be all that is needed to maintain cooperation. Each person knows that defecting would raise his or her profit from $1800 to $2000. But this benefit would last for only one week. Thereafter, profit would fall to $1600 and stay there. As long as the players care enough about future profits, they will choose to forgo the one-time gain from defection. Thus, in a game of repeated prisoners' dilemma, the two players may well be able to reach the cooperative outcome.

IN THE
news

The Prisoners' Dilemma in Action

*Sports involve some sort of game, but perhaps not always the game that
you might think. In this article on performance-enhancing drugs, we see
that there are often various "players" involved, and game theory can help us
understand their choices.*

Athlete's Dilemma

TWO sprinters may have got caught doing it
this week. And a cyclist didn't do it, but it is so
common in his sport that what he did do without
doing it is even more astonishing. "It" is taking
performance-enhancing drugs. The sprinters
were Tyson Gay and Asafa Powell, who both failed
drug tests (though both deny wrongdoing). The
cyclist was Chris Froome, who without pharmaceutical assistance managed a stunning ascent
of Mont Ventoux during the Tour de France.

Professional sport is rife with drug-taking.
Getting caught will get you banned, frequently for
life. Yet people carry on doing it regardless. Why?

Appropriately, the answer may lie in a branch
of mathematics called game theory. This deals
with conflicts of interest between parties who
know each other's preferences but not their actual intentions or decisions. It then deduces the
best course of action for any rational player.

Existing game-theory analyses of doping look
at things either from just the competitors' points
of view, or from the points of view of both competitors and organisers. Neither of these, though,
produces a perfect analysis of what is going on.
Berno Buechel of the University of Hamburg and
his colleagues have therefore introduced a third
factor—the one that allows sports to be professional in the first place. This factor is the customer.

The simplest game in game theory is "prisoner's dilemma". In the athletes' version, both
players will be better off if neither takes drugs,
but because neither can trust the other, both
have to take them to make sure they have a
chance of winning.

Introducing an authority figure, in what is
known as an inspection game, should deal with
this. If the inspector tests the athletes, and the
athletes trust the inspection process to catch
cheats, fear of getting caught should keep them
on the straight and narrow. Except that is not
what seems to happen in the real world. Clearly,
athletes do not think they will get caught. And
Dr Buechel and his colleagues think they know why.

In a working paper they started circulat-
ing among their peers earlier this year, they
suggest that the real game being played here
has yet another party in it—the fans and spon-
sors who pay for everything. In their view, the
inspector has several reasons to skimp on
testing. One is the cost. Another is the disrup-
tion it causes to the already complicated lives
of the athletes. A third, though, is fear of how
customers would react if more thorough testing
did reveal near-universal cheating, which an-
ecdotal evidence suggests that in some sports
it might. Better to test sparingly, and expose
from time to time what is apparently the odd
bad apple, rather than do the job thoroughly
and find the whole barrel is spoiled and your

sport has suddenly vanished in a hailstorm of
disqualifications.

This attitude, however, would result in precisely the outcome testing is supposed to obvi-
ate. It would be back to the prisoner's dilemma.
Anyone who seriously wanted to win would
have to cheat, even if his inclination was not to.
In these circumstances it would take a saint to
stay pure.

When the researchers turned their hypoth-
esis into maths, it seemed to stand up. The
only way out, the maths suggested, was for all
tests, and their results, to be reported—whether
negative or not. That would give customers a
real sense of how thorough the search for doping was, and thus how widespread the practice.
It would also help break the prisoner's dilemma
for the athletes.

The authorities in any given sport would no
doubt deny that Dr Buechel's analysis applied
to them. They would claim their testing regimes
were adequate—and would probably truly believe it themselves. But human capacity for self-
deception is infinite. It may thus be that the real
guilty parties in sports doping are not those who
actually take the drugs, but those who create a
situation where only a fool would not.

Source: Republished with permission of The Economist Group
Limited, from "Athlete's Dilemma," *The Economist*, July 20,
2013; permission conveyed through Copyright Clearance
Center, Inc.

case study · The Prisoners' Dilemma Tournament

Imagine that you are playing a game of prisoners' dilemma with a person
being "questioned" in a separate room. Moreover, imagine that you are
going to play not once but many times. Your score at the end of the game is the total
number of years in jail. You would like to make this score as small as possible. What
strategy would you play? Would you begin by confessing or remaining silent? How
would the other player's actions affect your subsequent decisions about confessing?

Repeated prisoners' dilemma is quite a complicated game. To encourage cooperation, players must penalize each other for not cooperating. Yet the strategy described earlier for Jack and Jill's water cartel—defect forever as soon as the other player defects—is not very forgiving. In a game repeated many times, a strategy that allows players to return to the cooperative outcome after a period of noncooperation may be preferable.

To see what strategies work best, political scientist Robert Axelrod held a tournament. People entered by sending computer programs designed to play repeated prisoners' dilemma. Each program then played the game against all the other programs. The "winner" was the program that received the fewest total years in jail.

The winner turned out to be a simple strategy called *tit-for-tat.* According to tit-for-tat, a player should start by cooperating and then do whatever the other player did last time. Thus, a tit-for-tat player cooperates until the other player defects; he then defects until the other player cooperates again. In other words, this strategy starts out friendly, penalizes unfriendly players, and forgives them if warranted. To Axelrod's surprise, this simple strategy did better than all the more complicated strategies that people had sent in.

The tit-for-tat strategy has a long history. It is essentially the biblical strategy of "an eye for an eye, a tooth for a tooth." The prisoners' dilemma tournament suggests that this may be a good rule of thumb for playing some of the games of life. ∎

 Tell the story of the prisoners' dilemma. Prepare a table showing the prisoners' choices and explain what outcome is likely. • What does the prisoners' dilemma teach us about oligopolies?

17-3 Public Policy toward Oligopolies

One of the ten principles of economics in Chapter 1 is that governments can sometimes improve market outcomes. This principle applies directly to oligopolistic markets. As we have seen, cooperation among oligopolists is undesirable from the standpoint of society as a whole because it leads to production that is too low and prices that are too high. To move the allocation of resources closer to the social optimum, policymakers should try to induce firms in an oligopoly to compete rather than cooperate. Let's consider how policymakers do this and then examine the controversies that arise in this area of public policy.

17-3a Restraint of Trade and the Competition Act

Freedom to make contracts is an essential part of a market economy. Businesses and households use contracts to arrange mutually advantageous trades, relying on the court system to enforce those contracts. Yet for many years, Canadian judges have refused to enforce agreements that restrain trade among competitors (reducing quantities and raising prices, or price-fixing) as being against the public interest.

Canada's Competition Act codifies and reinforces this policy. Section 45(1) of the act states:

Everyone who conspires, combines, agrees or arranges with another person (a) to limit unduly the facilities for transporting, producing, manufacturing, supplying, storing or dealing in any product, (b) to prevent, limit or lessen, unduly, the manufacture or production of a product or to enhance unreasonably the price thereof, (c) to prevent or lessen, unduly, competition in the production, manufacture, purchase, barter, sale, storage, rental, transportation or supply of a product, or in the price of insurance on persons or property, or (d) to otherwise restrain or injure competition unduly, is guilty of an indictable offence and liable to imprisonment for a term not exceeding five years or to a fine not exceeding ten million dollars or both.

The Competition Act contains both civil and criminal provisions. As we discussed in Chapter 15, the Competition Bureau is responsible for enforcing the act. The bureau may refer criminal cases to the Attorney General of Canada and civil cases to the Competition Tribunal. Mergers, also discussed in Chapter 15, are governed by the civil provisions of the act. Conspiracies in restraint of trade, such as those described in Section 45(1) above, fall under the criminal provisions of the act.

Other activities that are subject to criminal prosecution include bid-rigging, price discrimination, resale price maintenance, and predatory pricing. Bid-rigging occurs when potential bidders agree with other bidders to refrain from bidding on contracts, or rig bids in advance. Price discrimination occurs when a supplier charges different prices for similar quantities of goods sold to firms that compete with one another. Resale price maintenance occurs when a supplier "requires" retailers to sell its product at a specified (or minimum or maximum) price. Predatory pricing involves selling products at unreasonably low prices for the purpose of eliminating or substantially reducing competition. Criminal proceedings must be initiated by the commissioner, but individuals who have been harmed by criminal offences can sue for civil damages. These and other provisions of the Competition Act are used to prevent firms in oligopolistic industries from acting either individually or together in ways that make markets less competitive.

17-3b Controversies over Competition Policy

Over time, much controversy has centred on the question of what kinds of behaviour the competition laws should prohibit. Most commentators agree that price-fixing agreements among competing firms should be illegal. Yet the competition laws have been used to condemn some business practices whose effects are not obvious. Here we consider three examples.

Resale Price Maintenance One example of a controversial business practice is *resale price maintenance*. Imagine that Superduper Electronics sells Blu-ray Disc players to retail stores for $100. If Superduper requires the retailers to charge customers $150, it is said to engage in resale price maintenance. Any retailer that charged less than $150 would have violated its contract with Superduper.

At first, resale price maintenance might seem anticompetitive and, therefore, detrimental to society. Like an agreement among members of a cartel, it prevents the retailers from competing on price. For this reason, the courts have often viewed resale price maintenance as a violation of the competition laws.

Yet some economists defend resale price maintenance on two grounds. First, they deny that it is aimed at reducing competition. If Superduper Electronics wanted to exert its market power, it would do so by raising the wholesale price rather than controlling the resale price. Moreover, Superduper has no incentive to discourage competition among its retailers. Indeed, because a cartel of retailers sells less than a group of competitive retailers, Superduper would be worse off if its retailers were a cartel.

Let Them Eat Cake

Non-competitive behaviour on the part of companies affects all of us. One of the more high profile cases brought forward by the Competition Bureau in Canada involved bread price fixing on the part of some of our biggest retailers.

Prison Time and Billion-Dollar Lawsuits: Retailers Face Tough Outcomes in Bread Price-Fixing Scandal

By Naomi Powell

Imprisonment. Hefty government fines. Billion-dollar class action lawsuits.

A range of nasty outcomes await Canada's largest grocers and bread producers if they are convicted of participating in an industry-wide scheme to fix bread prices that lasted more than 14 years.

But a large-scale loss of business from outraged customers? Unlikely, analysts say. "The companies involved in this case control most of the market so it's not clear where people could shift their purchase," said Thomas Ross, a professor of regulation and competition policy in the University of British Columbia's Sauder School of Business. "Problems with food quality, like contamination, can be devastating for companies, but an economic offence? People really do just move on." In the legal arena however, the fight

facing Canada's grocers and bread-producers is just beginning.

Court documents made public this week allege Canada Bread Co. Ltd. and Weston Bakeries Ltd.—the country's top two bread producers—co-operated with major grocery retailers including Loblaw Companies Ltd., Walmart Canada, Empire Company Ltd. unit Sobeys, Metro Inc. and Giant Tiger Stores Ltd. to fix prices on an array of bread products. The allegations from the Competition Bureau cite 15 instances of co-ordinated actions.

The allegations have not been proven in court.

Financial penalties for price fixing are generally calculated at 20 cents on every dollar of sales affected by the scheme, to a maximum of $25 million, though the Bureau could attach a penalty to each type of bread product involved, Ross said. Given the nationwide scope and the length of time during which bread price fixing is alleged to have played out, that figure is unlikely to recoup the full profit the companies would have made.

Prices of bread rose at an average annual rate of 5.25 per cent between 2002 and

2014, compared to an annual inflation rate of 2.57 per cent for all other food purchased from stores, according to an analysis of Statistics Canada data by Kevin Grier, a food industry analyst. Those increases could not be linked to underlying factors such as the cost of ingredients. By 2015, a loaf of bread cost nearly a dollar more than it would have if prices had followed the same rate of inflation as all other food bought in stores, he found.

There is no way to know what grocers would have charged in a truly competitive market. Nevertheless, class action suits will certainly make an attempt to figure it out. Multiple class action suits seeking billions in damages have already been launched against the targeted companies. "In private actions, the big fight is to recover the total profit that came from price fixing," Ross said.

The most serious consequence facing executives and other employees involved in such schemes is prison time. Canada is one of about two dozen countries, including the United States, which allows imprisonment as punishment for individuals convicted of price fixing.

Second, economists believe that resale price maintenance has a legitimate goal. Superduper may want its retailers to provide customers with a pleasant showroom and a knowledgeable sales force. Yet, without resale price maintenance, some customers would take advantage of one store's service to learn about the Blu-ray player's special features and then buy the item at a discount retailer that does not provide this service. Good customer service can be viewed as a public good among the retailers that sell Superduper products. As we discussed in Chapter 11, when one person provides a public good, others are able to enjoy it without paying for it. In this case, discount retailers would free-ride on the service provided by other retailers, leading to less service than is desirable. Resale price maintenance is one way for Superduper to solve this free-rider problem.

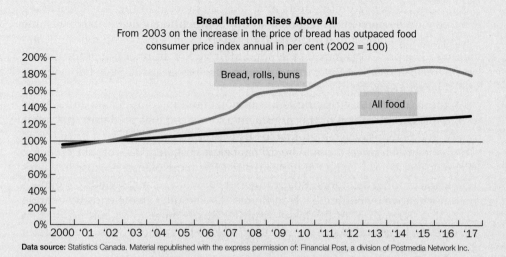

Bread Inflation Rises Above All
From 2003 on the increase in the price of bread has outpaced food
consumer price index annual in per cent (2002 = 100)

Data source: Statistics Canada. Material republished with the express permission of: Financial Post, a division of Postmedia Network Inc.

"It is a very different and more effective deterrent and punishment to take away someone's liberty, particularly a businessperson who's used to a decent life," said Spencer Waller, director of the Institute for Consumer Antitrust Studies at Loyola University in Chicago. "It's bigger than imposing a monetary fine on a company that can usually pay it and then pass it along later in the form of higher prices or reduced dividends to shareholders."

While U.S. employees and senior executives routinely receive two-year jail sentences for price fixing, the penalty isn't often applied in Canada unless some form of coercion, false testimony or obstruction of justice is involved, analysts say.

However, the size and duration of the alleged scheme and the large number of people it affected—particularly people on low incomes—make it a unique case, said Joseph Wilson, an expert in competition law at McGill University.

"Bread is a basic food item, an essential staple food. For someone living on welfare, with a very small weekly budget, an inflated price on that bread could mean the difference between getting by and not getting by. So yes, I think it's very possible and these considerations do go into the Bureau's analysis."

Just how bruised corporate reputations will be at the end of the scandal—and who will take the biggest hit in terms of public relations—is a matter of debate, though analysts say prices fixing cases are most often forgotten.

Unlike the other companies targeted in the Bureau's case, Loblaw and its parent George Weston were granted immunity from prosecution after tipping the bureau off to what they say was an "industry-wide" scheme. Giant Tiger, Sobeys, and Metro have all denied participating in the alleged price-fixing scheme while Walmart Canada has declined to comment, citing the ongoing investigation. Michael Medline, chief executive of Sobeys parent Empire, has vowed to fight the allegations in court.

Loblaw subsequently offered free $25 gift cards to customers as a goodwill gesture. "They got out in front of the situation and they may get some credit for being the whistleblower," Ross said. "It's not a great advantage, but it's something." Others were less optimistic.

"All the players have a PR problem to be sure but I don't know what the public perception will ultimately be of Loblaw," said Richard Janda, a law professor at McGill University. "They're off the hook because they tattled on the others, will that give them a black eye in terms of reputation? I myself don't get a lot of comfort from hearing a company admitting to years of criminal activity."

Source: Naomi Powell, "Prison time and billion-dollar lawsuits: Retailers face tough outcomes in bread price-fixing scandal," *Financial Post*, February 2, 2018. Material republished with the express permission of: Financial Post, a division of Postmedia Network Inc.

The example of resale price maintenance illustrates an important principle: *Business practices that appear to reduce competition may in fact have legitimate purposes.* This principle makes the application of the competition laws all the more difficult. The economists, lawyers, and judges in charge of enforcing these laws must determine what kinds of behaviour public policy should prohibit as impeding competition and reducing economic well-being. Often that job is not easy.

Predatory Pricing Firms with market power normally use that power to raise prices above the competitive level. But should policymakers ever be concerned that firms with market power might charge prices that are too low? This question is at the heart of a second debate over competition policy.

Imagine that a large airline, call it Coyote Air, has a monopoly on some route. Then Roadrunner Express enters and takes 20 percent of the market, leaving Coyote with 80 percent. In response to this competition, Coyote starts slashing its fares. Some competition analysts argue that Coyote's move could be anticompetitive: The price cuts may be intended to drive Roadrunner out of the market so Coyote can recapture its monopoly and raise prices again. Such behaviour is called *predatory pricing.*

Although predatory pricing is a common claim in competition suits, some economists are skeptical of this argument and believe that predatory pricing is rarely, and perhaps never, a profitable business strategy. Why? For a price war to drive out a rival, prices have to be driven below cost. Yet if Coyote starts selling cheap tickets at a loss, it had better be ready to fly more planes, because low fares will attract more customers. Roadrunner, meanwhile, can respond to Coyote's predatory move by cutting back on flights. As a result, Coyote ends up bearing more than 80 percent of the losses, putting Roadrunner in a good position to survive the price war. As in the old Roadrunner–Coyote cartoons, the predator suffers more than the prey.

Economists continue to debate whether predatory pricing should be a concern for anticompetition policymakers. Various questions remain unresolved. Is predatory pricing ever a profitable business strategy? If so, when? Are the courts capable of telling which price cuts are competitive and thus good for consumers and which are predatory? There are no simple answers.

Tying   A third example of a controversial business practice is *tying*. Suppose that Makemoney Movies produces two new films—*The Avengers* and *Hamlet*. If Makemoney offers theatres the two films together at a single price, rather than separately, the studio is said to be tying its two products.

The practice of tying is banned under the civil provisions of the Competition Act. The commonly used justification for the ban goes as follows: Imagine that *The Avengers* is a blockbuster, whereas *Hamlet* is an unprofitable art film. By tying, the studio could use the high demand for *The Avengers* to force theatres to buy *Hamlet*. It seems that the studio could use tying as a mechanism for expanding its market power.

Many economists are skeptical of this argument. Imagine that theatres are willing to pay $20 000 for *The Avengers* and nothing for *Hamlet*. Then the most that a theatre would pay for the two movies together is $20 000—the same as it would pay for *The Avengers* by itself. Forcing the theatre to accept a worthless movie as part of the deal does not increase the theatre's willingness to pay. Makemoney cannot increase its market power simply by bundling the two movies together.

Why, then, does tying exist? One possibility is that it is a form of price discrimination. Suppose there are two theatres. City Theatre is willing to pay $15 000 for *The Avengers* and $5000 for *Hamlet*. Country Theatre is just the opposite: It is willing to pay $5000 for *The Avengers* and $15 000 for *Hamlet*. If Makemoney charges separate prices for the two films, its best strategy is to charge $15 000 for each film, and each theatre chooses to show only one film. Yet if Makemoney offers the two movies as a bundle, it can charge each theatre $20 000 for the movies. Thus, if different theatres value the films differently, tying may allow the studio to increase profit by charging a combined price closer to the buyers' total willingness to pay.

Tying remains a controversial business practice. The commonly heard argument that tying allows a firm to extend its market power to other goods is not well founded, at least in its simplest form. Yet economists have proposed more elaborate theories for how tying can impede competition. Given our current economic knowledge, it is unclear whether tying has adverse effects for society as a whole.

case study **Is More Always Better?**

As suggested above, public policy regarding oligopolies can be complicated, and overly simplistic analysis can lead to questionable conclusions. A recent example of this in Canada is the federal government's approach to the wireless industry. Currently the wireless market in Canada is dominated by the "big three": Rogers, Telus, and Bell. Critics of the structure of the wireless industry in Canada point to our high average revenue per user and the low wireless penetration rate (mobile connections per capita) as evidence of insufficient competition. They say that the low penetration rate is due to high prices, and that those prices are high because of a cozy oligopoly. The solution to this problem, they say, is to encourage more entry into the industry: "More is surely better."

On the basis of this argument, the federal government has implemented policies to encourage new entrants and increase competition in the wireless market in Canada, including implementing caps on the wholesale roaming rates the "big three" can charge other providers, and preferential access to new wireless spectrum for new entrants.

In a study published by The School of Public Policy at the University of Calgary, economists Jeff Church and Andrew Wilkins question this policy, challenging the conventional wisdom that "more is always better."

First, they argue that international performance comparisons focusing on the penetration rate of cell phones in Canada and average revenue per user are not valid. With respect to the former, they argue that in many countries individuals often have more than one SIM card to take advantage of cheaper calls to numbers on the same carrier and avoid higher costs for calls that cross networks—many of those are pay-as-you-go plans. Canadians, on the other hand, prefer monthly plans, so each mobile consumer will have only one SIM card. That does not mean fewer mobile users in Canada, just fewer SIM cards.

With respect to average revenue per user, a proxy for the price of wireless services, Church and Wilkins emphasize that it is important to compare apples to apples. It turns out that while Canadians' per capita mobile voice usage is very similar to other countries when it comes to smartphone data usage per subscriber, Canadians are world leaders; we stream more data through our cell phones than most other countries. Demand for the latest devices, data service, and lots of data minutes means higher average revenue per user. Using average revenue per user as a proxy for the "price" of wireless services is therefore misleading: We spend more on wireless service because we use more, particularly on the data front.

Capital investment by the "big three" wireless providers in Canada also was high by world standards. The reason, of course, is that the heavy data usage so loved by Canadians requires more investment in high-speed networks: Without this investment the heavy data usage desired by Canadians would not be possible.

Church and Wilkins therefore argue that comparing "prices" internationally without factoring in the quality of the product (the network) makes standard international comparisons invalid. Rather, what matters is how closely prices track costs in a country. This requires a comparison of costs and prices in a country, not a comparison of prices between countries.

They therefore study whether prices track long-run average costs, and determine whether wireless providers in Canada are in fact making profits consistent with a cozy oligopoly (recall that firms earn profits when the price of their product exceeds their long-run average costs). Their examination of the leading firm's cash flow over the life cycle of the wireless investments suggests that rates of return on wireless capital investments in Canada are not consistent with them earning excessive oligopoly profits. For example, they calculate that over the period 1986–2012 Rogers Wireless's real, pre-tax rate of return was just under 10 percent. This, they argue, is hardly consistent with either the inefficient exercise of market power or the presence of oligopoly profits. They suggest instead that there is a "natural limit" to the number of carriers due to economies of scale.

Church and Wilkins argue that policy efforts to artificially increase the number of carriers will squeeze profit margins in the short run and will not likely be sustained in the long run as carriers exit and consolidate to reduce competition and restore margins consistent with profitability and the natural limit. They conclude that while consumers might gain in the short run from lower prices, everyone is likely worse off in the long run from the misallocation of spectrum, the reduction in scale of carriers, and the associated reduction in incentives to invest in expanding the network. ■

 QUICK Quiz   *What kind of agreement is illegal for businesses to make? • Why are the competition laws controversial?*

17-4   Conclusion

Oligopolies would like to act like monopolies, but self-interest drives them closer to competition. Where oligopolies end up on this spectrum depends on the number of firms in the oligopoly and how cooperative the firms are. The story of the prisoners' dilemma shows why oligopolies can fail to maintain cooperation, even when cooperation is in their best interest.

Policymakers regulate the behaviour of oligopolists through the anticompetition laws. The proper scope of these laws is the subject of ongoing controversy. Although price-fixing among competing firms clearly reduces economic welfare and should be illegal, some business practices that appear to reduce competition may have legitimate if subtle purposes. As a result, policymakers need to be careful when they use the substantial powers of the anticompetition laws to place limits on firms' behaviour.

summary

- Oligopolists maximize their total profits by forming a cartel and acting like a monopolist. Yet, if oligopolists make decisions about production levels individually, the result is a greater quantity and a lower price than under the monopoly outcome. The larger the number of firms in the oligopoly, the closer the quantity and price will be to the levels that would prevail under perfect competition.

- The prisoners' dilemma shows that self-interest can prevent people from maintaining cooperation, even

when cooperation is in their mutual interest. The logic of the prisoners' dilemma applies in many situations, including advertising, common-resource problems, and oligopolies.

- Policymakers use the anticompetition laws to prevent oligopolies from engaging in behaviour that reduces competition. The application of these laws can be controversial, because some behaviour that may seem to reduce competition may in fact have legitimate business purposes.

KEY **concepts**

oligopoly, *p. 374*
game theory, *p. 374*
collusion, *p. 376*

cartel, *p. 376*
Nash equilibrium, *p. 377*

prisoners' dilemma, *p. 379*
dominant strategy, *p. 380*

QUESTIONS FOR **review**

1. If a group of sellers could form a cartel, what quantity and price would they try to set?

2. Compare the quantity and price of an oligopoly to those of a monopoly.

3. Compare the quantity and price of an oligopoly to those of a competitive market.

4. How does the number of firms in an oligopoly affect the outcome in its market?

5. What is the prisoners' dilemma, and what does it have to do with oligopoly?

6. Give two examples other than oligopoly that show how the prisoners' dilemma helps to explain behaviour.

7. What kinds of behaviour do the competition laws prohibit?

8. What is resale price maintenance, and why is it controversial?

QUICK CHECK **multiple choice**

1. What is the key feature of an oligopolistic market?
   a. each firm produces a different product from other firms
   b. a single firm chooses a point on the market demand curve
   c. each firm takes the market price as given
   d. a small number of firms are acting strategically

2. If an oligopolistic industry organizes itself as a cooperative cartel, it will produce a quantity of output that is _____ the competitive level and _____ the monopoly level.
   a. less than, more than
   b. more than, less than
   c. less than, equal to
   d. equal to, more than

3. If an oligopoly does not cooperate and each firm chooses its own quantity, the industry will produce a quantity of output that is _____ the competitive level and _____ the monopoly level.
   a. less than, more than
   b. more than, less than
   c. less than, equal to
   d. equal to, more than

4. As the number of firms in an oligopoly grows large, the industry approaches a level of output that is _____ the competitive level and _____ the monopoly level.
   a. less than, more than
   b. more than, less than

   c. less than, equal to
   d. equal to, more than

5. The prisoners' dilemma is a two-person game that illustrates which of the following?
   a. the cooperative outcome could be worse for both people than the Nash equilibrium
   b. even if the cooperative outcome is better than the Nash equilibrium for one person, it might be worse for the other
   c. even if cooperation is better than the Nash equilibrium, each person might have an incentive not to cooperate
   d. rational, self-interested individuals will naturally avoid the Nash equilibrium because it is worse for both of them

6. What does competition policy aim to do?
   a. facilitate cooperation among firms in oligopolistic industries
   b. encourage mergers to take advantage of economies of scale
   c. discourage firms from moving production facilities overseas
   d. prevent firms from acting in ways that reduce competition

PROBLEMS AND **applications**

1. Some years ago, the *New York Times* reported that "the inability of OPEC to agree last week to cut production has sent the oil market into turmoil … [leading to] the lowest price for domestic crude oil since June 1990."
   a. Why were the members of OPEC trying to agree to cut production?
   b. Why do you suppose OPEC was unable to agree on cutting production? Why did the oil market go into "turmoil" as a result?
   c. The newspaper also noted OPEC's view "that producing nations outside the organization, like Norway and Britain, should do their share and cut production." What does the phrase "do their share" suggest about OPEC's desired relationship with Norway and Britain?

2. A large share of the world supply of diamonds comes from Russia and South Africa. Suppose that the marginal cost of mining diamonds is constant at $1000 per diamond, and the demand for diamonds is described by the following schedule:

Price	Quantity
$8000	5000
7000	6000
6000	7000
5000	8000
4000	9000
3000	10 000
2000	11 000
1000	12 000

   a. If there were many suppliers of diamonds, what would be the price and quantity?
   b. If there was only one supplier of diamonds, what would be the price and quantity?
   c. If Russia and South Africa formed a cartel, what would be the price and quantity? If the countries split the market evenly, what would be South Africa's production and profit? What would happen to South Africa's profit if it increased its production by 1000 while Russia stuck to the cartel agreement?
   d. Use your answer to part (c) to explain why cartel agreements are often not successful.

3. This chapter discusses companies that are oligopolists in the market for the goods they sell. Many of the same ideas apply to companies that are oligopolists in the market for the inputs they buy.
   a. If sellers who are oligopolists try to increase the price of goods they sell, what is the goal of buyers who are oligopolists?
   b. National Hockey League team owners have an oligopoly in the market for hockey players. What is the owners' goal regarding players' salaries? Why is this goal difficult to achieve?
   c. Hockey players went on strike in 2004 because they would not accept the salary cap that the owners wanted to impose. If the owners were already colluding over salaries, why did the owners feel the need for a salary cap?

4. Consider trade relations between Canada and Mexico. Assume that the leaders of the two countries believe the payoffs to alternative trade policies are as follows:

   a. What is the dominant strategy for Canada? For Mexico? Explain.
   b. Define *Nash equilibrium*. What is the Nash equilibrium for trade policy?
   c. In 1993, Parliament ratified the North American Free Trade Agreement (NAFTA), in which Canada, the United States, and Mexico agreed to reduce trade barriers simultaneously. Do the perceived payoffs shown here justify this approach to trade policy?
   d. Based on your understanding of the gains from trade (discussed in Chapters 3 and 9), do you think that these payoffs actually reflect a nation's welfare under the four possible outcomes?

5. You and a classmate are assigned a project on which you will receive one combined grade. You each want to receive a good grade, but you also want to avoid hard work. In particular, here is the situation:

   • If both of you work hard, you both get an A, which gives each of you 40 units of happiness.

   • If only one of you works hard, you both get a B, which gives each of you 30 units of happiness.

   • If neither of you works hard, you both get a D, which gives each of you 10 units of happiness.

   • Working hard costs 25 units of happiness.

a. Fill in the payoffs in the following decision box:

Your Decision

	Work	Shirk
Work	You: Classmate:	You: Classmate:
Shirk	You: Classmate:	You: Classmate:

Classmate's Decision

b. What is the likely outcome? Explain your answer.

c. If you get this classmate as your partner on a series of projects throughout the year, rather than only once, how might that change the outcome you predicted in part (b)?

d. Another classmate cares more about good grades: She gets 50 units of happiness for a B and 80 units of happiness for an A. If this classmate were your partner (but your preferences were unchanged), how would your answers to parts (a) and (b) change? Which of the two classmates would you prefer as a partner? Would she also want you as a partner?

6. The chapter described an advertising game between Molson and Labatt. Suppose the federal government is considering a law prohibiting beer commercials on television.

a. Would you expect the beer companies to oppose this law? Why?

b. Would you expect beer company profits to rise or fall? Why?

7. Farmer Singh and Farmer Vu graze their cattle in the same field. If there are 20 cows grazing in the field, each cow produces $4000 of milk over its lifetime. If there are more cows in the field, then each cow can eat less grass, and its milk production falls. With 30 cows in the field, each produces $3000 of milk; with 40 cows, each produces $2000 of milk. Cows cost $1000 apiece.

a. Assume that Farmer Singh and Farmer Vu can each purchase either 10 or 20 cows, but that neither knows how many the other is buying when she makes her purchase. Calculate the payoffs of each outcome.

b. What is the likely outcome of this game? What would be the best outcome? Explain.

c. There used to be more common fields than there are today. Why? (For more discussion of this topic, reread Chapter 11.)

8. Little Kona is a small coffee company that is considering entering a market dominated by Big Brew. Each company's profit depends on whether Little Kona enters and whether Big Brew sets a high price or a low price:

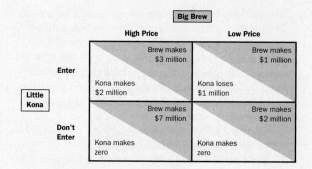

Big Brew

		High Price	Low Price
Little Kona	**Enter**	Brew makes $3 million Kona makes $2 million	Brew makes $1 million Kona loses $1 million
	Don't Enter	Brew makes $7 million Kona makes zero	Brew makes $2 million Kona makes zero

Big Brew threatens Little Kona by saying, "If you enter, we're going to set a low price, so you had better stay out." Do you think Little Kona should believe the threat? Why or why not? What do you think Little Kona should do?

9. Jeff and Steve are playing tennis. Every point comes down to whether Steve guesses correctly whether Jeff will hit the ball to Steve's left or right. The outcomes are:

Steve Guesses

		Left	Right
Jeff Hits	**Left**	Steve wins point Jeff loses point	Steve loses point Jeff wins point
	Right	Steve loses point Jeff wins point	Steve wins point Jeff loses point

Does either player have a dominant strategy? If Jeff chooses a particular strategy (Left or Right) and sticks with it, what will Steve do? Can you think of a better strategy for Jeff to follow?

10. Let's return to the chapter's discussion of Jack and Jill's water duopoly (page 375). Suppose that Jack and Jill are at the duopoly's Nash equilibrium (total production of 80 L) when a third person, John, discovers a water source and joins the market as a third producer.

a. Jack and Jill propose that the three of them continue to produce a total of 80 L, splitting the market three ways. If John agrees to this, how much profit will he make?

b. After agreeing to the proposed deal, John is considering increasing his production by 10 L. If he does, and Jack and Jill stick to the agreement, how much profit will John make? What does this tell you about the proposed agreement?

c. What is the Nash equilibrium for this market with three producers? How does it compare to the Nash equilibrium with two producers?

11. Two athletes of equal ability are competing for a prize of $10 000. Each is deciding whether to take a dangerous performance-enhancing drug. If one athlete takes the drug and the other does not, the one who takes the drug wins the prize. If both or neither take the drug, they tie and split the prize. Taking the drug involves health risks that are equivalent to a loss of X dollars.

    a. Draw a 2 × 2 decision box describing the decisions the athletes face and fill in the payoffs.
    b. For what X is taking the drug the Nash equilibrium?
    c. Does making the drug safer (that is, lowering X) make the athletes better or worse off? Explain.

12. Synergy and Dynaco are the only two firms in a specific high-tech industry. They face the following payoff matrix as they decide upon the size of their research budget:

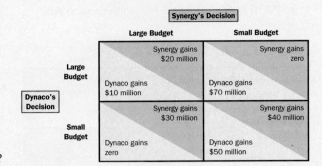

    a. Does Synergy have a dominant strategy? Explain.
    b. Does Dynaco have a dominant strategy? Explain.
    c. Is there a Nash equilibrium for this scenario? Explain. (*Hint:* Look closely at the definition of Nash equilibrium.)

Norm Betts/Bloomberg/Getty images

CHAPTER

18

LEARNING
objectives

The Markets for the Factors of Production

In this chapter, you will ...

1 Analyze the labour demand of competitive, profit-maximizing firms

2 Consider the household decisions that lie behind labour supply

3 Learn why equilibrium wages equal the value of the marginal product of labour

4 Consider how the other factors of production—land and capital—are compensated

5 Examine how a change in the supply of one factor alters the earnings of all the factors

When you finish school, your income will be determined largely by the kind of job you take. If you become a computer programmer, you will earn more than if you become a gas station attendant. This fact is not surprising, but it is not obvious why it is true. No law requires that computer programmers be paid more than gas station attendants. No ethical principle says that programmers are more deserving. What then determines which job will pay you the higher wage?

Your income, of course, is a small piece of a larger economic picture. In 2016, the total income of all Canadian residents was about $2.0 trillion. People earned this income in various ways. Workers earned about two-thirds of it in the form of wages and fringe benefits. The rest went to landowners and to the owners of *capital*—the economy's stock of equipment and structures—in the form of rent, profit, and interest. What determines how much goes to workers? To landowners? To the owners of capital? Why do some workers earn higher wages than others, some landowners higher rental income than others, and some capital owners greater profit than others? Why, in particular, do computer programmers earn more than gas station attendants?

The answers to these questions, like most in economics, hinge on supply and demand. The supply and demand for labour, land, and capital determine the prices paid to workers, landowners, and capital owners. To understand why some people have higher incomes than others, therefore, we need to look more deeply at the markets for the services they provide. That is our job in this and the next two chapters.

factors of production

the inputs used to produce goods and services

This chapter provides the basic theory for the analysis of factor markets. As you may recall from Chapter 2, the **factors of production** are the inputs used to produce goods and services. Labour, land, and capital are the three most important factors of production. When a computer firm produces a new software program, it uses programmers' time (labour), the physical space on which its offices are located (land), and an office building and computer equipment (capital). Similarly, when a gas station sells gas, it uses attendants' time (labour), the physical space (land), and the gas tanks and pumps (capital).

In many ways factor markets resemble the markets for goods and services we analyzed in previous chapters, but they are different in one important way: The demand for a factor of production is a *derived demand*. That is, a firm's demand for a factor of production is derived from its decision to supply a good in another market. The demand for computer programmers is inseparably linked to the supply of computer software, and the demand for gas station attendants is inseparably linked to the supply of gasoline.

In this chapter we analyze factor demand by considering how a competitive, profit-maximizing firm decides how much of any factor to buy. We begin our analysis by examining the demand for labour. Labour is the most important factor of production, because workers receive most of the total income earned in the Canadian economy. Later in the chapter, we will see that our analysis of the labour market also applies to the markets for the other factors of production.

The basic theory of factor markets developed in this chapter takes a large step toward explaining how the income of the Canadian economy is distributed among workers, landowners, and owners of capital. Chapter 19 will build on this analysis to examine in more detail why some workers earn more than others. Chapter 20 will examine how much inequality results from this process and then consider what role the government should and does play in altering the distribution of income.

18-1 The Demand for Labour

Labour markets, like other markets in the economy, are governed by the forces of supply and demand. This is illustrated in Figure 18.1. In panel (a) the supply and demand for apples determine the price of apples. In panel (b) the supply and demand for apple pickers determine the price, or wage, of apple pickers.

As we have already noted, labour markets are different from most other markets because labour demand is a derived demand. Most labour services, rather than being final goods ready to be enjoyed by consumers, are inputs into the production of other goods. To understand labour demand, we need to focus on the firms that hire the labour and use it to produce goods for sale. By examining the link between the production of goods and the demand for labour to make those goods, we gain insight into the determination of equilibrium wages.

18-1a The Competitive, Profit-Maximizing Firm

Let's look at how a typical firm, such as an apple producer, decides what quantity of labour to demand. The firm owns an apple orchard and each week must decide how many apple pickers to hire to harvest its crop. After the firm makes its hiring decision, the workers pick as many apples as they can. The firm then sells the apples, pays the workers, and keeps what is left as profit.

We make two assumptions about our firm. First, we assume that our firm is *competitive* both in the market for apples (where the firm is a seller) and in the market for apple pickers (where the firm is a buyer). A competitive firm is a price taker. Because there are many other firms selling apples and hiring apple pickers, a single firm has little influence over the price it gets for apples or the wage it pays apple pickers. The firm takes the price and the wage as given by market conditions. It only has to decide how many apples to sell and how many workers to hire.

FIGURE 18.1

The Versatility of Supply and Demand

The basic tools of supply and demand apply to goods and to labour services. Panel (a) shows how the supply and demand for apples determine the price of apples. Panel (b) shows how the supply and demand for apple pickers determine the wage of apple pickers.

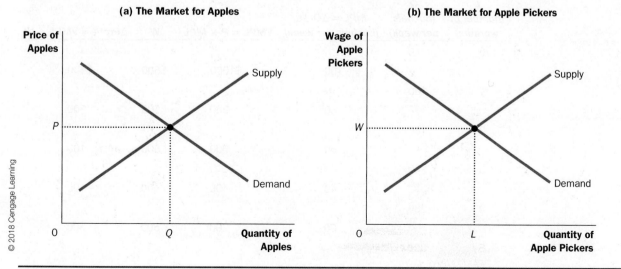

(a) The Market for Apples

(b) The Market for Apple Pickers

© 2018 Cengage Learning

Second, we assume that the firm is *profit-maximizing*. Thus, the firm does not directly care about the number of workers it employs or the number of apples it produces. It cares only about profit, which equals the total revenue from the sale of apples minus the total cost of producing them. The firm's supply of apples and its demand for workers are derived from its primary goal of maximizing profit.

18-1b The Production Function and the Marginal Product of Labour

To make its hiring decision, a firm must consider how the size of its workforce affects the amount of output produced. In our example, the apple producer must consider how the number of apple pickers affects the quantity of apples it can harvest and sell. Table 18.1 gives a numerical example. Column (1) shows the number of workers. Column (2) shows the quantity of apples the workers harvest each week.

production function

the relationship between the quantity of inputs used to make a good and the quantity of output of that good

These two columns of numbers describe the firm's ability to produce apples. Recall that economists use the term **production function** to describe the relationship between the quantity of the inputs used in production and the quantity of output from production. Here the "input" is the apple pickers and the "output" is the apples. The other inputs—the trees themselves, the land, the firm's trucks and tractors, and so on—are held fixed for now. This firm's production function shows that if the firm hires 1 worker, that worker will pick 100 bushels of apples per week. If the firm hires 2 workers, the two workers together will pick 180 bushels per week, and so on.

Figure 18.2 graphs the data on labour and output presented in Table 18.1. The number of workers is on the horizontal axis, and the amount of output is on the vertical axis. This figure illustrates the production function.

TABLE 18.1

How the Competitive Firm Decides How Much Labour to Hire

(1) Labour	(2) Output	(3) Marginal Product of Labour	(4) Value of the Marginal Product of Labour	(5) Wage	(6) Marginal Profit
L (number of workers)	Q (bushels per week)	$MPL = \Delta Q / \Delta L$ (bushels per week)	$VMPL = P \times MPL$	W	$\Delta Profit = VMPL - W$
0	0				
		100	$1000	$500	$500
1	100				
		80	800	500	300
2	180				
		60	600	500	100
3	240				
		40	400	500	−100
4	280				
		20	200	500	−300
5	300				

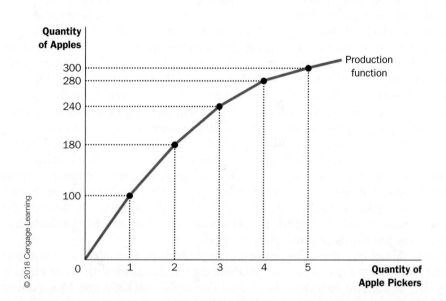

© 2018 Cengage Learning

FIGURE 18.2

The Production Function

The production function is the relationship between the inputs into production (apple pickers) and the output from production (apples). As the quantity of the input increases, the production function gets flatter, reflecting the property of diminishing marginal product.

One of the ten principles of economics introduced in Chapter 1 is that rational people think at the margin. This idea is the key to understanding how firms decide what quantity of labour to hire. To take a step toward this decision, column (3) in Table 18.1 shows the **marginal product of labour**, the increase in the amount of output from an additional unit of labour. When the firm increases the number of workers from 1 to 2, for example, the amount of apples produced rises from 100 to 180 bushels. Therefore, the marginal product of the second worker is 80 bushels.

Notice that as the number of workers increases, the marginal product of labour declines. That is, the production process exhibits **diminishing marginal product**. At first, when only a few workers are hired, they can pick the low-hanging fruit. As the number of workers increases, additional workers have to climb higher up the ladders to find apples to pick. Hence, as more and more workers are hired, each additional worker contributes less to the production of apples. For this reason, the production function in Figure 18.2 becomes flatter as the number of workers rises.

marginal product of labour

the increase in the amount of output from an additional unit of labour

diminishing marginal product

the property whereby the marginal product of an input declines as the quantity of the input increases

18-1c The Value of the Marginal Product and the Demand for Labour

Our profit-maximizing firm is concerned not about apples themselves but rather about the money it can make by producing and selling them. As a result, when deciding how many workers to hire to pick apples, the firm considers how much profit each worker will bring in. Because profit is total revenue minus total cost, the profit from an additional worker is the worker's contribution to revenue minus the worker's wage.

To find the worker's contribution to revenue, we must convert the marginal product of labour (which is measured in bushels of apples) into the *value* of the marginal product (which is measured in dollars). We do this using the price of apples. To continue our example, if a bushel of apples sells for $10 and if an additional worker produces 80 bushels of apples, then the worker produces $800 of revenue.

value of the marginal product

the marginal product of an input times the price of the output

The **value of the marginal product** of any input is the marginal product of that input multiplied by the market price of the output. Column (4) in Table 18.1 shows the value of the marginal product of labour in our example, assuming the price of apples is $10 per bushel. Because the market price is constant for a competitive firm while the marginal product declines with more workers, the value of the marginal product diminishes as the number of workers rises. Economists sometimes call this column of numbers the firm's *marginal revenue product:* It is the extra revenue the firm gets from hiring an additional unit of a factor of production.

Now consider how many workers the firm will hire. Suppose that the market wage for apple pickers is $500 per week. In this case, as you see in Table 18.1, the first worker that the firm hires is profitable: The first worker yields $1000 in revenue, or $500 in profit. Similarly, the second worker yields $800 in additional revenue, or $300 in profit. The third worker produces $600 in additional revenue, or $100 in profit. After the third worker, however, hiring workers is unprofitable. The fourth worker would yield only $400 of additional revenue. Because the worker's wage is $500, hiring the fourth worker would mean a $100 reduction in profit. Thus, the firm hires only three workers.

Figure 18.3 graphs the value of the marginal product. This curve slopes downward because the marginal product of labour diminishes as the number of workers rises. The figure also includes a horizontal line at the market wage. To maximize profit, the firm hires workers up to the point where these two curves cross. Below this level of employment, the value of the marginal product exceeds the wage, so hiring another worker would increase profit. Above this level of employment, the value of the marginal product is less than the wage, so the marginal worker is unprofitable. Thus, *a competitive, profit-maximizing firm hires workers up to the point where the value of the marginal product of labour equals the wage.*

Having explained the profit-maximizing hiring strategy for a competitive firm, we can now offer a theory of labour demand. Recall that a firm's labour demand curve tells us the quantity of labour that a firm demands at any given wage.

FIGURE 18.3

The Value of the Marginal Product of Labour

This figure shows how the value of the marginal product (the marginal product times the price of the output) depends on the number of workers. The curve slopes downward because of diminishing marginal product. For a competitive, profit-maximizing firm, this value-of-marginal-product curve is also the firm's labour demand curve.

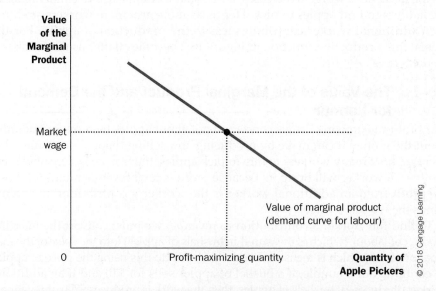

© 2018 Cengage Learning

We have just seen in Figure 18.3 that the firm makes that decision by choosing the quantity of labour at which the value of the marginal product equals the wage. As a result, *the value-of-marginal-product curve is the labour demand curve for a competitive, profit-maximizing firm.*

18-1d What Causes the Labour Demand Curve to Shift?

We now understand the labour demand curve: It reflects the value of the marginal product of labour. With this insight in mind, let's consider a few of the things that might cause the labour demand curve to shift.

The Output Price The value of the marginal product is marginal product times the price of the firm's output. Thus, when the output price changes, the value of the marginal product changes, and the labour demand curve shifts. An increase in the price of apples, for instance, raises the value of the marginal product of each worker who picks apples and, therefore, increases labour demand from the firms that supply apples. Conversely, a decrease in the price of apples reduces the value of the marginal product and decreases labour demand.

Technological Change Between 1961 and 2016, the amount of output a typical Canadian worker produced in an hour rose by about 128 percent. Why? The most important reason is technological progress: Scientists and engineers are constantly figuring out new and better ways of doing things. This has profound implications for the labour market. Technological advance typically raises the marginal product

---

Input Demand and Output Supply: Two Sides of the Same Coin

In Chapter 14 we saw how a competitive, profit-maximizing firm decides how much of its output to sell: It chooses the quantity of output at which the price of the good equals the marginal cost of production. We have just seen how such a firm decides how much labour to hire: It chooses the quantity of labour at which the wage equals the value of the marginal product. Because the production function links the quantity of inputs to the quantity of output, you should not be surprised to learn that the firm's decision about input demand is closely linked to its decision about output supply. In fact, these two decisions are two sides of the same coin.

To see this relationship more fully, let's consider how the marginal product of labour (*MPL*) and marginal cost (*MC*) are related. Suppose an additional worker costs $500 and has a marginal product of 50 bushels of apples. In this case, producing 50 more bushels costs $500; the marginal cost of a bushel is $500/50, or $10. More generally, if *W* is the wage, and an extra unit of labour produces *MPL* units of output, then the marginal cost of a unit of output is $MC = W/MPL$.

This analysis shows that diminishing marginal product is closely related to increasing marginal cost. When our apple orchard becomes crowded with workers, each additional worker adds less to the production of apples (*MPL* falls). Similarly, when the apple firm is producing a large quantity of

apples, the orchard is already crowded with workers, so it is more costly to produce an additional bushel of apples (*MC* rises).

Now consider our criterion for profit maximization. We determined earlier that a profit-maximizing firm chooses the quantity of labour so that the value of the marginal product ($P \times MPL$) equals the wage (*W*). We can write this mathematically as

$$P \times MPL = W$$

If we divide both sides of this equation by *MPL*, we obtain

$$P = W/MPL$$

We just noted that W/MPL equals marginal cost *MC*. Therefore, we can substitute to obtain

$$P = MC$$

This equation states that the price of the firm's output is equal to the marginal cost of producing a unit of output. Thus, when a competitive firm hires labour up to the point at which the value of the marginal product equals the wage, it also produces up to the point at which the price equals marginal cost. Our analysis of labour demand in this chapter is just another way of looking at the production decision we first saw in Chapter 14.

of labour, which in turn increases the demand for labour, which in turn shifts the labour demand curve to the right.

It is also possible for technological change to reduce labour demand. The invention of a cheap industrial robot, for instance, could conceivably reduce the marginal product of labour, shifting the labour demand curve to the left. Economists call this *labour-saving* technological change. History suggests, however, that most technological progress is instead *labour-augmenting*. Such technological advance explains persistently rising employment in the face of rising wages: Even though wages (adjusted for inflation) increased by over 100 percent during the last half-century, firms nonetheless increased by over 50 percent the amount of labour they employed.

The Supply of Other Factors The quantity of one factor of production that is available can affect the marginal product of other factors. The productivity of apple pickers depends, for instance, on the availability of ladders. If the supply of ladders declines, the marginal product of apple pickers will decline as well, reducing the demand for apple pickers. We consider this linkage among the factors of production more fully later in the chapter.

 QUICK **Quiz** *Define marginal product of labour and value of the marginal product of labour.* • *Describe how a competitive, profit-maximizing firm decides how many workers to hire.*

18-2 The Supply of Labour

Having analyzed labour demand in detail, let's turn to the other side of the market and consider labour supply. A formal model of labour supply is included in Chapter 21, where we develop the theory of household decision making. Here we informally discuss the decisions that lie behind the labour supply curve.

18-2a The Tradeoff between Work and Leisure

One of the ten principles of economics in Chapter 1 is that people face tradeoffs. Probably no tradeoff in a person's life is more obvious or more important than the tradeoff between work and leisure. The more hours you spend working, the fewer hours you have to watch TV, browse social media, enjoy dinner with friends, or pursue your favourite hobby. The tradeoff between labour and leisure lies behind the labour supply curve.

Another of the ten principles of economics is that the cost of something is what you give up to get it. What do you give up to get an hour of leisure? You give up an hour of work, which in turn means an hour of wages. Thus, if your wage is $15 per hour, the opportunity cost of an hour of leisure is $15. And when you get a raise to $20 per hour, the opportunity cost of enjoying leisure goes up.

The labour supply curve reflects how workers' decisions about the labour–leisure tradeoff respond to a change in that opportunity cost. An upward-sloping labour supply curve means that an increase in the wage induces workers to increase the quantity of labour they supply. Because time is limited, more hours of work means less leisure. That is, workers respond to the increase in the opportunity cost of leisure by taking less of it.

It is worth noting that the labour supply curve need not be upward sloping. Imagine you got that raise from $15 to $20 per hour. The opportunity cost of leisure is now greater, but you are also richer than you were before. You might decide that with your extra wealth you can now afford to enjoy more leisure. That is, at the higher wage, you might choose to work fewer hours. If so, your labour supply curve would slope backward. In Chapter 21, we discuss this possibility in terms of conflicting effects on your labour supply decision (called *the income and substitution effects*). For now, we ignore the possibility of backward-sloping labour supply and assume that the labour supply curve is upward sloping.

18-2b What Causes the Labour Supply Curve to Shift?

The labour supply curve shifts whenever people change the amount they want to work at a given wage. Let's now consider some of the events that might cause such a shift.

Changes in Tastes In 1950, 34 percent of working-age women were employed at paid jobs or looking for work. By 2016, the number had risen to 82 percent. Although there are many explanations for this development, one of them is changing tastes, or attitudes toward work. A generation or two ago, it was the norm for women to stay at home while raising children. Today, family sizes are smaller, and more mothers choose to work. The result is an increase in the supply of labour.

Changes in Alternative Opportunities The supply of labour in any one labour market depends on the opportunities available in other labour markets. If the wage earned by pear pickers suddenly rises, some apple pickers may choose to switch occupations. The supply of labour in the market for apple pickers falls.

Immigration Movement of workers from region to region, or country to country, is another important source of shifts in labour supply. When immigrants come to Canada, for instance, the supply of labour in Canada increases and the supply of labour in the immigrants' home countries contracts. In fact, much of the policy debate about immigration centres on its effect on labour supply and, thereby, equilibrium wages in the labour market.

 QUICK Quiz *Who has a greater opportunity cost of enjoying leisure—a janitor or a brain surgeon? Explain. Can this help explain why doctors work such long hours?*

18-3 Equilibrium in the Labour Market

So far we have established two facts about how wages are determined in competitive labour markets:

1. The wage adjusts to balance the supply and demand for labour.
2. The wage equals the value of the marginal product of labour.

At first, it might seem surprising that the wage can do both of these things at once. In fact, there is no real puzzle here, but understanding why there is no puzzle is an important step to understanding wage determination.

FIGURE 18.4

Equilibrium in a Labour Market

Like all prices, the price of labour (the wage) depends on supply and demand. Because the demand curve reflects the value of the marginal product of labour, in equilibrium, workers receive the value of their marginal contribution to the production of goods and services.

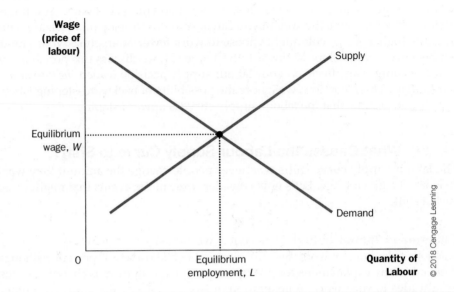

Figure 18.4 shows the labour market in equilibrium. The wage and the quantity of labour have adjusted to balance supply and demand. When the market is in this equilibrium, each firm has bought as much labour as it finds profitable at the equilibrium wage. That is, each firm has followed the rule for profit maximization: It has hired workers until the value of the marginal product equals the wage. Hence, the wage must equal the value of the marginal product of labour once it has brought supply and demand into equilibrium.

This brings us to an important lesson: Any event that changes the supply or demand for labour must change the equilibrium wage and the value of the marginal product by the same amount, because these must always be equal. To see how this works, let's consider some events that shift these curves.

18-3a Shifts in Labour Supply

Suppose that immigration increases the number of workers willing to pick apples. As Figure 18.5 shows, the supply of labour shifts to the right from S_1 to S_2. At the initial wage W_1, the quantity of labour supplied now exceeds the quantity demanded. This surplus of labour puts downward pressure on the wage of apple pickers, and the fall in the wage from W_1 to W_2 in turn makes it profitable for firms to hire more workers. As the number of workers employed in each apple orchard rises, the marginal product of a worker falls, and so does the value of the marginal product. In the new equilibrium, both the wage and the value of the marginal product of labour are lower than they were before the influx of new workers.

An episode in Israel, studied by MIT economist Joshua Angrist, illustrates how a shift in labour supply can alter the equilibrium in a labour market. During most of the 1980s, many thousands of Palestinians regularly commuted from their homes in the Israeli-occupied West Bank and Gaza Strip to jobs in Israel, primarily in the construction and agriculture industries. In 1988, however,

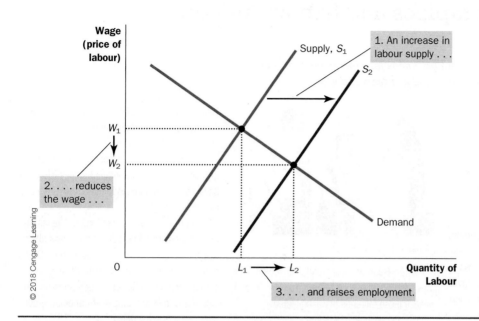

© 2018 Cengage Learning

FIGURE 18.5

A Shift in Labour Supply

When labour supply increases from S_1 to S_2, perhaps because of an immigration of new workers, the equilibrium wage falls from W_1 to W_2. At this lower wage, firms hire more labour, so employment rises from L_1 to L_2. The change in the wage reflects a change in the value of the marginal product of labour: With more workers, the added output from an extra worker is smaller.

political unrest in these occupied areas induced the Israeli government to take steps that, as a by-product, reduced this supply of workers. Curfews were imposed, work permits were checked more thoroughly, and a ban on overnight stays of Palestinians in Israel was enforced more rigorously. The economic impact of these steps was exactly as theory predicts: The number of Palestinians with jobs in Israel fell by half, while those who continued to work in Israel enjoyed wage increases of about 50 percent. With a reduced number of Palestinian workers in Israel, the value of the marginal product of the remaining workers was much higher.

When considering the economics of immigration, keep in mind that the economy consists not of a single labour market but rather a variety of labour markets for different kinds of workers. A wave of immigration may lower wages in those labour markets in which the new immigrants seek work, but it could have the opposite effect in other labour markets. For example, if the new immigrants look for jobs as apple pickers, the supply of apple pickers increases and the wage of apple pickers declines. But suppose the new immigrants are physicians who use some of their income to buy apples. In this case, the wave of immigration increases the *supply* of physicians but increases the *demand* for apples and thus apple pickers. As a result, the wages of physicians decline, and the wages of apple pickers rise. The linkages among various markets—sometimes called *general equilibrium effects*—make analyzing the full effect of immigration more complex than it first appears.

18-3b Shifts in Labour Demand

Now suppose that an increase in the popularity of apples causes their price to rise. This price increase does not change the marginal product of labour for any given number of workers, but it does raise the *value* of the marginal product.

Demographics and Labour Markets

As the following article discusses, recent graduates face mounting challenges in the labour market due to demographics and just plain bad luck.

Generation Unlucky

By Tim Shufelt

Graduating members of the Millennial Generation find themselves leaving the comforts of campus for what seems, by historical standards, the bleakest of futures: limited job prospects, prohibitive housing prices, schizophrenic financial markets, the ravages of a global recession and one giant bill from decades of excess.

Landing that first career position has never been easy. But the labour force's youngest cohort seems to have some legitimate grievances.

Older workers are clinging to their jobs longer, eating up available salary and squeezing the job market from the top. That's exacerbating competition for junior vacancies, which high youth unemployment indicates are already in short supply.

iStockphoto.com/Pamela Moore

When Boomers eventually do leave their jobs en masse, the capacity of the workforce to finance those retirements will be tested.

And the dwindling of defined-benefit pension plans will make it more difficult for Millennials to save for their own retirements, which can't even begin until they reconcile their record-high student debt loads.

Having enjoyed a stretch of relative economic prosperity, Boomers are now committing younger generations to a fate of austerity and stagnancy—an intergenerational transfer dubbed "fiscal child abuse" by one pundit.

Is this the unluckiest generation? According to research … graduating into a recession can have permanent consequences for income and job quality.

"There is a risk that the longer it takes, the more their skills depreciate, and the less attractive they are to employers," said Philip Oreopoulos, labour economist at the University of Toronto and co-author of a study analyzing the incomes of a large number of Canadian graduates over a 20-year period.

The central finding of the much-cited study: Luck matters.

Those unlucky enough to graduate into a recession face an average initial income shortfall of almost 10%. It takes an average of 10 years after graduation to overcome the initial damages.

With a higher price of apples, hiring more apple pickers is now profitable. As Figure 18.6 shows, when the demand for labour shifts to the right from D_1 to D_2, the equilibrium wage rises from W_1 to W_2, and the equilibrium employment rises from L_1 to L_2. Once again, the wage and the value of the marginal product of labour move together.

This analysis shows that prosperity for firms in an industry is often linked to prosperity for workers in that industry. When the price of apples rises, apple producers make greater profit, and apple pickers earn higher wages. When the price of apples falls, apple producers earn smaller profit, and apple pickers earn lower wages. This lesson is well known to workers in industries with highly volatile prices. Workers in oil fields, for instance, know from experience that their earnings are closely linked to the world price of crude oil.

From these examples, you should now have a good understanding of how wages are set in competitive labour markets. Labour supply and labour demand together determine the equilibrium wage, and shifts in the supply or demand curve for labour cause the equilibrium wage to change. At the same time, profit maximization by the firms that demand labour ensures that the equilibrium wage always equals the value of the marginal product of labour.

"They're significant and real and long-term," Mr. Oreopoulos said. "For some people, there are lifetime effects."

While contending with the effects of a recessionary employment market, what's known interchangeably as Generation Y, the Millennial Generation or the Echo Boomers also must wrestle with a macroeconomic albatross that could persist long into their working lives.

More and more, Baby Boomers are indicted by analysts as having handed off to future taxpayers a monumental bill for years of unsustainable finances.

Through their control of politics and elections, Boomers "have rationally chosen a path of more consumption today at the expense of future generations," Jason Hsu, chief investment officer at Research Affiliates, said in a recent report.

The resulting "new normal" he envisions features "an extended period of lower economic and return expectations for the aging and debt-ridden developed world."....

Compound that with the effect of changing demographics, particularly the retirement cycle

of the Boomers, and a substantial increase in the tax burden seems inescapable.

In developed countries, the support ratio of working-age adults per retiree was 5.3 to 1 in 1970, Mr. Hsu said. By 2050, that ratio is expected to fall to 2 to 1. In the United States, there will be "10 new retirees for each new entrant to the workforce," he said.

"Not only does the future appear unenviably poor in aggregate, it also appears predictably unproductive," he concluded.

Entitlement programs in the United States, including Social Security and Medicare, need profound reform to avoid a drastic increase to the taxes of the future American workers. In *The Coming Generational Storm*, Laurence Kotlikoff and Scott Burns likened the trend to fiscal child abuse.

Canada's public pensions, by contrast, are fairly well-funded. But retirement security is no less a concern for younger and future entrants to the workforce.

Between 1991 and 2009, the proportion of Canadian employees covered by a private

pension plan fell from 45% to 33%. Of those, about 75% are members of defined-benefit plans. But the discrepancy between the public and private sectors is vast, with only 56% of private-sector pension members covered by defined benefits.....

Unemployment of younger workers remains at about 14%, the product of the recession, which tends to disproportionately punish youth, as well as the unsteady recovery, during which older workers have postponed retiring.

Many workers near retirement saw the value of their investment portfolios sink over the past few years and decided to stay on the job to top up their savings, said Eric Cousineau, founder of OC Group, a human resources consultancy.

Meanwhile, just to rise to the point of zero net worth will take students years, given that student debt has soared over the past two decades.

For many, that will mean "postponement of milestones of life, like having children or owning a house," Paul Cappon, president of the Canadian Council on Learning, said in a document.

Source: "Generation Unlucky: From Boom to Gloom" by Tim Shufelt, *National Post*, October 15, 2011, p. F1. Material reprinted with the express permission of: National Post, a division of Postmedia Network Inc.

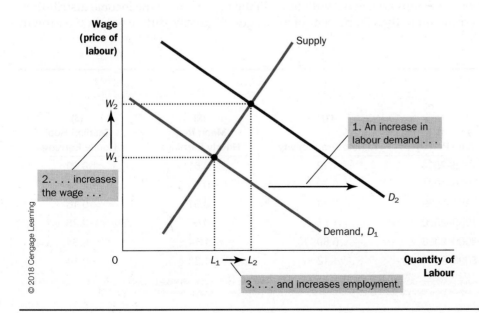

FIGURE 18.6

A Shift in Labour Demand

When labour demand increases from D_1 to D_2, perhaps because of an increase in the price of the firms' output, the equilibrium wage rises from W_1 to W_2, and employment rises from L_1 to L_2. Again, the change in the wage reflects a change in the value of the marginal product of labour: With a higher output price, the added output from an extra worker is more valuable.

© 2018 Cengage Learning

case study   Productivity and Wages in Canada

One of the ten principles of economics in Chapter 1 is that our standard of living depends on our ability to produce goods and services. In particular, our analysis of labour demand shows that wages equal productivity as measured by the value of the marginal product of labour. Put simply, highly productive workers are highly paid, and less productive workers are less highly paid. This lesson is key to understanding why workers today are better off than workers in previous generations.

However, things are not quite that simple in the real world, as several factors can affect the relationship between productivity and wages. Table 18.2 presents some data on annual growth rates in productivity and real wages (that is, wages adjusted for inflation) in Canada. The data, and subsequent analysis, are based on work produced by economists at the Centre for the Study of Living Standards, an institute dedicated to research on the determinants of living standards in Canada.

Column (1) shows the average growth rate per year in labour productivity from 1976 to 2014, and over several periods; the cut-off points for the sub-periods are picked to coincide with the peaks of the business cycle. We see that productivity growth averaged 1.12 percent per year over the entire period, which indicates that Canadian workers have indeed become more productive over the 38-year period. Our theory suggests that this should lead to higher wages. Two measures of the annual average growth rate in real wages are shown in the table, the growth rate in *mean* real wages (column (2)) and the growth rate in *median* real wages (column (3)).

The distinction between mean and median wages is important because it relates to the distribution of wages across income groups. The mean wage is a simple arithmetic average of wages over all workers. The median wage is the wage "in the middle," such that half of workers earn more than the median wage and half earn less. As we will discuss in more detail in Chapter 20, if the median wage is lower than the mean wage, which is indeed the case in Canada and in other countries, this indicates that the distribution of wages across income groups is skewed, with those in the upper half of the income distribution earning more than 50 percent of all wages. Similarly, differences in the growth

TABLE 18.2

Annual Productivity and Wage Growth in Canada

Time Period	(1) Labour Productivity	(2) Mean Real Hourly Earnings	(3) Median Real Hourly Earnings
1976–2014	1.12	0.61	0.09
1976–1981	0.90	−0.73	−0.32
1981–1989	0.94	0.31	0.16
1989–2000	1.51	0.65	−0.28
2000–2008	0.89	1.14	0.94
2008–2014	1.12	1.38	−0.14

Source: James Uguccioni, Andrew Sharpe, and Alexander Murray, Labour Productivity and the Distribution of Real Earnings in Canada, 1976 to 2014, Centre for the Study of Living Standards (November 2016) CSLS Research Report 2016–15. http://www.csls.ca/reports/csls2016-15.pdf.

FYI   Monopsony

On the preceding pages, we built our analysis of the labour market with the tools of supply and demand. In doing so, we assumed that the labour market was competitive. That is, we assumed that there were many buyers of labour and many sellers of labour, so each buyer or seller had a negligible effect on the wage.

Yet imagine the labour market in a small town dominated by a single large employer. That employer can exert a large influence on the going wage, and it may well use that market power to alter the outcome. Such a market in which there is a single buyer is called a *monopsony*.

A monopsony (a market with one buyer) is in many ways similar to a monopoly (a market with one seller). Recall from Chapter 15 that a monopoly firm produces less of the good than would a competitive firm; by reducing the quantity offered for sale, the monopoly firm moves along the product's demand curve, raising the price and also its profits. Similarly, a monopsony firm in a labour market hires fewer workers than would a competitive firm; by reducing the number of jobs available, the monopsony firm moves along the labour supply curve, reducing the wage it pays and raising its profits. Thus, both monopolists and monopsonists reduce economic activity in a market below the socially optimal level. In both cases, the existence of market power distorts the outcome and causes deadweight losses.

This book does not present the formal model of monopsony because, in the real world, monopsonies are rare. In most labour markets, workers have many possible employers, and firms compete with one another to attract workers. In this case, the model of supply and demand is the best one to use.

---

rates in mean and median wages indicate whether inequality is increasing or decreasing—if mean wages grow faster than median wages income inequality is increasing, and vice-versa. As is evident from the table, real mean wages grew at rate of 0.61 percent per year over the entire period, while median wages barely grew at all, at 0.09 percent per year; this suggests that income inequality increased in Canada over the period.

Also evident from the table is that the relationship between the growth rate in labour productivity and real wages is far from perfect. Our analysis suggests that they should move together, with higher productivity leading to higher wages. Over the entire period productivity growth averaged 1.12 percent per year while the growth in mean real wages averaged 0.61 percent. Though not perfect, mean real wages and productivity are indeed positively correlated. However, it is noteworthy that the relationship is not perfect. For example, an interesting exception is the period from 1976 to 1981 when productivity grew by 0.90 percent per year but mean wages actually fell by 0.73 percent per year. The gap between the growth rates in productivity and mean wages is not completely understood and is the subject of considerable ongoing research.

We also see from the table that there is very little relationship between the growth rate in productivity and the growth rate in median wages. One possible explanation for this is that productivity gains have tended to be concentrated in occupations at the higher income levels. However, as indicated, we do not have a complete understanding of the complex relationship between productivity and wage growth. ∎

QUICK **Quiz** *How does an immigration of workers affect labour supply, labour demand, the marginal product of labour, and the equilibrium wage?*

18-4 The Other Factors of Production: Land and Capital

We have seen how firms decide how much labour to hire and how these decisions determine workers' wages. At the same time that firms are hiring workers, they are also deciding about other inputs to production. For example, our apple-producing firm might have to choose the size of its apple orchard and the number of ladders for its apple pickers. We can think of the firm's factors of production as falling into three categories: labour, land, and capital.

capital

the equipment and structures used to produce goods and services

The meaning of the terms *labour* and *land* is clear, but the definition of *capital* is somewhat tricky. Economists use the term **capital** to refer to the stock of equipment and structures used for production. That is, the economy's capital represents the accumulation of goods produced in the past that are being used in the present to produce new goods and services. For our apple firm, the capital stock includes the ladders used to climb the trees, the trucks used to transport the apples, the buildings used to store the apples, and even the trees themselves.

18-4a Equilibrium in the Markets for Land and Capital

What determines how much the owners of land and capital earn for their contribution to the production process? Before answering this question, we need to distinguish between two prices: the purchase price and the rental price. The *purchase price* of land or capital is the price a person pays to own that factor of production indefinitely. The *rental price* is the price a person pays to use that factor for a limited period of time. It is important to keep this distinction in mind because, as we will see, these prices are determined by somewhat different economic forces.

Having defined these terms, we can now apply the theory of factor demand that we developed for the labour market to the markets for land and capital. Because the wage is the rental price of labour, much of what we have learned about wage determination applies also to the rental prices of land and capital. As Figure 18.7 illustrates, the rental price of land, shown in panel (a), and the rental price of capital, shown in panel (b), are determined by supply and demand. Moreover, the demand for land and capital is determined just like the demand for labour. That is, when our apple-producing firm is deciding how much land and how many ladders to rent, it follows the same logic as when deciding how many workers to hire. For both land and capital, the firm increases the quantity hired until the value of the factor's marginal product equals the factor's price. Thus, the demand curve for each factor reflects the marginal productivity of that factor.

We can now explain how much income goes to labour, how much goes to landowners, and how much goes to the owners of capital. As long as the firms using the factors of production are competitive and profit-maximizing, each factor's rental price must equal the value of the marginal product for that factor. *Labour, land, and capital each earn the value of their marginal contribution to the production process.*

Now consider the purchase price of land and capital. The rental price and the purchase price are related: Buyers are willing to pay more for a piece of land or capital if it produces a valuable stream of rental income. And, as we have just seen, the equilibrium rental income at any point in time equals the value of that factor's marginal product. Therefore, the equilibrium purchase price of a piece of land or capital depends on both the current value of the marginal product and the value of the marginal product expected to prevail in the future.

FIGURE 18.7

The Markets for Land and Capital

Supply and demand determine the compensation paid to the owners of land, as shown in panel (a), and the compensation paid to the owners of capital, as shown in panel (b). The demand for each factor, in turn, depends on the value of the marginal product of that factor.

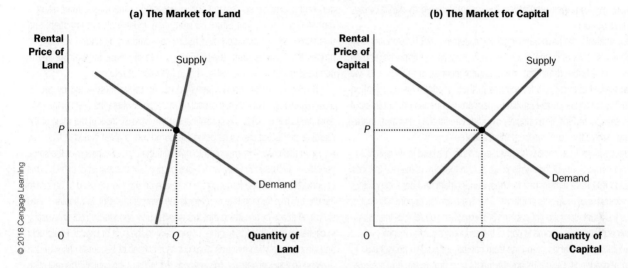

18-4b Linkages among the Factors of Production

We have seen that the price paid to any factor of production—labour, land, or capital—equals the value of the marginal product of that factor. The marginal product of any factor, in turn, depends on the quantity of that factor that is available. Because of diminishing marginal product, a factor in abundant supply has a low marginal product and thus a low price, and a factor in scarce supply has a high marginal product and a high price. As a result, when the supply of a factor falls, its equilibrium factor price rises.

When the supply of any factor changes, however, the effects are not limited to the market for that factor. In most situations, factors of production are used together in a way that makes the productivity of each factor dependent on the quantities of the other factors available for use in the production process. As a result, when some event changes the supply of any one factor of production, it will typically affect not only the earnings of that factor but also the earnings of all the factors as well.

For example, suppose a hurricane destroys many of the ladders that workers use to pick apples from the orchards. What happens to the earnings of the various factors of production? Most obviously, when the supply of ladders falls, the equilibrium rental price of ladders rises. Those owners who were lucky enough to avoid damage to their ladders now earn a higher return when they rent out their ladders to the firms that produce apples.

Yet the effects of this event do not stop at the ladder market. Because there are fewer ladders with which to work, the workers who pick apples have a smaller marginal product. Thus, the reduction in the supply of ladders reduces the demand for the labour of apple pickers, and this shift in demand causes the equilibrium wage to fall.

What Is Capital Income?

Labour income is an easy concept to understand: It is the paycheque that workers get from their employers. The income earned by capital, however, is less obvious.

In our analysis, we have been implicitly assuming that households own the economy's stock of capital—ladders, drill presses, warehouses, and so on—and rent it to the firms that use it. Capital income, in this case, is the rent that households receive for the use of their capital. This assumption simplified our analysis of how capital owners are compensated, but it is not entirely realistic. In fact, firms usually own the capital they use and, therefore, they receive the earnings from this capital.

These earnings from capital, however, eventually are paid to households in a variety of forms. Some of the earnings are paid in the form of interest to those households that have lent money to firms. Bondholders and bank depositors are two examples of recipients of interest. This is the explicit opportunity cost of capital to the firm discussed in Chapter 13. Thus, when you receive interest on your bank account, that income is part of the economy's capital income.

In addition, some of the earnings from capital are paid to households in the form of dividends. Dividends are payments by a firm to the firm's shareholders. A shareholder is a person who has bought a share in the ownership of the firm and, therefore, is entitled to share in the firm's profits.

A firm does not have to pay out all its earnings to households in the form of interest and dividends. Instead, it can retain some earnings within the firm and use these earnings to buy additional capital. Unlike dividends, these retained earnings do not yield a direct cash payment to the firm's shareholders, but the shareholders benefit from them nonetheless. Because retained earnings increase the amount of capital the firm owns, they tend to increase future earnings and, thereby, the value of the firm's stock. This is known as a *capital gain*. The earnings of shareholders therefore consist of the dividends they receive plus the capital gains on their shares. Dividing these earnings (dividends plus capital gains) by the purchase price of the shares determines the rate of return on the shares.

Capital markets are very complex. In particular, capital earnings, whether they are in the form of interest, dividends, or capital gains, are risky. However, if we abstract from these complexities (such as risk) we can see that the rate of return on shares must equal the interest rate on money loaned to the firm. If this were not the case, households would prefer to receive their earnings from capital completely in one form or the other. So, in what follows, we will simply refer to the interest rate.

In a sense, rather than renting capital to firms and receiving the capital income in the form of rental payments, households can be viewed as renting money to firms, which in turn use this money to purchase capital. The rental payments on this money take the form of interest, dividends, and capital gains.

What determines the interest rate (and the rate of return on shares)? The supply and demand of money invested in capital, of course! Without going into details, the supply of household funds to firms to invest in capital is determined by the tradeoff that individuals are willing to make between consuming now versus saving and consuming in the future. After all, current saving is really just future consumption. Individuals are impatient and prefer current consumption over future consumption. In order to save their money to consume later, they require a rate of return on their money to compensate them for the delay; this is the interest rate.

The demand for money invested in capital is determined by profit-maximizing firms that invest in capital up to the point where the value of the marginal product is equal to the cost of capital. We typically think of the value of the marginal product of capital as being measured over a given period of time, say a year. In this case, it is important to measure the cost of capital over the same period. As discussed in Chapter 13, one component of the cost of capital is the opportunity cost of the forgone rate of return on the money used to purchase the capital. This forgone rate of return is the interest rate. But, in Chapter 13 we simplified things by assuming that this was the only opportunity cost of investing in capital. In fact, there is another component to the cost of capital. Equipment and structures owned by firms wear out as it is used or becomes obsolete due to technological innovations. This reduces the value of the capital. This reduction in the value of the capital over time due to wear and tear and obsolescence is called *depreciation*. Depreciation is another component of the cost of capital. The *depreciation rate* is the annual rate at which capital depreciates.

With this in mind, now consider a profit-maximizing firm considering how much capital to purchase. The value of the marginal product of capital can be written as ($P \times MPK$), where P is the price of the additional output produced by an incremental unit of capital and MPK is the marginal product of that capital (economists, somewhat strangely, use the letter K to denote capital). As discussed above, the opportunity cost of capital consists of two components: the interest rate and the depreciation rate. Let P_K be the purchase price of a unit of capital, i the interest rate, and d the depreciation rate on that capital. A profit-maximizing firm thus demands capital up to the point where the value of the marginal product is equal to the opportunity cost of capital, or

$$P \times MPK = P_K \times (i + d)$$

For example, say the purchase price of a machine used in production is $300 000; this is P_K. If the interest rate (i) is 5 percent and the depreciation rate on the capital (d) is also 5 percent, the opportunity cost of capital (the right-hand side of the above equation) is $30 000 ($300 000 $\times$ (0.05 + 0.05) = $30 000). A profit-maximizing firm will purchase additional machines up to the point where the value of purchasing another (the value of the marginal product) is just equal to $30 000 per year.

These institutional details are interesting and important, but they do not alter our conclusion about the income earned by the owners of capital. Capital is paid according to the value of its marginal product, regardless of whether this income is transmitted to households in the form of interest, dividends, or capital gains.

This story shows a general lesson: An event that changes the supply of any factor of production can alter the earnings of all the factors. The change in earnings of any factor can be found by analyzing the impact of the event on the value of the marginal product of that factor.

QUICK Quiz *What determines the income of the owners of land and capital? • How would an increase in the quantity of capital affect the incomes of those who already own capital? How would it affect the incomes of workers?*

18-5 Conclusion

This chapter explained how labour, land, and capital are compensated for the roles they play in the production process. The theory developed here is called the *neoclassical theory of distribution.* According to the neoclassical theory, the amount paid to each factor of production depends on the supply and demand for that factor. The demand, in turn, depends on that particular factor's marginal productivity. In equilibrium, each factor of production earns the value of its marginal contribution to the production of goods and services.

The neoclassical theory of distribution is widely accepted. Most economists begin with the neoclassical theory when trying to explain how the Canadian economy's $2.0 trillion of income is distributed among the economy's various members. In the following two chapters, we consider the distribution of income in more detail. As you will see, the neoclassical theory provides the framework for this discussion.

Even at this point you can use the theory to answer the question that began this chapter: Why are computer programmers paid more than gas station attendants? It is because programmers can produce a good of greater market value than can gas station attendants. People are willing to pay dearly for a good computer game, but they are willing to pay little to have their gas pumped and their windshield washed. The wages of these workers reflect the market prices of the goods or services they produce. If people suddenly got tired of using computers and decided to spend more time driving, the prices of these goods and services would change, and so would the equilibrium wages of these two groups of workers.

summary

- The economy's income is distributed in the markets for the factors of production. The three most important factors of production are labour, land, and capital.

- The demand for factors, such as labour, is a derived demand that comes from firms that use the factors to produce goods and services. Competitive, profit-maximizing firms hire each factor up to the point at which the value of the marginal product of the factor equals its price.

- The supply of labour arises from individuals' tradeoff between work and leisure. An upward-sloping labour supply curve means that people respond to an increase in the wage by enjoying less leisure and working more hours.

- The price paid to each factor adjusts to balance the supply and demand for that factor. Because factor demand reflects the value of the marginal product of that factor, in equilibrium, each factor is compensated according to its marginal contribution to the production of goods and services.

- Because factors of production are used together, the marginal product of any one factor depends on the quantities of all factors that are available. As a result, a change in the supply of one factor alters the equilibrium earnings of all the factors.

KEY **concepts**

factors of production, *p. 398*
production function, *p. 400*
marginal product of labour, *p. 401*

diminishing marginal product, *p. 401*
value of the marginal product, *p. 402*
capital, *p. 412*

QUESTIONS FOR **review**

1. Explain how a firm's production function is related to its marginal product of labour, how a firm's marginal product of labour is related to the value of its marginal product, and how a firm's value of marginal product is related to its demand for labour.

2. Give two examples of events that could shift the demand for labour, and explain why they do so.

3. Give two examples of events that could shift the supply of labour, and explain why they do so.

4. Explain how the wage can adjust to balance the supply and demand for labour while simultaneously equalling the value of the marginal product of labour.

5. If the population of Canada suddenly grew because of a large immigration, what would happen to wages? What would happen to the rents earned by the owners of land and capital?

QUICK CHECK **multiple choice**

1. Approximately what percentage of Canadian national income is paid to workers, as opposed to owners of capital and land?
   a. 30 percent
   b. 50 percent
   c. 67 percent
   d. 90 percent

2. If firms are competitive and profit-maximizing, the demand curve for labour is determined by which of the following?
   a. the opportunity cost of workers' time
   b. the value of the marginal product of labour
   c. offsetting income and substitution effects
   d. the value of the marginal product of capital

3. A bakery operating in competitive markets sells its output for $20 per cake and hires labour at $10 per hour. To maximize profit, it should hire labour until the marginal product of labour is how many cakes per hour?
   a. 1/2 cake per hour
   b. 2 cakes per hour
   c. 10 cakes per hour
   d. 15 cakes per hour

4. A technological advance that increases the marginal product of labour shifts the labour _____ curve to the _____.
   a. demand, left
   b. demand, right
   c. supply, left
   d. supply, right

5. Around 1976, the Canadian economy experienced a significant _____ in productivity growth, coupled with a(n) _____ in the growth of real wages.
   a. acceleration, acceleration
   b. acceleration, slowdown
   c. slowdown, acceleration
   d. slowdown, slowdown

6. A storm destroys several factories, thereby reducing the stock of capital. What effect does this event have on factor markets?
   a. Wages and the rental price of capital both rise.
   b. Wages and the rental price of capital both fall.
   c. Wages rise, and the rental price of capital falls.
   d. Wages fall, and the rental price of capital rises.

PROBLEMS AND **applications**

1. Suppose that the prime minister proposes a new law aimed at reducing heath care costs: All Canadians are to be required to eat one apple daily.
   a. How would this apple-a-day law affect the demand and equilibrium price of apples?
   b. How would the law affect the marginal product and the value of the marginal product of apple pickers?
   c. How would the law affect the demand and equilibrium wage for apple pickers?

2. Show the effect of each of the following events on the market for labour in the computer manufacturing industry.
   a. The government buys personal computers for all college and university students.
   b. More postsecondary students major in engineering and computer science.
   c. Computer firms build new manufacturing plants.

3. Your enterprising uncle opens a sandwich shop that employs 7 people. The employees are paid $15 per hour, and a sandwich sells for $3. If your uncle is maximizing his profit, what is the value of the marginal product of the last worker he hired? What is that worker's marginal product?

4. Suppose a freeze in British Columbia destroys part of the apple crop.
   a. Explain what happens to the price of apples and the marginal product of apple pickers as a result of the freeze. Can you say what happens to the demand for apple pickers? Why or why not?
   b. Suppose the price of apples doubles and the marginal product falls by 30 percent. What happens to the equilibrium wage of apple pickers?
   c. Suppose the price of apples rises by 30 percent and the marginal product falls by 50 percent. What happens to the equilibrium wage of apple pickers?

5. During the 1980s and 1990s Canada experienced a significant inflow of capital from other countries.
   a. Using a diagram of the Canadian capital market, show the effect of this inflow on the rental price of capital in Canada and on the quantity of capital in use.
   b. Using a diagram of the Canadian labour market, show the effect of the capital inflow on the average wage paid to Canadian workers.

6. Suppose that labour is the only input used by a perfectly competitive firm that can hire workers for $50 per day. The firm's production function is as follows:

Days of Labour	Units of Output
0	0
1	7
2	13
3	19
4	25
5	28
6	29

Each unit of output sells for $10. Plot the firm's demand for labour. How many days of labour should the firm hire? Show this point on your graph.

7. This chapter has assumed that labour is supplied by individual workers acting competitively. In some markets, however, the supply of labour is determined by a union of workers.
   a. Explain why the situation faced by a labour union may resemble the situation faced by a monopoly firm.
   b. The goal of a monopoly firm is to maximize profits. Is there an analogous goal for labour unions?

   c. Now extend the analogy between monopoly firms and unions. How do you suppose that the wage set by a union compares to the wage in a competitive market? How do you suppose employment differs in the two cases?
   d. What other goals might unions have that make unions different from monopoly firms?

8. Leadbelly Co. sells pencils in a perfectly competitive product market and hires workers in a perfectly competitive labour market. Assume that the market wage rate for workers is $150 per day.
   a. What rule should Leadbelly follow to hire the profit-maximizing amount of labour?
   b. At the profit-maximizing level of output, the marginal product of the last worker hired is 30 boxes of pencils per day. Calculate the price of a box of pencils.
   c. Draw a diagram of the labour market for pencil workers (as in Figure 18.4) next to a diagram of the labour supply and demand for Leadbelly Co. (as in Figure 18.3). Label the equilibrium wage and quantity of labour for both the market and the firm. How are these diagrams related?
   d. Suppose some pencil workers switch to jobs in the growing computer industry. On the side-by-side diagrams you prepared in part (c), show how this change affects the equilibrium wage and quantity of labour for both the pencil market and for Leadbelly. How does this change affect the marginal product of labour at Leadbelly?

9. Smiling Cow Dairy can sell all the milk it wants for $4 a litre, and it can rent all the robots it wants to milk the cows at a capital rental price of $100 a day. It faces the following production schedule:

Number of Robots	Total Product
0	0 litres
1	50
2	85
3	115
4	140
5	150
6	155

   a. In what kind of market structure does the firm sell its output? How can you tell?
   b. In what kind of market structure does the firm rent robots? How can you tell?
   c. Calculate the marginal product and the value of the marginal product for each additional robot.
   d. How many robots should the firm rent? Explain.

10. Policymakers sometimes propose laws requiring firms to give workers certain fringe benefits, such as paid parental leave. Let's consider the effects of such a policy on the labour market.
    a. Suppose that a law required firms to give each worker $3 of fringe benefits for every hour that the worker is employed by the firm. How does this law affect the marginal profit that a firm earns from each worker at a given cash wage? How does the law affect the demand curve for labour? Draw your answer on a graph with the cash wage on the vertical axis.
    b. If there is no change in labour supply, how would this law affect employment and wages?
    c. Why might the labour-supply curve shift in response to this law? Would this shift in labour supply raise or lower the impact of the law on wages and employment?
    d. As discussed in Chapter 6, the wages of some workers, particularly the unskilled and inexperienced, are kept above the equilibrium level by minimum-wage laws. What effect would a fringe-benefit mandate have for these workers?

11. Only labour is used to produce mugs, which sell for $5 each. Labour is hired under perfectly competitive conditions and the market wage is $22.50 per hour. The production function for mugs is given by the following table:

Number of Workers	Mugs per Hour
0	0
1	12
2	22
3	28
4	33
5	37
6	40

    a. Augment the table by calculating the marginal product of labour, total revenue, and marginal revenue product of labour. (Remember to put marginal items in between units.)
    b. At the market wage, how many workers will the firm hire in order to maximize profit?
    c. Suppose that a shortage of workers causes the competitive wage for workers who can make coffee mugs to rise to $27.50 per hour. Now how many workers will this firm hire?

    d. Suppose that schools that teach pottery skills increase the supply of workers that can make coffee mugs, which lowers the competitive wage for coffee mug workers to $17.50 per hour. Now how many workers will the firm hire? Does this represent a shift in the firm's demand for labour curve or a movement along the firm's demand for labour curve?
    e. Suppose instead that the demand for coffee mugs rises, pushing up the price of coffee mugs to $10 per mug. If the competitive wage for coffee mug workers remains at $27.50 per hour, how many workers will this firm hire now? Does this represent a shift in the firm's demand for labour curve or a movement along the firm's demand for labour curve?

12. The nation of Ectenia has 20 competitive apple orchards, which sell apples at the world price of $2. The following equations describe the production function and the marginal product of labour in each orchard:

$$Q = 100L - L^2$$
$$MPL = 100 - 2L$$

where Q is the number of apples produced in a day, L is the number of workers, and MPL is the marginal product of labour.
    a. What is each orchard's labour demand as a function of the daily wage W? What is the market's labour demand?
    b. Ectenia has 200 workers who supply their labour inelastically. Solve for the wage W. How many workers does each orchard hire? How much profit does each orchard owner make?
    c. Calculate what happens to the income of workers and orchard owners if the world price of apples doubles to $4.
    d. Now suppose the price of apples is back at $2, but a hurricane destroys half the orchards. Calculate how the hurricane affects the income of each worker and of each remaining orchard owner. What happens to the income of Ectenia as a whole?

Earnings and Discrimination

In this chapter, you will ...

1 Examine how wages compensate for differences in job characteristics

2 Learn and compare the human-capital and signalling theories of education

3 Examine why in some occupations a few superstars earn tremendous incomes

4 Learn why wages rise above the level that balances supply and demand

5 Consider why it is difficult to measure the impact of discrimination on wages

6 See when market forces can and cannot provide a natural remedy for discrimination

7 Consider the debate over comparable worth as a system for setting wages

In Canada today, the typical physician earns about $225 000 per year, the typical police officer about $75 000, and the typical fast-food cook about $20 000. These examples illustrate the large differences in earnings that are so common in our economy. They also explain why some people live in mansions, ride in limousines, and vacation on the French Riviera, while other people live in small apartments, ride the bus, and vacation in their own backyards.

Why do earnings vary so much from person to person? Chapter 18, which developed the basic neoclassical theory of the labour market, offers an answer to this question. There we saw that wages are governed by labour supply and labour demand. Labour demand, in turn, reflects the marginal productivity of labour. In equilibrium, each worker is paid the value of his or her marginal contribution to the economy's production of goods and services.

This theory of the labour market, although widely accepted by economists, is only the beginning of the story. To understand the wide variation in earnings that we observe, we must go beyond this general framework and examine more precisely what determines the supply and demand for different types of labour. That is our goal in this chapter.

19-1 Some Determinants of Equilibrium Wages

Workers differ from one another in many ways, as do jobs. In this section, we consider how the characteristics of workers and jobs affect labour supply, labour demand, and equilibrium wages.

19-1a Compensating Differentials

When a worker is deciding whether to take a job, the wage is only one of many job attributes that the worker takes into account. Some jobs are easy, fun, and safe; others are hard, dull, and dangerous. The better the job as gauged by these nonmonetary characteristics, the more people there are who are willing to do the job at any given wage. In other words, the supply of labour for easy, fun, and safe jobs is greater than the supply of labour for hard, dull, and dangerous jobs. As a result, "good" jobs will tend to have lower equilibrium wages than "bad" jobs.

For example, imagine you are looking for a summer job in a local beach community. Two kinds of jobs are available. You can take a job as a beach-badge checker, or you can take a job as a garbage collector. The beach-badge checkers take leisurely strolls along the beach during the day and check to make sure the tourists have bought the required beach permits. The garbage collectors wake up before dawn to drive dirty, noisy trucks around town to pick up garbage. Which job would you want? If the two jobs paid the same wage, most people would prefer the badge-checker job. To induce people to become garbage collectors, the town has to offer higher wages to garbage collectors than to beach-badge checkers.

compensating differential

a difference in wages that arises to offset the nonmonetary characteristics of different jobs

Economists use the term **compensating differential** to refer to a difference in wages that arises from nonmonetary characteristics of different jobs. Compensating differentials are prevalent in the economy. Here are some examples:

- Coal miners are paid more than other workers with similar levels of education. Their higher wage compensates them for the dirty and dangerous nature of coal mining, as well as the long-term health problems that coal miners experience.

- Workers who work the night shift at factories are paid more than similar workers who work the day shift. The higher wage compensates them for having to work at night and sleep during the day, a lifestyle that most people find undesirable.
- Professors are paid less than lawyers and doctors, who have similar amounts of education. The higher wages of lawyers and doctors compensates them for missing out on the great intellectual and personal satisfaction that professors' jobs offer. (Indeed, teaching economics is so much fun that it is surprising that economics professors are paid anything at all!)

19-1b Human Capital

As we discussed in the previous chapter, the word *capital* usually refers to the economy's stock of equipment and structures. The capital stock includes the farmer's tractor, the manufacturer's factory, and the teacher's chalkboard. The essence of capital is that it is a factor of production that itself has been produced.

There is another type of capital that, while less tangible than physical capital, is just as important to the economy's production. **Human capital** is the accumulation of investments in people. The most important type of human capital is education. Like all forms of capital, education represents an expenditure of resources at one point in time to raise productivity in the future. But, unlike an investment in other forms of capital, an investment in education is tied to a specific person, and this linkage is what makes it human capital.

Not surprisingly, workers with more human capital on average earn more than those with less human capital. University graduates in Canada, for example, earn about 60 percent more than workers who end their education with a high-school diploma. This large difference has been documented in many countries around the world. It tends to be even larger in less-developed countries, where educated workers are in scarce supply.

From the perspective of supply and demand it is easy to see why education raises wages. Firms—the demanders of labour—are willing to pay more for highly educated workers because highly educated workers have higher marginal products. Workers—the suppliers of labour—are willing to pay the cost of becoming educated only if there is a reward for doing so. In essence, the difference in wages between highly educated workers and less educated workers may be considered a compensating differential for the cost of becoming educated.

human capital

the accumulation of investments in people, such as education and on-the-job training

case study **The Value of Education**

"The rich get richer and the poor get poorer." Like many adages, this one is not always true, but has been in Canada in recent years. We'll talk more about income distribution in the next chapter, but at this point we will address what many feel is an important determinant of the distribution of income in an economy: the wage gap between workers with high skills and workers with low skills, as measured by their education.

Figure 19.1 shows the median wages income of men and women in Canada as a whole, and for all of the provinces, in 2016 for different levels of education. The median income is the income "in the middle," such that half of workers earn more than the median and half earn less. It is clear that higher education is associated with higher incomes. For all of Canada, for every dollar earned by a man with just a high school diploma, a man with a bachelor's degree earns $1.47; for women the education premium for a bachelor's degree is even higher, at $1.57. There are

FIGURE 19.1

**Median Earnings by
Level of Education, 2016**

Source: Statistics Canada, Census of
the Population, 2016.

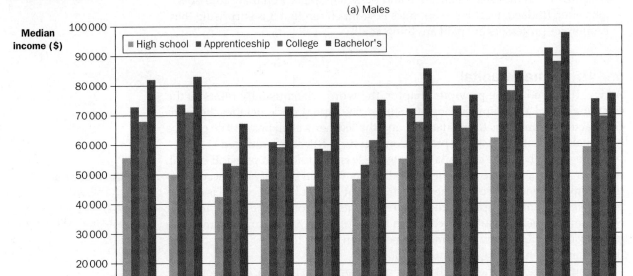

(a) Males

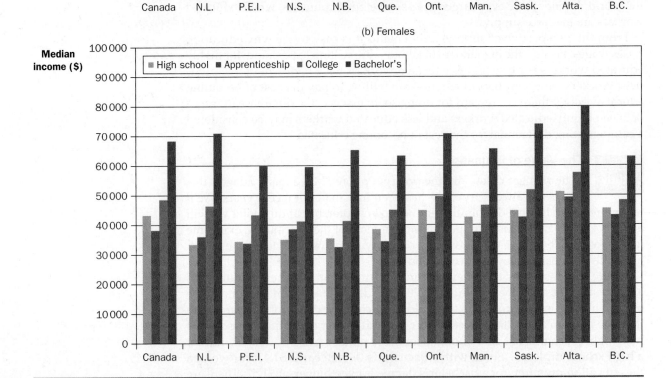

(b) Females

other differences between men and women evident in the figures. For example, for men with an apprenticeship certificate median earnings are quite close to those with a bachelor's degree. This is particularly true in the western provinces, presumably because of relatively high-paying jobs in the resource sector. This is not the case for women, where the education premium for a bachelor's degree is significantly higher in all of the provinces.

Recent research from the Education Policy Research Initiative, funded in part by the federal government, sheds some light on the earnings associated with different fields of postsecondary study. A study entitled "Barista or Better?" confronts the familiar barista trope—the suggestion that going to university or college, particularly in a non-STEM (science, technology, engineering, mathematics) field of study, is a "waste of time" and will leave graduates stuck in "barista-type" jobs with low earnings and little opportunity for career advancement or income growth. Figure 19.2 shows the mean and median earnings from years of graduation for the class of 2005 graduates for four general fields of study—social sciences, business, math and computer science, and fine arts. The picture that emerges belies the barista story. While there is no question that earnings tend to be higher for those with business and STEM degrees, the earnings profile of those with social science degrees is not that different, especially at the medians, and shows significant growth over time. Moreover, even the earnings profile for those with fine arts degrees is above the $22 000 salary (at best) that a barista might be expected to earn! ■

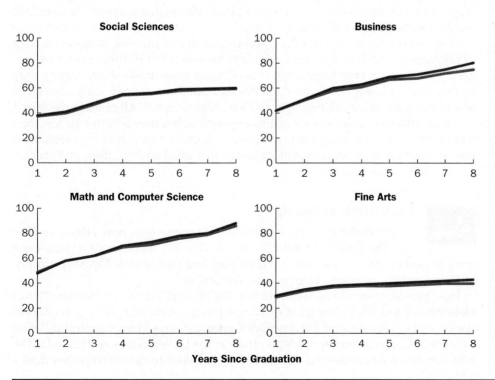

FIGURE 19.2

Mean and Median Wages by Broad Field of Study, Years Since Graduation, 2005 Cohort

The blue line is mean earnings and the green line is median earnings.

Source: "Barista or Better? New Evidence on the Earnings of Post-Secondary Education Graduates: A Tax Linkage Approach." Education Policy Research Initiative at https://static1.squarespace.com/static/5557eaf0e4b0384b6c9b0172/t/57a3595eb8a79b06bc686cbf/1470323048183/EPRI-ESDC+Tax+linkage_Report.pdf

Years Since Graduation

Ask the Experts

Inequality and Skills

"One of the leading reasons for rising income inequality over the past three decades is that technological change has affected workers with some skill sets differently than others."

What do economists say?

4% disagree — 8% uncertain

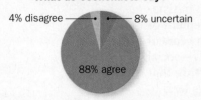

88% agree

Source: IGM Economic Experts Panel, January 24, 2012.
Figure © 2018 Cengage Learning.

19-1c Ability, Effort, and Chance

Why do NHL hockey players get paid more than those in the minor leagues? Certainly, the higher wage is not a compensating differential. Playing in the NHL is not a less pleasant task than playing in the minor leagues; in fact, the opposite is true. The NHL does not require more years of schooling or more experience. To a large extent, players in the NHL earn more just because they have greater natural ability.

Natural ability is important for workers in all occupations. Because of heredity and upbringing, people differ in their physical and mental attributes. Some people are strong, others weak. Some people are smart, others less so. Some people are outgoing, others awkward in social situations. These and many other personal characteristics determine how productive workers are and, therefore, play a role in determining the wages they earn.

Closely related to ability is effort. Some people work hard, others are lazy. We should not be surprised to find that those who work hard are more productive and earn higher wages. To some extent, firms reward hard work directly by paying people based on what they produce. Salespeople, for instance, are often paid a percentage of the sales they make. At other times, hard work is rewarded less directly in the form of a higher annual salary or a bonus.

Chance also plays a role in determining wages. If a person attended a trade school to learn how to repair televisions with vacuum tubes and then found this skill was made obsolete by the invention of solid-state electronics, she would end up earning a low wage compared to others with similar years of training. The low wage of this worker is due to chance—a phenomenon that economists recognize but do not shed much light on.

How important are ability, effort, and chance in determining wages? It is hard to say because these factors are difficult to measure. But indirect evidence suggests that they are very important. When labour economists study wages, they relate a worker's wage to those variables that can be measured, such as years of schooling, years of experience, age, and job characteristics. All of these measured variables affect a worker's wage as theory predicts, but they account for less than half of the variation in wages in our economy. Because so much of the variation in wages is left unexplained, omitted variables, including ability, effort, and chance, must play an important role.

case study **The Benefits of Beauty**

People differ in many ways. One difference is in how attractive they are. The Canadian actor Ryan Gosling, for instance, is a handsome man. In part for this reason, his movies attract large audiences. Not surprisingly, the large audiences mean a large income for Gosling.

How prevalent are the economic benefits of beauty? Labour economists Daniel Hamermesh and Jeff Biddle tried to answer this question in a study published in the December 1994 issue of *The American Economic Review*. Hamermesh and Biddle examined data from surveys of individuals in the United States and Canada. The interviewers who conducted the survey were asked to rate each respondent's

Good looks pay.

s_bukley/Shutterstock.com

physical appearance. Hamermesh and Biddle then examined how much the wages of the respondents depended on the standard determinants—education, experience, and so on—and how much they depended on physical appearance.

Hamermesh and Biddle found that beauty pays. People who are deemed to be more attractive than average earn 5 percent more than people of average looks. People of average looks earn 5 to 10 percent more than people considered less attractive than average. Similar results were found for men and women.

What explains these differences in wages? There are several ways to interpret the "beauty premium."

One interpretation is that good looks are themselves a type of innate ability determining productivity and wages. Some people are born with the attributes of a movie star; other people are not. Good looks are useful in any job in which workers present themselves to the public—such as acting, sales, and waiting on tables. In this case, an attractive worker is more valuable to the firm than an unattractive worker. The firm's willingness to pay more to attractive workers reflects its customers' preferences.

A second interpretation is that reported beauty is an indirect measure of other types of ability. How attractive a person appears depends on more than just heredity. It also depends on dress, hairstyle, personal demeanour, and other attributes that a person can control. Perhaps a person who successfully projects an attractive image in a survey interview is more likely to be an intelligent person who succeeds at other tasks as well.

A third interpretation is that the beauty premium is a type of discrimination, a topic to which we return later. ■

19-1d An Alternative View of Education: Signalling

Earlier we discussed the human-capital view of education, according to which schooling raises workers' wages because it makes them more productive. Although this view is widely accepted, some economists have proposed an alternative theory, which emphasizes that firms use educational attainment as a way of sorting between high-ability and low-ability workers. According to this alternative view, when people earn a college or university degree, for instance, they do not become more productive, but they do *signal* their high ability to prospective employers. Because it is easier for high-ability people to earn a college or university degree than it is for low-ability people, more high-ability people get postsecondary degrees. As a result, it is rational for firms to interpret a postsecondary degree as a signal of ability.

The signalling theory of education is similar to the signalling theory of advertising discussed in Chapter 16. In the signalling theory of advertising, the advertisement itself contains no real information, but the firm signals the quality of its product to consumers by its willingness to spend money on advertising. In the signalling theory of education, schooling has no real productivity benefit, but the worker signals his innate productivity to employers by his willingness to spend years at school. In both cases, an action is being taken not for its intrinsic benefit but because the willingness to take that action conveys private information to someone observing it.

Thus, we now have two views of education: the human-capital theory and the signalling theory. Both views can explain why better-educated workers tend to earn more than less-educated ones. According to the human-capital view, education makes workers more productive; according to the signalling view, education is correlated with natural ability. But the two views have radically different predictions for the effects of policies that aim to increase educational attainment. According to the human-capital view, increasing educational levels for all workers would raise all workers' productivity and thereby their wages. According to the signalling view, education does not enhance productivity, so raising all workers' educational levels would not affect wages.

Most likely, truth lies somewhere between these two extremes. The benefits to education are probably a combination of the productivity-enhancing effects of human capital and the productivity-revealing effects of signalling. The relative size of these two effects is an open question.

19-1e The Superstar Phenomenon

Although most actors earn very little and often have to take other jobs to support themselves, Canadian actor Rachel McAdams has earned millions of dollars making movies. Similarly, although most people who play hockey do it for free as a hobby, Connor McDavid earns millions as an NHL hockey player. McAdams and McDavid are superstars in their fields, and their great public appeal is reflected in astronomical incomes.

Why do Rachel McAdams and Connor McDavid earn so much? It is not surprising that there are differences in incomes within occupations. Good carpenters earn more than mediocre carpenters, and good plumbers earn more than mediocre plumbers. People vary in ability and effort, and these differences lead to differences in income. Yet the best carpenters and plumbers do not earn the many millions that are common among the best performers and athletes. What explains the difference?

To understand the tremendous incomes of Rachel McAdams and Connor McDavid, we must examine the special features of the markets in which they sell their services. Superstars arise in markets that have two characteristics:

1. Every customer in the market wants to enjoy the good supplied by the best producer.
2. The good is produced with a technology that makes it possible for the best producer to supply every customer at low cost.

If Rachel McAdams is one of the best actors around, then everyone will want to see her next movie; seeing twice as many movies by an actor half as good is not a good substitute. Moreover, it is *possible* for everyone to enjoy the acting of Rachel McAdams. Because it is easy to make multiple copies of a movie, McAdams can provide her service to millions of people simultaneously. Similarly, because hockey games are broadcast on television, millions of fans can enjoy the extraordinary athletic skills of Connor McDavid.

We can now see why there are no superstar carpenters and plumbers. Other things equal, everyone prefers to employ the best carpenter, but a carpenter, unlike an actor, can provide his services to only a limited number of customers. Although the best carpenter will be able to command a somewhat higher wage than the average carpenter, the average carpenter will still be able to earn a good living.

19-1f Above-Equilibrium Wages: Minimum-Wage Laws, Unions, and Efficiency Wages

Most analyses of wage differences among workers are based on the equilibrium model of the labour market—that is, wages are assumed to adjust to balance labour supply and labour demand. But this assumption does not always apply.

For some workers, wages are set above the level that brings supply and demand into equilibrium. Let's consider three reasons why this might be so.

One reason for above-equilibrium wages is minimum-wage laws, as we first saw in Chapter 6. Most workers in the economy are not affected by these laws because their equilibrium wages are well above the legal minimum. But for some workers, especially the least skilled and least experienced, minimum-wage laws raise wages above the level they would earn in an unregulated labour market.

A second reason why wages might rise above their equilibrium level is the market power of labour unions. A **union** is a worker association that bargains with employers over wages and working conditions. Unions often raise wages above the level that would prevail without a union, perhaps because they can threaten to withhold labour from the firm by calling a **strike**. Studies suggest that union workers earn about 10 to 20 percent more than similar nonunion workers.

A third reason for above-equilibrium wages is based on the theory of **efficiency wages**. This theory holds that a firm can find it profitable to pay high wages because doing so increases the productivity of its workers. In particular, high wages may reduce worker turnover, increase worker effort, and raise the quality of workers who apply for jobs at the firm. If this theory is correct, then some firms may choose to pay their workers more than they would normally earn.

Above-equilibrium wages, whether caused by minimum-wage laws, unions, or efficiency wages, have similar effects on the labour market. In particular, pushing a wage above the equilibrium level raises the quantity of labour supplied and reduces the quantity of labour demanded. The result is a surplus of labour, or unemployment. The study of unemployment and the public policies aimed to deal with it is usually considered a topic within macroeconomics, so it goes beyond the scope of this chapter. But it would be a mistake to ignore these issues completely when analyzing earnings. Although most wage differences can be understood while maintaining the assumption of equilibrium in the labour market, above-equilibrium wages play a role in some cases.

union
a worker association that bargains with employers over wages and working conditions

strike
the organized withdrawal of labour from a firm by a union

efficiency wages
above-equilibrium wages paid by firms in order to increase worker productivity

QUICK Quiz *Define compensating differential and give an example. • Give two reasons why more-educated workers earn more than less-educated workers.*

19-2 The Economics of Discrimination

Another source of differences in wages is discrimination. **Discrimination** occurs when the marketplace offers different opportunities to similar individuals who differ only by race, ethnic group, sex, age, or other personal characteristics. Discrimination reflects some people's prejudice against certain groups in society. Although discrimination is an emotionally charged topic that often generates heated debate, economists try to study the topic objectively in order to separate myth from reality.

discrimination
the offering of different opportunities to similar individuals who differ only by race, ethnic group, sex, age, or other personal characteristics

19-2a Measuring Labour-Market Discrimination

How much does discrimination in labour markets affect the earnings of different groups of workers? This question is important, but answering it is not easy.

It might seem natural to gauge the amount of discrimination in labour markets by looking at the average wages of different groups. For example, Canadian studies show that the average hourly wage of female workers is about 87 percent of the average wage of male workers. Studies have found that Indigenous people living off reserves earn about 10 percent less than non-Indigenous people. There is also some evidence that earnings differences exist among workers of different language origins. In particular, some studies find a significant unilingual-francophone earnings disadvantage, although more recent evidence suggests that the size of the disadvantage is decreasing. Taken at face value, these wage differentials are sometimes presented as evidence that many employers discriminate against minority groups and women.

Yet there is a potential problem with this inference. Even in a labour market free of discrimination, different people earn different wages. People differ in the amount of human capital they have and in the kinds of work they are able and willing to do. People also differ in the amount of experience they have and the extent to which that experience is continuous or uninterrupted. The wage differences we observe in the economy are, to some extent, attributable to the determinants of equilibrium wages we discussed in the previous section. Simply observing differences in wages among broad groups—minorities and nonminorities, women and men—does not prove that employers discriminate.

Consider, for example, the role of human capital. The proportion of individuals with high-school, college, and university degrees differs substantially across various groups. For example, the proportion of white males and females with high-school, college, and university degrees in Canada exceeds the proportion of Indigenous people with these degrees. Moreover, a greater proportion of males than females have college and university degrees, although this is changing as more females than males are now enrolled in Canadian universities. With the sizable wage gap between skilled and unskilled labour discussed earlier in this chapter, no doubt some of the wage differences between groups can be attributed to differences in education levels.

Differences in human capital may themselves be a function of discrimination of a more subtle form. "Pre-market differences" in productive characteristics, such as schooling, may be influenced by various social factors, and these social influences may themselves be the result of systemic pre-market discrimination that affects people's choices and opportunities. For example, for many years schools directed girls away from science and math courses even though these subjects may have had greater value in the marketplace than some of the alternatives.

Human capital acquired in the form of job experience can also help explain wage differences. In particular, women are more likely to interrupt their careers to raise children. Among the population aged 25 to 44 (when many people have children at home), about 83 percent of women are in the labour force, compared to about 92 percent of men. As a result, female workers at older ages tend to have less job experience than male workers.

In this regard, access to affordable child care seems to be an important determinant of female labour force participation. Figure 19.3 shows the labour force participation rates for women in Quebec, Ontario, and Alberta with an employed spouse and child younger than 6 years. Prior to 1997 the participation rates were roughly the same in the three provinces. In 1997 Quebec introduced a policy of providing inexpensive government subsidized child care. Since then, the labour force participation rate of mothers with an employed spouse increased substantially in Quebec relative to Ontario and Alberta. Particularly relevant in this regard is the comparison to Ontario, which is right next door and (perhaps arguably) subject to similar economic conditions. What about Alberta, where the participation of women in this group in the labour market has flattened and even dropped

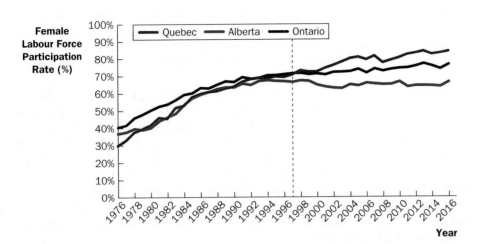

FIGURE 19.3

**Labour Force
Participation Rates,
Women with an
Employed Spouse
and Child Younger Than
6 Years**

Source: Statistics Canada CANSIM
Table 2820211.

slightly? It is difficult to say, but one explanation is that household incomes in Alberta increased significantly over this period because of the expansion of the oil sector, which may have allowed households to rely on only one income earner.

Yet another source of wage differences is compensating differentials. Men and women do not always choose the same type of work, and this fact may help explain some of the earnings differential between men and women. For example, the data show that women are more likely to be administrative assistants, and men are more likely to be truck drivers. The relative wages for these jobs depend in part on the working conditions of each job. Because these nonmonetary aspects are hard to measure, it is difficult to gauge the practical importance of compensating differentials in explaining the wage differences that we observe.

In the end, the study of wage differences among groups does not establish any clear conclusion about the prevalence of discrimination in Canadian labour markets. Most economists believe that some of the observed wage differentials are attributable to discrimination, but there is no consensus about how much. The only conclusion about which economists are in consensus is a negative one: *Because the differences in average wages among groups in part reflect differences in human capital and job characteristics, they do not by themselves say anything about how much discrimination there is in the labour market.*

19-2b Discrimination by Employers

Let's now turn from measurement to the economic forces that lie behind discrimination in labour markets. If one group in society receives a lower wage than another group, even after controlling for human capital and job characteristics, who is to blame for this differential?

The answer is not obvious. It might seem natural to blame employers for discriminatory wage differences. After all, employers make the hiring decisions that determine labour demand and wages. If some groups of workers earn lower wages than they should, then it seems that employers are responsible. Yet many economists are skeptical of this easy answer. They believe that competitive, market economies provide a natural antidote to employer discrimination. That antidote is called the *profit motive*.

Imagine an economy in which workers are differentiated by their hair colour. Blondes and brunettes have the same skills, experience, and work ethic. Yet, because of discrimination, employers prefer not to hire workers with blonde hair. Thus, the demand for blondes is lower than it otherwise would be. As a result, blondes earn a lower wage than brunettes.

How long can this wage differential persist? In this economy, there is an easy way for a firm to beat out its competitors: It can hire blonde workers. By hiring blondes, a firm pays lower wages and thus has lower costs than firms that hire brunettes. Over time, more and more "blonde" firms enter the market to benefit from this cost advantage. The existing "brunette" firms have higher costs and, therefore, begin to lose money when faced with the new competitors. These losses induce the brunette firms to go out of business. Eventually, the entry of blonde firms and the exit of brunette firms cause the demand for blonde workers to rise and the demand for brunette workers to fall. This process continues until the wage differential disappears.

Put simply, business owners who care only about making money are at an advantage when competing against those who also care about discriminating. As a result, firms that do not discriminate tend to replace those that do. In this way, competitive markets have a natural remedy for employer discrimination.

case study   ### Explaining the Gender Wage Gap

Figure 19.4 shows the female-to-male gender pay ratio in Canada from 1993 to 2015 using two metrics. The first is based on the annual earnings of full-time workers. Measured in this way, the gender pay ratio was .74 in 2015; thus, for every dollar earned by males employed full time, females earned 74 cents, a gap of 26 cents. Note that on the basis of this measure, the gender gap has remained relatively constant over time.

FIGURE 19.4

Female-to-Male Gender Pay Ratios, Canada, 1993–2015

Source: Statistics Canada, http://www.statcan.gc.ca/pub/89-503-x/2015001/article/14694/c-g/c-g017-eng.htm

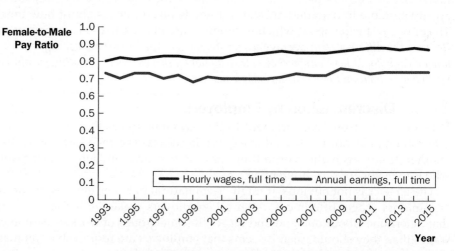

TABLE 19.1

Decomposition of the Gender Wage Gap

Raw Wage Gap	26.0 cents
Explained by:	
Hours	13.0
Occupation	3.9
Industry	2.8
Other	−1.4
Total Explained	18.3
Total Unexplained	7.7

Source: Author calculations based on http://www.statcan.gc.ca/pub/89-503-x/2015001/article/14694/c-g/c-g017-eng.htm and http://www.statcan.gc.ca/pub/11f0019m/11f0019m2013347-eng.pdf

One problem with this approach is that total earnings are the product of the hourly wage rate and total hours worked. Differences in male and female earnings could therefore arise due to differences in either, or both, of the wage rate and hours worked. And indeed, it turns out that men do tend to work more hours than women on average. The second metric therefore computes the gender pay ratio using average hourly wages for females and males. In this case the ratio in 2015 was .87, a gap of 13 cents. Note that using this metric the gender ratio has been growing slightly over time (the wage gap decreasing), rising from .80 in 1993 to .87 in 2015.

A sizable amount of research has been devoted to explaining the gender pay gap. We have seen that one explanation can be found in differences in hours worked. Are there others? Economists have used statistical techniques to determine the extent to which the gender pay gap may be "explained" by various other factors. Table 19.1 uses analysis undertaken by economists at Statistics Canada to break this down, starting with the "raw" earnings gap identified above of 26 cents.

As discussed, 13 cents of this gap can be explained by differences in the number of hours worked by full-time males and females. Another 3.9 cents can be explained by differences in male and female occupations, 2.8 cents by differences in the industries in which men and women tend to be employed, and a small amount (−1.4 cents) by other factors (differences in education, experience, etc.). Thus, of the total raw wage gap of 26 cents, 18.3 cents can be "explained" by various measurable factors, leaving 7.7 cents, or about 8 cents, "unexplained."

Some analysts interpret the "unexplained" 8-cent wage gap as evidence of gender discrimination, which may well be true. Note, however, that of the 18.3-cent "explained" part of the wage gap, 6.7 cents is due to differences in occupations and industries between men and women. This means that women tend to be employed in lower-wage occupations and in lower-paid industries, which may also reflect some degree of discrimination and stereotyping. ∎

19-2c Discrimination by Customers and Governments

The profit motive is a strong force acting to eliminate discriminatory wage differentials, but there are limits to its corrective abilities. Two important limiting factors are customer preferences and government policies.

IN THE news

Language and Wages in Canada

In this article, the author (who is an economist at McGill University) discusses some research on the wage gap between anglophones and francophones. The conclusion? It's complicated. . . .

While Francophones Get Richer, Anglophones Get Poorer

By William Watson

What is now almost official history in this province is that Bill 101... righted historic wrongs by increasing the demand for French-speaking workers and closing the wage gap between English- and French-speakers in Quebec, mainly by raising the wages of historically underpaid francophones.

A new study by David Albouy, a young Franco-American economist who was an undergraduate at McGill University and is now teaching at the University of Michigan, suggests the official history isn't quite right. It seems the wage gap was closed more by lowering the relative wages of Quebec anglophones than raising those of Quebec francophones, who weren't actually that badly off to begin with.

Albouy uses census data to look at the employment income of males 20 to 59 who worked full time. Unlike other researchers, who typically compared anglo and franco Quebecers, he divides wage-earners into four groups: anglophones and francophones both inside and outside Quebec. That lets him see how Quebec wage rates compared with those in the rest of the country.

His results are intriguing. In 1970, Quebec francophones averaged $16.40 an hour (measured in the purchasing power of year-2000 dollars). That was only three per cent less than francophones in the rest of the country, who averaged $16.90 an hour. The similarity

© All Canada Photos/Alamy

suggests Canadian labour markets were pretty integrated and francophone Quebecers didn't regard themselves as stuck in Quebec, an argument often used to rationalize lower wages here than elsewhere.

In 1970, however, anglophones in the rest of the country averaged $18.70 an hour,

---

To see how customer preferences for discrimination can affect wages, consider again our imaginary economy with blondes and brunettes. Suppose that restaurant owners discriminate against blondes when hiring servers. As a result, blonde servers earn lower wages than brunette servers. In this case, a restaurant could open up with blonde servers and charge lower prices. If customers care only about the quality and price of their meals, the discriminatory firms would be driven out of business, and the wage differential would disappear.

On the other hand, it is possible that customers prefer being served by brunette waiters. If this discriminatory preference is strong, the entry of blonde restaurants need not succeed in eliminating the wage differential between brunettes and blondes. That is, if customers have discriminatory preferences, a competitive market is consistent with a discriminatory wage differential. An economy with such discrimination would contain two types of restaurants: Blonde restaurants would hire blondes, have lower costs, and charge lower prices. Brunette restaurants would hire brunettes, have higher costs, and charge higher prices. Customers who did not care about the hair colour of their servers would be attracted to the lower prices at the blonde restaurants. Bigoted customers would go to the brunette restaurants. They would pay for their discriminatory preference in the form of higher prices.

Another way for discrimination to persist in competitive markets is for the government to mandate discriminatory practices. If, for instance, the government passed a law stating that blondes could wash dishes in restaurants but could not

11 per cent more than non-Quebec franco-phones and 14 per cent more than Quebec francophones. How come? Could be differences in education or experience. Could be the usefulness of English in the world market. Could be simple, old-fashioned discrimination. The raw data don't say.

Quebec anglophones are the real surprise. In 1970, they made $22.20 an hour, fully 35 per cent more than Quebec francophones, a gap that prompts thoughts of Westmount Rhodesians, "speak white!" and all the rest.

But it was also 19 per cent more than anglophones in the rest of the country. How was it that Quebec anglophones had such an advantage over English-speakers in other provinces? And if the pickings were so easy in anglo Quebec, why didn't anglos from the rest of the country come here and drive down anglo wages?

What happened after 1970? In relative terms, Quebec anglophones got hammered. Their average wages in 2000 were $22.30, still the highest in the country, but only 10 cents more than in 1970. By contrast, non-Quebec anglophones had risen to $21.90, non-Quebec francophones to $21.20, and Quebec francophones to $20.60. Wage differences essentially collapsed. There was only an eight-per-cent difference between top and bottom, vs. 35 per cent in 1970.

Why did Quebec's anglophones still lead the pack, despite all that has happened over the last three decades? Very likely because they were much better educated than the other three groups. In 2000, fully 24 per cent held at least a bachelor's degree. That compares with just 17 per cent of anglos outside Quebec and just 15 per cent of francophones in Quebec.

In fact, if you control for differences in education, in 2000 there was an unexplained wage gap favouring Quebec francophones. Yes, they made less on average than anglos, but, given their lower average education, they made more than they "should have"—about four per cent more. That's a big change since 1970, when they made almost 14 per cent less than expected, given their education and experience.

It's always tempting to ascribe wage differences that differences in education, training, experience can't explain to discrimination. But it's probably not wise. Wages may depend on more things than even the smartest economists, like Albouy, can squeeze into their equations. There might not have been discrimination in favour of anglos in 1970 and there might not be discrimination against them now.

What is clear is that for whatever reason, the big losers in Quebec, relatively speaking, over the last three decades have been anglophones.

Source: "While francophones get richer, anglophones get poorer; New study by a Franco-American challenges some old myths about Quebec" by William Watson, *Montreal Gazette*, October 16, 2007, page A19. Material reprinted with the express permission of: The Montreal Gazette, a division of Postmedia Network Inc.

work as servers, then a wage differential could persist in a competitive market. For example, before South Africa abandoned its system of apartheid, black people were prohibited from working in some jobs. Discriminatory governments pass such laws to suppress the normal equalizing force of free and competitive markets.

To sum up: *Competitive markets contain a natural remedy for employer discrimination. The entry into the market of firms that care only about profit tends to eliminate discriminatory wage differentials. These wage differentials persist in competitive markets only when customers are willing to pay to maintain the discriminatory practice or when the government mandates it.*

case study Discrimination in Sports

As we have seen, measuring discrimination is difficult. To determine whether one group of workers is discriminated against, a researcher must correct for differences in productivity between that group and other workers in the economy. Yet, in most firms, it is difficult to measure a particular worker's contribution to the production of goods and services.

One type of firm in which measurement is easier is the sports team. Professional teams have many objective measures of productivity. In baseball, for example, we can measure a player's batting average, home runs, stolen bases, and so on. In hockey, we can measure a player's goals, assists, plus–minus, and Corsi statistics.

Economists focus on three main types of potential discrimination in sports: (1) salary discrimination; (2) position segregation, where certain positions are systematically assigned to certain groups; and (3) hiring, or entry, discrimination, where only the most productive elements of the discriminated group are hired.

U.S. studies have tended to focus on wage discrimination on racial grounds. These studies suggest that racial discrimination has indeed existed in sports teams, and that much of the blame may lie with customers. For example, a study published in the *Journal of Labor Economics* in 1988 (6:1) found that black basketball players earned 20 percent less than white players of comparable ability. The study also found that attendance at basketball games was larger for teams with a greater proportion of white players. A similar situation also existed for baseball players, although more recent studies of salaries have found no evidence of discriminatory wage differentials. One interpretation of these findings is that customer discrimination makes black players less profitable than white players for team owners. In the presence of such customer discrimination, a discriminatory wage gap can persist, even if team owners care only about profit.

A series of studies that appeared in *Canadian Public Policy* between 1987 and 1995 examined the existence of discrimination against francophone hockey players in the NHL. Early work focused on hiring discrimination. Using various performance measures for NHL players, it was determined that francophone players are underrepresented in the NHL and have tended to outperform their anglophone counterparts. One interpretation of this evidence is that francophones have been subjected to hiring discrimination. As a result of discrimination, francophones must outperform anglophones by a significant margin to get into the league in the first place.

Subsequent studies have questioned this interpretation. For example, an alternative interpretation is that the inability of marginal francophone players to communicate well in English impedes their ability to adapt to the needs of the team. Thus, for marginal players, selecting partially on the basis of language maximizes the success of the team both on and off the ice.

Other work has emphasized differences in playing styles between junior hockey teams in Quebec (the primary providers of francophone players to the NHL) and junior hockey teams in English-speaking provinces. In particular, the Quebec-based teams tend to favour smaller players with offensive abilities, whereas NHL teams tend to favour bigger players with defensive abilities, especially for marginal or "role" players. This suggests that the underrepresentation of francophones in the NHL is not due to hiring discrimination but to different preferences in playing styles. Yet another study, using updated data, has found no evidence of either hiring or wage discrimination against francophones.

A recent salvo in the debate introduces the role of the location of NHL cities. The premise of this study is that the historical tensions between English Canadians and French Canadians suggests that francophones playing for teams based in English Canada may face salary discrimination, while francophones playing for teams based in the United States, where no such tensions exist, do not. Using this approach, the study finds evidence that francophones playing in English Canada do indeed suffer significant salary discrimination.

 QUICK Quiz *Why is it hard to establish whether a group of workers is being discriminated against? • Explain how profit-maximizing firms tend to eliminate discriminatory wage differentials. • How might a discriminatory wage differential persist?*

19-3 Conclusion

In competitive markets, workers earn a wage equal to the value of their marginal contribution to the production of goods and services. There are, however, many things that affect the value of the marginal product. Firms pay more for workers who are more talented, more diligent, more experienced, and more educated because these workers are more productive. Firms pay less to those workers against whom customers discriminate because these workers contribute less to revenue.

The theory of the labour market we have developed in this chapter and the previous two chapters explains why some workers earn higher wages than other workers. The theory does not say that the resulting distribution of income is equal, fair, or desirable in any way. That is the topic we take up in Chapter 20.

summary

- Workers earn different wages for many reasons. To some extent, wage differentials compensate workers for job attributes. Other things equal, workers in hard, unpleasant jobs get paid more than workers in easy, pleasant jobs.

- Workers with more human capital get paid more than workers with less human capital. The return to accumulating human capital is high and has increased over the past two decades.

- Although years of education, experience, and job characteristics affect earnings as theory predicts, there is much variation in earnings that cannot be explained by things that economists can measure. The unexplained variation in earnings is largely attributable to natural ability, effort, and chance.

- Some economists have suggested that more-educated workers earn higher wages not because education raises productivity but because workers with high natural ability use education as a way to signal their high ability to employers. If this signalling theory is correct, then increasing the educational attainment of all workers would not raise the overall level of wages.

- Wages are sometimes pushed above the level that brings supply and demand into balance. Three reasons for above-equilibrium wages are minimum-wage laws, unions, and efficiency wages.

- Some differences in earnings are attributable to discrimination on the basis of race, sex, or other factors. Measuring the amount of discrimination is difficult, however, because one must correct for differences in human capital and job characteristics.

- Competitive markets tend to limit the impact of discrimination on wages. If the wages of a group of workers are lower than those of another group for reasons not related to marginal productivity, then nondiscriminatory firms will be more profitable than discriminatory firms. Profit-maximizing behaviour, therefore, can reduce discriminatory wage differentials. Discrimination persists in competitive markets, however, if customers are willing to pay more to discriminatory firms or if the government passes laws requiring firms to discriminate.

KEY **concepts**

compensating differential, *p. 420*
human capital, *p. 421*

union, *p. 427*
strike, *p. 427*

efficiency wages, *p. 427*
discrimination, *p. 427*

QUESTIONS FOR **review**

1. Why are coal miners paid more than other workers with similar amounts of education?

2. In what sense is education a type of capital?

3. How might education raise a worker's wage without raising the worker's productivity?

4. What conditions lead to economic superstars? Would you expect to see superstars in dentistry? In economics? Explain.

5. Give three reasons why a worker's wage might be above the level that balances supply and demand.

6. What difficulties arise in deciding whether a group of workers has a lower wage because of discrimination?

7. Do the forces of economic competition tend to exacerbate or ameliorate discrimination on the basis of race?

8. Give an example of how discrimination might persist in a competitive market.

QUICK CHECK **multiple choice**

1. Ricky leaves his job as a high school math teacher and returns to school to study the latest developments in computer programming, after which he takes a higher-paying job at a software firm. This is an example of which of the following?
   a. a compensating differential
   b. human capital
   c. signalling
   d. efficiency wages

2. Lucy and Ethel work at a local department store. Lucy, who greets customers as they arrive, is paid less than Ethel, who cleans the bathrooms. This is an example of which of the following?
   a. a compensating differential
   b. human capital
   c. signalling
   d. efficiency wages

3. Fred runs a small manufacturing company. He pays his employees about twice what other firms in the area pay, even though he could pay less and still recruit all the workers he wants. He believes that higher wages make his workers more loyal and hard-working. This is an example of which of the following?
   a. a compensating differential
   b. human capital
   c. signalling
   d. efficiency wages

4. A business consulting firm hires Vivian because she was a math major in college. Her new job does not require any of the mathematics she learned, but the firm believes that anyone who can graduate with a math degree must be very smart. This is an example of which of the following?
   a. a compensating differential
   b. human capital
   c. signalling
   d. efficiency wages

5. Why is it difficult to measure how much discrimination affects labour market outcomes?
   a. data on wages are crucial but not readily available
   b. firms misreport the wages they pay to hide discriminatory practices
   c. workers differ in their attributes and the types of jobs they have
   d. the same minimum-wage law applies to workers in all groups

6. The forces of competition in markets with free entry and exit tend to eliminate wage differentials that arise from discrimination by which of the following groups?
   a. employers
   b. customers
   c. government
   d. employees

PROBLEMS AND **applications**

1. University and college students sometimes work as summer interns for private firms or the government. Many of these positions pay little or nothing.
   a. What is the opportunity cost of taking such a job?
   b. Explain why students are willing to take these jobs.
   c. If you were to compare the earnings later in life of workers who had worked as interns and those who had taken summer jobs that paid more, what would you expect to find?

2. As explained in Chapter 6, a minimum-wage law distorts the market for low-wage labour. To reduce this distortion, some economists advocate a two-tiered minimum-wage system, with a regular minimum wage for adult workers and a lower, "sub-minimum"

wage for teenaged workers. Give two reasons why a single minimum wage might distort the labour market for teenaged workers more than it would the market for adult workers.

3. A basic finding of labour economics is that workers who have more experience in the labour force are paid more than workers who have less experience (holding constant the amount of formal education). Why might this be so? Some studies have also found that experience at the same job (called *job tenure*) has an extra positive influence on wages. Explain why this might occur.

4. At some colleges and universities, economics professors receive higher salaries than professors in some other fields.
   a. Why might this be true?
   b. Some other colleges and universities have a policy of paying equal salaries to professors in all fields. At some of these schools, economics professors have lighter teaching loads than professors in some other fields. What role is played by the differences in teaching loads?

5. Sara works for Steve, whom she dislikes because of his snobbish attitude. Yet when she looks for other jobs, the best she can do is find a job paying $10 000 less than her current salary. Should she take the job? Analyze Sara's situation from an economic point of view.

6. A current debate in education is whether teachers should be paid on a standard pay scale based solely upon their years of training and teaching experience, or whether part of their salary should be based upon their performance (called "merit pay").
   a. Why might merit pay be desirable?
   b. Who might be opposed to a system of merit pay?
   c. What is a potential challenge of merit pay?
   d. A related issue: Why might a school district decide to pay teachers significantly more than the salaries offered by surrounding districts?

7. Imagine that someone offers you a choice: You could spend four years studying at the world's best university, but you would have to keep your attendance there a secret. Or you could be awarded an official degree from the world's best university, but you couldn't actually attend. Which choice do you think would enhance your future earnings more? What does your answer say about the debate over signalling versus human capital in the role of education?

8. When recording devices were first invented almost 100 years ago, musicians could suddenly supply their music to large audiences at low cost. How do you suppose this development affected the income of the best musicians? How do you suppose it affected the income of average musicians?

9. A case study in this chapter described how customer discrimination in sports seems to have an important effect on players' earnings. Note that this is possible because sports fans know the players' characteristics, including their race. Why is this knowledge important for the existence of discrimination? Give some specific examples of industries where customer discrimination is and is not likely to influence wages.

10. Suppose that all young women were channelled into careers as secretaries, nurses, and teachers; at the same time, young men were encouraged to consider these three careers and many others as well.
    a. Draw a diagram showing the combined labour market for secretaries, nurses, and teachers. Draw a diagram showing the combined labour market for all other fields. In which market is the wage higher? Do men or women receive higher wages on average?
    b. Now suppose that society changed and encouraged both young women and young men to consider a wide range of careers. Over time, what effect would this change have on the wages in the two markets you illustrated in part (a)? What effect would the change have on the average wages of men and women?

11. This chapter considers the economics of discrimination by employers, customers, and governments. Now consider discrimination by workers. Suppose that some brunette workers did not like working with blonde workers. Do you think this worker discrimination could explain lower wages for blonde workers? If such a wage differential existed, what would a profit-maximizing entrepreneur do? If there were many such entrepreneurs, what would happen over time?

Income Inequality and Poverty

In this chapter, you will ...

1 Examine the degree of economic inequality in our society

2 Consider some problems that arise when measuring economic inequality

3 See how political philosophers view the government's role in redistributing income

4 Consider the various policies aimed at helping poor families escape poverty

The great British Prime Minister Winston Churchill once summarized alternative economic systems as follows: "The inherent vice of capitalism is the unequal sharing of blessings. The inherent virtue of socialism is the equal sharing of miseries." Churchill's quip draws attention to two important facts. First, nations that use market mechanisms to allocate resources usually achieve greater prosperity than those that do not. This is the result of Adam Smith's invisible hand in action. Second, the prosperity that market economies produce is not shared equally. Incomes can differ greatly between those at the top and those at the bottom of the economic ladder. The gap between rich and poor is a fascinating and important topic of study—for the comfortable rich, for the struggling poor, and for the aspiring and worried middle income earners.

From the previous two chapters you should have some understanding about why different people have different incomes. A person's earnings depend on the supply and demand for that person's labour, which in turn depend on natural ability, human capital, compensating differentials, discrimination, and so on. Because labour earnings make up about two-thirds of the total income in the Canadian economy, the factors that determine wages are also largely responsible for determining how the economy's total income is distributed among the various members of society. In other words, they help determine who is rich and who is poor.

In this chapter we discuss the distribution of income—a topic that raises some fundamental questions about the role of economic policy. One of the ten principles of economics in Chapter 1 is that governments can sometimes improve market outcomes. This possibility is particularly important when considering the distribution of income. The invisible hand of the marketplace acts to allocate resources efficiently in markets where there are no market failures, but it does not necessarily ensure that resources are allocated fairly. As a result, many economists believe that the government should redistribute income to achieve greater equality. In doing so, however, the government runs into another of the ten principles of economics: People face tradeoffs. As we have discussed at various points in the previous chapters, when the government enacts policies to make the distribution of income more equitable, it distorts incentives, alters behaviour, and makes the allocation of resources less efficient, giving rise to an equity–efficiency tradeoff.

Our discussion of the distribution of income proceeds in three steps. First, we assess how much inequality there is in our society. Second, we consider some different views about what role the government should play in altering the distribution of income. Third, we discuss various public policies aimed at helping society's poorest members.

20-1 The Measurement of Inequality

We begin our study of the distribution of income by addressing four questions of measurement:

1. How much inequality is there in our society?
2. How many people live in poverty?
3. What problems arise in measuring the amount of inequality?
4. How often do people move among income categories?

These measurement questions are the natural starting point from which to discuss public policies aimed at changing the distribution of income.

20-1a Canadian Income Inequality

Imagine that you lined up all of the families in the economy according to their annual family income. Then you divided the families into five equal groups: the bottom fifth, the second fifth, the middle fifth, the fourth fifth, and the top fifth. Table 20.1 shows the average income for each of these groups as well as the share of total income that each group of families received in Canada in 2016.

These numbers give us a way of gauging how the economy's total income is distributed. If income were equally distributed across all families, each one-fifth of families would receive one-fifth (20 percent) of income. If all income were concentrated among just a few families, the top fifth would receive 100 percent and the other fifths would receive 0 percent. The actual economy, of course, is between these two extremes.

Using family market income before taxes and transfers as the income measure, Table 20.1 shows that in 2016, the bottom fifth of all families received only 2.5 percent of all market income and the top fifth of all families received 45.7 percent. In other words, even though the top and bottom fifths include the same number of families, the top fifth has about 18 times as much income as the bottom fifth.

Figure 20.1 shows the distribution of market income over time, from 1976 to 2016. As can be seen, the share of market income (before taxes and transfers)

TABLE 20.1

Distribution of Market Income in Canada, 2016

Source: Statistics Canada, CANSIM 206-0032.

Group	(1) Average Income in Group	(2) % of Total Canadian Market Income
Bottom Fifth	$ 6 800	2.5
Second Fifth	26 650	10.1
Middle Fifth	44 350	16.8
Fourth Fifth	65 250	24.7
Top Fifth	120 700	45.7

FIGURE 20.1

Share of Market Income in Canada by Quintile, 1976–2016

Source: Statistics Canada, CANSIM 206-0032.

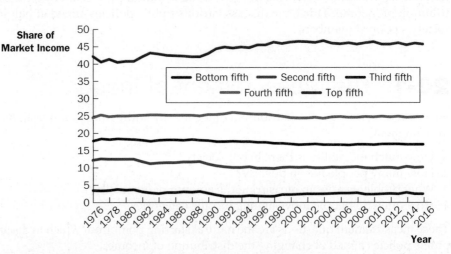

earned by the top 20 percent in Canada increased over this period, from about 42 percent in 1976 to 46 percent in 2016. This came primarily at the expense of the bottom half of the income distribution. In particular, the share of the bottom fifth of the income distribution fell from 3.5 percent in 1976 to 2.5 percent in 2016.

Income Redistribution in Canada

case study Various government policies are specifically designed to redistribute income. One way that governments do this is via income tax and transfer programs, which are not taken into account in Table 20.1. Table 20.2 shows how these programs affect the distribution of income in Canada.

Column (1) in the table replicates Table 20.1, showing average market income for each group and (in parentheses) the percentage of total market income received from that group. Column (2) shows the average amount of government monetary transfers received by each group. As can be seen from the table, transfer payments tend to fall with income, as does the percentage of total payments received.

Another way the government redistributes income is through the tax system. Income taxes play a particularly important role in this regard. As can be seen from column (3) of the table, average income taxes paid increased markedly with income. The richest income group paid an average of $27 700 in income taxes, accounting for over 57 percent of income taxes paid, while the lowest income group paid an average of $550 in taxes, accounting for about 1 percent of income taxes.

Column (4) of the table shows the average income for each group after transfers and income taxes, which is computed by adding transfers to market income and subtracting income taxes. Note that the distribution of after-tax/transfer income is more equal, although the highest income group still accounts for about 38 percent of income. Also, note that for the bottom three income groups (representing the lowest 60 percent of family income earners), their income after transfers and taxes is greater than their market income. In contrast, for the highest income groups (the richest 40 percent of income earners), combined income taxes and transfers lower their income.

Another way of measuring income inequality is by calculating the Gini coefficient (named after the Italian statistician Corrado Gini). The Gini

TABLE 20.2

Distribution of Income in Canada, Including Transfers and Income Taxes (percentage shares in parentheses), 2016

Source: Statistics Canada, Author calculations adapted from CANSIM 206-0032.

Group	(1) Average Market Income	(2) Average Transfers Received	(3) Average Income Taxes Paid	(4) Average Income after Transfers and Taxes
Bottom Fifth	$ 6 800 (2.5)	$ 12 500 (33.3)	$ 550 (1.1)	$ 18 750 (7.4)
Second Fifth	26 650 (10.1)	9 450 (25.2)	2 800 (5.8)	33 300 (13.2)
Middle Fifth	44 350 (16.8)	7 250 (19.3)	6 300 (13.1)	45 300 (17.9)
Fourth Fifth	65 250 (24.7)	5 000 (13.3)	11 000 (22.8)	59 250 (23.4)
Top Fifth	120 700 (45.7)	3 300 (8.8)	27 700 (57.5)	96 300 (38.1)

FIGURE 20.2

Gini Coefficients for Canada, Market and After-Tax/Transfer Income, 1976–2016

Source: Statistics Canada, CANSIM 206-0033.

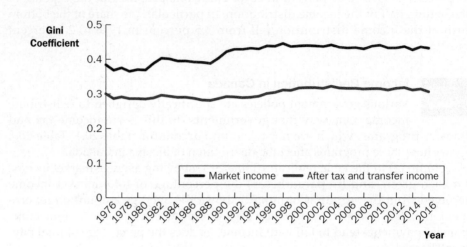

coefficient is a widely used measure of inequality that calculates the extent to which the distribution of income among individuals within a country deviates from a perfectly equal distribution. A Gini coefficient of 0 represents perfect equality (that is, every person in society has the same amount of income). In this case, each of the five income groups in the previous tables, each representing 20 percent of the population, would earn 20 percent of income. A Gini coefficient of 1 represents perfect inequality (that is, one person has all the income and the rest of society has none). So, the higher the Gini coefficient, the less equal the income distribution.

Figure 20.2 presents the Gini coefficient for Canada from 1976 to 2016. Gini coefficients for both market income and after-tax/transfer income are shown. As we would expect, the Gini coefficient for after-tax/transfer income is lower than the Gini coefficient for market income, because the tax/transfer system redistributes income from higher income groups to lower income groups. So the distribution of after-tax/transfer income is more equal, or less unequal, than the distribution of market income. However, both Gini coefficients have been increasing slightly over time, which indicates that the distribution of both types of income in Canada has become slightly less equal over this period.

It is also interesting to consider the extent of redistribution due to the tax and transfer system. This can be done by calculating what is known as the "R-factor" (R is for redistribution). The R-factor is the percentage difference between the Gini coefficient based on market income and the coefficient based on after-tax/transfer income. Thus, it is the difference between the Gini coefficients for market income and after-tax/transfer income, divided by the Gini coefficient for market income. An increase of the R-factor indicates an increase in redistribution through the tax/transfer system.

The R-factor from 1976 to 2016 for Canada is shown in Figure 20.3. Over this period it is evident that the amount of redistribution in the Canadian tax/transfer system increased, as the R-factor increased from about 22 in 1976 to about 29 in 2016. However, from the mid-1990s to the mid-2000s the degree of redistribution has declined somewhat from its peak of about 33 in 1994. This coincides with a period of fiscal consolidation on the part of both the federal and provincial

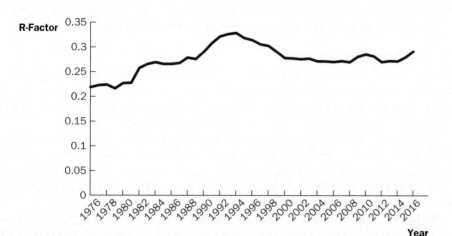

FIGURE 20.3

Redistribution in Canada (the R-factor), 1976–2016

Source: Statistics Canada, Author's calculations based on CANSIM 206-0033.

governments, which saw transfers decline. There are signs of a modest increase in redistribution beginning in 2012. ■

20-1b Income Inequality around the World

How does income inequality in Canada compare to that in other countries? This question is interesting, but answering it is problematic. For some countries, data are not available. Even when they are, not every country collects data in the same way; for example, some countries collect data on individual incomes, whereas other countries collect data on family incomes, and still others collect data on expenditure rather than income. As a result, whenever we find a difference between two countries, we can never be sure whether it reflects a true difference in the economies or merely a difference in the way data are collected.

With this warning in mind, consider Figure 20.4, which compares income inequality in 15 selected countries using after-tax and transfer Gini coefficients. Of

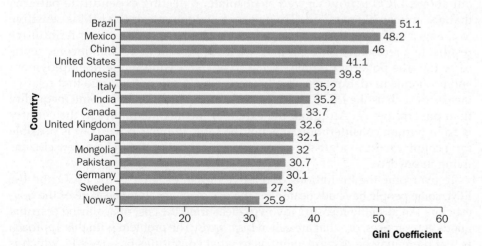

FIGURE 20.4

Income Inequality around the World (Gini coefficients), 2018

Source: United Nations Development Programme, Human Development Report, 2018. Table 3: Inequality-adjusted Human Development Index, http://hdr.undp.org/en/composite/IHDI.

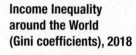

the 15 countries in the figure, the most equal (with the lowest Gini coefficient) is Norway and the most unequal is Brazil. Of the countries in the figure, we see that inequality in Canada is in the middle of the pack. Of particular note is the United States, which has quite a bit more income inequality than Canada.

20-1c The Poverty Rate

In assessing income inequality in Canada, we may be interested not only in the distribution of income but also in the number of Canadians living in poverty. Being relatively worse off is different from living in poverty, and government policies regarding income distribution should recognize the distinction.

poverty rate
the percentage of the population whose family income falls below an absolute level called the *poverty line*

poverty line
an absolute level of income set by the federal government for each family size, below which a family is deemed to be in poverty

The **poverty rate** is the percentage of the population with family income below the poverty line. The **poverty line** is the level of family income below which a family is considered poor. Unfortunately, the poverty line is not a well-defined concept. Indeed, until recently Canada did not even have an official measure of the poverty line. This changed in 2019.

Statistics Canada produces three income measures that have historically been used to calculate poverty rates. The first is called the Low Income Cut-offs (LICO). The LICO is calculated as the level of income at which a household of a given size in a community with a given population spends 20 percent more than average on food, shelter, and clothing. This measure has not been updated since 1992 except to adjust for inflation. This has rendered the measure problematic. It does not take into consideration, for instance, the fact that currently expenditures on transportation and communications surpass those on clothing. Nor does it measure regional variations in costs (for housing in particular). In addition, the LICO is used only in Canada, and it cannot allow international comparisons. Though this measure of poverty was widely used in the past, it is now viewed as being somewhat obsolete.

Another income concept used to measure poverty is the Low Income Measures (LIM). This measure is used much more widely in many countries, which allows for international comparisons. The LIM establishes the poverty threshold as a given proportion of median income, usually 50 percent (though the European Union uses 60 percent). The poverty rate based on the LIM thus reflects the percentage of people living on less than half of the median national income.

As Statistics Canada is quick to point out, the problem with using the LICO and LIM to measure poverty is that they are both relative measures that are defined in relation to some notion of average or median income. As pointed out above, LICO is now viewed as obsolete, reflecting expenditure patterns that are almost 30 years old. Though more widely used, the LIM is sensitive to changes in the median income, which sometimes produces counterintuitive results. In a recession, for example, when the growth in median income tends to be flat, the poverty rate may seem to be decreasing while unemployment and economic hardship are actually increasing. Critics also argue that relative measures such as the LICO and LIM are more a reflection of income inequality than poverty per se. Although the extent of income inequality in the country is an important consideration, it is not the same thing as poverty. It is possible for a country to have a great deal of income inequality but to have few citizens living in poverty.

To overcome the limitations of relative measures such as the LICO and the LIM, some people have advocated for the use of an absolute measure of the poverty line. An absolute measure involves measuring the cost of acquiring essential goods and services, or what are called *basic needs*. The problem with this approach is that there may be disagreement as to what constitutes basic needs, which is

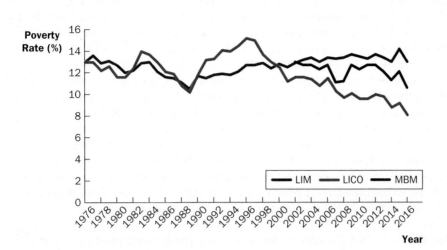

FIGURE 20.5

Poverty Rates in Canada, Different Income Measures, 1976–2016

Source: Statistics Canada, CANSIM 206-0041.

bound to be at least somewhat subjective and arbitrary (but perhaps no more so than any other measure of poverty).

Since 2002 Statistics Canada has reported another income measure, called the Market Basket Measure (MBM), based on the cost of goods and services deemed to be basic needs for families of various sizes in four categories—food, clothing and footwear, shelter, and transportation—as well as an "other goods and services" category. The MBM is therefore an absolute measure of poverty based on expenditures that people actually make and is sensitive to regional differences in the cost of living.

Figure 20.5 shows the poverty rate for all of Canada using the three approaches from 1976 to 2016 (the MBM since 2002). As is evident from the figure, the three measures can lead to quite different results. Since 2002, the LICO poverty rate has been lower than the MBM rate, which has in turn been lower than the LIM rate. In 2016 the LICO poverty rate was 8.1 percent, the MBM poverty rate was 10.6 percent, and the LIM poverty rate was 13 percent. Moreover, since the early 2000s the LIM suggests that the poverty rate has increased slightly, the LICO that it has fallen significantly, and the MBM that it has modestly declined.

Because of these discrepancies, the government announced in 2018 that going forward Canada would use the MBM as the official poverty rate. This decision was based on extensive consultations, and was made in large part because it best reflects what those with experience living in poverty indicated best reflect the underlying challenges. A key challenge arising from the new MBM of the official poverty line in Canada will be the need to constantly update the consumption basket underlying the method across the many communities in Canada.

20-1d Problems in Measuring Inequality

Although data on the income distribution and the poverty rate help to give us some idea about the degree of inequality in our society, interpreting these data is not as straightforward as it might first appear. The data are based on households' annual incomes. What people care about, however, is not their incomes but their ability to maintain a good standard of living. For various reasons, data on the income distribution and the poverty rate give an incomplete picture of inequality in living standards. We examine these reasons below.

in-kind transfers
transfers to the poor given
in the form of goods and
services rather than cash

In-Kind Transfers Measurements of the distribution of income and the poverty rate are based on families' *money* income. Through various government programs, however, the poor receive many nonmonetary items, including food, housing vouchers, and other services. Transfers to the poor given in the form of goods and services rather than cash are called **in-kind transfers**. Standard measurements of the degree of inequality do not take account of these in-kind transfers.

Because in-kind transfers are received mostly by the poorest members of society, the failure to include in-kind transfers as part of income greatly affects the measured poverty rate. Unfortunately, it is difficult to obtain data on the value of these in-kind transfers.

The important role of in-kind transfers makes evaluating changes in poverty more difficult. Over time, as public policies to help the poor evolve, the composition of assistance between cash and in-kind transfers changes. Some of the fluctuations in the measured poverty rate, therefore, reflect the form of government assistance rather than the true extent of economic deprivation.

life cycle
the regular pattern of income
variation over a person's life

The Economic Life Cycle Incomes vary predictably over people's lives. A young worker, especially one in school, has a low income. Income rises as the worker gains maturity and experience, peaks at around age 50, and then falls sharply when the worker retires at around age 65. This regular pattern of income variation is called the **life cycle**.

Because people can borrow and save to smooth out life cycle changes in income, their standard of living in any year depends more on lifetime income than on that year's income. The young often borrow, perhaps to go to school or to buy a house, and then repay these loans later when their incomes rise. People have their highest saving rates when they are middle-aged. Because people can save in anticipation of retirement, the large declines in incomes at retirement need not lead to similar declines in the standard of living.

This normal life cycle pattern causes inequality in the distribution of annual income, but it does not represent true inequality in living standards. To gauge the inequality of living standards in our society, the distribution of lifetime incomes is more relevant than the distribution of annual incomes. Unfortunately, data on lifetime incomes are not readily available. When looking at any data on inequality, however, it is important to keep the life cycle in mind. Because a person's lifetime income smooths out the highs and lows of the life cycle, lifetime incomes are surely more equally distributed across the population than are annual incomes.

permanent income
a person's normal income

Transitory versus Permanent Income Incomes vary over people's lives not only because of predictable life cycle variation but also because of random and transitory forces. One year, freezing rain may damage maple trees in Quebec, causing the income of Quebec maple syrup producers to decline temporarily. Over time the damaged trees will recover, and the incomes of maple syrup producers will rise again.

Just as people can borrow and lend to smooth out life cycle variations in income, they can borrow and lend to smooth out transitory variation in income. When maple syrup producers have a good year, they would be foolish to spend all of their additional income. Instead, they will likely save some of it against a "rainy day." Similarly, they respond to temporarily low incomes by drawing on their savings or by borrowing.

To the extent that a family saves and borrows to buffer itself from transitory changes in income, these changes do not affect its standard of living. A family's ability to buy goods and services depends largely on its **permanent income**, which is its normal, or average, income.

To gauge inequality of living standards, the distribution of permanent income is more relevant than the distribution of annual income. Although permanent income is hard to measure, it is an important concept. Because it excludes transitory changes in income, permanent income is more equally distributed than is current income.

20-1e Economic Mobility

People sometimes speak of "the rich" and "the poor" as if these groups consisted of the same families year after year. In fact, this is not at all the case. Economic mobility, the movement of people among income categories, is substantial in the Canadian economy. Movements up the income ladder can be due to good luck or hard work, and movements down the ladder can be due to bad luck or laziness. Some of this mobility reflects transitory variation in income, while some reflects more persistent changes in income.

A key measure of economic mobility is intergenerational mobility, which concerns the persistence of economic success from generation to generation. Three Canadian economists (Miles Corak, Lori Curtis, and Shelley Phipps) have sought to measure and compare the amount of intergenerational mobility across countries. This is a difficult task that is fraught with measurement problems, but one way of doing this is to calculate the intergenerational elasticity of earnings between fathers and sons (comparable calculations for daughters and mothers are not possible, given data limitations). The intergenerational elasticity measures the percentage change in the earnings of sons divided by the percentage change in the earnings of their fathers. The lower the intergenerational elasticity, the lower the extent to which economic outcomes are transmitted across generations and the higher the degree of economic mobility.

Corak, Curtis, and Phipps have assembled comparable estimates of the intergenerational elasticity of earnings between fathers and sons for several high-income countries. These estimates are shown in Figure 20.6. As can be seen from the figure, there is a wide variation in the degree of intergenerational mobility across the countries. The United Kingdom, Italy, and the United States exhibit a

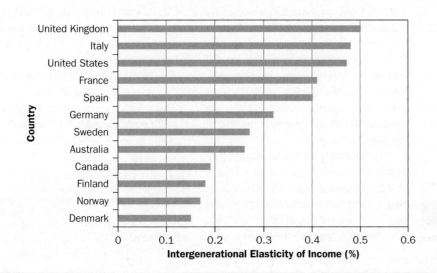

FIGURE 20.6

Intergenerational Mobility: The Intergenerational Elasticity of Earnings between Fathers and Sons for Selected Rich Countries

Source: Republished with permission of ABC-CLIO Inc., from "Inequality from Generation to Generation: The United States in Comparison" by Miles Corak, in *The Economics of Inequality, Poverty, and Discrimination in the 21st Century* by Robert S. Rycroft. © 2013; permission conveyed through Copyright Clearance Center, Inc.

The American Dream Is in Canada

*The so-called American dream—of rising from humble beginnings to high
income in a generation is much more likely in Canada than in the United States.*

In Canada, Unlike the U.S., the American Dream Lives On

By Barrie McKenna

We know the gap between rich and poor in Canada is large and growing.

One need look no further than Attawapiskat and other northern communities for evidence that not all Canadians are living the dream.

But income disparity shouldn't be confused with equality of opportunity.

And guess what? Canada is a world leader in economic mobility, right up there with Denmark, Norway and other Scandinavian countries.

A recent front-page story in *The New York Times* highlighted new research that "turns conventional wisdom on its head"—namely, that Americans enjoy less economic mobility than their peers in, gasp, Canada.

Yes, the U.S. is richer, but it's also significantly more unequal, and a lot less mobile. Inequality is inherited, much like hair and eye colour.

The conclusion is based partly on the work of University of Ottawa professor Miles Corak, a social policy economist and former director of family and labour research at Statistics Canada.

Prof. Corak has quantified the opportunity divide between the two countries and his conclusions are startling. Canadians are up to three times

more economically mobile than Americans, and it's almost entirely due to the conditions faced by those living at the very top and bottom of society, according to a new study he co-authored: Economic Mobility, Family Background, and the Well-Being of Children in the United States and Canada.

"What distinguishes the two countries is what's happening at the tails," Prof. Corak explained in an interview. "Rich kids grow up to be rich adults and poor kids stay poor. In Canada, that's not so much the case."

The American dream that anyone can rise from humble beginnings to vast wealth has become a myth. And as the gap between rich and poor widens, the middle class is shrinking.

For now, at least, the dream of upward mobility in Canada is still alive. Canadians can thank a legacy of sound public policy and a more progressive tax system.

Even the poorest of Canadian children have access to good schools, quality health care and decent homes (Attawapiskat notwithstanding).

A new Finance Department analysis found that seven million mainly low-income Canadians out of 24 million tax filers got a net cash transfer from the federal income tax regime in 2008. The Child Tax Credit, for example, has successfully mitigated poverty by shifting federal tax dollars to poor families.

The labour market, thanks partly to the paid parental leave benefits of Employment Insurance, likewise encourages parents to be parents. Canadian children are also more likely to grow up in two-parent homes and in homes where at least one parent works part-time to provide home care.

Compare that to the United States, where schools are financed primarily by wildly variable local property taxes rather than state income taxes. Neighbourhoods with low home values and marginal businesses have underfunded and failing schools, which become magnets for perpetual failure.

But it's a country of extremes, and life is good if you're at the top in the United States. A child's chance of staying at the wealth pinnacle is much greater than in Canada.

The divergence of opportunity in the U.S. grows even more pronounced with higher education. Tuition fees, which can easily run into the tens of thousands of dollars per year, essentially put the best schools out of reach for many Americans. Wealthy Americans, on the other hand, can literally buy opportunity for their children, paying their way through the best colleges, hiring tutors and providing access to family connections.

"It's not that the fathers are getting their sons jobs, but they are getting them into the right college and networks, and that pays off a lot more in the U.S.," Prof. Corak said.

Canadians shouldn't be complacent. Ottawa and most of the provinces are running large budget deficits, and education and health care are already targets as governments hunt for savings.

There's another cause for concern. Rising income inequality is chipping away at the opportunities of future generations. Prof. Corak worries that wealthy Canadians may be forming exclusionary institutions in a drift toward Americanization. It's reflected in increasingly polarized cities such as Toronto, where neighbourhoods are becoming more sharply divided along income and ethnic lines, he said.

The dream of upward mobility may be alive for the current crop of young Canadians.

That dream is an essential component of a healthy economy, and policy makers should ensure it's passed on to future generations.

Marie-Reine Mattera/Photononstop/Getty Images

relatively low degree of economic mobility, while in Denmark, Norway, Finland, and Canada intergenerational economic mobility is much higher. In Canada, the intergenerational elasticity of income between fathers and sons is only 0.19, which means that a 10 percent increase in the earnings of a father is associated with only a 1.9 percent increase in the earnings of the son. This suggests a very high degree of economic mobility across generations. In the United States, on the other hand, the elasticity is 0.50—a 10 percent increase in father earnings is associated with a 5 percent increase in son earnings.

QUICK **Quiz** *What does the poverty rate measure? • Describe three potential problems in interpreting the measured poverty rate.*

20-2 The Political Philosophy of Redistributing Income

We have just seen how the economy's income is distributed and have considered some of the problems in interpreting measured inequality. This discussion was *positive* in the sense that it merely described the world as it is. We now turn to the *normative* question facing policymakers: What should the government do about economic inequality?

This question is not just about economics. Economic analysis alone cannot tell us whether policymakers should try to make our society more egalitarian. Our views on this question are, to a large extent, a matter of political philosophy. Yet because the government's role in redistributing income is central to so many debates over economic policy, here we digress from economic science to consider a bit of political philosophy.

20-2a Utilitarianism

A prominent school of thought in political philosophy is **utilitarianism**. The founders of utilitarianism are the English philosophers Jeremy Bentham (1748–1832) and John Stuart Mill (1806–1873). To a large extent, the goal of utilitarians is to apply the logic of individual decision making to questions concerning morality and public policy.

The starting point of utilitarianism is the notion of **utility**—the level of happiness or satisfaction that a person receives from his or her circumstances. Utility is a measure of well-being and, according to utilitarians, is the ultimate objective of all public and private actions. The proper goal of the government, they claim, is to maximize the sum of utility of everyone in society.

The utilitarian case for redistributing income is based on the assumption of *diminishing marginal utility*. It seems reasonable that an extra dollar of income to a poor person provides that person with more additional utility than does an extra dollar to a rich person. In other words, as a person's income rises, the extra well-being derived from an additional dollar of income falls. This plausible assumption, together with the utilitarian goal of maximizing total utility, implies that the government should try to achieve a more equal distribution of income.

The argument is simple. Imagine that Peter and Paul are the same, except that Peter earns $80 000 and Paul earns $20 000. In this case, taking a dollar from Peter to pay Paul will reduce Peter's utility and raise Paul's utility. But, because of diminishing marginal utility, Peter's utility falls by less than Paul's utility rises.

utilitarianism
the political philosophy according to which the government should choose policies to maximize the total utility of everyone in society

utility
a measure of happiness or satisfaction

Thus, this redistribution of income raises total utility, which is the utilitarian's objective.

At first, this utilitarian argument might seem to imply that the government should continue to redistribute income until everyone in society has exactly the same income. Indeed, that would be the case if the total amount of income—$100 000 in our example—were fixed. But, in fact, it is not. Utilitarians reject complete equalization of incomes because they accept one of the ten principles of economics presented in Chapter 1: People respond to incentives.

To take from Peter to pay Paul, the government must pursue policies that redistribute income, such as the Canadian income tax and welfare system. Under these policies, people with high incomes pay high taxes, and people with low incomes receive income transfers. Yet, if the government takes away additional income a person might earn through higher income taxes or reduced transfers, both Peter and Paul have less incentive to work hard. As they work less, society's income falls, and so does total utility. The utilitarian government has to balance the gains from greater equality against the losses from distorted incentives. To maximize total utility, therefore, the government stops short of making society fully egalitarian.

A famous parable sheds light on the utilitarian's logic. Imagine that Peter and Paul are thirsty travellers trapped at different places in the desert. Peter's oasis has much water; Paul's has little. If the government could transfer water from one oasis to the other without cost, it would maximize total utility from water by equalizing the amount in the two places. But suppose that the government has only a leaky bucket. As it tries to move water from one place to the other, some of the water is lost in transit. In this case, a utilitarian government might still try to move some water from Peter to Paul, depending on how thirsty Paul is and how leaky the bucket is. But, with only a leaky bucket at its disposal, a utilitarian government will not try to reach complete equality.

20-2b Liberalism

liberalism
the political philosophy according to which the government should choose policies deemed to be just, as evaluated by an impartial observer behind a "veil of ignorance"

A second way of thinking about inequality might be called **liberalism**. Philosopher John Rawls develops this view in his book *A Theory of Justice*. This book was first published in 1971, and it quickly became a classic in political philosophy.

Rawls begins with the premise that a society's institutions, laws, and policies should be just. He then takes up the natural question: How can we, the members of society, ever agree on what justice means? It might seem that every person's point of view is inevitably based on that person's particular circumstances—whether he or she is talented or less talented, diligent or lazy, educated or less educated, born to a wealthy family or a poor one. Could we ever *objectively* determine what a just society would be?

To answer this question, Rawls proposes the following thought experiment. Imagine that before any of us is born, we all get together in the beforelife (the pre-birth version of the afterlife) for a meeting to design the rules that will govern society. At this point, we are all ignorant about the station in life each of us will end up filling. In Rawls's words, we are sitting in an "original position" behind a "veil of ignorance." In this original position, Rawls argues, we can choose a just set of rules for society because we must consider how those rules will affect every person. As Rawls puts it, "Since all are similarly situated and no one is able to design principles to favor his particular conditions, the principles of justice are the result of fair agreement or bargain." Designing public policies and institutions in this way allows us to be objective about what policies are just.

Rawls then considers what public policy designed behind this veil of ignorance would try to achieve. In particular, he considers what income distribution a person would consider fair if that person did not know whether he or she would end up at the top, bottom, or middle of the distribution. Rawls argues that a person in the original position would be especially concerned about the possibility of being at the *bottom* of the income distribution. In designing public policies, therefore, we should aim to raise the welfare of the worst-off person in society. That is, rather than maximizing the sum of everyone's utility, as a utilitarian would do, Rawls would maximize the minimum utility. Rawls's rule is called the **maximin criterion**.

Because the maximin criterion emphasizes the least fortunate person in society, it justifies public policies aimed at equalizing the distribution of income. By transferring income from the rich to the poor, society raises the well-being of the least fortunate. The maximin criterion would not, however, lead to a completely egalitarian society. If the government promised to equalize incomes completely, people would have no incentive to work hard, society's total income would fall substantially, and the least fortunate person would be worse off. Thus, the maximin criterion still allows disparities in income, because such disparities can improve incentives and thereby raise society's ability to help the poor. Nonetheless, because Rawls's philosophy puts weight on only the least fortunate members of society, it calls for more income redistribution than does utilitarianism.

Rawls's views are controversial, but the thought experiment he proposes has much appeal. In particular, this thought experiment allows us to consider the redistribution of income as a form of *social insurance*. That is, from the perspective of the original position behind the veil of ignorance, income redistribution is like an insurance policy. Homeowners buy fire insurance to protect themselves from the risk of their housing burning down. Similarly, when we as a society choose policies that tax the rich to supplement the incomes of the poor, we are all insuring ourselves against the possibility that we might have been a member of a poor family. Because people dislike risk, we should be happy to have been born into a society that provides us with this insurance.

It is not at all clear, however, that rational people behind the veil of ignorance would truly be so averse to risk as to follow the maximin criterion. Indeed, because a person in the original position might end up anywhere in the distribution of outcomes, he or she might treat all possible outcomes equally when designing public policies. In this case, the best policy behind the veil of ignorance would be to maximize the average utility of members of society, and the resulting notion of justice would be more utilitarian than Rawlsian.

20-2c Libertarianism

A third view of inequality is called **libertarianism**. The two views we have considered so far—utilitarianism and liberalism—both view the total income of society as a shared resource that a social planner can freely redistribute to achieve some social goal. By contrast, libertarians argue that society itself earns no income—only individual members of society earn income. According to libertarians, the government should not take from some individuals and give to others in order to achieve any particular distribution of income.

maximin criterion
the claim that the government should aim to maximize the well-being of the worst-off person in society

libertarianism
the political philosophy according to which the government should punish crimes and enforce voluntary agreements but not redistribute income

For instance, philosopher Robert Nozick writes the following in his famous 1974 book *Anarchy, State, and Utopia*:

> We are not in the position of children who have been given portions of pie by someone who now makes last minute adjustments to rectify careless cutting. There is no *central* distribution, no person or group entitled to control all the resources, jointly deciding how they are to be doled out. What each person gets, he gets from others who give to him in exchange for something, or as a gift. In a free society, diverse persons control different resources, and new holdings arise out of the voluntary exchanges and actions of persons.

Whereas utilitarians and liberals try to judge what amount of inequality is desirable in a society, Nozick denies the validity of this very question.

The libertarian alternative to evaluating economic *outcomes* is to evaluate the *process* by which these outcomes arise. When the distribution of income is achieved unfairly—for instance, when one person steals from another—the government has the right and duty to remedy the problem. But, as long as the process determining the distribution of income is just, the resulting distribution is fair, no matter how unequal.

Nozick criticizes Rawls's liberalism by drawing an analogy between the distribution of income in society and the distribution of grades in a course. Suppose you were asked to judge the fairness of the grades in the economics course you are now taking. Would you imagine yourself behind a veil of ignorance and choose a grade distribution without knowing the talents and efforts of each student? Or would you ensure that the process of assigning grades to students is fair without regard for whether the resulting distribution is equal or unequal? For the case of grades at least, the libertarian emphasis on process over outcomes is compelling.

Libertarians conclude that equality of opportunities is more important than equality of incomes. They believe that the government should enforce individual rights to ensure that everyone has the same opportunity to use his or her talents and achieve success. Once these rules of the game are established, the government has no reason to alter the resulting distribution of income.

 QUICK Quiz *Pam earns more than Pauline. Someone proposes taxing Pam in order to supplement Pauline's income. How would a utilitarian, a liberal, and a libertarian evaluate this proposal?*

20-3 Policies to Reduce Poverty

As we have just seen, political philosophers hold various views about what role the government should take in altering the distribution of income. Political debate among the larger population of voters reflects a similar disagreement. Despite these continuing debates, however, most people believe that, at the very least, the government should try to help those most in need. According to a popular metaphor, the government should provide a "safety net" to prevent any citizen from falling too far.

Poverty is one of the most difficult problems that policymakers face. Poor families are more likely than the overall population to experience homelessness, drug dependency, domestic violence, health problems, teenage pregnancy, illiteracy, unemployment, and low educational attainment. Members of poor families are both more likely to commit crimes and more likely to be victims of crimes. Although it is hard to separate the causes of poverty from the effects, there is no doubt that poverty is associated with various economic and social ills.

Suppose that you were a policymaker in the government, and your goal was to reduce the number of people living in poverty. How would you achieve this goal? Here we consider some of the policy options that you might consider. Although each of these options does help some people escape poverty, none of them is perfect, and deciding which is best is not easy.

20-3a Minimum-Wage Laws

Laws setting a minimum wage that employers can pay workers are a perennial source of debate. Advocates view the minimum wage as a way of helping the working poor without any cost to the government. Critics view it as hurting those it is intended to help.

The minimum wage is easily understood using the tools of supply and demand, as we first saw in Chapter 6. For workers with low levels of skill and experience, a high minimum wage forces the wage above the level that balances supply and demand. It therefore raises the cost of labour to firms and reduces the quantity of labour that those firms demand. The result is higher unemployment among those groups of workers affected by the minimum wage. Although those workers who remain employed benefit from a higher wage, those who might have been employed at a lower wage are worse off.

The magnitude of these effects depends crucially on the elasticity of demand. Advocates of a high minimum wage argue that the demand for unskilled labour is relatively inelastic, so that a high minimum wage depresses employment only slightly. Critics of the minimum wage argue that labour demand is more elastic, especially in the long run when firms can adjust employment and production more fully. They also note that many minimum-wage workers are teenagers from middle-income families, so that a high minimum wage is imperfectly targeted as a policy for helping the poor.

20-3b Welfare

One way to raise the living standards of the poor is for the government to supplement their incomes. The primary way in which the government does this is through the welfare system. **Welfare** is a broad term that encompasses various government programs. In Canada, welfare programs are the responsibility of provincial/territorial governments, which receive some help in funding the programs from the federal government.

welfare
government programs that supplement the incomes of the needy

The features of welfare programs and the levels of benefits vary significantly across Canada. However, the programs share some common features. Most programs distinguish between people who are considered employable and those who are not. People who are considered employable typically receive lower benefits. Individuals who are not considered employable, families with dependent children, and individuals with disabilities receive higher benefits.

A common criticism of welfare programs is that they reduce the incentive to work. One way in which they do this is by reducing welfare benefits when an individual earns other income. In the past many provinces/territories reduced welfare payments dollar for dollar when an individual earned other income. This resulted in a marginal tax rate on earned income of 100 percent. This reduces the incentive for welfare recipients to find work to supplement their welfare cheques, and results in what many refer to as a "welfare trap." In response to this criticism, many provinces and territories have lowered the implicit tax-back rates on welfare benefits, but they are still very high—in excess of 70 percent in most provinces/territories.

20-3c Basic Minimum Income

Whenever the government chooses a system to collect taxes, it affects the distribution of income. This is clearly true in the case of a progressive income tax, whereby high-income families pay a larger percentage of their income in taxes than do low-income families. As we discussed in Chapter 12, equity across income groups is an important criterion in the design of a tax system.

Many economists have advocated implementing a basic minimum income scheme, which guarantees individuals a minimum annual amount of income. These programs go under various names, including guaranteed basic income and negative income tax. The details vary but the basic idea is that every family would report its income to the government. High-income families would pay a tax based on their incomes. Low-income families would receive a subsidy. In other words, they would "pay" a "negative tax," thereby guaranteeing them a basic minimum income. Under such a program, poor families would receive financial assistance without having to demonstrate need. The only qualification required to receive assistance would be a low income.

Proponents of these programs argue that they could replace the myriad complicated and confusing programs that currently exist, and would provide a basic level of income required to lift families out of poverty. Critics counter with claims that they are very expensive and could give rise to disincentive effects such as lower work effort.

20-3d In-Kind Transfers

Another way to help the poor is to provide them directly with some of the goods and services they need to raise their living standards. For example, charities provide the needy with food, shelter, and children's toys for special occasions. In Canada, in-kind transfers supplied by the government include subsidized housing and daycare. Publicly funded health care, financed by income taxes and payroll taxes, can also be thought of as an in-kind transfer to the poor.

Is it better to help the poor with these in-kind transfers or with direct cash payments? There is no clear answer. Advocates of in-kind transfers argue that such transfers ensure that the poor get what they need most. Among the poorest members of society, alcohol and drug addiction is more common than it is in society as a whole. By providing the poor with food and shelter, society can be more confident that it is not helping to support such addictions. This is one reason why in-kind transfers are more politically popular than cash payments to the poor.

Advocates of cash payments, on the other hand, argue that in-kind transfers are inefficient and disrespectful. The government does not know what goods and services the poor need most. Many of the poor are ordinary people down on their luck. Despite their misfortune, they are in the best position to decide how to raise their own living standards. Rather than giving the poor in-kind transfers of goods and services that they may not want, it may be better to give them cash and allow them to buy what they think they need most.

20-3e Employment Insurance

Employment Insurance (EI) is one way the government provides some income support to people who find themselves temporarily out of work.

EI is available to workers who lose their jobs through no fault of their own; those who quit their jobs for no good reason or who are fired for cause receive no benefits. To qualify for EI, people must have worked a certain number of hours since their last spell of unemployment. Benefit levels are set at 55 percent of the individual's previous salary, up to a maximum equal to the average industrial wage. Unemployed workers can receive benefits for a maximum of 45 weeks.

There is ongoing debate in Canada on whether the EI system should be organized along the principles of an insurance program, or whether it should be operated as simply an income-transfer program. Those who argue that the EI system should embody insurance principles focus on various features of the current system. The EI system is funded from payroll taxes paid by both employees and employers. The payroll tax rates are the same for employees and employers in all industries, even though some industries and occupations have a much higher risk of unemployment than others. The construction industry, for example, tends to be both cyclical and seasonal. As a result, construction workers are more likely to be laid off than, say, university professors. Yet if a construction worker earns the same salary as a university professor, the construction worker and her employer will pay the same amount in EI payroll taxes as the university professor and his employer.

This equality in payroll tax payments contravenes one of the most important principles of insurance: High-risk individuals should pay higher insurance premiums than low-risk individuals. For example, young, single males pay much higher car insurance premiums than older, married males because they are more likely to have a car accident; similarly, people with poor driving records pay higher premiums than people with good driving records.

In effect, EI provides an implicit wage subsidy to industries that employ workers with a high risk of unemployment. In the absence of EI, construction workers would demand higher wages to compensate them for the higher risk of unemployment (recall our discussion of compensating differentials in Chapter 19). However, in the presence of EI, construction companies can pay their workers relatively lower wages because EI benefits provide a cushion if workers are laid off: Workers do not demand as much to compensate them for the risk of unemployment because their income will not fall by as much. For this reason, it is argued that EI payroll tax rates should be experience-rated. Under an experience-rated system, EI payroll tax rates would be higher in industries with a high risk of unemployment than in industries with a low risk of unemployment. Experience rating, it is claimed, would make the EI system more like true insurance and eliminate the implicit wage subsidies granted to some industries under the current system.

Not only is there currently no experience rating of EI in Canada, but some aspects of the EI system actually act as a sort of negative experience rating. For example, EI qualifying periods are shorter and benefit periods are longer in areas with persistently high unemployment rates. Sound insurance principles would require that workers in areas with high unemployment rates pay higher payroll taxes or receive lower benefits than workers in areas with low unemployment rates. However, by reducing the qualifying period and lengthening the benefit period in regions with high unemployment, the EI system does just the opposite. In this regard, the EI system acts as an income-transfer system to regions with high unemployment.

The debate over how closely the EI system in Canada should reflect insurance principles is a complicated and ongoing one.

IN THE news   EI and Work Incentives

Government programs designed to address poverty may also reduce the incentive to work. The following article explains how this can happen.

EI Claimants Bough Out

By David Johnston

The economy is going from bad to worse on the Gaspé peninsula, but people aren't grasping at straws just yet. In fact, they're grasping at Christmas-tree branches, and it's putting money in people's pockets.

In recent weeks, 250 people have been out in the woods, snipping small branches off balsam fir trees and hauling them to a new company that makes Christmas wreaths and other festive products.

When the company, WreathsPlus, was founded last fall in the industrial park outside the town of Gaspé, people took notice. New businesses are rare in the region, and seasonal workers who hadn't worked enough during the summer to get Employment Insurance over the winter saw an opportunity to qualify.

And so WreathsPlus had no trouble finding workers when it opened for a two-month

production run last fall. Even Emploi-Québec got in the act, agreeing to pay half the wages of 40 of the 70 original workers, under a job-training scheme.

The provincial subsidy was good for Wreaths Plus, good for the workers, and even good for the government, as it helped the 40 qualify for Employment Insurance and kept them from falling onto welfare rolls.

But then something remarkable happened: The wreaths the workers made sold like mad. Wholesalers loved them. This year, they put in orders for tens of thousands of them, as well as for other related balsam and cedar decorative products.

And so when three WreathsPlus facilities in Gaspé, Murdochville, and Rivière au Renard opened last month for another two-month run, there was work for 170 people, not just 70.

That's when the trouble started. Try as it did, the company could find only 150 people willing to work, even though the region's official unemployment rate is 19 percent, the highest

in Quebec. The problem, said WreathsPlus co-owner Bruce Jones, is that most of the people he tried to recruit said they'd already qualified for EI and didn't want to work. WreathsPlus had outgrown the local economy's demand for EI qualifying weeks....

WreathsPlus's seasonal production employees earn a minimum wage of $6.90 per hour, plus a small bonus that sees the most productive earn $8.50 per hour. This compares with the $7.10 per hour for people on EI, when you consider that the average Quebec EI recipient received a weekly cheque of $284.

People on EI would be looking at a 20-cent-per-hour pay cut if they went out to work for WreathsPlus instead of staying at home.

And so it is that one of the fastest-growing companies in the Gaspé faces an unofficial labour shortage.

Source: David Johnston, "EI Claimants Bough Out," *Montreal Gazette*, November 11, 2000, p. A19. Material reprinted with the express permission of: Montreal Gazette, a division of Postmedia Network Inc.

QUICK **Quiz**   *List three policies aimed at helping the poor, and discuss the pros and cons of each.*

20-4 Conclusion

People have long reflected on the distribution of income in society. Plato, the ancient Greek philosopher, concluded that in an ideal society the income of the richest person would be no more than four times the income of the poorest person. Although the measurement of inequality is difficult, it is clear that our society has much more inequality than Plato recommended.

One of the ten principles of economics discussed in Chapter 1 is that governments can sometimes improve market outcomes. There is little consensus, however, about how this principle should be applied to the distribution of income. Philosophers and policymakers today do not agree on how much income inequality is desirable, or even whether public policy should aim to alter the distribution of income. Much of public debate reflects this disagreement.

Whenever taxes are raised, for instance, lawmakers argue over how much of the tax hike should fall on the rich, with "middle income earners, and the poor.

Another of the ten principles of economics is that people face tradeoffs. This principle is important to keep in mind when thinking about economic inequality. Policies that penalize the successful and reward the unsuccessful reduce the incentive to succeed. Thus, policymakers often face a tradeoff between equality and efficiency.

summary

- Data on the distribution of income show wide disparity in our society. The richest fifth of families earn about 18 times as much income as the poorest fifth.

- Because in-kind transfers, the economic life cycle, transitory income, and economic mobility are so important for understanding variation in income, it is difficult to gauge the degree of inequality in our society using data on the distribution of income in a single year. When these other factors are taken into account, they tend to suggest that economic well-being is more equally distributed than is annual income.

- Political philosophers differ in their views about the role of government in altering the distribution of income. Utilitarians (such as John Stuart Mill) would choose the distribution of income to maximize the sum of utility of everyone in society. Liberals (such

as John Rawls) would determine the distribution of income as if we were behind a "veil of ignorance" that prevented us from knowing our own stations in life. Libertarians (such as Robert Nozick) would have the government enforce individual rights to ensure a fair process but then not be concerned about inequality in the resulting distribution of income.

- Various policies aim to help the poor—minimum-wage laws, welfare, negative income taxes, and in-kind transfers. Although each of these policies helps some families escape poverty, they also have unintended side effects. Because financial assistance declines as income rises, the poor often face effective marginal tax rates that are very high. Such high effective tax rates discourage poor families from escaping poverty on their own.

KEY concepts

poverty rate, *p. 444*
poverty line, *p. 444*
in-kind transfers, *p. 446*
life cycle, *p. 446*

permanent income, *p. 446*
utilitarianism, *p. 449*
utility, *p. 449*
liberalism, *p. 450*

maximin criterion, *p. 451*
libertarianism, *p. 451*
welfare, *p. 453*

QUESTIONS FOR review

1. Does the richest fifth of the Canadian population earn 4, 8, 18, or 50 times the income of the poorest fifth?

2. How does the extent of income inequality in Canada compare to that of other nations around the world?

3. What groups in the population are most likely to live in poverty?

4. When gauging the amount of inequality, why do transitory and life cycle variations in income cause difficulties?

5. How would a utilitarian, a liberal, and a libertarian determine how much income inequality is permissible?

6. What are the pros and cons of in-kind (rather than cash) transfers to the poor?

7. Describe how antipoverty programs can discourage the poor from working. How might you reduce this disincentive? What are the disadvantages with your proposed policy?

QUICK CHECK **multiple choice**

1. In Canada, the poorest fifth of the population earns about _____ percent of all income, while the richest fifth earns about _____ percent.
   a. 2, 45
   b. 4, 45
   c. 10, 35
   d. 15, 25

2. When income inequality is compared across countries, what is revealed about Canada?
   a. Canada is one of the most equal nations in the world.
   b. Canada is one of the least equal nations in the world.
   c. Canada has more equality than most advanced nations but less equality than many developing countries.
   d. Canada has less equality than most advanced nations but more equality than many developing countries.

3. A utilitarian believes that the redistribution of income from the rich to the poor is worthwhile as long as which of the following is true?
   a. the worst-off members of society benefit from it
   b. those contributing to the system are in favour of it
   c. each person's income, after taxes and transfers, reflects his marginal product
   d. the distortionary effect on work incentives is not too large

4. Which fact is Rawls's thought experiment of the "original position" behind the "veil of ignorance" meant to draw attention to?
   a. most of the poor do not know how to find better jobs and escape poverty
   b. the station of life each of us was born into is largely a matter of luck
   c. the rich have so much money that they don't know how to spend it all
   d. outcomes are efficient only if everyone begins with equal opportunity

5. Which of the following occurs under a negative income tax policy?
   a. individuals with low income get transfers from the government
   b. the government raises tax revenue without distorting incentives
   c. everyone pays less than under a conventional income tax
   d. some taxpayers are on the wrong side of the Laffer curve

6. What happens when the benefits from an antipoverty program are phased out as an individual's income increases?
   a. The program will encourage greater work effort from the poor.
   b. The program will lead to an excess supply of labour among unskilled workers.
   c. The program will increase the effective marginal tax rate that the poor face.
   d. The program will cost the government more than a program that benefits everyone.

PROBLEMS AND **applications**

1. By most measures, over the past 20 years income inequality in the United States has increased relative to income inequality in Canada. Some factors that may explain this difference were discussed in Chapter 19. What are they?

2. What do you think would happen to wage rates in the construction industry if Canada introduced full experience rating to the EI system? Explain.

3. Economists often view life cycle variation in income as one form of transitory variation in income around people's lifetime, or permanent, income. In this sense, how does your current income compare to your permanent income? Do you think your current income accurately reflects your standard of living?

4. The chapter discusses the importance of economic mobility.
   a. What policies might the government pursue to increase economic mobility *within* a generation?
   b. What policies might the government pursue to increase economic mobility *across* generations?
   c. Do you think we should reduce spending on current welfare programs in order to increase spending on programs that enhance economic mobility? What are some of the advantages and disadvantages of doing so?

5. Consider two communities. In one community, ten families have incomes of $100 each and ten families have incomes of $20 each. In the other community, ten

families have incomes of $200 each and ten families have incomes of $22 each.

   a. In which community is the distribution of income more unequal? In which community is the problem of poverty likely to be worse?

   b. Which distribution of income would Rawls prefer? Explain.

   c. Which distribution of income do you prefer? Explain.

6. This chapter uses the analogy of a "leaky bucket" to explain one constraint on the redistribution of income.

   a. What elements of the Canadian system for redistributing income create the leaks in the bucket? Be specific.

   b. Do you think that the NDP or Conservative political parties generally believe that the bucket used for redistributing income is more leaky? How does that belief affect their views about the amount of income redistribution that the government should undertake?

7. Suppose there are two possible income distributions in a society of ten people. In the first distribution, nine people would have incomes of $30 000 and one person would have an income of $10 000. In the second distribution, all ten people would have incomes of $28 000.

   a. If the society had the first income distribution, what would be the utilitarian argument for redistributing income?

   b. Which income distribution would Rawls consider more equitable? Explain.

   c. Which income distribution would Nozick consider more equitable? Explain.

8. Most measures of the poverty rate do not include the value of in-kind transfers in family income. Yet the value of in-kind transfers can be substantial. An example of an in-kind transfer is a housing subsidy. Let's say that the value of the housing subsidy is $5000 for each recipient family.

   a. If the government gave each recipient family an amount of cash equal to $5000 instead of the housing subsidy, do you think that most of these families would spend an additional $5000 on housing? Why or why not?

   b. How does your answer to part (a) affect your view about whether we should determine the poverty rate by valuing in-kind transfers at the price the government pays for them? Explain.

   c. How does your answer to part (a) affect your view about whether we should provide assistance to the poor in the form of cash transfers or in-kind transfers? Explain.

9. Suppose that a family's tax liability equalled its income multiplied by one-half, minus $10 000. Under this system, some families would pay taxes to the government, and some families would receive money from the government through a "negative income tax."

   a. Consider families with pre-tax incomes of $0, $10 000, $20 000, $30 000, and $40 000. Make a table showing pre-tax income, taxes paid to the government or money received from the government, and after-tax income for each family.

   b. What is the marginal tax rate in this system? (See Chapter 12 if you need to review the definition of marginal tax rate.) What is the maximum amount of income at which a family *receives* money from the government?

   c. Now suppose that the tax schedule is changed, so that a family's tax liability equals its income multiplied by one-quarter, minus $10 000. What is the marginal tax rate in this new system? What is the maximum amount of income at which a family receives money from the government?

   d. What is the main advantage of each of the tax schedules discussed here?

10. John and Jeremy are utilitarians. John believes that labour supply is highly elastic, whereas Jeremy believes that labour supply is quite inelastic. How do you suppose their views about income redistribution differ?

CHAPTER
21

LEARNING
objectives

The Theory of Consumer Choice

In this chapter, you will ...

1 See how a budget constraint represents the choices a consumer can afford

2 Learn how indifference curves can be used to represent a consumer's preferences

3 Analyze how a consumer's optimal choices are determined

4 See how a consumer responds to changes in income and changes in prices

5 Decompose the impact of a price change into an income effect and a substitution effect

6 Apply the theory of consumer choice to three questions about household behaviour

When you walk into a store, you are confronted with thousands of goods that you might buy. Because your financial resources are limited, you cannot buy everything that you want. You therefore consider the prices of the various goods being offered for sale and buy a bundle of goods that, given your resources, best suits your needs and desires.

In this chapter, we develop a theory that describes how consumers make decisions about what to buy. Thus far in this book, we have summarized consumers' decisions with the demand curve. As we have seen, the demand curve for a good reflects consumers' willingness to pay for it. When the price of a good rises, consumers are willing to pay for fewer units, so the quantity demanded falls. We now look more deeply at the decisions that lie behind the demand curve. The theory of consumer choice presented in this chapter provides a more complete understanding of demand, just as the theory of the competitive firm in Chapter 14 provides a more complete understanding of supply.

One of the ten principles of economics discussed in Chapter 1 is that people face tradeoffs. The theory of consumer choice examines the tradeoffs that people face as consumers. When a consumer buys more of one good, she can afford less of other goods. When she spends more time enjoying leisure and less time working, she has lower income and can afford less consumption. When she spends more of her income in the present and saves less of it, she reduces the amount she will be able to consume in the future. The theory of consumer choice examines how consumers facing these tradeoffs make decisions and how they respond to changes in their environment.

After developing the basic theory of consumer choice, we apply it to three questions about household decisions. In particular, we ask:

1. Do all demand curves slope downward?
2. How do wages affect labour supply?
3. How do interest rates affect household saving?

At first, these questions might seem unrelated. But, as we will see, we can use the theory of consumer choice to address each of them.

21-1 The Budget Constraint: What the Consumer Can Afford

Most people would like to increase the quantity or quality of the goods they consume—to take longer vacations, drive fancier cars, or eat at better restaurants. People consume less than they desire because their spending is *constrained*, or limited, by their income. We begin our study of consumer choice by examining this link between income and spending.

To keep things simple, we examine the decision facing a consumer who buys only two goods: pizza and Pepsi. Of course, real people buy thousands of different kinds of goods. Assuming there are only two goods greatly simplifies the problem without altering the basic insights about consumer choice.

We first consider how the consumer's income constrains the amount she spends on pizza and Pepsi. Suppose that the consumer has an income of $1000 per month and she spends her entire income each month on pizza and Pepsi. The price of pizza is $10, and the price of a litre of Pepsi is $2.

The table in Figure 21.1 shows some of the many combinations of pizza and Pepsi that the consumer can buy. The first line in the table shows that if the consumer spends all her income on pizza, she can eat 100 pizzas during the month, but she would not be able to buy any Pepsi at all. The second line shows another possible consumption bundle: 90 pizzas and 50 L of Pepsi. And so on. Each consumption bundle in the table costs exactly $1000.

The graph in Figure 21.1 illustrates the consumption bundles that the consumer can choose. The vertical axis measures the number of litres of Pepsi, and the horizontal axis measures the number of pizzas. Three points are marked on this figure. At point A, the consumer buys no Pepsi and consumes 100 pizzas. At point B, the consumer buys no pizza and consumes 500 L of Pepsi. At point C, the consumer buys 50 pizzas and 250 L of Pepsi. Point C, which is exactly at the middle of the line from A to B, is the point at which the consumer spends an equal amount ($500) on Pepsi and pizza. Of course, these are only three of the many combinations of Pepsi and pizza that the consumer can choose. All the points on the line from A to B are possible. This line, called the **budget constraint**, shows the consumption bundles that the consumer can afford. In this case, it shows the tradeoff between Pepsi and pizza that the consumer faces.

budget constraint
the limit on the consumption bundles that a consumer can afford

The slope of the budget constraint measures the rate at which the consumer can trade one good for the other. Recall that the slope between two points is calculated as the change in the vertical distance divided by the change in the horizontal distance (rise over run). From point A to point B, the vertical distance is 500 L, and the horizontal distance is 100 pizzas. Thus, the slope is 5 L per pizza. (Actually, because the budget constraint slopes downward, the slope is a negative number. But for our purposes we can ignore the minus sign.)

FIGURE 21.1

The Consumer's Budget Constraint

The budget constraint shows the various bundles of goods that the consumer can afford for a given income. Here the consumer buys bundles of Pepsi and pizza. The table and graph show what the consumer can afford if her income is $1000, the price of Pepsi is $2 per litre, and the price of a pizza is $10.

Litres of Pepsi	Number of Pizzas	Spending on Pepsi	Spending on Pizza	Total Spending
0	100	$ 0	$ 1000	$ 1000
50	90	100	900	1000
100	80	200	800	1000
150	70	300	700	1000
200	60	400	600	1000
250	50	500	500	1000
300	40	600	400	1000
350	30	700	300	1000
400	20	800	200	1000
450	10	900	100	1000
500	0	1000	0	1000

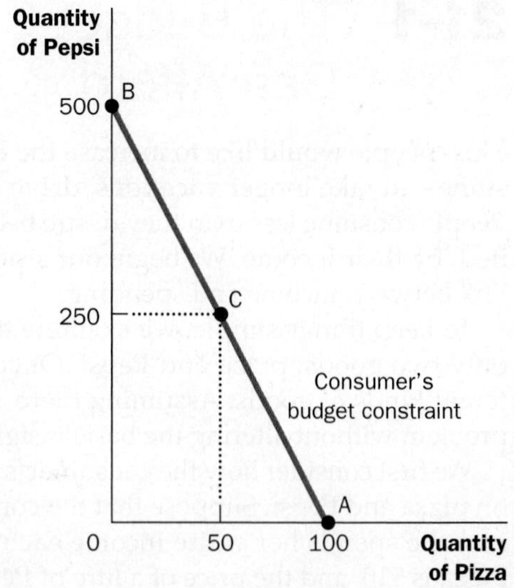

© 2018 Cengage Learning

Notice that the slope of the budget constraint equals the *relative price* of the two goods—the price of one good compared to the price of the other. A pizza costs five times as much as a litre of Pepsi, so the opportunity cost of a pizza is 5 L of Pepsi. The budget constraint's slope of 5 reflects the tradeoff the market is offering the consumer: 1 pizza for 5 L of Pepsi.

QUICK Quiz *Draw the budget constraint for a person with income of $1000 if the price of Pepsi is $5 per litre and the price of a pizza is $10. What is the slope of this budget constraint?*

21-2 Preferences: What the Consumer Wants

Our goal in this chapter is to understand how consumers make choices. The budget constraint is one piece of the analysis: It shows what combination of goods the consumer can afford given her income and the prices of the goods. The consumer's choices, however, depend not only on her budget constraint but also on her preferences regarding the two goods. Therefore, the consumer's preferences are the next piece of our analysis.

21-2a Representing Preferences with Indifference Curves

The consumer's preferences allow her to choose among different bundles of pizza and Pepsi. If you offer the consumer two different bundles, she chooses the bundle that best suits her tastes. If the two bundles suit her tastes equally well, we say that the consumer is *indifferent* between the two bundles.

Just as we have represented the consumer's budget constraint graphically, we can also represent her preferences graphically. We do this with indifference curves. An **indifference curve** shows the various bundles of consumption that make the consumer equally happy. In this case, the indifference curves show the combinations of pizza and Pepsi with which the consumer is equally satisfied.

Figure 21.2 shows two of the consumer's many indifference curves. The consumer is indifferent among combinations A, B, and C because they are all on the same curve. Not surprisingly, if the consumer's consumption of pizza is reduced, say from point A to point B, consumption of Pepsi must increase to keep her equally happy. If consumption of pizza is reduced again, from point B to point C, the amount of Pepsi consumed must increase yet again.

The slope at any point on an indifference curve equals the rate at which the consumer is willing to substitute one good for the other. This rate is called the **marginal rate of substitution** (*MRS*). In this case, the marginal rate of substitution measures how much Pepsi the consumer requires to be compensated for a one-unit reduction in pizza consumption. Notice that because the indifference curves are not straight lines, the marginal rate of substitution is not the same at all points on a given indifference curve. The rate at which a consumer is willing to trade one good for the other depends on the amounts of the goods she is already consuming. In other words, the rate at which the consumer is willing to trade pizza for Pepsi depends on whether she is hungrier or thirstier, which in turn depends on how much pizza and Pepsi she is consuming.

The consumer is equally happy at all points on any given indifference curve, but she prefers some indifference curves to others. Because she prefers more consumption to less, higher indifference curves are preferred to lower ones. In Figure 21.2, any point on curve I_2 is preferred to any point on curve I_1.

indifference curve
a curve that shows consumption bundles that give the consumer the same level of satisfaction

marginal rate of substitution
the rate at which a consumer is willing to trade one good for another

FIGURE 21.2

The Consumer's Preferences

The consumer's preferences are represented with indifference curves, which show the combinations of Pepsi and pizza that make the consumer equally satisfied. Because the consumer prefers more of a good, points on a higher indifference curve (I_2 here) are preferred to points on a lower indifference curve (I_1). The marginal rate of substitution (*MRS*) shows the rate at which the consumer is willing to trade Pepsi for pizza.

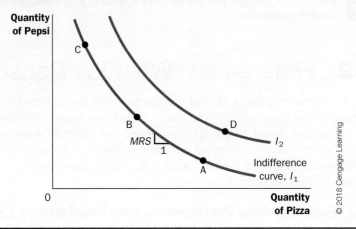

© 2018 Cengage Learning

A consumer's set of indifference curves gives a complete ranking of the consumer's preferences. That is, we can use the indifference curves to rank any two bundles of goods. For example, the indifference curves tell us that point D is preferred to point A because point D is on a higher indifference curve than point A. (That conclusion may be obvious, however, because point D offers the consumer both more pizza and more Pepsi.) The indifference curves also tell us that point D is preferred to point C because point D is on a higher indifference curve. Even though point D has less Pepsi than point C, it has more than enough extra pizza to make the consumer prefer it. By seeing which point is on the higher indifference curve, we can use the set of indifference curves to rank any combinations of pizza and Pepsi.

21-2b Four Properties of Indifference Curves

Because indifference curves represent a consumer's preferences, they have certain properties that reflect those preferences. Here we consider four properties that describe most indifference curves:

- *Property 1: Higher indifference curves are preferred to lower ones.* People usually prefer more of something to less of it. This preference for greater quantities is reflected in the indifference curves. As Figure 21.2 shows, higher indifference curves represent larger quantities of goods than lower indifference curves. Thus, the consumer prefers being on higher indifference curves.
- *Property 2: Indifference curves are downward sloping.* The slope of an indifference curve reflects the rate at which the consumer is willing to substitute one good for the other. In most cases, the consumer likes both goods. Therefore, if the quantity of one good is reduced, the quantity of the other good must increase for the consumer to be equally happy. For this reason, most indifference curves slope downward.

FIGURE 21.3

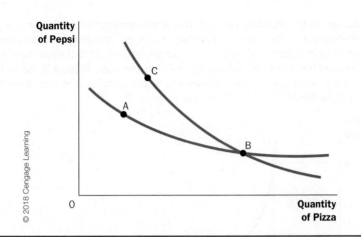

The Impossibility of Intersecting Indifference Curves

A situation like this can never happen. According to these indifference curves, the consumer would be equally satisfied at points A, B, and C, even though point C has more of both goods than point A.

- *Property 3: Indifference curves do not cross.* To see why this is true, suppose that two indifference curves did cross, as in Figure 21.3. Then, because point A is on the same indifference curve as point B, the two points would make the consumer equally happy. In addition, because point B is on the same indifference curve as point C, these two points would make the consumer equally happy. But these conclusions imply that points A and C would also make the consumer equally happy, even though point C has more of both goods. This contradicts our assumption that the consumer always prefers more of both goods to less. Thus, indifference curves cannot cross.

- *Property 4: Indifference curves are bowed inward.* The slope of an indifference curve is the marginal rate of substitution—the rate at which the consumer is willing to trade off one good for the other. The marginal rate of substitution (*MRS*) usually depends on the amount of each good the consumer is currently consuming. In particular, because people are more willing to trade away goods that they have in abundance and less willing to trade away goods of which they have little, the indifference curves are bowed inward toward the graph's origin. As an example, consider Figure 21.4. At point A, because the consumer has a lot of Pepsi and only a little pizza, she is very hungry but not very thirsty. To induce the consumer to give up 1 pizza, she has to be given 6 L of Pepsi: The *MRS* is 6 L per pizza. By contrast, at point B, the consumer has little Pepsi and a lot of pizza, so she is very thirsty but not very hungry. At this point, she would be willing to give up 1 pizza to get 1 L of Pepsi: The *MRS* is 1 L per pizza. Thus, the bowed shape of the indifference curve reflects the consumer's greater willingness to give up a good that she already has in large quantity.

21-2c Two Extreme Examples of Indifference Curves

The shape of an indifference curve tells us about the consumer's willingness to trade one good for the other. When the goods are easy to substitute for each other, the indifference curves are less bowed; when the goods are hard to substitute, the indifference curves are very bowed. To see why this is true, let's consider the extreme cases.

Perfect Substitutes Suppose that someone offered you bundles of nickels and dimes. How would you rank the different bundles?

FIGURE 21.4

Bowed Indifference Curves

Indifference curves are usually bowed inward. This shape implies that the marginal rate of sub-stitution (*MRS*) depends on the quantity of the two goods the consumer is consuming. At point A, the consumer has little pizza and much Pepsi, so she requires a lot of extra Pepsi to induce her to give up one of the pizzas: the *MRS* is 6 L of Pepsi per pizza. At point B, the consumer has much pizza and little Pepsi, so she requires only a little extra Pepsi to induce her to give up one of the pizzas: the *MRS* is 1 L of Pepsi per pizza.

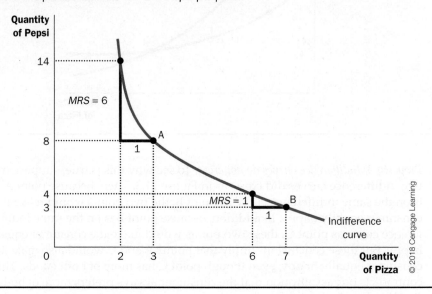

Most likely, you would care only about the total monetary value of each bundle. If so, you would always be willing to trade 2 nickels for one dime. Your marginal rate of substitution between nickels and dimes would be a fixed number: $MRS = 2$, regardless of the number of nickels and dimes in the bundle.

We can represent your preferences over nickels and dimes with the indifference curves in panel (a) of Figure 21.5. Because the marginal rate of substitution is constant, the indifference curves are straight lines. In this extreme case of straight indifference curves, we say that the two goods are **perfect substitutes**.

Perfect Complements Suppose now that someone offered you bundles of shoes. Some of the shoes fit your left foot, others your right foot. How would you rank these different bundles?

In this case, you might care only about the number of pairs of shoes. In other words, you would judge a bundle based on the number of pairs you could assemble from it. A bundle of 5 left shoes and 7 right shoes yields only 5 pairs. Getting 1 more right shoe has no value if there is no left shoe to go with it.

We can represent your preferences for right and left shoes with the indifference curves in panel (b) of Figure 21.5. In this case, a bundle with 5 left shoes and 5 right shoes is just as good as a bundle with 5 left shoes and 7 right shoes. It is also just as good as a bundle with 7 left shoes and 5 right shoes. The indifference curves, there-fore, are right angles. In this extreme case of right-angle indifference curves, we say that the two goods are **perfect complements**.

perfect substitutes
two goods with straight-line indifference curves

perfect complements
two goods with right-angle indifference curves

FIGURE 21.5

**Perfect Substitutes and
Perfect Complements**

When two goods are easily substitutable, such as nickels and dimes, the indifference curves are straight lines, as shown in panel (a). When two goods are strongly complementary, such as left shoes and right shoes, the indifference curves are right angles, as shown in panel (b).

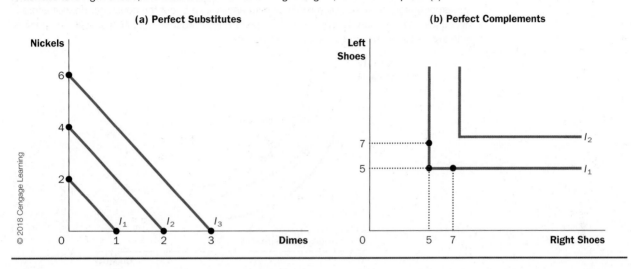

(a) Perfect Substitutes

(b) Perfect Complements

In the real world, of course, most goods are neither perfect substitutes (like nickels and dimes) nor perfect complements (like right shoes and left shoes). More typically, the indifference curves are bowed inward, but not so bowed that they become right angles.

QUICK
Quiz   *Draw some indifference curves for Pepsi and pizza. Explain the four properties of these indifference curves.*

21-3 Optimization: What the Consumer Chooses

The goal of this chapter is to understand how a consumer makes choices. We have the two pieces necessary for this analysis: the consumer's budget constraint (how much she can afford to spend) and the consumer's preferences (what she wants to spend it on). Now we put these two pieces together and consider the consumer's decision about what to buy.

21-3a The Consumer's Optimal Choices

Once again, consider our pizza and Pepsi example. The consumer would like to end up with the best possible combination of pizza and Pepsi for her—that is, the combination on her highest possible indifference curve. But the consumer must also end up on or below her budget constraint, which measures the total resources available to her.

Figure 21.6 shows the consumer's budget constraint and three of her many indifference curves. The highest indifference curve that the consumer can reach (I_2 in the figure) is the one that just barely touches the budget constraint. The point at which this indifference curve and the budget constraint touch is called the *optimum*. The consumer would prefer point A, but she cannot afford that point

FIGURE 21.6

The Consumer's Optimum

The consumer chooses the point on her budget constraint that lies on the highest indifference curve. At this point, called the *optimum*, the marginal rate of substitution equals the relative price of the two goods. Here the highest indifference curve the consumer can reach is I_2. The consumer prefers point A, which lies on indifference curve I_3, but the consumer cannot afford this bundle of Pepsi and pizza. By contrast, point B is affordable, but because it lies on a lower indifference curve, the consumer does not prefer it.

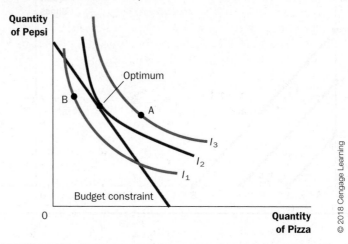

because it lies above her budget constraint. The consumer can afford point B, but that point is on a lower indifference curve and, therefore, provides the consumer less satisfaction. The optimum represents the best combination of consumption of Pepsi and pizza available to the consumer.

Notice that, at the optimum, the slope of the indifference curve equals the slope of the budget constraint. We say that the indifference curve is *tangent* to the budget constraint. The slope of the indifference curve is the marginal rate of substitution between pizza and Pepsi, and the slope of the budget constraint is the relative price of pizza and Pepsi. Thus, *the consumer chooses consumption of the two goods so that the marginal rate of substitution equals the relative price.*

In Chapter 7 we saw how market prices reflect the marginal value that consumers place on goods. This analysis of consumer choice shows the same result in another way. In making her consumption choices, the consumer takes as given the relative price of the two goods and then chooses an optimum at which her marginal rate of substitution equals this relative price. The relative price is the rate at which the *market* is willing to trade one good for the other, whereas the marginal rate of substitution is the rate at which the *consumer* is willing to trade one good for the other. At the consumer's optimum, the consumer's valuation of the two goods (as measured by the marginal rate of substitution) equals the market's valuation (as measured by the relative price). As a result of this consumer optimization, market prices of different goods reflect the value that consumers place on those goods.

21-3b How Changes in Income Affect the Consumer's Choices

Now that we have seen how the consumer makes the consumption decision, let's examine how this decision responds to changes in the consumer's income. To be specific, suppose that income increases. With higher income, the consumer can

FYI

Utility: An Alternative Way to Describe Preferences and Optimization

We have used indifference curves to represent the consumer's preferences. Another common way to represent preferences is with the concept of *utility*. Utility is an abstract measure of the satisfaction or happiness that a consumer receives from a bundle of goods. Economists say that a consumer prefers one bundle of goods to another if one provides more utility than the other.

Indifference curves and utility are closely related. Because the consumer prefers points on higher indifference curves, bundles of goods on higher indifference curves provide higher utility. Because the consumer is equally happy with all points on the same indifference curve, all these bundles provide the same utility. You can think of an indifference curve as an "equal-utility" curve.

The *marginal utility* of any good is the increase in utility that the consumer gets from an additional unit of that good. Most goods are assumed to exhibit *diminishing marginal utility*: The more of the good the consumer already has, the lower the marginal utility provided by an extra unit of that good.

The marginal rate of substitution between two goods depends on their marginal utilities. For example, if the marginal utility of good X is twice the marginal utility of good Y, then a person would need 2 units of good Y to compensate for losing 1 unit of good X, and the marginal rate of substitution equals 2. More generally, the marginal rate of substitution (and thus the slope of the indifference curve) equals the marginal utility of one good divided by the marginal utility of the other good.

Utility analysis provides another way to describe consumer optimization. Recall that, at the consumer's optimum, the marginal rate of substitution equals the ratio of prices. That is,

$$MRS = P_X/P_Y$$

Because the marginal rate of substitution equals the ratio of marginal utilities, we can write this condition for optimization as

$$MU_X/MU_Y = P_X/P_Y$$

Now rearrange this expression to become

$$MU_X/P_X = MU_Y/P_Y$$

This equation has a simple interpretation: At the optimum, the marginal utility per dollar spent on good X equals the marginal utility per dollar spent on good Y. (Why? If this equality did not hold, the consumer could increase utility by spending less on the good that provided lower marginal utility per dollar and more on the good that provided higher marginal utility per dollar.)

When economists discuss the theory of consumer choice, they sometimes express the theory using different words. One economist might say that the goal of the consumer is to maximize utility. Another economist might say that the goal of the consumer is to end up on the highest possible indifference curve. The first economist would conclude that at the consumer's optimum, the marginal utility per dollar is the same for all goods, whereas the second would conclude that the indifference curve is tangent to the budget constraint. In essence, these are two ways of saying the same thing.

---

afford more of both goods. The increase in income, therefore, shifts the budget constraint outward, as in Figure 21.7. Because the relative price of the two goods has not changed, the slope of the new budget constraint is the same as the slope of the initial budget constraint. That is, an increase in income leads to a parallel shift in the budget constraint.

The expanded budget constraint allows the consumer to choose a better combination of pizza and Pepsi, one that is on a higher indifference curve. Given the shift in the budget constraint and the consumer's preferences as represented by her indifference curves, the consumer's optimum moves from the point labelled "initial optimum" to the point labelled "new optimum."

Notice that in Figure 21.7 the consumer chooses to consume more Pepsi and more pizza. The logic of the model does not require increased consumption of both goods in response to increased income, but this situation is the most common. As you may recall from Chapter 4, if a consumer wants more of a good when her income rises, economists call it a **normal good**. The indifference curves in Figure 21.7 are drawn under the assumption that both pizza and Pepsi are normal goods.

normal good
a good for which, other things equal, an increase in income leads to an increase in demand

FIGURE 21.7

An Increase in Income

When the consumer's income rises, the budget constraint shifts out. If both goods are normal goods, the consumer responds to the increase in income by buying more of both of them. Here the consumer buys more pizza and more Pepsi.

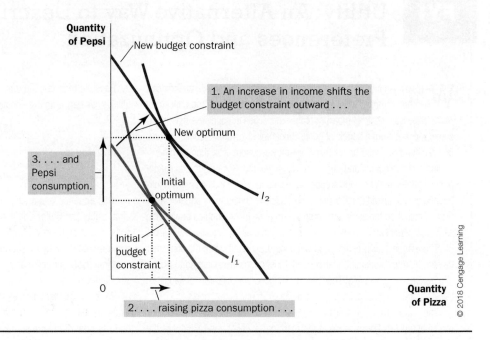

Quantity of Pepsi

New budget constraint

1. An increase in income shifts the budget constraint outward . . .

New optimum

3. . . . and Pepsi consumption.

Initial optimum

I_2

Initial budget constraint

I_1

0

2. . . . raising pizza consumption . . .

Quantity of Pizza

© 2018 Cengage Learning

inferior good
a good for which, other things equal, an increase in income leads to a decrease in demand

Figure 21.8 shows an example in which an increase in income induces the consumer to buy more pizza but less Pepsi. If a consumer buys less of a good when her income rises, economists call it an **inferior good**. Figure 21.8 is drawn under the assumption that pizza is a normal good and Pepsi is an inferior good.

FIGURE 21.8

An Inferior Good

A good is an inferior good if the consumer buys less of it when her income rises. Here Pepsi is an inferior good: When the consumer's income increases and the budget constraint shifts outward, the consumer buys more pizza but less Pepsi.

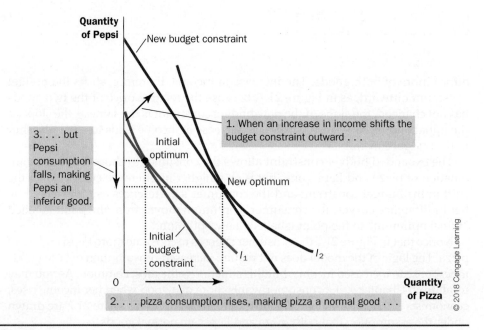

Quantity of Pepsi

New budget constraint

1. When an increase in income shifts the budget constraint outward . . .

3. . . . but Pepsi consumption falls, making Pepsi an inferior good.

Initial optimum

New optimum

Initial budget constraint

I_1

I_2

0

2. . . . pizza consumption rises, making pizza a normal good . . .

Quantity of Pizza

© 2018 Cengage Learning

Although most goods in the world are normal goods, there are some inferior goods as well. One example is bus rides. As income increases, consumers are more likely to own cars or take taxis and less likely to ride the bus. Bus rides, therefore, are an inferior good.

21-3c How Changes in Prices Affect the Consumer's Choices

Let's now use this model of consumer choice to consider how a change in the price of one of the goods alters the consumer's choices. Suppose, in particular, that the price of Pepsi falls from $2 to $1 per litre. It is no surprise that the lower price expands the consumer's set of buying opportunities. In other words, a fall in the price of any good shifts the budget constraint outward.

Figure 21.9 considers more specifically how the fall in price affects the budget constraint. If the consumer spends her entire $1000 income on pizza, then the price of Pepsi is irrelevant. Thus, point A in the figure stays the same. Yet if the consumer spends her entire income of $1000 on Pepsi, she can now buy 1000 L rather than only 500 L. Thus, the end point of the budget constraint moves from point B to point D.

Notice that in this case the outward shift in the budget constraint changes its slope. (This differs from what happened previously, when prices stayed the same but the consumer's income changed.) As we have discussed, the slope of the budget constraint reflects the relative price of pizza and Pepsi. Because the price of Pepsi has fallen to $1 from $2, while the price of pizza has remained $10, the consumer can now trade a pizza for 10 L rather than 5 L of Pepsi. As a result, the new budget constraint has a steeper slope.

How such a change in the budget constraint alters the consumption of both goods depends on the consumer's preferences. For the indifference curves drawn in this figure, the consumer buys more Pepsi and less pizza.

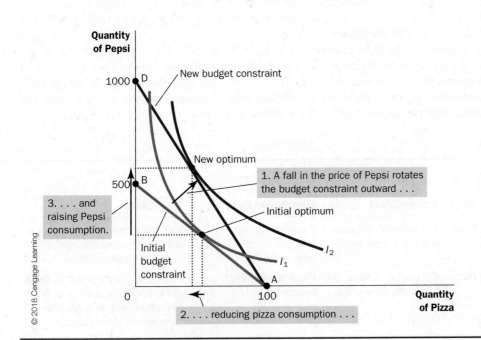

© 2018 Cengage Learning

FIGURE 21.9

A Change in Price

When the price of Pepsi falls, the consumer's budget constraint shifts outward and changes slope. The consumer moves from the initial optimum to the new optimum, which changes her purchases of both Pepsi and pizza. In this case, the quantity of Pepsi consumed rises, and the quantity of pizza consumed falls.

21-3d Income and Substitution Effects

The impact of a change in the price of a good on consumption can be decomposed into two effects: an **income effect** and a **substitution effect**. To see what these two effects are, consider how our consumer might respond when she learns that the price of Pepsi has fallen. She might reason in the following ways:

- "Great news! Now that Pepsi is cheaper, my income has greater purchasing power. I am, in effect, richer than I was. Because I am richer, I can buy both more pizza and more Pepsi." (This is the income effect.)
- "Now that the price of Pepsi has fallen, I get more litres of Pepsi for every pizza that I give up. Because pizza is now relatively more expensive, I should buy less pizza and more Pepsi." (This is the substitution effect.)

Which statement do you find more compelling?

In fact, both of these statements make sense. The decrease in the price of Pepsi makes the consumer better off. If pizza and Pepsi are both normal goods, the consumer will want to spread this improvement in her purchasing power over both goods. This income effect tends to make the consumer buy more pizza and more Pepsi. Yet at the same time, consumption of Pepsi has become less expensive relative to consumption of pizza. This substitution effect tends to make the consumer choose less pizza and more Pepsi.

Now consider the result of these two effects working at the same time. The consumer certainly buys more Pepsi, because the income and substitution effects both act to raise purchases of Pepsi. But for pizza, the income and substitution effects work in opposite directions. As a result, whether the consumer buys more or less pizza is not clear. The outcome could go either way, depending on the sizes of the income and substitution effects. Table 21.1 summarizes these conclusions.

We can interpret the income and substitution effects using indifference curves. The income effect is the change in consumption that results from the movement to a higher indifference curve. The substitution effect is the change in consumption that results from being at a point on an indifference curve with a different marginal rate of substitution.

Figure 21.10 shows graphically how to decompose the change in the consumer's decision into the income effect and the substitution effect. When the price of Pepsi falls, the consumer moves from the initial optimum, point A, to the new optimum, point C. We can view this change as occurring in two steps. First, the consumer moves *along* the initial indifference curve I_1 from point A to point B. The

---

income effect

the change in consumption that results when a price change moves the consumer to a higher or lower indifference curve

substitution effect

the change in consumption that results when a price change moves the consumer along a given indifference curve to a point with a new marginal rate of substitution

---

TABLE 21.1

Income and Substitution Effects When the Price of Pepsi Falls

Good	Income Effect	Substitution Effect	Total Effect
Pepsi	Consumer is richer, so she buys more Pepsi.	Pepsi is relatively cheaper, so consumer buys more Pepsi.	Income and substitution effects act in same direction, so consumer buys more Pepsi.
Pizza	Consumer is richer, so she buys more pizza.	Pizza is relatively more expensive, so consumer buys less pizza.	Income and substitution effects act in opposite directions, so the total effect on pizza consumption is ambiguous.

FIGURE 21.10

Income and Substitution Effects

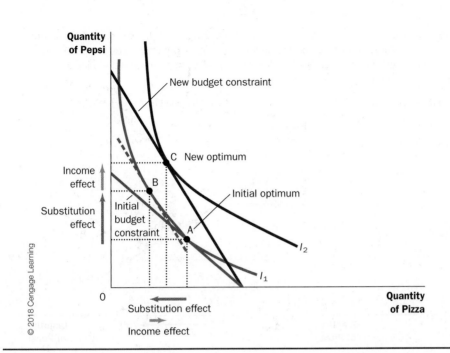

The effect of a change in price can be broken down into an income effect and a substitution effect. The substitution effect—the movement along an indifference curve to a point with a different marginal rate of substitution—is shown here as the change from point A to point B along indifference curve I_1. The income effect—the shift to a higher indifference curve—is shown here as the change from point B on indifference curve I_1 to point C on indifference curve I_2.

consumer is equally happy at these two points, but at point B, the marginal rate of substitution reflects the new relative price. (The dashed line through point B is parallel to the new budget constraint and thus reflects the new relative price.) Next, the consumer *shifts* to the higher indifference curve, I_2, by moving from point B to point C. Even though point B and point C are on different indifference curves, they have the same marginal rate of substitution. That is, the slope of the indifference curve I_1 at point B equals the slope of the indifference curve I_2 at point C.

The consumer never actually chooses point B, but this hypothetical point is useful to clarify the two effects that determine the consumer's decision. Notice that the change from point A to point B represents a pure change in the marginal rate of substitution without any change in the consumer's welfare. Similarly, the change from point B to point C represents a pure change in welfare without any change in the marginal rate of substitution. Thus, the movement from A to B shows the substitution effect, and the movement from B to C shows the income effect.

21-3e Deriving the Demand Curve

We have just seen how changes in the price of a good alter the consumer's budget constraint and, therefore, the quantities of the two goods that she chooses to buy. The demand curve for any good reflects these consumption decisions. Recall that a demand curve shows the quantity demanded of a good for any given price. We can view a consumer's demand curve as a summary of the optimal decisions that arise from her budget constraint and indifference curves.

For example, Figure 21.11 considers the demand for Pepsi. Panel (a) shows that when the price of a litre falls from $2 to $1, the consumer's budget constraint shifts outward. Because of both income and substitution effects, the consumer increases

FIGURE 21.11

Deriving the Demand Curve

Panel (a) shows that when the price of Pepsi falls from $2 to $1, the consumer's optimum moves from point A to point B, and the quantity of Pepsi consumed rises from 250 L to 750 L. The demand curve in panel (b) reflects this relationship between the price and the quantity demanded.

(a) The Consumer's Optimum

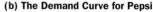

(b) The Demand Curve for Pepsi

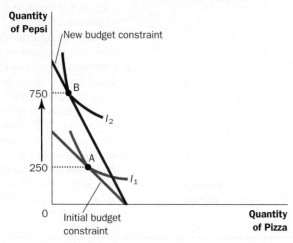

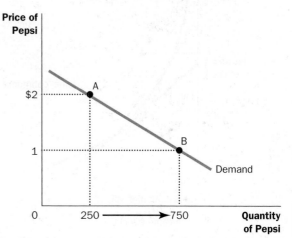

© 2018 Cengage Learning

her purchases of Pepsi from 250 L to 750 L. Panel (b) shows the demand curve that results from this consumer's decisions. In this way, the theory of consumer choice provides the theoretical foundation for the consumer's demand curve.

It may be comforting to know that the demand curve arises naturally from the theory of consumer choice, but this exercise by itself does not justify developing the theory. There is no need for a rigorous, analytic framework just to establish that people respond to changes in prices. The theory of consumer choice is, however, very useful in studying various decisions that people make as they go about their lives, as we see in the next section.

Draw a budget constraint and indifference curves for Pepsi and pizza. Show what happens to the budget constraint and the consumer's optimum when the price of pizza rises. In your diagram, decompose the change into an income effect and a substitution effect.

21-4 Three Applications

Now that we have developed the basic theory of consumer choice, let's use it to shed light on three questions about how the economy works. These three questions might at first seem unrelated. But because each question involves household decision making, we can address it with the model of consumer behaviour we have just developed.

21-4a Do All Demand Curves Slope Downward?

Normally, when the price of a good rises, people buy less of it. This usual behaviour, called the *law of demand*, is reflected in the downward slope of the demand curve.

FIGURE 21.12

A Giffen Good

In this example, when the price of potatoes rises, the consumer's optimum shifts from point C to point E. In this case, the consumer responds to a higher price of potatoes by buying less meat and more potatoes.

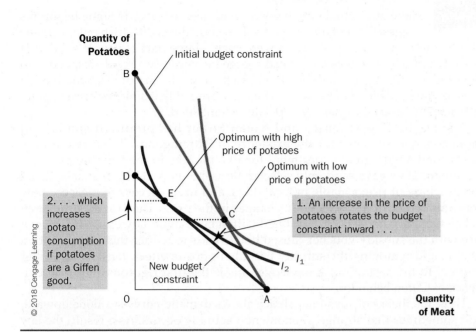

As a matter of economic theory, however, demand curves can sometimes slope upward. In other words, consumers can sometimes violate the law of demand and buy *more* of a good when the price rises. To see how this can happen, consider Figure 21.12. In this example, the consumer buys two goods—meat and potatoes. Initially, the consumer's budget constraint is the line from point A to point B. The optimum is point C. When the price of potatoes rises, the budget constraint shifts inward and is now the line from point A to point D. The optimum is now point E. Notice that a rise in the price of potatoes has led the consumer to buy a larger quantity of potatoes.

Why is the consumer responding in this strange way? In this example, potatoes are a strongly inferior good; that is, potatoes are a good that a person buys a lot less of when her income rises and a lot more of when her income falls. In Figure 21.12, the increase in the price of potatoes makes the consumer poorer; that is, the higher price puts her on a lower indifference curve. Because she is poorer and potatoes are an inferior good, the income effect makes her want to buy less meat and more potatoes. At the same time, because the potatoes have become more expensive relative to meat, the substitution effect makes the consumer want to buy more meat and fewer potatoes. If the income effect is much larger than the substitution effect, as it is in this example, the consumer responds to the higher price of potatoes by buying less meat and more potatoes.

Economists use the term **Giffen good** to describe a good that violates the law of demand. (The term is named for economist Robert Giffen, who first noted this possibility.) In this example, potatoes are a Giffen good. Giffen goods are inferior goods for which the income effect dominates the substitution effect. Therefore, they have demand curves that slope upward.

Giffen good

a good for which an increase in the price raises the quantity demanded

case study

The Search for Giffen Goods

Have any actual Giffen goods ever been observed? Some historians suggest that potatoes were a Giffen good during the Irish potato famine of the nineteenth century. Potatoes were such a large part of people's diet that when the price of potatoes rose, it had a large income effect. People responded to their reduced living standard by cutting back on the luxury of meat and buying more of the staple food of potatoes. Thus, it is argued that a higher price of potatoes actually raised the quantity of potatoes demanded.

A study by Robert Jensen and Nolan Miller has produced similar but more concrete evidence for the existence of Giffen goods. These two economists conducted a field experiment for five months in the Chinese province of Hunan. They gave randomly selected households vouchers that subsidized the purchase of rice, a staple in local diets, and used surveys to measure how consumption of rice responded to changes in the price. They found strong evidence that poor households exhibited Giffen behaviour. Lowering the price of rice with the subsidy voucher caused households to reduce their consumption of rice, and removing the subsidy had the opposite effect. Jensen and Miller wrote, "To the best of our knowledge, this is the first rigorous empirical evidence of Giffen behavior."

Thus, the theory of consumer choice allows demand curves to slope upward, and sometimes that strange phenomenon actually occurs. As a result, the law of demand we first saw in Chapter 4 is not completely reliable. It is safe to say, however, that Giffen goods are very rare. ∎

21-4b How Do Wages Affect Labour Supply?

So far we have used the theory of consumer choice to analyze how a person allocates income between two goods. We can use the same theory to analyze how a person allocates time. People spend some of their time enjoying leisure and some of it working so they can afford to buy consumption goods. The essence of the time-allocation problem is the tradeoff between leisure and consumption.

Consider the decision facing Carrie, a freelance software designer. Carrie is awake for 100 hours per week. She spends some of this time enjoying leisure—riding her bike, watching television, and studying economics. She spends the rest of this time at her computer developing software. For every hour she works developing software, she earns $50, which she spends on consumption goods—food, clothing, and music downloads. Her hourly wage of $50 reflects the tradeoff Carrie faces between leisure and consumption. For every hour of leisure she gives up, she works one more hour and gets $50 of consumption.

Figure 21.13 shows Carrie's budget constraint. If she spends all 100 hours enjoying leisure, she has no consumption. If she spends all 100 hours working, she earns a weekly consumption of $5000 but has no time for leisure. If she works a 40-hour week, she enjoys 60 hours of leisure and has weekly consumption of $2000.

Figure 21.13 uses indifference curves to represent Carrie's preferences for consumption and leisure. Here consumption and leisure are the two "goods" between which Carrie is choosing. Because Carrie always prefers more leisure and more consumption, she prefers points on higher indifference curves to points on lower ones. At a wage of $50 per hour, Carrie chooses a combination of consumption and leisure represented by the point labelled "Optimum." This is the point on the budget constraint that is on the highest possible indifference curve, which is curve I_2.

FIGURE 21.13

The Work–Leisure Decision

This figure shows Carrie's budget constraint for deciding how much to work, her indifference curves for consumption and leisure, and her optimum.

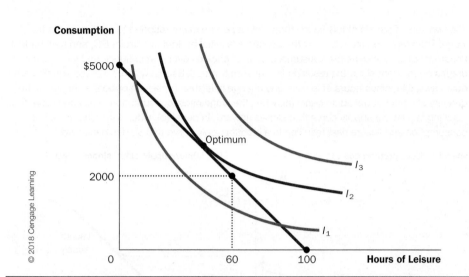

Now consider what happens when Carrie's wage increases from $50 to $60 per hour. Figure 21.14 shows two possible outcomes. In each case, the budget constraint, shown in the left-hand graph, shifts outward from BC_1 to BC_2. In the process, the budget constraint becomes steeper, reflecting the change in relative price: At the higher wage, Carrie earns more consumption for every hour of leisure that she gives up.

Carrie's preferences, as represented by her indifference curves, determine how her choice regarding consumption and leisure responds to the higher wage. In both panels, consumption rises. Yet the response of leisure to the change in the wage is different in the two cases. In panel (a), Carrie responds to the higher wage by enjoying less leisure. In panel (b), Carrie responds by enjoying more leisure.

Carrie's decision between leisure and consumption determines her supply of labour because the more leisure she enjoys, the less time she has left to work. In each panel, the right-hand graph in Figure 21.14 shows the labour supply curve implied by Carrie's decision. In panel (a), a higher wage induces Carrie to enjoy less leisure and work more, so the labour supply curve slopes upward. In panel (b), a higher wage induces Carrie to enjoy more leisure and work less, so the labour supply curve slopes "backward."

At first, the backward-sloping labour supply curve is puzzling. Why would a person respond to a higher wage by working less? The answer comes from considering the income and substitution effects of a higher wage.

Consider first the substitution effect. When Carrie's wage rises, leisure becomes more costly relative to consumption, and this encourages Carrie to substitute away from leisure and toward consumption. In other words, the substitution effect induces Carrie to work more in response to higher wages, which tends to make the labour supply curve slope upward.

Now consider the income effect. When Carrie's wage rises, she moves to a higher indifference curve. She is now better off than she was. As long as consumption and leisure are both normal goods, she tends to want to use this increase in well-being to enjoy both higher consumption and greater leisure. In other words, the income effect induces her to work less, which tends to make the labour supply curve slope backward.

FIGURE 21.14

An Increase in the Wage   The two sets of panels of this figure show how a person might respond to an increase in the wage. The graphs on the left show the consumer's initial budget constraint BC_1 and new budget constraint BC_2, as well as the consumer's optimal choices over consumption and leisure. The graphs on the right show the resulting labour supply curve. Because hours worked equal total hours available minus hours of leisure, any change in leisure implies an opposite change in the quantity of labour supplied. In panel (a), when the wage rises, consumption rises and leisure falls, resulting in a labour supply curve that slopes upward. In panel (b), when the wage rises, both consumption and leisure rise, resulting in a labour supply curve that slopes backward.

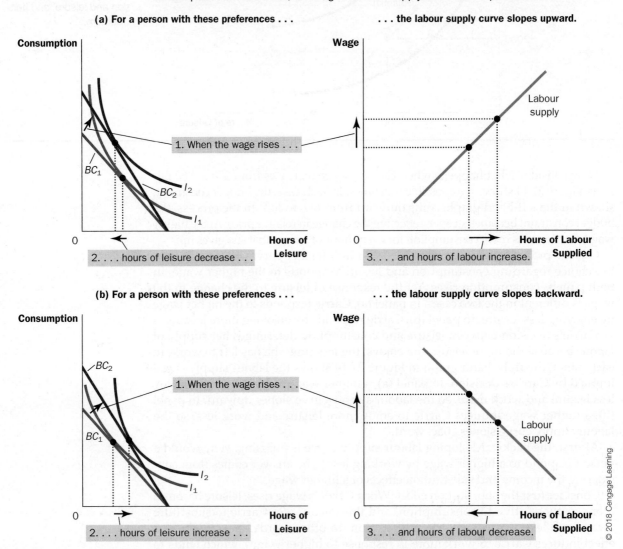

In the end, economic theory does not give a clear prediction about whether an increase in the wage induces Carrie to work more or less. If the substitution effect is greater than the income effect for Carrie, she works more. If the income effect is greater than the substitution effect, she works less. The labour supply curve, therefore, could be either upward or backward sloping.

| case study | **Income Effects on Labour Supply: Historical Trends, Lottery Winners, and the Carnegie Conjecture** |

"No more 9-to-5 for me."

The idea of a backward-sloping labour supply curve might at first seem like a mere theoretical curiosity, but in fact it is not. Evidence indicates that the labour supply curve, considered over long periods of time, does in fact slope backward. A hundred years ago many people worked six days a week. Today five-day workweeks are the norm. At the same time that the length of the workweek has been falling, the wage of the typical worker (adjusted for inflation) has been rising.

Here is how economists explain this historical pattern: Over time, advances in technology raise workers' productivity and, thereby, the demand for labour. This increase in labour demand raises equilibrium wages. As wages rise, so does the reward for working. Yet rather than responding to this increased incentive by working more, most workers choose to take part of their greater prosperity in the form of more leisure. In other words, the income effect of higher wages dominates the substitution effect.

Further evidence that the income effect on labour supply is strong comes from a very different kind of data: winners of lotteries. Winners of large prizes in a lottery see large increases in their incomes and, as a result, large outward shifts in their budget constraints. Because the winners' wages have not changed, however, the *slopes* of their budget constraints remain the same. There is, therefore, no substitution effect. By examining the behaviour of lottery winners, we can isolate the income effect on labour supply.

The results from studies of lottery winners are striking. Of those winners who win more than $50 000, almost 25 percent quit working within a year, and another 9 percent reduce the number of hours they work. Of those winners who win more than $1 million, almost 40 percent stop working. The income effect on labour supply of winning such a large prize is substantial.

Similar results were found in a 1993 study, published in the *Quarterly Journal of Economics*, of how receiving a bequest affects a person's labour supply. The study found that a single person who inherits more than $150 000 is four times as likely to stop working as a single person who inherits less than $25 000. This finding would not have surprised the nineteenth-century American industrialist Andrew Carnegie. Carnegie warned that "the parent who leaves his son enormous wealth generally deadens the talents and energies of the son, and tempts him to lead a less useful and less worthy life than he otherwise would." That is, Carnegie viewed the income effect on labour supply to be substantial and, from his paternalistic perspective, regrettable. During his life and at his death, Carnegie gave much of his vast fortune to charity. ∎

21-4c How Do Interest Rates Affect Household Saving?

An important decision that every person faces is how much income to consume today and how much to save for the future. We can use the theory of consumer choice to analyze how people make this decision and how the amount they save depends on the interest rate their savings will earn.

Consider the decision facing Saul, a worker planning for retirement. To keep things simple, let's divide Saul's life into two periods. In the first period, Saul is young and working. In the second period, he is old and retired. When young, Saul earns $100 000. He divides this income between current consumption and saving. When he is old, Saul will consume what he has saved, including the interest that his savings have earned.

Suppose the interest rate is 10 percent. Then for every dollar that Saul saves when young, he can consume $1.10 when old. We can view "consumption when

Backward-Sloping Labour Supply in Kiribati

In the island nation of Kiribati, when the coconut industry pays more, people spend less time working (picking coconuts) and more time enjoying leisure (fishing).

Reef Conservation Strategy Backfires

By Richard Harris

Tischenko Irina/Shutterstock.com

Aid organizations concerned about overfishing on tropical reefs often try to encourage fishermen out of their boats by offering them better-paying jobs on shore. But this strategy actually may make matters worse.

Take, for example, the story of Kiribati, an island nation in the central Pacific. Kiribati (pronounced KIR-a-bahs) has a simple economy. People either catch fish or they pick coconuts from their trees and produce coconut oil. Sheila Walsh, a postdoctoral researcher at Brown University, says most people do a bit of each.

The Kiribati government was concerned about overfishing. So it came up with a plan: It would subsidize the coconut oil industry.

"The thought was that by paying people more to do coconut agriculture, they would do less fishing," says Walsh. "And this would fulfill two goals: One, they would reduce overfishing; and two, people would be better off. They would have higher incomes."

Walsh wanted to know whether this plan was working, and the government invited her to study

the issue. So, as part of her graduate work at the Scripps Institution of Oceanography, she flew to Kiribati to interview fishermen.

"And it turned out that, actually, the result of paying people more to do coconut agriculture was to increase fishing," she says. In fact, fishing increased by a startling 33 percent. The reef fish population dropped by an estimated 17 percent, putting the whole ecosystem at risk.

"It was a bit of a surprise, and we were wondering: What's going on here?"

The answer was simplicity itself. Walsh's study concludes that people earned more money making coconut oil, which meant they could work less to support themselves. And they spent their new leisure time fishing.

"It hit us like a bumper sticker saying—a bad day fishing is better than a good day working. And that's sort of the story here," Walsh says.

It turns out she had stumbled into a universal truth about fishing: Fishermen aren't just in it for the money. Anthropologist Richard Pollnac of the University of Rhode Island says, just think of those snazzy sport-fishing excursions.

"People pay big money to go sports-fishing," he notes. There aren't very many occupations that people will actually pay money to do in their leisure time, he says.

So fishing as an occupation provides psychic benefits, as well as money. Pollnac argues that not just individuals but whole cultures get hooked on the thrill of being out on the water, and the gamble of coming back with either a boatload or empty-handed. ...

Walsh says she's trying to help the government figure out how to fix the problem of overfishing, which they'd accidentally made worse. Maybe, she says, the government can create new jobs out on the water by hiring the fishermen to patrol newly created nature preserves.

young" and "consumption when old" as the two goods that Saul must choose between. The interest rate determines the relative price of these two goods.

Figure 21.15 shows Saul's budget constraint. If he saves nothing, he consumes $100 000 when young and nothing when old. If he saves everything, he consumes nothing when young and $110 000 when old. The budget constraint shows these and all the intermediate possibilities.

Figure 21.15 uses indifference curves to represent Saul's preferences for consumption in the two periods. Because Saul prefers more consumption in both periods, he prefers points on higher indifference curves to points on lower ones. Given his preferences, Saul chooses the optimal combination of consumption in both periods of life, which is the point on the budget constraint that is on the highest possible indifference curve. At this optimum, Saul consumes $50 000 when young and $55 000 when old.

FIGURE 21.15

The Consumption–Saving Decision

This figure shows the budget constraint for a person deciding how much to consume in the two periods of his life, the indifference curves representing his preferences, and the optimum.

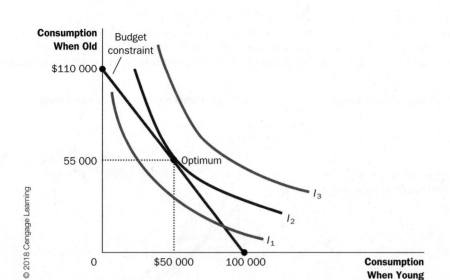

Now consider what happens when the interest rate increases from 10 percent to 20 percent. Figure 21.16 shows two possible outcomes. In both cases, the budget constraint shifts outward and becomes steeper. At the new higher interest rate, Saul gets more consumption when old for every dollar of consumption that he gives up when young.

The two panels show the results given different preferences for Saul. In both cases, consumption when old rises. Yet the response of consumption when young to the change in the interest rate is different in the two cases. In panel (a), Saul responds to the higher interest rate by consuming less when young. In panel (b), Saul responds by consuming more when young.

Saul's saving is his income when young minus the amount he consumes when young. In panel (a), an increase in the interest rates reduces consumption when young, so saving must rise. In panel (b), an increase in the interest rate induces Saul to consume more when young, so saving must fall.

The case shown in panel (b) might at first seem odd: Saul responds to an increase in the return to saving by saving less. Yet this behaviour is not as peculiar as it might seem. We can understand it by considering the income and substitution effects of a higher interest rate.

Consider first the substitution effect. When the interest rate rises, consumption when old becomes less costly relative to consumption when young. Therefore, the substitution effect induces Saul to consume more when old and less when young. In other words, the substitution effect induces Saul to save more.

Now consider the income effect. When the interest rate rises, Saul moves to a higher indifference curve. He is now better off than he was. As long as consumption in both periods consists of normal goods, he tends to want to use this increase in well-being to enjoy higher consumption in both periods. In other words, the income effect induces him to save less.

The result depends on both the income and substitution effects. If the substitution effect of a higher interest rate is greater than the income effect, Saul saves more. If the income effect is greater than the substitution effect, Saul saves less.

FIGURE 21.16

An Increase in the Interest Rate

In both panels, an increase in the interest rate shifts the budget constraint outward. In panel (a), consumption when young falls, and consumption when old rises. The result is an increase in saving when young. In panel (b), consumption in both periods rises. The result is a decrease in saving when young.

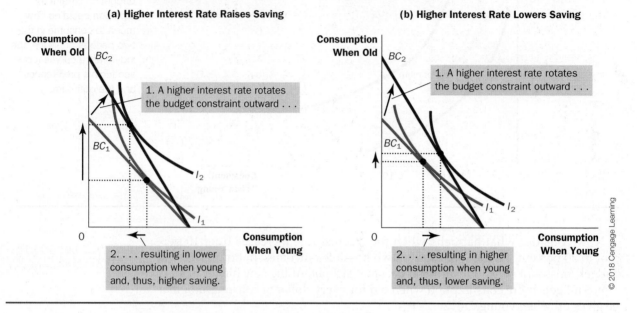

(a) Higher Interest Rate Raises Saving

Consumption When Old

BC_2

1. A higher interest rate rotates the budget constraint outward . . .

BC_1

I_2

I_1

0

Consumption When Young

2. . . . resulting in lower consumption when young and, thus, higher saving.

(b) Higher Interest Rate Lowers Saving

Consumption When Old

BC_2

1. A higher interest rate rotates the budget constraint outward . . .

BC_1

I_1 I_2

0

Consumption When Young

2. . . . resulting in higher consumption when young and, thus, lower saving.

© 2018 Cengage Learning

Thus, the theory of consumer choice says that an increase in the interest rate could either encourage or discourage saving.

This ambiguous result is interesting from the standpoint of economic theory, but it is disappointing from the standpoint of economic policy. It turns out that an important issue in tax policy hinges in part on how saving responds to interest rates. Some economists have advocated reducing the taxation of interest and other capital income. They argue that such a policy change would raise the after-tax interest rate that savers can earn and thereby encourage people to save more. Other economists have argued that because of offsetting income and substitution effects, such a tax change might not increase saving and could even reduce it. Unfortunately, research has not led to a consensus about how interest rates affect saving. As a result, there remains disagreement among economists about whether changes in tax policy aimed to encourage saving would, in fact, have the intended effect. ■

QUICK **Quiz**

Explain how an increase in the wage can potentially decrease the amount that a person wants to work.

21-5 Conclusion: Do People Really Think This Way?

The theory of consumer choice describes how people make decisions. As we have seen, it has broad applicability. It can explain how a person chooses between pizza and Pepsi, work and leisure, consumption and saving, and on and on.

At this point, however, you might be tempted to treat the theory of consumer choice with some skepticism. After all, you are a consumer. You decide what to buy every time you walk into a store. And you know that you do not decide by writing down budget constraints and indifference curves. Doesn't this knowledge about your own decision making provide evidence against the theory?

The answer is no. The theory of consumer choice does not try to present a literal account of how people make decisions. It is a model. And, as we first discussed in Chapter 2, models are not intended to be completely realistic.

The best way to view the theory of consumer choice is as a metaphor for how consumers make decisions. No consumer (except an occasional economist) goes through the explicit optimization envisioned in the theory. Yet consumers are aware that their choices are constrained by their financial resources. And, given those constraints, they do the best they can to achieve the highest level of satisfaction. The theory of consumer choice tries to describe this implicit, psychological process in a way that permits explicit, economic analysis.

Just as the proof of the pudding is in the eating, the test of a theory is in its applications. In the last section of this chapter we applied the theory of consumer choice to three practical issues about the economy. If you take more advanced courses in economics, you will see that this theory provides the framework for much additional analysis.

summary

- A consumer's budget constraint shows the possible combinations of different goods he can buy given his income and the prices of the goods. The slope of the budget constraint equals the relative price of the goods.

- The consumer's indifference curves represent his preferences. An indifference curve shows the various bundles of goods that make the consumer equally happy. Points on higher indifference curves are preferred to points on lower indifference curves. The slope of an indifference curve at any point is the consumer's marginal rate of substitution—the rate at which the consumer is willing to trade one good for the other.

- The consumer optimizes by choosing the point on his budget constraint that lies on the highest indifference curve. At this point, the slope of the indifference curve (the marginal rate of substitution between the goods) equals the slope of the budget constraint (the relative price of the goods) and the consumer's valuation of the two goods (measured by the marginal rate of substitution) equals the market's valuation (measured by the relative price).

- When the price of a good falls, the impact on the consumer's choices can be broken down into an income effect and a substitution effect. The income effect is the change in consumption that arises because a lower price makes the consumer better off. The substitution effect is the change in consumption that arises because a price change encourages greater consumption of the good that has become relatively cheaper. The income effect is reflected in the movement from a lower to a higher indifference curve, whereas the substitution effect is reflected by a movement along an indifference curve to a point with a different slope.

- The theory of consumer choice can be applied in many situations. It can explain why demand curves can potentially slope upward, why higher wages could either increase or decrease the quantity of labour supplied, and why higher interest rates could either increase or decrease saving.

KEY concepts

budget constraint, *p. 462*
indifference curve, *p. 463*
marginal rate of substitution, *p. 463*
perfect substitutes, *p. 466*

perfect complements, *p. 466*
normal good, *p. 469*
inferior good, *p. 470*
income effect, *p. 472*

substitution effect, *p. 472*
Giffen good, *p. 475*

QUESTIONS FOR **review**

1. A consumer has income of $3000. Wine costs $3 per glass, and cheese costs $6 per kilogram. Draw the consumer's budget constraint. What is the slope of this budget constraint?

2. Draw a consumer's indifference curves for wine and cheese. Describe and explain four properties of these indifference curves.

3. Pick a point on an indifference curve for wine and cheese and show the marginal rate of substitution. What does the marginal rate of substitution tell us?

4. Show a consumer's budget constraint and indifference curves for wine and cheese. Show the optimal consumption choice. If the price of wine is $3 per glass and the price of cheese is $6 per kilogram, what is the marginal rate of substitution at this optimum?

5. A person who consumes wine and cheese gets a raise, so his income increases from $3000 to $4000. Show what happens if both wine and cheese are normal goods. Now show what happens if cheese is an inferior good.

6. The price of cheese rises from $6 to $10 per kilogram, while the price of wine remains $3 per glass. For a consumer with a constant income of $3000, show what happens to consumption of wine and cheese. Decompose the change into income and substitution effects.

7. Can an increase in the price of cheese possibly induce a consumer to buy more cheese? Explain.

QUICK CHECK **multiple choice**

1. Emilio buys pizza for $10 and soda for $2. He has income of $100. His budget constraint will experience a parallel outward shift if which of the following events occur?
   a. The price of pizza falls to $5, the price of soda falls to $1, and his income falls to $50.
   b. The price of pizza rises to $20, the price of soda rises to $4, and his income remains the same.
   c. The price of pizza falls to $8, the price of soda falls to $1, and his income rises to $120.
   d. The price of pizza rises to $20, the price of soda rises to $4, and his income rises to $400.

2. At any point on an indifference curve, the slope of the curve measures the consumer's level of which of the following?
   a. income
   b. willingness to trade one good for the other
   c. perception of the two goods as substitutes or complements
   d. elasticity of demand

3. Matthew and Susan are both optimizing consumers in the markets for shirts and hats, where they pay $100 for a shirt and $50 for a hat. Matthew buys 4 shirts and 16 hats, while Susan buys 6 shirts and 12 hats. From this information, we can infer that Matthew's marginal rate of substitution is ___ hats per shirt, while Susan's is ___.
   a. 2, 1
   b. 2, 2
   c. 4, 1
   d. 4, 2

4. Charlie buys only milk and cereal. Milk is a normal good, while cereal is an inferior good. What does Charlie do when the price of milk rises?
   a. buys less of both goods
   b. buys more milk and less cereal
   c. buys less milk and more cereal
   d. buys less milk, but the impact on cereal is ambiguous

5. If the price of pasta increases and a consumer buys more pasta, what can we infer?
   a. Pasta is a normal good, and the income effect is greater than the substitution effect.
   b. Pasta is a normal good, and the substitution effect is greater than the income effect.
   c. Pasta is an inferior good, and the income effect is greater than the substitution effect.
   d. Pasta is an inferior good, and the substitution effect is greater than the income effect.

6. Under which of the following conditions does the labour supply curve slope upward?
   a. when leisure is a normal good
   b. when consumption is a normal good
   c. when the income effect on leisure is greater than the substitution effect
   d. when the substitution effect on leisure is greater than the income effect

PROBLEMS AND **applications**

1. Jennifer divides her income between coffee and croissants (both of which are normal goods). An early frost in Brazil causes a large increase in the price of coffee in Canada.
   a. Show the effect of the frost on Jennifer's budget constraint.
   b. Show the effect of the frost on Jennifer's optimal consumption bundle, assuming that the substitution effect outweighs the income effect for croissants.
   c. Show the effect of the frost on Jennifer's optimal consumption bundle, assuming that the income effect outweighs the substitution effect for croissants.

2. Compare the following two pairs of goods:
   • Coke and Pepsi
   • Skis and ski bindings
   a. In which case are the two goods complements? In which case are they substitutes?
   b. In which case do you expect the indifference curves to be fairly straight? In which case do you expect the indifference curves to be very bowed?
   c. In which case will the consumer respond more to a change in the relative price of the two goods?

3. Mario consumes only cheese and crackers.
   a. Could cheese and crackers both be inferior goods for Mario? Explain.
   b. Suppose that cheese is a normal good for Mario while crackers are an inferior good. If the price of cheese falls, what happens to Mario's consumption of crackers? What happens to his consumption of cheese? Explain.

4. Jim buys only milk and cookies.
   a. In 2019, Jim earns $100, milk costs $2 per litre, and cookies cost $4 per dozen. Draw Jim's budget constraint.
   b. Now suppose that all prices increase by 10 percent in 2020 and that Jim's salary increases by 10 percent as well. Draw Jim's new budget constraint. How would Jim's optimal combination of milk and cookies in 2020 compare to his optimal combination in 2019?

5. Consider your decision about how many hours to work.
   a. Draw your budget constraint assuming that you pay no taxes on your income. On the same diagram, draw another budget constraint assuming that you pay a 15 percent income tax.
   b. Show how the tax might lead to more hours of work, fewer hours, or the same number of hours. Explain.

6. Draw the indifference curve for someone deciding how much to work. Suppose the wage increases. Is it possible that the person's consumption would fall? Is this plausible? Discuss. (*Hint:* Think about income and substitution effects.)

7. Anya is awake for 100 hours per week. Using one diagram, show Anya's budget constraints if she earns $12 per hour, $16 per hour, and $20 per hour. Now draw indifference curves such that Anya's labour-supply curve is upward-sloping when the wage is between $12 and $16 per hour and backward-sloping when the wage is between $16 and $20 per hour.

8. The welfare system provides income to some needy families. Typically, the maximum payment goes to families that earn no income; then, as families begin to earn income, the welfare payment declines gradually and eventually disappears. Let's consider the possible effects of this program on a family's labour supply.
   a. Draw a budget constraint for a family assuming that the welfare system did not exist. On the same diagram, draw a budget constraint that reflects the existence of the welfare system.
   b. Adding indifference curves to your diagram, show how the welfare system could reduce the number of hours worked by the family. Explain, with reference to both the income and substitution effects.
   c. Using your diagram from part (b), show the effect of the welfare system on the well-being of the family.

9. Economist George Stigler once wrote that, according to consumer theory, "if consumers do not buy less of a commodity when their incomes rise, they will surely buy less when the price of the commodity rises." Explain this statement.

10. A college student has two options for meals: eating at the dining hall for $6 per meal, or eating a Cup O' Soup for $1.50 per meal. His weekly food budget is $60.
    a. Draw the budget constraint showing the tradeoff between dining hall meals and Cups O' Soup. Assuming that he spends equal amounts on both goods, draw an indifference curve showing the optimum choice. Label the optimum as point A.
    b. Suppose the price of a Cup O' Soup now rises to $2. Using your diagram from part (a), show the consequences of this change in price. Assume that our student now spends only 30 percent of his income on dining hall meals. Label the new optimum as point B.
    c. What happened to the quantity of Cups O' Soup consumed as a result of this price change? What does this result say about the income and substitution effects? Explain.
    d. Use points A and B to draw a demand curve for Cup O' Soup. What is this type of good called?

11. Consider a couple's decision about how many children to have. Assume that over a lifetime a couple has 200 000 hours of time to either work or raise children. The wage is $10 per hour. Raising a child takes 20 000 hours of time.

a. Draw the budget constraint showing the tradeoff between lifetime consumption and number of children. (Ignore the fact that children come only in whole numbers!) Show indifference curves and an optimum choice.

b. Suppose the wage increases to $12 per hour. Show how the budget constraint shifts. Using income and substitution effects, discuss the impact of the change on number of children and lifetime consumption.

c. We observe that, as societies get richer and wages rise, people typically have fewer children. Is this fact consistent with this model? Explain.

12. Five consumers have the following marginal utility of apples and pears:

	Marginal Utility of Apples	Marginal Utility of Pears
Jerry	12	6
George	6	6
Elaine	6	3
Kramer	3	6
Newman	12	3

The price of an apple is $2, and the price of a pear is $1. Which, if any, of these consumers are optimizing over their choice of fruit? For those who are not, how should they change their spending?

13. You consume only soda and pizza. One day, the price of soda goes up, the price of pizza goes down, and you are just as happy as you were before the price changes.

a. Illustrate this situation on a graph.

b. How does your consumption of the two goods change? How does your response depend on income and substitution effects?

c. Can you afford the bundle of soda and pizza you consumed before the price changes?

14. State whether each of the following statements is true or false. Explain your answers.

a. "All Giffen goods are inferior goods."

b. "All inferior goods are Giffen goods."

15. Daniel is a diligent student who loves getting As, but he also loves watching movies. Daniel is awake for 100 hours each week, and studying and watching movies are his only two activities. Daniel must study for 20 hours per week for each A he earns. Each movie is 2 hours long.

a. Draw Daniel's budget constraint that shows the tradeoff between the number of As he can receive and the number of movies he can watch. Assuming that he is happiest when he earns three As, draw an indifference curve that marks his optimal choice of studying and movie watching. How many movies does he watch each week? With a new semester beginning, Daniel decides to get his difficult requirements out of the way. Each class now requires him to study for 25 hours per week to get an A.

b. Draw the new budget constraint on your graph. Show one possible outcome on your diagram. How will the relative strengths of the income and substitution effects determine whether Daniel makes better or worse grades and whether he watches more or fewer movies?

CHAPTER

22

LEARNING
objectives

Frontiers of Microeconomics

In this chapter, you will ...

1 Learn how to examine problems caused by asymmetric information

2 Examine the market solutions to asymmetric information

3 Consider why democratic voting systems may not represent the preferences of society

4 Realize why people may not always behave as rational maximizers

Economics is a study of the choices that people make and the resulting interactions they have with one another. As the preceding chapters demonstrate, the field has many facets. Yet it would be a mistake to think that all the facets we have seen make up a finished jewel, perfect and unchanging. Like all scientists, economists are always looking for new areas to study and new phenomena to explain. This final chapter on microeconomics offers an assortment of three topics at the discipline's frontier to show how economists are trying to expand their understanding of human behaviour and society.

The first topic is the economics of *asymmetric information*. In many different situations, some people are better informed than others, and the imbalance in information affects the choices they make and how they deal with one another. Thinking about this asymmetry can shed light on many aspects of the world, from the market for used cars to the custom of gift-giving.

The second topic we examine in this chapter is *political economy*. Throughout this book we have seen many examples in which markets fail and government policy can potentially improve matters. But "potentially" is a necessary qualifier: Whether this potential is realized depends on how well our political institutions work. The field of political economy applies the tools of economics to understand the functioning of government.

The third topic in this chapter is *behavioural economics*. This field brings some of the insights from psychology into the study of economic issues. It offers a view of human behaviour that is more subtle and complex than that found in conventional economic theory, a view that may be more realistic.

This chapter covers a lot of ground. To do so, it offers not a full helping of these three topics but, instead, a taste of each. One goal of this chapter is to show a few of the directions economists are heading in their effort to expand knowledge of how the economy works. Another goal is to whet your appetite for more courses in economics.

22-1 Asymmetric Information

"I know something you don't know." This statement is a common taunt among children, but it also conveys a deep truth about how people sometimes interact with one another. Many times in life, one person knows more about what is going on than another. A difference in access to knowledge that is relevant to an interaction is called an *information asymmetry*.

moral hazard
the tendency of a person who is imperfectly monitored to engage in dishonest or otherwise undesirable behaviour

Examples abound. A worker knows more than his employer about how much effort he puts into his job. A seller of a used car knows more than the buyer about the car's condition. The first is an example of a *hidden action*, whereas the second is an example of a *hidden characteristic*. In each case, the party in the dark (the employer, the car buyer) would like to know the relevant information, but the informed party (the worker, the car seller) may have an incentive to conceal it.

agent
a person who is performing an act for another person, called the *principal*

Because asymmetric information is so prevalent, economists have devoted much effort in recent decades to studying its effects. Let's discuss some of the insights that this study has revealed.

principal
a person for whom another person, called the *agent*, is performing some act

22-1a Hidden Actions: Principals, Agents, and Moral Hazard

Moral hazard is a problem that arises when one person, called the **agent**, is performing some task on behalf of another person, called the **principal**. If the principal cannot perfectly monitor the agent's behaviour, the agent tends to undertake less effort than the principal considers desirable. The phrase *moral hazard* refers to the risk, or "hazard," of inappropriate or otherwise "immoral" behaviour by the agent. In such a situation, the principal tries various ways to encourage the agent to act more responsibly.

The employment relationship is the classic example. The employer is the principal, and the worker is the agent. The moral-hazard problem is the temptation of imperfectly monitored workers to shirk their responsibilities. Employers can respond to this problem in various ways:

- *Better monitoring:* Employers may plant hidden video cameras to record workers' behaviour. The aim is to catch irresponsible actions that might occur when supervisors are absent.
- *High wages:* According to *efficiency-wage theories* (discussed in Chapter 19), some employers may choose to pay their workers a wage above the level that balances supply and demand in the labour market. A worker who earns an above-equilibrium wage is less likely to shirk, because if she is caught and fired, she might not be able to find another high-paying job.

FYI Corporate Management

Much production in the modern economy takes place within corporations. Like other firms, corporations buy inputs in markets for the factors of production and sell their output in markets for goods and services. Also, like other firms, they are guided in their decisions by the objective of profit maximization. But a large corporation has to deal with some issues that do not arise in, say, a small family-owned business.

What is distinctive about a corporation? From a legal standpoint, a corporation is an organization that is granted a charter recognizing it as a separate legal entity, with its own rights and responsibilities, distinct from those of its owners and employees. From an economic standpoint, the most important feature of the corporate form of organization is the separation of ownership and control. One group of people, called the *shareholders,* own the corporation and share in its profits. Another group of people, called the *managers,* are employed by the corporation to make decisions about how to deploy the corporation's resources.

The separation of ownership and control creates a principal–agent problem. In this case, the shareholders are the principals, and the managers are the agents. The chief executive officer and other managers, who are in the best position to know the available business opportunities, are charged with the task of maximizing profit for the shareholders. But ensuring that they carry out this task is not always easy. The managers may have goals of their own, such as taking life easy, having a plush office and having a private jet, throwing lavish parties, or presiding over a large business empire. The managers' goals may not always coincide with the goal of profit maximization.

iStock/Thinkstock

The corporation's board of directors is responsible for hiring and firing top management. The board monitors the managers' performance, and it designs their compensation packages. These packages often include incentives aimed at aligning the interest of shareholders with the interest of management. Managers might be given bonuses based on performance or options to buy the company's stock, which are more valuable if the company performs well.

Note, however, that the directors are themselves agents of the shareholders. The existence of a board overseeing management only shifts the principal–agent problem. The issue then becomes how to ensure that the board of directors fulfills its own legal obligation of acting in the best interest of the shareholders. If the directors become too friendly with management, they may not provide the required oversight.

The corporation principal–agent problem has been in the news in recent years. The top managers of several prominent companies, such as Enron, Tyco, and WorldCom, were found to be engaging in activities that enriched themselves at the expense of their shareholders. In these cases, the actions were so extreme that they were criminal, and the corporate managers were not just fired but also sent to prison. In some cases, shareholders sued directors for failing to monitor management sufficiently.

Fortunately, criminal activity by corporate managers is rare. But in some ways, it is only the tip of the iceberg. Whenever ownership and control are separated, as they are in most large corporations, there is an inevitable tension between the interests of shareholders and the interests of management.

- *Delayed payment:* Firms can delay part of a worker's compensation, so if the worker is caught shirking and is fired, he suffers a larger penalty. One example of delayed compensation is the year-end bonus. Similarly, a firm may choose to pay its workers more later in their lives. Thus, the wage increases that workers get as they age may reflect not just the benefits of experience but also a response to moral hazard.

Employers can use any combination of these various mechanisms to reduce the problem of moral hazard.

There are many other examples of moral hazard beyond the workplace. A homeowner with fire insurance will likely buy too few fire extinguishers because the homeowner bears the cost of the extinguisher while the insurance company receives much of the benefit. A family may live near a river with a high risk of flooding because the family enjoys the scenic views, while the government bears the cost of disaster relief after a flood. Many regulations are aimed at addressing the problem: An insurance company may require homeowners to buy fire extinguishers, and the government may prohibit building homes on land with high risk of flooding. But the insurance company does not have perfect information about how cautious homeowners are, and the government does not have perfect information about the risk that families undertake when choosing where to live. As a result, the problem of moral hazard persists.

22-1b Hidden Characteristics: Adverse Selection and the Lemons Problem

adverse selection

the tendency for the mix of unobserved attributes to become undesirable from the standpoint of an uninformed party

Adverse selection is a problem that arises in markets in which the seller knows more about the attributes of the good being sold than the buyer does. In such a situation, the buyer runs the risk of being sold a good of low quality. That is, the "selection" of goods being sold may be "adverse" from the standpoint of the uninformed buyer.

The classic example of adverse selection is the market for used cars. Sellers of used cars know their vehicles' defects while buyers often do not. Because owners of the worst cars are more likely to sell them than are the owners of the best cars, buyers are worried about getting a "lemon." As a result, many people avoid buying vehicles in the used-car market. This lemons problem can explain why a used car only a few weeks old sells for thousands of dollars less than a new car of the same type. A buyer of the used car might surmise that the seller is getting rid of the car quickly because the seller knows something about it that the buyer does not.

A second example of adverse selection occurs in the labour market. According to another efficiency-wage theory, workers vary in their abilities, and they know their own abilities better than do the firms that hire them. When a firm cuts the wage it pays, the more talented workers are more likely to quit, knowing they are better able to find employment elsewhere. Conversely, a firm may choose to pay an above-equilibrium wage to attract a better mix of workers.

A third example of adverse selection occurs in markets for insurance. For example, buyers of life insurance know more about their own health problems than do insurance companies. Because people with greater hidden health problems are more likely to buy life insurance than are other people, the price of life insurance reflects the costs of a sicker-than-average person. As a result, people in average health may observe the high price of insurance and decide not to buy it.

When markets suffer from adverse selection, the invisible hand does not necessarily work its magic. In the used-car market, owners of good cars may choose to keep them rather than sell them at the low price that skeptical buyers are willing to pay. In the labour market, wages may be stuck above the level that balances supply and demand, resulting in unemployment. In insurance markets, buyers with low risk may choose to remain uninsured because the policies they are offered fail to reflect their true characteristics. Advocates of government-provided insurance sometimes point to the problem of adverse selection as one reason not to trust the private market to provide the right amount of insurance on its own.

22-1c Signalling to Convey Private Information

Although asymmetric information is sometimes a motivation for public policy, it also motivates some individual behaviour that otherwise might be hard to explain. Markets respond to problems of asymmetric information in many ways. One of them is **signalling**, which refers to actions taken by an informed party for the sole purpose of credibly revealing his private information.

signalling
an action taken by an informed party to reveal private information to an uninformed party

We have seen examples of signalling in previous chapters. As we saw in Chapter 16, firms may spend money on advertising to signal to potential customers that they have high-quality products. As we saw in Chapter 19, students may earn postsecondary and postgraduate degrees to signal to potential employers that they are high-ability individuals. Recall that the signalling theory of education contrasts with the human-capital theory, which asserts that education increases a person's productivity, rather than merely conveying information about innate talent. These two examples of signalling (advertising, education) may seem very different, but below the surface they are much the same: In both cases, the informed party (the firm, the student) uses the signal to convince the uninformed party (the customer, the employer) that the informed party is offering something of high quality.

What does it take for an action to be an effective signal? Obviously, it must be costly. If a signal were free, everyone would use it, and it would convey no information. For the same reason, there is another requirement: The signal must be less costly, or more beneficial, to the person with the higher-quality product. Otherwise, everyone would have the same incentive to use the signal, and the signal would reveal nothing.

Consider again our two examples. In the advertising case, a firm with a good product reaps a larger benefit from advertising because customers who try the product once are more likely to become repeat customers. Thus, it is rational for the firm with the good product to pay for the cost of the signal (advertising), and it is rational for the customer to use the signal as a piece of information about the product's quality. In the education case, a talented person can get through school more easily than a less talented one. Thus, it is rational for the talented person to pay for the cost of the signal (education), and it is rational for the employer to use the signal as a piece of information about the person's talent.

The world is replete with instances of signalling. Magazine ads sometimes include the phrase "as seen on TV." Why does a firm selling a product in a magazine choose to stress this fact? One possibility is that the firm is trying to convey its willingness to pay for an expensive signal (a spot on television) in the hope that you will infer that its product is of high quality. For the same reason, graduates of elite schools are always sure to put that fact on their résumés.

Thinkstock

"Now we'll see how much he loves me."

screening

an action taken by an uninformed party to induce an informed party to reveal information

case study

Gifts as Signals

A man is debating what to give his girlfriend for her birthday. "I know," he says to himself, "I'll give her cash. After all, I don't know her tastes as well as she does, and with cash, she can buy anything she wants." But when he hands her the money, she is offended. Convinced he doesn't really love her, she breaks off the relationship.

What's the economics behind this story?

In some ways, gift-giving is a strange custom. As the man in our story suggests, people typically know their own preferences better than others do, so we might expect everyone to prefer cash to in-kind transfers. If your employer substituted merchandise of his choosing for your paycheque, you would likely object to the means of payment. But your reaction is very different when someone who (you hope) loves you does the same thing.

One interpretation of gift-giving is that it reflects asymmetric information and signalling. The man in our story has private information that the girlfriend would like to know: Does he really love her? Choosing a good gift for her is a signal of his love. Certainly, the act of picking out a gift, rather than giving cash, has the right characteristics to be a signal. It is costly (it takes time), and its cost depends on private information (how much he loves her). If he really loves her, choosing a good gift is easy because he is thinking about her all the time. If he doesn't love her, finding the right gift is more difficult. Thus, giving a gift that suits the girlfriend is one way for him to convey the private information of his love for her. Giving cash shows that he isn't even bothering to try.

The signalling theory of gift-giving is consistent with another observation: People care most about the custom when the strength of affection is most in question. Thus, giving cash to a girlfriend or boyfriend is usually a bad move. But when students receive a cheque from their parents, they are less often offended. The parents' love is less likely to be in doubt, so the recipient probably won't interpret the cash gift as a signal of lack of affection. ■

22-1d Screening to Uncover Private Information

When an informed party takes actions to reveal private information, the phenomenon is called *signalling*. When an uninformed party takes actions to induce the informed party to reveal private information, the phenomenon is called **screening**.

Some screening is common sense. A person buying a used car may ask that it be checked by an auto mechanic before the sale. A seller who refuses this request reveals his private information that the car is a lemon. The buyer may decide to offer a lower price or to look for another car.

Other examples of screening are more subtle. For example, consider a firm that sells car insurance. The firm would like to charge a low premium to safe drivers and a high premium to risky drivers. But how can it tell them apart? Drivers know whether they are safe or risky, but the risky ones won't admit to it. A driver's history is one piece of information (which insurance companies in fact use), but because of the intrinsic randomness of car accidents, history is an imperfect indicator of future risks.

The insurance company might be able to sort out the two kinds of drivers by offering different insurance policies that would induce the drivers to separate themselves. One policy would have a high premium and cover the full cost of any accidents that occur. Another policy would have low premiums but would have, say, a $1000 deductible. (That is, the driver would be responsible for the first $1000 of damage, and the insurance company would cover the remaining risk.) Notice that the deductible is more of a burden for risky drivers because they are more likely to have an accident. Thus, with a large enough deductible, the low-premium policy with a deductible would attract the safe drivers, while the high-premium policy without a deductible would attract the risky drivers. Faced with these two policies, the two kinds of drivers would reveal their private information by choosing different insurance policies.

22-1e Asymmetric Information and Public Policy

We have examined two kinds of asymmetric information—moral hazard and adverse selection. And we have seen how individuals may respond to the problem with signalling or screening. Now let's consider what the study of asymmetric information suggests about the proper scope of public policy.

The tension between market success and market failure is central in microeconomics. We learned in Chapter 7 that the equilibrium of supply and demand is efficient in the sense that it maximizes the total surplus that society can obtain in a market. Adam Smith's invisible hand seemed to reign supreme. This conclusion was then tempered with the study of externalities (Chapter 10), public goods (Chapter 11), imperfect competition (Chapters 15 through 17), and income distribution and poverty (Chapter 20). In those chapters, we saw that government can sometimes improve market outcomes.

The study of asymmetric information gives us a new reason to be wary of markets. When some people know more than others, the market may fail to put resources to their best use. People with high-quality used cars may have trouble selling them because buyers will be afraid of getting a lemon. People with few health problems may have trouble getting low-cost health insurance because insurance companies lump them together with those who have significant (but hidden) health problems.

Asymmetric information may call for government action in some cases, but three facts complicate the issue. First, as we have seen, the private market can sometimes deal with information asymmetries on its own, using a combination of signalling and screening. Second, the government rarely has more information than the private parties. Even if the market's allocation of resources is not first-best, it may be second-best. That is, when there are information asymmetries, policymakers may find it hard to improve upon the market's admittedly imperfect outcome. Third, the government is itself an imperfect institution—a topic we take up in the next section.

QUICK Quiz *A person who buys a life insurance policy pays a certain amount per year and receives for his family a much larger payment in the event of his death. Would you expect buyers of life insurance to have higher or lower death rates than the average person? How might this be an example of moral hazard? Of adverse selection? How might a life insurance company deal with these problems?*

22-2 Political Economy

As we have seen, markets left on their own do not always reach a desirable allocation of resources. When we judge the market's outcome to be either inefficient or inequitable, there may be a role for the government to step in and improve the situation. Yet before we embrace an activist government, we need to consider one more fact: The government is also an imperfect institution. The field of *political economy* (sometimes called the field of *public choice*) applies the methods of economics to study how government works.

22-2a   The Condorcet Voting Paradox

Most advanced societies rely on democratic principles to set government policy. When a city is deciding between two locations to build a new park, for example, we have a simple way to choose: The majority gets its way. Yet, for most policy issues, the number of possible outcomes far exceeds two. A new park could be placed in many possible locations. In this case, as the eighteenth-century French political theorist Marquis de Condorcet famously noted, democracy might run into some problems trying to choose the best outcome.

For example, suppose there are three possible outcomes, labelled A, B, and C, and there are three voter types with the preferences shown in Table 22.1. The mayor of our town wants to aggregate these individual preferences into preferences for society as a whole. How should she do it?

At first, she might try some pairwise votes. If she asks voters to choose first between B and C, voter types 1 and 2 will vote for B, giving B the majority. If she then asks voters to choose between A and B, voter types 1 and 3 will vote for A, giving A the majority. Observing that A beats B, and B beats C, the mayor might conclude that A is the voters' clear choice.

But wait: Suppose the mayor then asks voters to choose between A and C. In this case, voter types 2 and 3 vote for C, giving C the majority. That is, under pairwise majority voting, A beats B, B beats C, and C beats A. Normally, we expect preferences to exhibit a property called *transitivity*: If A is preferred to B, and B is preferred to C, then we would expect A to be preferred to C. The **Condorcet paradox** is that democratic outcomes do not always obey this property. Pairwise voting might produce transitive preferences for a society in some cases, but as our example in the table shows, it cannot be counted on to do so.

Condorcet paradox
the failure of majority rule to produce transitive preferences for society

One implication of the Condorcet paradox is that the order in which things are voted on can affect the result. If the mayor suggests choosing first between A and B and then comparing the winner to C, the town ends up choosing C. But if the voters choose first between B and C and then compare the winner to A, the town ends up with A. And if the voters choose first between A and C and then compare the winner to B, the town ends up with B.

The Condorcet paradox teaches two lessons. The narrow lesson is that when there are more than two options, setting the agenda (that is, deciding the order in which items are voted) can have a powerful impact on the outcome of a

TABLE 22.1

The Condorcet Paradox

If voters have these preferences over outcomes A, B, and C, then in pairwise majority voting A beats B, B beats C, and C beats A.

	Voter Type		
	Type 1	**Type 2**	**Type 3**
Percentage of electorate	35	45	20
First choice	A	B	C
Second choice	B	C	A
Third choice	C	A	B

democratic election. The broad lesson is that majority voting by itself does not tell us what outcome a society really wants.

22-2b Arrow's Impossibility Theorem

Since political theorists first noticed Condorcet's paradox, they have spent much energy studying voting systems and proposing new ones. For example, as an alternative to pairwise majority voting, the mayor of our town could ask each voter to rank the possible outcomes. For each voter, we could give 1 point for last place, 2 points for second to last, 3 points for third to last, and so on. The outcome that receives the most total points wins. With the preferences in Table 22.1, outcome B is the winner. (You can do the arithmetic yourself.) This voting method is called a *Borda count,* for the eighteenth-century French mathematician and political scientist who devised it. It is often used in polls that rank sports teams.

Is there a perfect voting system? Economist Kenneth Arrow took up this question in his 1951 book *Social Choice and Individual Values.* Arrow started by defining what a perfect voting system would be. He assumes that individuals in society have preferences over the various possible outcomes: A, B, C, and so on. He then assumes that society wants a voting scheme to choose among these outcomes that satisfies several properties:

- *Unanimity:* If everyone prefers A to B, then A should beat B.
- *Transitivity:* If A beats B, and B beats C, then A should beat C.
- *Independence of irrelevant alternatives:* The ranking between any two outcomes A and B should not depend on whether some third outcome C is also available.
- *No dictators:* No person always gets his or her way, regardless of everyone else's preferences.

These all seem like desirable properties for a voting system to have. Yet Arrow proved, mathematically and incontrovertibly, that *no voting system can satisfy all of these properties.* This amazing result is called **Arrow's impossibility theorem**.

The mathematics needed to prove Arrow's theorem is beyond the scope of this book, but we can get some sense of why the theorem is true from a couple of examples. We have already seen the problem with the method of majority rule. The Condorcet paradox shows that majority rule fails to produce a ranking of outcomes that always satisfies transitivity.

As another example, the Borda count fails to satisfy the independence of irrelevant alternatives. Recall that, using the preferences in Table 22.1, outcome B wins with a Borda count. But suppose that suddenly C disappears as an alternative. If the Borda count method is applied only to outcomes A and B, then A wins. (Once again, you can do the arithmetic on your own.) Thus, eliminating alternative C changes the ranking between A and B. The reason for this change is that the result of the Borda count depends on the number of points that A and B receive, and the number of points depends on whether the irrelevant alternative, C, is also available.

Arrow's impossibility theorem is a deep and disturbing result. It doesn't say that we should abandon democracy as a form of government. But it does say that, no matter what voting scheme society adopts for aggregating the preferences of its members, in some way it will be flawed as a mechanism for social choice.

22-2c The Median Voter Is King

Despite Arrow's theorem, voting is how most societies choose their leaders and public policies, often by majority rule. The next step in studying government is

Arrow's impossibility theorem
a mathematical result showing that, under certain assumed conditions, there is no scheme for aggregating individual preferences into a valid set of social preferences

FIGURE 22.1

The Median Voter Theorem: An Example

This bar chart shows how 100 voters' most-preferred budget is distributed over five options, ranging from zero to $20 billion. If society makes its choice by majority rule, the median voter (who here prefers $10 billion) determines the outcome.

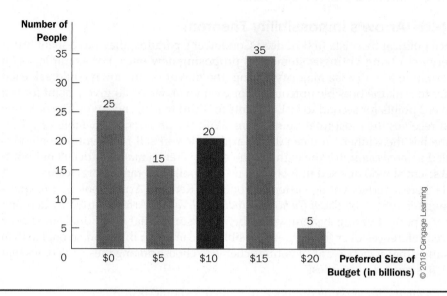

Number of People

© 2018 Cengage Learning

Preferred Size of Budget (in billions)

median voter theorem

a mathematical result showing that if voters are choosing a point along a line and each voter wants the point closest to his most preferred point, then majority rule will pick the most preferred point of the median voter

to examine how governments run by majority rule work. That is, in a democratic society, who determines what policy is chosen? In some cases, the theory of democratic government yields a surprisingly simple answer.

Let's consider an example. Imagine that society is deciding how much money to spend on some public good, such as the CBC. Each voter has his own most preferred budget, and he always prefers outcomes closer to his most preferred value to outcomes farther away. Thus, we can line up voters from those who prefer the smallest budget to those who prefer the largest. Figure 22.1 is an example. Here there are 100 voters, and the budget size varies from zero to $20 billion. Given these preferences, what outcome would you expect democracy to produce?

According to a famous result called the **median voter theorem**, majority rule will produce the outcome most preferred by the median voter. The *median voter* is the voter exactly in the middle of the distribution. In this example, if you take the line of voters ordered by their preferred budgets and count 50 voters from either end of the line, you will find that the median voter wants a budget of $10 billion. By contrast, the average preferred outcome (calculated by adding the preferred outcomes and dividing by the number of voters) is $9 billion, and the modal outcome (the one preferred by the greatest number of voters) is $15 billion.

The median voter rules the day because his preferred outcome beats any other proposal in a two-way race. In our example, more than half the voters want $10 billion or more, and more than half want $10 billion or less. If someone proposes, say, $8 billion instead of $10 billion, everyone who prefers $10 billion or more will vote with the median voter. Similarly, if someone proposes $12 billion instead of $10 billion, everyone who wants $10 billion or less will vote with the median voter. In either case, the median voter has more than half of the voters on his side.

What about the Condorcet voting paradox? It turns out that when the voters are picking a point along a line and each voter aims for his own most preferred point, the Condorcet paradox cannot arise. The median voter's most preferred outcome beats all challengers.

One implication of the median voter theorem is that if two political parties are each trying to maximize their chance of election, they will both move their positions toward the median voter. Suppose, for example, that the Liberal party advocates a budget of $15 billion, while the Conservative party advocates a budget of $10 billion. The Liberal position is more popular in the sense that $15 billion has more proponents than any other single choice. Nonetheless, the Conservative party gets more than 50 percent of the vote: It will attract the 20 voters who want $10 billion, the 15 voters who want $5 billion, and the 25 voters who want zero. If the Liberals want to win, they will move their platform toward the median voter. Thus, this theory can explain why the parties in a two-party system are similar to each other: They are both moving toward the median voter.

Another implication of the median voter theorem is that minority views are not given much weight. Imagine that 40 percent of the population wants a lot of money spent on the national parks, and 60 percent wants nothing spent. In this case, the median voter's preference is zero, regardless of the intensity of the minority's view. Such is the logic of democracy. Rather than reaching a compromise that takes into account everyone's preferences, majority rule looks only to the person in the exact middle of the distribution.

22-2d Politicians Are People Too

When economists study consumer behaviour, they assume that consumers buy the bundle of goods and services that gives them the greatest level of satisfaction. When economists study firm behaviour, they assume that firms produce the quantity of goods and services that yields the greatest level of profits. What should they assume when they study people involved in the practice of politics?

Politicians also have objectives. It would be nice to assume that political leaders are always looking out for the well-being of society as a whole, that they are aiming for an optimal combination of efficiency and equity. Nice, perhaps, but not realistic. Self-interest is as powerful a motive for political actors as it is for consumers and firm owners. Some politicians, motivated by desire for re-election, are willing to sacrifice the national interest to solidify their base of voters. Others are motivated by simple greed. If you have any doubt, you should look at the world's poor nations, where corruption among government officials is a common impediment to economic development.

This book is not the place to develop a theory of political behaviour. But when thinking about economic policy, remember that this policy is made not by a benevolent king (or even by benevolent economists), but by real people with their own all-too-human desires. Sometimes they are motivated to further the national interest, but sometimes they are motivated by their own political and financial ambitions. We shouldn't be surprised when economic policy fails to resemble the ideals derived in economics textbooks.

 QUICK Quiz *A school board is voting on the school budget and the resulting student–teacher ratio. A poll finds that 35 percent of the voters want a ratio of 9:1, 25 percent want a ratio of 10:1, and 40 percent want a ratio of 12:1. What outcome would you expect the school board to end up with?*

22-3 Behavioural Economics

Economics is a study of human behaviour, but it is not the only field that can make that claim. The social science of psychology also sheds light on the choices that people make in their lives. The fields of economics and psychology usually proceed independently, in part because they address a different range of questions. But recently a field called *behavioural economics* has emerged in which economists are making use of basic psychological insights. Let's consider some of these insights here.

22-3a People Aren't Always Rational

Economic theory is populated by a particular species of organism, sometimes called *Homo economicus.* Members of this species are always rational. As firm managers, they maximize profits. As consumers, they maximize utility (or equivalently, pick the point on the highest indifference curve). Given the constraints they face, they rationally weigh all the costs and benefits and always choose the best possible course of action.

Real people, however, are *Homo sapiens.* Although in some ways they resemble the rational, calculating people assumed in economic theory, they are far more complex. They can be forgetful, impulsive, confused, emotional, and shortsighted. These imperfections of human reasoning are the bread-and-butter of psychologists, but until recently, economists have neglected them.

Herbert Simon, one of the first social scientists to work at the boundary of economics and psychology, suggested that humans should be viewed not as rational maximizers but as *satisficers.* Rather than always choosing the best course of action, they make decisions that are merely good enough. Similarly, other economists have suggested that humans are only "near rational" or that they exhibit "bounded rationality."

Studies of human decision making have tried to detect systematic mistakes that people make. Here are a few of the findings:

- *People are overconfident.* Imagine that you were asked some numerical questions, such as the number of African countries in the United Nations, the height of the tallest mountain in North America, and so on. Instead of being asked for a single estimate, however, you were asked to give a 90 percent confidence interval—a range such that you were 90 percent confident the true number falls within it. When psychologists run experiments like this, they find that most people give ranges that are too small: The true number falls within their intervals far less than 90 percent of the time. That is, most people are too sure of their own abilities.
- *People give too much weight to a small number of vivid observations.* Imagine that you are thinking about buying a car of brand X. To learn about its reliability, you read *Consumer Reports,* which has surveyed 1000 owners of car X. Then you run into a friend who owns car X, and she tells you that her car is a lemon. How do you treat your friend's observation? If you think rationally, you will realize that she has increased your sample size only from 1000 to 1001, which does not provide much new information. But because your friend's story is so vivid, you may be tempted to give it more weight in your decision making than you should.
- *People are reluctant to change their minds.* People tend to interpret evidence to confirm beliefs they already hold. In one study, subjects were asked to read

and evaluate a research report on whether capital punishment deters crime. After reading the report, those who initially favoured the death penalty said they were surer in their view, and those who initially opposed the death penalty also said they were surer in their view. The two groups interpreted the same evidence in exactly opposite ways.

Think about decisions you have made in your own life. Do you exhibit some of these traits?

A hotly debated issue is whether deviations from rationality are important for understanding economic phenomena. An intriguing example arises in the study of tax-advantaged retirement savings accounts that some firms offer their workers. In some firms, workers can choose to participate in the plan by filling out a simple form. In other firms, workers are automatically enrolled and can opt out of the plan by filling out a simple form. It turns out many more workers participate in the second case than in the first. If workers were perfectly rational maximizers, they would choose the optimal amount of retirement saving, regardless of the default offered by their employer. In fact, workers' behaviour appears to exhibit substantial inertia. Understanding their behaviour seems easier once we abandon the model of rational man.

Why, you might ask, is economics built on the rationality assumption when psychology and common sense cast doubt on it? One answer is that the assumption, even if not exactly true, may be true enough that it yields reasonably accurate models of behaviour. For example, when we studied the differences between competitive and monopoly firms, the assumption that firms rationally maximize profit yielded many important and valid insights. Incorporating complex psychological deviations from rationality into the story might have added realism, but it also would have muddied the waters and made those insights harder to find. Recall from Chapter 2 that economic models are not meant to replicate reality but are supposed to show the essence of the problem at hand as an aid to understanding.

Another reason why economists so often assume rationality may be that economists are themselves not rational maximizers. Like most people, they are overconfident, and they are reluctant to change their minds. Their choice among alternative theories of human behaviour may exhibit excessive inertia. Moreover, economists may be content with a theory that is not perfect but is good enough. The model of rational man may be the theory of choice for a satisficing social scientist.

case study Left-Digit Bias

You may have noticed that prices often end in .99. In some ways, this phenomenon is odd. Why charge $4.99, instead of an even $5.00? If people were truly rational, sellers wouldn't have a good reason to focus on prices ending in .99. But in fact, it turns out that sellers are smart for using this approach to pricing. Various studies suggest that buyers are excessively sensitive to a price's left-most digit. Even though $4.99 is only one penny less than $5.00, buyers may not perceive it that way. Because adding the extra penny changes the left-most digit from a 4 to a 5, the change may exert a surprisingly large impact on consumer behaviour. An irrational focus on the left-most digit is called *left-digit bias*.

In one study, participants were given the choice of buying two different pens, a cheap one and a better, more expensive one. When the pens were priced at

Why not add a penny to this price?

$2.00 and $3.99, 44 percent bought the higher-priced pen. When the prices were $1.99 and $4.00, only 18 percent bought the more expensive one. Such a large change in behaviour in response to such tiny changes in the prices seems hard to square with standard models of rationality. But it is easier to understand if one imagines a consumer that focuses excessively on the left-most digit. To such a consumer, the prices would look like $2 and $3 in the first scenario and $1 and $4 in the second, and so the changes from the first to the second scenario would appear larger than they really are.

Another study of left-digit bias examined how the number of miles on a used car's odometer affected the price at which the car sold. The study examined data on millions of used cars sold at auction. Not surprisingly, cars that had been driven more miles sold for less. But the effect was not smooth. For example, when the odometer reading increased from 78 000 to 79 000 (leaving the left-most digit the same), the price of the car fell by about $10. But when the odometer reading increased from 79 000 to 80 000 (increasing the left-most digit), the price fell by $210. The prices of used cars jumped down at every 10 000-mile mark, when the left-most digit on the odometer changed.

When looking at either prices or odometers, buyers seem to be irrationally influenced by the left-most digit. ■

22-3b People Care about Fairness

Another insight about human behaviour is best illustrated with an experiment called the *ultimatum game*. The game works like this: Two volunteers (who are otherwise strangers to each other) are told that they are going to play a game and could win a total of $100. Before they play, they learn the rules. The game begins with a coin flip, which is used to assign the volunteers to the roles of player A and player B. Player A's job is to propose a division of the $100 prize between himself and the other player. After player A makes his proposal, player B decides whether to accept or reject it. If he accepts it, both players are paid according to the proposal. If player B rejects the proposal, both players walk away with nothing. In either case, the game then ends.

Before proceeding, stop and think about what you would do in this situation. If you were player A, what division of the $100 would you propose? If you were player B, what proposals would you accept?

Conventional economic theory assumes in this situation that people are rational wealth-maximizers. This assumption leads to a simple prediction: Player A should propose that he gets $99 and player B gets $1, and player B should accept the proposal. After all, once the proposal is made, player B is better off accepting it as long as he gets something out of it. Moreover, because player A knows that accepting the proposal is in player B's interest, player A has no reason to offer him more than $1. In the language of game theory (discussed in Chapter 17), the 99–1 split is the Nash equilibrium.

Yet when experimental economists ask real people to play the ultimatum game, the results differ from this prediction. People in the player B role usually reject proposals that give them only $1 or a similarly small amount. Anticipating this, people in the role of player A usually propose giving player B much more than $1. Some people will offer a 50–50 split, but it is more common for player A to propose giving player B an amount such as $30 or $40, keeping the larger share for himself. In this case, player B usually accepts the proposal.

What's going on here? The natural interpretation is that people are driven in part by some innate sense of fairness. A 99–1 split seems so wildly unfair to many people that they reject it, even to their own detriment. By contrast, a 70–30 split is still unfair, but it is not so unfair that it induces people to abandon their normal self-interest.

Throughout our study of household and firm behaviour, the innate sense of fairness has not played any role. But the results of the ultimatum game suggest that perhaps it should. For example, in Chapters 18 and 19 we discussed how wages were determined by labour supply and labour demand. Some economists have suggested that the perceived fairness of what a firm pays its workers should also enter the picture. Thus, when a firm has an especially profitable year, workers (like player B) may expect to be paid a fair share of the prize, even if the standard equilibrium does not dictate it. The firm (like player A) might well decide to give workers more than the equilibrium wage for fear that the workers might otherwise try to punish the firm with reduced effort, strikes, or even vandalism.

22-3c People Are Inconsistent over Time

Imagine some dreary task, such as doing your laundry, shovelling snow off your driveway, or filling out your income tax forms. Now consider the following questions:

1. Would you prefer (A) to spend 50 minutes doing the task immediately or (B) to spend 60 minutes doing the task tomorrow?
2. Would you prefer (A) to spend 50 minutes doing the task in 90 days or (B) to spend 60 minutes doing the task in 91 days?

When asked questions like these, many people choose B for question 1 and A for question 2. When looking ahead to the future (as in question 2), they minimize the amount of time spent on the dreary task. But faced with the prospect of doing the task immediately (as in question 1), they choose to put it off.

In some ways, this behaviour is not surprising: Everyone procrastinates from time to time. But from the standpoint of the theory of rational person, it is puzzling. Suppose that, in response to question 2, a person chooses to spend 50 minutes in 90 days. Then, when the 90th day arrives, we allow him to change his mind. In effect, he then faces question 1, so he opts for doing the task the next day. But why should the mere passage of time affect the choices he makes?

Many times in life, people make plans for themselves but then they fail to follow through. A smoker promises herself that she will quit, but within a few hours of smoking her last cigarette, she craves another and breaks her promise. A person trying to lose weight promises that he will stop eating dessert, but when the waiter brings the dessert cart, the diet goes out the window. In both cases, the desire for instant gratification induces the decision maker to abandon his own past plans.

Some economists believe that the consumption–saving decision is an important instance where people exhibit this inconsistency over time. For many people, spending provides a type of instant gratification. Saving, like passing up the cigarette or the dessert, requires a sacrifice in the present for a reward in the distant future. And just as many smokers wish they could quit and many overweight individuals wish they ate less, many consumers wish they saved more. According to one survey, more than 50 percent of Canadians were concerned that they were not saving enough for retirement.

An implication of this inconsistency over time is that people should try to find ways to commit their future selves to following through on their plans. A smoker trying to quit may throw away her cigarettes, and a person on a diet may put a

Can Brain Science Improve Economics?

Some scholars believe that studying the biology of the brain may improve our understanding of economic behaviour.

The Neuroeconomics Revolution

By Robert J. Shiller

Economics is at the start of a revolution that is traceable to an unexpected source: medical schools and their research facilities. Neuroscience—the science of how the brain, that physical organ inside one's head, really works—is beginning to change the way we think about how people make decisions. These findings will inevitably change the way we think about how economies function. In short, we are at the dawn of "neuroeconomics."

Efforts to link neuroscience to economics have occurred mostly in just the last few years, and the growth of neuroeconomics is still in its early stages. But its nascence follows a pattern: revolutions in science tend to come from completely unexpected places. A field of science can turn barren if no fundamentally new approaches to research are on the horizon. Scholars can

become so trapped in their methods—in the language and assumptions of the accepted approach to their discipline—that their research becomes repetitive or trivial.

Then something exciting comes along from someone who was never involved with these methods—some new idea that attracts young scholars and a few iconoclastic old scholars, who are willing to learn a different science and its different research methods. At a certain moment in this process, a scientific revolution is born.

The neuroeconomic revolution has passed some key milestones quite recently, notably the publication last year of neuroscientist Paul Glimcher's book *Foundations of Neuroeconomic Analysis*—a pointed variation on the title of Paul Samuelson's 1947 classic work, *Foundations of Economic Analysis*, which helped to launch an earlier revolution in economic theory. And Glimcher himself now holds an appointment at New York University's economics department (he also works at NYU's Center for Neural Science).

To most economists, however, Glimcher might as well have come from outer space. After all, his doctorate is from the University of Pennsylvania School of Medicine's neuroscience department. Moreover, neuroeconomists like him conduct research that is well beyond their conventional colleagues' intellectual comfort zone, for they seek to advance some of the core concepts of economics by linking them to specific brain structures.

Much of modern economic and financial theory is based on the assumption that people are rational, and thus that they systematically maximize their own happiness, or as economists call it, their "utility." When Samuelson took on the subject in his 1947 book, he did not look into the brain, but relied instead on "revealed preference." People's objectives are revealed only by observing their economic activities. Under Samuelson's guidance, generations of economists have based their research not on any physical structure underlying thought and behavior, but only on the assumption of rationality.

lock on the refrigerator. What can a person who saves too little do? He should find some way to lock up his money before he spends it. Some retirement accounts, such as retirement saving plans, do exactly that. A worker can agree to have some money taken out of his paycheque before he ever sees it. The money is deposited in an account that can be used before retirement only with a penalty. Perhaps that is one reason why these retirement accounts are so popular: They protect people from their own desires for instant gratification.

 Describe at least three ways in which human decision making differs from that of the rational individual of conventional economic theory.

22-4 Conclusion

This chapter has examined the frontier of microeconomics. You may have noticed that we have sketched out ideas rather than fully developing them. This is no accident. One reason is that you might study these topics in more detail in advanced

As a result, Glimcher is skeptical of prevailing economic theory, and is seeking a physical basis for it in the brain. He wants to transform "soft" utility theory into "hard" utility theory by discovering the brain mechanisms that underlie it.

In particular, Glimcher wants to identify brain structures that process key elements of utility theory when people face uncertainty: "(1) subjective value, (2) probability, (3) the product of subjective value and probability (expected subjective value), and (4) a neuro-computational mechanism that selects the element from the choice set that has the highest 'expected subjective value'. . . ."

While Glimcher and his colleagues have uncovered tantalizing evidence, they have yet to find most of the fundamental brain structures. Maybe that is because such structures simply do not exist, and the whole utility-maximization theory is wrong, or at least in need of fundamental revision. If so, that finding alone would shake economics to its foundations.

Another direction that excites neuroscientists is how the brain deals with ambiguous situations, when probabilities are not known, and when other highly relevant information is not available. It has already been discovered that the brain regions used to deal with problems

A neuroeconomist at work

when probabilities are clear are different from those used when probabilities are unknown. This research might help us to understand how people handle uncertainty and risk in, say, financial markets at a time of crisis.

John Maynard Keynes thought that most economic decision-making occurs in ambiguous situations in which probabilities are not known. He concluded that much of our business cycle is driven by fluctuations in "animal spirits," something in the mind—and not understood by economists.

Of course, the problem with economics is that there are often as many interpretations of any crisis as there are economists. An economy is a remarkably complex structure, and fathoming it depends on understanding its laws, regulations, business practices and customs, and balance sheets, among many other details.

Yet it is likely that one day we will know much more about how economies work—or fail to work—by understanding better the physical structures that underlie brain functioning. Those structures—networks of neurons that communicate with each other via axons and dendrites—underlie the familiar analogy of the brain to a computer—networks of transistors that communicate with each other via electric wires. The economy is the next analogy: a network of people who communicate with each other via electronic and other connections.

The brain, the computer, and the economy: all three are devices whose purpose is to solve fundamental information problems in coordinating the activities of individual units—the neurons, the transistors, or individual people. As we improve our understanding of the problems that any one of these devices solves—and how it overcomes obstacles in doing so—we learn something valuable about all three.

Mr. Shiller is an economics professor at Yale University.

Source: Robert J. Shiller, "The Neuroeconomics Revolution," Project Syndicate, November 21, 2011.

courses. Another reason is that these topics remain active areas of research and, therefore, are still being fleshed out.

To see how these topics fit into the broader picture, recall the ten principles of economics from Chapter 1. One principle states that markets are usually a good way to organize economic activity. Another principle states that governments can sometimes improve market outcomes. As you study economics, you can more fully appreciate the truth of these principles as well as the caveats that go with them. The study of asymmetric information should make you more wary of market outcomes. The study of political economy should make you more wary of government solutions. And the study of behavioural economics should make you wary of any institution that relies on human decision making—including both the market and the government.

If there is a unifying theme to these topics, it is that life is messy. Information is imperfect, government is imperfect, and people are imperfect. Of course, you knew this long before you started studying economics, but economists need to understand these imperfections as precisely as they can if they are to explain, and perhaps even improve, the world around them.

summary

- In many economic transactions, information is asymmetric. When there are hidden actions, principals may be concerned that agents suffer from the problem of moral hazard. When there are hidden characteristics, buyers may be concerned about the problem of adverse selection among the sellers. Private markets sometimes deal with asymmetric information with signalling and screening.

- Although government policy can sometimes improve market outcomes, governments are themselves imperfect institutions. The Condorcet paradox shows that majority rule fails to produce transitive preferences for society, and Arrow's impossibility theorem shows that no voting scheme will be perfect. In many situations, democratic institutions will produce the outcome desired by the median voter, regardless of the preferences of the rest of the electorate. Moreover, the individuals who set government policy may be motivated by self-interest rather than the national interest.

- The study of psychology and economics reveals that human decision making is more complex than is assumed in conventional economic theory. People are not always rational, they care about the fairness of economic outcomes (even to their own detriment), and they can be inconsistent over time.

KEY concepts

moral hazard, *p. 488*
agent, *p. 488*
principal, *p. 488*

adverse selection, *p. 490*
signalling, *p. 491*
screening, *p. 492*

Condorcet paradox, *p. 494*
Arrow's impossibility theorem, *p. 495*
median voter theorem, *p. 496*

QUESTIONS FOR review

1. What is moral hazard? List three things an employer might do to reduce the severity of this problem.

2. What is adverse selection? Give an example of a market in which adverse selection might be a problem.

3. Define *signalling* and *screening,* and give an example of each.

4. What unusual property of voting did Condorcet notice?

5. Explain why majority rule respects the preferences of the median voter rather than the average voter.

6. Describe the ultimatum game. What outcome from this game would conventional economic theory predict? Do experiments confirm this prediction? Explain.

QUICK CHECK multiple choice

1. Because Elaine has a family history of significant medical problems, she buys health insurance, whereas her friend Jerry, who has a healthier family, goes without. This is an example of which of the following?
   a. moral hazard
   b. adverse selection
   c. signalling
   d. screening

2. George has a life insurance policy that pays his family $1 million if he dies. As a result, he does not hesitate to enjoy his favourite hobby of bungee jumping. This is an example of which of the following?
   a. moral hazard
   b. adverse selection
   c. signalling
   d. screening

3. Before selling anyone a health insurance policy, the Kramer Insurance Company requires that applicants undergo a medical examination. Those with significant pre-existing medical problems are charged more. This is an example of which of the following?
   a. moral hazard
   b. adverse selection
   c. signalling
   d. screening

4. The Condorcet paradox illustrates Arrow's impossibility theorem by showing which characteristic of pairwise majority voting?
   a. it is inconsistent with the principle of unanimity
   b. it leads to social preferences that are not transitive
   c. it violates the independence of irrelevant alternatives
   d. it makes one person in effect a dictator

5. Two political candidates are running for mayor, and the key issue is how much to spend on the town's annual Canada Day fireworks. Among the 100 voters, 40 want to spend $30 000, 30 want to spend $10 000, and 30 want to spend nothing at all. What is the winning position on this issue?
   a. $10 000
   b. $15 000
   c. $20 000
   d. $30 000

6. What is illustrated by the experiment called the "ultimatum game"?
   a. People are overconfident in their own abilities.
   b. People play the Nash equilibrium in strategic situations.
   c. People care about fairness, even to their own detriment.
   d. People make inconsistent decisions over time.

PROBLEMS AND **applications**

1. Each of the following situations involves moral hazard. In each case, identify the principal and the agent, and explain why there is asymmetric information. How does the action described reduce the problem of moral hazard?
   a. Landlords require tenants to pay security deposits.
   b. Firms compensate top executives with options to buy company stock at a given price in the future.
   c. Car insurance companies offer discounts to customers who install antitheft devices in their cars.

2. Suppose that the Live-Long-and-Prosper Life Insurance Company charges $5000 annually for an insurance policy. The company's president suggests that the company raise the annual price to $6000 in order to increase its profits. If the firm followed this suggestion, what economic problem might arise? Would the firm's pool of customers tend to become more or less healthy on average? Would the company's profits necessarily increase?

3. A case study in this chapter describes how a boyfriend can signal to a girlfriend that he loves her by giving an appropriate gift. Do you think saying "I love you" can also serve as a signal? Why or why not?

4. Some AIDS activists believe that life insurance companies should not be allowed to ask applicants if they are infected with HIV, the virus that causes AIDS. Would this rule help or hurt those who are HIV-positive? Would it help or hurt those who are not HIV-positive? Would it exacerbate or mitigate the problem of adverse selection in the market for life insurance? Do you think it would increase or decrease the number of people without life insurance? In your opinion, would this be a good policy?

5. The government is considering two ways to help the needy: giving them cash, or giving them free meals at soup kitchens. Give an argument for giving cash. Give an argument, based on asymmetric information, for why the soup kitchen may be better than the cash handout.

6. Ken walks into an ice-cream parlour.

   WAITER: We have vanilla and chocolate today.

   KEN: I'll take vanilla.

   WAITER: I almost forgot. We also have strawberry.

   KEN: In that case, I'll take chocolate.

   What standard property of decision making is Ken violating? (*Hint:* Reread the section on Arrow's impossibility theorem.)

7. Why might a political party in a two-party system choose not to move toward the median voter? (*Hint:* Think about abstentions from voting and political contributions.)

8. Two ice-cream stands are deciding where to locate along a one-kilometre beach. Each person sitting on the beach buys exactly one ice-cream cone per day from the stand nearest to him. Each ice-cream seller wants the maximum number of customers. Where along the beach will the two stands locate?

9. After a widely reported earthquake in British Columbia, many people call their insurance company to apply for earthquake insurance. Might this reaction reflect some deviation from rationality? Discuss.

10. Three friends are choosing a restaurant for dinner. Here are their preferences:

	Rachel	Ross	Joey
First choice	Italian	Italian	Chinese
Second choice	Chinese	Chinese	Mexican
Third choice	Mexican	Mexican	French
Fourth choice	French	French	Italian

   a. If the three friends use a Borda count to make their decision, where do they go to eat?
   b. On their way to their chosen restaurant, they see that the Mexican and French restaurants are closed, so they use a Borda count again to decide between

the remaining two restaurants. Where do they decide to go now?

c. How do your answers to parts (a) and (b) relate to Arrow's impossibility theorem?

11. Three friends are choosing a TV show to watch. Here are their preferences:

	Chandler	Phoebe	Monica
First choice	Dexter	Glee	House
Second choice	Glee	House	Dexter
Third choice	House	Dexter	Glee

a. If the three friends try using a Borda count to make their choice, what would happen?

b. Monica suggests a vote by majority rule. She proposes that first they choose between *Dexter* and *Glee*, and then they choose between the winner of the first vote and *House*. If they all vote their preferences honestly, what outcome would occur?

c. Should Chandler agree to Monica's suggestion? What voting system would he prefer?

d. Phoebe and Monica convince Chandler to go along with Monica's proposal. In round one, Chandler dishonestly says he prefers *Glee* over *Dexter*. Why might he do this?

12. Five roommates are planning to spend the weekend in their dorm room watching movies, and they are debating how many movies to watch. Here is their willingness to pay:

	Quentin	Spike	Ridley	Martin	Steven
First film	$14	$10	$8	$4	$2
Second film	12	8	4	2	0
Third film	10	6	2	0	0
Fourth film	6	2	0	0	0
Fifth film	2	0	0	0	0

Buying a DVD costs $15, which the roommates split equally, so each pays $3 per movie.

a. What is the efficient number of movies to watch (that is, the number that maximizes total surplus)?

b. From the standpoint of each roommate, what is the preferred number of movies?

c. What is the preference of the median roommate?

d. If the roommates held a vote on the efficient outcome versus the median voter's preference, how would each person vote? Which outcome would get a majority?

e. If one of the roommates proposed a different number of movies, could his proposal beat the winner from part (d) in a vote?

f. Can majority rule be counted on to reach efficient outcomes in the provision of public goods?

A

Ability-to-pay principle the idea that taxes should be levied on a person according to how well that person can shoulder the burden

Absolute advantage the comparison among producers of a good according to their productivity

Accounting profit total revenue minus total explicit cost

Adverse selection the tendency for the mix of unobserved attributes to become undesirable from the standpoint of an uninformed party

Agent a person who is performing an act for another person, called the principal

Arrow's impossibility theorem a mathematical result showing that, under certain assumed conditions, there is no scheme for aggregating individual preferences into a valid set of social preferences

Average fixed cost fixed cost divided by the quantity of output

Average revenue total revenue divided by the quantity sold

Average tax rate total taxes paid divided by total income

Average total cost total cost divided by the quantity of output

Average variable cost variable cost divided by the quantity of output

B

Benefits principle the idea that people should pay taxes based on the benefits they receive from government services

Budget constraint the limit on the consumption bundles that a consumer can afford

Budget deficit an excess of government spending over government receipts

Budget surplus an excess of government receipts over government spending

Business cycle fluctuations in economic activity, such as employment and production

C

Capital the equipment and structures used to produce goods and services

Cartel a group of firms acting in unison

Circular-flow diagram a visual model of the economy that shows how dollars flow through markets

Club goods goods that are excludable but not rival

Coase theorem the proposition that if private parties can bargain without cost over the allocation of resources, they can solve the problem of externalities on their own

Collusion an agreement among firms in a market about quantities to produce or prices to charge

Common resources goods that are rival but not excludable

Comparative advantage the comparison among producers of a good according to their opportunity cost

Compensating differential a difference in wages that arises to offset the nonmonetary characteristics of different jobs

Competitive market a market in which there are many buyers and many sellers so that each has a negligible impact on the market price

Competitive market a market in which there are many buyers and many sellers so that each has a negligible impact on the market price

Complements two goods for which an increase in the price of one leads to a decrease in the demand for the other

Condorcet paradox the failure of majority rule to produce transitive preferences for society

Constant returns to scale the property whereby long-run average total cost stays the same as the quantity of output changes

Corrective taxes taxes enacted to correct the effects of negative externalities

Cost–benefit analysis a study that compares the costs and benefits to society of providing a public good

Cross-price elasticity of demand a measure of how much the quantity demanded of one good responds to a change in the price of another good, computed as the percentage change in quantity demanded of the first good divided by the percentage change in the price of the second good

D

Deadweight loss the fall in total surplus that results from a market distortion, such as a tax

Demand curve a graph of the relationship between the price of a good and the quantity demanded

Demand schedule a table that shows the relationship between the price of a good and the quantity demanded

Diminishing marginal product the property whereby the marginal product of an input declines as the quantity of the input increases

Diminishing marginal product the property whereby the marginal product of an input declines as the quantity of the input increases

Discrimination the offering of different opportunities to similar individuals who differ only by race, ethnic group, sex, age, or other personal characteristics

Diseconomies of scale the property whereby long-run average total cost rises as the quantity of output increases

Dominant strategy a strategy that is best for a player in a game regardless of the strategies chosen by the other players

Dconomic profit total revenue minus total cost, including both explicit and implicit costs

Dconomics the study of how society manages its scarce resources

Dconomies of scale the property whereby long-run average total cost falls as the quantity of output increases

E

Efficiency the property of society getting the most it can from its scarce resources

Efficiency wages above-equilibrium wages paid by firms in order to increase worker productivity

Efficient scale the quantity of output that minimizes average total cost

Elasticity a measure of the responsiveness of quantity demanded or quantity supplied to one of its determinants

Elasticity of the tax base the sensitivity of the tax base to changes in the tax rate

Equilibrium a situation in which the price has reached the level where quantity supplied equals quantity demanded

Equilibrium price the price that balances quantity supplied and quantity demanded

Equilibrium quantity the quantity supplied and the quantity demanded at the equilibrium price.

Equity the property of distributing economic prosperity fairly among the members of society

Excludability the property of a good whereby a person can be prevented from using it

Explicit costs input costs that require an outlay of money by the firm

Exports goods and services produced domestically and sold abroad

Externality the impact of one person's actions on the well-being of a bystander

Externality the uncompensated impact of one person's actions on the well-being of a bystander

F

Factors of production the inputs used to produce goods and services

Fixed costs costs that do not vary with the quantity of output produced

Free rider a person who receives the benefit of a good but avoids paying for it

G

Game theory the study of how people behave in strategic situations

Giffen good a good for which an increase in the price raises the quantity demanded

H

Horizontal equity the idea that taxpayers with similar abilities to pay taxes should pay the same amount

Human capital the accumulation of investments in people, such as education and on-the-job training

I

Implicit costs input costs that do not require an outlay of money by the firm

Imports goods and services produced abroad and sold domestically

In-kind transfers transfers to the poor given in the form of goods and services rather than cash

Income effect the change in consumption that results when a price change moves the consumer to a higher or lower indifference curve

Income elasticity of demand a measure of how much the quantity demanded of a good responds to a change in consumers' income, computed as the percentage change in quantity demanded divided by the percentage change in income

Indifference curve a curve that shows consumption bundles that give the consumer the same level of satisfaction

Inferior good a good for which, other things equal, an increase in income leads to a decrease in demand

Inferior good a good for which, other things equal, an increase in income leads to a decrease in demand

Inflation an increase in the overall level of prices in the economy

Internalizing the externality alter incentives so that people take account of the external effects of their actions

L

Law of demand the claim that, other things equal, the quantity demanded of a good falls when the price of the good rises

Law of supply the claim that, other things equal, the quantity supplied of a good rises when the price of the good rises

Law of supply and demand the claim that the price of any good adjusts to bring the quantity supplied and the quantity demanded for that good into balance

Liberalism the political philosophy according to which the government should choose policies deemed to be just, as evaluated by an impartial observer behind a "veil of ignorance"

Libertarianism the political philosophy according to which the government should punish crimes and enforce voluntary agreements but not redistribute income

Life cycle the regular pattern of income variation over a person's life

Lump-sum tax a tax that is the same amount for every person

M

Macroeconomics the study of economy-wide phenomena, including inflation, unemployment, and economic growth

Marginal benefit of public funds the value that society places on one more dollar of expenditure on a government program

Marginal changes small incremental adjustments to a plan of action something that induces a person to act an economy that allocates resources through the decentralized decisions of many firms and households as they interact in markets for goods and services

Marginal cost the increase in total cost that arises from an extra unit of production

Marginal cost of public funds the total cost to society of raising one more dollar in tax revenue

Marginal product the increase in output that arises from an additional unit of input

Marginal product of labour the increase in the amount of output from an additional unit of labour

Marginal rate of substitution the rate at which a consumer is willing to trade one good for another

Marginal revenue the change in total revenue from an additional unit sold

Marginal tax rate the extra taxes paid on an additional dollar of income

Market a group of buyers and sellers of a particular good or service

Market failure a situation in which a market left on its own fails to allocate resources efficiently

Market power the ability of a single economic actor (or small group of actors) to have a substantial influence on market prices

Maximin criterion the claim that the government should aim to maximize the well-being of the worst-off person in society

Median voter theorem a mathematical result showing that if voters are choosing a point along a line and each voter wants the point closest to his most preferred point, then majority rule will pick the most preferred point of the median voter

Microeconomics the study of how households and firms make decisions and how they interact in markets

Monopolistic competition a market structure in which many firms sell products that are similar but not identical

Monopoly a firm that is the sole seller of a product without close substitutes

Moral hazard the tendency of a person who is imperfectly monitored to engage in dishonest or otherwise undesirable behaviour

N

Nash equilibrium a situation in which economic actors interacting with one another each choose their best strategy given the strategies that all the other actors have chosen

Natural monopoly a monopoly that arises because a single firm can supply a good or service to an entire market at a smaller cost than could two or more firms

Normal good a good for which, other things equal, an increase in income leads to an increase in demand

Normal good a good for which, other things equal, an increase in income leads to an increase in demand

Normative statements claims that attempt to prescribe how the world should be

O

Oligopoly a market structure in which only a few sellers offer similar or identical products

Oligopoly a market structure in which only a few sellers offer similar or identical products

Opportunity cost whatever must be given up to obtain some item

Opportunity cost whatever must be given up to obtain some item

P

Perfect complements two goods with right-angle indifference curves

Perfect substitutes two goods with straight-line indifference curves

Permanent income a person's normal income

Positive statements claims that attempt to describe the world as it is

Poverty line an absolute level of income set by the federal government for each family size, below which a family is deemed to be in poverty

Poverty rate the percentage of the population whose family income falls below an absolute level called the poverty line

Price ceiling a legal maximum on the price at which a good can be sold

Price discrimination the business practice of selling the same good at different prices to different customers

Price elasticity of demand a measure of how much the quantity demanded of a good responds to a change in the price of that good, computed as the percentage change in quantity demanded divided by the percentage change in price

Price elasticity of supply a measure of how much the quantity supplied of a good responds to a change in the price of that good, computed as the percentage change in quantity supplied divided by the percentage change in price

Price floor a legal minimum on the price at which a good can be sold

Principal a person for whom another person, called the agent, is performing some act

Prisoners' dilemma a particular "game" between two captured prisoners that illustrates why cooperation is difficult to maintain even when it is mutually beneficial

Private goods goods that are both excludable and rival

Production function the relationship between quantity of inputs used to make a good and the quantity of output of that good

Production function the relationship between the quantity of inputs used to make a good and the quantity of output of that good

Production possibilities frontier a graph that shows the combinations of output that the economy can possibly produce given the available factors of production and the available production technology

Productivity the quantity of goods and services produced from each hour of a worker's time

Profit total revenue minus total cost

Progressive tax a tax for which high-income taxpayers pay a larger fraction of their income than do low-income taxpayers

Property rights the ability of an individual to own and exercise control over scarce resources

Proportional tax a tax for which high-income and low-income taxpayers pay the same fraction of income

Public goods goods that are neither excludable nor rival

Q

Quantity demanded the amount of a good that buyers are willing and able to purchase

Quantity supplied the amount of a good that sellers are willing and able to sell

R

Rational people those who systematically and purposefully do the best they can to achieve their objectives

Regressive tax a tax for which high-income taxpayers pay a smaller fraction of their income than do low-income taxpayers

Rival in consumption the property of a good whereby one person's use diminishes other people's use

S

Scarcity the limited nature of society's resources

Screening an action taken by an uninformed party to induce an informed party to reveal information

Shortage a situation in which quantity demanded is greater than quantity supplied

Signalling an action taken by an informed party to reveal private information to an uninformed party

Strike the organized withdrawal of labour from a firm by a union

Substitutes two goods for which an increase in the price of one leads to an increase in the demand for the other

Substitution effect the change in consumption that results when a price change moves the consumer along a given indifference curve to a point with a new marginal rate of substitution

Sunk cost a cost that has already been committed and cannot be recovered

Supply curve a graph of the relationship between the price of a good and the quantity supplied

Supply schedule a table that shows the relationship between the price of a good and the quantity supplied

Surplus a situation in which quantity supplied is greater than quantity demanded

T

Tariff a tax on goods produced abroad and sold domestically

Tax incidence the manner in which the burden of a tax is shared among participants in a market the study of how the allocation of resources affects economic well-being the maximum amount that a buyer will pay for a good a buyer's willingness to pay minus the amount the buyer actually pays the value of everything a seller must give up to produce a good the amount a seller is paid for a good minus the seller's cost the property of a resource allocation of maximizing the total surplus received by all members of society the fairness of the distribution of well-being among the members of society

Total cost the market value of the inputs a firm uses in production

Total revenue (for a firm) the amount a firm receives for the sale of its output

Total revenue (in a market) the amount paid by buyers and received by sellers of a good, computed as the price of the good times the quantity sold

Tragedy of the Commons a parable that illustrates why common resources get used more than is desirable from the standpoint of society as a whole

Transaction costs the costs that parties incur in the process of agreeing to and following through on a bargain

U

Union a worker association that bargains with employers over wages and working conditions

Utilitarianism the political philosophy according to which the government should choose policies to maximize the total utility of everyone in society

Utility a measure of happiness or satisfaction

V

Value of the marginal product the marginal product of an input times the price of the output

Variable costs costs that do vary with the quantity of output produced

Vertical equity the idea that taxpayers with a greater ability to pay taxes should pay larger amounts

W

Welfare government programs that supplement the incomes of the needy

world price the price of a good that prevails in the world market for that good